RELIGIOUS SYSTEMS AND PSYCHOTHERAPY

RELIGIOUS SYSTEMS
AND
PSYCHOTHERAPY

Edited by

RICHARD H. COX, Ph.D.
*Medical—Consulting Psychologist
and Clergyman*

With a Foreword by

E. Mansell Pattison, M.D.
*Department of Psychiatry and Human Behavior,
University of California, Irvine*

CHARLES C THOMAS • PUBLISHER
Springfield • Illinois • U.S.A.

Published and Distributed Throughout the World by
CHARLES C THOMAS • PUBLISHER
Bannerstone House
301-327 East Lawrence Avenue, Springfield, Illinois, U.S.A.

This book is protected by copyright. No part of it
may be reproduced in any manner without written
permission from the publisher

© 1973, by CHARLES C THOMAS • PUBLISHER
ISBN 0-398-02753-6
Library of Congress Catalog Card Number: 72-93207

With THOMAS BOOKS careful attention is given to all details of manufacturing and design. It is the Publisher's desire to present books that are satisfactory as to their physical qualities and artistic possibilities and appropriate for their particular use. THOMAS BOOKS will be true to those laws of quality that assure a good name and good will.

Printed in the United States of America
CC-11

CONTRIBUTING AUTHORS

RICHARD H. COX, PH.D., Editor
Medical and Consulting Psychologist,
Private Practice, La Jolla, California;
Professor, Clinical Psychology and Human Behavior;
Chairman, Program of Marriage, Family and Child Study,
United States International University,
San Diego, California

ROY C. AMORE, PH.D.
Assistant Professor, Department of Theology,
University of Windsor, Windsor, Ontario, Canada

JULES BARRON, PH.D.
Private Practice,
Consultant in Psychotherapy, V. A. Hospital,
Consultant, Riverdell Regional High School,
Westwood, New Jersey

ROBERT L. BERGMAN, M.D.
Chief, Mental Health Programs, Indian Health Service,
Department of Health, Education, and Welfare,
Window Rock, Arizona

AGEHANANDA BHARATI, PH.D.
Professor and Chairman, Department of Anthropology,
Syracuse University, Syracuse, New York

CH'U CHAI, PH.D.
Professor Emeritus, Chinese Culture and Philosophy,
New School for Social Research,
New York, New York

WINBERG CHAI, PH.D.
Coordinator, Department of Government,
University of Redlands, Redlands, California

PAUL W. CLEMENT, PH.D.
Director, Clinical Training, Associate Professor, Graduate
School of Psychology, Fuller Theological Seminary,
Pasadena, California

CHARLES A. CURRAN, PH.D.
Professor, Department of Psychology, Loyola University,
Chicago, Illinois

BINGHAM DAI, PH.D.
Professor Emeritus, Department of Psychiatry and Psychology,
Duke University, Durham, North Carolina

EDGAR DRAPER, M.D.
*Professor, Psychiatry and Post-Graduate Medicine,
Director, Resident Education, University of Michigan,
Ann Arbor, Michigan*

SYLVANUS M. DUVALL, PH.D.
*Professor Emeritus, Social Science and Religion,
George Williams College, Downers Grove, Illinois*

TRUMAN G. ESAU, M.D.
*Psychiatry, Private Practice
Park Ridge, Illinois*

HARRISON S. EVANS, M.D.
*Professor and Chairman, Department of Psychiatry,
Loma Linda University, School of Medicine,
Loma Linda, California*

JOAN HALIFAX, B.A.
*Instructor, Department of Psychiatry,
University of Miami School of Medicine,
Miami, Florida*

JOHN A HAMMES, PH.D.
*Professor and Associate Head, Department of Psychology,
University of Georgia, Athens, Georgia*

JOSEPH HAVENS, PH.D.
*Psychotherapy and Counseling, Private Practice,
Amherst, Massachusetts*

EMANUEL M. HONIG, M.D.
*Psychiatry, Private Practice,
Beverly Hills, California*

PAUL E. JOHNSON, PH.D.
*Professor Emeritus, Psychology of Religion and Pastoral
Counseling, Boston University, Boston, Massachusetts*

SIDNEY M. JOURARD, PH.D.
*Professor, Department of Psychology,
University of Florida, Gainesville, Florida*

ISSA J. KHALIL, PH.D.
*Assistant Professor, Religious Studies,
California State University, San Diego, California*

ARI KIEV, M.D.
*Head, Program in Social Psychiatry, The New York
Hospital, Cornell Medical Center,
New York, New York*

ROGER M. LAUER, M.D.
*Staff Psychiatrist, Mental Health Study Center,
National Institute of Mental Health, Adelphi, Maryland*

Contributing Authors

WOLFGANG LEDERER, M.D.
Psychiatry, Private Practice,
San Francisco, California

C. MARSHALL LOWE, PH.D.
Assistant Professor, Division of Counseling Psychology,
School of Education, University of California,
Berkeley, California

O. HOBART MOWRER, PH.D.
Research Professor of Psychology, University of Illinois,
Champaign, Illinois

E. MANSELL PATTISON, M.D.
Associate Professor, Department of Psychiatry and Human
Behavior, University of California, Irvine, California;
Deputy Director, Training, Orange County Department of
Mental Health

RAYMOND PRINCE, M.D.
Research Director, The Mental Hygiene Institute Inc.
Montreal, Quebec, Canada

JOHN RACY, M.D.
Associate Professor, Psychiatry, University of
Rochester School of Medicine and Dentistry
Rochester, New York

WILLIAM R. ROGERS, PH.D.
Professor, Religion and Psychology, The Divinity School,
Harvard University, Cambridge, Massachusetts

VIN ROSENTHAL, PH.D.
Psychotherapy, Private Practice;
Professor, Northeastern Illinois State University,
Chicago, Illinois

DELWIN BYRON SCHNEIDER, PH.D.
Associate Professor, Religious Studies,
Coordinator, Ecumenical Center for World Religions,
University of San Diego, San Diego, California

IRMA LEE SHEPHERD, PH.D.
Professor, Department of Psychology,
Director, Laboratory for Psychological Services,
Georgia State University, Atlanta, Georgia

C. JAY SKIDMORE, ED.D.
Professor, Department of Family and Child Development,
Utah State University, Logan, Utah

HARRY C. STAMEY, M.D.
Associate Medical Director; Associate, Psychiatry,
Geisinger Medical Center, Danville, Pennsylvania

E. MARK STERN, ED.D.
Associate Professor and Coordinator, Sequence in Psychology
and Theology, Graduate Division of Pastoral Counseling,
Iona College, New Rochelle, New York;
Adjunct Associate Professor, Division of Humanistic Studies,
Seton Hall University, South Orange, New Jersey

JOHN M. VAYHINGER, PH.D.
Professor, Psychology and Pastoral Care,
Anderson School of Theology, Anderson, Indiana

WALTER I. WARDWELL, PH.D.
Professor, Department of Sociology,
University of Connecticut, Storrs, Connecticut

NEIL CLARK WARREN, PH.D.
Assistant Professor and Director of Research,
Graduate School of Psychology, Fuller Theological
Seminary, Pasadena, California

HAZEL H. WEIDMAN, PH.D.
Associate Professor of Social Anthropology,
Department of Psychiatry, University of Miami School of
Medicine, Miami, Florida

A FOREWORD

Making Paths through the Forest of Life and through the
Cultural Cloudedness of Consciousness

MOST OF US WHO HAVE WRITTEN for this book, and most of those who will be reading it are children of our times, products and reflections of the modern world of scientific thought. Although many of the authors herein represented descry more than one world in which we exist, we are all academicians, professionals, and intellectuals. We participate and work in a world view infused with the notions of logic, reason, thought, with objective and observable data confirmed as true by the published data of others. We live within this Western technological, scientific world, and we cannot deny that we are part of it, if for no other reason than that we partake in writing and reacting to the chapters in this book!

In one sense this is a book about the relationship between psychiatry or psychotherapy, and religion. We might say: what, another one? For there is a plethora of books on psychiatry and religion. And often there does not seem to be much that is new to be said. But let us stop for a moment and look back at the context of almost three quarters of the twentieth century. Let us look at the way we have lived and thought and felt in all that time. And we may see that the way we have lived, and thought, and felt, and existed is no more. The age of "cultural innocence" is lost.

In Retrospect

Let us look at America at the turn of the twentieth century for a moment. At that time the majority of the population lived in small towns, or if they lived in urban areas, the ethnic neighborhood community functioned effectively as a small town. People grew up where they were born, married in the place where they were raised, bore children and raised them in the same place, followed a vocation most likely in their parents' pattern, grew aged as grandparents to observe *their* grandchildren follow the same pattern. And, often as not, they died and were buried in the place where they had been born.

This was a "mono-valued" culture. Everyone lived the same way, felt the same way, thought the same way, existed the same way.

Although these small cultures changed, they changed slowly, almost imperceptibly, naturally, as if things were meant to be as they were.

Born into such a small, or restricted, culture, one grew up with an experience of the world about him that was consistent, and uniform. Without awareness, the values, styles, mores, the patterns of *being*ness were taken in by the child, laid down and cemented into his ego-structuring of the world. So that like an arrow shot from a sure bow, the child grew the way he should become, and became, a "good" person.

As a result, the person growing up in this "world" acquired an ego structure of reality that was firm and sure. There was an intrinsic sense of rightness and truth. One knew what was right and wrong, acceptable and vile, desirable and loathsome. When decisions were to be made in those days, one did not appeal to logic, to evidence, to experimentation first of all. No, he looked inside himself, to his feelings, to his own internal sense of *"known*ness"—to that which cannot be gainsaid by all external new ideas. Then he knew what the right decision should be. For how can anything controvert the reality that is a part of oneself?

Let us pause for a psychoanalytic parenthesis. What I am describing here is not just the internalized superego or "ego ideal" structure. Rather, I am talking about the nature of so-called autonomous ego structures—the way in which the ego constructs a view of external reality, paints a picture for oneself that portrays the world so that the individual person can go about the business of living life. One *must* have an "ego-picture" of the world in order to live, to act, to decide, to derive satisfaction and meaning from his own style of being-in-the-world. (1)

To return to our person of 1900. Being born, growing up, and living out his life in a mono-valued culture provided certainty, security, and meaning. When the stranger came to town, when the politician or speculator arrived, he might be greeted with curiosity, but not with incorporation—*not* with an invitation to form a part of that town. The reaction was probably: Here is a person from the "outside" world, "another world," but certainly not "my world." And the newcomer either chose to become a part of the mono-valued world, or was extruded. For two worlds did not exist within the same ego.

Sinclair Lewis catches the flavor of cultural constraint in his preface to *Main Street* (1920), wherein he remarks: "God made the country, and Man made the city, but the Devil must have surely made the small town!" In other words, the newcomer, representing a different world of existence, brought cognitive dissonance to the lives of our people of 1900. And the ego does not well tolerate cognitive dissonance (not, at least, unless trained to do so). So that, to reduce cognitive dissonance, there must be constraint to conformity.

To be sure, changes were brewing. Young men and women were leaving the small town, and they left also their urban ghettos and boroughs. They got educated—got smart! They learned that the world view of their upbringing was chauvinistic—was provincial, was naive, was religious! And so they learned a *new* world view. They learned a world view of rationalism, empiricism, scientism. Forsaking the faith of their elders, they followed the faith of the new prophets. Thus we arrive at the world view of the scientific professional man. This man of the twentieth century was not beholden to the myths, fantasies, and superstitions of his religious forbears. He was free! He had traded the mono-valued culture of the small town for the mono-valued culture of cosmopolitan science.

But something else was happening. After 1940 the social structure of America began to move at a quickening pace. In a scant quarter-century the established patterns of cultural change accelerated. Now children grow up in a place which is not the one where they were born. One out of seven American families moves every year. The typical family will now live in four different houses as a family unit. Children do not follow the vocations of their fathers. It is predicted that technological change will require that workers change vocations every ten years. It can safely be foretold: Your children will move away and you will not see your grandchildren. You will retire some place different from where you worked. And you will die among strangers.

And look! The majority of Americans now live in a handful of large megalopolises. People who came from different mono-valued cultures find themselves living, working, existing, side-by-side with people who are different from themselves—people whom they do not understand, people whom they do not agree with, people who do not live as they do. And so it happens that my next-door neighbor calls into question *the very essence of my existence.* How do I reconcile my "cognitive dissonance"? How do I make sense out of the fact that other people around me live according to different values, different styles, different mores? What is happening to the world? Is everyone going crazy? Or *am I?*

And so we look for answers, for guidance, for reinforcement, for reassurance that our way of living life is right, is true, is valuable, is meaningful. And we look to our friends, we look to our church, we look to our psychotherapist.

Then we have to decide how to raise our children. It is a bewildering affair. We can demand that they follow precisely in our footsteps. But that is gauche. So we say to them: make up your own mind, we cannot guide you. As a result, children grow up sans parental commitment to a "life style" of their own, with a *carte blanche, laissez-faire* opportunity to choose their own life. And our children are lost, bewildered, confused. They look for a way to be. They reach out grasping for a way of being-in-the-world that will give them direction, certainty, satisfaction, and meaning. (2) And so they join the ecology movement, they support the latest political white hope, the Jesus-freaks, the Hare Krishnas, the organic food club. Or they eschew the freakish, and commit themselves to becoming teachers, engineers, scientists, or psychotherapists.

And in all of this effort, we engage in a style of bewildered behavior that I call the "cultural cloudedness of consciousness." Most of us, at least in my generation, grew up knowing only one way of being. But today we are confronted with many ways of being. It is now clear that the scientific way of being is the one we—sage authors of the present volume—have elected as one way of being. But this way is not necessarily better or worse than other ways of being. The scientific-academic way is *one* way. (3) We are no happier, no more fulfilled, nor better adjusted, nor more successful, than the aborigine. (4) Different? Yes. Better? No.

Looking Ahead

We have grown up with the assumption that there was *one way to be*. And many of us traded off a religiously defined way-to-be for a scientifically defined way-to-be. And we have been unaware—our consciousness has been clouded—that there are *many* ways of being-in-the-world.

BUT. In order to exist. In order to function. In order to derive satisfaction and meaning from life, we cannot exist in a relativistic ennui. We must be able to construct an ego-picture of the world. We must be able to frame a "weltanschauung"—a world view. And here we face a new task, a new ego-coping skill, a new style of existence. We must learn how to become "multi-cultural." By this I mean, we must, each one, acquire the ability to commit ourselves to *A* style of life, with the conscious recognition that it is not *The* style of life.

Heretofore, in the history of the human race, ego development and the ego sense of reality have been based upon a normative view of the world. And now we are faced with the plurality of human existence. There are *many ways* to be-in-the-world. But *I must* choose *one way* to be. And that way must be normative *for me,* although it may not be normative for others.

So how do we decide to live out our lives? How do we pick our way through the jungled maze of existence? How do we make a path through the forest?

In the earliest times, in the primary societies of man, in the major cultures of society, the way to live life was spelled out in terms of religion. Religion was the overarching superstructure that contained the embodiment of the *how* man should live. Clyde Kluckhohn sums it up in apt fashion:

> There is the need for a moral order. Human life is necessarily a moral life precisely because it is a social life, and in the case of the human animal the minimum requirements for predictability of social behavior that will insure some stability and continuity are not taken care of automatically by biologically inherited instincts, as is the case with the bees and the ants. Hence there must be generally accepted standards of conduct, and these values are more compelling if they are invested with divine authority and continually symbolized in rites that appeal to the senses. (5)

Within this context, we can observe that religious frames of reference have served to structure human existence from the earliest times to the present. (6)

However, with the advent of the scientific age, religion was seen as superfluous, constricting, destructive. Science would replace religion. Freud viewed religion as a destructive force in society. And morality was viewed as synonymous with religion. This type of culture was oppressive. Morality added a negativistic quality to life. For Freud psychotherapy was an *amoral* enterprise: it made no demands, held no standards, conducted no judgements. But while psychotherapy, as a science of human behavior, was promoting a nonnormative view of human behavior, it was thereby undercutting the very basis of human existence. (7)

In his book, *The Triumph of the Therapeutic: Uses of Faith After Freud*, sociologist Philip Rieff notes that by undercutting the notion of normative commitment, the psychotherapeutic movement contributed to the symbolic impoverishment of society, to the notion of "negative" communities that required no commitment and offered no symbolic integrative values. Heretofore, people had lived within "positive" communities that demanded a commitment and that provided a type of salvation through participation in the community. To Rieff the notion of an amoral life is antithetical to human communal existence:

> To speak of a moral culture would be redundant. Every culture has two main functions: (1) to organize the moral demands that make men intelligible and

trustworthy to each other, thus rendering also the world intelligible and trustworthy; (2) to organize the expressive remissions by which men release themselves in some degree from the strain of conforming to the controlling symbolic, internalized variant readings of culture that constitute individual character. The process by which a culture changes at its profoundest levels may be tracted in the shifting balance of controls and releases which constitute a system of moral demands. (8)

To twentieth century scientific professional man, the idea of religion was atavistic. Religion was a structure that spelled out the way in which people should live; psychotherapy was a method that did *not* spell out how people should live. However, that may turn out to be a false conclusion. Psychotherapy is merely an alternative methodology. It is the contemporary faith of the scientific man. In a recent philosophical study, Joseph Margolis (9) concludes: "Psychotherapy, then, is primarily concerned with a technical goal, the preservation and restoration of mental health; nevertheless, its own development leads it, inevitably, to take up the role of moral legislator."

Research on psychotherapy indicates that therapists are not amoral. (10) Psychotherapists *do* transmit their values to their patients. That is not at question. Rather, the issues are as follows: (1) How does this transmission of values influence the course of therapy? (2) What *are* the values a therapist holds to and transmits? (3) How then does the therapist influence the values of his patient? Surely these are questions not yet fully answered.

For psychotherapy is the religious system of contemporary modern man. It defines how one should be, how one should live one's life. But is contemporary psychotherapy applicable beyond the pale of scientific twentieth century man? Contemporary studies of non-western cultures suggest that scientific psychotherapy is not necessarily the most useful way to respond to problems of the human condition. Psychotherapy is part of a world view; it is useful *within* that world view. Outside that world view other modes of human guidance may be more appropriate. (11)

In the traditional religious systems of the world, sin is sickness, and sickness is sin. The priest is the physician, and the physician is the priest. Religious systems define the nature of man, how he should live, and how to restore a man to function. Religious systems are systems of human guidance. Psychotherapy is a system of human guidance. Thus we can visualize psychotherapy as *one* system among *other* systems of human guidance.

Heretofore, discussions on psychiatry and religion have been framed in terms of mono-valued worlds of existence. Representatives from both sides put forth their interpretations of human beings as the more adequate. Or one group would interpret all the perspectives of the other group as merely variants of their own view—"We are doing the same thing but using a different language," they might say. Or both groups would propose ways to collaborate. But the basic problem remained: man's life was seen, interpreted, experienced within a mono-valued sphere of being. (12)

However, this era has now come to an end. Whereas the various religious systems of human guidance offered man a certainty of life and a security of truth, the modern age of science, with psychotherapy as its handmaiden, offered a new certainty and a new truth. Yet the progress of the scientific study of man reveals that we are inverted upon ourselves. Our science tells us that we cannot attain certainty and we cannot know truth. And so the psychotherapeutic way turns out to be as arbitrary as the religious way.

Our fellow psychoanalytic colleague, Allan Wheelis, concludes his recent observations on the nature of man thus:

> At the beginning of the Modern Age science did, indeed, promise certainty. It does no longer. Where we now retain the conviction of certainty we do so on our own presumption, while the advancing edge of science warns that absolute truth is a fiction, is a longing of the heart, and not to be had by man. . . . Our designations of evil are as fallible now as they were ten thousand years ago; we simply are better armed now to act on our fallible vision. (13)

So where does that leave us? We can no longer pretend. The cultural cloudedness has been blown away. We see clearly in our consciousness that we stand naked in the world. Nietzche is said to have run in the streets, crying: Fall on your knees and weep, for God is dead! And after him the preeminent philosopher of our times, Jean Paul Sartre, looked out on the streets of science. And Sartre saw that science too was dead! So after all this, man is alone, desolate, forlorn. He has nowhere to turn to find out how to be.

What shall we do? Shall we turn out the clergy, depose the scientists, shun the psychotherapist?

Nihilism and pessimism, ennui and despair are one answer. Frantic and frenetic activity to drown out consciousness is another. Or we can go on with our myths of religion and our myths of science, playing a game with our consciousness to the effect that we really don't know what we know.

Yet still another way exists—or is it ways? Paul Tillich called it *the Courage to Be*. It is the willingness to look at man in full consciousness. It is learning to become a "multi-cultural" man. It is the acquisition of new ego-coping skills not dependent on certainty and truth. It is the recognition that there are many ways (for me) to paint a picture of man, and many ways to live in accord with the picture I paint. (14)

In order to live life, to decide and act, to extract satisfaction and meaning, I must paint *A* picture of man. I must commit myself to *A* way of life. But I cannot and will not confuse *A* way with *THE* way. To walk through the dim lit forest of life I must hack out a path, while others hack out theirs.

Finding A Way

This then leads us to the focus of this book. Man does not exist unto himself. We fall in the forest and we are stymied by the thickets. Human societies are bands of wanderers who aid each other. This book is about the various bands of humans, about the way each band describes their path, about the way each band provides guidance and assistance, one member to another.

In the modern age the human helping profession of psychotherapy has developed within the amoral, areligious world of science and technology. It would be tempting to view the psychotherapeutic structure of helping as normative. But it is not. The intent of this book is to describe the human systems of guidance. Sometimes these systems involve large bands of wanderers—those who live within the world views of the great religions. Sometimes the bands of wanderers are small—and their systems of guidance seem to us esoteric because they are unfamiliar. We are asked to compare these systems of guidance with the psychotherapy system of guidance. Let us, however, remember that comparison is not a normative judgment.

One final question confronts us. To what extent are we bound within the system to which we are committed? How far can we stray from our path through the forest, how far can we stray from our own band of wanderers? And then, how effectively can we help a member of another band struggling along in his way that is not my way?

Lest we rush into judgement, based on our own psychotherapeutic experience, we should recall that the patients we see are self-selected. They know the path of psychotherapy. Nor perhaps should we look with envy and naïve admiration at the helpers and gurus, going along tracks in other systems, as if they had somehow held on to truths and skills that we have lost in the scientific quest.

As I read the chapters of this book one after another, I kept wanting to draw conclusions and to make interpretations from my spot in the forest. Yet I know this misses the point. Perhaps that is the overweaning hubris of the psychotherapist, or any other healer. We *need* to do things our way, we *need* to believe in what we are doing, we *need* to be committed to our path and our way of helping. Let us continue to be committed; we cannot function without that commitment. But let us also look at ourselves with a clear consciousness as we trudge through the forest.

Irvine, California   E. MANSELL PATTISON, M.D.

REFERENCES AND FOOTNOTES

1 Cf. E. M. Pattison: Ego Morality: An Emerging Psychotherapeutic Concept. In *Psychoanalytic Review*, 55: 187–222, 1968. Also J. H. van den Berg: *The Changing Nature of Man. Introduction to a Historical Psychology*. New York, Delta Books, 1961.
2 Needleman, J.: *The New Religions*. Garden City, Doubleday, 1970.
3 See S. Z. Klausner (ed.): *The Quest for Self-Control. Classical Philosophies and Scientific Research*. New York, Free Press, 1965.
4 Levi-Strauss, C.: *The Savage Mind*. Chicago, University of Chicago Press. 1966.
5 See C. Kluckhohn's Introduction to *Reader in Comparative Religion: An Anthropological Approach* (W. A. Lessa and E. Z. Vogt, eds.). New York, Harper & Row, 1966.
6 Wallace, A. F. C.: *Religion: An Anthropological View*. New York, Random House. 1966.
7 Pattison, E. M.: Ego Morality: An Emerging Psychotherapeutic Concept. From *Psychoanalytic Review*, 55: 187–222, 1968.
8 Rieff, P. *The Triumph of the Therapeutic: Uses of Faith After Freud*. New York, Harper & Row, 1966.
9 Margolis, J.: *Psychotherapy and Morality: A Study of Two Concepts*. New York, Random House, 1966.
10 Pattison, E. M.: Social and Psychological Aspects of Religion in Psychotherapy. From *J Nerv Ment Dis*, 141: 586–597, 1966.
11 For examples see the following: J. D. Frank: *Persuasion and Healing*; A. Kiev (ed.): *Magic, Faith and Healing*; and A. W. Watts: *Psychotherapy East and West*.
12 Cf. E. M. Pattison: Social and Psychological Aspects of Religion in Psychotherapy; and E. M. Pattison (ed.): *Clinical Psychiatry and Religion*, Boston, Little Brown, 1969.
13 Wheelis, A.: *The End of the Modern Age*. New York, Basic Books, 1971.
14 In this connection see in the Bibliography the books edited by I. Galdston and S. Z. Klausner; together with F. R. Kluckhohn and F. L. Strodtbeck: *Variations in Value Orientations*; C. Levi-Strauss: *The Savage Mind*; J. Needleman: *The New Religions*; and B. G. Rosenthal: *The Images of Man*.

BIBLIOGRAPHY

1. Frank, J. D.: *Persuasion and Healing*. Baltimore, Johns Hopkins Press, 1961.
2. Galston, I. (ed.): *Man's Image in Medicine and Anthropology*. New York, International Universities Press, 1963.
3. Kiev, A. (ed.): *Magic, Faith, and Healing*. New York, Free Press, 1964.
4. Klausner, S. Z. (ed.): *The Quest for Self-Control. Classical Philosophies and Scientific Research*. New York, Free Press, 1965.
5. Kluckhohn, C.: Introduction to *Reader in Comparative Religion: An Anthropological Approach* (W. A. Lessa and E. Z. Vogt, eds.), 2nd ed. New York, Harper & Row, 1966.
6. Kluckhohn, F. R. and Strodtbeck, F. L.: *Variations in Value Orientations*. Evanston, Row, Peterson, 1961.
7. Levi-Strauss, C.: *The Savage Mind*. Chicago, University of Chicago Press, 1966.
8. Margolis, J.: *Psychotherapy and Morality: A Study of Two Concepts*. New York, Random House, 1966.

9. Needleman, J.: *The New Religions.* Garden City: Doubleday, 1970.
10. Pattison, E. M. (ed.): *Clinical Psychiatry and Religion.* Boston, Little Brown, 1969.
11. Pattison, E. M.: Ego Morality: An Emerging Psychotherapeutic Concept. From *Psychoanalytic Review, 55:* 187–222, 1968.
12. Pattison, E. M.: Social and Psychological Aspects of Religion in Psychotherapy. From *J Nerv Ment Dis, 141:* 586–597, 1966.
13. Rieff, P.: *The Triumph of the Therapeutic: Uses of Faith After Freud.* New York, Harper & Row, 1966.
14. Rosenthal, B. G.: *The Images of Man.* New York, Basic Books, 1971.
15. van den Berg, J. H.: *The Changing Nature of Man. Introduction to a Historical Psychology.* New York, Delta Books, 1961.
16. Wallace, A. F. C.: *Religion: An Anthropological View.* New York, Random House, 1966.
17. Watts, A. W.: *Psychotherapy East and West.* New York, Pantheon Books, 1961.
18. Wheelis, A.: *The End of the Modern Age.* New York, Basic Books, 1971.

PREFACE

Man's search for answers to the problems of human existence has led him from soothsayers to psychotherapists. He has sought guidance on an individual and a group basis. This guidance has often resulted in organized institutions of a religious, political or philosophical nature. Man has attempted to have "right" and "wrong" defined and promises of "happiness here and hereafter" assured. As we know very well, such insatiable needs have led to many religions and systems of human guidance. No doubt many people have found hope, while others have only been further confused and some perhaps even exploited. Such systems have affected both the rich and the poor from all educational and social strata. In spite of the innumerable systems the world has known, attempts at new methods and revisions of old methods are continually being advanced. Twentieth century man can no longer make the simplistic inquiry as to which single system offers the whole truth, but must take parts of many systems and integrate them into an individually redemptive gestalt which allows his real person to find expression in a philosophy that is both pragmatic and existential.

It is the editor's desire that this volume present many systems of guidance by which various groups of peoples attempt to answer their questions about human existence. Each author has been encouraged to use his own style and present his material in his own way. Although all of the degrees, positions, status and experience of the individual contributors are not listed, they all have highly specialized credentials in their respective fields, as well as expertise with regard to the particular chapter relating religion and psychotherapy herein presented. Through such ecumenical understanding it is hoped that both the science and art of living will become individually transcended to that which makes us mortal creatures.

This volume has been undertaken as a result of grappling with religion and psychotherapy as companion disciplines for many years and as a result of serving as Chairman of the Committee on Religion and Psychotherapy for the Division of Psychotherapy (Division 29) of the American Psychological Association.

As editor, I am grateful to the international organizations which have been responsible for utilizing my consultative services in many parts of the world, thus allowing a first-hand experience with numerous religious systems. The creative thinking of the many contributors to this volume, as well as the assistance of my wife and office staff, is gratefully acknowledged.

La Jolla, California
RICHARD H. COX, PH.D.

CONTENTS

	Page
Foreword: Making Paths Through the Forest of Life E. Mansell Pattison	ix
Preface Richard H. Cox, *Editor*	xix

Chapter

1. AN INTRODUCTION TO HUMAN GUIDANCE ... 3
   Richard H. Cox

PART ONE
MAJOR RELIGIOUS SYSTEMS

2. COUNSELING AND THE INTEGRATION OF RELIGIOUS VALUES—
   ROMAN CATHOLICISM ... 15
   Charles A. Curran

3. LIBERAL PROTESTANT THEOLOGY AND HUMANISTIC
   THEORIES OF PSYCHOTHERAPY ... 32
   William R. Rogers

4. PROTESTANTISM AND PSYCHOTHERAPY ... 46
   Paul E. Johnson

5. PROTESTANTISM (CONSERVATIVE–EVANGELICAL) AND THE THERAPIST ... 56
   John M. Vayhinger

6. CHRISTIAN SCIENCE AND SPIRITUAL HEALING ... 72
   Walter I. Wardwell

7. THE SEVENTH-DAY ADVENTIST FAITH AND PSYCHOTHERAPY ... 89
   Harrison S. Evans

8. MORMONISM AND PSYCHOTHERAPY ... 98
   C. Jay Skidmore

9. JUDAISM: A PSYCHOLOGICALLY ORIENTED PHILOSOPHY ... 108
   Emanuel M. Honig

Chapter	Page
10. MAHAYANA BUDDHISM	117
Delwin Byron Schneider	
11. ZEN AND PSYCHOTHERAPY	132
Bingham Dai	
12. THERAVADA BUDDHISM AND PSYCHOTHERAPY	142
Roy C. Amore	
13. ISLAM	156
John Racy	
14. HINDUISM, PSYCHOTHERAPY, AND THE HUMAN PREDICAMENT	167
Agehananda Bharati	
15. CONFUCIANISM AND TAOISM	180
Ch'u Chai and Winberg Chai	
16. EASTERN ORTHODOXY AND PSYCHOTHERAPY	195
Issa J. Khalil	

PART TWO
INDIGENOUS AND EMERGENT RELIGIOUS SYSTEMS

17. MAGIC, FAITH AND HEALING IN MODERN PSYCHIATRY	225
Ari Kiev	
18. PRIMITIVE PSYCHOTHERAPY	236
Wolfgang Lederer	
19. MASTERS OF METAPHYSICS	254
Roger M. Lauer	
20. GESALT, BIOENERGETICS AND ENCOUNTER: NEW WINE WITHOUT WINESKINS	268
Joseph Havens	
21. EXORCISM AND PSYCHOTHERAPY: A CASE OF COLLABORATION	284
E. Mansell Pattison	
22. THE PEYOTE RELIGION AND HEALING	296
Robert L. Bergman	

Chapter	Page
23. MYSTICAL EXPERIENCE AND THE CERTAINTY OF BELONGING: AN ALTERNATIVE TO INSIGHT AND SUGGESTION IN PSYCHOTHERAPY Raymond Prince	307
24. RELIGION AS A MEDIATING INSTITUTION IN ACCULTURATION Joan Halifax and Hazel H. Weidman	319

PART THREE
PLURALISM: MULTIPLE SYSTEMS

25. THE MAN UPSTAIRS Harry C. Stamey	335
26. PSYCHOTHERAPY AND THE "NEW MORALITY" AS SOURCES OF PERSONAL VALUES C. Marshall Lowe	344
27. HUMANISTIC PSYCHOLOGY, THERAPY, RELIGION, AND VALUES John A. Hammes	355
28. PSYCHOANALYSIS AND RELIGION: A METAPSYCHOLOGICAL APPROACH TO RELIGIOUS DATA Edgar Draper	369
29. RELIGIOUS PROBLEMS OF COLLEGE STUDENTS Truman G. Esau	388
30. ETHICS AS THE MORAL CODES MEN LIVE BY AND THE ESSENTIALS OF HUMAN WELL-BEING Sylvanus M. Duvall	403
31. CAN RELIGION AND PSYCHOTHERAPY BE HAPPILY MARRIED?— AN EXPERIMENT IN EDUCATION Paul W. Clement and Neil Clark Warren	417
32. TRANSCENDING THE ROLE OF PSYCHOTHERAPIST Vin Rosenthal	427
33. THE PSYCHOTHERAPIST AS PRIEST, PROPHET, HOLY MAN, "RELIGIOUS" EDUCATOR AND PERSON Jules Barron	435

Chapter	Page
34. Prophets as Psychotherapists, and Psychotherapists as Prophets	439
Sidney M. Jourard	
35. Is the Small–Groups Movement a Religious Revolution?	447
O. Hobart Mower	
36. The Psychotherapist as Priest	452
E. Mark Stern	
37. There's No Turning Back	458
Irma Lee Shepherd	
Index	461

RELIGIOUS SYSTEMS AND PSYCHOTHERAPY

CHAPTER 1

AN INTRODUCTION TO HUMAN GUIDANCE

RICHARD H. COX

SINCE MAN HAS, from his beginning, sought guidance, it can be safely assumed that he has felt lost. The feeling of being lost has led him into untold insecurity, frustration and pain. In his search for direction, he has turned from one philosophy to another and from one leader to another. Of all the systems of human guidance to which man has turned, he has most consistently and relentlessly returned to religion as offering "ultimate truth." In actuality, "truth" has come to mean security. Security against ignorance—i.e. "*God* knows, I don't *have to* know"; security against fear—i.e. "an all powerful God," etc. Hence, a theology of an omniscient, omnipotent, omnipresent and indestructible Supreme Being.

It is my belief that all of man's problems are basically religious. Whether the problems are defined as physical, philosophical or spiritual, it has been demonstrated that whatever pain they bring, it is relative: relative to when and how relief will come, and to the assurance of the permanence of that relief. Herein lies the essential difference between philosophy and religion: religion differs from philosophy in that it requires faith. Man discusses *philosophies* of pain, but he turns to *religion* for the relief of that pain in accordance with that which is consistent with his internal value system. Man turns to that which he believes is truth and to that which through his faith offers hope. The problems of human existence have to do with values—i.e. with what he believes is "right" and " wrong." In other words, man searches for what to him is ego-syntonic, ethno-syntonic and socio-syntonic.

It has been demonstrated in primitive cultures that persons in extreme physical pain will not accept a cure which is not in accord with what they and their fellow men believe to be "right." I have personally observed patients in "primitive" societies who have refused what might have been a life-saving operation because it was not consistent with their value system. For instance, to some peoples it is not "right" to mutilate the body even in a life-saving surgical operation since it will leave the body scarred. Many of the chapters in this volume help us to understand the complexities of interrelating faith and human suffering. We seek to transcend pain, sorrow and death. These and many more miseries frustrate, inhibit, and prohibit man from reaching not only that which to him would be ideal but also that which to him would be most gratifying.

Institutions have traditionally developed in an attempt to meet man's needs as well as his hopes and dreams. Of all institutions, religious institutions have more than any other single societal unit attempted to promise and fulfill our hopes and dreams for transcendence. The attempt to rise above the enemies of life, and the endeavor to overcome inhibitions and prohibitions thus become a *religious* effort. These attempts and endeavors may be considered religious in that they reach for transcendence via faith. Another way to put it, is to say that we seek something we can worship, something to which we can commit ourselves, and to which we can entrust our present and future well-being. Religion is that unique system which promises continuity to man, linking his past with his future, thus making his existence here and now truly valuable. Faith in this continuity is a religious value. All systems of human guidance must of necessity, recognize man's history and future. It is man's feeling that he is caught in space and time with the accumulations of the past and the hopes of the future, that makes him basically a religious creature.

THE PROBLEM

Man's basic problem is the fear of never being whole. He feels fragmented, always putting parts together, but never finding a satisfactory totality. Fragmentation results in the unavailability of man's internal and external resources at any simultaneous moment.

This fragmentation produces an inability to solve even his own individual problems. There is, of course, no promise that if such cumulative resources were available, a meaningful answer could be found. It seems that mankind requires in varying amounts mysticism, faith, and even ambiguity. Man is, therefore, attempting to offer solutions to his fellow man in the form of a religion, philosophy, guidance, etc. while at the same time struggling to find the path of hope for himself. This bifurcation causes the most painful and damaging kind of hypocrisy and dishonesty.

The fear of "*un*-wholeness" can be discussed in a variety of ways.

One way is to discuss the fear of pain. The concept of "pain" is most ambiguous in that one may say that he feels pain from a fresh wound, or one may equally well say that he feels pain from a recent death in his family. Pain is a concept, a descriptive word, a definition for that which is going on in life that fragments and tears the soul apart. In this context there is no need to differentiate between physical and emotional pain. Research has demonstrated well that one's pain threshold is relative to one's state of mind, to one's physical surroundings, and essentially to the extent to which the rest of one's life offers hope for wholeness. In some civilizations, people seek relief for minor physical discomfort. In other societies great amounts of discomfort and even excrutiating pain are endured before one would consider seeking relief from a "professional." I have witnessed persons in primitive society who wait nearly until death before believing it legitimate to seek relief.

It seems that one's consciousness of pain increases with the knowledge of available relief. In primitive societies, when there is no relief for pain available, it is accepted as part of the human situation. In modern societies, when no relief for pain is available, it is blamed on the lack of sufficient medical knowledge. In Western civilization, we are taught that man need not endure so much as a minor headache, but should reach for a pill to relieve it. Our society has attempted to alleviate pain at all levels. The poor are given financial aid, the illiterate are educated, the sorrowing are comforted, and we work to abolish "skid rows." There are no "wrongs" in such attempts to better mankind. And certainly I am not advocating that we should endure pain simply for the sake of doing so. To alleviate pain at all levels is perhaps the least that we can do for our fellow man. The problem is in gaining full understanding that such pain is ever-present and that to relieve one pain is only to expose many more. We are dealing with fragments of life, and to relieve *a* pain is not to deal with the multi-faceted aspects of the etiology of that pain. Pain, as I understand it, is the result of fragmentation. Therefore, we are not only dealing with fragments when we attack a given pain, but perhaps add to pain in the ultimate sense by dealing with it in such fragmentary ways. Man is not necessarily any more whole because he is unaware of hurt. All pain cannot be understood as "bad." Someone has said that without pain a person could die without ever knowing he was ill.

It is at this point that the problem of human existence deepens. Most of us can endure a fair amount of pain, whether it be physical or emotional. Our fear mounts because we cannot be certain of finding any person or any means to relieve the *cause* of that pain. The relief from one pain only exposes us to the next one, and the ultimate distress comes in the knowledge that one day we will have a pain that will kill us. Each pain, therefore, serves as a constant reminder of our human mortality. The knowledge of death again demonstrates our un-wholeness. It presents mankind with a predicament that is insurmountable except for some system of transcendence.

The irrevocable knowledge of pain and death are antithetical to our wishes. These facts are beyond our control and, therefore, chip away at our ego. Every human being wishes control of his destiny, both here and hereafter. Some persons by denying belief in an "hereafter" have been able to circumvent eschatology, but only the psychotic individual can deny the presence of today. Every day brings human pain and suffering and one day will bring death. With this the human situation deepens. Death not only threatens our wholeness, but creates a fear that we won't exist at all. To be less than whole *and* hurt, is one thing, but to not exist at all so that one cannot even feel hurt, is a greater threat still. The fear of "non-beingness" is simply beyond the human imagination and is psychologically intolerable.

We are earth-bound creatures. Being earth-bound means that man has only temporal methods to deal with that which is beyond his control. This simply means that we have very limited methods to deal with that which is limitless and only *micro*scopic understandings of that which is *macro*scopic. We do not want to be controlled, we want to control. We do not always want to be searching for vital knowledge, but would one day like to have the basic answers to man's great questions and be able to do research just for fun! In our attempt to find answers and to gain control, we search for cures for cancer, make attempts to reach the moon and other planets, and continue to write philosophies. Such attainments are not anti-religious, but quite the contrary. They are very religious in that these illustrations and many more are attempts at transcendence.

Conflict is evident in that so few methods have been discovered for the amelioration of the pain of fragmentation, and that no methods have been discovered to prevent death. We have not found pragmatic ways to transcend ultimate pain, for ultimate pain involves every facet of human existence, physical, emotional, environmental and interpersonal, to name only a few. Many of the elements of our fateful human existence are still unknown. It is here that the human predicament deepens even further. To be human is to suffer ambiguity and uncertainty.

Man likes to define. He likes to predict. For in definition and prediction he can plan and he can control. That which is ambiguous escapes planning and refutes reasoning. We pride ourselves on being "rational creatures." But to be human is to wrestle with ambiguity. To reason is to understand, and to understand is to gain control. But how is man to reason, understand *or* control when the only constancy seems to be change? We say that we "think," but thinking is only a matter of being able to state minutiae in a finite moment, and to know that by the time these have been stated, the very circumstances which led to a tentative truth regarding them have changed, thus making them at best only relatively true. As we all know, research is out of date by the time it is published, and technological advances are often passé by the time they can be put into production.

Religions have often capitalized on the fact that man is the victim of ambiguity and tentativeness. Often religions have simply offered their own brand of positivism which, in reality, is also ambiguous and tentative. However, the difference between science and religion is that science builds upon that which is believed to be *fact* while religion cannot survive without ambiguity, for its very basis is *faith*. Religions have appealed to faith and hope, which offer constancy, sameness, and permanence. For the most part, religion promises to leave very little to ambiguity and uncertainty. Although most religions state rather clearly that we never know the complete answer, the ambiguity and uncertainty are taken away by the demand for *total faith*. Religion states the problem, prescribes the method of salvation, and promises with absolute certainty a happy ending for the unstintingly faithful follower. But here again, the human predicament deepens. Man does not want to be a blind follower. He desires meaning and purpose for his life.

Theology is an intellectual, academic, literary construct. There is no such thing as "theology," per se. Theology is the study of God as man defines him. Nowhere is there *a theology* written down. There are *many* theologies written. Man is much more concerned with epistemology than he is with theology. That is to say, he is far more interested in *his* purpose for being than he is in the purpose of *God's* being. Thus, from the time of the early philosophers we have had libraries of books written, worded in different ways, of course, on the subject: where did man come from, what is he doing here, and where is he going? Most books on religion, philosophy, psychology, and psychiatry (as well as this book and this chapter) are no exception.

Man, then, is forced paradoxically even by his own achievements to battle with his fragmentation and to hope for wholeness, while at the same time he continues to speak of his own ultimate despair.

DIAGNOSIS

Medical students are taught that a proper diagnosis leads to a proper treatment. To diagnose man's ills as being religious is relatively simple for one trained in theology. It is a bit more difficult sometimes for one trained in both theology and psychology. Such a diagnosis is not only difficult, but often impossible for individuals trained solely in psychology, psychiatry, and other behavioral science fields.

Without attempting to discuss the "Freudian" theories, it may be stated that certainly the psychoanalytic school of thought would not accept man's basic problem as being religious in origin. Nor would most other psychological theories of personality support such a view. In his most recent book, *Beyond Freedom And Dignity*, B. F. Skinner believes man's basic problem to be environmental. However, it does not seem correct to fragment man from his environment or the enevironment from man. Nor does it seem proper to state that man's basic problem is found in a childhood fixation, or in man's self-polluted environment, but in a combination of these and of many other factors which produce a total greater than the sum of all the parts. It is my belief that man's ills lie deeply within the realization that he is a mortal creature and in his constant struggle to transcend that inevitable fate known as death, thus destroying for him the possibility of permanent wholeness.

We are at odds with our internal value systems. It is the law within that condemns. When a person transgresses a law in which he does not believe, he does not feel guilty. He may cease to transgress that law simply because the results are painful, but his "conscience" does not condemn him. The more rigid the system and the greater one's belief in it, the more difficult it is to find absolution and the greater is the condemnation which is forthcoming. Persons wholeheartedly believing in systems that demand specific penalties for specific transgressions, have no alternatives for the reduction of guilt. In most religions the *sinner* seeks conversion to become a *saint* but finds that as a saint he continues to be a sinner and must constantly pay various prices in an attempt to reach and maintain "sainthood."

Every man has some kind of an internal value system. It is impossible to function without such. Some actions and beliefs demand priority over others, thus producing a system. Some individuals have more deeply imbedded value systems than others, and it is impossible to know the origin of most values. It is not sufficient to say of a man's value system that "it depends upon his upbringing." Rigid value structures are found among persons reared in the most so-called "non-religious" backgrounds, and conversely, very limited feelings of guilt are often found among these from the most "religious" backgrounds.

The diagnosis of an individual's problem is most difficult. Furthermore, the diagnosis varies according to the nature of the practitioner making the diagnosis. Illustrative of this is the person who presents himself to the minister and confesses a theft. The minister as a religious man utilizes a theological nosology and treats the problem as "sin." The same person may present the same problem to a psychotherapist and in the psychological framework be treated as a "sick" person who needs psychotherapy. Actually, both are doing the same thing. They are diagnosing the problem, defining it, labeling it, as well as allowing the person to accept himself as being in need of help. Both professionals are attempting to reach similar goals, but they utilize different vocabularies and diagnostic labels. Both professionals set out to do exactly the same thing, namely, structure a method by which the individual can transcend his problem. This is done by a variety of means and by the remedial person "prescribed" within their system. Within some systems it will be the witch doctor and in other systems a minister, while in still other systems a psychotherapist. The means will vary from walking barefoot on beds of hot coals to lying on a couch free-associating. Vocabularies will range from simply saying that the problem must be *resolved,* to asserting that the individual must gain *forgiveness,* to saying, finally, that the wrongdoer must claim simple *acceptance* of the wrongdoing.

All of these systems, however, attempt to build a method by which the individual deals with his *guilt,* not the deed. The deed has been committed and even with the most extreme restitution, that original deed remains. It is the *value* with which man must grapple, regardless of what he calls it. It is his understanding of the consequences of his deed, and the meaning of that deed. The label he puts upon it will not substitute in any way for the value he ascribes to the actual deed itself. The language of diagnosis is complex and interesting. Different disciplines use various terms to designate the same action. In modern medicine a diagnosis is arrived at by the accumulation of symptoms. The more clinically proven those symptoms can be, the more accurate the diagnosis. In psychodiagnosis, the symptoms are often much less important. The interpretation of the symptoms is more important, and it is that interpretation which leads to a diagnosis.

It is most interesting to study Jesus' method of diagnosis. He most often simply accepted the patient's (or family member's) diagnosis. He did not redefine people's problems in a new language. He took their language for their problem. He didn't even argue as to what they called it. We really don't know whether the man that was called *blind* was blind, as we would define the word in medical language today. We only know that he called his affliction "blindness" and that, after Christ's healing, he called his new state of being, the ability to see. Jesus never assumed that there was any kind of healing power in the diagnosis.

As one reads the chapters in this book, he becomes keenly aware that most religions deal with evil as a very specific entity rather than as a result of man's problems. It seems to me that the primary reason for insisting upon a diagnosis that fits a given religious, philosophical, psychological, or other vocabulary, is that without a specific semantic label it is difficult, if not impossible, to fit an individual's problem into a consistent nomenclature. It is not really important in the long run whether a man's problem is called sickness or sin if that individual can be helped to transcend the crippling effects and the pain of that problem.

TREATMENT

Whatever the method of treatment, it must allow the human to transcend his own human predicament. In other words, that treatment must allow man to find continuity. By continuity I mean a method of relating his past with his present and his present with his future. Ultimate health and happiness for man comes in believing that he is part of a whole greater than himself. Whether the end result is called "health," "salvation," or simply "peace of mind," the final end must allow man to come to grips with his real human-ness and to find relief from the pangs of guilt and the depths of sorrow. The treatment must offer at least the following ingredients: the attainment of one's ego-ideal, some reasonable explanation of how things fit together, and the possibility of dealing with both the absurdities and the purposes of being.

Psychotherapy utilizes a cognitive-insight-emotive framework as treatment. Whether the framework be psychoanalysis or behavior modification, the patient comes to understand that his actions and his feelings must correlate if he is to live at peace with himself and his fellow man. His internal value system must match his exterior behavior pattern. When this goal is achieved, man is probably the closest to what religionists would call *redemption* and what psychotherapists would call *health*.

Religion treats the human predicament by prescribing certain methods of behavior as well as certain dogmas of belief. These methods and ideologies often include restitution. The transcendence is forthcoming in the knowledge of having completed a prescribed ritual which then makes one acceptable to his fellow man and, by his own religious dogma, acceptable to God.

The treatment is not a matter of transcending one's value system. We cannot rise above that which we believe. We can only transcend the *judgement* of the value system. Protestant Christians, for instance, often state that Christ transcended the law for them, meaning that Christ has established a method of redemption on a higher order than legalism. It could easily be argued that Christ did exactly what every man must do for himself, namely, learn how to transcend the judgement of the law for himself. The Biblical concept of "grace" was not invented by Jesus. He demonstrated what is termed "God's grace," but the elaborate rituals of the Old Testament testify so well to the effectiveness of man's attainment of grace, by showing how to transcend the judgement of their own law. One only has to read the accounts of the offerings and sacrifices in the Old Testament to substantiate this.

Many of the chapters in this book further illustrate how religions much older than Christianity have found methods of releasing what might be called "grace" upon their followers when certain rituals are accompanied by prescribed beliefs. It is my belief, however, that to accept the totally mystical theory of forgiveness and grace is to deny man his responsible place in his own actions and destiny. Further, it seems that man must be a responsible partner in the act of his own redemption. Modern man often assumes that he has moved beyond primitive religions in that he no longer sacrifices his children or his animals in an attempt to assure his own salvation. This is a serious mistake from both psychological and theological points of view. Anyone who has had much experience with psychotherapy and with religious institutions, realizes full well that many monetary and physical prices are extracted and paid for that which, in our modern jargon, is called "health" or "redemption."

By what channel the "treatment" comes is probably not important. It is of ultimate importance that man establish a line of integrity between that which he believes and himself. It is also imperative that man establish a line of integrity between himself and his past. It is equally important that that line of integrity be established between himself and his future. Furthermore, that line of integrity must be established between man himself and his fellow men, individually and collectively. The interception of those lines of integrity promises the greatest fulfillment and the greatest possibility for transcendence. The establishment of such a consistent and all-encompassing system affords a congruence between what "I think," what I "feel," and how I "behave."

What man calls his problem is therefore probably not important. It may not even be terribly important who treats his problem. It is not important whether he knows the correct social, psychological, religious or medical jargon with which to assign a technical diagnosis to it. Certainly we have learned that a vast variety of treatment methods seem to produce similar results. The important thing is that man recognizes that he *has a problem*, and that the problem is in the very structure of his being and not the result of things which go wrong around him.

BIBLIOGRAPHY

1. Brantl, George (ed.): *Catholicism*. New York, Braziller, 1962.
2. Castaneda, Carlos: *The Teachings of Don Juan: A Yaqui Way Of Knowledge*. New York, Ballantine, 1969.
3. Dunstan, J. Leslie (ed.): *Protestantism*. New York, Braziller, 1962.
4. Gard, Richard A. (ed.): *Buddhism*. New York, Braziller, 1962.
5. Heideggar, Martin: *An Introduction to Metaphysics*. Anchor Books edition. Garden City, Doubleday, 1961.
6. Henry, William E., Sims, John H., and Spray, S. Lee: *The Fifth Profession*. San Francisco, Jossey-Bass, 1971.
7. Hertzberg, Arthur (ed.): *Judaism*. New York, Braziller, 1962.
8. Holmes, Ernest: *The Science of Mind* (Rev. and enlarged). New York, Dodd, Mead, 1966.
9. Jones, W. T.: *A History of Western Philosophy, Kant to Wittgenstein and Sartre*, 2nd ed. New York, Harcourt, 1952.
10. May, Rollo: *Man's Search for Himself*. New York, Norton, 1953.
11. Pattison, E. Mansell (ed.): *Clinical Psychiatry and Religion*. Boston, Little, 1969.
12. Renou, Louis (ed.): *Hinduism*. New York, Braziller, 1962.
13. Teilhard de Chardin, Pierre: *The Phenomenon of Man*. New York, Harper, 1959.
14. Williams, John Alden: *Islam*. New York, Braziller, 1962.

Part One

MAJOR RELIGIOUS SYSTEMS

CHAPTER 2

COUNSELING AND THE INTEGRATION OF RELIGIOUS VALUES

Roman Catholicism

CHARLES A. CURRAN

LIKE MANY AREAS of both religious and daily living, Roman Catholicism is undergoing significant changes. There is, therefore, no simple viewpoint that represents it. We cannot, then, claim that this presentation or any other, for that matter, would be authoritative or official. What we propose to do, rather, is to take one basic tradition around the concept of counsel and extend it into the modern realm of counseling, psychotherapy and personality integration.

This approach will certainly not be complete. It leaves out many elements and is more focussed on counseling normal people than on therapy. But it does represent one significant aspect of counseling and therapy related to personal values as it has developed recently in Catholic counseling and guidance circles.

We can perhaps best approach a discussion of the relationship between religion and psychotherapy from the viewpoint of Roman Catholicism then, by considering it under the general heading of counseling. In Section I we will discuss the basic aspects of counseling and its extension as a therapeutic aid in the resolution of personal and interpersonal emotional conflict and confusion. But we do not see counseling as being limited only to people who are in emotional conflict and confusion and, consequently, in need of therapy. In a far broader application, it relates to the whole of life and to the individual's entire value system. In Section II, therefore, we will consider counseling in its relationship to the whole spectrum of learning, where learning is viewed as the internalizing of meanings, resulting in the acquisition of unique values. For it is a man's value system, that which he invests in, that is ultimately therapeutic or nontherapeutic for him.

SECTION I: GENERAL ASPECTS OF COUNSELING

Clarification Of Terms

One of the complexities in a discussion of counsel in its traditional sense, and of counseling in the modern sense, is the confusion that exists in the meaning of the term itself. Words like "guidance" and "counseling" have been, and still are, often used interchangeably in much of educational literature. While in general these two terms are distinguished from education as such, they are increasingly becoming an important and even an essential part of the education process. This has been recognized and encouraged by government-sponsored Institutes for teachers held in large University centers throughout the United States.

In the fields of psychology and psychiatry, moreover, the terms "counseling" and "psychotherapy" are often used without any clear distinction. While psychotherapy is generally considered to be the domain of the psychiatrist it is, in fact, also practiced by psychologists. And while psychologists are perhaps more commonly thought to practice counseling, this term is sometimes used to refer to the work of the psychiatrist, particularly in the area of marriage counseling.

Because of the evident confusion and ambiguity that still exist in the use of the word "counseling," applied either to an educational, psychological, psychiatric, or social work setting, it is premature to attempt its final definition. We will therefore not attempt to differentiate it too sharply from guidance on the one hand or psychotherapy on the other. Nor will we attempt to relate counseling to any precise background, training, or professional setting. Both its meaning and its use are still so broad at the present time that such precise application, in a general discussion such as this, seems unfitting.

One distinction, however, that might be made—at the risk of oversimplification—between counseling and psychotherapy would be to say that psychotherapy is concerned with the greater complexity of personality problems, whereas counseling is primarily concerned with those issues and conflicts more related to the normal personality. And the distinction of counseling from guidance and education can be seen in the anomaly of a person who possesses sufficient knowledge of what he should do and is yet unable to put into practice what he knows. This conflict between knowing and doing is continually encountered by people in education, guidance, counseling, social case work, and other similar relationships, so much so that it seems to be a universal aspect of the normal personality. While the same conflict exists in extremely disturbed persons and so has to be dealt with in psychotherapy, it seems to give counseling a more general application to people everywhere—in schools, in hospitals, in industry, and in other social institutions.

A brief glance at the historical development of counseling and psychotherapy can also be of aid in seeing a distinction between the two terms. Counseling, concomitant with guidance, seems to be almost exclusively an American development, whereas psychotherapy, particularly in its psychoanalytic aspects, was originally almost exclusively European. While these two developments have fused and mutually affected one another now, some basis for their separate growth might be found in the social and cultural attitudes of America as contrasted with those of Europe. Universal education in America had as its ideal a concern for each person in the educative process. Included in this concern was the need to offer help to those faced with academic problems, vocational choices, and personality difficulties. In light of this it is understandable that guidance and counseling should have had a largely educational origin in the United States. In Europe, on the other hand, medical practice has tended to include both psychiatry and psychology as parts of its area of concern. One can see, then, that concern for personality conflicts would stem out of a medical background in Europe rather than an educational one, since the effort to educate everyone was never so completely undertaken in Europe as in the United States.

The Nature Of Counseling

With the above clarifications in mind we can examine more specifically the nature of counseling as it relates to the traditional concept of "counsel." A major factor in personal conflict and unhappiness, as Aristotle and Aquinas pointed out, is the fact that a person can seek an apparent good which satisfies one or another of his needs but which is actually contrary to the overall *reasonable* good of his whole person. Personal problems arise because an individual's craving for particular personal, emotional, or sensual satisfactions lead him away from the reasonable goals which he ultimately seeks. A man is, therefore, capable of a complex self-deception. He can allow himself to be misled by particular urges to objects and goals which he knows will not really satisfy him nor ultimately be good for him.

It is at this point that counsel, the first act of prudence, is needed. Aquinas tells us:

> Prudence is the right reason applied to action. . . . Hence that which is the chief act of reason in regard to action must needs be the chief act of prudence. Now

> there are three such acts. The first is to *take counsel*, which belongs to discovery, for counsel is an act of inquiry. . . . The second act is *to judge of what one has discovered*, and this is an act of the speculative reason. But the practical reason, which is directed to action, goes further, and its third act is *to command*, which act consists in applying to action the things counseled and judged. . . . (1)

Personal difficulties usually come from the disorder of our emotions at war and in conflict with our reason. Either we guide our emotions or we are guided by them. The mass of details of life are apt at times to overwhelm us and leave us confused and disorganized. We need to reorganize ourselves. The core of this self-organization is prudence. But prudence is often popularly misunderstood. It is not simply caution, hesitancy in action, or mere passivity to avoid trouble; nor is it just a kind of inborn cleverness, as is sometimes supposed. Prudence is the ability to act reasonably and it can be acquired. But, because of the individual character of our actions, prudence as such cannot be taught.

The first act of prudence, as we noted in quoting Aquinas, is called *counsel* and it consists of a process of survey and inquiry. This process will be different for each person because of the almost infinite variety of possible conditions, circumstances, situations, and personalities that can in one way or another affect our choice of methods or means. And while prudence itself cannot be taught, its development through counsel can be greatly aided by the skill of a counselor. But the skill of the counselor does not of itself consist in giving advice or providing direct information. Both facts and general knowledge of the speculative and practical sciences are taken for granted since the purpose of counsel is directly related to immediate action.

The counseling relationship as such, therefore, is for the purpose of integrating the knowledge of one's past and present in those circumstances and events that are so intimately related to a person that he alone can adequately know and control them. It is this function that is particularly the field of counsel as the first phase of man's prudential judgement and action. To advance and aid this is the main characteristic of counseling.

In developing counsel and prudence, then, those skills are needed by the counselor which further responsibility, self-direction, and self-control in the individual coming for help. The problems of each person's life are so interwoven with the many minute factors in his own past and present that a completely prudent judgement about them could hardly be made by any one but himself. An approach to the process of survey and inquiry where by the counselor tends to take over and make decisions about another's personal problems, appears to weaken rather then further a person's prudential judgement. The person seeking help may quietly acquiesce to the counselor's judgement, but he is no better off when he must face new problems alone.

The Process Of Counseling

Having briefly considered how counsel is related to prudence as its first act, we can now discuss the process by which a person arrives at more reasonable and adequate choices. The change in personal values resulting from the counseling relationship invariably involves a shift in focus from the self of the client to others. Such change includes an increasingly broader realization of all the factors involved. This, in turn, results in a changing perception of what is truly good, and thus one's choices and actions change. To illustrate this, we will present an excerpt from a second counseling interview and contrast it with the insight stage of the tenth interview with the same person.

The data we will present were drawn from a series of interviews, the main point of which centered around a married woman in a serious infatuation with another man. In the second interview, the only thing the woman considers beyond herself and the man (John) is seen in the brief phrase: "I've got people I don't want to hurt either." In the whole of the first and second interview the above statement represents the only expression of consideration for anyone or anything outside of herself and John. But if we contrast this limited view with the insight stage of the tenth interview, we see a striking change in perception. The superimposed image of John and herself has given way to a vastly different picture of the total situation:

> When John and I were together it just sort of pushed everything else into the background. But you just can't turn aside and say, "Well, I'm going back to where I was," even though if I really wanted to I couldn't do that. It's hard to give up John after all the good times we've had and the things we've done, but when you stop and think what could have happened why you see things different. (Long pause) But I know even now, just by not seeing John, I'm better physically and spiritually too. Yes, the way it was before I wasn't really happy. It was just a state of conflict and misery and fear of being found out, and thinking of the kids and all. . . . No, it really wasn't happy, even when it seemed most enjoyable. There's no happiness in it. You're always under a constant strain. (Pause) I'll lose a lot in a worldly way, but I'll gain too. I would gain more than I would lose spiritually.

One might observe here the perceptual language in the phrase, "When John and I were together it just sort of pushed everything into the background." This statement seems to suggest that the superimposed image of "John and I" blocked out the overall awareness of her responsibilities to her husband, family, and God. The second phrase, "But when you stop and think what could have happened why you see things different," suggests that the thinking process of the counseling interviews also brought about a different self-perception. When we look for the difference in perceptions, it seems to be the removal of the superimposed, narrowed focus on "John and I", replaced by a broad reality awareness of responsibilities to husband, children, and God. Now, even though giving up John is a severe sacrifice when she reflects on the pleasure John brought her, she sees herself to be better off physically and spiritually when her perceptions are clearly on the total field of responsibilities.

Stated in goal-directed language, the superimposed image is itself an *apparent* good. The self tends to move toward this apparent good until its perceptions are broadened and the reasoning and insightful action of the personality, in this case engendered through counseling, brings out from the background the *real* good, the total perceptual field. This puts into its proper perceptual organization the *immediate* good which, in this case, was the relationship with John. When the immediate good is measured against the total perceptual field of all values involved, the self chooses and moves towards the relationship of husband, children, and God as the *real* good, and rejects the apparent good which was the narrow focus on "John and I".

The Skill Of The Counselor

Considerable skill on the part of the counselor is required for the above process to be realized. Because a long process of training and supervision is necessary to produce an adequate counselor in the professional sense, this skill can only be hinted at here. The counselor's accurate understanding and verbalization of the client's conflict and confusion aids the client in the clarification and objectification of himself. Somewhat as a mirror helps one to see himself from a different perspective and far more clearly, so each response of the counselor adds to self-awareness and gives the client courage and help in examining himself and his situation further. The following comment of a person after a counseling interview demonstrates this effect:

> I've never been listened to so well before—no one before ever cared so much about what I was saying. I have confidence in speaking. Even if what I say is foolish or stupid, I am not made to feel foolish or stupid. I trust the counselor to hold what I say and not to let it slip or become blurred. In such a situation I can react to myself and my own thoughts and feelings much as I might react to those of someone else. There is an objectivity about the counselor's responses that is freeing.

Another person said:

> When I finished last time I thought I was too confused to say anything more. Then, as I heard your responses, I somehow understood what I had said and it seemed very easy to say something further. I didn't sound really as foolish as I thought. I began to become more understandable to myself.

This reasonable objectivity about oneself in counseling does not mean a cold and mechanical analysis. On the contrary, it is only possible to a maximum degree because of the mutually deep commitment to the relationship. The commitment is made possible by a love on the counselor's part which the Greek and medieval philosophers called *amor benevolentiae*—a love that concerns only the other and his good. This they contrasted with *amor concupiscentiae* in which the person is seeking some self-determined gratification from the other. But in the commitment of mutual love of *amor benevolentiae*, the counselor is not only a catalytic agent of emotions; he is at the same time, and even more essentially, a warm, understanding, auxiliary reasoning power.

The Counseling Relationship

Counseling, at its deepest level, is both a profound relationship between the self of the counselor and the client, and an intensely searching and probing dialogue. Interwoven and mutually dependent are the understanding process itself—the dialogue—and the deepening relationship it produces—the commitment. The relationship and dialogue together aim at greater self-understanding, orientation to more adequate goals and values, and more complex operational integration and efficiency. The relationship between counselor and client is unquestionably one of great emotional and somatic significance, but it is most of all a dynamism of the giving or withholding of the selves of both counselor and client. The degree to which both commit themselves to the relationship seems to determine much of the ultimate significance of the relationship itself.

The manner in which this mutual commitment comes about, while evident to the experienced counselor, is difficult to communicate to another. On the part of the counselor it is, first of all, a genuine and complete willingness not only to see the client for a stated time at set intervals, but also, during this time, to divest himself as much as he can of all those preoccupations that ordinarily concern him. Analogous to the manner in which the surgeon "scrubs" himself before performing surgery, the counselor would enter the counseling relationship "scrubbed" of his own self-concern. Secondly, the counselor attempts to enter the "world" of the client and to identify with him as completely as possible. This does not mean that he becomes emotionally involved with the client; rather, through his empathetic sharing, he "feels with" the client and in this way enables him to clarify and objectify his emotions.

In the counseling relationship, therefore, there must be a true gift of the self—first of the self of the counselor to the client, and then, more slowly, the genuine commitment of the client. This is what constitutes a relationship of both loving and being loved, and it is the heart of the counseling relationship. Obviously, this is not love in the popular emotional or romantic sense. Rather, it seems to approximate that high kind of spiritual love which gives of itself entirely and seeks no return except the best fulfillment of the other.

Inextricably bound up with the mutual commitment in the counseling relationship is the counselor's "understanding heart". We use this expression to designate the special skill in understanding that constitutes the counselor's most difficult art. To understand another at the deepest level of his feelings and reactions is an immeasureably more profound, complex, and delicate kind of understanding than simply knowing the meaning of what a person says. While the kind of understanding that comes "from the heart" may appear simple and easy of application when one reads excerpts from skilled interviews, it is in fact a complicated and difficult skill. There are many ways in which our tendency to diagnose and judge can distort and impede our real understanding of what a person is trying to tell us.

Auxiliary Reasoning Power

We have previously referred to the skill of the counselor as providing an auxiliary reasoning power to aid the client in his self-search. We may say, in general, that when people begin to communicate personal disturbances to us we can be of great help to them if, in addition to being an empathetic listener, we can also act as an auxiliary reasoning power. It is a common experience that when a person is uninvolved in an issue, he can see its implications more clearly than one who is directly involved in it. The involved person sees the issue from an "innerview", and his presentation of it will often be interwoven with a deep feeling reaction to the experience. The value of the counselor's response is that it is also given from the "innerview", but it is uninvolved and reasonable.

Such a response will invariably be accepted by the client. It will often elicit even an enthusiastic reaction, such as, "Yes, that's it, exactly," or "Yes, that's just the way I feel." From the client's tone it would seem evident that he has gotten something significant out of himself and that he has been helped by the way his initial confused expression of himself flowed through and was understood by the counselor. Simple agreement with another, or even a neutral accepting or echoing response, seldom produces so strong an affirmation of being completely understood. Even when the counselor does choose to give guidance or direction, its acceptance by the client is more likely after an understanding atmosphere has been established. Outside of such an understanding atmosphere the advice may be quickly rejected, even though in itself it is good. Moreover, the client may be made so resistant that he does not return again. The relationship that might have been very constructive can thus be broken, perhaps permanently. Or, if the counselor disagrees and tries to "set the client straight," the client may feel that he is not understood and show increased resistance and irritation. A misunderstood person will often continue to insist on his point of view, adding still more details in an attempt to communicate.

An important point to be noted here is that the counselor responses are not interpretations of what the client is saying. They are responses to the expression of feelings and attitudes actually implied in the client statements themselves at the moment he makes them. Once a feeling or attitude, contained in the client's expression, has been clarified through the counselor's response, it continues to be subject to the client's own reasonable evaluation. This often leads to the eventual unfolding of a complex interweaving of basic life-patterns and goals which in some way conflict with one another.

Core Response

As the client begins to put together a series of causes and relationships as seen from an "innerview" of himself, he is best helped when the counselor can respond to the "hub" or core of the communication, rather than to the "spokes" or peripheral aspects of the communication. For example, if the client is speaking of previous failure to reach desired personal goals, the core communication would be his personal *inadequacy*; or if his expression is positive and hopeful, he may be communicating *satisfaction*.

The kind of counselor response that reaches the core of the communication is not simply a parroting or echoing of what the client said. Rather it is a refined, synthesized, and precise delineation of what is still very often a complex issue as the client tries to reason it out from his "innerview". The final stages of this kind of joint reasoning process often involves certain steps towards self-reorganization and a new way of acting, as well as new personal goals. This usually involves a discussion of:

Acquiring and Accepting: new views and attitudes towards self, others, and various life situations.
Changes in Fundamental Motive Patterns: as a result of new self-understanding.
Balancing and Weighing: alternate new ways of coping more effectively with personal conflicts and disorders in the way of desired goals.
Choice: of some new plans of action.
Success in Action: as a result of new plans.
Re-evaluation: of why plans succeeded or failed.
Changes in Plans: to improve performance and increase success.

Conclusion: Section I

The above schema of the general aspects of counseling and brief explanation of the counseling skill may prove helpful, especially to those readers who have not had the opportunity to acquaint themselves in detail with recent psychological research. But, as one quickly learns in studying excerpts from actual interviews, personal statements seldom appear in so orderly a fashion. They are often intricately interwoven in a complex web of intimate and often disturbing and painful circumstances.

Unless this has become clear from what has already been said, the use of categories such as those above may obstruct rather than improve the counselor's effectiveness. Such categories may only produce mechanical responses which lack a genuinely deep personal understanding and acceptance, and consequently contain no real warmth. Such responses seem seldom, if ever, to result in penetrating self-clarifications.

SECTION II: COUNSELING RELATED TO LEARNING

In Section I we discussed counseling both as it related to the traditional virtue of counsel and as an aid to people seeking the resolution of primarily emotional conflicts and confusion. In our discussion we noted the necessity of several crucial developments in the counseling relationship if the counseling process itself is to succeed. Among these developments, the main one was the mutual self-investment of the client and counselor in the search for satisfactory goals and solutions. From this mutual self-investment, not only did the client receive a sense of his own worth and dignity in being "redeemed"; but the counselor also received convalidation of his gift of self to the client.

We now wish to apply some of these counseling concepts to learning. We have called this an "incarnate-redemptive learning theory". Like our discussion of counseling we cannot, of course, claim any special "Catholic" designation for these concepts. They do, however, involve a basic incarnate and redemptive personal relationship in learning which is both new yet represents a fundamental respect for and regard of the worth and value of the whole person in the learning process. This could surely be regarded as "Catholic". In this limited sense, then, we have included this development here.

As a result of recent research in learning, (2) it has become clear that if the same deep mutual self-investment, as well as the other aspects of the counseling relationship, could be incorporated into the learning relationship, a similar mutually redemptive encounter would occur between the teacher and the students. In Section II, therefore, we will discuss learning as an incarnate-redemptive self-investment process modelled on counseling.

Change In Models

What this essentially involves is a change in the model of learning. This change is from an intellectual model or a conditioning model to one based on the concepts of counseling, psychotherapy and recent personality theory. In this model we do not think of learning as an intellectual, abstractive, reflective and symbolic process alone, nor simply as a conditioned reaction. We think of it rather as an "engagement"—as a personal self-commitment. The whole person—soma, instincts, and emotions—is involved in such self-commitment.

We are also contrasting this self-committed, whole-person learning with a learning process that is the result of competitive motivation and is often simply defensive learning. While a student's academic grades may indicate that he is learning well under competitive and emotional stress, in fact he will often later have an extremely negative reaction about what he has learned. This can sometimes result not merely in a negative attitude about learning, but a student can be so traumatized by the learning experience itself that he remains hostile to the subject matter of learning. When this happens he may turn away, in aversion, from the whole area of knowledge that the negative learning experience represents for him.

In contrast to this, we are speaking of learning which is measured finally by the degree to which the learner has genuinely invested himself in the learning process and has internalized the subject matter of learning.

Counseling And Learning Parallel

By considering the self-investment aspect of the whole person in learning, and not simply what he knows intellectually and can give back to the teacher in rote form, we are also bringing closer together the counseling and the learning process. The process by which a person invests himself in what he learns, and the counseling therapy process by which he invests in *what he wants to be* and begins to fulfill it, are very similar. We no longer see a sharp dividing line between counseling therapy and learning. Rather we are calling them both learning, either at a personal level, or at a broader educational, social and cultural level.

This idea is not necessarily new. If we consider the ancient axiom that "whatever is received is received according to the manner of the one receiving," it becomes quite evident that the whole personality structure of the learner is basic to what he finally learns as a personal self-investment. We are proposing that the degree of student self-investment would be the main focus of learning rather than simply whether adequate knowledge has been presented and intellectually understood. Basic to the measurement of real learning is not what the student gives back in evidence that he knows, but what he has personally invested in and identified with. This would involve the teacher in fundamental concepts that are not only conscious but unconscious in the student. From the learning process, as from the counseling process, implicit and explicit value systems would emerge which would aid or impede the student's cooperation in the learning experience.

Incarnate-Redemptive Learning

These conceptions bring the learning process closer to the intense somatic, instinctive, and emotional involvement of the client in counseling. The student's degree of self-worth seems to determine the extent to which he can learn openly and without defense. He sees learning, not as something attacking him and from which he must defend himself, but as something positively invoking his genuine self-investment and permanent self-identification. We have called this positive learning an incarnate as well as a redemptive self-investment process. In order for it to occur, there must often be the acceptance not simply of an intellectual and judgemental self, but also of an instinctual and emotional self. Only after such incarnate-redemptive self-acceptance can a genuine investment take place. We see this as similar to the struggle with conflicting aspects of the self that is often revealed in the process of counseling.

Language Learning Model

Considering a counseling model of learning and learning as persons, we will focus on those characteristics of learning which are seen to be basic to the learning process. For this presentation we will draw heavily from linguistic research carried out over a period of several years, and to which we referred previously. In the linguistic model, the emphasis is not so much on the learning of grammar and vocabulary as such, but on the process by which a person learns to speak a foreign language through and in the presence of natives of that language. Learning is thought of as a personal relationship similar to the counseling relationship. We have used the phrase "learning is persons" to capture the intense relationship that exists as people speak together in a foreign language. We have tried to incorporate into this kind of group learning experience the deep rapport, understanding, and sensitivity that has to exist if the counseling process is to be effective.

Looking at counseling from a language learning model, we would propose that on a level of self-knowledge, the knowing teacher is, in fact, the "I." There is a blocking between the "I" and the "myself" when the acting self, the "myself," does not carry out what the 'I" proposes. It is this blocking that causes the conflict, confusion, pain, and guilt which the client often expresses at the beginning of counseling with expressions such as, "I am disgusted with myself."

In the educative process a similar blocking often occurs between the teacher who knows and the student who, in his state of confusion and conflict, is unable to learn what the teacher knows and is trying to communicate to him.

Stages Of Learning

In the learning of foreign languages, the learning process was marked by a transition from extreme dependency, anxiety, fear, and a kind of primitive, almost embryonic state in the learner, to a growing independence and security. The struggle to become independent was indicated by the learner's almost dramatic determination to express in the foreign language those words or phrases that he knew without the help of the native expert. This expression was often accompanied by feelings of anger and aggressive self-assertion. There existed, then, in the groups a continuum from a highly dependent state beginning at Stage I and extending through Stage V. In Stage V there was a basic self-determination, self-esteem, and forceful self-assertion against being dependent on the knower. At this point the learning of the foreign language has become internalized.

In the dependency of Stage I, one might think of ignorance as similar to illness. Both force one into a kind of invalid state of regression where he is fearful, anxious, and dependent. Gaining health, like acquiring knowledge, involves the gradual mobilization of forces within the self, pushing the person into independent existence.

As we noted, the learning continuum began, in Stage I, with dependency and anxiety and extended, in Stage V, to aggression and self-determination. The contrasting states of submissive anxiety and aggressive independence characterize an inner growth in the self. The self will only tolerate the initial state of dependency and anxiety, in which help is needed, until it can gain sufficient knowledge, courage and self-assertion to reach an independent state. One can expect this growth continuum in learning provided nothing is done to impede, interrupt, or conflict with it.

Internalization Of Knowledge

Learning, viewed as a growth process from Stage I through Stage V, can be seen as a process of giving birth to a new self. In this process the teacher would be the "midwife" of learning, according to Plato's conception. The physician is often thought of as someone who has simply learned to do the things that do not impede nature's process. In this sense the teacher would be like the physician. He would do only those things which further the internal forces of the learner that lead toward independent learning.

This process is what we would call the internalization of knowledge in contrast to its initial external state. Merely to assert knowledge from the outside so that it is intellectually understood is, at best, a beginning process. For genuine internalization to take place, the self must invest totally. To do this, one's anxieties, fears, and dependency needs all must be understood and engaged as in the initial stages of counseling. As these forces are assuaged and understood, new forces of self-assertion and desire for independence begin to emerge. At the final stage, it is this independent self-assertion that marks the internalization of knowledge. There is no longer a dependency on the outside knower because now what the knower represents has been internalized and constitutes aspects of a new self for the learner.

We are applying, then, to learning what a generation ago we began to apply to the relationships of guidance, counseling, and therapy. As counseling skills developed, they focused not on external knowledge but on the internal self-awareness of the client. His struggle with himself to carry out what he was told, or what he already knew, was far more important than extrinsic advice or additional, but often unnecessary, information. Similarly in learning, the mere increment of facts, if it fails to take cognizance of the learner's struggle to digest and personalize these facts, leaves them inoperational.

A Mimetic Bind

To explicate the process from externalization to internalization of knowledge, we use the phrase "mimetic internalization." Learning begins with a mimetic bind between the learner and the knower (from Plato's idea of *mimesis* or representation as fundamental to learning.) A learning contract is established, similar to the counseling contract, when a person (teacher) knows in an organized way what someone else (student) wishes to learn. The knower is thus mimetic to or representative of what the learner ultimately wishes to become. The presence of this mimetic bind can be implied in so simple an act as the learner having paid a fee and enrolled in a certain course, or even just by his presence in class. This would seem to indicate that much of the conflict and resistance in the initial stages of learning do not imply unwillingness to learn, as is sometimes thought, but rather are similar to the conflict and resistance often experienced in the early stages of counseling. They are part of the disorganized psychosomatic state of the learner and, rightly understood, evidence of his genuine self-investment. He simply needs help in the learning experience, as he does in counseling, to make the self-investment operationally effective.

CONCLUSION

We are suggesting that our present educative process has been primarily intellectual, reflective, and abstractive, and thus largely removed from personal engagement. In recalling the use of two words that have disappeared from our English vocabulary, namely, "tract" (used in *attract*) and "flect" (used in *reflect*), we might again arrive at the original conception of learning in which we first engage ourselves *as persons* with one another, in contrast to disembodied intellects. Instead of the overemphasis on *reflecting* and *abstracting*, we have to be aware of the need to "tract" and "flect" first before any abstraction and reflection is possible.

Thus, for example, in our foreign-language model, when we dealt with rules of grammar or extension of vocabulary, we did so out of the experiences of the group in which individual members had deeply invested their feelings and somatic reactions. From the material of the group experiences, which was recorded and written so that it became a kind of "lesson plan," it was pointed out that certain consistent rules were being used in the speaking of the foreign language. Upon reflection of the experience ("flecting"), the group could grow to recognize and gradually internalize vocabulary changes and better implementation of the rules.

What emerged from this was the realization that while life, in terms of such foreign language communication, is spontaneous, free, personal, and intense, and so is emotional and somatic as well as intellectual, it is not without some internal form and order. Upon abstraction and reflection, one grows to see this internal form and order as basically necessary for adequate communication and understanding. In this sense the rules of grammar and vocabulary, while dead structures when they have been memorized outside the range of reference to any communication, were contained in the spontaneous expressions of the group. Somewhat as people may be surprised in the study of anatomy to discover that skeletal structures are contained in the living people whom they know and love, so our students were surprised and excited to see that the grammar and vocabulary of a language could be alive and basic to warm human communication.

To continue the analogy, one might conclude that while no one loves a skeleton, yet skeletons are basic to our whole body structure. By always proceeding from abstraction, remoteness, a certain "nonhumaness" in human learning, we force the learner into the inhuman experience of finding a skeleton lovable! But, in fact, he usually finds it fearful or comic.

This corresponds to an ancient sense of two words that have lost their original meaning: *science* and *discipline*. Perhaps no two words have changed their meaning so much as these. "Science" originally meant "that which the person knows," from the Latin *scire*—to know. Science, then, simply meant the orderly presentation of knowledge. Only since the seventeenth century has this word had the narrower, more mathematical or precise, and certainly more accurate meaning of its present connotation.

As for the axiom that "whatever is received is received according to the manner of the one receiving," while the knower taught "scientia", the learner—the one receiving—filtered this through his own uniqueness. The learner received, then, not "scientia," but what was characteristic of the disciple, namely, "disciplina." This is obviously a very different meaning from the present "law and order" connotation of the word *discipline*. Originally it simply meant what the disciple received as a function of his own uniqueness as a learner. This was, therefore, different from what the knower-teacher taught—"scientia."

In these original Latin meanings of the words *science* and *discipline*, we also see evidence of another and different tradition and theory of learning. As a theory, the whole-person uniqueness of each learner was stressed. It is this entire connotation that clearly relates it to our present "incarnate-redemptive" learning concepts.

We are suggesting, too, that the incarnation-redemption dynamic by which the abstract God of the intellectual Greeks became the humanly incarnate God of the Jews and Christians, might have a further learning dynamic parallel. The removed (as on a pedestal) and near god-like image of the teacher must become man and must incarnately present himself in a deep, genuine total-person relationship with the learner. Only then, perhaps, can learning become truly redemptive and convey a new sense of worth and self-esteem to the learner. The teacher must decrease, *and the learner increase*.

This process should continue until a "new man", in the Pauline sense, or a "new self" in the learning sense, comes into being. This would be the result of a positive self-investment, of an internalization of knowledge on the part of the learner, who will then no longer need the external knower. And this is the teacher's greatest achievement—to be no longer needed.

REFERENCES AND FOOTNOTES

1 *Summa Theologica,* II-II, Q. 47, a–8.
2 This has been reported in detail by Curran, C. A.: *Counseling and Psychotherapy, the Pursuit of Values.* New York, Sheed and Ward, 1968, pp. 295–351.

CHAPTER 3

LIBERAL PROTESTANT THEOLOGY AND HUMANISTIC THEORIES OF PSYCHOTHERAPY

WILLIAM R. ROGERS

Focus And A Note Of Caution

THE FOCUS OF THIS CHAPTER will be on an issue of central concern within both liberal Protestant theology and Humanistic theories of psychotherapy: namely, attempts to understand and facilitate the dynamic process of human transformation. Not only is this appropriate to the intent of this present volume, but it is in fact the greatest point of increasing convergence within these two perspectives. Over and over, those writers who have attempted to be faithful to both liberal protestant theology and clinical understandings of personality change (Roberts, Outler, Hiltner, Tillich, Williams, Browning, Oden, Clinebell, etc.) have focused on the relationship of "salvation" and "psychotherapy." This essay will explore issues related to three critical dimensions of this relationship:

1. **Presuppositions**, with attention to increasing areas of convergence between psychology and liberal protestant theology
2. **Goals** of personal change in the two perspectives
3. **Processes** involved, with particular attention to the question of guidance

The note of caution is simply a qualification that any brief attempt at an overview of issues involving such complexity, such a wealth of clinical and theological analysis, runs a severe risk of oversimplification. The issues considered here are narrowed somewhat by the exclusion of psychoanalytic and behavioristic material on the psychological side and the exclusion of more conservative perspectives on the religious side since these matters are taken up in other chapters of this volume. What remains is still a large area within which we can only designate some of the primary integrative issues.

An Historical Perspective On Converging Presuppositions

The initial relationships between religion and psychology at the beginning of this century were marked by suspicion, defensiveness and hostility. On the side of religious persons there was apprehension that the psychological attacks on religious motivation as wish fulfillment, illusion, regression, repetition compulsion—in short a massive defense against insecurity, a projection of a desired order, and a dependent wish for a benevolent father—would seriously undermine the faith of the believers. Notions of men's spiritual depth appeared threatened by the analysis of unconscious motivations designed to disguise man's suffering and weakness.

On the psychological side there was suspicion that religious attempts to maintain a belief system repressive of fundamental human experiences would threaten both the mental health of men and women, and the legitimacy of an emerging science of the unconscious. The energy of the psychoanalytic attacks on neurotic components of religious experience betrays an apprehension that traditional beliefs might overweigh and deny the new clinical discoveries as well as the general scientific method.

Following such an inauspicious beginning, it is the more surprising that developments through the twentieth century within both religious understandings and psychological understandings have tended to move major streams of those two perspectives much closer together. It is instructive to examine some of these changes, particularly as they bear on fundamental presuppositions about the nature of man and of personality change.

The developments in humanistic psychology and psychotherapy which have been particularly conducive to more compatible relationships with theological concerns could be enumerated as follows:

Psychology has become increasingly concerned with the *whole* person, not just with partial processes of a perceptual or cognitive sort, nor simply with unconscious dynamics, defense mechanisms, or reinforcement schedules in learning.

Psychology has become increasingly concerned with matters of *change and personal growth*, rather than remaining with static studies of faculties, structures, or descriptive states. Stated broadly, psychotherapy is as concerned with movement from situations of human predicament or dysfunction to new possibilities (new "becoming") as are many religious endeavors.

Implied in this is also an increasing attempt in psychology to understand and facilitate the human quest for *meaning* and *direc-*

tional striving. Therapy is seen as inadequate if it only involves insight into personal history, the analyzing of pathology, catharsis, or adaptation. In the multiple forms of psychosynthesis, logotherapy, client-centered therapy, reality therapy, etc. there is evidence of concern with what Allport termed "propriate striving" or with what Maslow deals with as "self-actualization." In each there is the assumption that men can and should move toward identifiable goals of maturation. Since this obviously implies significant normative judgements, it has a direct bearing on theological concerns.

This suggests that psychology is also concerned then with *value* issues insofar as the norms of health or the goals of psychotherapy imply a good. Psychology particularly in its humanistic dimensions abandons simple attempts to describe behavior, and is unwilling to say that all life solutions are healthy or good. Critique is brought against egoistic power-seeking, self-effacement, ennui, irresponsibility and multiple forms of defensive denial or distortion of reality.

Together with this concern there is also psychology's attempt to deal increasingly with issues of human *responsibility for decision and action*. Such notions of responsibility grow partly out of the existentialist influences on psychology and mark a refinement in earlier understandings of psychological reductionism or determinism based on rigid genetic or social learning theories. It is important to see that both humanistic psychology and behaviorism, at least in its therapeutic utilization by Bandura and Wolpe, hold that in the process of goal setting and in the reduction of specific unwanted behaviors, the individual may take increased responsibility for his behavior.

Psychology, especially in the stream of humanistic psychotherapy, has placed increasing emphasis on the therapeutic significance of human *relationship* involving empathy, supportive understanding, attentiveness, caring and unconditional positive regard. The therapeutic relationship itself, involving these qualities, is seen as the critical element facilitating both personal growth and an immediate experiential reeducation in the possibilities for human interaction. This has superseded earlier understandings of catharsis, abreaction, intellectual analysis, or insight, as the pivotal facilitating variable in human transformation.

A further amplification of the significance of the quality of the relationship in therapy is also to be noted in formulations of the role of the researcher as *participant-observer*. There is recognition not only in therapy but in research on therapy that the individual is motivated in both the vision (hypotheses) and depth of his work by his own interest and predispositions. The fruitfulness of one's encounter with the individuals he is engaged with depends largely on the degree of his own genuineness and authenticity, as opposed to cold objectivity, detachment, or noninvolvement. Humanistic psychology in this sense exemplifies the insights of Dilthey, of Polanyi in his conception of "personal knowledge," and the more traditional theological insights of persons like Augustine that the most profound knowledge emerges in the union of cognition and affection.

Psychology has also recognized its increasing dependence on *models, symbol-building* and *myth* in understanding human personality, admitting that it is no more dealing with sheer facts than is religion, though both may have their foundation in disciplined observation of significant human experiences. In each case there is interpretation through imaginative attempts to give coherence and intelligibility often through the illumination of metaphonic imagery or mythological symbols—an observation which is also valid in psychoanalytic theory. These elements, coupled with rational analysis, point to greater compatibility with theological methods than was previously acknowledged.

Finally humanistic psychology is increasingly attentive to the integrity of the *unique frame of reference* of individual apperceptions of reality. This attention to the idiosyncratic marks a movement away from broadscale generalizations (nomothetic abstractions) toward an insight similar to the theological concerns with individual redemption, vocation, and the transvaluation of vaules that comes in the recognition that God speaks in unique ways in and through the life of each person.

On the side of liberal protestant theology there have also been a number of developments which involve presuppositions increasingly conducive to compatible relations with humanistic psychotherapy. Liberal protestantism no longer assumes that the only proper object of theology is the investigation of the sacred; but it is, instead, acutely focused on the *secular involvement of the Spirit,* assuming a transcendence of the old sacred-secular dichotomy. There is in theologians like Tillich, Bonhoeffer, Vahanian, Van Buren and Cox a sense of eternal presence in the everyday events of life—clearly a recognition that insights from the social sciences, particularly psychology and sociology—must be incorporated into any responsible or profound understanding of Christ and culture.

Theology, like psychology, has been extensively influenced by *existential concerns* with an emphasis on *particularity* and *immediacy* in human experience. With this influence there is the recognition that blanket answers cannot be given for the predicament of each. There is a reassertion of the protestant understanding that each individual must work out his own salvation "in fear and trembling," though this is invariably tied also to a recognition of the supports which one receives from the covenanted community.

Liberal protestant theology has also emphasized the pretentiousness and idolatrous nature of any attempt to say that one person, however prophetic or charismatic, can give final answers to individual life dilemmas. This denial of paternalism and authoritarianism as inappropriate to religious or personal interaction, and the simultaneous affirmation of a mode of humility, even chastity, with respect for each person's wrestling with the Spirit, parallels the humanistic, psychological concern for the integrity of individual growth and the view of the role of the therapist as that of a facilitator and catalyst in change, not as that of a director.

Liberal protestant theology has also recognized more of a place for empirical theological method, or for *naturalistic theology,* than traditional protestantism allowed herefore. This methodology recognizes that all human knowledge including theological knowledge has its base in human experience, particularly experiences in times of crisis or personal breakthrough. There is, of course, generally an affirmation that the implications of these experiences involve a process which transcends the individual. This recognition of ontological or transcendent processes may move the theological presuppositions beyond most humanistic psychologies, though even within the psychological sphere there is often a stance of awe and humility before profoundly moving experiences in which one discovers releasing therapeutic sustenance in the midst of depression and helplessness.

There is a view of *revelation* in liberal protestantism which also assumes the importance of psychological realities. Revelation is not seen simply as an event in which God manifests himself, but rather as an interaction in which there is a "coincidence of event and appreciation" (Temple). It is not as though propositional truths are thrown down from heaven, but rather that truth emerges in the relationship of objective events and subjective appropriation, when there is the recognition or appreciation of profound meaning in phenomena such as the Christ event. Furthermore such appreciation depends in part on the relative degree of non-defensive openness, clarity, self-acceptance, and freedom from neurotic distortion in the perceptual processes of the individual. Psychotherapy, insofar as it facilitates greater perceptual clarity by reducing unconscious needs to distort, may thus be seen as enabling greater receptivity to spiritual depth rather than inviting enmity and suspicion regarding such depth.

Liberal protestantism, as all Christian theology, recognizes the *creation as good* and also the inevitability of the *"fall,"* or sin. The nature of sin however is understood more in terms of alienation, separation, estrangement, and the failure to achieve human potential rather than in terms of obliteration of potentialities for growth through disobedience or disbelief. Not only is the liberal view of sin parallel to existential psychological notions of separation and alienation (though it involves an ontological perspective in addition to intrapsychic and interpersonal alienation), but also the protestant affirmation of the importance of individual responsibility in moving toward reunification is affirmed in ways similar to the humanistic affirmation.

The critical difference between protestantism and humanistic psychology may come with regard to the question of "grace." Whereas protestant theology recognizes that it is not man's work alone which leads to transformation, it may appear that many humanistic psychologists are willing to make such an affirmation. Psychological presuppositions regarding principles like the "self-actualizing tendency" or the "organismic valuing process," (Rogers) may be read as a trust in inherent autonomous capabilities of the individual. But they could also be seen to imply that there is a level of affirmation of some reality operative in the transformation process not necessarily contained within, or controlled through, the energies of the individual.

Taken together, these presuppositions in recent liberal protestant theology, coupled with the trends in humanistic psychology and psychotherapy, point the way to increased collaboration and mutual interest. There is common concern with facilitating the growth of individuals, assuming fundamental constructive potentialities operative within and through the self, recognizing our common dilemma as broken and separated persons, asserting that ways of addressing our common dilemma must recognize the distinctiveness of individual life experiences, envisioning the goal as reunification or restored wholeness of the self within itself, in community, and in relationship to the depths of reality, recognizing also individual responsibility and ethical decision, but acknowledging that a caring relationship is critical, along with a reliance on the healing resources which emerge in the midst of crisis and which are not finally to be controlled by even the most imaginative therapist or pastor.

Goals

Following from many of these presuppositions concerning both the predicament and potentiality within persons, comes a common concern for the normative development of general characteristics which are articulated as anticipated outcomes of either the process of salvation or psychotherapy. These goals are frequently stated in terms relevant to characteristics of individual life though they also explicitly and implicitly involve new possibilities in a communal sense, as well as a reconceived perspective on the rootedness of the self and the nature of reality most broadly understood. The following is an attempt to articulate in somewhat neutral terms the main features of such goals having concurrent importance in both liberal protestant theological conceptions of salvation and humanistic views of the outcomes of psychotherapy. Following the statement of more common concerns, we can also look at the points where these goals differ.

The most overarching understanding of the common goal is the widely expressed concern for *restored relationship, reunification* or *reconciliation*. Over against the internal and external manifestations of brokenness, estrangement or alienation, the possibilities for reunification have meaning in terms of the integrity of self, the renewed possibilities for genuine human relationships, and the restored sense of one's context within the processes and structures of being itself.

In relation to the self, the integration is seen as the drawing together of elements unnecessarily separated in the defensive protection of a pseudo security based on dishonest or partial conceptions of the self. The separated elements may be understood as "conscious" and "unconscious," or "self-concept" and "organismic striving," or "self-image" and "repressed feelings." The psychological statements of the goal are in terms of increased capacity for "congruence" (Rogers), self-integration (Allport), "individuation" through the assimilations of unconscious and conscious contents (Jung), "identity" (Erikson), "self-consistency" (Lecky) or simply the emergence of an "authentic self" (Jourard, Moustakas, etc.). The theological formulation of this integration comes in concerns to "restore a right heart within us," in which the "purity of heart is to will one thing." (Kierkegaard) It is envisioned as the unity of intent through the remediation of the privations of the will (Augustine), or as "centeredness" in the reunification of the self (Tillich).

Directly related to this goal or reunification is the notion of *relinquishing egoistic claims* for the self which were grounded on neurotic defensiveness or sinful pride. Theologically this is recognized as a mode of humility that emerges both in a person's sense that he is not the invincible master of his fate but is ultimately dependent, particularly in those moments of healing and self-discovery, on ontological forces which transcend his personal existence. And in psychological terms this relinquishing is seen as an openness to deeper levels of awareness which confound and contradict the easy pretense of a partial self-image. The possibility of this awareness is seen as coming about under the conditions of a particular form of therapeutic relationship in which there is understanding, caring and interpersonal warmth which again the individual self does not control. There is a critical movement here, however, from infantile dependence to responsibility in mutual interdependence.

To state this goal somewhat differently, there is from both perspectives a sense of the self having been *received, prized* or *accepted.* In this there is an affirmation of one's genuine experience under the conditions of human existence—that it is alright to be oneself. Acceptance may also lead to release from the anxiety of self-doubt, loneliness and separation. The context of this acceptance is understood somewhat differently by some theologians and psychologists, particularly along the lines of whether the acceptance is seen as simply interpersonal or whether it is more profoundly experienced as a right relationship within the ontological context of a more universal love and forgiveness. The role of judgement in confrontation with the most demonic, destructive elements of human experience is also debated in relation to the function and qualities of such acceptance.

Directly related to the release from bondage to an egoistic self is also the common goal of an increased *capacity to live in love* toward others. Theologically the ethic of love is conceived more as a response in faith to the experience of having been received or renewed through a forgiving and understanding relationship, than as a demand, the accomplishment of which would be a prerequisite for forgiveness and renewal. Psychologically, there are similar understandings that love as an understanding, caring, knowing, fulfilling and responsible relationship with others comes only as one is freed from the protective mechanisms which deny or distort perceptions of other people. Such distortions frequently stem from the need to maintain either power over others with its implied narcissism, or self-diminution which can also be seen as a reflexive narcissism and interpersonally manipulative—in either case antithetical to love and calculated to maintain a defensive self-image. Stated more neutrally, openness to others and care for their well-being is directly related to openness to one's experience internally. The goal of a *beloved community* is associated with the genuineness, honesty and dependability of relationships that are freed from self-striving or self-effacement (Horney).

Psychotherapeutic goals may be conceived as differing from views of salvation in that therapy focuses on matters of symptom reduction, and emphasizes the role of sexuality and anger in human experience in ways that some critics claim are neglected by the theological tradition. Within the humanistic view of psychotherapy. however, symptom reduction is clearly seen as a secondary component, subordinated to the primary importance of the reorientation of the self to its own deepest reality and to genuine human relationships. Such reorientation, it would be argued, can reframe a sense of personal identity in such a way that anxiety, duplicity, and incongruent strivings, coupled with related physiological manifestations, are significantly reduced. It is true that theology pays little attention to specific symptomatology, but like humanistic psychology it assumes that salvation will restore inner integrity and communal relationships in a way that is instrumental to health.

As health (wholeness) is clearly valued in relation to the actualization of human patentiality, a responsible theology needs to incorporate the significant dimensions of human sexuality and aggressiveness. They should neither be ignored nor dutifully repressed. At the same time, theologians like psychologists are concerned with saefguarding against distortion and manipulation in the possible sexual or aggressive tyrannies of one person over another.

It would also appear that the theological goals of an increased capacity for relationship between man and God, as well as for attention to the truth of God's revelatory activity might be neglected in the psychotherapeutic understandings of change. If, however, God is understood in relation to the creative power of renewal and healing, then any therapeutic act which puts the person in touch with experiences involving healing (especially involving the transcendence of former anticipations and perceptions of reality) could have a theological dimension. Granted some psychologists would disallow such an interpretation; but even when they do, the other terms in which they speak of the creative actualization in therapy could be translated into theological categories of the ultimate as "creative event" (Wieman) or "empowerment of Being" (Tillich). Clearly the therapeutic relationship, insofar as it extends consciousness beyond defensively conceived, self-protective limits, broadens a person's awareness not only of interpersonal realities but of realities generative of, and exemplary of the very possibility of being and becoming.

It is in this ontological context that we might speak of all forms of personal and interpersonal life as participating in the structure and processes of Being. And therapy can certainly be seen as facilitating the quality of this participation and as enhancing the actualization of Being.

Revelation, as discussed, implies not cataclysmic acts of God but involves a relational view of truth in which the acts of giving and receiving must be coincident. Therapeutic reintegration and expanded awareness may make possible the greater apprehension of truth and hence be complementary to the revelatory event. Modalities of therapy, like the emergence of salvation, drive toward greater accuracy and comprehension in one's awareness of reality—both the reality of the self and the reality of the broadest context in which life proceeds.

Processes

Movement toward the above goals is understood as a dynamic process in which certain components play a critical role. Again we can look at these components from both a theological and a psychological point of view, observing *how similarly* they are perceived by liberal protestantism and humanistic psychotherapy.

The *qualities of the therapist or religious leader* who facilitates the process are seen from both points of view as a significant, though not as the most critical determinant of change. The congruence, genuineness, integrity and depth of experience of such a facilitator is regarded highly from both perspectives. It is important that such a person has *himself* progressed through the process which he is enabling other persons to experience. But the profoundest enabling power for growth and change is not perceived as coming from the facilitator or therapist so much as from resources in or beyond the person himself. Psychologically speaking this is conceptualized as a "self-actualizing principle" or a person's "powers." Theologically it may be perceived as a transcendent power. In either case, there is the acknowledgment of an emergence, at critical points of insight or transformation, of some resources which are not under the direct control of either the individual, the therapist or the spiritual guide.

The activity of "guidance" in both perspectives is viewed *not as explicit direction,* advice-giving, or the formulation of answers for the other person, but rather as the encouragement of a quality of relationship in which there is understanding, empathy, and respect for the mutuality of engagement in facing serious personal and ultimate questions. Humanistic psychotherapy is very clear in its disavowal of the efficacy of advice-giving. The problems involved are multiple: (a) the therapist may have inadequate information about the life situation of an individual and hence give inappropriate advice; (b) the therapist may have adequate information but have poor judgment regarding the effects of certain behaviors and hence give advice which in the long run is both unhelpful to the person and may damage further possibilities for the individual seeking help; (c) the therapist may have adequate information and give good advice which the person can successfully follow, but even when this occurs the process perpetuates or increases dependency on external authority, robbing the individual of the precious opportunity to discover modes of resolving personal and social dilemmas in more independent and creative ways. Theologically speaking conceptions of "guidance" and advice-giving fall prey to a pretentious idolatry which would suppose that the skill of the therapist or religious leader has more ultimate authority than it really does.

Liberal protestantism is particularly wary of any idolatry that suggests that some persons have more of a right than anyone else to interpret divine will or to direct the path of another person's life. Protestantism generally affirms a humility before all existing formulations of the truth of God's will for individual life. Certainly liberal protestantism reemphasizes the "protestant principle" of the priesthood of all believers, and acknowledges the high priority that must be given to the integrity of *individual* discoveries of truth and meaning, in recognition of, but not in obedience to, external forms of dogma or tradition. This affirmation of the emergence of meanings which have personal significance in terms of the experiential frame of reference of the individual is perhaps one of the most distinguishing marks of both the liberal protestant and the humanistic psychological interpretations of human growth.

The *beginning of the process* of human transformation, understood from both these perspectives, is also similar. Readiness for therapy or for entry in the process of salvation involves an initial recognition on the part of the individual that something is wrong and that something must be done. Psychologically speaking, this may be thought of as an awareness of one's incongruence or neurotic distortion of reality, and a corresponding desire to change. Theologically speaking, it is conceived of as contrition or "conviction of sin" and similarly involves the inference of personal responsibility for inadequacy or for the violation of the potentially constructive and integrative possibilities of life.

In both perspectives, there is in addition an understanding of the process of change going from the expression of *negative* feelings toward an awareness of *positive* resources and *positive* feelings toward the self and others. The expression of personal dilemmas, confusion, guilt, brokenness, and so on must be understood and "worked through" before the possibilities for deeper integration and interpersonal communication are realized. Stated theologically this is the insight that confession must be an antecedent of reconciliation and renewal.

Both perspectives also emphasize the importance of attention to the crippling effects of *anxiety*, self-deceit, and dishonesty. These experiences must be dealt with directly in the healing relationship, as the individual concerned reliquishes the safety of evasion or denial. However in the concern to reduce anxiety, the theological awareness of man's ultimate finitude and of the precariousness of our human existence, suggests that honest recognition of a continuing form of ontological anxiety needs to be preserved (Tillich). It is important to note that humanistic psychotherapy has also become conscious of this ontological dimension and attempts to discriminate between neurotic anxiety and ontological anxiety, the second being acknowledged as ultimately a constructive dimension of human awareness (May, Laing).

Both perspectives also recognize the process of change as involving *a rediscovery of primary meanings* in experience, especially primary *emotional* meaning—though the connotation of "meaning" itself involves integration of cognitive and affective elements. Emotional reeducation, or access to the existential realities of ambivalence, guilt, alienation or pain, however, is not seen as the end of the process. It is rather seen both theologically and within existential psychotherapy as instrumental to a deeper level of integration and meaning. One moves from an awareness of the loss of significance toward the regaining of a sense of more profound significance, or from the sense of deep hurt and pain to the discovery that even in the sharing of that pain there is healing and renewed courage. A new sense of personal hope and integrity frequently emerges in the midst of a deeply shared recognition of the agony or absurdity of experience.

Both liberal protestant theology and humanistic psychotherapy pay considerable attention to the dynamics of those *critical moments* when individuals experience transition from such times of crisis or despair to a sense of recovery, renewed hope, new release. This is to say there are critical incidents in psychotherapy and critical junctures in the salvatory process when people experience a dipping down to the bottom, as it were, and a final shedding of the pretenses and mummylike shrouds that have disguised their elementary realities from themselves and other people. These moments of nakedness and profound vulnerability may overwhelm the person with a fear of engulfment (Laing) or annihilation of the self-concept (Rogers); or they may be the potent harbingers of new honesty, growth and a solid sense of building from the most fundamental levels of reality toward new authenticity and personhood. Some streams of liberal protestantism emphasize such points as moments of "conversion," whereas other streams may minimize these points or acknowledge their repetition in views of salvation as "nurture." In either case, however, these moments of alteration are seen as both painful and joyful—painful in the excruciating acknowledgment of failure, weakness, deception and loss, but joyful in the discovery of an unexpected strength and self-transcedence through which the person is enabled to begin anew with greater confidence in his honest appraisal of himself, in the abiding worth of his experience of a caring relationship, and in his own apprehension of those realities on which life itself is based. In therapeutic discussions this moment is often seen as a moment of "breakthrough" or life-affirmation, or as "peak experience" or "being-cognition" (Maslow). The profound and lasting vision of the potency of life and the very sources that sustain life coming from such experiences have not only personal relevance, but also are frequently experienced as guiding one's perception of the profound dignity and worth of all life.

Conclusion

The merging of so many common concerns between liberal protestantism and humanistic psychotherapy, as they view the process of human transformation, bodes well for continuing cooperation. Even the chief point of past disjunction—the issue concerning the ultimate source of transforming power—has been modified as theologians renounce the sacred/secular dichotomy and acknowledge the relational character of revelatory truth, and as psychologists look further at the ontological context of human potentiality and anxiety and at the peculiar potency revealed in the critical moments of healing in therapy. With more time, one could employ greater precision in designating the variant interpretations of particular theorists analyzing the points of diversion and continuity in these two general perspectives. At the center, however, they are united in their view that "guidance" must rest finally on a trust in the illumination or meaning that is made manifest when one becomes increasingly open to the profound depths of experience within the context of caring, durable, and receptive relationships.

BIBLIOGRAPHY

1. Allport, Gordon W.: *The Individual and His Religion.* New York, Macmillan, 1954.
2. Bonhoeffer, Dietrich: *Life Together.* New York, Harper and Bros., 1954.
3. Browning, Donald: *Atonement and Psychotherapy.* Philadelphia, Westminster Press, 1966.
4. Clinebell, Howard: *Basic Types of Pastoral Counseling.* Nashville, Abingdon, 1966.
5. Cox, Harvey: *The Secular City,* New York, Macmillan, 1963.
6. Erikson, Erik: *Identity and the Life Cycle,* Psychological Issues Monograph, 1. New York, International Universities Press, 1959.
7. Hiltner, Seward: *Preface to Pastoral Theology.* New York, Abingdon Press, 1958.
8. Homans, Peter (ed.): *The Dialogue Between Theology and Psychology.* Chicago, University of Chicago Press, 1968.
9. Laing, Ronald: *Politics and Experience.* New York, Ballantine, 1968.
10. Maslow, Abraham: *Motivation and Personality.* New York, Harper and Bros., 1954.
11. May, Rollo, et al.: *Existence.* New York, Basic Books, 1958.
12. Oden, Thomas: *Contemporary Theology and Psychotherapy.* Philadelphia, Westminster Press, 1967.
13. Outler, Albert: *Psychotherapy and the Christian Message.* New York, Harper and Bros., 1954.
14. Roberts, David: *Psychotherapy and a Christian View of Man.* New York, Charles Scribner's Sons, 1953.
15. Rogers, Carl: *Client Centered Therapy.* Boston, Houghton Mifflin, 1951.
16. Temple, William: *Nature, Man and God.* London, Macmillan, 1934.
17. Tillich, Paul: *The Courage to Be.* New Haven, Yale University Press, 1952.
18. Tillich, Paul: *Systematic Theology,* 3 Vols. Chicago, University of Chicago Press, 1963.
19. Vahanian, Gabriel: *The Death of God.* New York, Braziller, 1961.
20. Van Buren, Paul: *The Secular Meaning of the Gospel.* New York, Macmillan, 1966.
21. Wieman, Henry Nelson: *The Source of Human Good.* Chicago, University of Chicago Press, 1946.
22. Williams, Daniel Day: *The Minister and the Care of Souls.* New York, Harper, 1961.

CHAPTER 4

PROTESTANTISM AND PSYCHOTHERAPY

Paul E. Johnson

Christianity is a tree of many branches. The central vitality rises through the trunk, and as it continues to grow, new shoots and branches spring forth. The main stream of vitality flows outward from the life and teachings of Jesus. When Jesus speaks of the vine and branches he affirms two criteria of growing life: (1) to bear fruit and (2) to remain united with the vine. It is only as vine and branches are united that they are able to bear fruit (John 15:1-6).

Protestantism is one of the branches of Christianity that springs forth to bear fruit. It has multiplied its life in many other branches known as denominations. There is great diversity in these 250 branches of Protestantism, and no little separation of one from another. We may see in this diversity a freedom and healthy moving out in new directions. Yet if separatism is the chief purpose of any branch, it may wither for want of unity with the main stream of vitality in Jesus, who is the central unifying and vitalizing source of the Christian life.

When rivalries develop between the branches of Christianity, one may claim to be purer or truer than others. Jesus did not recognize any inherent superiority of one branch over another, for each is an outgrowth of one trunk which carries one life to all. Yet there are differences in the way this life may be expressed. If a branch is fruitful it is to be pruned and cleansed that it may bear more fruit. If it is barren it will wither away for lack of vitality and unity with the creative source of fruitfulness.

In this chapter we desire to look at Protestantism as a whole, as it bears fruit in the healing power and guiding wisdom of psychotherapy. We acknowledge that healing and wisdom may be manifest in any religion or branch of Christianity. And we do not claim that our branch is greater in either healing or wisdom in contrast to others. Yet there are distinctive features to be noted in the aims and beliefs of Protestants. And these characteristics will influence the nature of its guiding principles and approach to healing.

I. A COMMUNITY OF FAITH AND LOVE

From an outside view Protestantism may appear as a structure with specific forms of social-religious organization. But from an inside view this is a dynamic spiritual life. Bringing together the inner and outer view, we find ourselves participating in a spiritual community of faith and love. This is the essence of Protestantism, as it is of any religion in its dynamic spirit. This spirit is deeper and wider than any particular church or any religion in its visible structure. If we are to understand the relation of Protestantism to psychotherapy, we will need to see this spiritual community living by faith and reaching out in love.

What is the Protestant movement? The historic mission is a creative protest in facing the limits of each situation, impelling a new search for the ultimate meaning of life. (1) Here is the prophetic spirit questioning the finality of the past and the inertia of the present and seeking a new life in the potentiality of the future. How does this Protestant mission come to expression in a community of faith and love? We may note four dynamic principles of this motivating purpose in Protestantism.

1. We begin with the resolve to *live by faith*. Martin Luther, after many penances and pilgrimages in search of a new life, was lecturing at the University of Wittenberg on Paul's letters to the Romans when he discovered new meaning in the text, "The just shall live by faith." (Romans 1:17) Before this the righteousness of God was a judgement against him, for he knew in his tragic conscience that he fell short of the perfection of God. Now it dawned upon him that to be just is not to do good works, but to accept God's spirit of justice freely given to us here and now. By accepting this Spirit dwelling in us we can henceforth live by faith. Instead of relying upon the mediation of a priest to grant him penance and offer him formal absolution to begin a new life, he found the new life of Christ dwelling in him. He could now live as Christ's man with freedom to change and become a new person. This was a revolution in his relationship to God, to other persons and to himself. He discovered the power of new beginnings not by virtue of his own works, but by the grace of God freely flowing to him as a loving Spirit.

2. This *freedom to initiate* is the outcome of a dynamic faith through direct access to God. Finding that God will accept and guide

him by his loving Spirit, Luther is able to decide who he will become and begin a new life. He is more autonomous and independent as a free person. Yet he is more related and interdependent as he becomes aware of the potentiality within him that develops by this mutual response. God shows him the New Being in Christ and calls him to enter this new life. Every man is a priest before God, and as he accepts the new being freely offered to him, this faith and love will overflow to others in the community of the Spirit. This is a second principle of Protestantism.

3. A third principle is *openness to truth* from whatever source it comes. God speaks to a faithful seeker not only through a particular church and a particular book, but in all the avenues of awareness to meet the creative Spirit everywhere. For God is both distant and near. He is remote in the distant heavens, and present in all nature and growing life, to be encountered in each situation and met in every person, nation and religion. He reveals his truth along the advancing frontiers of science and invention, in the mysterious order of the stars and planets, the atoms, and electrons, in the procreation and heredity of life in every species and individual. If truth is everywhere open to us, we should seek in every event for meaning, and not discount the reason and intuition of anyone who speaks from his own experience.

The radical evangelists like Thomas Münzer were all dependent on Luther, yet they went beyond him. They felt that he was standing half way in the Reformation. They declared that God not only speaks in the past in the Bible, but in the present in the heart and depths of any person who is prepared to hear. But to receive the Spirit one must accept the cross to suffer for others and give his life that others may be saved from despair and enter a new life. The sacraments are not the only road to the new being in Christ, and the office of the ministry is to be shared among all who are willing to be disciples of this new life. Zwingli declared that the Spirit is at work everywhere, and God may give his truth through non-Christians also. The Quakers lived by the "Inner Light," which is the light of God in every man.

4. A fourth principle of Protestantism is the call to a *vocation in the world*. John Calvin believed in the urgency of God's call to every man to deny himself and go forth to serve by faithful labor in the world. If we would glorify God, we are to be partners with him in creative labors to produce goods and make the world a better place for all. In this way honor is given to the secular as well as the sacred vocations. The fellowship of believers is not a closed

community or an aristocracy of the privileged few, but an open democratic society where every person is at work and has a voice in the shaping of a new community for all. The pietistic awakening of Christian experience in response to the call of God was not otherworldly. Zinzendorf and Wesley set forth to care for the poor, the sick and the orphans; and gathered momentum in outgoing mission to persons in special need.

II. INNER SOURCES OF HEALING

Psychotherapy unites two Greek words to designate mind-healing. In a general term of such dimensions, many associations are called forth. If the mind is in need of healing, how is this to be accomplished? Healing is to come through the mind and its potential resources. Who is authorized to provide healing of the mind? Special qualifications and training will evidently be needed for this delicate task. This is becoming a matter of public concern, and many states are now defining a procedure by which to license authorized healers who meet specific qualifications. Even from primitive times the healer has been authorized by his community to practice healing.

In our time there are quite a few forms of healing. The practice of medicine is developing many branches and specializations, which through rigorous training and refined procedures bring healing to specific ills. Increasingly other professions are called into health work as the complex needs of human life are seen in larger perspective. If the whole person is involved in either illness or health in all his social relationships, we must be drawn together in seeking to maintain health for all persons. There are religious dynamics in health and illness. The spirit as well as body and mind are joined in every experience of *good*ness and *ill*ness. Ever since Jesus called on his disciples to carry on his work of healing and teaching, Christians have been concerned in an endeavor to heal.

Is there a Protestant psychotherapy? There is no specific method of healing that is distinctive of Protestantism. What we do find is an attitude of mind emerging into a Protestant culture. (2) And attitudes of mind are very important in health and illness. Psychotherapy acknowledges the inner sources of healing, and undertakes to work with them in the dynamic process with which we move toward the goals we seek. Let us look into these attitudes of mind in Protestantism to see if they may be favorable resources conducive to healing.

To live by faith is the first principle of the Protestant way of life. Here is an essential inner resource for healing. Erikson finds in his psychoanalytic study of childhood that, in the first year of life, the crisis of every infant is basic trust *vs* basic distrust. If the child's primary relation to his mother is conducive to basic trust, he will be freer from crippling anxieties and able to grow more successfully in every subsequent stage of his development. Basic distrust on the other hand, is a crippling emotion that retards and constricts the human life style, producing acute anxiety and the many stresses that distort relationships into neuroses and psychoses.

Luther suffered a deep depression due to his negative conscience and the inner conflicts he was unable to resolve, until he discovered that the way of health and wholeness was *to live by faith*. Erikson shows us the significance of this creative breakthrough to faith in the reformer's struggle.

This revelation, which Erikson calls "a sudden inner flooding with light," brought Luther into a new life. "He changed from a highly restrained and retentive individual into an explosive person; he had found an unexpected release of self-expression, and with it, of the many-sided power of his personality." (3)

It is this going forward in faith that enables a person to hope in a new life. Faith is essential for anyone to enter a course in psychotherapy, and even more so to progress into enlarging health. Without faith we can do nothing; we cannot even accept the love that is offered to us. Trust is therefore basic to all the values and goals that one may hope for. Religion is one of our greatest providers of hope and trust, as Erikson shows. "Trust born of care is, in fact, the touchstone of the *actuality* of a given religion." (4) All religions have in common this motive power of trust in a Provider; and with it the insight that individual trust is to become a common faith in a sustaining community.

Freedom to *initiate a new life* is the second Protestant principle, one we find emerging from faith. But such freedom can be restricted by anxiety, and depressed by apathy or despair. Many scientists and psychologists for example, are committed to a theory of determinism which may act as a deterrent to hope and faith in our human ability to bring on change or to enter a new life. Yet in practice most scientists act as if they were free to initiate experiments, invent new machines, and break forth into new theory. Every psychotherapist acts as a change agent to promote initiative in persons within his care. His entire vocation is devoted to helping persons grow into a new life, through choices which they are to initiate in a healthy release of personal freedom. Even behavioral therapists who rely on operant conditioning are free to select the conditions by which persons will choose to respond in a new behavior.

The most overpowering neurosis of our time is a loss of the meaning of life. Viktor Frankl, (5) influential Viennese psychiatrist, finds this loss of meaning in eighty per cent of the persons who report their condition to him. Actually, this is not a disease of mind or body, but a spiritual condition of confusion and doubt in our whole existence today. In the prevalent mood of our times we are captured by a deterministic belief that we are helpless in the grip of impersonal forces too vast to cope with by any decisive act of freedom. If our freedom to make decisions is overcome by helplessness, we consequently see no meaning or purpose in life.

For this spiritual condition of emptiness, or existential vacuum, he offers logotherapy. *Logos* refers to the meaning of life, which we seek to discover by liberating the spirit at the decisive center of each person. Here we need not retreat from life, but instead respond to whatever concrete situation life presents to us. The real question is not what we ask of life, but what life is asking of us. The spirit can act in spite of difficult circumstances, and counteract the downward pull of gravity. For example, I can decide how I will respond to each situation and so become a responsible person acting freely and heroically in the midst of illness or loss, by turning the adversity into a new and challenging frontier of growth. There are inner resources deeper than we know, and potentialities to reach higher summits than we have yet climbed. Let us seek a *height* psychology as well as a *depth* psychology.

III. THE CHALLENGE OF MENTAL HEALTH

It is now recognized in the life sciences that most of us are using only five or ten per cent of our human potential. Why are we so inert and depressed, when these vast inner resources are so largely unused? Voices are now being lifted to call us back to ourselves and away from our obsession with machines. Is man destined to defeat his great human potential by reacting to fear and hostility? How long will we turn the earth's amazing resources into weapons of destruction, and our social resources into the sorry tragedy of keeping other persons out—excluding them from the values we clutch so frantically to ourselves?

Are we ready for the new revolution in personal consciousness? It is high time to ask if we are sound in mind and wise in the priorities to which we commit ourselves. This is the time, as we are caught in mounting conflict and violence, to turn our course toward mental health and to unite to fulfill the aspirations of free persons who care enough to help one another.

At such a time we need to re-enact the third Protestant principle of *openness to truth* from whatever source it comes. In our haste to speak up and control others, we are slow to listen to or care what other persons feel and want. It is *our failure to listen* that turns off the other person and drives him to desperation. When nations stop listening to each other, they are hurled precipitously into war and mutual destruction. When leaders rely on propaganda to put over their program, they do not listen to the people, who thereupon turn from negotiation to violent revolt. When parents and teachers forget to listen, they are alienated from youth, and communication breaks down into a hopeless generation gap.

The challenge of mental illness is the needless suffering and defeat that close in upon us when we are unwilling to listen to one another. Then we are cut off from living relationships, out of touch and isolated, anxious and insecure, distressed and disturbed by pent-up emotions of guilt and anger, grief and despair. When Anton Boisen (6) was seized by a mental illness, he was given solitary confinement in a mental hospital in "the wilderness of the lost" to battle his way through alone. When he recovered, he was told he would no longer be fit to serve as minister of a church. So he asked if he might be a chaplain to other mental patients in the Worcester State Hospital. He was encouraged by the hospital staff to do this and, at the doctors' urging, to study mental illness with patients. In 1925 he invited theological students to leave their books and cloistered halls long enough to serve these patients face to face and, together with interprofessional staff workers, seek to guide them into larger health. So began the historic movement of Clinical Pastoral Education, now approved by most of our theological schools and taught by chaplain supervisors in teamwork with all cooperating mental health professions.

Now we are turning away from remote isolation in secluded hospital wards to nearby community mental health centers. The long separation of commitment to a mental hospital then would provide incarceration in a place very like a tomb behind barred windows and locked doors, making re-entry into society all the more difficult. Instead of isolating a distressed person with the stigma of "insanity," the new approach is to listen to and to minister to each person in a community center, where he can live at home, stay on the job or in school, and learn to work through his stress in the normal context of his ongoing social relationships. In this way mutual listening to accept and understand, to respond with loving concern and faithful caring, we are enabled to meet better and more promptly that person's needs and to uphold his momentum of unbroken learning and growth in an open society.

At this time we may also respond to the fourth Protestant principle—*the call to a vocation in the world*. Whoever and wherever we are, there is work for us to do in the world, to serve those who journey with us and to share with them on our great planetary voyage. Mental health is everybody's business: we are all involved in healthy and unhealthy attitudes and relations one with another in our world. We are therefore called to care for each other in a community of open and sustaining relations.

Religious leaders in most Protestant churches are deeply involved in family and community life. The pastor is expected to call upon the sick and the dying to sustain them with resources of hope, faith and love. Persons under emotional stress are apt to turn to him for counsel in time of crisis, uncertainty or family conflict. A nationwide survey by the Joint Commission on Mental Illness and Health reported in 1960 that forty-two per cent of those who seek help with emotional problems come first to the pastor, because they know and trust him. (7) This has led to a Pastoral Counseling movement in which pastors ask for special training to qualify as better counselors.

Since 1941 it has been my privilege to help pastors learn the principles of pastoral care and counseling. Here we have relied constantly upon the expert knowledge and dedicated teamwork of leaders in mental health professions. Coming to general and mental hospitals for clinical pastoral education, we have learned ministry to the sick and the distressed from the devotion and skill of these physicians and nurses, chaplains and social workers, who welcomed us into their healing team and invited us to share an interchange of insights and experiences.

From psychologists, like Carl Rogers to whom we are deeply indebted, we have been learning the significance of an accepting relationship, the patience of unwearied listening, faith in the inner wisdom of self-guidance, the right of each person to decide for himself, and the healing power of basic respect and positive regard for the other person.

From psychiatrists, like J. L. Moreno and Viktor Frankl, to whom we are also indebted, we have been learning the principles of spontaneity and creativity, the need for face to face encounter, the profound influence of interpersonal relations, the freedom of the spirit to rise above illness and adversity, the release of feeling in open dialogue and psychodrama, the value of a new perspective and training through responsible action in the world.

From such encounters we are coming to see the multiplied learning effect of intensive group experiences. The discovery of the group is one of the most significant openings in our time, from anxious separation and defensive resistance to a community of shared experience. In the open communication of person with person we come to know ourselves and each other better, as we learn to listen to and accept each other. Carl Rogers describes an open group experience in these words:

> A climate of mutual trust develops out of this mutual freedom to express real feelings, positive and negative. Each member moves toward greater acceptance of his total being—emotional, intellectual, and physical—as it is, including its potential. . . . Individuals can hear each other, can learn from each other, to a greater extent. (8)

He continues to show how feedback from one person to another promotes learnings in the group which carry over in all the ongoing relationships of life. We are drawn together by "a hunger for relationships which are close and real," (9) where feelings are more open, deep experiences can be shared, and new behavior can be risked with more hope and confidence.

In this era of rapid change when a whole new society is being formed, we may wonder about the future of Protestantism. But whatever surprises and revolutions the future may unveil before us, we need not be fearful or empty-handed. If we have a faith to live by, life can find meaning and purpose. If we are free to learn and initiate new beginnings, we are not impoverished by change that may leave the past for an unknown future. If we are open to listen and accept truth from any source, we will discover what we may learn together. And if we respond to the call of a vocation in the world, we may join with our fellows in seeking and sharing, building and creating a world that is open to all.

REFERENCES AND FOOTNOTES

1 See Tillich, Paul: *The Protestant Era.* Chicago, University of Chicago Press, 1948. *Systematic Theology,* Vol. 3. Chicago, University of Chicago Press, 1963. Braaten, Carl E. (ed.): *A History of Christian Thought.* New York, Harper, 1968.

2 See Oates, Wayne E.: *Protestant Pastoral Counseling.* Philadelphia, Westminster Press, 1962. Also Hiltner, Seward: *Pastoral Counseling.* Nashville, Abingdon, 1949.
3 Erikson, Erik: *Young Man Luther.* New York. Norton. 1958, p. 205.
4 Erikson, Erik: *Childhood and Society.* New York, Norton, 1950, rev. 1963, p. 250.
5 Frankl, Viktor: *Man's Search for Meaning,* Boston, Beacon, rev. 1962; *The Doctor and the Soul,* New York, Knopf, rev. 1965; and *The Will to Meaning,* New York, World, 1969.
6 Boisen, Anton T.: *Out of the Depths.* New York, Harper, 1960.
7 Ewalt, Jack R.: *Action for Mental Health.* New York, Basic Books, 1965. Clinebell, Howard J. Jr. (Ed.): *Community Mental Health.* Nashville, Abingdon, 1970.
8 Rogers, Carl: *Carl Rogers on Encounter Groups.* New York, Harper, 1970, p. 7.
9 *Ibid.,* p. 11.

CHAPTER 5

PROTESTANTISM (CONSERVATIVE–EVANGELICAL) AND THE THERAPIST

JOHN M. VAYHINGER

ANY PERSON, ESPECIALLY AS A PATIENT needing psychotherapy, is a full human being. His adaptations to living—psychological, sociological, spiritual—are all involved in his resources and his past experiences, as well as in the symptoms indicative of his basic pathological problem. So, when a "hurting person" seeks professional help in resolving his psychological conflicts, his values (religious experiences, spiritual failures, hopes, and resources) are all as much involved as his power strivings, his sexual and pleasure responses, his relationships with significant persons, his suffering and confusion.

The Christian who is also a psychotherapist, whether medical or psychological or sociological, brings his particular value system to apply in the treatment of this person. The patient, whether in point of faith a Christian, a non-Christian, or a non-believer, also complicates his needs and his emotional condition with his personal religious beliefs and faith or value structures.

We could keep in mind here that, although psychiatry became a specialty of medicine a little more than a hundred years ago, the "care of souls" (from *iatros tes psuches*—"healer of the soul") dates back a lot further. Not only has it been a primary responsibility of clergy since AD 30, but it has its roots in ancient Israel's Wise Men (*Hakhamin*), who counseled their fellows of all ranks and callings on the principles of personal conduct and the good life. Indeed "therapists" may be found among the clergy of all religions, ancient as well as modern.

It is Charlotte Buhler who insists one cannot live without encountering the problem of values, implicitly or explicitly, especially so when practicing psychotherapy. Nor, she adds,

> can one engage in psychotherapy as a therapist without bringing certain convictions about values into one's work. These convictions may or may not be

specifically communicated to the patient, but they underlie the therapist's activities; they help determine the goal he sets for himself and his patient; and they are consciously or unconsciously reflected in his questions, statements or other reactions.[1]

Any psychologist or psychiatrist who has watched Carl Rogers or Albert Ellis work or has read about Sigmund Freud's or Carl Jung's practice, is quite aware how much the therapist conveys to the patient of his thinking forms and his values. These may include, as Karl Menninger specifies, his attitudes of patience, consistency, poise, kindliness, rationality and respect—in short, his real love for the patient—as well as other aspects of his very own personality characteristics.

The Christian therapist simply makes known the source of his values and, as in Frankl's Logotherapy, is consciously aware of his influence on his patient. While some psychotherapists and psychoanalysts and some behavior-modifiers may purport to leave the "freed patient" to find his own *Weltanschauung,* most therapists consciously or unconsciously move easily from the role of screen or "rational director" or reinforcer to that of *educator* when called upon, at some points during the therapy. True, many of us believe in encouraging patients to work through their own values with regard to decisions about right and wrong in matters of personal behavior. Referred to here are, for example, the expression of anger or hostility, the expression of sex drives, the handling of authority and discipline in family life, work activities, or situations like divorce, extra- or pre-marital sexual intercourse, and so on. We generally believe in encouraging the patient to work out his own decisions, but without neglecting his past training and value systems or the value systems of the society and of religion.

The rationale for insisting that the patient make his own value decisions comes from the belief that every person has indeed been created "in the image of God" and therefore will, with personality conflicts resolved, have the capacity to work through what, to him or her, will be best in the life situations to be confronted.

Some of us feel sad when we hear that a patient's personal spiritual or religious beliefs are being overlooked by therapists, or being specifically attacked as illusory, even though this attitude would not be surprising in a therapist antagonistic toward religion or having himself no personal religious convictions.

DEFINITION OF A "CONSERVATIVE-EVANGELICAL CHRISTIAN"

Now the term "Christian" needs a word of explanation. *Christian* is used in this chapter in a restricted way. It does not just mean anyone who is not a Jew, Moslem, Buddhist, Hindu, animist or unbeliever; nor does it refer to one living in a Western country who was raised in a nominally Christian or religious family. *Christian* is used here to describe a person who has made an individual commitment to Jesus Christ as personal Saviour and Lord. This individual further "believes in" the life and death and resurrection of Jesus Christ and beyond that believes that God will empower him to live a Christian life in this world and that Christ's love will enable him to love and serve his fellowmen.

Furthermore we are defining the Conservative Evangelical Christian, as Professor A. E. Taylor does, as being one who places religion in human experience not as *primarily* concerned with social or moral reform, but rather as, first of all, throwing new light upon God and His relations with men—with moral and social reformation following as a consequence. For moral reform and relief from anxiety should occur as a natural result "from the consciousness of a new relation to God." (2)

Where do the terms "evangelical" and "conservative" fit into theological forms? As in other systems of thought, *liberal, conservative-evangelical,* and *orthodox* schools of thought exist on a continuum. The designation "evangelical-conservative" was minted by one group of Christians to indicate persons who believed firmly in an authentic historic-Biblical faith. After the term "Fundamentalist" was stigmatized and caricatured by its "modernistic" enemies beyond its original meaning of "believers in the basics or fundamentals of the Christian faith," it has been pretty well dropped by most conservative thinkers. For purposes of this chapter, let us define the evangelical-conservative Christian as one who believes in an authentic and authoritative Holy Scriptures, in the life, teachings, sacrificial death and resurrection of Jesus Christ, and in an eternal life. A psychiatrist describes his beliefs in these words: "The facts of history have not changed; Christ was crucified, is risen and coming again." (3)

Evangelicals emphasize knowledge by involvement—as do the behaviorists—but with differing presuppositions. Evangelicals seek to realize Christ through experience. In the experience of the forgiveness of sin, for example, sin is not rationalized away by explaining its harmlessness or its relativity; but rather, through faith in God's forgiveness, one is released from the consequences of sin, from guilt, and is restored through repentance, restitution, and a change of heart and attitude.

The Evangelical is quite aware that a great many psychotherapists are deeply religious and are helped in their understanding of religious experience (healthy and pathological) through their own spiritual development. Just as the psychotherapist insists that part of his training should be his own personal experiencing of psychotherapy or analysis, as he knows that the probing and analysis of inner conflicts will make the therapist more sensitive to his patients' conflicts and needs; so, therapists by coming to terms with their own religious needs, can improve treatment of their patients who have like religious concerns.

The Evangelical believes that man has worth, not only in his own right, but also because he was "created in the image of God," and this defines his relations both to nature and to other humans. A description of existential anxiety is an account of man's creatureliness and occurs when he lacks "faith." For instance, one of the commonest symptom complexes appearing in the therapist's office is "guilt" or "guilt feelings." Both are seen as "real" or "actual" by the therapist. Guilt will be discussed at greater length later in this chapter.

The Evangelical therapist rejects the tendency of many writers, both secular and religious, to completely bifurcate psychotherapy into secular and sacred healing. Granted that there are differences of focus dictated by the individual's need and condition, the therapist need not lose sight of the implicit theological presupposition of psychotherapy, as if God heals in *some* situations and natural forces do so in others. Our belief is that it is *God* who heals *always,* although through differing modalities and persons and techniques (depending upon the hurting person's need and the openness of the healer). This would seem to mean that the Christian therapist does not so much dilute Christ into the world or abstract Him out into theology, but rather that he, as Thomas Oden would say, "by a deeper Christology that celebrates Christ's concrete formation in the world," *lives out* the implications of his faith, therefore trusting that Christ loves all persons and desires their healing regardless of the channels through which the healing comes. Specifically, Dr. Oden rephrases this radical authenticity and possibility in this way:

> One might better speak of effective psychotherapy as a dekerygmatized soteriology with an implicit Christology than a natural theology, in the strict sense of a theology that intends to speak explicitly of God from some analogy with being. (4)

The Evangelical therapist not only believes that every conflict between his faith and the assumptions of his skills is resolvable, but agrees with Dr. Oden when he writes, further:

> There is an *implicit* ontological assumption hidden in all effective psychotherapy which is made *explicit* in the Christian proclamation, and (that) by means of the analogy of faith the process of psychotherapy may be understood as an arena of God's self-disclosure. (5)

And he explores the implications for theology in an era of "rapid secularization, and for psychotherapy in a time when theology is grasping a deeper perception of the worldliness of the word of God." (6)

Certainly the Evangelical therapist believes as much as does the non-Christian in a non-capricious, regularized behavior on the part of persons, healthy or pathological. No apparent irregularities or inconsistencies are ultimately unpredictable or "capricious," though they may be beyond our understanding of the moment or the age. In fact, Christian belief, as well as the teachings of the Bible, leads one to believe that the behavior of men and animals would exhibit the lawfulness, orderliness and regularity of the rest of the universe. Created "from the dust of the earth" (Genesis 2:7), man, according to Christian doctrine, would not behave in other than an orderly and lawful way, just like the rest of God's Creation. In fact, "reaping what one sows" is consistent with both the Scriptures and science. Yet none of this would indicate that man acts in a *passive* way, from the classification of the animals to man's part in scientific research and cybernetics; rather man is shown to play an active part in determining large sections of his attitudes and behaviors. (7)

This participation is often called "responsibility" by most psychotherapists, Christian and non-Christian alike. Though trained in radical behaviorism which emphasizes the necessity for empirical confirmation of any statement, I could never discard words like *choice, responsibility, beauty, truth,* and *concern for persons,* let alone concepts like *God, the worth of persons, forgiveness* and *love* (beyond *Eros* to *Agape*). While certainly the decription of *efficient cause* rests mainly upon empirical research, the discovery of *final cause* rests ultimately on religion and even on revelation. And neither excludes the other; rather one or the other is dominant in each given situation—like cold, which (short of theoretical absolute zero) includes a fraction of heat, and (masculine) males who possess some feminine characteristics.

The Christian therapist, then, sees and interprets the over-all pattern of behavior—normal and abnormal, adjusted and non-adjusted, healthy and sick—in terms of bio-chemical, physiological and psychological principles, and also in accordance with conditions of sin and grace, to use more religious terminology. All are necessary to do full justice to every aspect of human experience under consideration.

THE CHRISTIAN AS THERAPIST

The Christian therapist has no magical or illusory view of his faith. Believing Christians are as susceptible to mental illness as are non-Christians, and that, when emotionally maladjusted, Christians need help like anyone else, he nevertheless holds to a set of resource beliefs that speak to certain kinds of stress. To believe that "in everything God works for good with those who love him, who are called according to his purpose," (Romans 8:28, RSV) may undergird a person under pressure; and so the Christian Therapist, as well as the patient, is able to accept his situation positively with perseverance, with trust, with assurance and an ability, in many instances, to see his way through the experience.

It is indeed unfortunate that Sigmund Freud apparently came in contact mainly with "sick" kinds of religion and that many of his followers approach religious belief with distrust. The Christian feels more sad than angry at the Freudian mésalliance with agnostic if not anti-religious forces. The therapist recalls Oskar Pfister's reply to Freud, printed in *Imago*, and entitled "The Illusion of a Future," in which the Swiss psychoanalytic pastor refuted Freud's claims that religion stifles open thinking (one might think of some psychological orthodoxies here) and in which he pointed out that Christianity required: the giving up of wishful thinking, a positive love of truth, a total lack of compromise in relation to the ultimate and highest values, and love as the central factor in understanding humans and their behavior. It was Dalbiez who suggested that the breadth of competence that Freud's dictum embodied, i.e. "the illusional character of all religion," was itself a specific example of "psychiatric totalitarianism."

A CONTEMPORARY DIALOGUE

It is my observation that a real dialogue between psychotherapists generally and Christians specifically is under way in our generation. Two decades ago David Roberts wrote *Psychotherapy and a Christian View of Man,* insisting that no person can be brought into harmony with himself, nature and his fellow persons without reaching a harmonious relationship with God. To help psychiatry understand its task, he declared, psychotherapists need at least to understand a Christian view of God and man. Albert Outler, in *Psycho-*

therapy and the Christian Message, described psychotherapy and religious faith as natural allies except when therapists "believe" in reductive naturalism and secular humanism. "Christianity," Outler states, "offers the truest wisdom about human nature and destiny, providing an adequate context for the scientific study of man." (8)

The Evangelical psychotherapists are in agreement with a Catholic Father who, after discussing the human needs of religious (and non-religious) persons, avers that, by the grace of God and human resources, many persons overcome serious anxieties and insecurities without outside help. Also many persons mature through their relationship with friends or within religious institutions. Nevertheless, he continues, in many instances

> Christianity has need today of specialists who are well trained in spirituality, psychology and psychotherapy; men and women of deep and genuine spiritual life and of excellent psychological training who are willing to fulfill the humble role of John the Baptist to other Christians. They are not called to help people in the full flowering of their presence to Christ. They have the far more humble vocation of preparing the way for Christ by helping their fellow Christians to explore neurotic tendencies which poison their holy motives and cripple the development of their religious mode of existence." (9)

The Christian therapist is well aware that, as in this description of the therapeutic process,

> In all forms of psychotherapy a patient seems to acquire a conviction, a faith, or a system of beliefs that sustains him in the struggle against his neurotic trends and his relationships with other people and the environment at large. The essence of this faith is difficult to define and may take multiple forms. It may express itself as a sense of trust in the benevolence of a superior being (a personal God); a conviction of the strength of one's own powers, a belief that one can master adversity. It may also express itself in an ability to cope with the vicissitudes of life, and the ability to retain a sense of integrity and wholeness, a conviction of the truth of a set of scientific principles. All of this may express the fact that *one is not alone in a hostile world."* (10)

The obvious similarity of the child's trust in his parents was not overlooked by Sigmund Freud who saw this as the prototype of the Judeo-Christian belief in "Our Father," the God Who is a Good Father. The Christian insists this is most probably one psychological source of "fatherly belief," but would point out that this no more reduces the real Good Father God from consideration than an understanding of the mechanism of conditioning and reinforcement destroys learning experience. No "sneering reductionism" for the Christian! Rather, this basic belief in a loving Father may result also in the trust, love and interrelating between therapist and patient, culminating in another relationship which ultimately finds its most perfect expression in the relationship between God and person. In this connection, Strupp points out that the as yet unclear *HOW* of the therapeutic change, explained in terms like introjection and identification, transference and insight, behavior modification and stimulus-response replacement, and other differing terms, may show that psychotherapy is not necessarily to be set apart from religious experience and other psychological influences which may also result in the improvement of a person's condition.

A BASIC NEED: FAITH

Hans Strupp further insists that psychotherapy is not intended to *take the place* of religious faith, nor to be a philosophy of living, nor can it be a solace for the inescapable fact of man's existential mortality, his strictly limited powers, and the suffering, loneliness and anxiety inherent in his human condition. Religious experience and brotherhood are set apart from psychoanalytic therapy mainly in their attempts to discover and make application of psychological laws and prescriptions to problems in human adjustment. (11)

The Christian, here, sees psychoneurosis as only one way of dealing with a psychological conflict between two incompatible motives or with inadequately learned adjustment skills, and sees religious conversion as another psychological way of handling these difficulties. Since a neurosis is primarily a symptomatic way of escape from an intolerable situation or the consequence of *a denial of consequences of behavior,* one might say that conversion in the religious sense is often *a facing of the consequences,* a making of restitution for wrong doing, a restoration of relationships between persons, and a faith for living in the present and the anticipated future.

Often the Christian as a therapist is asked about his use of specifically Christian symbols and language (prayer, communion, Church attendance, religious holidays, Scripture, etc.) Do you pray in your therapy? I'm sometimes asked. My invariable answer is, Yes, continuously. Not out loud of course but in a prayer deep within my own self, something like, "Help me, Lord, to be sensitive to this person, to hear what he says and what he omits. Help me to be perceptive to the interference of my own needs and hopes and conflicts when seeking to understand his true self. Refine my skill that I may respond to this individual as a *person,* that he may not be manipulated to conform to my standards but rather be 'self-actualized' in his finest creative self-hood."

Such a prayer atmosphere seems to sharpen appreciation of my own self-hood and truly deepens confidence in my own skills as a therapist; increases my patience when the patient's acting out (backsliding) disappoints both of us; and further increases my flexibility in accepting and being involved in the patient's experimenting in and developing his own life-style and standards of conduct.

How does the Evangelical therapist deal with the obvious fact that many fine behavioral scientists do not see eye-to-eye with him on the causes or dynamics of behavior? Here William Klassen suggests that

> perhaps the new form of the behavioral sciences was sent to us as a reminder that God does not always get the response he wishes from those who confess Him and must then turn to other instruments who serve Him unknowingly. (12)

Then, too, one could not assert that psychotherapy is a stable science. Far from it, as the strife of its sects and systems would indicate—with almost as many "schools of thought" in psychology as there are denominations in the Protestant church. Yet, all the schools form a common company, as does the Church, of persons seeking to understand and repair human breakdown, with their proper datum of living human persons. Since an understanding of the world is far too vast and complex for any one person to encompass, the Christian simply allows for "other points of view," inviting dialogue and conversation and exchange of information, showing charity as he seeks fellowship with all those who serve mankind.

None of this therapy is performed in a vacuum. For the Christian therapist it presupposes congregations and parishes and pastors and theological and ecclesiastical institutions, which in turn include sacraments and pastoral care and religious education and concerned "brothers and sisters" in Christ. J. Stanley Glen points out that "only those persons who have acute problems come for psychotherapy," (13) and nearly half of all those disturbed persons seek out first their spiritual pastor (priest, rabbi, minister). So the Evangelical therapist has an immense advantage in being able to encourage a patient, when appropriate and at critical times, and in being able to see his patient involved in a "healing community." For seven years I was chief clinical psychologist in a psychiatric clinic in a catchment area of 250,000 persons. During those same years I was pastor of a small Methodist Church on the edge of the city. At no time did we have fewer than two patients, and sometimes as many as five or six, who found an accepting community in this parish. None, except for one pre-teen age boy who was adopted by a church family, joined the congregation formally, but after the recovery period returned to their own or a newly chosen congregation.

The Evangelical therapist may use specific resources from his faith in his treatment. One Evangelical psychiatrist in private practice, describes his technique as follows:

> The actual psychotherapy I had given him [the patient] was not significantly different from that which he would have gotten from a non-Christian psychiatrist. However, there were three factors which were different. First, he felt more easily able to express his problems in Biblical terms and knew that I understood what he was trying to say. Second, being assured that I was myself a committed Christian believer, he was much more readily able to accept my explanation and respond to my suggestions. Third, I was able to read a few relevant passages of Scripture to him and we often concluded our sessions with prayer together. My prayers invoking the healing power of the Holy Spirit, I am certain, were a major contributing factor in his recovery. (14)

GUILT: REAL AND NEUROTIC, AS UNDERSTOOD BY CHRISTIAN THERAPISTS

Christians have always believed in the power of the spoken word. As William Klassen insists, psychotherapy has certainly confirmed what is already clear in Biblical thought: words are effective carriers of great healing power. Jesus spoke to individuals, saying "Your sins are forgiven you," and the persons experienced dynamic changes in their attitudes and their bodies. The minister receives some of the greatest satisfactions and joys of his work when confession has been made and a human being has turned himself over to God; and, in order to bring this about, the pastor needs do only one thing; assure the penitent that God has already turned to him and forgiven him.

Hyder quotes Glasser as making the point that all society is based on moral and religious principles, and that the individual must responsibly judge his own standards of behavior to bring them into conformity with the society in which he lives. Dr. Hyder continues with the thought that

> as Christians we have absolute standards as our guidelines. The Holy Scriptures are for the Christian a handbook of daily living. They are our guide to what is right and wrong according to God's perfect and holy standard. The Ten Commandments and the Golden Rule are still valid. So, for the Christian, are several others of the laws of Moses, the Sermon on the Mount, and the admonitions of Paul and the other New Testament writers. "Thy word is a lamp unto my feet and a light unto my path." (Psalms 119:105) Jesus said: "If ye love me, keep my commandments." (John 14:15) (15)

However, commandments and laws and rules get broken, and the cumulative experience of pastors and psychotherapists is that *guilt* has caused a great many people to function ineffectively. Freud, with his background in Judaism, was much impressed by the many difficulties caused by pointing to man's sin, but without providing him with a viable means of expiating his sin or enabling him to be clearly reassured that his sins had been forgiven. The ancient Hebrews had a clear and forceful way of experiencing God's forgiving nature; Roman Catholicism has its confessional, and Protestantism its mourners' bench. To meet this need for forgiveness, psychiatry has, from its beginnings, seen itself, at least in part, in the role of a worldly father confessor. Freud wrote that the most powerful impediment to recovery from an emotional illness was an unconscious sense of guilt (i.e. guilt feelings), which leads to a negative therapeutic reaction, stronger even than narcissistic inaccessibility. Alfred Adler corrected this view, maintaining that all personality difficulties or behavior disorders are overcompensations for deficiencies, environmental repressions, or feelings of inferiority. He felt that the patient, by setting himself up as the one who condemns the act, can dissociate himself from the one who committed the guilt-producing acting out.

Guilt feelings may be described, first of all on a common sense level, as an uncomfortable sensation, a mixture of feelings which destroys inner peace. Secondly, *guilt* is the unpleasant information that something has been thought or done which violates a law or standard. *Guilt feelings* include the fear of punishment, the feelings of shame, remorse and regret, as well as resentment and anger toward the authority against whom the wrong has been committed. Finally, *guilt feelings* may be a sensation of inferiority or low self-worth. Inevitably, guilt and guilt feelings both lead to isolation and alienation—from others and from self.

So, in addition to "guilt feelings," *real* or *value guilt* has actual existence. Breaking the law of man or society is also called a *crime*, and violating a spiritual or religious standard is a *sin*. While any experienced guilt may be partly depression or anxiety, that is, partly real and partly feelings, for the religious person guilt is also compounded by a felt separation from communion with God, felt at times as some form of punishment coming from a certain failure, dishonesty, or lack of love or from a selfish action.

Ruth Benedict distinguished those cultures which controlled their populations by guilt (internalized and self-directed) and shame (from the influence of the society). Super-ego and conscience could helpfully be distinguished in somewhat the same way. Super-ego, developing during the child's period of socialization, is formed by the introjection of the child's primary care-takers' standards of conduct and belief, resulting in "those intra-individual processes that mediate the acquisition of the child's basic set of values." Sarnoff conceived of the super-ego as "a repository of all the different types of values which we may acquire as members of a culture." (16) These have some basic underlying forms consistent from culture to culture, i.e. incest, but may vary quite broadly in performance ways.

Conscience, on the other hand, refers to a spiritual capacity for discerning the person's destiny, for developing spiritual wholeness—holiness—and for achieving social health. "To know oneself altogether," is the aim. Conscience in this sense, holds standards of behavior which are defined in terms of wholeness and rationality, rather than as rigid perfection of action and thought. St. Paul summarizes the citizen's responsibiilty to the social order with the words, "It is an obligation imposed not merely by fear of retribution but by conscience." (Romans 13:5, NEB) The Christian asserts that the Holy Spirit informs the believer mainly through the conscience, only indirectly within the super-ego.

These two definitions of the "behavior-director" of the personality are not mutually independent; in fact they may be two levels of the same psychological function. But one derives primarily from society's reinforcing of behavior, while the other comes through rationality and choice and "inward integrity of heart," as C. V. Brister puts it. Charles A. Curran describes guilt as the internalization of "sin" and of "conscience" as the responsible agent which faces the prophetic call with its demand for holiness. Karl A. Menninger, though using the term "archaic conscience" for the superego, clearly distinguishes it from the "mature conscience" which mediates responsibility and broader perception and regard of self and others.

The Christian therapist would insist that even this integrity of conscience needs education to enlighten and apply its guidelines to complex personal and social concerns. And even this mature conscience benefits both through a confession of its real (or forensic) guilt and/or an effective experience of psychotherapy.

While psychotherapists generally prefer to talk about guilt *feelings*, not guilt itself, and even sometimes deny that real guilt exists, with its assumed moral standards which are permanent and real, the Christian therapist insists that treatment is limited and sometimes ineffective which ignores the reality of law-breaking and resulting guilt. Charles Curran in "Religious Values in Counseling and Psychotherapy," points out that removing pain by drugs or neurosurgery when the source of the pain remains, ultimately does the patient grave damage and even handicaps him by leading him to believe he is well, when actually he only doesn't suffer.

One therapist declares that

any psychological theory which denies the Biblical concept that there is in fact a divine standard for man's behavior is limited in its therapeutic effectiveness precisely because it is impossible virtually to forget about serious past guilt-provoking transgressions. . . . Only forgiveness can give peace. Forgiveness from the man who has been wronged can help greatly; forgiveness from God can eradicate guilt feelings completely. . . . No psychotherapy of any sort can effectively remove true guilt. Only forgiveness by the man who has been wronged or by God who has been sinned against can do this. True guilt is both a legal and theological issue. It is a feeling a man gets when his conscience condemns him. It cannot be analyzed away by a thousand sessions with a psychiatrist. It can be removed instantaneously and permanently once restitution and apology or repentance is followed by forgiveness. . . . Because Christ died on the cross for us we can receive total cleansing from every sin, and this can lead to complete restoration of fellowship with God and man, and to tranquility and peace within. This is the best psychotherapy there is, and it is not magical. . . . John, the apostle of love, said in his first letter: "If we say that we have no sin, we deceive ourselves, and the truth is not in us. If we confess our sins, he is faithful and just, and will forgive our sins and cleanse us from all unrighteousness." (I John 1:8–9) (17)

SOME GENERAL OBSERVATIONS

Let me say at this point that, in spite of the oft-repeated caricature of the clergyman as rigidly moralistic, most of us have found him—and the dedicated Christian in general—as close or closer to having Roger's "unconditional positive regard" for persons as anyone. Pastors, and Christian therapists, seek to involve a genuine willingness for the parishioner-patient to *be* whatever is present at the moment of encounter and to care for the person in a non-possessive way, taking a warm and positive attitude toward whatever is motivating the patient at his point of need.

An important facet of this fact lies in a dialectical combination of a very elevated concept of the potential of man (imago Dei) with an equally profound description of man's estrangement from himself and God (original sin). As Tom Oden points out, the therapist's conception of these possibilities is amazingly like the Pauline-Augustinian-Protestant dialectic of the estranged person created for authentic life in relationship with God, yet existing in wretched alienation from his own best possibility; and this statement holds true regardless of the therapist's religious point of view. The hiatus here may be bridged in one of three ways: normal development and maturing; psychotherapy; or religious experience—or by various combinations of any two or all three of these alternatives. While Freud's dismal view of human potentiality would fit into the original sin end of the scale, and Rogers' (with the humanistic therapists) within the imago Dei expectations, the Evangelical therapist can understand *both* within his fuller explanation of man.

Does any therapist, knowingly or unwittingly, encourage tolerant attitudes toward action which the Christian characterizes as sinful? Not necessarily. Let us look at a twenty-five year old white male, a graduate student in religion who was referred for treatment of his "homosexuality." Psychological testing and a few hours of exploratory therapy quickly revealed that homosexuality was not the, or even a, basic concern. The individual's emotional development was about age two, i.e. prephallic. An overprotective but demanding mother who was out of the home following a career much of her life, and a rigid and domineering father had contributed to an emotional fixation on a childish pre-genital level. The fellatio he unwittingly courted in the public toilets of a metropolitan subway system was more accurately described as a "suckling" or "nursing" experience than a genital sexual act. After nearly two years of treatment the patient arrived at an average adolescent curiosity about heterosexual "love." Where he worked there were several women who were not only available but aggressively sexual. The normal heterosexual interest was a therapeutic triumph, but the fornication was a threat to his religious and moral system.

What does an Evangelical therapist do in such a situation? I did what nearly any therapist would do, I rejoiced and thanked God for the progress, and placed with the patient the decision as to whether or not to practice fornication, trusting to his growing maturity to do what would be best for him, and continued the therapeutic hours.

What did he do? Today, he is a trusted professional religious worker and an effective one. He worked through his masculine identity and matured into an adult and Christian set of values that respected, rather than exploited, the sad women in his office. But shouldn't the therapist be interested in "protecting" his patient against "evil?" Obviously I did not encourage him to experiment sexually in ways that were foreign to and against his own moral values, nor would I encourage anyone to transgress the commonly held Judeo-Christian values of human worth and moral behavior. However, my own faith includes the profound respect for human beings which is founded in the Biblical teaching that man is made in God's own image and, when he is ready, can therefore be trusted to make his own decisions. And profit by his own mistakes.

While these are only a few of the areas available for exploration of the Christian attitudes in therapy, they do perhaps indicate some general trends in treatment. First, the Christian respects persons and their freedom; second, God's laws and nature's regularities are permanent and not situational or transient, so the therapist has a firm base of belief from which to work; and third, all healing comes eventually from God and is available for all therapists to use.

CONCLUSIONS

Finally, the Christian Evangelical therapist, somewhat selfconsciously explored in this chapter, feels at home as a Psychotherapist and as a Christian. It's as Tom Oden says,

> The Christian's uniqueness in contrast to the untheological views of the world and unworldly view of theology is its equal insistence both upon high Christology and upon the worldly character of the love of God, understood not as two different commitments but as a single one, *single-mindedly* dealing with the Christ who always shares in the life of the world and the world which already shares in the life of the Christ. (18)

The goal of psychotherapy seems generally to be an inner organization and tranquility in which the environment is realistically fitted into a supportive or subordinate role. The Christian therapist, seeing psychotherapy originating in the Judeo-Christian faith historically, could contrast therapy and its results with "pragmatism and behaviorism which imply drives converted to direct action and moral behavior," with wholesomeness in three broad areas of human functioning—*inward* toward the self, *outward* toward others, and *upward* toward God. A right personal relationship with Jesus Christ as Saviour and Lord, writes O. Quentin Hyder, would be necessarily included in the whole person—and this would be demonstrated by the quality of his life.

"Therapeia" (a Greek term implying *service* as used in the New Testament) suggests that all psychotherapy embodies an expectation for deliverance which is, gently points out Dr. Oden, analogous to the Christ hopes of the Judeo-Christian tradition with its expectation of deliverance from human bondage, from compulsions, anxieties, guilts—from all those experiences called by pre-scientific man, demonic powers.

Without minimizing the differences, or overlooking the disagreements, or undervaluing the conflicts, the Evangelical psychotherapist believes that his, and all, helping and healing comes ultimately from God.

REFERENCES AND FOOTNOTES

1 Buhler, Charlotte: *Values in Psychotherapy.* New York, Free Press, 1962, p. 1.
2 Quoted by McKenzie, J. G.: *Psychology, Psychotherapy and Evangelicalism.* London, George Allen & Unwin, Ltd, 1941, p. 4.
3 Hyder, O. Quentin: *The Christian's Handbook of Psychiatry.* Old Tappan (N.J.), Fleming H. Revell, 1971, p. 23.

4 Oden, Thomas C.: *Contemporary Theology and Psychotherapy*. Philadalphia, Westminster Press, 1967, p. 80.
5 *Ibid.*, p. 12.
6 *Ibid.*, p. 12.
7 For a further development of this point, see Jeeves, Malcolm A.: *The Scientific Enterprise and Christian Faith*. Downer's Grove (Ill.), Inter-Varsity Press, 1969, p. 126 ff.
8 Quoted by Orville S. Walters: Have Psychiatry and Religion Reached a Truce? In *Christianity Today*, vol. 10, no. 1 (Oct. 8, 1965), p. 21.
9 van Kaam, Adrian: *Religion and Personality*. Garden City, Doubleday, 1968, p. 186.
10 Strupp, Hans H.: Psychoanalytic Psychotherapy and Research (ch. 2) in *The Relation of Theory to Practice in Psychotherapy* (Leonard D. Eron and Robert Callahan, eds.) Chicago, Aldine Publishing Co., 1969. See esp. pp. 28, 29.
11 *Ibid.*, p. 27.
12 Klassen, William: *The Forgiving Community*. Philadelphia, Westminster Press, 1966, p. 16.
13 Glen, J. Stanley: *Erich Fromm: A Protestant Critique*. Philadelphia, Westminster Press, 1966, p. 16.
14 Hyder, *op. cit.*, p. 148.
15 *Ibid.*, pp. 172, 173.
16 Sarnoff, Irving: *Personality Dynamics and Development*. Salt Lake City and Somerset, John Wiley & Sons, 1962, pp. 282, 283.
17 Hyder, *op. cit.*, pp. 118, 119, 120.
18 Oden, *op. cit.*, p. 140. Italics are this writer's.

CHAPTER 6

CHRISTIAN SCIENCE AND SPIRITUAL HEALING

Walter I. Wardwell

> She has delivered to them a religion which has revolutionized their lives, banished the glooms that shadowed them, and filled them and flooded them with sunshine and gladness and peace; religion which has no hell; a religion whose heaven is not put off to another time, with a break and a gulf between, but begins here and now, and melts into eternity as fancies of the working day melt into the dreams of sleep.
> —Mark Twain, *Christian Science*, p. 268.

A PROVOCATIVE CHARACTERIZATION of Christian Science is that it is "neither Christian nor scientific." Such playing with words is only possible because these words have different meanings in different contexts. Christian Science is Christian in some senses but not in others. While it grew out of the Unitarian-Universalist Christianity of nineteenth century New England, it bears the distinctive imprint of Mary Baker Eddy, who founded it in 1866. It honors the Christian Bible as scripture, but it treats Mrs. Eddy's *Science and Health with Key to the Scriptures* as at least equal, if not superior, to the Bible in doctrinal authority. (1) It recognizes the role of Jesus, especially his achievement as a healer, but it does not consider him divine, at least no more divine than Mary Baker Eddy herself. The Lord's Prayer in Christian Science usage begins: "Our Father and Mother who art in heaven. . . ." In these and other ways Christian Science has modified fundamentally traditional Christian doctrine.

The word "Science" is often capitalized in Christian Science writing to distinguish it from empirical science in the modern sense. Because the latter is based on human observation, it is necessarily tentative, partial, and subject to future correction, whereas Science as a religious doctrine is absolute, perfect, and final. It is *Truth* rather than *truth*.

It cannot be tested in scientific experiment, but only demonstrated, as in Christian Science healing. Thus *Science* is clearly not *scientific*. However, it is only fair to point out that in earlier English usage the word *science*, like the Latin *scientia* and the German *Wissenschaft*, referred to any systematic body of knowledge whether or not it could be validated by observation of sense data. Thus Christian Scientists have a perfect right to these terms provided that their special meanings are recognized.

VALUES AND RELIGIOUS ORIENTATIONS

What are the fundamental bases of Christian Science as a religion and as a system of healing? To use Mary Baker Eddy's own words, they are metaphysical. The fundamental reality is mental or spiritual, not material: "God is incorporeal, divine, supreme, infinite Mind, Spirit, Soul, Principle, Life, Truth, Love." (2) The opposites of these—matter, body, evil, error, disease, and death—do not exist but are the products of mortal mind, which is in error.

Nevertheless, the human drama of mortal man unfolds, even though it be illusion for him to think of himself as material and subject to disease and death. Such subjective impressions of the ills that man is heir to, while erroneous, are to be combatted. The pragmatic considerations of money, fame, social relationships, fears, pain, and suffering should not divert mortal man from true belief in his own perfection as an idea of God. The challenge, and the solution, is for man to reject the false "claims" which mortal mind and the material world make upon him, and to accept the absolute reality of God with His many synonyms—Good, Truth, Mind, Principle, Life, and Love. "Since God is good, there can be no reality in evil nor in the testimony of the material senses." (3) Furthermore, "Christian Science teaches that all maladies, whether of mind or body, are of mental origin and are to be cured by substituting for the beliefs of the human mind the recognition of the omnipresence and omnipotence of the Mind which is God." (4) These are the basic theological principles of Christian Science.

Despite popular impressions, Christian Science healing is not narrowly limited to diseases of man's body or mind in the medical sense but applies "to the whole spectrum of human sins, fears, griefs, wants, and ills." (5) Observers have particularly noted that the fears and wants conquered in Christian Scientists' testimonials reflect ordinary Americans' concern with material success and happiness. Pierre Janet very early observed that Christian Science has "an eminently practical character, well adapted to please persons of an ambitious and active type and whose main concern was with material success. It is not a religion for weaklings and repiners. . . . Christian Science has a message of joy for all; it exalts health, vanity, and material prosperity, as lofty virtues . . . It thus ministers to the sense of satisfaction and well-being characteristic of the prosperous classes of the United States." (6) The cures achieved include sickness, loneliness, poverty, and alcoholism. Bryan Wilson observes: "Christian Scientists are realists by the world's standards, despite their idealistic philosophy. . . . Its followers may enjoy, and the religion should help them enjoy, the blessings of the material world. The material world is an illusion but at least it should be a pleasant, and not a painful, illusion." (7) He notes that there is little concern about an afterlife and no doctrine of the soul.

Hence there is no notion in Christian Science of separation from the world, despite verbal denial of its unreality. Indeed, "there is no antinomian bias in Christian Science," since the claims of sin, disease, and death are illusion, the result of false belief. "Man is not seen as perfectible but as already perfect . . . . Christian Science holds that in the absolute sense man is spiritual and therefore cannot be sick." (8) In this sense there is no problem of theodicy in Christian Science.

A central value of Christian Science is that of the "wholeness" of man. Man is not a summation of parts but an integral being. Not only is there no mind-body problem, since the body is only an illusion of mortal mind, but there is "a sense of the interrelatedness of physical, mental, and spiritual health." (9)

Perhaps as a result, although it is never mentioned in their literature, Christian Scientists reveal some empathy for such types of drugless healing as osteopathy (particularly earlier when it taught that "the body is its own laboratory" and abjured drugs), naturopathy, and chiropractic. When Christian Scientists succumb to the "claims" of their material selves (i.e. suffer an illness in which their faith fails them), they often prefer to go to one of the above-named practitioners rather than to a medical doctor who would be more likely to employ drugs or surgery. Even though such natural methods of healing include dietary regulation and bodily manipulation, they derive from theories of the innate, self-regulatory power of the body to attain perfect health provided foreign substances like medicines and anti-toxins are not introduced into the body. They thus share with Christian Science the principle that man can cope with assaults from outside (e.g. resist bacterial invasion) through inner resources and strengths. Hence it should not be surprising that Christian Scientists often prefer such therapists to orthodox physicians. (10)

CHRISTIAN SCIENCE AND MENTAL ILLNESS

The reason why Christian Science reveals little specific concern with mental illness as a distinctive malady is probably that for the Christian Scientist all illness and all healing are mental. In strictly theological terms there can be no difference for Christian Science between mental and physical disability. But just as Christian Science "maintains a commonsense distinction between sickness and sin," (11) one would expect it to maintain at least a commonsense distinction between physical disability, especially where somatic lesions are apparent, on the one hand, and functional neuroses and psychoses, on the other. The problem is further confused by the fact that the vast proportion of Christian Science cures ("demonstrations") of physical complaints ("claims") involve vague aches and pains, often internal or afflicting muscles, bones, or joints (e.g. arthritis). Improved mobility is a major manifestation in Christian Science cures. Many such physical disabilities are presumably partly psychogenic or psychosomatic in origin. Since critics have frequently alleged that Christian Science cures by suggestion, it could be a source of embarrassment to call attention to the benefits that Christian Science provides to the psychologically ill.

In any case, despite abundant evidence of emotional problems in Christian Science testimonials, references to mental illness as such are nearly absent from the Christian Science literature. The secondary status of mental illness is revealed in the following statement by Robert Peel: "It is impossible to say what part of a practitioner's time is devoted to the healing of physical disease and what part to the dealing with emotional disturbances, family problems, questions of employment, schooling, professional advancement, environmental adjustment, theological confusion, existential anxiety, and so forth. The proportion differs with individuals, and in any case, the two classes of problems are too closely interrelated to be logically separable." (12) Thus Peel distinguishes physical disease from all other disabilities and places emotional disturbances in the residual group. Even the dramatic concreteness of financial success, promotion, or finding a lost object apparently cannot compete with relief from physical suffering as a demonstration of the effectiveness of Christian Science.

However, in many published testimonials it is clear that no particular social or somatic trauma has occurred but that a problem requiring nothing more than a change of attitude has been coped with. The person is enabled to experience God's love or see his problem in a new light, pulls himself together and is "healed." The very vague conception of what constitutes healing permits a wide variety of interpretations of it. The poor, dirty Arab boy who learned to wash his clothes and to work for money and acquired property in the form of a bicycle is reported as "healed." (13) A woman "suffering from an internal growth, totally blind, almost completely paralyzed, and finally in a semi-coma . . . later explained, 'the fear of dying left me in the realization that what I really wanted was to know God better—to know Him as He actually is—to know the truth.' " (14) Her "instantaneous healing" apparently consisted in her changed mental attitude toward her fate. Inasmuch as this testimonial appears on nearly the last page of a 256-page book summarizing a century of Christian Science healing, it presumably is considered a representative, if not an outstanding, example of Christian Science healing. When "healing" has such a wide variety of meanings it is difficult to know whether it is mental, somatic, or neither.

It is ironic that the strongest evidence of the power of Christian Science to heal should come from awareness of one's bodily state. Wilson properly asks "why the testimony of the senses should be accepted as an evidence of health (which an examination of Christian Science testimonies will reveal to be the case) but denied as evidence of disease." His answer does not satisfy, however: "The answer must be that, on Christian Science premises, health, and anything beneficial, is a normal condition and to be expected, whilst any disruption is abnormal and not to be tolerated." (15) The dilemma inheres in the postulates of Christian Science and no amount of semantic legerdemain will eliminate it.

PRACTITIONERS

Christian Science has no clergy. However, it recognizes two or three types of specialists at the local level plus a governing Board of Directors and other officers in Boston.

Practitioners are lay members with a commitment to Christian Science who according to Peel are basically self-taught, although they must take two weeks of "primary class instruction" from a qualified teacher. If they have "met basic church standards and given evidence of effectiveness in healing, high moral character, and readiness to meet the challenges of the task they are undertaking," they may be listed in the directory of practitioners included each month in the *Christian Science Journal,* which constitutes certification as a practitioner. They then place the letters "C. S." (Christian Scientist) after their name, hold regular office hours, and accept no other employment.

Teachers, in addition to having had primary class instruction, are graduates of the Normal Course, which lasts one week and is given only once every three years by the Christian Science Board of Education. Originally both the Primary Course and the Normal Course, plus a course in Metaphysical Obstetrics, were taught in the Massachusetts Metaphysical College, which Mrs. Eddy founded in 1881 and closed in 1889. A graduate of the Normal Course is certified as a "teacher," places the letters C.S.B. (Bachelor of Christian Science) after his name, and may offer primary class instruction (for a fee of three hundred dollars) once a year to not more than thirty pupils. Instruction in both courses is based on a single chapter ("Recapitulation") from Mrs. Eddy's *Science and Health with Key to the Scriptures.*

Teachers are also often practitioners, and both teachers and practitioners may held local, regional or national offices in the Church. Upon Mrs. Eddy's death in 1910 the Board of Directors of the Mother Church succeeded to absolute power. Doctrine, finances, and publications are rigidly controlled by this self-perpetuating group of five. Each week the central office in Boston prescribes the lessons to be studied in every local Church.

Readers in the local churches (one male and one female), who serve limited terms, are forbidden to comment on the text they read. Discussion of doctrine is permitted only during class instruction or at the annual get-together of the pupils of a particular teacher. Divergence from doctrine can lead to excommunication. If a teacher is excommunicated all his former pupils must be retrained by an approved teacher in order to regain good standing as practitioners. (16) However, healing is definitely more important than teaching, as Mrs. Eddy clearly states in her Church manual. (17)

In 1971 there were 4785 Christian Science practitioners in the United States, and another 1115 in other parts of the world, nearly all in countries of Western European Protestant culture. In 1953 eighty-eight per cent of all practitioners were women, eleven per cent of the total unmarried women. Men outnumber women as teachers and are much more prominent in policy-making positions in the Mother Church in Boston. Nevertheless, there is a strong feminine bias in the religion—in its founder, in its adherents, in its near deification of Mary Baker Eddy as the prophesied Woman of the Apocalypse, and in its emphasis on the feminine values of love in interpersonal relationships and denial of aggression and hostility. (18)

Mrs. Eddy urged practitioners to charge fees equivalent to those charged by local physicians, but advised them to reduce their charges where a cure is not effected or where recovery is slow. However, the Church Manual prohibits a practitioner from suing patients for payment of fees. (19) Braden reports that "practitioners are authorized by statute to sign certificates for sick leave and for disability claims in seven states . . . and for federal employees. In health, accident, and hospitalization policies, some insurance companies today recognize the services of a Christian Science practitioner in lieu of a physician or surgeon." (20)

THE THERAPEUTIC PROCESS

Although Christian Science treats all types of human wants and disabilities, it is clearly the healing of body and mind that is central to its philosophy and practice. The Church Manual prescribes that "each member of this Church shall strive to demonstrate by his or her practice that Christian Science heals the sick quickly and wholly, thus proving this Science to be all that we claim for it." (21) As this is a church of laymen, there is in principle no esoteric knowledge or technique that is not accessible to each member, Wilson states: "The patient is eventually encouraged to read *Science and Health* for himself, and simply reading the book is confidently asserted to have a beneficial effect." (22) Not only does reading occupy half the time of the Sunday church service, but it is part of the daily life of the faithful. "Christian Science is unique in the extent to which it relies on the printed word; it is a religion of reading—Mrs. Eddy even designated the Bible and the textbook as 'our only preachers' . . . . It is also private reading . . . . First and foremost a Christian Scientist needs his books, and regards them as very sacred, devoting hours of study each week to the textbook." (23)

However, the rank and file may need help. The class-instructed Christian Scientist frequently offers his assistance "to those newer in the faith . . . . The practitioner, on the other hand, does not offer services: he (or, more usually, she) is consulted very much as a doctor is consulted, gives 'treatment,' and makes a charge for services." (24) But in other respects the practitioner does not function like a medical doctor. According to Peel,

> The practitioner's diagnosis is neither medical nor psychological, in the accepted sense of the word, but spiritual. The same thing is true of his treatment. Essentially it is prayer, as the word is understood in Christian Science, and such discussion or counseling as he may carry on with the patient is distinctly subservient to his silent prayer, or metaphysical treatment." (25)

Wilson explains that "prayer means something other than what is usually meant by Christians. It is neither praise nor supplication, but an attempt to bring subjective attitudes into accord with what Science proclaims to be objective reality. It is largely silent affirmation, the application of logic to certain given premises." (26)

Braden presents the most extensive description of Christian Science practice, identifying three levels of therapeutic treatment. (27) The first is concerned with the patient's consciousness, and uses the technique of "affirmation and denial"; the practitioner employs audible argument to destroy the patient's belief of suffering. Although in her earliest experimentation with healing Mrs. Eddy used " 'manipulation of the head and solar plexus' - a sort of massage" as an aid to healing, she soon discarded such laying on of hands from her therapy, possibly because it focused attention on the body as the material self.

The second level of treatment includes, in addition to audible affirmation and denial, mental or silent argument by the practitioner—"a mental salutation, in which the patient is told silently that he is well and that he knows it." Mrs. Eddy says: "If their belief of suffering is real to you it will be more difficult to make it unreal to them, which you must do in order to heal them." (This shrewd observation has been proved many times—the physician's belief in his own therapy is a most important element in its effectiveness.) Known as "addressing the thought," such invasion of another person's mental privacy would constitute mental malpractice if it were done without the person's knowledge and consent. But with the patient's consent the practitioner can treat him without being in his physical presence. Hence Christian Science healers often treat patients while both stay in their own homes. There can be meaningful communication between them, since mind is the only reality and "space is a false belief to which mind is not subject." Braden states that Christian Scientists disavow belief in thought transference, or telepathy, despite the fact that Mrs. Eddy wrote about transference of thought and that mental argument logically requires it.

At the third level, known as "impersonal treatment," the practitioner works primarily on his own thought rather than on that of the patient. Braden quotes Mrs. Eddy as saying: "If the *healer realizes* the truth, it will free his patient," and "Our *patients* manifest health after and in proportion to *our* consciousness of perfection." A *Journal*-listed practitioner provides the most extreme statement of this position: "It is the knowing of the practitioner that determines the healing. It does not depend upon the belief or the faith of the patient." Arthur Corey, a devout though disaffected and excommunicated Christian Scientist, argues in justifying this position that "Mentation is one and indivisible, and this mentation is the universe . . . . In no sense do you ever treat 'another mind'." (28)

As logically consistent as this third level of treatment is with Christian Science first principles, it remains inaccessible to ordinary minds and even to most practitioners of Christian Science. Thus Will B. Davis, Manager of the Committee on Publication of the Christian Science Church (in a personal communication to the writer) objects to Braden's distinguishing three levels of treatment, saying, "These are certainly Braden's levels and not Mrs. Eddy's! If you went out and asked the first ten practitioners you met what 'levels' of Christian Science treatment they knew of, probably all ten of them would refer to the only two levels that have meaning for Christian Scientists, namely, the level of what Mrs. Eddy calls 'argument' and that of the absolute consciousness of good, as explained in her *Miscellaneous Writings*." (29)

In any case, whatever is conceived as transpiring in Christian Science therapy, it is unlike other spiritual healing. First, the Christian Scientist does not mean by prayer the rote repetition of ritual appeals to God that other religions sometimes use; rather, the practitioner instructs and exhorts the client in right thinking. Secondly, it is private rather than public; in fact, even the practitioner can be absent. Thirdly, as it is private, there are no group rituals or organized processions with singing or chanting such as characterize the ceremonies at the healing shrine of Lourdes or the cures of Oral Roberts. Fourthly, there is no laying on of hands, so frequently found in systems of healing involving faith or psychological suggestion. And finally, related to its emphasis on reading, the impact of Christian Science is abstract and intellectual rather than emotional. With all these differences from other forms of religious healing, the question arises as to what really occurs in Christian Science treatment. Since thousands of believers have testified to its effectiveness, the problem is to discover and interpret why and how it heals people.

INTERPRETATION

The most obvious fact about Christian Science is its denial of reality. The most immediate things that are denied are the material world, one's body, pain, and death, but so also are fear, sin, wickedness, and the evil that man does to his fellow man. A well-known psychodynamic defense mechanism, denial protects the ego against threats (principally one's own impulses) unacceptable to consciousness. We may inquire then into the nature of these threats. Since empirical data on Christian Scientists as believers, patients, and practitioners are essentially non-existent, we are forced to use indirect measures to discover the meaning which Christian Science has for its adherents and the functions it serves in their lives and in therapy.

Edwin Dakin's book, *Mrs. Eddy: The Biography of a Virginal*

Mind, is a superbly documented biography of the founder of Christian Science. In it he analyzes the meaning that Christian Science had for Mrs. Eddy and some of her early followers. Basically he finds that Mary Baker Eddy was motivated by fear—"fear of inferiority, fear of disease and pain, fear of poverty and dependence, fear of reality, fear of self." (30) At times Mrs. Eddy was self-consciously aware of the role of fear, as when she wrote: "Always begin your treatment by allaying the fear of patients," and "To succeed in healing, you must conquer your own fears as well as those of your patients, and rise into higher and holier consciousness." (31) But Dakin says that "such moments of intellectual logic, however, never served to deliver Mrs. Eddy from the terrors to which she became more and more enslaved." (32)

What Mrs. Eddy most feared was "malicious animal magnetism," usually abbreviated M.A.M. Having lived during the period when the mysterious phenomenon of hypnotism was little understood, and having received physical relief as well as instruction from Phineas Quimby, the pioneering mental healer, she was impressed by the power of one mind to influence another, even at a distance. Most of all she feared the harm that could be done by malicious mental malpractice. She blamed M.A.M. for all the pain, suffering, and misfortunes she suffered throughout her career. Viewing as enemies those of her followers who became disenchanted and left Christian Science, or whom she had excommunicated for displeasing her, she often accused them of practicing M.A.M. against her or her Church. There is no doubt that behind Mrs. Eddy's expressions of love was much ill-concealed rage. Dakin refers to the "strange sleeping volcano within herself with its streams of suppressed bitterness and anger that were ever waiting some opportunity to break through the thin crust of the conscious to wreak havoc in her life." (33) M.A.M. at times became a very real and frightening thing to her as the big red dragon, the serpent, the devil, and the personification of evil, although at other times and in recent Christian Science writing it seems to be little more than mortal mind or error. (34) She taught her students how to defend themselves against M.A.M., and when she felt threatened she posted mental guardians on two-hour watches throughout the night to ward off the evil thoughts of her enemies.

Dakin indicates that M.A.M. can also be redirected against one's enemies, since "one could even assert that the human embodiment of the 'Fiend' was himself suffering from the very ills he sought to induce." (35) And he writes: "A regular society called the 'Private Meeting' and usually referred to as 'P.M.' was formed to gather in

Mrs. Eddy's parlor and to 'take up the enemy' in thought. . . . In 1888 Mrs. Eddy took occasion in the *Christian Science Journal* to deny some of the stories, admitting that she did organize 'a secret society known as the P.M.' but insisting that its 'workings' were not 'terrible and too shocking to relate.' " (36) The purpose in pushing the point this far is not merely to understand the workings of Mrs. Eddy's mind, but to indicate that beyond the possibility of denying and projecting one's impulses onto others lies the potential use of mental practice for the explicit purpose of hurting another person. Few Christian Scientists today would admit that such a possibility inheres in their religion, and probably most Christian Scientists have never contemplated that such a possibility exists. But nonetheless the Church Manual still includes a by-law titled "No Malpractice" under Discipline, Section 8:

> Members will not intentionally or knowingly mentally malpractise, inasmuch as Christian Science can only be practised according to the Golden Rule: "All things whatsoever ye would that men should do to you, do ye even so to them." (Matt. 7:12)
>
> A member of The Mother Church who mentally malpractices upon or treats our Leader or her staff without her or their consent shall be disciplined, and a second offense as aforesaid shall cause the name of said member to be dropped forever from The Mother Church. (37)

Thus the psychological mechanisms of denial and projection of hostile impulses were clearly characteristic of Mrs. Eddy. It is difficult to assess how frequently they have characterized her followers as well. One wonders about the meaning of M.A.M. to a paranoid patient. Dakin says: "It is undeniable that many converts attracted first to Mrs. Eddy's fold by her presentation of God as Love were later held there by an induced fear of M.A.M. as the devil. It would be unfair, however, not to emphasize that most followers took the good in Mrs. Eddy's Science and ignored the bad." (38)

There is clearly a sexual dimension to M.A.M. ("malicious animal magnetism"). Reference to it as the serpent and the big red dragon involve obvious sexual symbolism. More explicit is Mrs. Eddy's teaching regarding sex: "These words of Saint Matthew have special application to Christian Scientists, namely, 'It is good not to marry.' " (39) She is reported to have advised a woman that she would show greater affection for her husband "in the proportion that you withhold the conjugal claim," (40) and she held that spiritual propagation, rather than biological lust, would provide all the children wanted. Since this ideal is impractical among mortal men, she recognized that marriage must continue, but urged that coitus be limited to the purpose of procreation (not an unusual idea at the time and in the puritanical culture in which she was reared).

The subtitle of Dakin's book, *Mrs. Eddy: The Biography of a Virginal Mind*, underscored Mrs. Eddy's sexual repressions, which seem to have infected some of her followers as well. "The New York *World* asserted that many of her practitioners, married or single, led an almost nun-like existence." (41). One of her early followers, a Mrs. Woodbury, insisted that she had conceived her own child by virginal conception. Later, after Mrs. Woodbury had been excommunicated from the Church, she revealed that in private Mrs. Eddy taught that a woman could become pregnant not only by divine thought but also by a malign spirit, by which, of course, she meant the red dragon of M.A.M. (42) The obvious interpretation is that repressed sexual desires created in Mrs. Eddy unconscious conflicts, resulting in projection onto others of hostile and sexual impulses.

The sole passage in the Church Manual on relations between the sexes is the following twenty words: "If a Christian Scientist is to be married, the ceremony should be performed by a clergyman who is legally authorized." (43) It is never performed in a Christian Science Church. Thus marriage is simply not a sacrament for Christian Scientists; although tolerated, marriage is not really condoned. It is difficult to discover whether there has occurred any attenuation of Mrs. Eddy's strictures against sex among Christian Scientists with the passage of time.

Nevertheless, animal magnetism and malpractice continue as preoccupations of Christian Scientists. The technique for defending oneself against mental practice is the one component of class instruction that is specifically required in the Church Manual. (44) Braden concludes that although M.A.M. may be "less emphasized in the present day, . . . it has not disappeared by any means." (45) The student "comes more and more to the conclusion that correct handling of animal magnetism is the real crux of Christian Science practice." (46)

A related effect among Christian Scientists is a kind of alienation of the individual from the world of men, deriving from several sources. First, denial of the reality of the world, sin, and suffering separates the individual from his own bodily senses and thus from others. Secondly, although there is much concern with the material things of this world (called "supply" in Christian Science jargon), despite denial of their reality, there is little religious basis for concern with other people. Not only is matter not real, but other people don't really matter. This thought is clearly expressed in a passage attributed to the Scientist Bicknell Young: "It does not matter what someone else is thinking, but it does matter what I am thinking. What is going on is pure Mind—my Mind. And all that appears to be going on will undergo redemption if, called to a case, I know that the only man there is is already well." (47) Thirdly, specific Church practices symbolize the lack of communal bonds between fellow members at the same time that they inhibit their development. The (symbolically) most social of all religious sacraments—communion—is held only twice a year, and then without bread and wine. No weddings, funerals, baptisms, or social gatherings ever occur in Christian Science churches. Even personal acts of charity to those in need are not encouraged; indeed, the word "charity" is not even indexed in the Church Manual. Gatherings of the faithful to discuss Science are forbidden. Because "students develop strong affection for the teacher from whom they have chosen to receive instruction, and the annual association meetings serve as a re-kindling of strong personal sympathies between those who have learned their Science from the same teacher, Mrs. Eddy . . . quite early converted the original quarterly association meetings into annual meetings, and forbade the more frequent assembling of pupils by their teacher." (48) In all these ways the formal structure of the Church discourages the development of strong social bonds between members. Wilson concludes in a sociological vein that "the Christian Science Church has much more the elements of *Gesellschaft* than of *Gemeinschaft* . . . . It is an almost impersonal institution, and this is the way that Christian Scientists are taught to keep it." (49)

Mark Twain writes: "Personally I have not known a Scientist who did not seem serene, contented, unharassed." (50) This mask-like composure has been noticed particularly in Christian Science practitioners, who are professionally more involved in denying illness and evil than are the rank and file. Impersonal absorption in Mind, Spirit, divine Love floods Scientists with "sunshine and gladness and peace," but the heaven which it creates "melts into eternity as fancies of the working day melt into the dreams of sleep," as Mark Twain beautifully expresses it. Thus one somewhat withdraws from the world while he functions in the world. Or, rather, one can continue to function in the world precisely because he withdraws belief from a part of it—the bad part.

Hence the dilemma of Christian Science—how can man act in a material world when it is unreal?—is partially resolved. Wilson's answer to the question "why the testimony of the senses should be accepted as an evidence of health . . . but denied as evidence of disease," is not logically correct but it is psychologically correct, within the frame of reference of Christian Science thought. For only part of the world is unreal—the bad part. "Supply"—possessions and the means to live well—is not illusion. In this way Christian Science teaches man to adapt to those aspects of the world which he may not like but which he cannot change. And it directs attention away from many problems which he might otherwise try to do something about—sickness, poverty, war, etc.

Louis Rose offers a cynical characterization of Christian Science in his little book titled *Faith Healing*:

> In summary, "Christian Science" appeals to no reason and to only one authority, that of its founder. Its services lack the attraction of either Protestant rhetoric or Catholic ritual. Its philosophy is in essence simple to the point of banality: as developed it is incomprehensible to the simple-minded and ridiculous to the sophisticated. It is without the glamor of occult oriental theosophies or the easy comfort of the offer of an automatic life after death. Above all, it flatly contradicts our most intense everyday experience: for most of us do not need to "sit on a pin when it punctures our skin, to dislike what we fancy we feel" in order to reject its Berkeleyan idealism.
>
> Only one thing, indeed, can explain the lasting popularity of the cult, and that is the desperate need of mankind for help which the medical profession cannot give . . . .
>
> It should be stressed that Mrs. Eddy claimed to cure only the *illusion* of sickness and denied the reality of sickness itself—or even that there was a body to be sick. . . . In the strict sense, then, "Christian Science" does not form a curative discipline at all. (51)

Wilson, agreeing with Rose, states: "The system . . . in one sense is not curative at all, on its own premises, but rather preventative of ill-health, accident and misfortune, since it claims to lead into a state of consciousness where these things do not exist. What heals is the realization that there is nothing really to heal." (52)

The reason why Christian Science is not a curative discipline is that it deals with thought, not matter. Since thought can be changed even when matter cannot, Christian Science denial makes possible the belief that matter is other than it is. But since the material world is not easily changed in reality, believing that it is other than it really is makes it possible for one to accept it and live in it. More important, however, is the fact that the principle "thinking makes it so" is valid in many social contexts. A person who is convinced that he is capable of accomplishing something is far more likely to succeed in doing it. A person who denies he is sick is more likely to remain well (provided he is not so far out of contact with reality as to fail to take reasonable medical precautions). Conviction is infectious, and belief that something is so, frequently serves as a self-fulfilling prophesy.

CONCLUSION

Christian Science cures by changing belief. It employs ritualistically repeated denial of whatever is wrong—disease, evil, or lack of any kind—and compulsive reaffirmation of whatever is desired—health, love, or success of any kind. Where necessary, correct thinking is stimulated and supported by a practitioner. Whether supported by a practitioner or not, it is reinforced by reading authorized texts, especially Mary Baker Eddy's *Science and Health with Key to the Scriptures,* an equally repetitive mélange of denial of bad and affirmation of good. The spiritual force of the faith is intellectual and impersonal, not emotional and social. Whatever suggestion is involved in changing belief, it does not include emotional ecstasy or the imposition of irresistible group pressures on suggestible individuals. Christian Scientists believe because they *want* to believe.

Strong *will-power* is required to deny the reality of the senses and of bodily impairment and pain. And will-power was what the Calvinist, puritanical culture, from which Christian Science arose, most valued. Self-discipline has always depended on the mental mechanism of denial. The importance of self-reliant will-power, maintained by this defense mechanism, is undoubtedly one link between Christian Science and the American social values which observers have found very compatible with it. In this connection Thorner's insights into Christian Science are pertinent: "It is only verbally that the literature describes man as submissive to and dependent on the will of an omnipotent supernatural personality, while verbally and in action the believer proceeds upon the other view, that this 'personality' is an impersonal force which is at man's disposal." Thorner concludes that "Christian Science is the polar development of ascetic Protestant tendencies toward the transformation of the omnipotent and transcendental personal God of the Old Testament into a dependable impersonal and immanent force available for man's disposal." The net result is a "thoroughly self-reliant and responsible . . . type" of person who directs his energies in a pragmatic, this-worldly direction. (53)

REFERENCES AND FOOTNOTES

1 Dakin, Edwin F.: *Mrs. Eddy: The Biography of a Virginal Mind* (New York, Charles Scribner's Sons, 1930, p. 195) quotes Mrs. Eddy as writing: "Even the Scriptures gave no direct interpretation of the scientific basis for demonstrating the Spiritual Principle of healing, until our heavenly Father saw fit, through the Key to the Scriptures in Science and Health, to unlock this 'mystery of godliness.'"

2 Eddy, Mary Baker: *Science and Health with Key to the Scriptures.* Boston, Christian Science Publishing Society, 1934 (originally published in 1875), p. 587.
3 Healing (pamphlet). Boston, Christian Science Publishing Society, 1966, p. 1.
4 *Ibid.,* p. 13.
5 Peel, Robert: The Christian Science Practitioner. *Journal of Pastoral Counseling, 4:* 39–42, 1969. Esp. p. 40.
6 Janet, Pierre: *Psychological Healing* (trans. by Eden and Cedar Paul). New York, Macmillan, 1925, p. 88.
7 Wilson, Bryan R.: *Sects and Society: A Sociological Study of the Elim Tabernacle, Christian Science, and Christadelphians.* Berkeley, University of California Press, 1961, pp. 132–133.
8 *Ibid.,* p. 123.
9 *A Century of Christian Science Healing.* Boston, Christian Science Publishing Society, 1966, p. 243.
10 Historically, the main impact of Christian Science on medical practice was to focus attention on the mental factors in physical illness. Secondarily, Christian Science, along with homeopathy, which Mrs. Eddy claimed to have studied earlier, led to decreased reliance by allopathic physicians on massive doses of such drugs as calomel, which produces acute mercurial poisoning.
11 *A Century of Christian Science Healing,* p. 243.
12 Peel, *op. cit.,* p. 40.
13 *A Century of Christian Science Healing,* pp. 217–219.
14 *Ibid.,* pp. 254–255.
15 Wilson, *op. cit.,* p. 128.
16 See Charles S. Braden: *Christian Science Today.* Dallas, Southern Methodist University Press, 1958, ch. 7, for documentation.
17 Eddy, Mary Baker: *Manual of the Mother Church of the First Church of Christ Scientist in Boston, Massachusetts.* Boston, Christian Science Board of Directors, 1936, p. 92.
18 See the author's, Walter I. Wardell's, article: Christian Science Healing (*Journal for the Scientific Study of Religion, 4:* 175–181, 1965) for development of this theme.
19 *Manual of the Mother Church . . . ,* p. 46.
20 Braden, *op. cit.,* pp. 258–259.
21 *Manual,* p. 92.
22 Wilson, *op. cit.,* p. 129.
23 *Ibid.,* pp. 164–165.
24 *Ibid.,* p. 167.
25 Peel, *op. cit.,* p. 41.
26 Wilson, *op. cit.,* pp. 125–126.
27 Braden, *op. cit.,* ch. 13.
28 *Ibid.,* p. 352.
29 Eddy, Mary Baker: *Miscellaneous Writings.* Boston, Joseph Armstrong, 1902. See p. 352.
30 Dakin, *op. cit.,* p. 81.
31 *Ibid.,* p. 197.
32 *Ibid.,* p. 198.
33 *Ibid.,* p. 76.
34 What Is Animal Magnetism? (pamphlet) Boston, Christian Science Publishing Society, 1969.
35 Dakin, *op. cit.,* pp. 175–176.
36 *Ibid.,* p. 187.
37 *Manual,* p. 42.
38 Dakin, *op. cit.,* p. 216.
39 *Miscellaneous Writings,* p. 298.
40 Wilson, *op. cit.,* p. 187.
41 *Ibid.,* p. 188.
42 Dakin, *op. cit.,* p. 314.
43 *Manual,* p. 49.

44 *Ibid.*, p. 84.
45 Braden, *op. cit.*, p. 344.
46 *Ibid.*, p. 130.
47 *Ibid.*, p. 351.
48 Wilson, *op. cit.*, pp. 168–169.
49 *Ibid.*, p. 168.
50 Mark Twain (Samuel L. Clemens): *Christian Science*. New York, Harper and Bros., 1907, p. 268.
51 Rose, Louis: *Faith Healing*. Baltimore, Penguin Books, Inc., 1971, pp. 68–69.
52 Wilson, *op. cit.*, p. 125.
53 Thorner, Isador: Christian Science and Ascetic Protestantism. Harvard University (Unpublished Ph.D. Thesis, 1950), pp. 327–336.

BIBLIOGRAPHY

1. Braden, Charles S: *Christian Science Today*. Dallas, Southern Methodist University Press, 1958.
2. Clemens, Samuel L. (Mark Twain): *Christian Science*. New York, Harper and Bros., 1907.
3. Dakin, Edwin F.: *Mrs. Eddy: The Biography of a Virginal Mind*. New York. Charles Scribner's Sons, 1930.
4. Eddy, Mary Baker: *Miscellaneous Writings, 1883–1896*. Boston, Joseph Armstrong, 1902.
5. Eddy, Mary Baker: *Science and Health with Key to the Scriptures*. Boston, Christian Science Publishing Society, 1934.
6. Peel, Robert: The Christian Science Practitioner. *Journal of Pastoral Counseling*, 4: 39–42, 1969.
7. Wardwell, Walter I.: Christian Science Healing. *Journal for the Scientific Study of Religion*, 4: 175–181, 1965.
8. Wilson, Bryan R.: *Sects and Society: A Sociological Study of the Elim Tabernacle, Christian Science, and Christadelphians*. Berkeley, University of California Press, 1961.

CHAPTER 7

THE SEVENTH-DAY ADVENTIST FAITH AND PSYCHOTHERAPY

HARRISON S. EVANS

Introduction

ALTHOUGH RELIGION HAS ultimate goals and purposes that are greater than those ordinarily included within the framework of psychology, it does nevertheless constitute an important system of guidance and psychological support. Much that exists in religious faith is meaningful in the psychological and psychotherapeutic aspects of life as well as in the spiritual.

Religious contribution to psychological well-being: The many practical contributions that religious faith makes to the individual's psychological well-being are readily identified. A system of beliefs forms the basis of a meaningful philosophy of life, and when these beliefs are associated with an organized church there is added a sense of security in identity, the believer feeling that he is a part of something tangible, purposeful and enduring.

Further, inherent in most systems of faith are structured ways for the individual to deal with the common problems of living, such as loss, grief, guilt, loneliness and death. Faith and belief are, therefore, a source of sustenance in coping with life's vicissitudes. It is well accepted that one adjusts more adequately to the problems of living in the context of hope and faith. (1)

Religious contribution to psychological growth: In addition to the promulgation of its system of belief, the church offers inspiration and fellowship. People can feel loved and be moved to adopt a better pattern of living. Under the impact of the church's influence lives can be changed. No one can deny that the church has brought about changes in patterns of living that nothing else has or perhaps could have done.

Conversion and sanctification are religious terms, but their counterpart can be identified in the psychological processes of resistance resolution, insight and sublimation.

The church and psychotherapy: Although the church is a bulwark for good and has heavenly aspirations, it nevertheless remains an earthly institution, and therefore does not always satisfy every need or solve every problem of its members. Not infrequently, people of faith need to turn to scientifically trained persons, for example the psychotherapist, for assistance in resolving emotional and psychological conflicts. Certainly science has something to offer people in the psychological as well as the physical sphere of life.

It is true that the church has tended to be skeptical and fearful of psychiatry and psychotherapy. These feelings are understandable when one realizes that not infrequently psychotherapy has played a part in undermining faith or in directing the person away from his churchly orientation. It is easy for man to settle for an adjustment at the level of the purely psychological, interpersonal, and mundane.

However, it is my feeling that in the hands of a mature, objective, and ethical therapist who does not insist on insinuating his philosophy or style of life upon the patient, psychotherapy can be remarkably compatible with essential features of the christian faith and, indeed, faith can be strengthened through therapy. If religion and psychotherapy are viewed with understanding and tolerance, it is not difficult to see that they have much in common. There is a need to recognize how each relates to the other and how each contributes to the person's life and well-being.

The Seventh-Day Adventist Church—Its Origin And Distinctive Beliefs

I will not attempt to go into all of the doctrines of the Adventist church but will touch only upon those that seem to be most relevant to the general purpose and theme of this book. I do believe, however, that those doctrines that I will discuss represent what is most central to and distinctive of the Adventist faith.

First, a brief word about the church's origin. The church appeared on the scene in the northeastern part of the United States around the middle of the nineteenth century. It developed out of the ferment and change that was taking place in Protestant churches at that time. Its founders were seeking new truths and particularly a better understanding of man's relationship to God and his Commandments.

Two of its most distinctive features, both now and at the time of its origin, were (1) a belief in the imminent return of Christ to earth—His second coming, and (2) a belief that the seventh day of the week, Saturday, is sacred and that it—rather than Sunday, the first day of the week—should be kept as the Sabbath.

The church is fundamentalist in its orientation, and it is a recognized and accepted member of conservative protestantism. For the most part, the Bible is interpreted literally, it is looked upon as the revealed word of God, believed to be in itself a sufficient guide for man in his moral and spiritual life.

Areas that I will focus on are these: (1) the church's position regarding the role of the Ten Commandments in the life of man, (2) the seventh-day Sabbath, (3) the concept of a personal God, (4) the role of Christ in the plan of man's redemption, and (5) the holistic nature of man.

I will attempt to clarify how these points of doctrine serve as a basis for a system of human guidance and how they can, if rightly understood, add depth and meaning to human existence.

The Ten Commandments

The Ten Commandments are accepted as being of divine origin and as being the standard by which man should conduct his life. Further, it is believed that the Law is the standard against which each person's life is judged.

An orderly, lawful and responsible life: Health or wholeness is dependent upon an orderly life—a life that is responsible and that is lived out in conformity with nature's laws. In psychological circles today we are witnessing an increasing emphasis on the importance of attitudes of irresponsibility as one of the components of mental illness. This point of view suggests that in mental illness the person is not as helpless as we once tended to believe, but that indeed he can do much to be of help to himself.

Recovery from many illnesses and particularly from mental illness, usually requires an awareness on the part of the patient that he has failed to live up to certain standards and values—that indeed he has followed in some degree an immature and irresponsible pattern.

As statesmen desire a world of order based upon law and not man, so must the individual desire an ordered life based upon laws and principles abiding within. Criticism has been directed toward psychoanalysis when its emphasis seemed to be that of analyzing away guilt and conscience at the expense of recognizing the legitimate claims of conscience and healthy guilt.

The Commandments as a guide in relationships: For Adventists the peculiar and powerful import of the Law is that it is a basic guide for man in his relationship with God and his fellowmen. The Church recognizes that these relationships are most vital, and that mental and spiritual health or wholeness cannot exist in the context of faulty relationships. For the latter only bring alienation and sickness of soul and mind.

The Commandments not only serve as a guide in perfecting these relationships but point out to each individual where he has failed. "Wherefore the law was our schoolmaster to bring us unto Christ, that we might be justified by faith." (2) The Law and vital relationships, therfore, are inseparable, for it is the Law that defines what the relationships should and must be!

The Commandments and the law of love: Stressing the importance of the Commandments does not necessarily imply a legalistic frame of mind, for the church recognizes that man is saved by grace and not by works. Initially, requirements as laid down in the Law may seem restrictive and burdensome, but when their purpose is clearly understood, they will be followed according to the *spirit* rather than the letter of the Law and no longer will be onerous. The mature person lives a life of decency, concern, respect and love, not because he *has* to, but because he *wants* to, for "thy law is within my heart." (3) The Law is interpreted and obeyed in the context of the law of love: "If ye love me, keep my commandments." (4)

The Seventh Day as the Sabbath

The fourth Commandment ("Remember the sabbath day, to keep it holy. Six days you shall labor, and do all your work; but the seventh day is a sabbath to the Lord your God . . .") (5) is obeyed for two reasons. First, because it is an integral part of the Ten Commandments. Second, because it defines a relationship to God that the church considers to be of vital importance.

Adventists are creationists. Man is viewed as being the son of God, created in His own image. Therefore, there should be an acknowledged and meaningful relationship between the creator and the created, just as there is between a father and a son.

Keeping the seventh day as the Sabbath keeps alive in man's heart and mind the fact that he is a son of God and that by recognizing Him and learning to know Him he can become like Him. But one cannot become like another unless a relationship is preserved. Keeping the Sabbath makes it possible to establish or re-establish this much-needed relationship.

The Concept of a Personal God

The concept of a personal God is an integral part of the broader and more basic concept of creation. Sabbath keeping specifically emphasizes the personal nature of man's relationship to God—a relationship between the creator and the created.

The idea of a personal God, recognized and confirmed in Sabbath keeping, serves to keep man properly oriented in life. This idea enables him to be aware that he is personally significant; that he is not just a bit of flotsam on nature's impersonal stream of life, but that he is a part of a great purpose and plan; that indeed there is something personal at the center of existence—a concerned "Significant Other"—whom one is privileged to know and with whom one can experience and enjoy a vital relationship.

Christ in Adventist Theology

As is true in most Christian confessions, Christ occupies a role of central importance in Adventist theology. Much of what has been said above is dependent upon Christ and the significance of His earthly ministry.

Adventists accept Christ as being the Son of God and believe that during His time on earth He shared his divinity with humanity. To them Christ's sojourn on earth can be viewed as having a twofold purpose. First, his purpose in coming was to save fallen man. Christ is the redeemer, savior and the sacrificial lamb. He is the prototype of all acts of atonement and ritualistic restitution. Second, and more relevant to our subject, His purpose in coming was to present a correct image of God.

The idea of a personal God fulfilled in Christ: Christ was God's representative. Indeed He was God incarnate. He came to express God's concern for man and to establish a personal relationship between man and God. Through Christ God became involved with man in a very personal way. No longer was God a remote, impersonal idea or concept, but a real Person whom man could experience and know in the flesh by knowing Christ.

The restoration of God's image in man: Man was created in God's image. He was to be like God. But as a consequence of the Fall this image was seriously marred and defaced. Man had regressed and had become morally corrupt and evil.

Man is elevated by his aspirations and ideals. There is needed in every man an *ego ideal.* An ego ideal is grounded in an inner image, an introjected figure, which one aspires to be like. To establish an inner image that is to be the *basis* of an ego ideal, there must first be an object for introjection and identification.

The image of God could only be re-established through *identification with a model* who accurately represented Him. This it is believed Christ did perfectly. "He that hath seen me hath seen the Father." (6) And again, "No man hath seen God at any time; the only begotten Son, which is in the bosom of the Father, he hath declared him." (7) In other words, God who created man in His own image did not leave man without the opportunity to have this image restored within him, and this (restoration) was accomplished through man's relationship and identification with Christ.

Christ was fully aware of the importance of identification in the moral elevation of man and in his acquisition of spiritual and psychological unity. For his stated wish was "That they all may be one; as thou, Father, art in me, and I in thee, that they also may be one in us. . . . I in them, and thou in me, that they may be made perfect in one." (8)

The impact of Christ's influence and the change through identification is further alluded to in a familiar passage from the New Testament:

> "That which was from the beginning, which we have heard, which we have seen with our eyes, which we have looked upon, and our hands have handled, of the word of life; For the life was manifested, and we have seen it, and bear witness, and show unto you that eternal life, which was the Father, and was manifested unto us; That which we have seen and heard declare we unto you, that you also may have fellowship with us; and truly our fellowship is with the Father and with His Son Jesus Christ." (9)

Corrective emotional experience in Christ's ministry: To man God was a remote, awesome and fearful figure. He could not be safely approached except through ritual or priestly mediation. Man approached God much as an anxiety-laden patient approaches the therapist, with fear and trembling.

The therapist's task is to provide a corrective emotional experience, to show that he is not as the patient imagines him to be.

Therefore, one of the significant things that Christ accomplished was to provide for man a corrective emotional experience—to reveal what God is really like, surely not as man had imagined Him to be.

Christ did not reject, judge, or condemn, but responded with attitudes of unconditional acceptance, understanding, forgiveness, love and compassion—as in the words, "Neither do I condemn thee: go, and sin no more." (10)

By responding to mankind differently than what they expected,

He provided a new concept of God and of Justice. Through His healing relationship man's sense of alienation was overcome; man no longer felt isolated, rejected or burdened down by guilt.

Man's relationship to man: In His ministry Christ not only revealed what God is like, but He also provided an example of how man should relate to his fellowman. He condemned pride, selfishness and indifference and constantly emphasized what is basic and meaningful in life and in man's interpersonal relations.

The Commandments and the law of love: Christ said He had not come to destroy the Law but to fulfill it. "Think not that I am come to destroy the law, or the prophets: I am not come to destroy, but to fulfill." (11) He came that man might have life more abundantly—not by doing away with the Law, but by fulfilling it completely in the context of a spirit of love. He made the purpose and the spirit of the Law come alive in the example of His own life. He did not diminish the Law but enhanced its value and meaning by demonstrating what it can accomplish for man if properly understood and carried out in the right spirit.

The Holistic Nature of Man

The Seventh-Day Adventist Church has been distinguished by its emphasis of the holistic nature of man. It takes the position that man is a unity—that body, mind, and spirit are aspects of the greater whole; and that if man is to be made whole—healthy or holy—each of these aspects must be given appropriate attention.

This philosophy explains why the Church has been active in the areas of health, nutrition and education as well as concerned with spiritual and religious matters. Unless laws pertaining to physical health are understood and obeyed, man cannot be whole, even though he might be ever so faithful in the religious sphere. The Adventist Church in its effort to promulgate this holistic view of man has supported a far-flung, world-wide network of hospitals, schools and colleges. Health education and health care have gone hand in hand with the education of the mind and the spreading of the Gospel.

Dynamic Psychotherapy and the Adventist System of Human Guidance

The essential features of dynamic psychotherapy are not in conflict with the essential features of what one can call the Adventist system of human guidance.

The individual's needs: In the framework of dynamic psychotherapy, the individual's needs and problems center in the area of interpersonal relations. The person is in conflict, both with others and within himself. There are problems of immaturity, distorted attitudes, hostility, rebellion, poor impulse control, and so on. The individual's life is far from being orderly and lawful. Neurotic and psychotic lives are characterized by varying degrees of fragmentation and chaos.

It is impossible, however, for the person to establish order or lawfulness within his life without personal help. He needs a "savior" who enters into a relationship with him and who in this relationship makes possible the kind of an experience that is healing and productive of health and wholeness or holiness.

The therapist's task: The therapist will (should) present himself as a mature person—lawful and orderly. His lawfulness will be demonstrated and not preached—demonstrated in the interpersonal process. He will attempt to reflect such qualities as indicate a respect and acceptance of those lawful behavioral patterns that undergird healthy living. These will include respect and unconditional acceptance of the patient as a person, decency and fair play, responsibility, the setting of limits when necessary, the value of maturity and the orderly management of life, and the greater worth of behaving on the basis of the reality principle rather than the pleasure principle.

In this therapeutic interplay the patient enjoys new and healing experiences. Corrective emotional experience brings new perspectives. The therapist's attitude of unconditional acceptance enhances self-esteem and self-respect; his reliable and responsible relationship develops trust and confidence; and his example of maturity, good will and orderliness stimulates the process of identification with the inevitable restructuring of the patient's ego and superego.

The therapeutic process brings order and lawfulness into the patient's life, not out of a categorical imperative, although lawfulness must be honored and obeyed if the person is to be whole. That sense of order and lawfulness will come to him because the law becomes written *in his heart* by the process of an ordered, loving relationship. Thus the person is bound to the law by love and not by a sense of duty.

The spiritual context of healing: Healing and therapy in the spiritual context must utilize the same steps and psychological processes that are used in dynamic psychotherapy. The mind can no more be by-passed in spiritual healing than it can in psychological healing.

Even though the steps in psychological healing are closely related to, if not identical with, spiritual healing there are basic philosophical differences between the two. In the spiritual context the therapist is attempting to represent a supernal model. He is pointing to Someone beyond himself. He acknowledges a law and an order that is not man-made and therefore not subject to human arbitration. He believes that spiritual healing leads not alone to a life of mental peace, but to a life that can experience and enjoy extra-earthly pleasures and joys (salvation). He also recognizes that although the therapist is vital to the healing process, there is something beyond and above him that heals, namely, a "Spirit" or a "Life Principle" working in and upon man. The ground in spiritual healing, therefore, is ultimately not just man, but God.

REFERENCES AND FOOTNOTES

1. Menninger, K. A., Mayman, M., and Pruyser, P.: *The Vital Balance*. New York, Viking, 1963, pp. 365–400.
2. Galatians 3:24
3. Psalms 40:8
4. John 14:15
5. Exodus 20:8 (R.S.V.)
6. John 14:9
7. John 1:18
8. John 17:21,23
9. I John 1:1-3
10. John 8:11
11. Matthew 5:17

CHAPTER 8

MORMONISM AND PSYCHOTHERAPY

C. Jay Skidmore

Introduction

Mormonism is a way of life for its members. The Church of Jesus Christ of Latter-Day Saints guides its members in a dynamic way toward a universal goal of "personal exaltation and eternal life." This means that Church members who are able to live the gospel plan believe they are being more "God-like" in this world; and after death, they will become Gods with their own eternal increase and worlds of their own. Active members are generally obedient to the guidance and teachings from their Church leaders.

The Mormon Church is concerned with both the spiritual and temporal affairs of its members. It is involved in influencing almost every aspect of human living. There are many programs and services which help each member grow toward his own goal of fulfillment. With the lay leadership practice within the Church, everyone is needed and has an opportunity to serve. The helping and teaching processes in the Church assist members in experiencing many of the feelings of "psychotherapeutic-like relationships," informally, formally, and professionally. The Church leadership is constantly looking for ways to bring health and happiness to its members. There is great concern to share with all peoples the joy which comes from living the gospel of Jesus Christ and serving God.

Values and Beliefs

The Mormon Church teaches the basic doctrines of the New Testament related to the development of the "whole man." Mormons are motivated toward eternal progression by such scriptures as: "Be ye therefore perfect, even as your Father which is in heaven is perfect," (Matthew 5:48) and "Thou shalt love the Lord thy God with all thy heart. . . . Thou shalt love thy neighbor as thyself" (Matthew 22:37,38) and "But he that is greatest among you shall be your servant." (Matthew 23:11) Modern Mormon scriptures say that "God's glory" is "to bring to pass the immortality and eternal life of man . . ." (*Pearl of Great Price,* Moses 1:39), "Man is that he might have joy" (*Book of Mormon,* II Nephi 2:25), and "The glory of God is intelligence, or in other words, light and truth" (*Doctrine and Covenants* 93:36-37). The thirteenth Article of Faith from the basic creed presented by Joesph Smith, reflects the attitude of Mormons: "We believe in being honest, true, chaste, benevolent, virtuous and in doing good to all men; indeed, we may say that we follow the admonition of Paul, we believe all things, we hope all things, we have endured many things and we hope to be able to endure all things. If there is anything virtuous, lovely, or of good report or praiseworthy, we seek after these things." The Mormon leaders claim to be divinely authorized and to be inspired in guiding the affairs of the Church.

Mormon Church Programs and Services

The Church has many programs and services whereby individuals may become more perfect in the sight of the Lord. It is common for members to spend several hours per week in meetings—spiritual, educational, and cultural—sponsored by the Church. Many hours are devoted to recreational activities and compassionate service.

There is a belief in the Church that persons in various positions of leadership will be inspired to perform their tasks and responsibilities. Individual members, through prayer, may get comfort and satisfaction for their personal health and well being. A father may gain inspiration as he guides and directs his family. A bishop for a ward (congregation) is blessed with powers to guide and direct the members under his supervision. The bishop is the key person offering guidance services in the Mormon Church as described by Elder Spencer W. Kimball, Church authority:

> A Bishop is ordained with an everlasting endowment. He is set apart as Bishop of a ward to provide its leadership. He becomes the spiritual adviser, inspirer, counselor, discipliner. He becomes by ordination and setting apart the father of his people and should know them individually by name and nature and weakness and strength. He should foresee and forestall possible problems and if some develop, be able and ready to help in their solution. His ward family should be his enlarged family and receive general interest as his own flesh and blood children.
> By virtue of his call and ordination and setting apart, he also becomes a "judge in Israel" and has the responsibility of making many decisions which affect their progress and development and their life. He has control over their spiritual activities so that he can give them opportunities for growth; and judge their ac-

complishments. He decides as to their worthiness and eligibility for certain blessings and privileges. He holds the key to all temples in the world and it is he who must turn the key to open the doors thereof and through eternal marriage to life eternal. . . . Accordingly, bishops may lack much in formal training or they may be specialists high in academic cirlces. But both will succeed in proportion to their dependence on Divine guidance and their humility, industry, love and consecration. (1)

The Bishop's Training Course and Self-Help Guide indicates a bishop may find that, along with courage and hope, "in his ordination was included the spiritual gift of discernment." (2)

The bishop visits families in their homes at least once a year and his representatives visit once a month.

He interviews members of all ages periodically. He encourages them toward worthiness and living a good gospel life. Boys and girls are interviewed at the age of eight, just before baptism. As they grow up, they are interviewed by the bishop a few times each year. He encourages them to stay close to the Church.

The bishop also counsels young people prior to the wedding ceremony. He has a commission to provide for the spiritual welfare of all the members of his congregation. Other officers assist him in carrying out this goal. He calls the priesthood to work on welfare projects. These efforts create wealth which can be used for needy families.

Guidance and instructions come to all members through conference sessions and printed materials presented by leaders above the ward level, such as stake leaders (over several wards), regional leaders (over several stakes), and the general authorities of the Church from Salt Lake City, Utah. The bishop receives instruction from these leaders and he can seek special help on difficult problems from them.

The bishop and priesthood members, men specially called, may give a special blessing in the household of faith for the sick—the practice of faith healing. This practice is common for persons with both physical and emotional illness. They receive comfort from this kind of blessing.

More and more, the bishops are utilizing the organized Latter-Day-Saints social service agencies. The functions of these agencies include adoption of children, foster home care, personal counseling, and marriage and family counseling. These agencies are being administered on a regional basis and are staffed by well-trained, experienced workers.

More than one hundred paid professional persons are in regional centers to consult with bishops, stake presidents and regional representatives, providing the services of a licensed welfare agency. They also coordinate a new voluntary services program from professional persons. They call on persons with professional skills in the region to donate their special services.

The Church maintains the Primary Children's hospital in Salt Lake City with its staff of physicians, psychiatrists, psychologists, and social workers who provide medical, psychological and psychiatric help to children from all over the world. The extensive Church hospital system features psychiatric wards on an out-patient care. Professional treatment may be rendered to members of families who are emotionally disturbed.

Love-inspired, compassionate service is the activity for which the Relief Society, the women's auxiliary, is best known and most highly respected. Sympathetic and tender merciful service to those in distress is and always has been a fundamental part of the work of the Relief Society. The visiting teaching program is a medium through which this compassionate service can be done. This organization is also under the direction of the Relief Society. The purposes of visiting teaching according to Belle S. Spafford, President of the Relief Society, are "to search out the poor and needy, to exercise watchcare over Latter-Day Saint sisters in their homes; to offer encouragement, help, solace and comfort to Latter-Day Saint women, to establish warm friendly relationships with them so that in time of need they instinctively will turn to the visiting teachers, knowing that through them necessary sisterly help is available." (General Conference Talk, 1971)

All this is done in conformity with the assignment given to the Society by the Prophet Joseph Smith to search out the poor and suffering.

A bishop has a great challenge and responsibility to assist all members in his ward toward exaltation. He is able to call on those persons and resources to help make this possible.

Helping Process-Psychotherapeutic-Type Relationships

If the psychotherapeutic-like process is broadly defined as all human relationships which enhance the adequacy and fulfillment of the individual's personal and social adjustments, then the relationships in the Mormon Church can be described in three categories—informal, formal, and professional.

The Informal Relationships

Each member of the Church throughout his lifetime cycle from birth to death has an opportunity for personal development and social skill enhancement. Mormons get a great deal of support in their association with Church members. A strong feeling of identification exists with Mormons wherever they are. It would be realistic to note that most experiences and relationships within the Mormon Church are healthy and positive. Yet some persons may be "turned off" for various personal reasons within themselves or by unsatisfactory experiences with the Church program. Feelings of importance, productivity and personal worth may be achieved in the interpersonal relationships through involvement. These relationships are therapeutically sound.

The Formal Relationships

It is feasible that Mormons may be active in the Church programs as long as they live. This means that many hours a week are devoted to meetings, activities, and services. Obedience to the ordinances brings satisfactions in building one's life. Leadership responsibilities usually indicate growth and development of the inner self. The result of a wide variety of good experiences in the various programs of the Church is the gaining of a testimony of God and the sound gospel principles. Members value church opportunities more than others. An example of how many persons feel about the monthly "fast and testimony" meeting would be deep emotional expression by those persons testifying to the meaning and value of the gospel in their lives. They experience feelings of catharsis, forgiveness, and appreciation. Those in attendance often empathize with the persons talking and they develop a sense of closeness and understanding.

Required as well as spontaneous interviews with the bishop encourage deep soul searching—what should I be like, and what am I really like? One result of this may be that of a spiritual feeling of belonging—someone cares!

Professional Services

The Church is concerned that truth, beauty, love, and the art of living be of the highest quality. Guide manuals are available for self training for bishops and others. Inservice training workshop materials are used in leadership training. The religious instruction through the seminary and institute system is under the direction of professional educators.

There is an increase in the use of professional persons in the psychotherapeutic professions of psychiatry, psychology, social work, and marriage counseling within the Church services and functions. Professional persons not directly part of the Church organizational structure are working more closely with Church leadership to provide effective, appropriate and meaningful guidance services for those in need.

Major Concerns and Special Problems in Counseling and Psychotherapy

Obedience, Conformity and Free Agency

A major doctrine of the Church is free agency. One has the freedom of choice to conform to the gospel plan and advice of the Church leaders, thus reaping the blessings and benefits of that style of living. One has the choice of deviating from the teaching of Christ as one perceives the meaning of living with results appropriate to these decisions. Church members may be classified in three ways: (1) Those who accept the commitment to the teachings and principles, finding great comfort and strength in living as suggested. (2) Those who use free agency and think through many of the religious decisions around conflicts and choices. They find comfort in a good life, but it would vary from the model "Christian plan." (3) Those who reject and rebel against the teachings of the Church, expressing patterns of behavior not in harmony with the Church standards. The degree of solution to personal problems depends on the basic commitment to values and laws. Peace of mind comes when one lives according to the laws, and the quest for the meaning of life is furthered.

Fear of Counseling or Therapeutic Help

Members of the Church who are suffering "emotional pain" whether it be guilt, anxiety, decision, depression, or others will most likely seek relief through an interview with the bishop. Yet there may be an attempt to understand these feelings by talking to friends, family, or the family physician. Often there are concerns of trying to understand the feeling as related to the behavior of obedience in living gospel principles. If the bishop is a close personal friend it may be hard to talk freely about one's intimate life. For some, then, it is a difficult decision, "Who do I go to for help?" One is free to seek help from professionals such as psychiatrists, psychologists, social workers, marriage counselors, teachers, and physicians. Members realize that real forgiveness and repentence must be worked through the bishop, yet many of these feelings may be resolved by counseling with professional persons. The fear associated with seeking help is not a sign of weakness or illness; it is a start on the path of growth toward greater health and maturity.

Dealing with Mental Illness

When a member of a family becomes mentally ill, usually the family will work with the bishop, but some families will seek professional help directly. The bishop will do everything within his power spiritually. Depending on the nature of the illness, much may be accomplished in this way. Until recently there has been much conflict and strain between the religious leaders and the professional person in the treatment of mental illness. Dr. Louis Moench, a Salt Lake psychiatrist, comments on how each may be most effective and how they might work together in bringing about health in the patient:

> President [Stephen L.] Richards and I accepted the premise that ideally the clergy and psychiatrists could and should work together, with common or at least compatible goals, but in actual practice the cooperation is far from ideal.
>
> I acknowledge the validity of President Richards' concern, and expressed the concern psychiatrists often have when encountering the clergy treating illness, often without recognizing it as illness. We agreed that each discipline tended to look on people's problems as belonging in his domain, and each often minimized the proper domain of the other, that cooperation between the two is often praised and much less often practiced.
>
> We agreed that guilt serves useful and constructive purposes in helping a person achieve inner control, and in converting a mistake into a learning and growth experience, but it may become pathological in amount (excessive or deficient), in duration, or may be distorted or symbolic. In some circumstances, it is appropriate to deal with guilt itself, but in others it becomes advisable to understand and deal with the underlying process.
>
> It is not appropriate for psychiatrists to forgive sin or to encourage behavior or attitudes contrary to the religious standards of the person or of the community. The psychiatrist should be familiar with and respectful of the patient's religion and encourage the healthy application of and participation in his religion. He is often much more aware of the pathological forms of religious involvement, such as entheomania, scrupulosity, asceticism, fantasy, denial, etc., than the wholesome forms of religious participation.
>
> The clergy should not treat mental illness (except where especially trained or as part of a professional team), should be aware of the pathological forms of religious belief, should be aware of the principles of mental health, and should recognize the more overt signs of psychiatric disorder. The psychiatrist and the clergyman can use each other as resource persons without competitive concern. In the enormous middle ground of human experience and relations, mutual respect and cooperation between the psychiatrist and clergyman enlarge the calling of both. (3)

Mormon bishops as they learn more about psychotherapeutic process may be more effective in their spiritual role. Professional therapists may need to be much more sensitive of the religious belief as related to motivation, causation, and treatment.

Spiritual Guidance and Psychiatry

It is difficult to evaluate the amount of help bishops may offer in the prevention and treatment of emotional difficulties. By the same token, not all psychiatrists help all of their patients. Psychiatrists Hunt and Blacker discuss some of the differences as they see them between Mormonism and psychiatry:

> Among many Mormons there exists a genuine distrust of psychiatry. Apprehensions arise partly from misconceptions about psychotherapy and partly from a stigma that many attach to anything associated with emotional disorders. Many believe "If you live your religion, you won't need a psychiatrist." For many, to visit a psychiatrist would be to admit emotional and spiritual failure. Mormons might enter psychotherapy with not only the usual fears and anxieties concerning an unknown experience that lies ahead, but also with questions and reservations concerning the relationship of their religion to the psychotherapeutic process. "Will I be instructed to do something which violates my own moral standards? "Will my faith in God or in modern prophetic revelation be threatened or ridiculed in psychotherapy?" "Will I lose my testimony?" "What are the differences in emphasis or the conflicts between psychiatry and Mormonism?"
>
> Most Mormons believe in the existence of moral absolutes—that there is a right and wrong to every moral question which is independent of the person and the situation. . . .
>
> Psychiatry generally considers moral values as being relative to the individuals, the circumstances, and the relationship involved. It does not attempt to establish a universal concept of morality. . . .
>
> Psychoanalytic psychology stresses that moral values arise from the integration of man's biological strivings, his experience, and his intellect. Man is capable of creating his own values and ethics through revelation and prayer, and believes that all men have access to it if they but seek. . . .
>
> The psychiatrist is more interested in exploring the nature of behavior and its effects on the individuals involved than in rendering any value judgment. . . .
>
> Mormonism is primarily concerned with the relationship of behavior to divine law. . . . The moral struggle for most Mormons lies not so much in the quest of moral principles, as in obedience to divine command.
>
> Finally, there is a difference in the goals for man as expressed by Mormonism and psychiatry. The psychiatrist's objective for the individual is for him to be a self-directed, self-knowing man, one whose decisions are authentically his own. In psychiatry, man is encouraged to be ultimately responsible to himself. This is not a simple task. It requires careful assessment of one's loyalties, responsibilities, and desires. Man must answer to himself for his actions. He can allow no organization or society to totally excuse or dictate his behavior. The goal of the gospel is for man to use his self-direction to follow Christ. To most Mormons man is ultimately responsible to God with the hope of becoming a god himself. He strives not only for a rational standard of goodness, but for a spiritual quality of righteousness. His ultimate prayer is not "Thy will be done," but "Make thy will my will." Thus, while psychiatry seeks health, Mormonism seeks exaltation. (4)

The understanding and use of true principles in both religion and psychiatry by the bishop or the psychiatrist may get appropriate results. Much depends on the personalities involved and the problems. Maturity of the counselor and religious leader and the way they build relationships is crucial to the helping process. The difference in so-called values is not so different if both parties could have a common understanding of needs, goals and the helping processes. The writer agrees with Hunt and Blacker that Mormons expect more than just health, they expect exaltation or perfection. Some areas of differences have not been resolved and they present a challenge to both for careful consideration.

Mormonism's Contribution to Mental Health

The Church is most influential in the lives of its members. There is a purpose in life and a meaning of life. The Church leaders and organizations exist to bring the growth and realization of the "good life" to all members. This is brought about by the experiencing of the development of self, of sound relationships with others, of performance of services, of gaining a sense of personal worth and productivity, and of achieving satisfaction and joy. Dr. Victor B. Cline, psychologist, emphasizes this:

> I am impressed by the positive impact of its [Mormon Church] philosophy and remarkable action program on people's lives, an impact akin to what I occasionally witness in psychotherapy. (5)

Dr. Stanton L. Hovey describes the scope of the influence of the Church:

> The potential influence of the Church in bringing about the development of healthy families may be found in three areas: (1) doctrine and practice aimed at members' families, (2) professional resources from both the Church and the secular world, and (3) political and social action aimed at all families. (6)

Summary and Trends

The Mormon Church is a dynamic force in the guidance of its members toward self-expression and fulfillment. It provides extensive programs and services for growth and enrichment of its members. It is sensitive to the need to alleviate human suffering and illness through the healing arts of the spiritual leaders. Professional persons from psychiatry, psychology, social work, and medicine will be called to work closely with the spiritual leaders in their own social service agencies. Private and public professional services may join hands appropriately to meet the needs of Church members.

REFERENCES AND FOOTNOTES

1 Talk given by Elder Spencer W. Kimball, November 1963, to Latter-Day Saint psychologists and psychiatrists in a class of Dr. G. Hugh Allred, Brigham Young University, Provo, Utah.
2 The Church of Jesus Christ of Latter-Day Saints: Bishop's Training Course and Self Help Guide. Salt Lake City, Utah, 1970, p. VI-13.
3 Louis G. Moench: Guilt: A Psychiatrist's Viewpoint. From *Dialogue*, vol. 3, Autumn 1970, pp. 50–54.
4 Robert D. Hunt and K. H. Blacker: Mormons and Psychiatry. From *Dialogue*, vol. 3, Winter 1968, pp. 13–24.
5 Victor B. Cline: The Faith of a Psychologist. From *Dialogue*, vol. 1, Spring 1966, pp. 54–67.
6 Stanton L. Hovey: Church Influence upon the Family. From *Dialogue*, vol. 2, Autumn 1967, pp. 53–63.

CHAPTER 9

JUDAISM: A PSYCHOLOGICALLY ORIENTED PHILOSOPHY

Emanuel M. Honig

JUDAISM AND the Jewish religion are not synonyms. The term Judaism is a more comprehensive one. The religion is only one aspect of Judaism which represents in its total structure a cultural orientation, a heritage, a history, and a philosophy of life. The creed and theology only serve as an inspiration and guiding force in the identification with spiritual values and ethical behavior patterns. In essence, it serves as a functional process for the humanization of man. Judaism must not be conceived of as a static religious structure but as a dynamic, evolving life process. It represents the full expression of the striving of the Jewish people.

The rabbis, the sages of Judaism, were obviously not psychologists or psychiatrists, nor were they trained in psychotherapeutic methods. They did not attempt to equate their function as teachers of religious values with psychotherapy, as is too often done by the present day clergy of all faiths. Certainly religion and psychiatry can not be equated in terms of function or purpose. The goal of psychiatry is to treat mental illness through definitive therapeutic techniques, and secondarily to offer dynamic insights into the nuclear factors within emotional illness which can serve as a prophylaxis against the psychological traumata which effect the neurotic conflict. By this definition certainly Judaism is not a curative or therapeutic process.

However, Jewish tradition expresses many insights into the character of man, and through an intuitive understanding of the art of living has created a psychologically healthy philosophy of life. Judaism has always sought to facilitate mental health through a system of values which contributes to the individual's self realization and to the good of humanity and society. For a long time, Judaism has been aware that there is such a thing as a pathological religion.

Extremist behavior of any kind exercised in the name of religious morality, is not looked upon as a positive value, and neither extreme abstinence, frequent fasting, nor any other form of self mortification has been prescribed or encouraged. Judaism has sought the proper balance between man's internal and external life.

In one sense there is a similarity between the goals of psychotherapy and Judaism in that they both attempt to broaden the individual's perspective to a point where he moves from a preoccupation with the self and his own problems, to a greater personal freedom and broad empathy with the needs of others. In short, man's achievement of a high level of integration in his relationship to himself, to others and to the world is paramount within both disciplines.

To understand how this goal of human integration is achieved within the framework of Judaism, one must examine its basic concepts and fundamental principles.

The God Idea

Sigmund Freud, in his attack against religion, was motivated by a profoundly humanistic approach to life. He perceived of man's creative forces and his strivings for a better life as the only true value. He condemned any influence which he deemed as *limiting* man's freedom of thought. Any religion or religious philosophy which would infantilize man and encourage dependency needs was rejected. He did not countenance any rigid fundamentalist theism which created fear and servile obedience.

Freud was not unaware of the profound contributions of the humanistic features of religion to man's emotional and spiritual growth and development. He avowed this openly in his statement in "Civilization and Its Discontents": "Nor may we allow ourselves to be misled by our own judgements concerning the value of these religious philosophic systems or of these ideals; whether we look upon them as the highest achievement of the human mind, or (whether) we deplore them as fallacious, one must acknowledge that where they exist and especially where they are in the ascendant, they testify to a high level of civilization."

An avowed faith in God is an essential element within the Jewish religion as in all religions. However, Jewish theology insists that the fulfillment of man's duty and obligations to God can be manifested only through his relationship to his fellow man. In the Talmud, the rabbis presented this concept by picturing God as stating, "Would that they forsake me, but keep my commandments, because if they keep my commandments, they will eventually find me." The emphasis in Judaism is not so much on a God-centered philosophy but on the realization that man's finest way of serving God and His religious ethic is through man's obligation to human society. On the Day of Atonement, a person cannot seek godly forgiveness before he seeks forgiveness from those of his fellow men whom he has wronged. Solomon Schechter, one of the founders of Conservative Judaism, succinctly summarized the Jewish concept of God: "The rabbis cared more about what God requires us to be, then about knowing what he is."

Certainly there are many Jews who believe in the God who hears and answers prayers, in a God upon whom they rely for retribution and rewards, and many who bear the conviction that God will intervene in human affairs to set all things right. However, Jewish theology warns against the childlike wish to weigh all moral considerations in the scales of reward and punishment. They stress that men are to be as "those who serve their masters without hope of reward." Judaism has always emphasized man's responsibility for his own actions and decisions and has encouraged self-reliance and individuality. In man's efforts to relate to himself and to the world, there is a great kinship between the Jewish God concept and the founder of psychoanalysis.

Sex

One of the psychological conflicts within society is the area of sex and love. Many neuroses are products of sexual inhibitions and taboos. Religions, in general, are considered to be inhibitory with regard to sexuality, Specifically, in earlier times the rights of women in sexual gratification were often denied. However, the sexual attitude of Judaism does not fit into the rigid mold of Puritanism. Judaism has traditionally always presented a most enlightened viewpoint relative to sex and marital relationships. Even for the ancient Jew, sex not only existed for the propagation of the race, but sexual play in marriage was highly recommended for increasing the gratification of both men and women.

The Old Testament and Talmudic tradition are replete with ideas which glorify the physical nature of sex. The "Song of Songs"—sanctified as sacred Scripture—depicts the sensual love of man and woman and poetically describes the beauties of the female body. "Oh that you would kiss me with the kisses of your mouth for your love is better than wine." (1:2) And "Behold, you are beautiful, my love; behold, you are beautiful; your eyes are doves. . . . Your lips are like a scarlet thread, and your mouth is lovely. Your cheeks are like halves of a pomegranate behind your veil. . . . Your two breasts are like two fawns, twins of a gazelle, that feed among the lilies." (1:15 and 4:3,5) Similarly the maiden speaks of love for her man. The poems are explicit not only as to the physical beauties of the two lovers, described in detail, but also their sexual play. The "Song of Songs" is a hymn in praise of sensual love with no prudery nor shame to disturb its beauty.

Many are the sayings in the Talmud which emphasize the importance of sex as one of the requisites for the happy union of man and wife. In fact, Talmudic law makes specific provisions for adequate satisfaction of the wife's sexual needs. For example, a husband was cautioned about embarking upon a long journey without first having intercourse with his wife, and he was required to have relations with her again as soon as possible after his return. According to Jewish law, sexual intercourse was a duty owed to the wife by the husband (Keth. 6lb; Nid. 71a) and if he did not fulfill this sexual duty, the wife could divorce him if she so desired. The Talmud further discusses the proper marital relationships according to the occupation of the husband so that the wife's sexual wishes could be gratified (Ketuboth 6lb.). Nachmanides in his treatise "Iggeret ha-Kodesh" presented the viewpoint that since all the functions of the body were the works of God, none of their impulses could be regarded as intrinsically objectionable. "The act of sexual union is holy and pure. The Lord created all things in accordance with his wisdom, and whatever he created can not possibly be shameful or ugly. When a man is in union with his wife in the spirit of holiness and purity, the Divine presence is with them." Historically and traditionally, the Jewish family has always been encouraged to become sexually mature through appropriate education within the home and in the school environment.

The Family

Psychiatry places great emphasis upon the integration of the family group and its influences upon the human personality. If there has been any one basic reason for the survival of the Jewish people, it has been its emphasis upon a stable family life.

For the Jewish family the home is the nursery of its value system. Synagogal activities are basically secondary to family observances. Judaism has consistently emphasized the importance of developing a sense of mutuality and togetherness between the parents and with the children. It is in this regard that the Talmud said (Sotah, 17a): "A husband and wife, when they are made one by common nobility, bear God's impress in them." The husband and wife are bound to each other by special duties. The marriage state, according to Jewish teachings, is an *ideal* state. It has been divinely instituted for the happiness of the individual and the well being of human society. Conjugal obligation is invested with the most sacred character. Nowhere in the Bible is the dignity of marriage more strikingly set forth that in the beautiful account of the creation of woman in the second chapter of Genesis. "It is not good that a man should be alone." And woman is created to be his complement. She is told in Scriptural phrase, to be his "help mate" and yet his equal. The superiority of either man or woman is not inherent within Jewish life. Each has a distinct place to fill in marriage and each has something to offer to the common stock of happiness that the other lacks. Jewish tradition in the Bible and the Talmud seems to express much of what would be mouthed by a present day marriage counselor.

In the Jewish family a woman can not more truly realize the ideal of wifely duty than when she seeks to be a husband's conscience, silently holding out to him a lofty pattern of conduct, to which, for her sake as well as for his own, he strives to conform. The rabbis of the Talmud were not unmindful of this lofty conception of woman's duty. In the Tractate Berachoth 17a, the sages say, "When a woman leads her children to the class room and saves her husband from transgression she thus fulfills her mission." "That man's life," they add, (Shabbath, 25b), "is indeed enriched who is wedded to a virtuous woman, for with the wife rests the power to make her husband noble or ignoble. . . . But if a wife must be energetic in all good suggestion, the husband must show himself considerate to her."

The importance of the fatherly role in the development of the child is emphasized by Erik H. Erikson in his *Childhood and Society*. He takes cognizance of the child's need for the patriarchal relationship by suggesting that it is often sought in the psychoanalytic process through the attachment to the psychoanalyst. In Judaism the patriarch occupies a position of dignity and respect. His vital influence in shaping the child's personality and in preparing the child for the task of developing his own individuality as a result of healthy identification is illustrated frequently in the Old Testament and other traditional Jewish sources. Here it is interesting to contrast the Hellenic and the Hebraic views on the father-son relationship. The Greek Oedipus myth ends in patricide. In the Biblical story Abraham, advised to offer his son Isaac as a sacrifice, withholds the knife. Abraham and Isaac, father and son, are thereafter bound together in a covenant of love. Biblical literature thus reflects a patriarchal system which enhanced the family cohesiveness. There are frequent comparisons between God who chastens his people out of His great love, and the father who chastises the son. In Proverbs 3:16, it is stated: "For whom the Lord loveth he correcteth even as a father the son in whom he delighteth." The father's love for his son appears in the words of David, mourning for Absalom: "O my son Absalom, my son, my son Absalom! Would I had died for thee, O Absalom, my son, my son!" (2 Samuel 18:33)

The parents are bound to their children by sacred obligations. With them rest the safe-guarding not only of their children's happiness, but of their moral destinies as well. The role of the parents as teachers of morality, the embodiment of the spiritual values, frequently appears in the book of Proverbs in such well-known verses as 22:6. "Train a child in the way he should go, and even when he is old, he will not depart from it." And in 23:15-16, "My son, if thy heart be wise, my heart will be glad, even mine; Yea, my reins will rejoice, when thy lips speak right things."

Daughters were joined with their brothers in the educational process within the family. In the Talmud (Yeb. 62b) it is stated: "Our masters have taught: He who loves his wife as himself, and honours her more than himself; who leads his sons and daughters in the straight path and marries them near their time of maturity, to his house the words of Job (5:24) apply, 'Thou shalt know that thy tent is peace.'" The parents offer a value system with which the children can identify and, since example is mightier than precept, the parents must present those values by their own behavior patterns. Jewish parents by tradition are bound to everything that will promote the physical and emotional welfare of their children, and the Jewish family has been structured to lay a psychologically healthy foundation for the personality development of the child.

Group Consciousness

Psychiatry emphasizes the need of the individual for healthy group identification. Eric Fromm stresses this in his book on *Psychoanalysis and Religion,* "It is the feeling of isolation, of being shut out which is the painful sting of every neurosis. Even the most irrational orientation, if it is shared by a considerable body of men, gives the individual the feeling of oneness with others, a certain amount of security and stability which the neurotic person lacks." We are told by Renan that a nation is a spiritual principle constituted essentially upon two things: "One is the possession in common of a rich legacy of memories; the other is actual consent, the desire to live together, the will to continue to make the best use of the invisible heritage received." Judaism has always stressed these two principles—(1) tradition, a rich legacy of the memories of the past, and (2) the desire to live together to make use of this legacy by symbol and ceremony.

Judaism has always represented a great source of shared experience, especially that of an historic past with which the Jew identifies. In this way the Jew of today feels himself united to the Judaism of the past and with the Judaism which is to be. He feels himself linked to the sages, the poets, the philosophers and the saints of yesterday and tomorrow. Abraham and Moses, Rabbi Akiba and Hillel, Miamonides and Nahmanides, all are united in one revelation. This sense of belonging to a specific way of life has been a great source of emotional strength and stability for the adherents of Judaism. However, Judaism does not only offer a sense of belonging to the brotherhood of Israel but it also widens its horizon and gives a greater essence of meaning to social consciousness by stressing the universality of man and the importance of being a part of the greater world community.

It is noteworthy that a significant part of the group conciousness of Judaism is its emphasis upon its ceremonial and ritual forms. Sigmund Freud in the second volume of his collected papers on "Obsessive Acts and Religious Practices" was struck by what he felt was the resemblance between obsessive acts in neurotics and the religious observances. "One might venture to regard the obsessional neurosis as a pathological counterpart to the formation of religion, to describe this neurosis as a private religious system and religion as a universal obsessional neurosis." One can only conjecture a resemblance between religious rites and obsessional ceremonies when they both express neurotic fear based on a rigid punitive Superego. However, the equation is no longer consistent when the religious ceremonies are symbolic expressions of a group philosophy manifested through group behavior. The religious formulations and symbols of Judaism are attempts to give expression to definitive religious experiences.

In Judaism, the milestones of human existence from birth to death are expressed in ritualistic behavior. The Jew takes the event of birth and invests it with a spiritual character. The Brith, the Circumcision, represents the symbolic act of the child becoming a part of the Covenant of Jewish life. The Bar Mitzvah is the ceremonial process during which the child enters into adulthood and wherein he assumes the obligation of a responsible member of society. In death, rituals are invoked not only to give reverence to the deceased, but specific techniques have been established to aid the individual in working through the depression following loss of a love object. Jewish tradition prescribes a series of cermonies to be performed by the bereaved that regulate his behavior during the period of bereavement. It allows him openly to express his grief. The psychological soundness of the rituals prescribed by Jewish tradition for the mourner has been empirically validated.

Catharsis or Abreaction

Catharsis, from a psychiatric viewpoint, is one of the most valuable means for the relief of emotional stress. The overt expression of pent-up emotion and feeling tones within a group setting, has been exemplified in the Holy days and the festivals of Judaism. Rosh-ha-Shonah and Yom Kippur are days during which the collective expression of sin and guilt is explored, and worshippers openly express their inadequacies and sins. They are periods of introspection and spiritual enlightenment. The festival of Pentecost, celebrating the harvest season, is made up of days of thanksgiving and rejoicing, the collective expression of gratitude. Pentecost is also the festival expressing joy in the acceptance of the law and emphasizing the significance of education. Passover, with its feasting and joy, is expressive of the Jewish passion for freedom and equality. Chanukah and Purim, unlike the other festivals which were basically those of joy and introspecting, enable the Jewish people to express their aggressive impulses in terms of identifying with the aggressor and emotionally uniting with their warriors of the past to "work through" their feelings of anger and hatred toward those who would deny them their freedom of thought and religious expression. Joshua Liebman, in his book *Peace of Mind,* sums up this theme by stating, "In prayers, in songs, and in dances, in the home festivals and synagogue rites, the Jews acted out in unison their own inner needs and passions, finding collective health and enormous powers of resistance as byproducts of this wise emotional strategy."

The Jewish people use their Holy Days as a form of group catharsis. There is no confessional for the individual in Judaism. However, there is a definite awareness of the emotional need of the human being for a confidant to whom he might express his thoughts and feelings. In Psalm 32, God is seen in this role, as a nondirective therapist, so to speak. "Happy is the man unto whom the Lord counteth not iniquity, and in whose spirit there is no guile. When I kept silence, my bones wore away through my groaning all the day long. For day and night, Thy hand was heavy upon me. . . . I acknowledged my sin unto Thee, and Thou forgavest the iniquity of my sin." (vss. 2-5)

The Chassidim, a Jewish sect of the eighteenth century, perceived of their Zaddik, a Holy one, as a therapist. Simcha Bunam said, "It is highly necessary for every human being to have at least one sincere friend, one true companion so close to us that we are able to tell him of (that) which we are ashamed."

Summary

As a dynamic religious philosophy, with a this-worldly emphasis, Judaism has always been hospitable to influences from other sources and has felt no reluctance in incorporating a new insight which can broaden its own philosophy of life. Judaism is very much in accord with William James who enunciated quite aptly, "What in the end are all of our verifications but experiences that agree with more or less isolated systems of ideas that our minds have framed? But why in the name of common sense must we assume that only one such system of ideas can be true?"

The early confrontation between Religion and Psychiatry which followed Freud's *Future of an Illusion,* did not threaten the adherents of Judaism. Since Judaism represents the composite of the concepts, sentiments and manifestations of the spiritual life of the Jewish people, Freud's attack on religion was not experienced as conflictful. Judaism, like psychiatry, has a humanistic assumption, and thus found an ally in the new discipline. Judaism experienced in the insights of psychiatry and psychoanalysis a reenforcement of its primary goal to aid its followers in their quest for meaning and purpose in life.

BIBLIOGRAPHY

1. Erikson, Erik H.: *Childhood and Society.* New York, W. W. Norton, 1950.
2. Freud, Sigmund: *Civilization and Its Discontents* (3rd ed.) London, Hogarth Press, 1946.
3. Freud, Sigmund: *Collected Papers,* Vol. 5. London, Hogarth Press and the Institute of Psychoanalysis, 1950.
4. Freud, Sigmund: *The Future of an Illusion.* London, Hogarth Press and the Institute of Psychoanalysis, 1929.
5. Fromm, Erich: *Psychoanalysis and Religion.* New Haven, Yale University Press, 1950.
6. *(The) Holy Scriptures.* Philadelphia, Jewish Publication Society of America, 1942.
7. James, William: *Varieties of Religious Experience.* New York, Longmans, Green and Co., 1902.
8. Liebman, Joshua Loth: *Peace of Mind.* New York, Simon and Schuster, 1946.
9. *The Talmud.* London, Soncino Press Ltd, 1951.

CHAPTER 10

MAHAYANA BUDDHISM

DELWIN BYRON SCHNEIDER

THEOLOGIANS TODAY in most of the religions of the world are aware of the unmistakable mark that psychotherapy has set on modern life. Psychotherapy has come to hold an undisputed place among the healing arts of the world. But through the years of its development it has become more than an healing or a clinical art. It has developed to the point where it has formulated theories of human growth and maturation which have become accepted as models throughout the world. As the emphasis on interpersonal relationships in psychotherapy has grown, it has been compelled to confront questions about the human self and its well-being. It has found itself commenting on the great issues of human nature and the right and wholesome ordering of human life. Thus it has come to bear a special relationship to philosophy and ethics and religion. Though it may have begun as a clinical technique, psychotherapy has grown to the point where it has developed an extensive practical wisdom about human values. From this practical wisdom about life, it has moved ahead to interpret the right ordering of life and the proper destiny of man.

It is inevitable, therefore, that theologians of all religious persuasions should be interested in psychotherapy. (1) The great religions of the world are compelled to take its import seriously. For Hinduism and Buddhism and Islam and Christianity and Judaism and Confucianism and Taoism have a common interest in the very same problems of psychotherapy, and that is, human health and well-being. The religions of mankind began as a "Way" of ordering human life. They began with a proclamation and a conviction about the fullness of life. Religion is interested in the means by which life becomes "full" or "abundant" or "ultimately transformed." Religion says that there is more to life than mere physical existence. Being "ultimately transformed" means having that quality of life that points to the "more than" character of human life that appears on the surface. (2) Psychotherapy's willingness today to pass beyond the level of practical wisdom to a wisdom-about-life thus brings it into vital relationship and intimate encounter with the world religions' wisdom and message.

Buddhism, along with other religions, finds itself in alliance with psychotherapy. This alliance is clearly indicated because of common concerns between the two. Modern psychotherapy illumines the study of human behavior as no other study can do. In fact, *the illumination of human behavior* lies at the core of its enterprise. It offers a perspective which is indispensable to any human wisdom about man. With its aim of self-knowledge and self-acceptance and self-expression, it is dealing with what matters most to men as they reach out to find meaning and goodness and fulfillment in their existence. Buddhism allies itself with psychotherapy at this core of its enterprise. Buddhism lays claim to be the wisdom about the ultimate questions men ask concerning self-knowledge, self-acceptance and self-expresion. Psychotherapy celebrates "man's own powers" and his capacities for self-realization. It proceeds on the assumption that all distinctively human meanings and values in life are supplied by man himself. The human possibility is man's achievement. It is a natural process. The human endeavor is sufficient, for it opens the door into life's largest room of freedom and realization.

Buddhism, perhaps as much as any other religion of the world, urges man on to celebrate his "own powers" and to realize his own capacities, but in addition, in Mahayana Buddhism, we find also an emphasis on the "divine authors of salvation" who aid men in their quest for *self*-acceptance and *self*-knowledge and *self*-realization. In these pages Dr. Dai will be writing of Zen Buddhism's understanding of its relationship to psychotherapy. (3) Zen is one of the five main schools into which Mahayana Buddhism eventually split—schools or sects which have become analogous to the major denominations within the Christian church. Zen stresses self-effort within Mahayana. Our chapter on Mahayana Buddhism will stress the resources available for making "salvation by grace" a possibility within Buddhism. It is the intent of this study to give a portrayal of the "authors of salvation" in Mahayana Buddhism and their message of salvation which embodies directives for the whole range of human needs and interests.

I.

Buddhism begins with the life of Gautama in the sixth Century B.C., the son of a head of the minor state of the Sakyas in Northern India now known as Nepal. The name Buddha by which Gautama is commonly known is a title, meaning "the Enlightened One." This title is applicable to him only after he had become successful in "becoming" a Buddha. His personal name may have been Siddhartha, that is, "One Who Achieves His Goal," although this too may have been a title of respect and reverence that the faithful put on him. Already at this time in India the religious question uppermost in men's minds was: how does one become released from the inevitable wheel of rebirth (*samsara*) and find liberation from the inexorable law of *karma* (cause and effect) to become one with the great and ultimate ocean of infinite being, awareness and joy? The idea of release (*moksha*) from the law of *karma* and *samsara* introduced in the period of the Upanishads had become widespread in India. (4) The desire of "escape" is present in all religions, but it appears to be particularly strong in the Indian tradition. In Northeastern India many had undertaken this quest either alone or in company with others, leaving home and adopting an ascetic discipline of life.

As a child and young man, Gautama spent his early life in his father's court, having married and having had a son. But the pleasures of his father's court and married life could not long hold him. He left home at the age of twenty-nine on the night of the "Great Going Forth" when he became a wandering ascetic. He placed himself under the rule of two Hindu spiritual *gurus* or teachers who taught him the methods of *yoga*, that is, the way of being "linked" or "yoked" with Brahman or Ultimate Reality. His efforts along the line of *yoga*, however, proved unsuccessful. Following the examples of his time, he and five other wandering mendicants who were following the same path of release and liberation started on another method that was to lead this time to severe bodily mortification. At one point, Gautama appeared to be on the verge of death. He reduced his diet to "one or two beans a day" and became exceedingly thin. The Buddhist scriptures say:

> Like dried cane now became my arms and legs, withered by this extremely scanty diet; like the foot of a camel became my buttocks; like a string of beads became my spinal column, with the vertebrae protruding through; just as the roofbeams of an old house sharply protrude, so protruded my ribs; just as in a deep well the little water-stars far beneath are scarcely seen, so now in my eye-balls the sunken pupils are scarcely seen; as a wild gourd, freshly cut, in the hot sun becomes empty and withered, so now became empty and withered the skin of my head.... And when I wished to touch my belly, I reached the back of my spine, and when I wished to touch my spine, I again reached to the belly. (5)

Recovering from this experience, and convinced that this was not the way to his goal of *moksha* or release, he altered his methods to a more moderate discipline. He continued to seek release, but this time in his own way. At least, after six years of struggle, the "Night of the Great Enlightenment or Awakening" occurred. He seated himself beneath the *bodhi* tree (tree of "enlightenment") and there he achieved success. From that night he could rightly be known as the *Buddha* or the "Enlightened One." This "Night of Enlightenment" signaled for Gautama and his followers the beginning of awakening from ignorance to knowledge, from darkness to light, from mortality to the undying. As the night passed he began to see with a clear vision how all things come and go, why all are circling in a never-ending process of life-death-rebirth. He gained a penetrating insight into the nature of suffering and its causes, and the way of deliverance from the conditioned misery of human existence. Rarely do Buddhas appear in man's lifetime or even in many men's lifetimes; consequently, this marked a stupendous event in the history of this era. From the Night of Enlightenment to his death, Buddha, the fully "Self-Awakened One," taught the eternal *Dharma* (the way by which man sees the "more than" character of human life) which he had penetrated and comprehended as he sat in deep meditation under the *bodhi* tree.

It is said that the Buddha debated with himself whether he should be satisfied with having made this discovery for himself or whether he should pass it on to others. He decided on imparting it to others, and in the Deer Park a few miles north of the present city of Benares, he won his first converts. His exposition of his teaching in the Deer Park at Sarnath is set forth in the *Dharma* ("of the law") *Cakra* ("of the wheel") *Pravartana* ("setting in motion") *Sutra*, which purports to be the contents of the Buddha's first sermon. (6) This *Sutra* sets in motion "the wheel of the *Dharma*" or the Buddhist faith, and it contains many of the teachings which later generations found central to the Buddhist religion.

While sitting in meditation under the *bodhi* tree, Buddha came to four great convictions about life. These four statements in regard to the universality of suffering, its origin, its eradication and the practical means to be taken towards that end are commonly known as the Four Noble or Holy Truths. One gains knowledge of the Middle Way (neither the way of hedonism nor the way of severe asceticism) by following the Four Holy Truths and the Holy Eightfold Path. This Way is known as the *Dharma* in Buddhism; it is the way of liberation and deliverance. (7)

II.

The preaching of Buddha's first sermon is regarded in Buddhism as one of the four great events of the Buddha's life, the other three being his birth, his enlightenment and his passing into *paranirvana*. His sermon began in this way:

> And the Blessed One thus addressed the five Bhikkus: There are two extremes, O Bhikkhus, which he who has given up the world, ought to avoid. What are these two extremes? A life given to pleasures, devoted to pleasures and lusts: this is degrading, sensual, vulgar, ignoble, and profitless; and a life given to mortifications: this is painful, ignoble and profitless. By avoiding these two extremes, O Bhikkhus, the Tathāgata has gained the knowledge of the Middle Path which leads to insight, which leads to wisdom, which conduces to calm, to knowledge, to the Sambodhi, to Nirvāna.
>
> Which, O Bhikkhus, is this Middle Path the knowledge of which the Tathāgata has gained, which leads to insight, which leads to wisdom, which conduces to calm, to knowledge, to the Sambodhi, to Nirvāna? It is the holy eightfold Path, namely, Right Belief, Right Aspiration, Right Speech, Right Conduct, Right Means of Livelihood, Right Endeavor, Right Memory, Right Meditation. This, O Bhikkhus, is the Middle Path the knowledge of which the Tathāgata has gained, which leads to insight, which leads to wisdom, which conduces to calm, to knowledge, to the Sambodhi, to Nirvāna.
>
> This, O Bhikkhus, is the Noble Truth of Suffering; Birth is suffering; decay is suffering; illness is suffering; death is suffering. Presence of objects we hate, is suffering; Separation from objects we love, is suffering; not to obtain what we desire, is suffering. Briefly, the fivefold clinging to existence is suffering.
>
> This, O Bhikkhus, is the Noble Truth of the Cause of suffering: Thirst, that leads to re-birth, accompanied by pleasure and lust, finding its delight here and there. (This thirst is threefold), namely, thirst for pleasure, thirst for existence, thirst for prosperity.
>
> This, O Bhikkhus, is the Noble Truth of the Cessation of suffering: (it ceases with) the complete cessation of this thirst—a cessation which consists in the absence of every passion—with the abandoning of this thirst, with the doing away with it, with the deliverance from it, with the destruction of desire.
>
> This, O Bhikkhus, is the Noble Truth of the Path which leads to the cessation of suffering: that holy eightfold Path, that is to say, Right Belief, Right Aspiration, Right Speech, Right Conduct, Right Means of Livelihood, Right Endeavor, Right Memory, Right Meditation. . . .
>
> Thus the Blessed One Spoke. The five Bhikkhus were delighted, and they rejoiced at the words of the Blessed One. And when this exposition was pronounced, the venerable Kondanna obtained the pure and spotless Eye of the Truth (that is to say, the following knowledge): "Whatsoever is subject to the condition of origination, is subject also to the condition of cessation."
>
> And as the Blessed One had founded the Kingdom of Truth (by propounding the four Noble Truths), the earth-inhabiting *devas* shouted: Truly the Blessed One has founded at Benares, in the deer park Isipatana, the highest kingdom of Truth, which may be opposed neither by a Samana nor by a Brāhmana, neither by a deva, nor by Māra, nor by Brahma, nor by any being in the world. (8)

This is the Middle Way and the core of the Buddha's teaching. We might sum up his teaching in this way:

A. All existence is suffering (*dukkha*). Sickness, old age and death come to all men in their transitory existence. All the splendor of life is but ephemeral and temporal and rests on the struggle with other lives.
B. Suffering springs from ignorant craving and desire (*tanha*) to preserve individual ego; suffering springs from one's own ego-desires.
C. The end of suffering is the extinction of desire or craving.
D. To achieve the end of desire, there is an Eightfold Path of conduct to follow.
   The eight steps of the Path are:
   1. Right views or correct insight, which begins with rational understanding and proceeds to an insight that permeates the whole being.
   2. Right will or motives or aspirations which begin with the compassionate renunciation of all the pleasures of life which are generally possible only at the expense of others.
   3. Right speech, the avoidance of untruths and mastery of one's own passions.
   4. Right conduct or action.
   5. Right pursuits or right livelihood.
   6. Right effort or perseverance in goodness.
   7. Right mindfulness or right use of the intellect.
   8. Right concentration and meditation on the Buddha and the *Dharma*.

III.

Several hundred years after the Buddha's death, we find the beginning of a movement which was to prove most important for the later history of Buddhism, not only in India but in many of the lands which are presently Buddhist today. At that time Buddhism split into two branches, called Theravada ("The Way of the Elders") and Mahayana ("Great Raft or Great Career"). The Buddhism which today goes by the name of Theravada is continuous with the Buddhism of the early disciples. It lays emphasis on the necessity of renouncing the world and aggressively pursuing the path of self-conquest irrespective of how many other people are prepared to follow one's lead in taking such a step. The spiritual ideal in Theravada is symbolized by the *Arhat*. An *Arhat* is the individual who in his own power and self-effort has overcome the power of *tanha* and has thrown aside the fetters which bind him to the cycle of birth and death. Now he gains the unutterable peace of Nirvana, the assurance that he has attained what he set out to do—no longer the subject of one weary round of rebirths after another. The rebirth cycle now comes to an end for him. And for his fellow man he has set an inspiring example of one who boldly explores ahead. He has pointed them the way to the spiritual goal. When they are ready in understanding and aspiration and determination, they, too, will follow.

The movement know as Mahayana embraces a whole series of movements which are often so different from the Pali or original Buddhism that one can almost regard them as separate religions. The followers of Mahayana Buddhism are generally found in China, Japan, Korea and Tibet, while those of Theravada are generally the southern Asians found in Ceylon, Burma, Laos, Cambodia and Thailand. The name *Maha-yana* was adopted by those who felt that the prospect of seeking only one's own release is selfish and inadequate. A *higher* ideal is that of seeking the release of others by postponing one's own entrance into Nirvana to make this possible. The Mahayana teaching, then, lays great stress upon the ideal of the *Bodhisattva*, that is, "one whose essence" (*sattva*) is "illumination" (*bodhi*). A Bodhisattva is the person, who, although capable of entering Nirvana immediately, refuses to do so in order that he may carry out his saving work for *others*. In Theravada, human self-reliance is insisted upon. In Mahayana, men are taught to trust not to themselves but to the saving power of one or the other of the cosmic authors of salvation.

Sir Charles Eliot in *Hinduism and Buddhism* sums up the characteristic features of Mahayana under seven categories:

1. A belief in Bodhisattvas and in the power of human beings to become Bodhisattvas.
2. A code of altruistic ethics which teaches that everyone must do good in the interest of the whole world and make over to others any merit he may acquire by his virtues. The aim of the religious life is to become a Bodhisattva, not to become an Arhat.
3. A doctrine that Buddhas are supernatural beings, distributed through infinite space and time, and innumerable. In the language of later theology a Buddha has three bodies and still later there is a group of five Buddhas.
4. Various systems of idealist metaphysics, which tend to regard the Buddha essence or Nirvana much as Brahmans regarded in the Vedanta.
5. A canon composed in Sanskrit and apparently later than the Pali Canon.

6. Habitual worship of images and elaboration of ritual. There is a dangerous tendency to rely on formulae and charms.
7. A special doctrine of salvation by faith in a Buddha, usually Amitabha, and invocation of his name. Mahayana can exist without this doctrine but it is tolerated by most sects and considered essential by some. (9)

The basic conviction of Mahayana at this point of salvation is expressed in John G. Whittier's little poem, "The Meeting":

> He findeth not who seeks his own;
> The soul is lost that's saved alone. (10)

This Mahayana ideal of the Bodhisattva has become theoretically clarified in doctrinal formulations. It has also been concretely embodied in the cosmic authors of salvation found in Mahayana. In Theravada the Buddha was generally regarded as a human being who after passing through the normal experiences of life, had by means of his own exertions attained enlightenment. In Mahayana, as theologians penetrated deeper into the transcendental reality behind the earthly appearance of the Buddha, they gradually evolved the doctrine of the *Trikaya*. (11) Accordingly, the Buddha is not merely a human being but Reality-Itself. This Reality-Itself is filled not only with wisdom but compassion. Out of compassion, for the purpose of preaching the *Dharma*, Reality assumes innumerable forms. These forms, of which Gautama is one of the best known to us, are all identical with Reality-Itself and are, therefore, wholly transcendental.

Thus in reality the Buddha is never born and never dies. He never attains enlightenment for he is eternally enlightened. His attainment under the *Bodhi* tree like all the other events of his life, is simply a skillful device for the encouragement of the ignorant. The historical personality of the Buddha is the particular mode in which unenlightened gods and men perceive the transcendental compassionate activity of the Reality-Itself or Absolute. Sangharakshita beautifully and accurately sums up the result of this attitude when he points out the fact that the devotion of the Mahayanists was so fervent, their spiritual imagination so exuberantly creative, and their artistic creativity so intensive that the spacious Mahayana heavens speedily became populated with a glorious company of transcendental beings—Buddhas, Bodhisattvas and a host of lesser divinities. (12)

IV.

As we look now to the "authors of salvation" in Mahayana, we find that we can categorize them, as John Noss has done, as three kinds. They are the *Manushi* Buddha, the *Dhyani* Buddhas and the Bodhisattvas. (13)

The *Manushi* or Historical Buddhas are men, who like Gautama, have appeared on earth in the past as human beings. They have attained enlightenment on the strength of their previous births and have instructed men in the true way of life by preaching to them the *Dharma*. But now their duty is done and they have passed off into Nirvana not to be reborn again. Prayers do not reach them nor do the pious words of their worshippers affect them. They have become part of the great ocean of bliss of Nirvana. As Mahayana theologians sought to clarify the role of the historical Buddhas in their doctrinal statements, Gautama becomes only one of several successive Buddhas who for convenience may be counted as four, seven or even twenty-four. The Buddhas form an infinite series extending without limit backwards into the past and forward into the future. As a result of this belief in a series of Buddhas, Mahayana theology has produced a plentiful number of personalities with Buddha-like qualities which has caused much speculation as to their alliance with one another, their connection with the phenomena of the world and the universe, and their relationship to the human soul.

Another class of savior beings is composed of the *Dhyani* or "Contemplative Buddhas." They are unlike Bodhisattvas because they have attained full Buddhahood. On the other hand, they stand in a different category from the "Historical Buddhas" because they have not achieved their Buddahood in human form. They dwell in the heavens and, in the interval between the present time and their compassionately postponed final entrance into Nirvana, they actively minister to men's needs.

Among the many of the "Contemplative Buddhas" in the Mahayana fold, there are two that need to be mentioned. They are Vairocana and Amitabha. Vairocana is a solar Buddha. He is the chief deity of the Shingon Sect in Japan and is represented by the great temple in Nara. Vairocana is a derivative of a recognized title of the sun in Sanskrit. (14) Eliot says that while the origins of this deity are not known, there is a connection between a Buddha and light which has long been recognized. Buddhas are clearly revealers and light-givers, conquerors of darkness and dispellers of ignorance. In Japan, the sun-goddess Amaterasu has been called the manifestation of Vairocana, the compassionate bringer of salvation.

The second, Amitabha (or the Buddha of limitless or measureless light), has become one of the great gods of Asia. Like Vairocana his origin is also obscure. As a Buddha of Healing he has a great following in Tibet, in China (where he is known as *O-Mi-To*) and in Japan (where he is known as *Amida*). Amitabha was once a monk who took the vow to become a Bodhisattva. And now he presides over the Western Paradise or "Buddha field." This is the domain which he has called into existence named *Sukhavati* or the "Happy Land," more generally known as the "Pure Land." The central theme of the Pure Land School is faith and devotion to Amitabha. Amitabha achieved Buddhahood on the express condition that he could receive at death all who sincerely call upon his name. At death, he would then carry his faithful ones to his Western Paradise or Pure Land, where they might pursue the quest for ultimate perfection under far happier circumstances than when surrounded by the conditions of this world's existence. In the Western Paradise the devotees would live in unbroken happiness until they obtain Nirvana.

At the core of Mahayana theology we find a proclamation that states unequivocably that at the heart of ultimate reality or Reality-Itself is the compassionate wisdom revealed in the infinite light of Amitabha. Here we have almost a complete reversal of what Gautama taught, for faith in Amitabha and prayers to him assures the devotee of being received by him after death in his paradise. "Beings are not born in that Buddha country as a reward and result of good works performed in this present life." (15) Though this teaching has had brilliant success in China and enjoys much popular acclaim in Japan, in Nepal and Tibet, Amitabha is only one in a pantheon of divine authors and in India this idea in Mahayana theology has almost completely died out.

The third class, and perhaps the most important, are the Bodhisattvas. Bodhisattva means, as we have seen, the essence of knowledge, the one who is in the process of obtaining Buddhahood. If the historical Buddha had not come on the scene, the idea of Bodhisattvas would have never become a vital concept. But as Sangharakshita reminds us:

> The Bodhisattva is not only himself the supreme exemplar of the devotional life: he is at the same time the highest object of devotion to the Mahayana devotee. Even as the New Moon . . . is worshipped in preference to the Full Moon, so are the Bodhisattvas worshipped more than the Buddhas. (16)

In the full bloom of Mahayana theology, the Bodhisattvas are part of a numberless company of supernatual beings who hear the petitions of the faithful and who bring assistance to those who call on them. The luxuriant fancy of India, which loves to multiply divinities, fashioned for itself in Mahayana beautiful images of benevolent beings who refuse the bliss of Nirvana that they may alleviate the suffering of others. They embody, as it were, the symbols belonging to the supra-historical realm of cosmic myth. They express in form accessible to human prayer and sympathetic to human emotions the forces which rule the universe. In Edward Conze's *Buddhist Texts Through the Ages* the infinite compassion of the Bodhisattva is seen in its full beauty:

> A Bodhisattva resolves: I take upon myself the burden of all suffering. I am resolved to do so, I will endure it. I do not turn or run away, do not tremble, am not terrified, nor afraid, do not turn back or despond.
>
> And why? At all costs I must bear the burdens of all beings, in that I do not follow my own inclinations. I have made the vow to save all beings. All beings I must set free. The whole world of living beings I must rescue, from the terrors of birth, of old age, of sickness, of death and rebirth, of all kinds of moral offence, of all states of woe, of the whole cycle of birth–and–death, of the jungle of false views, of the loss of wholesome dharmas, of the concomitants of ignorance—from all these terrors I must rescue all beings. . . . I walk so that the kingdom of unsurpassed cognition is built up for all beings. My endeavors do not merely aim at my own deliverance. For with the help of the boat of the thought of all-knowledge, I must rescue all these beings from the stream of Samsāra, which is so difficult to cross, I must pull them back from the great precipice, I must free them from all calamities. I must ferry them across the stream of Samsāra. I myself must grapple with the whole mass of suffering of all beings. To the limit of my endurance I will experience in all the states of woe, found in any world system, all the abodes of suffering. And I must not cheat all beings out of my store of merit. I am resolved to abide in each single state of woe for numberless aeons; and so I will help all beings to freedom, all the states of woe that may be found in any world system whatsoever.
>
> And why? Because it is surely better that I alone should be in pain that that all these beings should fall into the states of woe. There I must give myself way as a pawn through which the whole world is redeemed from the terrors of the hells, of animal birth, of the world of Yama, and with this my own body I must experience, for the sake of all beings, the whole mass of all painful feelings. And on behalf of all beings I give surety for all beings, and in doing so I speak truthfully, am trustworthy, and do not go back on my word, I must not abandon all beings.
>
> And why? There has arisen in me the will to win all-knowledge, with all beings for its object, that is to say, for the purpose of setting free the entire world of beings. And I have not set out for the supreme enlightenment from a desire for delights, not because I hope to experience the delights of the five-sense qualities, or because I wish to indulge in the pleasures of the senses. And I do not pursue the course of a Bodhisattva in order to achieve the array of delights that can be found in the various worlds of sense-desire.
>
> And why? Truly no delights are all these delights of the world. All this indulging in the pleasures of the senses belong to the sphere of Māra. (17)

Today millions of unnamed Bodhisattvas are freely mentioned in Buddhist scriptures. Few of them, however, have definite personalities. Two of them with personalities, *Avalokita* and *Manjusri,* tower above the rest. Avalokita in many forms and in many ages has been one of the principal deities of Asia, but like so many of the other Asian gods and goddesses, his origin is obscured by antiquity. He is portrayed as the personification of divine mercy and pity. In its full form the name of this author of salvation is *Avalokitesvara,* "the Lord who looks down from heaven." He watches over all who inhabit the world. And for this purpose it is said that he came to earth over three hundred times in human form. (18) In order to carry out his deeds of mercy and compassion, he is compelled to assume all manner of names and forms. He often appears in the guise of a Buddha or a Bodhisattva, or a Hindu deity, or in fact, in any shape. He is omnipresent. He saves those who call on him from shipwreck and execution, from robbers and violence and distress. He saves from moral evils such as passion, hatred and folly, and he grants children to women who worship him.

Avalokita is often portrayed as a prince in the costume of Indian royalty with a high jewelled crown on his head. His right hand is extended in a gesture of charity and compassion. In his left hand he carries a red lotus and he stands on a large lotus. He has sometimes four arms and sometimes many arms, all symbolizing his liberality and generosity. Besides the lotus he carries such objects as a book, a rosary and a jar of nectar. The images with many arms and eyes seem an attempt to represent him looking after the unhappy in all the world, and stretching out his hands in a gesture of helpfulness. In China Avalokita becomes transfigured and takes the name of *Kuan-Yin,* and in Japan he becomes *Kannon.* In China and Japan he becomes transformed also into a female form. Out of his desire to help, he assumes the shape of divine womanhood. The images of Kuan-Yin and Kannon assume a variety of gracious and winsome poses, symbolized in images found all over China, Korea and Japan. She is often shown seated on a lotus or standing on one, or she rides upon a cloud or glides on the waves of the sea. In her arms she often bears a child, for it is such she gives to women who worship her. On her hand she may wear a crown set with an image in miniature of Amitabha Buddha, the Lord of the Western Paradise to whom she takes those who are faithful with her.

The second great Bodhisattva is *Manjusri.* Unlike Avalokita, he is not so much the helper of human beings as the personification of thought and knowledge and meditation. His image is often found in Zen meditation halls. In his hand he has a sword of knowledge (logic) and in his other hand a book (the Buddhist Truth). He is the Bodhisattva who assists those who wish to know and follow the *Dharma* or the teaching or law of the Buddha.

After Avalokita and Manjsuri the most important Bodhisattva is *Maitreya*, or the Future Buddha. Maitreya is the Buddha who is still to come. Like Gautama, Maitreya has lived innumerable lives. Now having made himself worthy of Buddhahood, he awaits in the Tusita Heavens for the appropriate time of his next appearance. His images are found in all parts of the Buddhist world; the most famous of the statues is enshrined in Koryu-ji Temple in Kyoto. Maitreya, a bringer of salvation, is believed to watch over the propagation of the faith. In paintings he is usually depicted as golden in color. His statues show him standing or sitting in the European fashion and not in the cross-legged fashion of Asia. In Maitreya we have a symbol of the Buddhist truth that the attainment of enlightenment or awakening to what is Real is a constantly recurring event in the universe. Maitreya is the symbol of that truth which the Mahayana texts repeat over and over—the number of Buddhas are as "incalculable as the sands of the Ganges"—simply because the number of world systems and their duration are so many and varied. It is a reminder that the advent, after the elapsing of vast periods of time, of an enlightened human, is an integral part of the structure and workings of man, his history and the universe.

V.

As we conclude this survey of the authors of salvation in Mahayana Buddhism, we are aware of one fact that stands out most clearly—the Buddhist is freed to live life, freed from the inexorable wheel of rebirth because the authors of salvation have revealed the truth of the human situation to him. Buddhism concerns itself with ultimates, with what matters most to men, if they are to find the meaning and the goodness and the fulfillment of their existence. It is the wisdom about the ultimate questions that men ask about themselves and their world. Buddhism lays claim to the awareness and power and insight to distinguish between what is real or true and what is secondary, derivative or even false. This insight is called "wisdom" or "revelation" for it opens new horizons for man's self-realization, self-knowledge and self-acceptance. To know the truth then is to live an authentic life since truth is a part of the nature of things.

As man realizes who he is, he loses his marks of "secondary" existence, his destructive tensions, and his limitations whereby he defines himself at the expense of others. As he lives authentically he transforms this secondary existence because he is now participating in the structures and activity of human existence with a different perspective. As we have seen, psychotherapy celebrates man's own power and his capacities for self-realization. Distinctively human meanings and values in life are supplied by man himself. God and redemption are not prerequistites to the full life.

In Mahayana Buddhism, the good news is that there exists a multitude of saviors, real and potential, who can help men "help themselves" because they are beings whose chief desire is to cure the disabilities of men. They have come to show man the "truth" of the human situation. He does not have to walk alone. The Buddhists see life as a journey. This journey is like climbing a mountain. There are many mountain paths available for those willing to begin the journey. Which path should one chose? Shall it be grace and compassion and mutuality or shall it be the path of self-effort and individualism and wisdom? Ultimately whether one treads the path of knowledge and self-effort as in Theravada, or the path of intuition (Zen) or the path of faith as in Mahayana, the results according to Buddhism are the same. Though the paths may vary, when one reaches the mountain top all enjoy the same moonlight.

Mahayana Buddhism offers to its followers the pathway of faith, and it provides a satisfactory cosmological explanation of the universe to support this faith. As a result of this interpretation of the universe with its fullness of gods and its ethical interpretation of the world, Mahayana lays claim to providing a solution for human frailties and social ills. For the Mahayana believer, this wisdom or revelation brings the glad tidings which is able to transform suffering humanity into perfect beings in the Happy Land of the Western Paradise. The consequences of human frailty and sins are thus mitigated by the compassionate intervention of the authors of salvations.

REFERENCES AND FOOTNOTES

1 One of the early works, for example, that have sought with clarity and precision to define the problems of alliance and conflict between psychotherapeutic thought and the Western tradition as embodied in the Christian tradition is Albert C. Outler's *Psychotherapy and the Christian Message.* New York, Harper and Brothers, 1954. There are others, among them—David E. Roberts: *Psychotherapy and a Christian View of Man;* and Vanderveldt and Odenwald: *Psychoanalysis and Personality.*

2 For the scope and nature of religious life see Frederick J. Streng: *Understanding Religious Man.* Belmont, Dickensen Publishing Co., 1969. Especially Chapter I, "The Problem of Interpreting Religious Expression," pp. 1–11.

3 See Chapter 11 in this volume.

4 About 500 B.C. the Upanishads (the philosophic treatises of the Hindu scriptures known as *Vedas*) embody the earliest Indian attempts at abstract philosophical thought, seeking a profounder meaning behind the varied phenomena of the universe and re-interpreting the Vedic traditions accordingly.

5 E. H. Brewster: *The Life of Gotama the Buddha* (Compiled from the Pali Canon). London, Kegan Paul, Trench, Trubner and Co., Ltd., 1926, pp. 35–36. For the early years of

the Buddha, see Henry C. Warren: *Buddhism in Translation.* Cambridge, Harvard University Press, 1896, pp. 1–110. Also Paul Carus: *The Gospel of Buddha.* Chicago, The Open Court Publishing Co., 1915, pp. 1–259.

6. Nicol Macnicol: *The Living Religions of the Indian People.* New Delhi, Y.M.C.A. Publishing House, 1964, p. 218.

7. Buddha's teaching has been handed down first in the ancient Pali language, then in Sanskrit and Chinese, and preserved in the three great collections of books called *Tripitaka* or the Three Baskets, namely: the *Vinaya-Pitaka* or collection of discipline, containing the rules of the monastic order; the *Sutta Pitaka* or collection of discourses, consisting of various books of discourses, dialogues, verses, and stories dealing with the doctrine proper as summarized in the Four Holy Truths; and the *Abidharma Pitaka* or philosophical collection, presenting the teachings of the *Sutta Pitaka* in systematic and philosophical form.

8. Translation by T. W. Rhys Davids and Herman Oldenberg: *Vinaya Texts,* Part I, in *Sacred Books of The East,* XIII (Oxford, 1881), pp. 94–97. Quoted from Mircea Eliade: *From Primitives To Zen.* New York, Harper and Row, 1967, pp. 572–573.

9. Charles Eliot: *Hinduism and Buddhism.* New York, Barnes and Noble, 1921, Volume II, p. 6.

10. Quoted in E. A. Burtt: *The Teachings of the Compassionate Buddha.* New York, New American Library, 1955, p. 126. For a clear introduction to the Mahayana religious ideal, see Part IV, pp. 123–166.

11. The *Trikaya,* or the three-fold body of the Buddha, does not imply three separate bodies, but three aspects of the one body of Buddahood. Buddha as *Dharmakaya* (Body of Truth) resides in everything; it is the eternal principle, ultimate reality, the very truth of the universe. This reality is indescribable and inexpressible. The Buddha as *Sambhogakaya* (Accommodated Body) is personal and appears before man's religious awareness, for example, as Amida Buddha, as Wisdom and Compassion. Buddha as *Nirmanakaya* (Manifested Body) refers to the historical Buddha who appeared on earth as Gautama of the Sakya clan 2,500 years ago.

12. Bhikshu Sangharakshita: *A Survey of Buddhism.* Bangalore, Indian Institute of World Culture, 1957. Especially Part V, What Is Mahayana Buddhism? pp. 250–265.

13. John Noss: *Man's Religions.* New York, Macmillan Co., 1969, p. 162.

14. Eliot, *op. cit.,* p. 27.

15. *Ibid.,* p. 30.

16. Sangharakshita, *op. cit.,* p. 433.

17. Quoted in Eliade, *op. cit.,* pp. 48,49.

18. Eliot, *op. cit.,* p. 14.

BIBLIOGRAPHY

1. Berry, Thomas: *Religions of India.* New York, Bruce Publishing Co., 1971.
2. Ch'en, Kenneth K. S.: *Buddhism in The Light of Asia.* Woodbury, Barron's Educational Series, 1968.
3. Humphreys, Christmas: *Buddhism.* Baltimore, Penguin Books, 1951.
4. Morgan, Kenneth W. (ed.): *The Path of The Buddha.* New York, Ronald Press, 1956.
5. Rahula, Walpola: *What the Buddha Taught.* New York, Grove Press, 1959.
6. Robinson, Richard H.: *The Buddhist Religion.* Belmont, Dickenson Publishing Co., 1970.
7. Sangharakshita: *The Three Jewels.* Garden City, Doubleday, 1970.
8. Smith, Huston: *The Religions of Man.* New York, Harper and Row, 1958.
9. Suzuki, Daisetz Teitaro: *Studies in the Lankavatara Sutra.* London, Routledge and Kegan Paul, Ltd., 1930.
10. Zaehner, R. C. (ed.): *Living Faiths.* Boston, Beacon Press, 1959.

CHAPTER 11

ZEN AND PSYCHOTHERAPY †

BINGHAM DAI

ALTHOUGH ZEN, the teaching of a Chinese Buddhist sect, is generally thought of as a form of religious mysticism, it may also be considered as a system of psychotherapy. For Zen and psychotherapy share a common objective, and that is to enable man to enjoy the benefits of society and culture without losing his innate spontaneity and to live a full and creative life without being hampered by undue anxiety. It is on this basis that we will compare Zen with psychotherapy in regard to some major issues to be mentioned in the following.

1. *The Nature of Human Nature.* Perhaps the most authoritative and the most concise statement of the Zen theory of human nature is the following famous verse of Hui-neng (638-713 A.D.), which, according to legend, won him the recognition as the Sixth Patriarch:

> The mind is the Bodhi tree,
> The body is the mirror stand.
> The mirror is originally clean and pure,
> Where can it be stained by dust?

My understanding of this verse is that human nature is good and that the original mind of man is naturally perceptive, spontaneous and flexible; its immediate response to stimuli from the environment, within or without, is usually appropriate and adaptive, provided it is not "attached" to, and thereby unduly influenced by, egotistic cravings, passions and delusions. In Buddhist terminology, this original mind of man is called Buddha nature.

This view of human nature, it should be noted in passing, is as typically Chinese as it is Indian. It was first stated in the *I-Ching* (the *Book of Changes* compiled some 3000 years ago), and runs through all the teachings of Confucius and Laotze. In fact, it was

---

† A paper given at the annual meeting of the Southeastern Psychological Association, February 27, 1969.
Reprinted from *VOICES*, Fall-Winter, 1969 (used by permission).

mainly through the efforts of Chinese monks who were thoroughly versed in the Chinese philosophies, especially Taoism, that Indian Buddhism was transformed into Chinese Zen and its central focus was shifted from deliverance from the cycle of rebirths in the next world to the cultivation of an unfettered and joyous life here and now.

This theory of human nature may sound strange to some psychotherapists. But actually very few of us do not practice with the assumption that the homeostatic principle operating in the "inner environment" of man will somehow function equally well in his psychological environment. This tendency has been called by various names, such as the tendency toward consistency (Lecky), the urge toward the realization of the real self (Horney), the "organismic valuating process" (Rogers), or simply the tendency toward health in the broadest sense of the word (Sullivan).

EVEN THE FOUNDER OF MODERN PSYCHOTHERAPY, Freud, who is not usually associated in our mind with people who believe in the goodness of human nature, worked most consistently on this very assumption; namely, if we can help remove the obstacles standing in the patient's way so that he can say freely what comes to his mind, including dreams, the chances are that something in him will come up with the right answers to the perplexing problems of his life. Whatever one may choose to call this something—the unconscious or the subconscious—there is no denying the fact that it is the patient's mind or the patient himself who knows and who informs the therapist, even though he often does not know that he knows. In fact, to have tapped this innate source of insight for psychotherapy by the methods of free association and dream analysis may be considered as Freud's greatest contribution to the science of man.

In the light of these considerations, perhaps it is not farfetched to say that in regard to the theory of human nature, Zen and psychotherapy have surprisingly more in common than we would ordinarily expect.

2. *The Genesis of Human Suffering.* In regard to the genesis of human suffering, the *Platform Sutra* has this to say:

> In this teaching of mine . . . "no-thought" has been instituted as the main doctrine, "non-form" as the substance, and non-attachment as the foundation. What is meant by "non-form?" "Non-form" means to be detached from form even when associated with it. "No-thought" means not to be carried away by thought in the process of thinking. Non-attachment is the original nature of man.
>
> This state of non-attachment should characterize all thoughts . . . At no time should a single instant of thought be attached to anything. If one single instant of thought is attached to something, the successive thoughts will be similarly

> attached; the result is *bondage*. On the other hand, if no thought is attached to anything, there is *freedom*. Hence, non-attachment is the foundation of this teaching.

This passage can be best understood to mean that man's original spontaneity and adaptability is often stunted or ruined by what we may call his personal and cultural compulsives. By personal compulsives, we mean the compelling effects of one's previous personal experiences on one's perception of, and response to, a current life situation. By cultural compulsives, we mean the myriad ways in which the folkways and mores of one's society tend to mold one's thought patterns and value systems without one's awareness. As a result, what is not customary is often depreciated. While participation in society and culture is absolutely essential for the development of the indidual personality, these personal and cultural compulsives, nevertheless, do often breed shortsightedness, narrow-mindedness, bigotry, intolerance, unhealthy inhibitions, unfounded fears and irrational hostilities, and, in unfortunate cases, pathological behaviors of various kinds and of varying degrees of severity. This phenomenon is so familiar to all psychotherapists that there is no need for further eleboration.

What perhaps should be specifically mentioned is the fact that in both Zen and psychotherapy the most important source of human suffering has been found to be man's excessive ego-preoccupation. For people who are so preoccupied seldom see the world as it is; they can see it only in terms of their own needs. And their vision is often clouded by strong feelings, such as envy and jealousy, frustration and anger. For this reason, in order to restore man's original intuitive capacity and his adaptive flexibility, Zen emphasizes strongly the need for liberation from the compulsive cravings of the ego and constantly points to the regenerating freedom and creativity of what a Japanese Zennist, Koji Sato, has aptly called the "egoless ego."

SIMILARLY, PSYCHOTHERAPY has found narcissism, the morbid love of self, to be the most important source of neurotic anxiety and its opposite, the capacity to love, the most essential source of emotional health and strength.

3. *Methods Used to Alleviate Human Suffering and to Restore Spontaneity.* The principal method used by Zen to free man's mind from "attachments" or from his personal and cultural compulsives and to restore its pristine spontaneity and flexibility is meditation. In fact, the word Zen means meditation in Sanskrit (*dhyana*). It must be noted, however, that there are different kinds of meditation and that what was originally taught by the founders of the Zen sect

in China was very different from those practiced by the other Buddhist sects. In fact, compared with the latter, it can almost be said to be not meditation at all. This was explained by the well-known Chinese philosopher-historian, Hu Shih, as follows:

> For the first time in the history of Chinese Buddhism, Hui-neng revolted against *Dhyana* itself. He said, "In my teaching, *Ting* (*Samatha*, meditation) and *Hui* (Vipassana, insight) are one and not two. *Calm* (*Ting*) is the lamp and insight is the light. In all actions, talking or resting, sitting or sleeping, always act with a straightforward heart; that is the *samadhi* of one-mindedness. And in all places and all times, always act with intelligence; that is the *prajna paramita*. Sitting actionless is no dhyana; introspection of your own mind is no dhyana; and looking inward at your own calmness is no dhyana." In thus overthrowing the principal element in the Indian dhyana, Hui-neng was laying the foundation of Chinese Zen which was no Zen at all.

In practice, however, the early Chinese Zennists did not do away with meditation altogether. What was discarded was the traditional Indian way of restricting meditation by rigid ritualistic procedures and its conceiving of meditation and insight as two separate processes. What was advocated was that the Zen student should at all times and in all places learn to accept all thoughts that come to his mind but to be detached from them at the same time, so that his spontaneity and straightforwardness may function freely. This is known as the practice of "no-thought." On this point the *Platform Sutra* says:

> What is "no-thought?" It means even though you see all things, you do not attach to them, but, always, keeping your original nature, you come and go freely in the very midst of responding to stimuli from objects in the environment and from your own sense organs. This is wisdom or insight *(prajna samadhi)*, and to learn to be free and emancipated in this manner is called the practice of "no-thought."

The psychotherapeutic method that is comparable to meditation is free association. In fact, these two methods have a great deal in common. For what is meditation, if it is not a kind of marathon free association minus the presence of an analyst? But there are differences, of course. In addition to the fact that the Zen monk during meditation usually faces his problems alone, while the patient thinking aloud is always engaged in some form of communication with his therapist, Zen and psychotherapy differ fundamentally in their approach to certain biologic needs and ego strivings. Thus, when a Zen monk is troubled by sexual or aggressive impulses, he is generally taught either to suppress or in renounce them, whereas the patient in therapy is often encouraged to express them fully in words and to find the appropriate ways to satisfy them. Which way of dealing with such impulses is more effective and healthy can be an interesting subject for comparative study.

Some other methods used by the Zen masters that are different from the techniques of psychotherapy are the use of precepts and personal examples and the very unusual form of questions and answers, involving the use of *koans*.

Since *koans* are often puzzling, it may be worthwhile to mention one or two that are commonly used and see how a Chinese Zen scholar, C. C. Chang, makes sense out of them. A monk asked, "What is the meaning of Bodhidharma's coming from the West?" The master replied, "The cypress tree in the courtyard." The same question put before another master was answered, "The teeth of the board grew hair." What the masters tried to convey to, or to awaken in, the pupil is described by Chang as follows:

> ... the Zen Master had no intention of answering the questions; he was merely making a plain and straightforward statement of what he saw and felt at the moment the question was put. In this down-to-earth "plain feeling" in its primordial, genuine, and natural state lies the whole secret of Zen. Plain, yet marvelous, this feeling is the most cherished keystone of Zen—sometimes described as the *tang hsia i nien* or instantaneous thought. ... Never departing from this eternal "instantaneousness," the Zen master sees everything as the great *Tao*—from the cypress tree to a stick of dry dung. Thus, the master made no effort to give a relevant answer; he just plainly stated what he saw and felt at that moment.

IT IS INTERESTING TO NOTE THAT *tang hsia i nien* literally means the first thought that comes to mind, which, surprisingly enough, is also exactly what free association means. In other words, their differences in method notwithstanding, Zen and psychotherapy actually share a common goal, and that is to cultivate in the pupil or the patient the ability to respond to any given situation immediately and spontaneously without the interference of undue anxiety.

Perhaps the most spectacular method used in Zen training is the systematic induction of a trance or a trance-like state by the use of such devices as the setting of a time limit for the attainment of enlightenment—varying from five to seven days—and the monotonous repetition of a sound, such as *Mu*. Both devices can produce a psychological state, in which the individual loses his self-awareness and in which he completely identifies himself with his surroundings, including the sound, resulting in a momentary exhilarating feeling of oneness with Nature and with his fellow human beings. When such artificial means are used to speed up enlightenment, as Ernest Becker rightly pointed out, it becomes extremely difficult to draw the line between genuine enlightenment and the results of hypnotic experience or sensory deprivation.

It must be pointed out, however, that the use of such artificial means as a shortcut to enlightenment is not an essential part of Zen. It was not known in the first four hundred years of the Zen movement in China. Even the use of the *koan* did not become prevalent until the latter Sung Dynasty in the eleventh century. Many Zen devotees even now still prefer the less dramatic method of "serene reflection."

When genuine enlightenment comes, it is usually the end result of a long process, which follows the well-known stages of discovery either in science or religion, as pointed out by Hutchinson some years back. They are: first, an initial period of prolonged and sustained intellectual acitvity—in the case of the monks, often many years of searching and meditation; then a period of relaxation in which the sustained activity is suspended and the individual's attention is drawn to something entirely different—in the case of the Zen monks, listening to the temple bell, for example, or receiving a surprise blow from the Zen master; and finally, the sudden emergence of insight or enlightenment when it is least expected. And in both scientific and religious discoveries, there is the intuitive leap, which may appear mystical to the uninitiated but which, as suggested by the more recent studies of Westcott, may be a natural inference from observations that were previously made but that are now linked together in a meaningful relationship.

Although psychotherapy does not claim anything quite as dramatic as the *satori* experience, yet it is not entirely unfamiliar with the phenomenon of sudden insights. And when they come to a patient, they also follow the same stages of discovery as mentioned above.

There is another surprising similarity between Zen and psychotherapy. This has to do with the effectiveness or validity of the *satori* experience. Many Chinese Zen masters have taught that the *satori* experience or sudden insight alone is not sufficient: it has to be translated into everyday lining. Hence, they make a clear distinction between *chien* or insight and *hsing* or practice. The latter concept is equivalent to what is known as "working through" in psychotherapy. The distinction is important, for we know that the undesirable effects of a man's previous social and cultural experiences just do not disappear overnight. For this reason, the effects of the *satori* experience on the everyday behavior of the Zen pupils can be a fascinating area of study.

4. *The Goal of Zen and Psychotherapy*. The ultimate goal of the Zen discipline is a man who thinks, feels and acts with the degree of objectivity, sponstaneity, freedom and compassion that can come

only from having transcended what we call his personal and cultural compulsives and from feeling truly at one with all sentient beings and with Nature. Such a Zen man has been described in various ways. One Zen master calls him "the man of no rank," meaning not being attached to anything external. Another simply describes him as a man who eats when he is hungry and drinks when he is thirsty; no anxiety interferes with his functioning freely as a biosocial being. More picturesquely, Suzuki refers to him as a true artist of life, "whose every deed expresses originality and creativity," and whose response to any given situation in life manifests his full mastery of himself, just as any true artist has of his material and his instruments. Perhaps the simplest and the most down-to-earth description is given by Blyth, a student of Zen as well as world literature. He says simply that the enlightened man is one in whom the "self has decreased in quantity and importance, and other things correspondingly and inevitably increase in value and significance."

INTERESTINGLY ENOUGH, what Blyth says applies equally well to the results of effective psychotherapy; inevitably there is a decrease of ego-preoccupation, accompanied by a corresponding increase of genuine interest in other people. Similar observations have been made by writers who have made comparative studies of Oriental philosophies and psychotherapy. Fingarette, a philosopher, follows Federn and thinks of the transformation resulting from psychotherapy as a movement from egocentricity to the "self-forgetfulness" that is characteristic of a normal healthy personality. Arasteh, a psychotherapist, well versed in the mysticisms of the Far East and the Near East, maintains that liberation from the bondage of one's ego and one's culture is essential for the final integration of the adult personality.

5. *Ways in Which Zen and Psychotherapy Can Learn from Each Other.* Earlier in this paper I have pointed out several areas in which the analytic methods of psychotherapy can be of help to Zen training. It remains to be shown that psychotherapy, too, has a few things to learn from Zen.

First, in the course of my experience as a psychotherapist in this culture, I have come to the conclusion that the greatest obstacle to a patient's functioning freely and creatively as a person is his excessive ego-preoccupation and morbid competitiveness. This observation has led me to think that Zen's concept of selflessness—in the sense of being able to be totally and wholeheartedly involved in an on-going task or an interpersonal relationship without being fettered by compulsive egotistic concerns—is not just a religious or philosophical ideal, but also a practical goal for psychotherapy. Just imagine how free and spontaneous a man would be, if he could fully appreciate and apply the message of the following famous verse of an ancient Zen master:

> While alive,
> Be a deadman.
> Thoroughly dead,
> and act as you will
> and all is good.

The result of liberation from compulsive egotistic concerns is not a weak, passive or regressive ego as it may appear to a Western mind, but a much stronger and more creative one, for the liberated man, as the *Platform Sutra* puts it, "comes and goes freely" without being hampered by undue anxiety.

Secondly, meditation in a modified form can be used to supplement psychotherapy. My own experience indicates that a patient can definitely profit from spending 15 minutes a day on meditation or self-examination. It seems a good way for him to consolidate the gains he has made during therapy and to continue the process of self-discovery after therapy. The Zen practice of "no-thought," if carried out properly, should be even more useful, especially to those who have the problem of impulse control and who take themselves and their ego-extensions too seriously; the result could be a degree of detachment in the very midst of involvement that is the characteristic of a free spirit.

Finally, the most important lesson psychotherpy can learn from Zen is its teaching about the original mind as his immense capacity for intuitive insight and for appropriate action, which, alas! is too often stunted by learned fears and inhibitions. To tap, to release and to utilize this intuitive potentiality of the patient should also be the main objective of our therapeutic endeavor. This can be accomplished by placing the greatest emphasis, at all times, on the patient's intuitive insights and the least on the therapist's own theoretical preoccupations. The patient's intuitive insights often show themselves in the following forms: (1) his initial immediate reaction to a given life situation in the past, which he has ignored or suppressed because of anxiety; (2) his initial immediate reaction to a given life situation at present, which he hesitates to utilize or to carry through because of anxiety; (3) the first thought or feeling that comes to his awareness in response to a given stimulus in the therapeutic situation, which he has failed to mention; (4) his sudden rock-bottom realizations regarding his attitudes and feeling toward a given life situation; and (5) other relatively better known forms of self-revelation, such as the patient's non-verbal behavior in the therapeutic setting, his fantasies and, most important of all, his dreams. To make full and consistent use of such indices of the patient's intuitive insight may be called the intuitional approach to psychotherapy.

SPACE DOES NOT PERMIT a detailed discussion of the methods of the intuitional approach to psychotherapy. Suffice it to mention briefly that it has at least three distinct advantages: (1) It will reduce resistance, for the patient learns mainly by the process of self-discovery. (2) Because of minimal resistance, it will shorten the time for therapy. And (3) it will assuredly enhance the patient's self-esteem as well as his capacity for genuine independence. For he is constantly reminded by this approach that he is the leading partner in the therapeutic endeavor and that whatever progress he is making is largely due to his own effort.

BIBLIOGRAPHY

1. Arasteh, A. Reza: *Final Integration of the Adult Personality.* Leiden, E. J. Brill, 1963.
2. Becker, Ernest: *Zen: A Rational Critique.* New York, W. W. Norton, 1961.
3. Blyth, R. H.: *Zen in English Literature and Oriental Classics.* Tokyo, Hokuseido Press, 1942.
4. Chan Wing-tsit: *The Platform Scripture; The Basic Classic of Zen Buddhism.* Jamaica, New York, St. John's University Press, 1963.
5. Chang, C. C.: *The Practice of Zen.* New York, Harper & Bros., 1959.
6. Ch'en, Kenneth K. S.: *Buddhism the Light of Asia.* Woodbury, Barron's Educational Series, 1968.
7. Fingarette, Herbert: *The Self in Transformation: Psychoanalysis, Philosophy and the Life of the Spirit.* New York, Basic Books, 1963.
8. Horney, Karen: *Neurosis and Human Growth.* New York, W. W. Norton, 1950.
9. Hu Shih, The Development of Zen Buddhism in China, in Briggs, William (ed.): *Anthology of Zen:* New York, Evergreen Books, 1961.
10. Hutchinson, K. D.: Varieties of Insight in Humans. See *Psychiatry* (Washington, D.C.), August, 1939.
11. Lecky, P.: *Self Consistency: A Theory of Personality.* New York, Doubleday, 1945.
12. Rogers, Carl B. and Barry Stevens: *Person to Person: The Problems of Being Human.* Lafayette, Real People Press, 1967.
13. Sato, Koji: How Zen Conceives of Mind. In Murphy, Gardner and Lois B. Murphy (Eds.): *Asian Psychology.* New York, Basic Books, 1968.
14. Siu, R. O. H.: *The Man of Many Qualities: A Legacy of the I-Ching.* Cambridge, MIT Press, 1968.

15. Sullivan, H. S.: *Conceptions of Modern Psychiatry*. New York, Norton, 1946.
16. Watts, Alan: *Psychotherapy East and West*. New York, Pantheon Books, 1961.
17. Westcott, M. R.: *Toward a Contemporary Psychology of Intuition*. New York, Holt, Rinehart and Winston, 1968.
18. Yampolsky, Philip B.: *The Platform Sutra of the Sixth Patriarch*. New York, Columbia University Press, 1967.

CHAPTER 12

THERAVĀDA BUDDHISM AND PSYCHOTHERAPY

Roy C. Amore

INTRODUCTION

THE INDIAN WORD FOR ROAD or path comes from a verb meaning "to wipe clean," and this concept of a cleared passageway leading through difficult terrain encouraged the early Buddhists to call Gotama Buddha's teaching a "Path." This Path is the basis by which man may be made whole, and every devout Buddist is striving to follow the Path cleared by the Enlightened One through an existence full of hazards and pitfalls. Whereas the Western concept *religion* generally focuses on one's relationship to a god, the Buddhist concept *Path* focuses on a teaching which leads toward a goal. What we in the West call the Buddhist religion or Buddhism, the Buddhists themselves call the "teaching of the Buddha" (*Buddha-sāsana*).

Perhaps more than any other religion, Theravāda Buddhism is consciously psychological, and I do not think a Theravādin would be disturbed at our presentation of Buddhism as a system of human guidance. As we shall see, the Buddha presented his famous Four Truths teaching in the guise of a medical formulation, (1) and Theravādins sometimes suggest that the Buddha advocated a scientific approach to religion, calling upon his followers to not merely accept the teaching on his authority but to advance to the stage of full realization (*pativedha*) of the truth for themselves. (2) But before considering the psychology of the Buddhist Path, a brief history of Theravāda Buddhism might be helpful.

History of Theravāda

The Buddhist religious movement which began in Northern India in the sixth century B.C. had spread over nearly all of India by the reign of the emperor Ashoka during the third century B.C. During these early centuries variations occured within Buddhism concerning both practice and doctrine. Eventually certain areas of India became the centers for specific "schools" or sects within "Early Indian Buddhism." Later a liberal, creative movement which deified the Buddha took shape in Northern India. It called itself the Great Vehicle (Mahāyāna) and referred to all the earlier schools by the pejorative term Little Vehicle (Hinayāna). Buddhism gradually weakened in India and was eliminated completely by the Muslim conquest of India in the Middle Ages. But Buddhism survived in its foreign mission fields beyond India. The Mahāyāna movement had established itself in Central and East Asia, and one of the early Buddhist ("Hinayāna") schools had taken root in Ceylon, where Buddism was sheltered from the forces which had spelled its doom in India.

This branch of early Indian Buddhism which has existed in Ceylon since the time of Ashoka refers to itself as Theravāda, meaning the Way of the Elders. It has preserved its version of the early Buddhist scriptures and has added to this a rich collection of histories, commentaries, and stories. Like many religions it has managed to change and adapt to historical vicissitudes while nevertheless taking a strong conservative stance, as the name "way of the Elders" suggests. Since approximately 1000 A.D., Theravāda Buddhism has been adopted as the major religion of all the countries of Southeast Asia, except for Vietnam, which follows the Mahāyāna school of Buddhism brought by the Chinese. Theravāda remains today the major religion in Burma, Thailand, Laos, and Cambodia as well as in Ceylon.

Theravāda Buddhism does not exactly fit into the average Westerner's definition of religion as "believing in God." Although most Buddhists believe in a number of spirits and lesser gods, there is no God in Buddhism *per se*. One modern Buddhist writes that if one understands religion as a system of faith in and devotion to a god, then Buddhism is not a religion strictly speaking. But if religion is understood as "a teaching which takes a view of life that is more than superficial, . . . a teaching which furnishes men with a guide to conduct . . . , a teaching which enables those who give it heed to face life with fortitude and death with serenity," or a system to overcome the ills of life, then Buddhism is very much a religion. (3) To put the matter in the categories of this volume, Theravāda Buddhism is a non-theistic religious system of human guidance.

Theravāda Buddhists venerate and "take refuge in" their "three jewels," the three sacred branches of Buddhism:

1. the Buddha; the man Gotama who became "the Enlightened One"

2. the Dhamma; the truth about existence as realized and taught by the Buddha and contained in the canon
3. the Sangha; the collective name for the true disciples of the Buddha, and usually taken to refer to the Buddhist monks collectively.

Theravāda Buddhists, however, also typically believe in a variety of other supernatural beings such as (1) the *good spirits* of the rice fields, forests, waters; (2) the *malevolent spirits* (demons) which do such things as steal away the souls of babies (crib deaths), frighten people in the night, and attack those who intrude upon their territory in the wilderness; (3) and *guardian spirits* which reward proper behavior, but punish behavior which goes against traditional customs; (4) finally, *ancestral spirits* which guard the interests of the family lineage by rewarding proper behavior and bringing disease or death to offenders.

There are cultic specialists for the appeasement of the spirits or veneration of the "Grandfather," and each of the Theravādin countries has its (non-Buddhist) exorcists which village Buddhists call upon when needed. Descriptions of the psychosomatic healing rituals of these exorcists make fascinating reading (4) and form a part of the Buddhist culture, but I will confine myself to a description of the Buddhist Path proper.

This discussion of the Theravādins' belief in supernatural beings calls our attention to important ways in which the Theravādin's world view is similar to that of a medieval Christian but differs from that of a contemporary Westerner. In a village in Southeast Asia it is "normal" to believe in ghosts (spirits of the dead), demons who cause evil things to happen, and a "Grandfather" spirit of the village who sanctions behavior, like a village superego. In the contemporary Western worldview, the individual experiencing undeserved suffering has little explanation for the situation except perhaps to say that it is the will of God or that it is bad luck. The Theravādin, in contrast, has at his disposal a belief system which has an explanation for practically every unusual happening, whether good or bad. I am suggesting, then, that the Theravāda Buddhist has supernatural explanations for suffering not available to contemporary Westerners because they are no longer credible for them. In an earlier era of the West, when the belief in the devil still provided a vivid symbol accounting for the anomalies and evils of life, Christians and Buddhists were not so different on this matter as they now are. In contrast to many Westerners the Theravādins' means for dealing with anomalous situations are usually associated with religion, either with Buddhism proper or with the cults of the gods and demons.

With these introductory comments before us, let us turn to our fundamental question concerning the Theravāda Buddhist system of human guidance.

THE PATH

Concerning the Buddhist system of human guidance, let us consider each of the following: (a) the need for a Path, (b) the goal of the Path, (c) the teachings of the Path, and (d) the psychology of the Path.

The Need for a Path: There is for mankind a social and an individual need for a Path. The latter has received more attention from Buddhists and so I will begin with it.

Buddhism, like many other Indian teachings, understands human existence to be *samsāra*, an untranslatable term which embraces the following beliefs: Life is an ongoing process which does not really begin with the birth nor end with the death of an individual. A particular "person" stands within a "stream" of existences which may include hundreds of future existences as well as innumerable previous births on various planes of life (the animal, the "hell-being," the human, the ghost, the "heaven-being," etc.). One's moral actions (*karma*) help determine the circumstances of the rebirth—e.g., whether animal or human, or whether unfortunate or happy.

The need is for a path which will lead one out of *samsāra*, with its unending births accompanied by sickness, old age, and death. An important interpreter of Buddhism, Prof. O. H. de A. Wijesekera of Ceylon, writes that Buddhist ethics is clearly founded upon the analysis of *samsāra*, with the goal being release from the suffering (*dukkha*) filled chain of rebirths. "Thus we discover that the *raison d'être* of Buddhist ethics is the fundamental fact of samsāric *dukkha*." (5)

The other way of considering the need for a Path begins by analyzing man's inhumanity to man. This consideration lies within the sphere of what we usually call social ethics, but unfortunately this dimension of Theravādin ethics has usually been passed over by Western interpreters. The Buddhist critique of human evil distinguishes between a wrong (*micchā*) and right (*sammā*) path. The point is that everyone is on a path, but unfortunately many persons are following a path constituted by wrong opinions, wrong conceptions, wrong actions, etc. Those individuals on the wrong path are to be pitied because they can never be really happy and they are creating for themselves a wretched rebirth; but they are also a social problem since bandits, murderers, thieves, etc., come from among their ranks.

Gotama Buddha was concerned that his teaching be effective in converting the evil doers onto the right path. This pragmatic orientation led him to criticize severely many of the other famous teachers against whom he competed for followers. (6) One of these famous contemporaries of Gotama, Kassapa, took a position of completely denying karmic causation. Kassapa held that one could go all along the Ganges river harming persons in every village but accumulate no personal defilement at all, and conversely no merit accrued from doing good along the Ganges. Gotama argued against Kassapa and others who took the position of denying that ethical acts come to fruition, by noting that one who held such a position would have no way to dissuade the liar, murderer, etc., from continuing in his evil ways. To be a responsible teacher, Gotama warned, one must maintain that actions affect the actor.

For the same reason Gotama denounced as unhelpful any deterministic view because to preach determinism (by the gods or by fate) to a murderer for instance does not in any way encourage him to alter his life. By contrast with these irresponsible teachings, Gotama gives his own position, which is a middle path between overemphasizing the role of causation and understating the value of disciplined, habituated virtue. This middle path is intended to solve the interconnected needs for individual happiness and social morality.

The Goal of the Path

The goal of the Buddhist path is *nirvāna,* or *nibbāna.* The etymological meaning of the term *nirvāna* is "extinction," or blowing out, and many interpreters have misleadingly written that *nirvāna* means the extinction of the self. Buddhists do seek to overcome the delusion that the self is a permanent entity, but *nirvāna* itself means the state of mind in which the three unhealthy motivations (to be discussed later) have been extinguished. This is clear in passages of the Buddhist scriptures such as the following:

> Extinction of greed, extinction of hate, extinction of delusion: this is called *nirvāna.*[7]

> But if greed, hatred and delusion are given up, man aims neither at his own ruin, nor at the ruin of others nor at the ruin of both, and he experiences no mental pain and grief. Thus is *Nibbāna* visible in this life, immediate, inviting, attractive, and comprehensible to the wise. (8)

Stated in negative terms, then, *nirvāna* is the overcoming of man's evil motivations, which I will discuss elsewhere. Stated positively, *nirvāna* is happiness, the deep joy and peace which comes from eradicating craving, hatred, confusion, and anxiety. Theravādin commentators have enumerated ten fetters from which the saint becomes free. One who has entered the stream or path, the first stage, gains the freedom from the naive belief that the "self" is a permanent entity rather than merely a convenient designation for the on-going flux of mind-body, the freedom from doubt which could keep one from attempting to move to higher levels of spirituality, and the freedom from the tendency to rely upon mere rules and rituals for salvation. At the second stage of the spiritual progress one gains the freedom from sensuous craving and the freedom from ill will (repulsion). At the third stage these five lower freedoms are perfected and at the fourth stage, that of the Arahat (saint), one gains the five higher freedoms: freedom from the longing for the lower and the higher heavenly spheres, from conceit of all types, from restlessness, and from non-wisdom. Whereas an ordinary life is anxiety-ridden (*dukkha*-filled), progress on the path leads one into ever deepening realization of the profound peace called *nirvāna*, according to Theravādin psychology.

The Teachings of the Path

The famous Noble Eightfold Path is not to be thought of as a ladder with eight rungs which one ascends step by step, but perhaps as a pathway which is eight bricks wide. Spiritual progress on the Path is accomplished by moving from wrongness to rightness in eight related dimensions. These eight fall into three areas of instruction: morality, meditation, and wisdom.

All Buddhists must begin with the instruction in morality, which involves striving toward right speech, right actions, and right means of livelihood. Once a certain level of morality is achieved, the Buddhist may go on to the two higher instructions. Meditation embraces the dimensions of the Path known as right effort, right mindfulness, and right concentration. Wisdom includes the remaining two dimensions of the Path, right thought and right understanding.

Morality is the most important instruction for Buddhist laymen, and for the monk it is prerequisite to spiritual progress in meditation and wisdom. The Path is designed to lead its follower toward a lifestyle of "giving" rather than "harming." For example, "right thought" means having no harming thoughts; being free from sensuous desire, ill-will, and cruelty. "Right speech" involves avoiding these harmful practices! lying, talebearing, speaking harshly, and wasteful chattering. "Right action" means avoiding murder, theft, and unlawful sexual intercourse. "Right livelihood" is one that does not bring harm to men or animals.

The symbolism of evil forms an important background to any system of ethics, and for Buddhism the background symbols of evil are the Indian notions of defilement-versus-purity and of giving-versus-harming. Paul Ricoeur's view that (in the West) the concept of defilement is the most primitive layer of the consciousness of evil is true also for India. The older texts express the belief that one's evil actions (evil karma) become a corrupting substance which weighs down the soul, prohibiting its innate tendency to rise to the higher, purer realms of the universe. The specifically Buddhist understanding of evil occurs within the symbol system which contrasts meritorious actions with demeritorious actions. The Buddhists insist that in order for an act to be either meritorious or demeritorious, it must be done willfully, consciously. Thus, Theravādin psychology carefully distinguishes healthy and unhealthy dispositions.

The symbolism of merit and demerit is multi-layered. Ethically, Theravāda distinguishes between actions which are "giving" (helpful, non-harming, kind) and ones which in any way bring harm. Psychologically, it distinguishes between wildness and tameness; the mind, like an elephant, must be carefully tamed. Spiritually, it distinguishes between purity and impurity, as is true for other Indian religions as well. Thus the layman's meritorious practices make him more generous, more self-controlled, and purer.

Doing merit by thought, word and deed is the essence of the layman's morality. I prefer the translation "doing merit," which focuses attention on the act itself, to the usual "making merit," since in English "making merit" implies that the act is done primarily in order to stockpile merit (such a motive would neutralize the good deed according to Theravāda). "Doing merit" is intended to help control the mind and eliminate evil tendencies. This gradual taming of the mind is a matter of harmonizing the various bodily and mental functions toward the goal of perfect peace, harmony, non-aggression, etc.

In popular Buddhism the goal of taming oneself has been partially replaced by the quest for acquiring more and more merit with the goal of gaining worldly happiness and a pleasant rebirth in heaven—in Buddhism a rebirth in a heavenly realm is not permanent and one eventually is reborn on earth. The short range goal of attaining rebirth in heaven is not sharply opposed to the goal of *nirvāna,* it is argued, since the person dedicates himself to obtaining sainthood eventually. Since most Buddhists are in fact striving to do merit and eventually spend time in a heavenly realm, popular Buddhism is not so different from popular Christianity as one might expect a non-theistic, *nirvāna*-oriented religion to be.

Acts of merit include giving support in any form to the Order of monks, venerating the Buddha at a temple, giving to the needy, listening to sermons, observing the moral precepts, "transferring" (without loss) one's merit to ancestors, etc. Besides his spiritual development and the fact that he helps others with his gifts, the merit-doer reinforces his relationship with his fellow villagers, with his ancestors, and with Buddhists beyond his village—this has become especially important with the rise of nationalism and Buddhist internationalism in recent years.

Meditation, the second area of instruction, traditionally is practiced in some degree by all monks but not by laymen. However, recently some meditation masters have founded centers open to laymen and monks alike. More and more Buddhist business men, laborers, and others are setting aside an hour or two each day for meditation. Buddhist meditation has very little to do with unconscious trance states, as in certain forms of yoga, but instead is intended to heighten *conscious* awareness. The most popular form of Buddhist meditation is appropriately called "mindfulness" (*sati*), for example, and includes awareness of one's body, feelings, mind, and objects of consciousness.

Wisdom, the final instruction, involves deep realization of Buddhist doctrines and is essential for *nirvāna*. The fruits of accomplishment in wisdom are said to be a clear perception of oneself and of reality as it really is. The man of wisdom sees into the nature of reality, discerning these three important characteristics: entities are *impermanent* (not eternal) for which reason one should not become physically or psychologically dependent upon anything; human existence is filled with *suffering,* both physical and (especially) mental; and persons have *no self,* being devoid of a material or mental essence which is eternal and could be called a soul.

However, Buddhism is neither pessimistic in outlook nor nihilistic in doctrine, as has been charged, because it optimistically offers a Path to eternal peace, and the instruction in wisdom provides positive methods for overcoming unpleasant feelings, etc. One interpreter suggests that Western psychology could learn from the Buddhist observation that understanding (wisdom) can dissolve even dynamic factors such as desires or emotions. (9)

The Psychology of the Path

As an entrée into Buddhist psychology as it relates to our topic, we may consider the Buddhist understanding of "mental attitude" (*citta*). The English term *attitude* is too narrow in meaning to be an accurate translation, but perhaps it, better than other terms, suggests the state of one's mind as being determined by the past yet open to the future. As H. V. Guenther explains, "Having a certain attitude means to be ready for something, and this readiness for something is due to the presence of a certain subjective group-pattern, being a definite combination of many factors in the human psyche." (10) The Buddhist understanding is that bodily, mental, and vocal actions of the past (whether in this life or in former lives) have given shape to a frame of mind which favors certain ways of perceiving and acting in new situations.

This notion of a mental *attitude* or frame of mind leads to another important part of Buddhist psychology, the analysis of the mind's deep motivations, which the psychotherapist might call unconscious motives and which the Buddhists call "root causes" (*mūla*). Early Buddhism developed a sophisticated philosophical psychology that classified the numerous possible mental states according to which of these root causes was conditioning them. One system of analysis which is of interest here classified all mental states as healthy, unhealthy, or indeterminate.

The unhealthy states are those conditioned by the three unhealthy roots: greed, hatred, and delusion. These three root causes or deep motives have a very comprehensive meaning in Buddhist psychology, and taken together they account for all unhealthy mental states in man. "Greed" means longing for something, and it includes the full range of desire from a weak attraction to uncontrolled lust. "Hatred" is the opposite motive, that of avoidance in any degree. "Delusion" is a technical term denoting the mental state in which one's motives, however sincere, stem from "untruth." According to Buddhism, then, all evil acts have one or more of these unhealthy roots as their underlying cause. For example, one passage of the canon states that killing, stealing, unlawful sexual intercourse, lying, tale-bearing, harsh language, frivolous talk, covetousness, ill-will and wrong views are due to greed, hatred, or delusion. (11)

The healthy mental states are those conditioned by the opposite three root causes: non-greed, non-hatred, and non-delusion. The important term "healthy" here refers to those states of mind which are conducive to progress on the spiritual Path. As such, the Buddhist concept "healthy," is not a synonym for "normal" or "well"—for the goal of the Path is to bring one out of the normal state of consciousness (ignorance) into a healthy state. The Buddhist Path frees one from the "average," the state of being under the control of the evil root causes.

Thus the Theravādins see the Path as the means for a movement from ignorance to understanding, from bondage to freedom. The word *ignorance* in this context does not mean "stupidity" but "non-wisdom," the state of existing without the benefit of spiritual wisdom. An "ignorant" man is spiritually blind, whereas the saint has insight into all realities. The deluded man may think he is free, but from the saint's vantage point of perfect freedom, it can be seen that the ignorant man has scales over his eyes and psychological chains fettering his mind.

Buddhists hold that the Path begins where ordinary man really is, in a self-imposed state of bondage, and moves gradually toward freedom by the practice of morality and the development of calmness and insight. Wijesekera writes, ". . . Buddhism does not go against the basic psychology of man's nature, but endeavors to bring about its refinement and sublimation until it totally transcends the level at which it is found in samsāric existence. Thus Nibbānic Happiness must be considered as the ideal for every living being." (12)

CONCLUDING REMARKS

There is a similarity of purpose between the Buddhist Path and psychotherapy only if the objectives of the two are stated in very general terms. We can say, for instance, that both Buddhism and psychotherapy strive to eliminate mental problems with the goal of mental health. If we compare Buddhism and psychotherapy on their specific understandings of the mental problems and mental health, however, considerable differences emerge. I see the following areas of difference in which further investigation should prove fruitful.

Of primary importance is the area of the understanding of the *mind* itself. I do not anticipate that psychotherapy would take significant exception to the Buddhist insistence that there is "no-self" in the sense of an eternal soul, but would psychotherapy grant that insight the importance given to it in Buddhism? Psychotherapy might agree with Buddhism that the mind is an on-going mental flux, but would psychotherapy be as confident as Buddhism that a total transformation of personality is possible—i.e. that important dispositions can be completely eliminated? Furthermore, Buddhism has a complex set of explanations for the cause and effect relations within the mind, and it would be very difficult to correlate these satisfactorily with Western terms and explanations.

Another area for consideration is the understanding of **mental health.** The Buddhist goal of *nirvāna* has very little to do with adaptation, adjustment, or integration (of values and purpose) "to the world" but instead involves "departing from the world" into monastic life. Controlled aggressiveness and self-assertion are not a part of the Buddhist ideal, and Buddhism would be more likely to speak of eliminating deep desires rather than channeling them through socially acceptable outlets. The topic for dialogue here would be that concerning the nature of mental dispositions, with Buddhist psychology taking the position that even man's deep seated dispositions can be altered or even eliminated through careful habituation. The Buddhist notion of a completely calmed or tamed person probably does not have a parallel in Western psychology. The Buddhist notion of mental health is perhaps more confident in categorizing specific actions as good or bad—here Buddhism is comparable to the traditional Jewish or Christian ethic. The Buddha was quite concerned that his teaching (*dharma*) have the pragmatic effect of leading persons out of the harming frame of mind into the giving frame of mind. The Buddhist understanding of the better psychic life does not speak in terms of the absence of neurosis, but of the absence of unhealthy dispositions and the transcendence of normal ego-ality.

In **technique,** the third area for comparison, there are also important variations. We need to distinguish Buddhism as practiced by the monks from the Buddhism of the laymen at this point. For the laymen the Buddhist Path provides ethical guidelines and norms for individual development and social interaction. The laymen's ethic places a high value on the cultivation of a capacity for lovingkindness, compassion, altruistic joy, and equanimity, and for the meritorious there is the hope of a happy stay in a heaven before being reborn on earth. The universality of human needs and hopes is such that popular Buddhism has a great deal in common with popular Christianity, for instance, and any meaningful comparisons of Buddhist and Western thought would have to take into account the functional similarity of Buddhism and Western religion. On the other hand the Buddhist Path as practiced by the serious monks involves the practice of meditation and the development of wisdom, and it has *nirvāna* as a more immediate goal.

It is difficult to say just how comparable Buddhist meditation and psychotherapy are. Writers who see the two as quite comparable generally mean that Buddhist meditation has a therapeutic function. For example, Douglas Burns, in a Buddhist publication called "Buddhist Meditation and Depth Psychology," (13) sees many points of similarity. He claims that Gotama abandoned yogic trance for the same reason Freud abandoned hypnotism; namely, that therapy is harder when one is not conscious. Burns presumably sees agreement between the two approaches when he notes that the goal in meditational insight is *awareness of* rather than *elimination of* one's evil thoughts. As an example, he relates that one Buddhist he knew found that he could not overcome his hatred by meditating on love, but had to change to the correct Buddhist procedure of becoming aware of what gave rise to his hatred. Putting this Buddhist procedure in Western terms, Burns gives these three steps for meditational therapy for hatred: what is unconscious must become conscious; the unpleasant feelings must be confronted and fully acknowledged; and finally the egoistic desire of self-exaltation must be relinquished. Burns also raises the question of the scientific verifiability of meditational achievement when he cites experiments which establish that Buddhist meditators maintain an alpha wave (while awake and with the eyes open).

An historian of Buddhism, Glasenapp, also sees similarity between meditation and psychotherapy. He writes that the Buddhist technique of meditation, which is concerned with the latent forces of the unconscious is a forerunner of modern psychoanalysis. He holds that the Indian psychology of the unconscious, which far antedates its Western counterpart, describes the unconscious as the totality of the impressions which slumber in the individual as the inheritance from his previous existences.

In an essay on mindfulness, called "Buddhist Therapy," Ruth Walshe goes well beyond Burns and Glasenapp when she claims that Buddhism goes much deeper than any school of psychology: "While psychology helps you to understand yourself intellectually and, at best, emotionally, Buddhism helps you to get beyond the intellect to the actual experience of life itself." (14)

Other reputable scholars, however, have cautioned against any easy identification of Buddhist meditation and psychotherapy. Winston King, who has himself spent time in a Theravāda meditation center in Burma, points out that there are essential differences between the Buddhist and scientific approaches. However much meditation and psychotherapy have in common as they seek to exorcise evils from within the mind, they are quite different in that meditation is practiced within a religious context, which means that it assumes a world view and transcendent values in the context of which the healing must take place. In contrast psychotherapy as a discipline is not committed to bring the patient to a particular world view, theological beliefs, and moral convictions. (15) Perhaps King has overestimated the psychotherapists' moral neutrality, and some Buddhists might take issue with him about their alleged religiosity, but he has rightly identified the major difference between the two approaches.

Another famous Buddhologist, Edward Conze, strongly opposes any hastily drawn similarities between Buddhist meditation and psychotherapy. Except that they both have mental health as the goal, he writes, they have nothing in common. He calls attention to this major difference: psychotherapy guides people back into the world—the hectic modern world at that—while Buddhist meditation encourages one to withdraw from the everyday world. He notes also that psychotherapy is a product of the modern world, whereas the meditative life-style antedates such modern characteristics as (1) distaste for memorization and discipline; (2) hurried life, with no place for contemplation; (3) lack of quiet places for meditation; and (4) lack of qualified gurus. (16)

The Buddhist cultivation of *wisdom* is more comparable to psychotherapy than is the Buddhist meditation in that both Buddhist wisdom and psychotherapy employ the technique of analysis. But any attempt to compare the two systems of analysis would have to consider the differences brought about by the Theravādin understanding of karma and rebirth, (17) by its practice of meditation, and by its conservatism in adhering to a terminology which is over two thousand years old.

As one of the world's oldest living religions, Theravāda differs considerably from contemporary Western religion and psychotherapy in both theory and practice. For millions of Southeast Asians, from the rural villager to the urban businessman and from the temple boy to the meditation master, Theravāda continues to function as a system of human guidance.

REFERENCES AND FOOTNOTES

1 Cf. the first part of Chapter 10: "Mahayana Buddhism" by D. B. Schneider.
2 For statements by Buddhists on Buddhism as a scientific religion see, for example: Benz, Ernst: *Buddhism or Communism: Which Holds the Future of Asia?* (Htoon, T.M.T.S.); U Chan: *Buddhism—The Religion of the Age of Science* (Rangoon: Democracy Publishing Co., Ltd); King, Winston L.: *A Thousand Lives Away: Buddhism in Contemporary Burma* (Oxford, Bruno Cassierer, 1964).
3 Bhikkhu Silacara cited in Nanada Thera: *Buddhism in a Nutshell.* Pondicherry (India), Sri Aurobindo Ashram Press, p. 18.
4 For accounts of exorcist practices see, for example: Wirz, P.: *Exorcism and the Art of*

Healing in Ceylon (Leiden, E. J. Brill, 1954); Tambiah, S. J.: *Buddhism and the Spirit Cults in North-east Thailand* (Cambridge, Cambridge University Press, 1970), ch. 18; Spiro, Melford E.: *Burmese Supernaturalism* (Englewood Cliffs, Prentice-Hall, 1967), ch. 11; Nur Yalman: The Structure of Singhalese Healing Rituals (in *Religion in South Asia*, ed. by Edward B. Harper, Seattle, University of Washington Press, 1964), p. 115 ff.

5 Wijesekera, O. H. de A.: Buddhist Ethics. In *Knowledge and Conduct* (The Wheel Publications, no. 50), Kandy (Ceylon), Buddhist Publication Society, 1963, p. 13.
6 For example see the Anguttara Nikāya, Book VII, no. 61.
7 The Samyutta Nikāya, sutta no. 38.
8 The Anguttara Nikāya, Book II, p. 159. The translation given here is by Nyanatiloka.
9 Johansson, Rune E. A.: *The Psychology of Nirvāna*. London, George Allen and Unwin, Ltd, 1969, p. 91.
10 Guenther, H. V.: *Philosophy and Psychology in the Abhidhamma*. Lucknow (India), Buddha Vihara, 1957, p. 17.
11 The Anguttara Nikāya, Book X, no. 174.
12 Wijesekera: Buddhist Ethics, pp. 19–20.
13 Burns, Douglas M.: *Buddhist Meditation and Depth Psychology* (The Wheel Publications, nos. 88–89). Kandy (Ceylon), Buddhist Publication Society.
14 Walshe, Ruth: Buddhist Therapy (Bodhi Leaves, no. B 18). Kandy (Ceylon), Buddhist Publication Society, 1963.
15 King, Winston: *Buddhism and Christianity: Some Bridges of Understanding*. Philadelphia, Westminster Press, 1962, p. 172.
16 Conze, Edward: *Buddhist Meditation*. New York, Harper and Row, 1969, pp. 37–41.
17 Herbert Fingarette gives an interesting consideration of Karma and rebirth in his book, *The Self in Transformation: Psychoanalysis, Philosophy and the Life of the Spirit* (New York, Harper and Row, 1963), especially in Chapter 5, "Karma and the Inner World." Fingarette finds the three roots—he calls them "cravings"—to be markedly reminiscent of certain basic psychoanalytic conceptions, such as the libidinal drive and neurotic self-deception, and he maintains that the spiritual sources of reincarnationist doctrine lie close to the kind of experience touched by psychoanalysis.

BIBLIOGRAPHY

1. Amore, Roy C.: The Concept and Practice of Doing Merit in Early Theravāda Buddhism. Unpublished Ph.D. dissertation, Columbia University, 1970, available from University Microfilms.
2. Amore, Roy C., and Elrod, John: From Ignorance to Knowledge: A Study in the Kierkegaardian and Theravāda Buddhist Notions of Freedom. *Union Seminary Quarterly Review*, XXVI, no. 1 (Fall, 1970), 59–79.
3. Buddhaghosa: *The Path of Purity* (Translated by Pe Maung Tin). London, Luzac and Co. for the Pali Text Society, 1971.
4. Burns, Douglas M.: *Buddhist Meditation and Depth Psychology* (The Wheel Publication series, nos. 88–89). Kandy (Ceylon), Buddhist Publication Society.
5. Conze, Edward: *Buddhist Meditation*. New York, Harper and Row, 1969.
6. Govinda, Lama Anagarika: *The Psychological Attitude of Early Buddhist Philosophy and Its Systematic Representation According to Abhidhamma Tradition*. London, Rider and Company, 1961.
7. Guenther, Herbert: *Philosophy and Psychology in the Abhidhamma*. Lucknow (India), Buddha Vihara, 1957.
8. King, Winston L.: *Buddhism and Christianity: Some Bridges of Understanding*. Philadelphia, Westminster Press, 1962.
9. Wijesekera, O. H. de A.: *The Buddhist Concept of Mind* (The Wheel Publication series, no. A 9). Kandy (Ceylon): Buddhist Publication Society.

CHAPTER 13

ISLAM

John Racy

ISLAM IS THE YOUNGEST of the world's major religions. Commanding the loyalty of approximately half a billion people, it is second only to Christianity in its number of adherents and second to none in its rate of growth. (1) The very name, Islam, implies conversion through "surrender" to God's will. The prophet Muhammad regarded himself and was regarded by his followers as no more than a messenger of God's word. He professed no divinity in his person; while revered by Muslims as holy and regarded as closest of all the prophets to God, Muhammad is not God-like. For this reason, Muslims strongly disapprove of the terms "Mohammedan" and "Mohammedanism." Islam is vigorously monotheistic, abjuring all fragmentation or duplication of God's oneness: "Your God is one God; there is no God save him, the Beneficent, the Merciful." (*The Glorious Koran*, Surah II, *The Cow*: 163)

Islam, Judaism and Christianity

Islam's God is the same as the God of the Jews and the God of the Christians. In fact, the *Koran* (the Bible of Islam, God's message) includes much that is derivative from the other two religions and reflects the Middle Eastern Judaeo-Christian tradition in many of its aspects. Jews and Christians are regarded by Muslims with distinct ambivalence. As "readers of the scripture" Christians and Jews have received the same message from God; but they have also erred from the straight path and are in need of correction. "Allah will judge between them on the Day of Resurrection concerning that wherein they differ." (*The Glorious Koran*, Surah II, *The Cow*:113) Certain beliefs unite the three religions: "Say (O Muslims): We believe in Allah and that which is revealed unto Abraham and Ishmael and Isaac, and Jacob and the tribes, and that which Moses and Jesus received, and that which the Prophets received from the Lord. We make no distinction between any of them and unto Him we have surrendered." (*The Glorious Koran,* Surah II. *The Cow*: 136)

Much more than Christianity, Islam is a *code for living*. It deals with many mundane and practical aspects of life. One can find support for almost any point of view in the *Koran*: from the most liberal to the most bigoted, from the gentlest to the harshest, from the enterprising to the passive, from the worldly to the other-worldly. But in general, Islam, in comparison with Christianity, presents certain characteristics: (1) lays more emphasis on ritual and deeds (it should be recalled that the five pillars of Islam are all acts; they are prayer, witness, fasting, alms-giving, and pilgrimage to Mecca); (2) is more fatalistic ("What is written" will happen); (3) is more concrete in its rewards and punishments (heaven is described in florid detail); (4) is more tolerant of sexual activity, even regarding it as an obligation or good deed; and (5) is more of a legal code, with provisions for children, women, the ill, and the insane. Polygamy is permitted by the *Koran,* provided the husband is just to his wives and marries no more than four at a time. This last provision (justice to all four wives) is often used by modern reformers as an argument against polygamy. They claim that since it is impossible for a man to be just to four wives, he should not marry more than one.

Islam and The Arabic Tongue

An essential feature of Islam is its identification with the Arabic language. This stems not so much from the historical fact that Muhammad was an Arab (a fact no more significant than Buddha's identity as an Indian, Jesus' as a Palestinian, Paul's as a Syrian, or Luther's as a German), but from the belief that the *Koran* constituted God's literal, concrete message to humans. God spoke the *Koran* to Muhammad—and he spoke it in Arabic. Thus all practicing non-Arab Muslims (for example, Indonesians, Malayans, Pakistanis, and Persians) must recite the *Koran* in their prayers in the original Arabic, whether they understand it or not. In fact, the *Koran's* classical style is barely comprehensible to the Arab child who must memorize it. Jacques Berque in his book on the Arabs wrote:

> It was less a question of instructing the child than of adapting him to the absolute. The *Koran* is learned by heart, with superb disregard of intelligibility. The virtue of its words lies in their form and sound rather than in any sort of correspondence with the facts of everyday. They acquire greater power, thereby imprinted deep in men's memories. . . . It is easy to see how the great language, thus preserved in a vessel that was both childlike and godlike, offers a social symbol of tremendous intensity. (Berque, 1964)

Arabic is a rich, sonorous language, particularly apt for affective and descriptive expression. It manifests a tendency to overemphasis, hyperbole, and exaggeration. This phenomenon has been commented on by a number of writers and has been the subject of study by Prothro (1955) and others. Shouby, an Arab psychologist, in writing about the exaggerated use of the language states:

> Arabs are forced to overassert and exaggerate in almost all types of communication, as otherwise they stand a good chance of being gravely misunderstood. If an Arab says exactly what he means without the expected exaggeration, other Arabs may still think that he means the opposite. (Shouby, 1951)

In considering the effect of religion on psychiatric therapy, one needs to take into account all aspects of the culture. Powerful as its influence may be, religion is but a part of the mosaic. The remainder of this discussion will therefore concern itself with that section of the Muslim world with which the author is personally familiar and which constitutes a geographical-historical-political-cultural unit, namely the Arab countries of the Middle East. Fortunately, the close identification of Islam with Arabic makes a discussion of Arabs relevant to non-Arab Muslims. Furthermore, Arab land remains the acknowledged heart of the Muslim world. Islam's spiritual capital is Mecca, its second holiest city is Medina (both in Saudi Arabia), its third holiest city is Jerusalem, and its intellectual and theological capital is Cairo.

Arab Women

Arab culture being strongly masculine in its orientation, the Arab woman has suffered the burdens of second-class citizenship for several millennia. Modernization in the last hundred years has brought with it changes in woman's role that often lead to conflict. In a monograph on psychiatry in the Arab East (Racy, 1970), I recorded these impressions:

> The strongest taboos and most cherished values of Arab Muslim culture are expressed in terms of woman's role. It is therefore not surprising that the young Arab college-educated woman represents a particularly poignant example of the personal impact of cultural change. She often leads a double life and adheres to a double set of values: the traditional and the modern. Tradition requires of her that she subordinate herself completely to her husband, her family, her household, and even her children. As an educated person, on the other hand, she is tempted to consider herself as her husband's equal partner, as mistress of her home, and as a productive member of society (whether in the factory, the classroom, or the hospital). At times, and with remarkable agility, she succeeds in playing both roles, either simultaneously or alternately. More often, she renounces one role in favor of the other, usually the modern in favor of the tradi-

tional. She buys peace by renouncing the full implications of her education; for, along with all other considerations, she must contend with the fact that Arab men regard the educated young woman with reserve.

As Muhyi wrote, "The emancipated woman of the Middle East may derive satisfaction from her new freedom, but she is evidently not a very good bargain in the marriage market." (Hudson, 1959)

Sufism

Before discussing modern trends and practices, it may be of interest to dwell briefly on Sufism: Muslim mysticism which arose in the late tenth and early eleventh centuries. "The highly developed symbolism of the soul's union with God is expressed in exquisite lyric style. The movement . . . borrowed ideas from Neoplatonism, Buddhism, and Christianity . . . . Emphasis (is) on the immediate personal union of the soul with God. In some variations the beliefs of Sufism verge sharply toward pantheism, thus almost leaving Islam altogether." (*Columbia Encyclopedia,* 1967) In a series of articles for the Egyptian Journal of Psychology in 1949 and 1950, a Sufi Sheikh, A. Taftazani, explained the psychology of Sufism. The mystic experience, he indicated, is accomplished through three stages: (1) Doubt and anxiety; (2) "Zuhd", a state of resignation and renunciation; and (3) Love of God, which is of various degrees, leading to unity with God or loss of one's identity in Him. (Taftazani, 1949)

Thus, on his road to God, the seeker after truth (*Al-Mureed*) must suffer a long and strenuous struggle. He needs and must secure the guidance of a Sufi Sheikh. To the latter he must reveal all his thoughts and problems and from him obtain (and follow) certain spiritual "exercises." The wise Sheikh uses a combination of interpretation, counseling and suggestion, and must always maintain an individual approach adapted to the specific make-up of the seeker.

The human psyche is stratified in an ascending order of four faculties:

1. "The Self" (*Al-Nafs*)—the most primitive of these, the seat of all that is base, particularly desire and anger. It is ever rebellious, a source of temptation, and a guide to evil. It must be curbed and "broken".

2. "The Heart" (*Al-Kalb*) is the seat of knowledge. It is fed by the senses and acts as mediator between the lower "self" and higher "spirit." Its knowledge of things is intuitive, in contrast to the Mind (*Al-Akl*) which knows by deduction and observation. (It is not clear why the mind is not included in the classification. Conceivably, it may be regarded as a totally separate agency outside the psyche.)

3. "The Spirit" (*Al-Ruh*) —the seat of *good* qualities, and therefore opposed to the "self". It is the principle of life and is pure, kind, and humane. It impels to good deeds.

4. "The Secret" (*Al-Sirr*) —the highest faculty, the locus of "Witness" (*Markaz Al-Mushahada*). Such witness is the cardinal manifestation of the supreme state of bliss.

In his struggle, the seeker must move from one level to the next, finally attaining "the Secret." This struggle (*Al-Mujahada Al-Nafsiyya*) is a mortification of "the self" through denial of its desires—both through physical suffering (hunger, thirst, etc.) and psychological suffering (exercise of self-control, and the conversion into positive feelings of such base emotions as pride, anger, and envy). (Taftazani, 1950)

Native Treatment

The Arab world has its share of seers, fortune-tellers, mindreaders and clairvoyants. The line separating these from out-and-out charlatans and quacks is hard to establish. In either case, individuals resort to such practitioners not so much for mental illness as for relief of anxiety, of uncertainty or of fear attached to some realistic concern or physical ailment. For the treatment of mental disease as such, native methods may be broadly divided into "magical" and "religious", though here again, the distinction is somewhat vague and artificial. The use of such methods, according to local observers, appears to be on the decline. Not surprisingly, they are most prevalent in traditional areas, particularly in Arabia and the Sudan. Below are listed some of them:

I. **Magical Therapy** of various sorts has existed in the Near East since the dawn of history. Much of it is borrowed from adjoining regions, mainly Africa and Central Asia, and has been encrusted with multiple accretions over the ages. Thus a belief or practice may reveal traces of Mediterranean folklore, Judaic taboo, Christian faith, and Muslim ritual.

    A. Preventively, charms in the form of a blue bead, a cross, or Koranic verses may be hung about the neck to ward off evil influence. The frequent invocation of Allah by using one of his many names ("ya Hafeez," "ya Mu'een," etc.) is another magical device to avoid harm.

    B. Cautery ("Kayy") of the head or painful part of the body is a time-honored form of treatment.

    C. Undoing of an evil wish is achieved through the services of a religious leader, a Sheikh. After divining the source of pathology, he unties "the knot" causing a man's impotence, or erases the "writing" that is the source of his misfortunes.

D. "The Zar" ceremony, imported into Sudan and Egypt from Ethiopia around the turn of the century, is one of the more dramatic and expensive procedures. Designed to relieve the distress of unhappy women, it is a several-days affair involving a number of sufferers and their relatives and presided over by a woman, the "Sheikha". The latter leads a series of incantations, exhortations, and dancing that culminate in ecstasy and collapse. At that point, the Zar, or evil spirit possessing the woman, is called upon to indicate its price for leaving her alone. This is stated "through the patient's voice" as a direct wish. Considerable pressure is then brought to bear upon the husband, or relatives, to satisfy the demand, however outlandish, lest the Zar refuse to depart. It is obvious that relief of a number of neurotic and frustrated women is achieved through a combination of abreaction, suggestion, and direct or symbolic gratification.

II. **Religious Therapy.** In Europe and the Middle East, institutional religion has long been the warden of man's mind. Islam, like Christianity, has concerned itself with the mentally afflicted; Islamic law regards them as children who cannot be held responsible for their acts.

At their homes and in the Mosque, Sheikhs are often called upon to help resolve problems of a psychological nature, fulfilling a role similar to that of the Christian priest's tending to the needs of his congregation.

The historic and renowned Maristans of Cairo and Damascus that at one time provided amazingly humane and enlightened treatment of the mentally ill have long since disappeared (El-Mahi, 1959). In the Sudan today it is still possible to witness a humble form of Muslim institutional treatment. The Sufi "Maseed" at Umn-Dubban outside Khartoum is a complex of one-story buildings, consisting of a mosque, a shrine, a Koranic School for boys (run by a blind teacher), and a facility for the treatment of the insane. Patients are classified into two large categories:

A. "Mawhumoon," or those who have "wahm". They "imagine" disease and are probably neurotics. Given religious instruction and allowed to remain for several days or weeks at the Maseed, they help out with the daily routine and relax in the unusually calm and restful setting of the Maseed;

B. "Majnunoon," or those who have "Junun". Most of these are between eighteen and forty years of age and, from the description given by Sheikhs and some personal observation, appear to fall within the large category of "functional psychoses."

Senile dementia is regarded as a developmental stage and therefore not cause for intervention.

The treatment of psychotics is energetic. Patients are isolated in cubicles in the field, at times chained down, and fed solid or liquid nutriment, depending on tolerance. Religious readings, prayer, and water passed over the pages of Koranic verses and given orally are the major weapons in therapy. In effect, the psychotic episode is allowed to run its course and the patient returns home during remissions. The relatives are encouraged to leave the patient alone for the first few days; beyond that they are free to keep him or take him away at will. Fatalities do occur. The Sheikhs seem to be aware of, and are to a certain extent in favor of, the psychiatric clinic run by the Ministry of Health in Khartoum North.

A third group of patients, those who come for personal and family problems, are not considered ill. They discuss their affairs with the Sheikh, from whom they obtain guidance or intercession. In general, good service is rendered those who come with everyday problems in living, neurotics are provided a congenial setting for spontaneous recovery, but psychotics tend to suffer at the Maseed.

Support for the institution comes from voluntary contributions and treatment is free.

Modern Therapy

One way or another, all medical practitioners adapt their practice to their culture. Some do so with more imagination than others; a few are able to articulate these adaptations. Gadallah, an Egyptian physician, wrote of the utilization of traditional Islamic teachings to introduce modern principles of public health. He counseled the frequent use of prayers and the repeated mentioning of the prophet's name before examining or treating rural patients, thereby providing them with reassurance. Occasionally reference to a Koranic verse or a Hadeeth (the Prophet's sayings) may facilitate acceptance of a new program, for example, "Cleanliness is part of Islam," and "Fetch knowledge, even from China." (Gadallah, 1962)

A wise and enlightened Sudanese psychiatrist, Dr. Tigani El-Mahi, displayed a remarkable capacity of integrating the traditional and the modern, the religious and the secular; as a result of his initiative, psychiatric practice in the Sudan is perhaps the most imaginative and the best suited to its setting in the Arab world. Dr. El-Mahi, and more recently his student and successor Dr. Taha Baasher, have both expressed respect for native healers. Writing of them, Dr. El-Mahi attributed their effectiveness to the use of suggestion and persuasion.

Religious healers are often remarkably effective. They are in a position to use suggestion and persuasion based on an intense religious transference. Dr. Tigani explained the theory of mental illness on which such therapy is based: "Its psychopathology emphasizes sinfulness and stresses conflict between 'evil and good' and 'religious and irreligious' as productive of symptoms which are sometimes regarded as retributions. These 'evil and good' influences are no doubt the prototypes and personifications of the Id and Super-Ego which were later postulated by Freud." (El-Mahi, 1955)

In another communication Dr. El-Mahi quoted the fourth Caliph after Mohammad to the effect: "And Ali said, may God honour his face, 'People to their times bear greater resemblance than to their fathers.'" (El-Mahi, 1963)

At the conference on care of patients with fatal illness sponsored by the New York Academy of Sciences in New York City in February 1967, I said, "For the Arab, grief, like life and death, is not a private matter. Management of the dying must perforce include management of the family. Opportunities must be provided for reunion at the bedside, for the open display of sorrow, and for the formal presentation of condolences (which are probably the most binding social obligations in the Arab East)." (Racy, 1969)

In my monograph on Psychiatry in the Arab East mentioned above, I summarized my own experiences and observations of psychiatric treatment in Arab countries and ended with the following questions and statements which should serve to round out this chapter (Racy, 1970).

It is logical to extend the concept of cultural psychiatry to the field of treatment in order to ask: Are there modifications of standard treatment that have been introduced by local psychiatrists? Can one describe an "Arab style" in patient management? Is there a "cultural therapy"?

Here certain impressions and observations may be made, relevant to this issue, and again I refer to my earlier monograph:

1. The tendency to use somatic modes of therapy is particularly marked with the poorer and more conservative patients from traditional areas. The personal bias of psychiatrists toward organic approaches and the lack of time are doubtless involved. But we must also consider that to most patients, no therapy is worthy of the name (or their money) if it does not include colorful and painful injections,

or some large pills at least. (There is a tendency to disdain small hypodermic injections and tiny tablets.) Talking cannot replace a prescription.

2. Being a product of his own culture as much as of Western technological training, the Arab physician in general displays a striking combination of authoritarian dogmatism and tolerant realism. Observing him in action, one is impressed by his self-assured and highly pragmatic approach. He speaks to his patients, whether young or old, with patronizing finality, addressing them as "my son," "my daughter," "my sister," "my brother," "my uncle," "my aunt," and rarely "my father" or "my mother." To them this is both natural and welcome. There is little doubt that the physician is readily regarded, and regards himself, as the good, powerful, and all-knowing father. Kindness is in keeping with his role, but not humility.

3. As brought out earlier, Arabic is a remarkably emotive and hyperbolic language; while fairly uniform as a literary tool, it is highly variable in colloquial form. Words, phrases, and sounds of everyday speech tend to convey concepts that are fully comprehensible within a very small radius. Since these shadings of meaning are of great significance in psychiatric work, the physician may find himself best able to "understand"—in the emotional sense—patients who come from his own district. For their part, such patients tend to regard the psychiatrist's familiar accent as an indicator of emotional propinquity, and inflections of speech become a major factor in the establishment of rapport or the lack of it. The peculiar mixture of foreign and Arabic languages used by educated people can itself be regarded as a distinctive mode of communication and appears to facilitate the psychotherapy of such individuals (who, in any event, are the majority of candidates for expensive verbal forms of treatment).

4. The problems of youth in a changing society pose a specific challenge. Faced with them, the psychiatrist is called upon to do more than "ally himself with reality"; for there are multiple social realities. He cannot simply "lend his ego to the patient" because the latter needs to develop his own. To offer himself as a model is a questionable practice in a society that does not recognize that model as desirable. Yet, maintaining an attitude of strict neutrality frequently leaves the sufferer where one found him, paralyzed with indecision. In effect, the psychiatrist's dilemma is that of the youth he is trying to help: to encourage rebellion against tradition imposes risks upon the patient, to foster tradition sacrifices individual fulfillment, and to "stand pat" invites futility.

As members of the new generation themselves, most physicians, including psychiatrists, appear in subtle ways to ally themselves with the aspirations of youth and the processes of change; some, out of realism and caution, temper this attitude with a substantial measure of respect for traditional values, regarding them as a factor in stability and health. A few hope to utilize tradition in order to effect change (El-Mahi, 1960 and Gadallah, 1962).

Conclusion

Finally, we return to the original question: Is there a "cultural therapy"? In answering it, we should bear in mind that "Arab psychiatrists as a rule respond intuitively rather than deliberately to the cues and clues, verbal and non-verbal, of their patients; little effort is made to formalize or examine such response. Thus certain adaptations and alterations in psychiatric treatment are introduced but at a preconscious level. Under those conditions, 'cultural therapy' becomes both inevitable and ineffable." (Racy, 1970)

In conclusion, it is wise to recall that modernization is sweeping the Muslim world as well as its Arab portion. As a result, psychotherapy will inevitably change from a locally applicable and idiosyncratic form of treatment to a more universal communication understood by all. For, as Ali said, "People to their times bear greater resemblance than to their fathers."

REFERENCES AND FOOTNOTES

1 In all, more than 500,000,000 persons today, one-sixth of humanity, profess themselves to be Muslims, however minimal in practice. Of this number about 125,000,000 are in Africa and almost 400,000,000 in Asia, with scattered communities in Europe and the Americas.

Of perhaps greater significance than its present numbers is the fact that Islam, of all major religions, continues to show the most steady growth. "Particularly noteworthy is its progress in regions previously dominated by pagan tribal cultures. Its (strongest) appeal (is) to underprivileged or minority groups everywhere."

(*International Encyclopedia of the Social Sciences.* New York, Macmillan Co., 1968, Vol. 8, p. 204.)

For all other references in this study, consult the following Bibliography. Author and date indicate the monograph, article, or book referred to in the text (usually in parentheses).

BIBLIOGRAPHY

1. Berque, J.: *The Arabs, Their History and Future* (Translated by Jean Steward). London, Faber, 1964.
2. *Columbia Encyclopedia,* 3rd Edition, New York, Columbia University Press, 1967, esp. p. 2063.

3. Gadallah, F.: Some Cultural Implications in Medical and Public Health Practice in Egypt. *Journal Egyptian Public Health Association,* vol. 27, no. 3, p. 63, 1962.
4. Hudson, B. (Editor): Cross-Cultural Studies in the Arab Middle East and United States: Studies of Young Adults. *Journal Social Issues,* vol. 15, no. 3, 1959.
5. El-Mahi, T.: Psychiatry in the Light of Specific Cultures. *Sudan Medical Journal,* 1 (old series), no. 3, April 27, 1955.
6. El-Mahi, T.: *(An Introduction to the History of Arab Medicine.)* Sudan, Matba'at Misr Ltd., (Arabic). Summary in *Racy,* 1970, 1959.
7. El-Mahi, T.: Religion and Social Conformity. Paper for Mental Health Group Meeting, Alexandria, U.A.R., EM/MH. Gp./110, November 15. Summary in *Racy,* 1970, 1960.
8. El-Mahi, T.: (Human Relations and Their Influence in the Education of the Arab Citizen), Manuscript, (Arabic), Summary in *Racy,* 1970, 1963.
9. Pickthall, Mohammed Marmaduke (trans.): The Meaning of the Glorious Koran (A Mentor Religious Classic). New York: New American Library, 1953.
10. Prothro, E. T.: Arab-American Differences in the Judgment of Written Messages. *Journal Social Psychology, 42:* 3, 1955.
11. Racy, J.: The Conception of Death in an Arab Culture. *Annals of the New York Academy of Sciences, 164:* 871–880, 1969.
12. Racy, J.: Psychiatry in the Arab East. *Acta Psychiatricia Scandinavica,* Supplement 211, Munksgaard, Copenhagen, 1970.
13. Shouby: The Influence of the Arabic Language on the Psychology of the Arabs. *Middle East Journal, 5:* 284, 1951.
14. Taftazani, A.: (The Psychology of Sufism), *Egyptian Journal of Psychology,* 5, No. 2, p. 291 (Arabic). Summary in *Racy* 1970, 1949.
15. Taftazani, A.: (The Psychology of Sufism), *Egyptian Journal of Psychology,* 5, No. 3, p. 377, (Arabic). Summary in *Racy* 1970, 1950.

CHAPTER 14

HINDUISM, PSYCHOTHERAPY, AND THE HUMAN PREDICAMENT

Agehananda Bharati

TOTAL SOLUTIONS are for the birds and for old-time clerics. Both humanists and scientists disclaim their possibility as well as their desirability. Freudian reductionists as well as the Hindu Swamis' claim that their brand of Eastern wisdom will usher world peace are rejected by both. There has been some literature on total-solution Hinduism and total-solution therapy; (1) some of it makes good reading, nothing in it is verifiable or falsifiable, and nothing of it has provided the goods promised. Amazingly, today's best theologians who belong to traditions which had originally put up dogmatic claims of this sort, have reduced their stipulations, while religious teachers representing relatively non-dogmatic traditions have taken to pontificating universal panaceas. I am thinking of Bultmann, the late Tillich, and other Christian theologians of our day, vis-à-vis the roaming sadhus from India. The non- or anti-Christian humanist, and the social scientists of this day and age feel much more comfortable with the former than with the swamis and their Western votaries. This is due to the abandonment on the part of sophisticated, diversified theologians of total solution claims, which, by contrast, the Hindu preachers of today spew forth with an enthusiasm reminiscent of the Christian theologians of the past.

Only three decades ago, *engagé* Hindus knew infinitely more about the Mediterranean religions and Western thought than did Western scholars about Indian ideas. The ecumenical atmosphere in the Judaeo-Christian world today does not have a parallel in Hindu India. One reason for this lack is very banal and irksome: since Indian currency is not negotiable, Indian scholars can no longer buy foreign publications to keep up with Western thought. Indian college teachers have to rely on the old library material, bought in better days previous to 1950. More sinister, however, is the fact that Hindu apologists tend to be ideological totalitarians; their unabashed sympathy for Hitler—who, so they insist, was not only the promulgator of an Aryan creed, but also a celibate and a vegetarian—is but one of the many unwholesome aspects of what I call Hindu fascist tendencies. (2)

The sort of Hinduism today's English-speaking Hindus hold and talk about is simplistic, and highly alienated both from the grassroot Hinduism of the village, as well as from that of the indigenous scholars, the *pandits* and the *sannyasis* (monks). Reading the works and listening to the words of the agents of urban Hinduism, one gets the impression that they really cathect a Protestant Ethic with Hindu names replacing the Judaeo-Christian terms. Their Hinduism is antiaesthetical, non- and anti-sexual, naïvely monotheistic, normatively society-oriented. It has nothing of the rich, powerfully chthonic, experimental, and discursive features non-Westernized Hinduism used to have. I say "used to have," because the irrefragable fact is that grassroot Hinduism withers to the degree that modern India turns industrialist, unadmittedly Western, becoming subject to the Protestant Ethic as presaged by Max Weber (3) well before it happened. Let me state, therefore, quite categorically, that the Hinduism we hear about from people who speak English, who praise Gandhi, and who dissimulate the grassroot elements of the Hindu tradition in favor of the urban eclectic jargon of the alienate, is not the Hinduism I shall report here. It does not yield a viable set of human options or alternatives to psychotherapy; nor does it in any way assuage the toils and turmoils of our day.

The psychoanalysis and/or therapy which I want to juxtapose with genuine Hinduism is not Freudian. The Freudian model does not apply in the Indian situation unless we insist on forcing it into a procrustean bed. R. D. Laing, Th. Szasz, and the late Harry Stack-Sullivan have independently generated information of the kind which can be linked to Hinduism as practiced—namely, Hindu meditation.

The human predicament in the title of this chapter covers the symptoms which sociologists and literary people as well as some psychologists bracket as "alienation"; or, in Kierkegaardian language, the human predicament as nausea, fear, and anguish, existential uncertainty, and all those built-in, counter-operative modes of human existence which we somehow accept as inevitable.

In presenting the salient features of radical Hinduism to the readers of this anthology, I intend to show that selected Hindu teachings and praxes could indeed be an alternative to Western psychotherapy. Let me then adumbrate this Hinduism, bereft of its social and ethnic complexities.

Hinduism, like Buddhism and other religions with a written tradition, stipulates dissatisfaction with the mundane, empirical situation in which human beings find themselves. The remedy is sought in doctrinally determined praxis. Whereas the Mediterranean traditions—Judaism, Christianity, and Islam—roughly identify the good life as the method to achieve this remedy, as granting salvation when consummated in sainthood, etc., the Indian traditions teach that the morally good life alone is not an instrument toward the redemptory end. The person desirous of reaching deliverance from the shackles of birth, death, rebirth, and the agonies inevitable to the born, has to embark on a series of supererogatory efforts which are quite unrelated to moral goodness or sainthood. The overall term for these efforts, of course, is *yoga,* but it is important that its fatuous occidental connotations be eschewed—the millions of Westerners who practice "yoga" are not really doing anything the Indian theologian would consider as *yoga,* since the spiritual claims foisted on calisthenics by the Western yogis and their teachers (both Western and Eastern) are felt to be spurious by the Indian specialists who do not cater to Western lovers of the occult and of alleged Eastern mysteries. The proper definition of *yoga* was given by the father of systematized *yoga,* the Brahmin teacher Patanjali (about 300 B.C.), *yogashcitavrtti nirodhah*: "Yoga is the curbing of the outward-directed tendencies of the mind." Physical contortions, arcane gymnastics, and all the things that seem to fit the semantic *gestalt* of *yoga* to the Westerner today, are at best marginal to the purpose of *yoga,* and at worst fraudulent superimpositions.

Why should the "outward-directed tendencies of the mind" be curbed? The theological axiom—in all indigenous Indian religions—is that man remains in bondage, going through millions of births and rebirths, until he has learned to withdraw his mind from all sense objects. This is to be understood quite literally, not in any metaphorical way which might suggest itself to the Western student who first encounters this peculiar diction. The consummation of the Hindu's religious life is not some kind of a paradise which he could achieve through moral actions, through charity or through other things which go into the making of a saint. Rather he has to learn—preferably under the instruction of a preceptor, a guru—to withdraw his mind from the objects, to prevent sense impressions from getting to his mind: not only from affecting his mind one way or the other, but from being perceived. To some, this appears as some sort of a sleeping state or trance; however, the clinical, pejorative connotation must be taken out of the term; it means achieving a state of insight, in which the objects—the objective world—are either no longer present to the viewer at all, or else their presence is shadow-like, illusory, seeming imaginary, variously referred to as *māyā, samsāra* or other Sanskrit term. Always implied in these words is a distantiation of the yogi from the objects surrounding him.

The eschatological assumption is that once a person has broken the "outward going tendencies" of the mind, the effect of his past actions in millions of past lives no longer reaches him; he is then liberated from rebirth. Since birth and life are viewed as predominantly painful, there is no such thing, in the long run, as a happy life, a heaven, a paradise, because all these are evanescent; ephemerality being synonymous with pain in Hindu and Buddhist religious parlance, such seemingly pleasant states and abodes do not satisfy the criteria of perfection, and are not 'blissful' in any sense akin to the Christian homiletic. Good actions in the moral sense, as well as ritualistically correct actions including the proper religious observances, the Vedic sacrifice, and the whole lot of acts and deeds of merit accrue to more pleasant and more diversified existences in future lives—they may give wealth, power, sensual enjoyment; they may deliver heavens and paradise; they may even confer the status of gods as high up as the God Indra, supreme in the Aryan pantheon. Yet all these merits are exhausted when their momentum has been spent, and the circle of birth, death, and rebirth stays uninterrupted. Occidental believers in rebirth seem perfectly silly to the Hindu teacher, since these Westerners *like* the idea of rebirth. The Hindu rejects it once he steers toward consummation of the religious life, which is *not* one of good deeds and noble acts leading to further births, even though pleasant ones, but of contemplation of the true essence of one's self, and of renunciation of *all* acts, good and bad alike.

Contrary to the notion cherished by Westernized modern Hindus—which includes all Indian political leaders known in the West today—Hinduism is not society-oriented in its essence, though there are texts and traditions within its amorphous lore which lend themselves to activistic, sociocentric interpretations. But when the chips are down, either the learned Hindu or the learned Buddhist will want to quit society, to withdraw either into himself or into a circle of similarly oriented aspirants. This, of course, accounts for the wealth of monastic and para-monastic institutions, for the *ashram*-type life cherished and propagated by religiously *engagé* Hindus and their Western disciples.

The theological parameters here are sundry, and often blatantly incompatible with one another. Polytheism, monotheism, abstract monism, and even some sort of total atheism (4) exist side by side in Hindu thought. But all these disparate schools have one element in common: it is through *yoga,* through meditation—and not through discursive thought or moral effort of any kind, nor through a combination of these—that the theologically stipulated knowledge is gained: the knowledge that leads to freedom from rebirth, i.e. freedom from pain.

There are two meditational approaches available to the Hindu who seeks emancipation. The contrastive extremes are those of total asceticism such as practiced by certain recluses in the Hindu tradition, from very ancient days until now, *versus* total sensuous indulgence guided by certain esoteric controls—these are the least known, and in India, the most highly suspect Tantric traditions, to which we will turn further down. (5) In between these two extremes, there is a very large number of intermediary approaches, emphasizing or de-emphasizing the ascetic rule as the case may be. At any point, it is important to bear in mind that whether the rule is ascetic or sense-indulgent, or anything in between, the target is not "heaven" or "a better life," comparable either to Christian or secular Western notions; rather it is redemption from rebirth. Indian theologies differ radically with one another on matters which appear crucial to all Mediteranean systems (Judaic, Christian, and Islamic) : the existence of a supreme being, the number of gods, atheism *vs* theism, gnosticism *vs* agnosticism. All these are schools within the Hindu compass. But all Hindu schools—together with all the other indigenous Indian religions, viz. Buddhism and Jainism—take rebirth and the capacity to liberate oneself from it as axiomatic, and as somehow self-evident.

On the grassroot level, the villagers of India—and they account for over 90 per cent of the population—rebirth is not much talked about. Other causes of happiness and misfortune are quoted, such as witchcraft, curses, fate, evil stars, along with *karma,* and most Hindus do not seem to mind, or know, the contradiction implied. For either *I* am responsible for my fate in line with a strict reading of the inexorable laws of *karma* which generate a calculus of good and bad actions regulating pleasant and unpleasant births and events within millions of births which all individuals undergo; or *someone else* is—some more or less whimsical god with his anthropomorphic likes and dislikes, some demon, some witch, or some vaguely defined "fate." Religion as a belief system, however, is never a system of logic. The doctors of Hinduism usually stress *karma* as the main cause for a person's career; the Hindu commoners see *karma* as one of several concurrent, non-exclusive causes.

Yet, both the learned and the naïve hold that life is so radically permeated with suffering that the wise man wants to get out of it; which, of course, he cannot accomplish by suicide, since that would result in a painful rebirth without any gain, but only by *yoga*—highly structured meditation under the guidance of a *guru*. The morally good life is accepted by all as a condition, but never as a cause for salvation. There is no mediator for redemption: each seeker must do it by himself. The guru's task is strictly one of guidance and even where he is powerfully charismatic, it is not his charisma that somehow bestows salvation on his disciple—it may only impel him to intensifed efforts much like any good teacher prompts his student toward harder work and discipline. However, the concept of intercession on behalf of an aspirant or a devotee simply does not exist in the Indian tradition; there is no *ora pro nobis* category in the yogic quest.

The ascetic world-renouncing mode of meditation has been, and is, the prevalent one in India. It was espoused and presented in many guises—as the scholarly, stern, dialectic path of the Vedāntins [6] and the numerous scholastics of the Brahmin lore; as the humble, highly emotional, rustic effusions of the medieval saints of Hindu India, with their eclectic search and their poetic expression incorporating all the religious elements available in their days, not excluding Muslim and other non-Hindu themes. In this century, the latter style was adopted and urbanized, as it were, by the religious and the political leaders of nationalist India: Tilak, Gandhi, Vivekananda, and their followers. Since it was the urban middle-class which took a non-sophisticated, theologically naïve, highly puritanical and basically anti-intellectual posture, levelling the intricacies of learned grassroot Hinduism, we now find that this somewhat washed-out, asexual, anti-aesthetic type of belief system emerges as the Hinduism of tomorrow.

The city boy who has been exposed to Western models of formal education claims to be secular. He is not—in fact hardly any Hindu, modern or traditional, understands the meaning of "secular." [7] Modern Hindus invariably say such things as "the West is materialistic, the East is spiritual"; "Hinduism is not a religion, but a way of life." What all this means in actual fact, if it is not to be seen as pompous rubbish as Arthur Koestler thinks it should be, [8] is that the puritanical, naïvely monotheistic, anti-ritualistic as well as anti-scholastic Hinduism of the Hindu village saints who lived and sang between the fifteenth and the eighteenth centuries A.D., interiorized and translated into the schoolmasterly parlance of Victorian English, more recently retranslated from this sort of English into the Indian vernaculars, has come to stay. The simplistic disquisitions on Hindu doctrine as promulgated by fairly scholarly persons like Dr. S. Radhakrishnan, second President of the Indian Republic, illustrate a profound aversion both to the magico-mystical experimentalism of grassroot-Hinduism as well as to the sophisticated ritualism and the tough theologies of the Brahmin tradition. A pervasive example: Radhakrishnan and virtually all other Hindu scholars who write in English use the term "God" to translate a number of Sanskrit terms connoting a supreme being. Yet there is no "God" at all in any school of Hinduism; the term "God" implies a creator, one who formed the universe *ex nihilo*. This notion is absurd to the Indian theologian since the Hindu universe is without beginning and without end (*anādi-ananta*), which axiom precludes the concept of a creator god. What could he create since everything was always there, in one form or the other, cyclically formed, un-formed, and modified primordial matter?

This sort of Hinduism—let me call it the official Hinduism of modern India—is of no use at all for the analysis and the therapy which modern life necessitates. Modern Hindus see human problems very much like Protestant ministers used to around the turn of the century. Normatively, they define the good man as one who is abstemious in food and sex, pious, non-argumentative, and averse to any sort of ecstatic behavior. This pervasive attitude, generated by a Protestant Ethic incipient in India as in other parts of the Third World, militates against virtually all that is at the core of Hindu teachings unfiltered through the Colonial-Victorian and post-Colonial, modernistic-urban sieve. We now see the *Hare Krishna* people perform their arcane gymnastics on 42nd Street in New York, on Sunset Boulevard and in Piccadilly; their guru, Swami Bhaktivedanta, speaks in terms of ecstasy. The thespian mode of the cult—which has its roots in seventeenth century rural Northeastern India and was transplanted into the West with considerable managerial skill—might suggest a truly ecstatic framework. Such, however, is not the case at all.

This specific movement, together with over two dozen neo-Hindu movements which originated in the cities of India, is hypertrophically puritanical, anti-erotic, extolling ascetic and medieval values, albeit couched in quasi-modernistic terms. Hindu leaders today quote the *Bhagavadgītā* (9) to show that the religious life is compatible with scientific achievement, with commerce, industry, secular activity, and with citizenship. As a professional witness to neo-Hinduism, I can only state, and *re*state, (10) that the philistine, highly castrating message of modern Hinduism as enunciated by Gandhi and by the swamis since the first decades of this century, is psychologically counteroperative: its claim to total solutions of an eirenic sort perpetuates a systematic disregard for the human person as an empirical individual and does not yield any scope for the individual generating his own moral, intellectual, and decision-making norms.

To the Hindu—modern and traditional—nothing of real value is new: all that is good and commendable is contained in the Hindu tradition, and all that is stated can only be a commentary and a reiteration of the scriptures and their commentaries, if it is to be valid. This accounts for the sad state of humanistic and philosophical teaching at Indian universities. Radically intellectual ideas and the sort of philosophical analysis which forms the main thrust of modern professional philosophy in the West, are taboo in India, as these would undercut the once-and-for-all-valid doctrines of the tradition. Modern Hindu claims not withstanding, Hinduism is *not* tolerant, but highly authoritarian; it is, of course, less intolerant than the kind of Bible-thumping missionary teachings that got into India in the wake of the European conquest, and it is less intolerant than Islam, but that is not really saying much when standards are set by intellectual, secular humanism, rather than by various competing theologies.

There is a tradition, albeit clandestine *and* resented, in India, which "delivers the goods" needed for the radical standards of sanity postulated by the humanistic intellectuals of this day and age. It is to this tradition that I must now turn as I conclude this chapter. The paradigm, in all yogic traditions, is control—in order to escape from the travail of rebirth, the aspirant has to control his mind and his body. Let me stress that *mind* and *body* are not by any means as highly polarized in the Indian tradition as they are in the Mediterranean belief systems. The Sanskrit terms which can be translated as *mind* are distinct categories to the Indian thinker; and the terms referring to the *somatic* organization overlap with some of the semantic *mind* categories. In the higher reaches of meditational achievement, the distinction between "body" and "mind" becomes trivial or irrelevant, since the successful contemplative, the consummate yogi transcends both the mind and the body system, reaching identity with the Absolute, the *brahman*, the theologically postulated base of all that exists.

Perhaps the best analogy would be found in some of the more insightful reports on LSD-25 experiences of thinking people rather than by the run-of-the-mill groovers of the Western counter-culture. Here, too, the distinction between body and mind disappears progressively—no doubt a frightening experience ("a bad trip") for those not briefed in the theologies of numerical oneness of the individual and the divine. Here, too, some sort of transcending entity is sensed, which is neither physical nor mental, or which is both at the same time.

The *Taittirīya-Upanishad*, a canonical text of Hinduism, established a "measuring scale of ecstatic delight" (*Ananda-mimāmsa*). The positive, active, hedonic life of a healthy man who succeeds in the business of living is the unit of that scale. A thousand times more "delight" is experienced by certain celestial beings, another thousand times more by the "world gods," and another thousand times more pleasure, delight, ecstasy (*ānanda*) are realized by the person who has gained the intuition of oneness with the absolute, the divine, the *brahman*, along with cessation of rebirth.

The ascetic tradition of India was, however, predominant at all times. Retreat from the world, rejection of the senses, and the concomitant exclusion of the aesthetic was epitomized by the sadhus and sannyasis, the professional monastics of the land at all times, as well as by lay leaders like Mahatma Gandhi. The official culture of India is ascetic, puritanical, notwithstanding modern Indian disclaimers. Western sexual morality is feared, looked down upon, and coveted. In the Hindu mind, the West is *materialistic*, because Westerners eat meat, drink liquor, and have "open sex," whatever that means. Middle class Hindus also drink, some eat meat, and presumably, most have sex—but they feel guilty about it.

I always warn my students before they go there, not to confuse India with the erotic sculpture of Khajuraho, Konarak, and hundreds of Hindu shrines and their rich erotic display; and not to confuse India with the *kāmasūtra*. All these belong to long bygone ages, and even then, such indulgence was the prerogative of a very small, wealthy, feudal elite. All this is gone and has been fossilized in stone and in poems over half a millennium ago. When Gandhi was asked his views about the erotic temple sculpture, he said, "If I had the power, I would tear them down." (11) A famous Hindu swami, lecturing to a large, sophisticated audience in Colombo, Ceylon, a summer or so ago, had as his topic "The Sin of Carnality"—and his audience looked on eagerly and demurely. This sort of language had once been used by Christian sermonists—modern Hindu teachers picked it up at some point; they have never abandoned it. And now they look with great anger and disgust at the occidental counter-culture's attention to those elements of Hinduism and of the Indian tradition, which reveal a deep commitment to the senses and to aesthetic delight, coupled with a meditational, religious universe of discourse.

In the vernacular idiom of the majority, to *control* the mind implies "to kill the mind" (*man ko mārnā*); the esoteric minority, the tantrics argue to the contrary, that you cannot achieve anything by killing the mind, just as you cannot get to your destination by killing the wayward horse on which you are riding. It is guided, controlled indulgence which leads the tantric esotericist to the same target which the ascetic yogi approaches through self-mortification and sense denial. The central method of tantric yoga is called "the (method of) the five M's"—viz., the use of the five "ingredients" which begin with the letter M: meat (*māmsa*), fish (*matsya*), wine (*mada*), parched kidney beans (*mudrā*—a supposed aphrodisiac), and ritualistic copulation (*maithuna*) with the Shakti, the female initiate partner representing the cosmic energy. I have described this complex ritual in detail elsewhere (12)—suffice it to say here that the incorporation of these five "ingredients" is fully ritualized, and that it postulates a large set of previous spiritual and yogic qualifications as its prerequisite. The ascetically inclined majority has been challenging the tantric yogis for well over a thousand years, imputing that the latter use forbidden food and sex under the guise of religion. The tantrics' answer is that in order to have meat, fish, wine, and sexual intercourse one does not have to undergo these elaborate, expensive, and extremely complex rituals which presuppose mastery of an enormous quantity of theological learning, and of ceremonial knowhow, together with the rote knowledge of thousands of liturgical texts. "The most delightful prostitute, beautiful like the moon and consummate in the sixty four arts costs but a fraction of the ingredients required for the five M's, and she does not test her examiner in Sanskrit or in the holy texts," as a medieval tantric commentator aptly put it.

The key notion underlying tantric meditation is that the yogi who can perform the sexual act without ejaculation, and who can prevent orgasm in himself and in his female co-aspirant at the moment when orgasm would indeed occur in both, has achieved the power to destroy the effects of his and her past *karma*, and has crossed the threshold of emancipation by this act of supreme self-control. This is the explanation of the *linga*, the phallic representation of the God Shivā—for Shiva is not the god of creation or of worldly enjoyment (these are functions of other world gods, i.e. Brahmā and Visnu), but he is the preceptor of yogis, monks, ascetics. It also explains India's erotic temple sculpture. The ithyphallic shape of the *linga* is not priapic—on the contrary, it means total control: in the act of ritualistic copulation, the male practitioner achieves total erection, but the psychic power built up by him is not discharged. It is converted into *ojas*, the force which creates the momentum toward release from *karmic* bondage. To the non-initiate the act itself looks like *coitus revervatus*, but it isn't, since the aim of the process is yogic *enstasy*,(13) not worldly enjoyment or propagation of the species.

The four forbidden ingredients preceding *maithuna*—"forbidden" because the Hindu religious scene is highly vegetarian and teetotalling—are utilized in order to break down the impeding forces of custom and convention, obstacles to spiritual consummation in all esoteric tradition, across the world.

What are the non-Hindu, non-esoteric implications of this powerful system? Are there any spin-offs for modern man who is neither a Hindu, nor a yogi, and, *a fortiori*, not a tantric? And specifically, has the system got any potential therapeutic use? I strongly believe it has—let me present some of my conclusions.

Since much of the clinical psychologist's day-to-day work has to do with individual problems of alienation, and with the lack of meaningful self-reference to the world surrounding the patient's ego, a powerful, ideologically unshakable system of identification and of praxis leading to it may well be an alternative to therapeutic or analytic manipulations. It has all the elements of the therapeutic situation without its jargon and, of course, without the Western clinical parameters which psychiatrists like R. D. Laing, Th. Szasz, Ronald Leifer and a growing number of young men in the profession are trying to eschew in one way or the other. This alternative becomes all the more important at a time when so many more cognitive options are open to the erstwhile "patients." The classical patient knew nothing about Eastern cults; he was caught up in the Judaeo-Christian framework which he either accepted or rejected or, more often, which sat there as a catalyst with no supportive links to the patient who had no religious interest or commitment to begin with, but who was, nevertheless, hampered by the pervasive Judaeo-Christian value-orientation surrounding him—his family, the psychiatrist, the hospital.

Tantrism may well be a true break-away. I have long doubted that Freudian and post-Freudian clinical talk helps toward releasing salutary libidinal development. Whatever the jargon of emancipation, sex and religious communication are kept apart axiomatically, because sex has no place in the Judaeo-Christian ritual and belief systems, except as a disturbing factor. It has no such place in modern, urban, washed-out Hinduism either. But in the tantric practice, guided sexual indulgence, and guided sensual experimentation are directly harnessed as religious instruments. The patient need no longer heed the negative sanctions of his religious background, which he may or may not have rejected dialectically. It is no longer enough for a religion not to be punitive toward sex—it has to incorporate it, not as a permissible marginal practice, but in a central position within its ritual. There have been attempts in this direction in many religious systems in history, but they have all proved abortive; also, our knowledge of them is much too sketchy to make them in any way operative. Tantrism is there—there are some excellent Tibetan tantrics in North America and western Europe right now; and there are some tantric teachers in India—not the roaming swamis—but people who don't have to look for a clientele outside their own fold. They would have to be sought out to give instruction.

The monistic thrust of the Hindu theology provides an optimal cognitive frame of reference: once the individual *knows* that he or she is one, through and through, with the supreme cosmic being, which the texts describe as *satyam-sivam-sundaram* ("true, benign, and beautiful") or as *satyam-jñānam-anatam-brahma*) "true, intuition infinite, the absolute spirit"), the problem of identification, the painful quest of 'who am I,' the problem of role and status, or role play and role acceptance, of role rejection and alienation must become trivial and lapse. Regardless of whether mama and daddy regard their offspring as objects of castration, or whether peers regard him or her as competitive or dumb, the knowledge that these roles and statuses are trite superimpositions on the inalienable, enormous, cosmic essence which we *are,* must be therapeutic.

The most likely objection to all this will be that there is no guarantee about there being any such absolute, divine essence, or that this essence is coextensive with that of the individual. The Hindu teacher is not fazed by such remonstrance: he admits without a qualm that *brahman,* this absolute is not the object of discursive knowledge at all, and he will quote canonical scripture galore to show that it is not. Rather, this absolute is the target of the yogi's intuition—an intuition which does not, and need not, confer existential status on its content.

This is new to Jew, Christian, and Muslim and modern intellectual alike: that the ontological reality of divinity is totally unimportant to the religious way of the Hindu contemplative. Divinity is an experiential postulate, corroborated by the mystical experience of oneness with it. This is what aids the seeker, and perhaps the patient: what can be experienced through skilled meditation and its ramifying practices is what counts, in the long run, *not* what is actually there, in the ontological sense. Whether what is experienced *exists* in the sense in which the physical universe, or the objects of science exist, is irrelevant to this therapeutic quest.

REFERENCES AND FOOTNOTES

1 See Potter, K. H.: *Presuppositions of Indian Philosophy,* (Englewood Cliffs, Prentice Hall, 1963); and Jacobs, H.: *Western Psychology and Hindu Sadhana,* (London, Allen & Unwin, 1961).

2 See Bharati, Agehananda: "Hindu Scholars, Germany, and the *Third Reich*" in *Quest* No. 44, Bombay, 1965.

3 Especially in his (Max Weber's) *The Religions of India* (English translation by H. H. Gerth and D. Martindale). New York, Free Press, 1958. Also, his *Protestant Ethic and the Spirit of Capitalism* (translated by Talcott Parsons). London, Allen & Unwin, 1930.

4 See Riepe, D.: *The Naturalistic Tradition in Indian Thought.* Seattle, University of Washington Press, 1961.

5 See Bharati, Agehananda: *The Tantric Tradition.* New York, Anchor-Doubleday, 1970.

6 Lit. "the end of the Veda", a highly speculative, predominantly monistic interpretation of the Veoa, the canonical scripture of the Hindus. See Deutsch, E.: *Advaita Vedanta: A Philosophical Reconstruction.* Honolulu, East West Center, 1969.

7 Shah, A. B. (Ed.): *Jawaharlal Nehru: A Critical Tribute.* Bombay, Manaktalas, 1965. Especially the chapter by Agehananda Bharati, entitled: Prospects for Secularism in India.

8 Koestler, A.: *The Lotus and the Robot.* New York, Harper, 1966.

9 The most highly overrated text in the Hindu tradition. There are about a dozen bad translations on the market; the only scholarly, sober one is that by the late Edgerton, F.: *The Bhagavad Gita.* New York, Harper, 1964.

10 Bharati, Agehananda: *The Ochre Robe* (autobiography). New York, Anchor-Doubleday, 1970.

11 Personal communication by the late M. N. Roy, one of the most outstanding Marxist ideologues of India, a close associate of Gandhi at a much earlier time.

12 See Bharati: *Tantric Tradition,* p. 228 ff.

13 Mircea Eliade suggests this term to replace "ecstasy," since the experience is one of going-into-oneself rather than going-out-of-oneself. See his excellent *Yoga: Immortality and Freedom.* New York, Pantheon, 1958.

CHAPTER 15

CONFUCIANISM AND TAOISM

CH'U CHAI AND WINBERG CHAI

Pre-Confucian Religious Thought

CHINESE RELIGIOUS THINKING grew out of a mixture of animism. In addition to the worship of ancestors, there was reverence for the deities of the sun, moon, stars, wind, rain, and sacred mountains and rivers, whose blessings were regarded as necessary to the well-being of men. However, forces and objects of nature were not the only deities with whom the early Chinese related and to whom they offered sacrifices. Among other divine beings worshipped, there were deities of the earth and grain, which were symbolized by *she chi*, "the altar of land and grain," and exerted a very definite influence on human affairs. But *she chi* was also recognized as a religious and symbolic center of the state, where certain elaborate ceremonies, especially those in connection with military expeditions, were held.

In the ancient documents and on oracle bones, we find frequent reference to a Supreme Deity called *Ti* or *Shang Ti* (the Lord-on-High), whose sway extended over all deities and creations. The position of *Ti* in heaven was somewhat like that of the king on earth. The blessing and protection of the Supreme Deity, which was essential to the welfare of men, *especially* that of the ruling house, were to be secured by the proper performance of ritual and sacrifice in honor of him. Just how this Supreme Deity was originally conceived by the early Chinese, we cannot tell. In view of the close relationship between *Ti* and the ruling house, the possibility is that *Shang Ti* was the chief deity or even a deified ancestor of the ruling house. It was a basic belief of great antiquity that the spirits of ancestors seem to have lived in heaven, in a position sitting near *Ti,* for they were often spoken of in the oracle bones as descending, sending down blessings, and so forth.

All these were the basic relgious beliefs of the early Chinese—a belief in *Ti* or *Shang Ti* as a Supreme Deity, and a belief in a variety of heavenly and earthly deities, which had a good deal of influence over human affairs. However, it was still ancestor-cult that played the most significant role in the religious life of the early Chinese. It was interwoven into the very fabric of life that the main ritual activities of the state centered around the ancestral temple of the ruling house. According to the ancient records, the early kings had lavishly sacrificed to their ancestors and believed that the latter's blessings and protection in various undertakings were of utmost importance. The ceremonial rules and rites of ancestor worship were not merely religious, but contained legal obligations as well; any move to neglect them, or to perform them improperly, would bring about condemnation and even calamity.

In the last analysis, basic to the religious tradition of the early period was a belief in an intimate and mutual relationship between this world and the other world, as well as between various deities and spirits, and human beings. The spiritual beings shared a reciprocal dependence with men, bestowing blessings in return for sacrifices. The relationship of mutual dependence, with its expectation of blessings in exchange for sacrifices, has been a popular belief of the Chinese, which persists to this day.

Historically speaking, these religious beliefs had been transformed during the Chou period (1111-249 B.C.). As popularly practiced at that time, these beliefs contained a lot of both sophisticated ideas and gross superstition. In simplifying and modifying these ideas, however, the Chou gave them humanistic interpretations. In the Chou literature, we find an important concept of *T'ien* or Heaven, which was used interchangeably with *Shang Ti* as the Supreme Deity. Originally, these two concepts were probably distinct: *Shang Ti*, as the Supreme Deity over an elaborate hierarchy of spirits, having a nearer approach to a personal theistic significance, and the depersonalized *T'ien* representing a cosmic moral order and divine power, known as being concerned with the actions of men and as a source of "mandate" for the legitimacy of the ruling dynasty. Thus the *Shu Ching*, or the *Book of History*, says: *T'ien*, having produced people below, appointed for them rulers and teachers." (Bk I, Sec. 4) It was in this light that a Chou king was commonly called *T'ien Tzu* or "the Son of Heaven." This was the religious belief of the Chou, which was thus tinctured with ethical and political considerations.

In this connection, there was an important concept—that of *T'ien-ming*, or the Mandate of Heaven, which came to be the political creed of the Chou. As noted above, Heaven as a great deity of humanity did not come into direct contact with the people, but appointed as his medium on earth a line of kings to rule with his mandate. However, Heaven was believed to be displeased with the wickedness of the reigning house and resolved to transfer his mandate to another house to form a new dynasty, because of its virtue. It was in the light of this belief that the Chou rulers justified their conquest of the Shang and their royal rule over the country.

What is significant in the Chou religious thought is a basic belief in the divine sanction of political order and the grave responsibility of the ruler to fulfill his moral duties to Heaven and to the people. The king ruled with the Mandate of Heaven because of virtue in himself and the glory of his ancestors. In other words, he received the mandate in trust, subject to revocation if he proved unable to set up a good example and to glorify his ancestors. The way in which the king should set up a moral leadership so as not to lose the Mandate of Heaven became a major concern of the Chou statesmen and one of the key problems of Chinese thought.

In spite of what has been said, the Chou were no agnostics (denying the existence and power of intervention of Heaven). But virtue, they insisted, was far more important than sacrifices in getting the blessings and protection of Heaven. This belief was based on the assumption that Heaven would throw its weight on the side of the virtuous conduct of men. In this manner, the concept of Heaven as conceived came to be an impersonal ethical force, a cosmic counterpart of moral responsibility in man, a guarantee for rewarding virtue and punishing vice. This was a far cry from the origin of Heaven as a supreme deity over the destiny of man or the future of a dynasty, rewarding or punishing as He pleased. With this change in religious faith, it was to be expected that, with regard to religion, the Chinese during the Chou period would place their emphasis on moral code and not on purely ritual practices.

Meanwhile, religious ceremonies underwent an enormous change. The elaborate ceremonies, which were of many kinds and grades, contained much of superstition and mythology. During the Chou period, humanistic interpretations of these ceremonies and especially those of sacrifices were offered to purify these aspects and to germinate ethical ideas from the purely ceremonial practices. With the humanistic interpretations, Chinese religious beliefs had been rationalized and ritual practices had been transformed into a universal system of ethics.

Before the end of the Chou period, the various schools of thought developed within the stream of what may be called humanism—not the humanism that denied the existence and power of natural forces and objects, but one that placed emphasis on the interrelationship of man and nature. This is what is known as the theory of *the unity of Heaven and man* as enunciated by Chinese philosophers. How humanism came about and developed can best be told through the study of Confucianism.

Confucianism

Confucianism has long since become time-honored and yet has remained dominant in Chinese thought. The place which it has occupied in Chinese history has been comparable to that of religion in other countries. All educated Chinese have been brought up in accordance with Confucian teachings. The *Four Books,* which consist of the *Lun Yii (Confucian Analects)*, the *Meng Tzu (Book of Mencius)*, the *Ta Hsiieh (Great Learning)*, and the *Chung Yung (Doctrine of the Mean),* have been the "holy scriptures" of the Chinese people. It is in Confucianism that they live, move, and have their spiritual being. It is no exaggeration to say that China is the land of Confucianism and that the Chinese are essentially Confucian in their mentality and outlook on life.

The question often arises whether Confucianism is a religion. Confucianism, as is generally asserted, is *not* a religion, for it has no religious structure or sanction. It presents lofty intellectual ideals, but there is nothing to be feared by one who fails to live up to them. In competing with a religion that preaches the assurance of immortality, Confucianism suffers from its silence on the realm beyond life. Moreover, it attaches great importance to humanity and stays fairly close to ethical and political considerations. Nevertheless, Confucianism, though not a religion, is *religious* in some of its features. There has been reverence for *T'ien* or Heaven, which is assumed to throw its weight on the side of the virtuous. There have been ceremonial and sacrificial practices, which are considered to be essential to the welfare of man. There has been belief in moral order and values, which involve a concern for the whole of humanity, its suffering and its well-being. Even more important, there have been noble ethical teachings, which have permeated Chinese life in all its aspects, whether moral, political or social. This is how the Chinese people derive religious comfort from Confucianism.

In spite of its religious features, Confucianism remains to this day a philosophy and *a system of ethics.* Even as an ethical or philosophical system, it has undergone many changes as a consequence of interpretation and alien influences. Moreover, the place of Confucianism in Chinese history, though always influential, has changed considerably from one period to another. But we are not in a position here to trace the various stages of its development. What concerns us at present is the Confusian orthodoxy as founded by Confucius (551-479 B.C.) and developed by Mencius (c. 372-289 B.C.).

Under the influence of humanism, it was no wonder that Confucius' principal concern was man and his "duties which are proper to the people"; he had studiously shunned all questions that enter into ontological subtleties or partake of the supernatural. Taken as a whole, the thought of Confucius is more in the nature of an ethical system than a religion. As such, it is essentially this-worldly in outlook and rationalistic in approach. All his teachings are in fact undertaken in the interest of this central concern.

Let us first consider the life ideal of Confucius. The ideas through which his life ideal is expressed are not abstract ideas, but rather are visions of a cultivated mind, inbued with a profound sense of purpose and an intense concern for the well-being of his fellow men. These ideas are indeed reflected in his own life and embodied in the concept of *jen*, or human-heartedness. In the *Lun Yii*, we find that *jen* has a great scope and a great depth; yet it is familiar and appears to be simple and practical. It has flexibility and versatility; yet it stands out amid the thought of Confucius as the central thesis of the whole system. His ethics, his politics, his life ideal—all flow from this governing doctrine.

The ideography for *jen* is composed of two characters, "man" and "two," showing stress on the relationship between man and his fellow men. Confucius maintained that human relations should be based on the moral element of *jen* in the individual, the natural compassion of the human heart. In the *Lun Yii,* Confucius said that *jen* is "to love men." (XII-22) The idea of *jen* may be best expressed in the conceptions of *chung* or conscientiousness—i.e. to be faithful to one's self; and *shu* or altruism—i.e. to have proper regard for one's fellow men. The former means the state of mind when one is completely honest with one's self, while the latter is the state of mind when one is in complete understanding and sympathy with other men. The Chinese character for *chung* is made of two components "middle" and "heart." With one's *heart* in the middle, one will be faithful to one's *self*, so as to do one's very best *for the sake of others*. In Confucius' words, "A man of *jen*, desiring to be established himself, seeks to establish others; desiring himself to succeed, he helps others to succeed." This is the positive way to practice *jen*. The Chinese word *shu* has the meaning of "as one's heart"; that is, to do to others as your heart prompts you. It is indeed a sense of fellow-feeling with other men—to extend one's self to include others. As to the significance of *shu*, Confucius said: "Do not do to others what you do not want done to yourself" (XV-24). This is the negative way to practice *jen*.

In the proper sense of this word, as noted above, *jen* is the virtue of being faithful to one's self and having a sense of fellow-feeling with one's fellow men. These two aspects are the main ingredients of *jen*. However, we must remember that *jen* is a natural feeling that comes directly and spontaneously from the human heart. Men with this natural feeling recognize that they must live in a community of mutual friendship and joyful harmomy. Faith that such an idealistic state of affairs might become a reality, so Confucius contended, was based on the cultivation and perfection of goodness not only in one's self, but in and toward every one else, with whom the individual is inevitably bound and related.

As noted above, Confucius' life ideal is a vision of how *jen* is realized at large: it consists of doing one's very best for the sake of others. For Confucius, it is not sufficient to cultivate good in one's self; it is important to extend one's goodness to include others. For him, it is not sufficient to do what one ought to do, it is more important to disregard what is external to this moral obligation. Confucius offered a good example of a life dominated by the doctrine of *jen*. His itinerary through many states of his time was made with a purpose to seek opportunity to test this doctrine in actual practice. Although his efforts were in vain, he was not disappointed. Confucius said: "If my *tao* (a way of life) is to prevail, it is Fate. If my *tao* is to be rejected, it is also Fate" (XIV-38). While Confucius made his best effort to realize the ideal of his *tao,* at the same time he insisted that Fate would determine whether this ideal prevailed or failed. In other words, Confucius did his best for the sake of others, but he left his success or failure to Fate. The word "Fate" may be interpreted either as "the decree of Heaven," or as "the existent conditions of the universe." Whatever is meant by the word, Fate is something inevitable, independent of effort. Hence the best way of life, according to Confucius, is to do one's best, without regard for success or failure in the process. To act in this way, as Confucius said, is "to know Fate."

However, Confucius was not a fatalist, nor did he intend to rely on Fate. On the contrary, he repeatedly insisted on *the importance of effort* by the individual, the moral obligation to do one's best for the sake of others. Here is the key, then, to Confucius' attitude toward life. He believed in Fate, apparently, but he was not much concerned about it. He was interested in bringing order out of chaos; what could not be done did not concern him very much. What he was convinced of was that man should do his best while disregarding what is beyond his control, not that he should refrain from exerting himself and be dependent on Fate.

This brings us to the difference between Fate and *jen*. As a natural feeling of the human heart, *jen* is not only attainable, but also within the grasp of all. In other words, *jen* is within one's own heart. Let one but turn one's attention to oneself, and one shall be free from anxiety or fear, and so shall be happy. For it is in one's own heart, not in the external world, that one must seek for happiness. This is why Confucius said: "A wise man is free from doubts; a *jen* man, from anxiety; a brave man, from fear." (IX-28). As for himself, he said: "I do not complain against Heaven, nor do I blame man. I study things on the lower level but my understanding penetrates the higher level. The one who knows me is Heaven!" (XIV-37).

The last passage quoted above is sufficient for the wisdom of Confucius, which makes him a great philosopher and a great sage. Because of his knowledge of Fate, he had no resentment against Heaven or man. As a man of *jen,* he was sure to have good ability in considering others, and thence he discovered the ideal of life—this is what is known as the "lower level" of life. Moreover, his ideal of life led to a search for the fundamental reality and ultimate truth of the universe—this is what is known as the "higher level" of life. As noted above, *jen* is the virtue about how other virtues are to be attained and extended, so that it transcends the barriers of space and time. According to Confucius, to be *jen*-minded is not just to have a due regard for others; instead, to be *jen*-minded should involve a concern for the whole of humanity. In other words, not merely does a man of *jen* know his moral responsibility in society and particularly in his relations with others, but also he is conscious of something above human society and relations—a larger reality, Heaven, from which, for Confucius, man as a part is derived. It is through the affirmation of Heaven that man will transcend himself and possess a meaning which is not limited to human community. In this way, the level in which Confucius lived was one transcending the moral level. Hence Confucius' ideal of life seems simple and direct, and yet it has a great scope and a great depth. This is why he claimed: "The one who knows me, is Heaven!"

We will not dwell on these ideas any further. What is important here is to recognize that Confucius thought of men as related in "one world, one family", so that all shared a common destiny which was to be guided by the cultivation and extension of one's goodness to the service of mankind. It is in this process of self-cultivation that one will attain a sense of purpose, a sense of destiny, a sense of mission; it is also in this process that one will transcend one's ego, so as to enjoy a kind of spiritual life. This was exactly why Confucius had devoted his life to spiritual development and moral cultivation; as he worded it, "At fifteen, I set my mind on learning; at thirty, I could stand (on ceremony); at forty, I had no doubts (about the purpose of life); at fifty, I knew the Decree of Heaven; at sixty, I was ready to listen to it; and now, at seventy, I can follow my heart's desire, without transgressing (what is right)" (II-4).

Now let us turn to Mencius, who, as an apostle of the Confucian school, naturally made *jen* the focal point of his thought. However, he claimed that, for the cultivation of moral character, *jen* should be coupled with *yi* or righteousness. For Confucius, *yi* is an important moral force that, together with *li* or ceremony, guides and regulates one's conduct (*Analects,* XV-17). It was Mencius who gave *yi* the position of cardinal virtue equal to that of *jen*. As to the difference between *jen* and *yi*, Mencius said: "*Jen* represents the human heart; *yi* the human way" (The *Meng Tzu,* VA-11). In this light, *jen* is a natural feeling that comes from the human heart, whereas *yi* is the proper way to which one ought to conform. That is to say, *yi* involves a moral obligation, which is unconditional and absolute. In our community life, there are certain things which should be done for their own sake, because they are obligatory in themselves. If one does these things only because of other, nonmoral, considerations— say, as the means to achieve one's personal ends—one's action is no longer righteous, because one is then acting for profit, and not for *yi*. Confucian scholars laid special emphasis on the distinction between profit and *yi*—a distinction which Mencius considered to be paramount in moral importance. In his effort to develop the idea of *yi*, Mencius made his chief contribution to Chinese thought: his belief in the innate goodness of human nature.

Much controversy had arisen among the followers of Confucius as to the moral quality of human nature, and Mencius was the first to enunciate distinctly the doctrine that the nature of man inclines him to goodness and kindness. There is one passage from the *Meng Tzu* that serves as a general statement of the doctrine that man's nature is good:

> If left to follow its innate feelings, human nature will do good. This is what I mean by saying that human nature is good. If it becomes evil, it is not the fault of man's natural endowment. The feeling of compassion is common to all men; so is that of shame and dislike; that of reverence and respect; and that of right and wrong. The feeling of compassion is *jen*; that of shame and dislike is *yi*; that of reverence and respect is *li*; and that of right and wrong is *chih* (wisdom). *Jen, yi, li,* and *chih* are not imposed upon us from without; they are inherent in our nature. Only we give them no thought. As the saying goes, "Seek and you will find them; neglect and you will lose them" (VIA-6).

The above passage reveals three salient points: first, man is good by nature and will naturally do what is good; second, man possesses four good feelings which imply four great virtues—*jen, yi, li,* and *chih;* third, men differ in the development of their innate goodness. Mencius saw human nature as confounded by the externals of life. He insistently maintained that human nature is originally good, but that it may become depraved through man's environmental influences. This, of course, does not allow us to say that human nature is not good. Mencius extended this idea to maintain that men by nature are the same, their differences being due to environment. He compared men to crops of barley that are alike but only so long as they are grown under identical circumstances (VIA-7). While attention was thus focused on the goodness of human nature, Mencius did not fail to recognize that nurture could bring nature to its fruition and that environmental influences are important to the development of the individual.

When Mencius held that human nature is good, he meant that all men are born with an inclination toward goodness. As to the meaning of the term "good," Mencius seemed to believe that the "good" is that which is in harmony with human nature. In his discussion of human nature, he pointed out that "man's mouths agree in having the same relishes; their ears agree in enjoying the same sound; their eyes agree in recognizing the same beauty" (VIA-7); from this illustration, he reasoned that men's minds should approve similar principles of reason and *yi*. Hence Mencius concluded, in the same passage, that "the principles of reason and *yi* are agreeable to our minds just as the flesh of grass-fed and grain-fed animals is agreeable to our mouths."

For Mencius, as for Confucius, "the principles of reason and *yi*" are not imposed upon us from without; they are, on the contrary, something inherent in human nature. Like Confucius, Mencius emphasized what is in himself, as he said: "All things are already complete in oneself. There is no greater delight than to examine oneself and be sincere. If one acts with a vigorous effort at altruism (*shu*), *jen* is not far to seek, but right by him" (VIIA-4).

There is good reason for this. Mencius said: "All men have a heart which cannot bear (to see the suffering of) others" (IIA-6). Such a feeling of compassion leads to positive effort for the good of others. As an instance of this, Mencius said: "Now suppose that one suddenly sees a child about to fall into a well. One will immediately experience a feeling of alarm and distress. This is not so one will win (the) gratitude of the child's parents, nor so he may seek the praise of one's neighbors and friends, nor so one is distressed at the child's cries" (IIA-6). The feeling of compassion, as well as those of shame and dislike, reverence and respect, and right and wrong, are a part of man's nature that distinguishes men from other creatures. In other words, that which makes man a man is the innate goodness of the human heart.

Mencius pleaded eloquently that cultivation could bring innate goodness to fruition and that environmental influences are important to the development of the individual. Even more important, Mencius was characteristically Confucian in his concern for the interplay among human beings. For both Confucius and Mencius, one's life is to be guided by the cultivation and perfection of goodness, not only in oneself, but in every one else to whom one is inevitably bound and related. Mencius said: "Treat the aged in my family as they should be treated, and extend this treatment to the aged of others' families. Treat the young in my family as they should be treated, and extend this treatment to the young of others' families" (IA-7). Mencius called this "extending one's good heart to include others," and he viewed it as the ultimate development of *jen* and *yi*.

In the last analysis, the main objective of Mencius' system lies in the importance of the individual, his improvement, and his perfection. The individual was to be relied upon to have free play of his judgement and his good sense. Mencius said: "What we get by our seeking and lose by our neglecting, our seeking is of use to getting, and the thing sought is something inherent in ourselves. When our seeking is in accord with the *tao*, but the getting is determined by Fate, our seeking is of no use to getting, and the thing sought is something without us" (VIIA-3). Therefore, what man should do is to seek what is in himself and leave what is beyond his control to Fate. What one should do is to exert one's utmost in moral endeavor, and disregard such matters about which one can do little. At this point, Mencius was completely in harmony with Confucius' theory of "knowing Fate."

Mencius, however, carried his theory to, and even beyond, its logical conclusion. Thus he remarked: "All things are already complete in oneself" (VIIA-4). In other words, man is self-sufficient, if only he develops his inborn nature. This is why, as Mencius affirmed, *everyone* can be a sage. What is important here is to recognize that "seeking-in-oneself" involves the process of self-cultivation, leading to knowledge of the self in relation to other men and in relation to the universe; it is also in this process that a man not only knows Heaven, but also becomes one with Heaven so that all distinctions between the self and non-self, between what is external and what is internal, are obliterated.

Therefore, for Mencius, the ultimate goal of life is goodness, and the final objective, for him, is man in his perfection, the Great Man. We are told in a passage from the *Meng Tzu* about the man of perfection: "He who dwells in the broad house of the universe, stands firm on the right place of the universe, and walks in the great way of the universe; he who, if successful, walks in the way along with the people, and if unsuccessful, walks in the way all alone; he whom wealth and honor cannot corrupt, poverty and obscurity cannot move, threats and violence cannot subdue—he it is that may be called a great man" (IIIB-2). In this, Mencius was a man of faith and religious sentiment; so Confucianism, based on his teachings, may be regarded as a humanistic religion. The goodness of human nature is his religious faith; a complete devotion to the ends of human life is his religious spirit.

Taoism

Next to Confucianism the most important and influential thought for the Chinese has been that of the Taoist school. As we have already noted above, while Confucianism emphasizes social order and human relations, Taoism concentrates on individual life and the state of nature, suggesting a thought essentially naturalistic and antisocial. Ever since its beginning, the two streams of Chinese thought—Confucianism and Taoism—have been running counter (and yet complementary) to each other; and so they remain to this day.

The name "Taoist School" was first mentioned in the *Shih Chi (Historical Records)*, written two thousand years ago by Ssu-ma Ch'ien (c.145-86 B.C.). However, Taoist teachings must have been flourishing for centuries. The first members of the Taoist school may have had their origin in the anarchistic recluses, some of whom had confronted Confucius in the course of his travels. Reacting differently to the disorder of the age, they spurned as futile all Confucius' efforts at social and political reforms by means of elaborate ritual and carefully reasoned codes of ethics.

The recluses called themselves "the men who shunned the world, ... in order to maintain their personal purity." They regarded nature as their constant refuge, simple living their ideal of life, and farming their profession, if they ever had any. The recluses mentioned in the *Lun Yü* were the pioneers of the Taoist movement, even though they made no attempt to justify their conduct by formulating any systematic thought.

Yung Chu seems to have been the first recluse to develop a system of thought for the importance of life and self-interest which has a close connection with the Taoist school. We know little about his life, but from the scanty material now available we know that he was a prominent apostle of egoism of the fourth century B.C. He was also reported to have written a philosophical treatise, which has not survived today. The oldest Taoist books, as generally agreed, are the *Lao Tzu* (also known as *Tao-teh Ching*) and the *Chuang Tzu*. Much has been written about the authors and the authenticity of the books. This, however, is not the place to undertake an extended analysis of the controversy. What matters most to us is the Taoist philosophy, as illustrated in the *Lao Tzu* and *Chuang Tzu,* which represents the mind of a certain period in the past and which ever since has exerted great influence on the life and thought of the Chinese people.

So far as we know, the Taoist thought is based on the exaltation of the Tao and idealization of Nature. Here by "Nature" is meant what is self-sufficient and uncreated. In the *Lao Tzu*, we read: "Man follows the ways of the Earth, the Earth follows the ways of Heaven, Heaven follows the ways of the Tao, and the Tao follows the ways of *Tzu-jan*" (ch. 25). Here lies the essence of the Taoist thought. The key phrase is *tzu-jan* (literally, "spontaneous, natural"), by which is meant all coming into being by itself; that is, the totality of the spontaneity of things—the absolute freedom from artificiality. The best illustration of the expression is found in the passage:

> Penumbra said to unbra: "At one moment you move; at another you are at rest. At one moment you sit down; at another you stand up. Why this instability of purpose?"
>
> "Do I depend on something," answered unbra, "which causes me to do so? And does that something depend in turn upon something else, which causes it to do so? Is my dependence like (the unconscious movements of) the scales of a snake or the wings of a cicada? How can I tell why I do one thing, why I do not do another?" (*The Chuang Tzu* ch. 2)

This question will indicate the self-originating state of mind which is absolutely unconscious, natural, and spontaneous in all its doings. In the *Chuang Tzu*, the state of unconsciousness is often referred to under such phrases as *tzu-hua* (self-transforming) and *tzu-wang* the *Chuang Tzu*, when things are allowed to take their own natural (self-forgetting). According to Taoist teachings of the *Lao Tzu* and the *Chuang Tzu*, when things are allowed to take their own natural course, they move with perfection and harmony because they then do not hinder the Tao in its natural and spontaneous operation as the first principle of the universe. This is known as the way of *wu wei* (literally, non-action).

The doctrine of *we wei*, as Taoism is often called, belongs to the naturalistic school of Chinese thought, as we find it in the *Lao Tzu* and *Chuang Tzu*. *Wu wei* is by no means entirely negative in the sense of total absence of activity. What it really means is "refraining from action contrary to Nature"; that is, letting all things take their own course. This is the essence of the Tao, that "invariably refrains from action (contrary to Nature), and yet there is nothing that is not done" (The *Lao Tzu*, ch. 37). This is also the way of *wei wu wei*.

The significance of Taoism as a school of thought lies not only on its emphasis on the spontaneity of the Tao, but also in its intoxication with the wonder and power of Nature. But Nature itself is also self-sufficient and independent of human effort. The *Chuang Tzu* says: "Heaven (the natural) abides within, man (the artificial) without.... What is of Heaven? What is of man? Horses and oxen have four feet—that is what is of Heaven. Put a halter on a horse's head, and a string through a bullock's nose—that is what is of man" (ch. 17). It is evident that "Heaven" means something natural; "man" means something artificial. The Taoist philosophers see only the good aspects of what is of Nature. Every kind of "man's doings", including moral values and social institutions, is to them against Nature. The *Lao Tzu* says: "Banish wisdom; discard knowledge, and the people will be more benefited a hundredfold. Banish *jen*; discard *yi*, and the people will return to filial piety and parental love" (ch. 19). Likewise, the *Chuang Tzu* counsels: "Cherish what is within you, and shut off that which is without; for much knowledge is a curse."

According to the Taoist philosophers, the best way to be happy is to live true to Nature, intoxicated with its wonder and power, and revert to the state of pristine simplicity. The *Lao Tzu* expresses the Taoist ideal when it speaks of the ancient adept of the Tao who has attained the state of simplicity and purity: "He is cautious, like one crossing a stream in winter; he is hesitating, like one fearing his neighbors; he is modest, like one being a guest; he is yielding, like ice about to melt; he is simple as an uncarved block; he is hollow as a valley; he is obscure as a muddy stream" (ch. 15). These are the seven aspects of the Taoist ideal of life, signifying simplicity and purity in spirit and in heart.

The *Chuang Tzu,* however, goes much further to characterize the ideal of life as a state where a man "will bury gold in the hillside and cast pearls into the sea. He will not struggle for wealth, nor for fame. He will not rejoice at long life, nor will he grieve ever early death. He will not find pleasure in success, nor will he feel pain in failure. He will not account the throne of a state as his personal gain, nor will he claim the empire of the world as his personal glory. His glory is to have the insight that all are one and that life and death are the same." This blissful ecstasy marked by no will, no consciousness, no knowledge—where a man becomes one with Nature, knowing "not whence he comes into life nor where he goes in death." This ideal, suspended state is well illustrated in the following passage:

> Once upon a time, Chuang Chou (i.e., Chuang Tzu) dreamt that he was a butterfly fluttering about—to all intents and purpose a butterfly. It does not know that it was Chuang Chou. Suddenly, he awoke, and there he was Chuang Chou again. But he did not know whether he was Chuang Chou, dreaming he was a butterfly, or whether he was a butterfly, dreaming he was Chuang Chou (ch. 2).

Taking together what has been said, the Tao, by which is meant the order of Nature, may be comparable to the Judaeo-Christian God. However, God created the world with conscious design and conscious will, whereas the Tao acts by means of *wu wei* and operates unconsciously and naturally. Thus when we say that the Tao creates the world, we mean no more than that the world is created of itself: Taoist philosophy emphasizes this unconscious, natural, spontaneous element. It is so well ordered that there is no need for human exertion. As to its operation, the *Chuang Tzu* says: "Heaven cannot help being high, the Earth cannot help being wide, the sun and the moon cannot help being round, and all creations cannot help but live and multiply." (ch. 22)

Epilogue

Chinese thought, as illustrated in the teachings of Confucius and Mencius, as well as in those of the *Lao Tzu* and *Chuang Tzu,* is a blend of humanism and naturalism. It is ethical, yet metaphysical. It attaches importance to spiritual cultivation and yet has a deep concern for the ordering of the world. It has a vast scope and a great depth, and yet appears to be simple and direct. It has a flexibility and versatility, and yet forms a single thread of unity—one main tradition, one main stream of thought (i.e. to aim at a particular kind of highest life). This kind of highest life is "not divorced from daily regular activities," and yet at the same time, "it goes straight to what is beyond the Heaven." The first part of this expression represents the Tao of man, while the second part, the Tao of Heaven. Because it is of the Tao of man, it is concerned with human affairs; because it is the Tao of Heaven, it reaches up to the sublime.

In Chinese thought, the man who attains to this kind of highest life is called the "Sage", or the "Ideal Man." What is more significant lies in the fact that, although the sphere in which the "Sage" or the "Ideal Man" lives is a transcendental one, his achievements are in the main concerned with the business of the world. This is what is taught in Chinese thought, whether it be Confucianism or Taoism.

CHAPTER 16

EASTERN ORTHODOXY AND PSYCHOTHERAPY

Issa J. Khalil

THE OROTHODOX CHURCH has from early times practiced principles which today we ascribe to psychology, psychoanalysis or psychotherapy. However, it never looked at these principles in isolation from other elements of religious experience. That is to say, psychotherapeutic practices never existed autonomously or separate from the wholeness of the religious life. Nor, for that matter, did the Eastern Church ever define narrowly religious experience as an entity apart from the entirety of man's experience. Eastern Christians may speak of man as composed of "parts," yet they nevertheless consider him to be a unified whole. Consequently, man's various experiences and relationships with God and the world are never compartmentalized. They are, rather, generally interrelated with one another. That is why, in its anthropology, Orthodoxy does not neglect the viewpoints of medicine and biology, but rather takes them into consideration and allows for the acceptance of new scientific theories and discoveries.

Thus, although the orientation of Eastern Orthodox theology differs fundamentally from that of psychotherapy, the two are nevertheless compatible in their basic concern with the *whole* of man. Keeping this important similarity in mind, I shall, in the following discussion, focus on those doctrines and practices of the Eastern Orthodox churches (1) which relate most closely to the principles and goals of psychotherapy, either directly or indirectly. Indeed, these doctrines and practices, which provide the foundation for their therapeutic principles, are meant to treat not only the "ill" in the strict sense of the term, but also the "healthy" as a preventative medicine.

A DYNAMIC VIEW OF MAN

C. G. Jung once stated that the "goal of psychotherapy is not to bring the patient into an impossible state of happiness but to provide him strength and philosophical patience to endure suffering." (2) Indeed, modern psychology does not offer such variously defined and commonly sought benefits as happiness, effective living or successful social adaptation, and accordingly, it does not speak of "normality" in the popular sense. Nor does psychotherapy operate as do the traditional static anthropologies, i.e. the idealistic, materialistic and synthetic, from certain almost rigid perspectives. Each of these defines man from a set of abstract principles, and seeks to find what is "normal" through the analysis of given physiological and psychic states in which the "nature" of man appears more or less pure in its specificity and wholeness. In other words, man is viewed in terms of "essence" and man's nature is seen as an effective principle. Psychotherapists hold, rather, as do many others, that such abstractions do not do full justice to the individuality and creative spontaneity of man. For the particular historical situation helps to form each man in a singular way, thus allowing for greater or lesser individual freedom of action. Each man is unique and thus his individual situation and its historical dimension should be taken seriously into any consideration of his normality. This approach is one to which Eastern Christians are most sympathetic. We can see this understanding of the psychotherapeutic position especially well in the Orthodox doctrine of man.

The psychotherapist will find the Eastern Church's doctrine of man refreshing. For, in contract to Western Christianity, Eastern Christianity holds to a dynamic view of man. That is to say, the Eastern churches do not understand the Genesis account of man's creation "in the image of God" (1:27) to imply that man thereby attained realized perfection. They hold, rather, that the first man's potential destiny was to be realized in the future. In the words of a second century theologian, St. Irenaeus:

> ... Man, who is contingent and created, grows into the image and likeness of the eternal God.[3]
>
> The eternal is perfect; and this is God. Man has first to come into being, then to progress, and by progressing come to manhood, and thus increasing to persevere, and be glorified, and thus see his Lord.[4]
>
> We were not made gods at our beginning, but first we were made men, then in the end, gods.[5]

According to the Eastern view, God, in creating man, did not create a vicar, but a "being who shares in *his* own properties, who rules not 'in the *name* of God' but *in* God, and who, first of all shares in a quality which belongs properly to God alone: immortality." (6) In other words, man has a share in God's preservative and creative powers, and this affects his relationship to the whole of creation.

Indeed, man has been created in order to participate in the divine life. However, this participation had only a beginning at the moment of creation. Man is to receive the fullness of life in his state of becoming. He will participate more fully in the divine life as he, choosing to do so in freedom and with love, draws nearer to his Creator and continues on the course of his destiny. Thus man is in a state of *becoming*, for his existence is not a closed one. Such an idea of man's participation in God is not viewed with favor by the Western Christian tradition. For instance, in Reformed theology, God is conceived of solely in terms of His essence, but human participation in the essence cannot be reconciled with God's transcendence. Accordingly, a real participation in God would not be possible. The Eastern churches consider that participation in God is possible, not in His essence, but through His "energies," which they hold to be a part of God Himself, whereas in the West, God's "energies" are considered rather to be created. (7)

To go back to the Eastern view, although these "energies" are not created grace, they can become the possessions of the saints in their lives of union with God. In other words, Eastern Christians believe that man, who is created "in the image," can, in this life, attain to the "likeness" of God through the deifying grace. Man was, moreover, created in order to share in the Divine Life, in order to be deified.

Thus the Eastern churches, like those in the West, hold that there is a primordial correspondence between God and man, but they go farther than the Western churches in saying that this correspondence is to grow towards the deification which is the goal and destiny of man. Accordingly, the "image and likeness" is the norm of man's normality. This theological view of man is not identical either with that of the empirical sciences nor with that of philosophical speculation. But does this mean that the "norm" in the East is static? Not at all! Eastern theology merely asserts that man has a divine origin and that he is tending towards deification. This destiny of man is dynamic in character, for inasmuch as each man is a person, and thus unique, and inasmuch as deification is a process, the historical dimension and the individual situation must be incorporated into any concept of normality. That is why the theologians of the Eastern church, particularly the Fathers, do not agree on a single definition of the "image"! This does not mean, however, that the beliefs of the Fathers on this point are contradictory. It rather shows that they do not single out any *one* part of human nature which is supposed to be "in the image." Some of them speak in terms of the soul, others of soul and body, while still others talk of the spirit, intellect, mind or freedom of man, inasmuch as each may be "in the image." In other words, there is not one single part of man to which the "image" is confined. For to limit it to one part of man would imply a limitation of God, for "in the 'likeness' which is 'after the image' we have a summary of the characteristics of the divinity." (8) This is to say that the divine characteristics are given to man, with the difference that the former are uncreated, whereas the latter are created. In other words, man possesses these attributes by grace, but they are God's property by nature. Yet man did not fully share in this Divine life at the moment of his creation, but possessed it potentially; he was given the capacity to share in it in this life. Man is to actualize this "likeness" in his freedom. Gregory of Nazianzus (known as Gregory the Theologian) states this concept in the following words:

> Thus he (i.e. man) is a living creature under God's providence here, while in transition to another state, and (this is the consummation of the mystery [i.e. the fulfillment of God's hidden purpose, which has now been revealed]) in process of deification by reason of his natural tendency towards God. (9)

What is the "image," then, for the Eastern Orthodox? Insofar as the "image" is perfect, it is necessarily unknowable "for as it reflects the fullness of its archetype, it must also possess the unknowable character of the divine Being. This is the reason why it is impossible to define what constitutes the divine image in man. We can only conceive it through the idea of participation in the infinite goodness of God." (10) For God in His goodness, in creating man in His image, could not have bestowed only a part of his characteristics, withholding the rest. Rather, God made man *a potential sharer* in all His goodness. This does not mean that God and man may attain in time undifferentiated unity. Orthodoxy has never envisioned a unity between God and man in the sense of absorption. On the contrary, man will retain his individuality and personality.

The Orthodox approach to "the image," according to a modern theologian, V. Lossky, differentiates between the concepts of "person" and "individual." These two terms are not to be confused, ". . . the word individual expressing a certain mixture of the person with elements which belong to the common nature, while person, on the other hand, means that which distinguishes it from nature." (11) Individuality is generally viewed in terms of consideration that the human nature which one possesses is one's own property, and is to be regarded as the "me," being different from other natures. But such a view of individuality confuses nature and person. A human being as an individual nature is not to set up his nature against other natures, for he is only one among millions of human beings, and only one of the countless elements that make up the universe. Thus, individualism, instead of realizing the commonality of human nature, emphasizes the self-centeredness and isolation of man, and serves as the basis of egoism, competition, and conflict. But the Eastern Church considers that, insofar as a human being is a person, he is not simply a part of a whole, but a unique being in whom the whole is contained; he is a microcosm. The historical situation which cooperates in the concrete formation of a person is unique; so also are all the other elements that help to form a person. What makes a human being unique is not that which is held in common with others, i.e. nature. It is, rather, personhood. However, personhood without the individualized nature will not be realized. "The nature is the content of the person, the person the existence of the nature. A person who asserts himself as an individual, and shuts himself up in the limits of his particular nature," (12) will not be able to realize himself. Self-realization excludes individualism, for it is the "image" which is to be realized in the person. Thus there need not be conflict or competition between person and nature, but rather, harmonious and loving relationships. For the basis of conflict and egoism is gone, and since a person is going through a process of deification, the anxiety of extinction is overcome. The ideal of this doctrine is none other than the Trinity, in which each of the three persons (yet one in nature) retains his uniqueness without conflict or competition or absorption. The Life of the Trinity is the ideal for the life of man according to the Eastern Church, and forms the basis for its anthropology. In the pastoral sphere, as we shall see later, the Eastern Church brings this doctrine to bear on the concrete human situation.

Thus participation in the Divine Life is not relegated only to man's afterlife in Orthodoxy, but is rather to be begun here on earth. Nor is it only the ideal of the monastic life, for it permeates the life of all members of the church. This experience is deeply embedded in the life and practice of Orthodoxy. Nicholas Cabasilas, a distinguished humanist of the fourteenth century, affirmed that the supreme mystical experience is to be obtained not by withdrawal from the world, but by participation in the liturgy and sacraments. One may stay in his home, and keep his worldly goods, for

> God is everywhere around us and will come to us if we open the door by meditating upon his goodness and on the link that He has provided between Himself and man. Then we can reach him by sharing in the divine drama of His life and death and resurrection, which is the Holy Liturgy; and He will fill us with love, love of God and love for His creatures." (13)

Cabasilas taught that true Christocentric life is to be found in the world, and is not necessarily to be equated with eremitical life. He believed that the Liturgy provides the highest mystical experience. Although there were some writers, notably Gregory of Sinai, who took the extreme position that participation in the Liturgy was unnecessary for a true mystic, Eastern Christendom, on the whole, rejected such an approach. However, high respect and even reverence for the monastic life continued to exist in the churches. To the Orthodox, who is accustomed to look at reality in terms of wholeness, the monastic and the secular spheres interpenetrate each other. Again the question is not one of competition and conflict, but rather of different callings to share in the *one* Life.

In the same way the Eastern Church resolutely excludes the juxtaposition of the doctrines of nature and grace. "Nature and grace do not exist side by side, rather there is a mutual interpenetration of one another, the one exists in the other." (14) From the moment of his creation, man was given the capacity to receive the deifying energy of God. God gives freely and man receives freely. Orthodox rejects any doctrine that infringes upon man's freedom. Man *cooperates* with God in his attempt to achieve full fellowship with Him. But man can refues this cooperation and can reject the destiny which God set before him, as did Adam, with the result that, instead of achieving cooperation (*synergeia*) and harmony with God, man set himself up as a rival and a competitor. Man was to be deified by his cooperation with God's grace. But man believed Satan's deception that he can become "like God" through his own powers. Thus, by turning away from God, man turned to himself, becoming self-centered and setting in motion the processes of alienation (from God, from other men, and from nature), disintegration, competition and conflict. The consequences of Adam's fall extended to all his descendants by virtue of the mysterious unity of the human race.

This does not mean that the Orthodox believe that man lost the "image" of God. It was *distorted,* but never destroyed. Man never lost his freedom, as St. Augustine, Luther and other Christians from the West teach. Nor do the Orthodox say with Calvin that man has been utterly depraved and so is incapable of good desires. "Orthodoxy, holding as it does a less exalted idea of man's state before he fell, is also less severe than the West in its view of the consequences of the fall. Adam fell, not from a great height of knowledge and perfection, but from a state of undeveloped simplicity; hence he is not to be judged too harshly for his error." (15)

The Orthodox doctrine of salvation is to be understood in the same way. The "original guilt" of Adam did not pass to his descendants.

The Eastern Christians hold none of the descendants of Adam guilty because of his sin. Each is guilty insofar as in his freedom he imitates Adam. Thus, the Savior did not come to wash away the "original guilt" or the sins of the individual by dying on the Cross, but rather *to bestow upon man a new life* of unity, holiness and immortality by regeneration. Salvation is wrought by Christ in his victory over the powers of the enemies of man—notably Satan, sin and death. In its doctrine of Salvation, the Eastern Church does not separate between such concepts as justification, regeneration, sanctification and deification. To St. Anselm and many Western theologians who were influenced by him, humanity is the object of God's wrath because it is guilty on account of the sin of Adam. Man is to be punished because of his guilt through Adam, but Christ came to suffer in place of man and thus freed man from punishment. Thus, the doctrine of Justification came to be regarded in terms of the medieval penitential system, and preoccupation with suffering in the Middle Ages occupied a prominent place.

In the East, on the contrary, Salvation was viewed as a drama—a battle between God and the evil forces that surround man, among which death was one of the chief enemies. Such a view is to be distinguished, as Gustav Aulen has shown admirably, from others that conceive the Atonement either in forensic or exemplary terms. Rather, Salvation is a story of conflict and victory: Christ, the Divine Redeemer, fights against and is victorious over the evil powers of sin and death which usurped God's sovereignty over the world. "The drama is a cosmic drama, and the victory over the hostile powers brings to pass a new relation, a relation of reconciliation between God and the world." (16) The Eastern concept of Redemption deals not merely with man as an individual, but also with his entire world. It is a cosmic redemption. That is probably why the most popular pictorial representation of the cross in the East shows it empty, as the symbol of Christ's victory over death. (17) And the Easter Celebration—which is observed as the feast of feasts—is considered above all as a joyous and happy moment, imbued with the sense of victory over the evil powers. For instance, on Easter morning the clergy and congregation sing joyously the triumphant hymn:

> Christ is risen from the dead.
> He conquered death by dying
> And bestowed life upon those
> Who are in the graves.

This joyousness and feeling of victory is not limited to the church service, but extends also to the daily life of the believer. A visual symbol of this is the new light which is kindled at midnight at the Easter eve service, at which time the Priest first announces that Christ has risen. The worshippers have brought candles to be lit in church at this time, one bestowing upon another the flame which originated at the altar, until the entire church is ablaze. The faithful, who have extinguished all fires in their homes earlier in the evening, bring the new light to their homes, and many keep the Easter candle burning for the next forty days. Also, during these forty days—between the Resurrection and the Ascension—Eastern Christians salute each other with the joyous greeting: "Christ is risen" to which the traditional response is, "He is risen indeed." This helps to nurture hope for the believer.

MAN AND THE CHURCH

According to the Eastern Church, salvation is not possible for the individual apart from the community. As we have already seen, it is a process of transfiguration of the whole cosmos, "culminating in *'theosis'* or the deification in Christ of the members of the Church as representatives of the entire creation." (18) Man is not saved *from* the world but *along with* the world; salvation means incorporation into the redeemed community and the sharing in the gifts of the Spirit which are given to the whole community. Thus, man becomes whole by overcoming his alienation through reconciliation with (1) God, with (2) himself, with (3) his neighbor and with (4) nature. In caring for the welfare of its members, the Eastern Church keeps these relationships (which are, in fact, therapeutic in nature) in proper perspective. The Church believes that man is wounded by sin. (19) In order for one to be healed, a right relationship in all four spheres is necessary, for it is not possible to achieve this in only one (for example, with God, or with oneself) to the exclusion of the other relationships. This can be illustrated by the four sides of a cross, representing the four relationships.

If any of the four sides is missing, then there is no cross. So also it is not possible for man to be healed without reconciliation to all of the four relationships. For instance, the great commandment given by Christ to love God and to love one's neighbor as oneself points up the immediate and close interrelationships between God, the individual and others. (20) Loving God is not possible without loving oneself (the reverse is true, also), and loving oneself is not possible without loving one's neighbor and vice versa. Antony of Egypt, the father of monasticism, (251-356) said, "From our neighbor is life and from our neighbor is death. . . . If we win our neighbor we win God, but if we cause our neighbor to stumble we sin against Christ." (21) What is meant here is that one cannot have a right relationship with God without loving one's neighbor. Just as the Persons of the Trinity dwell in each other, so man must "dwell" in his fellow men, living not for and unto himself, but in and for others.

The Eastern Church in this way stresses togetherness, wholeness and community in the life of its members. The individual is always to be related to the community and the community to the individual. This integral relationship of the individual to the community is not carried out at the expense of the person. Rather the individual is part of the whole without being swallowed up by the whole, just as the parts relate to the whole organism of the body. And, indeed, Orthodox Christians, along with all Christians, speak of the Church as the Body of Christ! Yet the Eastern Christians do not press this simile. For the relationship of the individual believer to the whole is characterized by freedom and spontaneity and not by obedience. That is why the unity between the Eastern churches is based upon unity of faith, and not on unity of administration. There is no one individual—like the Pope—who is the supreme head of the churches. The Orthodox churches are a group of autonomous and independent churches that are united by one faith. The supreme authority in these churches is the unanimous decision of an Ecumenical council, as it is received by the laity. In other words, it is the entire church itself composed of clergy and laity as it is guided by the Holy Spirit, that forms the basis of authority. Thus authority in the East is much more flexible than it is in the West.

With this general theological framework in mind, let us proceed to see how these concepts are carried out in concrete practice, and how the Eastern Church applies them in pastoral care to her members—first by considering the relationship between worship and the individual.

1. Liturgy and the Worshipper

One of the first things a newcomer observes about the worship service in an Eastern Church is the freedom and spontaneity allowed the individual worshippers to express themselves within a structured liturgy. Though members of the congregation may participate at any time in the singing of the liturgy, they are not required to do so (except for reciting the Creed and the Lord's Prayer), as this is performed antiphonally by the priest or deacon and two choirs placed on either side of the church towards the front. (22) However, the congregation also participates in the liturgy in other ways. Some kneel, others prostrate themselves, others remain standing, and all cross themselves or bow at different times. There is no prescribed order of action. The presence of many children, including babies, contributes still further to the atmosphere of informality. Nevertheless, the service is well structured and not chaotic. Indeed, it is not unusual for some worshippers to come late to the service, an act which would be considered both inappropriate and disruptive in a Western Church. This is because in the Eastern Church the corporate act of worship is emphasized. The believer does not come primarily to be instructed by a sermon, (23) or for other similar reasons; his interest is, rather, in joining with the Saints to render worship to God.

The Orthodox Church building represents the joining of heaven and earth. The screen (iconostasis), on which are hung pictures (icons) (24) of the whole story of redemption, divides the sanctuary, representing heaven, from the rest of the building, which represents the earth. Accordingly, since the Church is heaven on earth, God is considered to live there, and thus the worshipper goes there to meet and worship Him. The Church's liturgy is itself an "icon" of the heavenly liturgy. Thus, in the Eastern Orthodox Church, the emphasis is on rendering right adoration and worship, (25) not by attending the performance of a rigid and controlled ritual, but by participating as the individual is moved in an atmosphere of freedom within a structured worship service, because each individual is considered to be in the presence of God and His saints.

The first thing that an Orthodox worshipper does upon entering the church is to light candles in front of some of the icons. Then he stands in the vicinity of his favorite saint to render praise and worship to God along with him. (26) However, the acts of lighting candles and venerating the saints represented by the various icons need not be limited to the time of entering the church, but may take place at almost any time while the liturgy is going on if the worshipper is so moved. And since a significant number of icons are placed in front of the congregation, one sees many of the devout going to these icons while the liturgy is going on. To a Westerner this spectacle may seem disorderly and confused. It is worth noting also that in an Orthodox church there are no pews except on the sides for the elderly and the sick. (27) The lack of pews allows worshippers to stand close to one another, thus enabling them to feel more keenly the sense of the corporateness of believers, and also helping them not to be necessarily conformed in their actions. One is reminded somewhat also of the Mosque, in which all these individual actions may take place in a free space—yet conformity is expected in the actual service. As we have seen, the emphasis in the liturgy is on the action of the individual within the structure of the corporate.

The emphasis and orientation of Orthodox worship is to free the individual from uniformity of action so that he may most effectively render his worship and adoration unto his Lord who is present before him, and to prepare for the Eucharist which is the high point of the liturgy. (28) The worshipper is not a passive spectator observing a drama or a musical. Rather he is actively participating in worship by following the course of the liturgy, attempting not only to be part of it, but also to interiorize and to appropriate it, so to speak. Thus, the creation of an environment conducive to worship facilitates personal involvement in the act of worship and, in fact, helps the individual to reach an ecstatic experience. This individual approach is well expressed in St. Basil's liturgy (which is celebrated a few times a year in place of the usual St. Chrysostom liturgy), where the Lord is entreated:

> Become Thou all things to all men,
> for Thou knowest each one
> and the petition of his soul.

And many of the faithful make the following Eucharistic prayer of St. Basil's theirs on those days on which it is sung:

> May Thou unite us all, as many as are partakers in the one bread and cup, one with another, in the participation of the one Holy Spirit: to suffer no one of us to partake of the Holy Body and the blood of thy Christ unto judgment or unto condemnation; but that thereby we may find mercy and grace together with all the saints which have been well-pleasing unto Thee since the world began, our forefathers and fathers, Patriarchs, Prophets, Apostles, Preachers, Gospellers, Martyrs, Confessors, Doctors, and with all the spirits of the just in faith made perfect.

Thus in their worship the Eastern Christians are individuals (though not individualistic) who are members of a great family composed of the living and the departed. In worship itself it is the saints and the faithful departed who lead the prayers of the congregation, while the living saints intermittently join their great company in its never-ceasing praise of God. Thus, the corporate sense of the church is extended in a very real way to all those who have departed this life. The worshipping members feel this strongly, so that when they come to worship, they come to share in the life of the whole body as it renders praise and worship to God. That is why they pay homage to the saints and stand next to the saints whose icons are represented in the church, for these departed saints are their leaders in acts of worship, and the icons are visible signs of their invisible presence.

In this way does the Eastern church services reflect the duality of Christian existence. The faith is personal and corporate at the same time. To be Christian means one is an integral part of the community; however, the "simile of the Body should never be misinterpreted and pressed too far. The church is composed of unique and irreplaceable personalities which can never be regarded merely as elements or cells of the whole, because each individual is in direct and immediate union with Christ and His Father—the personal is not to be dissolved in the corporate. Christian 'togetherness' should not degenerate into a kind of impersonalism." (29) So in the act of worship the individual comes in contact with the Lord in the most intimate and personal way, yet he can pray only as an integral member of the whole body. "Indeed, no true worshipper can ever forget that *his* Father is also the *common* Father of all believers and of the whole human race." (30)

One of the main aspects of the liturgy of the Eastern Church is its pastoral function, concerned as it is with the well-being of man, by providing possibilities for his integration with God and with his neighbor. But the pastoral care of the church is not limited to the liturgical aspects. It enters into all facets of the life of the individual from the cradle to the grave. The Church considers man to be a citizen of both worlds. Through the Incarnation of Christ the irruption of the Kingdom of God took place. Although this Kingdom will be perfected by Christ at the second coming, nevertheless it is here; it exists in the church, and in the believers. Accordingly, heaven and earth—the eternal and the temporal, in accordance with Eastern Christianity—are not two separate spheres alienated from each other; on the contrary, they penetrate each other. Thus all the rites that the church administers to each member stress this penetration: "The rites that attend his birth and his death stress the link between the two worlds and the fact that man lives in both at the same time." (31)

2. The Sacramental Rites

The term "sacrament" ("Mystery" in Greek) refers to an outward visible sign that carries with it an inward spiritual grace. The sacrament is considered a unity; the invisible grace and the visible material sign form *one* whole. In other words, matter is capable of becoming a means of grace, for the divine spirit can manifest His powers through it. Accordingly, the Eastern Church uses the sacraments in her pastoral care for each member. The new-born usually receives baptism between the ages of one and six months. Even baptism is not the first occasion on which the church begins her ministration to the child. The priest comes to say prayers over the mother and the child on the day following his birth, and again, a week later, when the child is given his Christian name. On the fortieth day the mother brings the child to the church so that prayers may be said for it and, if baptism has been administered, the priest carries the child through the church reciting special prayers.

The rite of baptism, which may take place at home or in the church, starts with exorcism and a short catechism, renouncing the devil and his powers and affirming the acceptance of Christ. It is the godparents who spit on the devil and speak for the infant, who is carried in the arms of the godfather or godmother. Then the infant is anointed with olive oil, which has been blessed. The priest first makes the sign of the cross on the brow of the child with his fingers dipped in the oil, saying: "The Servant of God, (name) is anointed with the oil of gladness in the Name of the Father, Son and Holy Spirit. Amen." Then, as he anoints the breast and back, he continues, "Unto the healing of soul and body"; and upon anointing the ears, "Unto hearing the faith." When he anoints the palms, he says, "Thy hands have made and fashioned him"; and upon anointing the feet he continues, "that he may walk in the way of the commandments."

Then the actual baptism takes place, with triple immersion, followed immediately afterwards by Chrismation (the equivalent of Confirmation). This rite entitles the infant to receive communion of both kinds (bread and wine), which is in fact given to him immediately after. Thereafter he is brought to church as a full-fledged member. For the Eastern church does not discriminate against the young by relegating them to nurseries or to Sunday schools, while the adults attend the regular service. (32) In the East there is no "generation gap" between members of the church.

The therapeutic function of the rite of baptism is apparent, but there are also two aspects of this rite which may be worthy of consideration, in that they may have some bearing on the welfare of the new-born. First of all, the Christian name which is given in connection with baptism is usually a name of one of the departed saints. This symbolizes the unity achieved by the initiate with both the earthly church and the heavenly church. The patron saint after whom the child is named receives a special place in the heart as well as in the home of the new church member. Usually he keeps an icon of this saint in his room, and celebrates the saint's festival as his Name Day, which is considered more important than one's actual birthday. Thus, the baby is immediately introduced meaningfully into th fellowship of the community of the saints, both living and dead. And he enters into the life of the church, because not only does the church invoke, on occasion, his particular patron saint, but also sets aside a special day of the year on which the memory of the saint is celebrated. This helps the member of the church to recognize that the grave is not the end of life, and that one's world encompasses the dead as well as the living. Thus, one is tied to roots in history that are at once ancient and alive.

Secondly, one must note the important functions that the godparents exert in the life of the child. One of these is to endeavor to bring up the baby in the faith, and to pay special attention to his welfare throughout life. In other words, the godparents "adopt" the child spiritually, without taking him away from his parents; consequently marriage between the god-child and the natural (or adopted) children of the godparents is forbidden. This new system or relationship brings the child into an immediate contact with people who are not necessarily connected by blood. It helps the child to be on his own, and can remove the threat of possessiveness by either of the parents. And it helps to provide continuity should one or both of the parents die. In times of crisis, especially illness, the godparents do their best to help, not only the child, but the whole family.

As at baptism, all major events of one's life are connected with the life of the church sacramentally. Space does not allow us to examine all the sacraments in detail. But I think that the brief discussion of baptism well illustrates the place and function of the sacraments as aspects of the church's pastoral care. The sacraments serve a double function, from a psychotherapeutic view: to help achieve individuation and integration at one and the same time. The process of individuation begins in the giving of a name, baptism, and the first Eucharist. These acts give equal status in the church to the three-month old baby and the thirty-year old man. The only difference is that the baby is unable to participate fully and effectively in the life of the church—particularly in those aspects that presuppose consciousness and rationality. Nevertheless, these and other sacraments help the new-born towards the achievement of his personhood. In the sight of the church, he is equal to the older members, for he received the grace of God through the sacraments just as any adult. The reception of grace does not depend on the development of rationality and consciousness. Moreover, the reception of grace is an individual thing; it is a solitary act, for the relationship is between the person and God. The Church plays the mediating role in this relationship. Indeed she considers this role to be important, for every human being that comes into the world needs the power of grace in order to achieve his personhood and his call. Moreover, the solemn participation of and witness by the community at each of the sacramental rites administered to the new-born helps to bring recognition of the independence of the baby.

But at the same time, the Church recognizes the possibilities for the processes of disintegration and alienation within the life of the individual, even in the relationships discussed above. The result of the fall of Adam, in accordance with Eastern Christianity, is the introduction into the life and destiny of man of various disruptive potentialities. However, these nagative forces are not in total control, because the image of God in man, which represents the positive forces of the good, has not been totally destroyed, but rather only tarnished, and its forces somewhat inhibited. Hence, the paradox of human existence: as soon as a baby is born, along with the powers of life and growth, the forces of disintegration are at work. These latter forces, as far as the organism of the body is concerned, culminate in physical death. The disintegrative forces are at work, in a very real sense, in the spiritual and psychic realms, producing alienation and isolation from God and the world. The basic motivations for such alienation and isolation are, according to theologians, pride and self-sufficiency. These are the basic motivations that impelled Adam and Eve to reject their Creator's plan for their lives.

Thus the Eastern Church believes that man needs the healing medicine of the Spirit of God, from the moment of birth, to help him overcome in the struggles, from within and from without, between the integrative and the disintegrative forces. The "new" nature (i.e. the nature of the new Adam-Christ) which is received, in accordance with Orthodox belief, is actualized, not punctiliously, but in a process which culminates in deification. Gregory Nazianzen exhorts, in reference to infant baptism, "Do not let wickedness seize it chance. Let him be sanctified from babyhood, and consecrated by the Spirit in his tender years." (33) Later on he affirms that even though infants cannot feel spiritual deprivation or grace, nevertheless they ought to be baptized, for "even if they cannot fully understand, their characters and minds are in process of formation. Then we should sanctify their souls and bodies by the great mystery of full initiation." (34)

The sacraments are neither isolated from each other nor are they magical. The cooperation, not only of the individual, but also of his community and—I dare say—of his environment, with God, is needed for the full actualization of the grace received through the sacraments. That is why the sacraments have a communal character. For the Church believes that the forces of isolation, individualism and alienation are indicative of the need of every human being, not only the obviously "sick," for the healing power of grace.

Does this imply that the Eastern churches have no special pastoral care for the sick? Not at all. Caring for the sick has a special place in the life of the Eastern Christians. Indeed, one of the important functions of the pastoral ministry of the Church is the healing, helping and comforting of the sick. First of all, the priest comes to the sick man to offer prayers over him. This is done several times—depending upon the length of the illness. Needless to say, consultation takes place and advice is given on such occasions. Moreover, in the case of grave sickness, the sacrament of Holy Unction is administered for the healing of both bodily and spiritual infirmities. (35) Since this service consists of seven lessons about the miracles of Jesus, it is preferable (but not necessary) that seven priests be present, each to read one lesson and anoint different parts of the body with oil. Also participating are some members of the household and as many as would attend from the congregation. Participation by more than one priest as well as laity tends to emphasize the corporate nature of the healing services. Prayers are also said for the sick during the Liturgy, in common with all Christian denominations, not only on Sundays but also on other days, whenever liturgies are conducted. Several times during the liturgy the priest or the deacon entreats the Lord, "For those that travel . . . for the sick, for those that suffer, for captives and for their salvation. . . ." Besides this general prayer for the sick, individual requests are usually made (by the one who is sick or by friends and relatives), and the sick person is prayed for by name.

By such attention paid to them in the church, Eastern Christians are reminded how important is the comfort of the sick. That is why visits to the sick are encouraged, not only by the priest, but also by members of the congregation. It is felt that the sick and the suffering, in their hour of need and loneliness, need not only prayers and medicine, but also the presence of concerned individuals. The sick person is thus helped to shatter the walls of loneliness.

Nevertheless, Orthodoxy encourages the care and healing of the sick by the secular art of medicine. Yet the latter is always viewed from the perspective of religion, which is concerned with the total man and his world. One of the greatest fathers of the fourth century Eastern Church, Basil the Great (ca. 330-379), in addition to being a fine theologian and an ascetic, was a great philanthropist concerned for the physical and material welfare of man. He established hospitals for the sick, asylums for the poor, and hospices for the traveler. These contributions were evaluated thus in the Panegyric of Gregory of Nazianzus:

> A noble thing is philanthropy, and the support of the poor, and the assistance of human weakness. Go forth a little way from the city, and behold the new city, the storehouse of piety, the common treasury of the wealthy . . . are stored, in consequences of his (i.e. Basil's) exhortations, freed from the power of the moth, no longer gladdening the eyes of the thief, and escaping both the emulation of envy and the corruption of time: where disease is regarded in a religious light, and disaster is thought a blessing, and sympathy is put to the test. (36)

In addition, there persists in the Eastern Church the practice of prayers for the healing of various diseases which are not strictly physical, particularly those that are labeled "possessions." Under the general category of "possessed" come patients who are believed to be inhabited or influenced by "outside" powers, those who suffer from psychic disturbances, and those who do not respond to doctor's treatments because the causes of their disorders are often psychological. There are various forms of exorcism practiced in the Eastern churches. In one, the simplest, sick people bow their heads under the Gospel while it is being read by the priest during liturgy. In another, when the priest removes his vestments after the liturgy, he piles them on the head of an afflicted person, lays his hands upon him, and utters certain prayers. These are common types of exorcism.

While all Orthodox priests can and, in fact, do pray for anyone "possessed," it is only a few who distinguish themselves as having special gifts of exorcism, to be effective in extreme cases. Consequently "patients" from far and wide are brought to such a priest, who performs the prayers without charge. The afflicted person is usually given a room in which to stay close to the residence of the priest. After meeting and praying several times with the "patient" and the relatives who accompanied him, the priest fasts, either totally for a period of one to three days, or partially for a longer period, depending upon his custom and upon the inspiration of the Spirit. The priest will meanwhile spend long periods in prayer and consultation with his patient. This relationship may continue for a period as long as a month, or even longer, but not necessarily until the person is healed. Sometimes the priest may send his "patient" back home with hope and prayers before any sign of recovery has been observed; in other cases, he may wait until a partial recovery has been seen, or even until full recovery has been achieved.

Exactly what transpires between priest and "patient" on these occasions is confidential between them. The Church provides sets of prayers and procedures to guide the healer, but the individual must rely heavily on the gifts of the Holy Spirit and on his own integrity and dedication. In some cases, prayers are said with a minimum of consultation and exhortation; in others, the reverse may be true. But whatever the emphasis may be, the prototype for this form of exorcism is to be found in the New Testament, where the disciples asked Jesus why they could not cast out the "dumb" spirit. Jesus' reply was, "This kind can come forth by nothing, but by prayer and fasting" (Mark 9:29). The Eastern churches adhered to this ancient practice in varying degrees from that time forth throughout the centuries.

Another important aspect of pastoral care by the Church is the hearing of "confessions," a practice which is encouraged. But as elsewhere, the Orthodox attitude is determined by "corporate mindedness". To the Orthodox, sincere and inward repentance is not sufficient without reconciliation to the rest of the community. For the sin of an individual affects others. That is why confession begins, not with a visit to the priest, but by becoming reconciled with one's neighbors. The general custom is for one to visit relatives and friends in order to ask their pardon, even for small things. Those who are approached usually respond, "May God pardon you." This is followed by the kiss of reconciliation. Then, the evening before communion, a bath is taken to symbolize the inner cleansing.

Then the penitent goes the next day to the priest, who takes him aside in the church, or even into a private room. The penitent does not kneel, but stands beside the priest. The situation is thus very different from what happens in the Roman Catholic Church, for instance, where he must kneel and where the priest, standing behind a small window, is heard but not seen. In the Eastern Church, the confessor is regarded not as a judge in the seat of authority, but rather as a witness. In fact, the priest begins by reminding the penitent, as both stand before an icon of Christ, that it is God who is the judge, while he is only a witness. Then he listens to the penitent and may question him. Such questioning, when performed by a gifted father confessor, can be of great help to the confessant. At the conclusion of this, the priest may offer advice and even prescribe penance. Then follows the prayer of absolution, in which the priest asks God to forgive, but does not pronounce forgiveness in his own person (except in the Russian churches, into which this practice was introduced during the seventeenth century under Roman Catholic influence), for the Eastern Christians believe that forgiveness comes only from God through the agency of the church.

What form the confessions take, and what actually transpires between priest and penitent varies according to the individuals concerned. The details of confessional procedure are not regulated by the Church, only its general form. But the Priest who is selected by a particular person to receive his or her confessions enters into a close spiritual relationship with that person and accordingly is called his "spiritual father," the confessant being a "spritiual son" (or "daughter"). The "spiritual father" is not necessarily one's local parish priest. In fact it is a tradition among Eastern Christians to have freedom of choice in selecting a father confessor, who may not be the same as he from whom one receives communion. Consequently, in a particular town or city, a certain priest may become very popular as a father confessor. In fact it is possible for laymen to become "spiritual fathers" for certain individuals, though in such cases the penitent must go to a priest after confession for the prayers of absolution. But whatever his calling, the confessor, like a doctor, usually tries to find out what is the spiritual disease of the penitent and attempts to see how deeply this is rooted in his soul. In cases where despair exists, the priest attempts to find out the reason and to lead the penitent to God for hope and confidence. Thus the sacrament of confession acts also for the healing of the soul, since the confessor gives advice in addition to his prayer of absolution. Consequently, the better the "father confessor" is acquainted with his spiritual children, the more pertinent are his questions and the more useful is his advice. That is why changing frequently from one spiritual father to another is not encouraged.

THE EASTERN CHURCH'S ATTITUDE TOWARDS NATURE

This chapter will not be complete without some demonstration of how Eastern Christians relate to nature. We have already seen that the theological doctrines emphasize cosmic redemption—i.e. salvation is to be viewed not only in terms of man alone, but in terms of the total environment of man and his world. The victory of Christ over death is the central fact of sacred history and affects the *whole* of creation. In other words, the Orthodox look with hope to the transfiguration of the entire natural order along with man. God regenerates not only man, but also beasts and all the natural order. Spirit and matter are not two antagonistic entities, but manifest this same reality. The Eastern Christian looks with reverence, love and awe towards nature. Natural objects not only are capable of becoming vehicles of grace, but in fact do become them. That is why material objects are used in sacraments. In fact, the Orthodox look at their whole world sacramentally. The limitation of the sacraments to the number seven seen in some Orthodox manuals is only a recent introduction, and must be regarded as an impoverishment of the sacramental life of the Church.

The tradition and practice of the Eastern Church is not to number the sacraments, because any enumeration sets arbitrary limitations. The church invokes the power of the Spirit upon the water (on the day of Christ's baptism), on church buildings, icons, houses, fields, animals and plants. It is true that not all these and similar acts are called sacraments in the full sense of the term; some are simple blessings. Nevertheless, the Orthodox believe that all natural objects can receive and in turn manifest the grace of the Spirit. That is why in worship, aspects of the entire natural environment—images, ideas, sounds, words, movements of the body, light, darkness, eating, kissing (though the "kiss of peace" is practiced in few Orthodox churches nowadays), water, earth and the fruits of the earth, etc.—are used in the worship of God. Moreover, the Orthodox liturgical cycles correspond closely to the cycles in nature, which fact helps man not only to be attuned to the rhythm of nature in his devotion, but helps him also to praise God and work with nature and not against it.

The Eastern attitude to nature is well illustrated by the Liturgy of Transfiguration which falls on August 6. We must remember that transfiguration, deification and seeing the Divine Light are the goals of Orthodox life and worship. In Canticle Six of the Matins of the Transfiguration, these goals are expressed in the following words:

> Awake ye sluggards, lie not forever on the ground, and ye thoughts . . ., arise and go up to the high slope of the divine ascent. Let us run to join Peter and the sons of Zebedee, and go with them to Mount Tabor, that with them we may see the glory of our God and hear the voice they heard from heaven; and they proclaimed that this is the Brightness of the Father. (37)

Now at the end of the liturgy in which the hopes and prayers for ascent are uttered, the priest blesses grapes which have been brought earlier and placed on a table in the center of the church, and says the following prayer:

> Bless, O Lord, this new fruit of the vine, which Thou has been pleased to bring to full ripeness through temperate seasons, showers of rain, and calm weather. May we who partake thereof be filled with joy. . . . (38)

Next to the sacraments and the icons, probably one of the best illustrations of the Eastern attitude to nature is the practice of fasting. The main periods of fasting during the year are: (1) Great Lent, culminating in Easter, and beginning seven weeks before; (2) the fast of the Apostles, which varies in length between one to six weeks;

(3) the Fast of the Assumption, lasting two weeks; and (4) the christmas Fast of forty days. In addition to these four periods, all Wednesdays and Fridays (with few exceptions) are fast days. It is estimated that more than half of the year is a time of fasting! The Orthodox fasts are very rigorous, in contrast to those of Western churches, as abstinence is demanded not only from meat, but also from all animal products, such as lard, butter, milk, cheese and eggs, and even fish. (39) Moreover, some of the faithful abstain totally from food from one to three days at the beginning and end of each of the four major periods, especially Great Lent.

The fast has important functions in the lives of Eastern Christians, in addition to its primary religious significance. Indeed, the Orthodox Church, regarding man as unity of soul and body, has always insisted that "the body must be trained and disciplined as well as the soul." (40) Moreover, the abstinence from meats and all animal products to a point far exceeding vegetarianism, expressing, indeed, the desire to abstain almost totally from food, has two symbolic meanings: humility and repentance, and reconciliation. That the time of fasting is a time for humility and repentance is seen, for instance, in the service of forgiveness immediately before Lent begins, when clergy and people kneel before each other asking each other's forgiveness one by one. The same thing is done afterwards at home and in Orthodox communities. It is a time when repentance towards the poor and the underprivileged is expressed by giving alms generously. Humility and repentance towards nature is also expressed.

By refraining from the use of animals and their products, the Orthodox acknowledge man's encroachment upon nature, in effect saying that living on and of the animal world is not the ideal state of man, but one which exists because man cannot help it. But in this time of humility and reconciliation—the time of fasting—the Eastern Christian recognizes the claims of the animal kingdom upon him, and does not injure or harm it. He performs a symbolic act of reconciliation in the hope of the final reconciliation—in the new earth and new heaven—when not only "the wolf shall dwell with the lamb," but also when the most destructive of creatures, man, shall not hurt or destroy any of the creatures of God. By fasting, the Orthodox Christian is, in effect, telling the animal kingdom that not only are their lives to be spared, but also that he is sparing their products for their young ones, for whom they were intended in the first place.

CONCLUSION

This study of the Eastern Orthodox Church from a psychotherapeutic perspective has emphasized that the Eastern Christians, like their Western brethren, are concerned with the basic problems of man's nature and existence. These problems and their derivatives face all human beings, in different degrees and with various effects. Yet the basis of spiritual and psychic help, according to the Eastern Church, is the achievement of integral relatedness to God, to neighbor and to nature. That is to say, it is a movement towards union (not based on absorption, but rather on differentiation) with God, with one's neighbor, with nature and, indeed, with oneself—the basis of integrity and identity. Indeed, this last relationship is tied to the first according to Eastern theology. Man is an icon of God; he is a "living theology," and God can be found within the depth of his soul.

By returning to oneself, one finds God. For Christ announced to his followers that the Kingdom of God is here and that it "is within you" (Luke 17:21). But from the very fact that it is a kingdom, and that each person is in the image, one's relationship with others becomes an integral one. Sin results in the breakup of these relationships, and thus man finds the various alienating forces at work right from the beginning of his life. Accordingly, the Eastern Church, in her theology and practice, considers man in his predicament to be in need of reconciliation and the power of healing which was brought by Christ. The church sees the God who became man as the center of all therapeutic processes. This does not mean, however, that the Church recognizes only itself as the agency of these healing powers. On the contrary, she sees a definite place for all agencies of healing. But as the Eastern Church views man in his totality (including his environment), she refuses to posit a dichotomy between the "secular" and the religious forms of healing—between priest and psychotherapist, for instance. Every healing art must have its roots in religious experience, and every religious experience its therapeutic dimension. The secular and the religious are not two separate spheres, but are interrelated and penetrate each other. So, also, the spiritual and the material, and the so-called "natural" and "supernatural," are not separate, clearly defined realities, but rather expressions of the same basic reality. In other words, as we have seen, the Eastern Church views the world sacramentally. God can and does reveal himself in and through material objects.

The Eastern Church, we have also seen, is concerned with the meaning of life, for without giving an account of the purpose of one's existence, any kind of therapy or healing is without foundation. Consequently, the individual who experiences the meaning of life through the Church is enabled to participate completely in the realities that transcend his life. Indeed, meaning and hope sustain biological and psychological functions. Thus man may gain wholeness, which achievement is part of God's greater plan for mankind. Yet the Eastern Christian, despite his faith, never forgets the tragic and transient nature of human existence. He cannot devote himself to a consistently optimistic outlook, for his expectation of the ultimate transfiguration of nature does not allow him to conclude that the disruptive forces no longer have their effect in his life. And the Church helps him to express this awareness of the tragic, as is well exemplified in the funeral rite. The following moving reflection, for example, expressed in a burial canticle, recognizes fully the tragedy of death:

> I weep and mourn when I look upon death,
> and when I see our beauty, created in the image of God,
> laid in the grave, formless, shapeless and without glory.
> What is the mystery that is our lot?
> Why are we given to corruption and yoked together with death?

And the Church further encourages the people to express their emotion when the choir sings, in the name of the deceased who is lying in their midst in an open coffin, saying:

> I lie voiceless and deprived of breath.
> Come all that love me, kiss me,
>   for never shall I converse with you again . . . . .
> Beholding me, bewail me, for yesterday I spake with you,
>   and suddenly came on me the dread hour of death.
> I beg you all, pray to Christ our God for me that for
>   my sins I be not bidden unto the place of torment,
>   but be granted the light of life.

Along with this sense of pathos there is also expressed hope and confidence in the life to come for the departed and for those who are alive also:

> What delight of life continues unmixed with sorrows? What glory on earth remains unutterable? All things are more fleeting than a shadow, all things are more illusive than dreams; one moment, and all these things are followed by death. But in the light of thy countenance, and in the sweetness of thy beauty, do thou, O Christ, in mercy, give rest to him whom thou hast chosen, for as much as thou art the lover of mankind.

Thus the Orthodox sees the tragedy in the human condition and expresses it without inhibition. He doesn't whitewash or minimize its effect. But at the same time the formidable power of death does not overcome or crush him. For he lives by faith and hope, always looking and sharing in the incorruptible reality in which he is participating and which he faces. Man is not alone, for God, to whom he is related, is with him.

But because the Church views man in his relatedness, her approach to the basic problems of man is founded upon the "I-Thou" encounter, not upon a deterministic and impersonal approach. And since man is isolated because of sin, the Church attempts to promote communication by enabling man to be open to God and to other men. For she endeavours to help each individual to be truly human, aiding him to break the walls of separation to get out of himself to reach the other. Thus her interest is in enabling man to overcome the exterior powers of dehumanization which attempt to submerge one individual identity into another, as well as the interior forces which impel the self to remain submerged in the crowd. Thus the Church helps each person to retain or to recover identity.

Since relatedness and effective participation are the bases of human becoming and identity, the Church sees herself as providing the matrix and the mediatorship to the achievement of these ends. And since the Eastern Church treats man not simply in terms of rational life, or alone in terms of bodily life, but rather in terms of the whole—i.e. the body-spirit continuum—she approaches healing and reconciliation also in terms of the whole. That is why the sacraments have such a prominent place in the life and function of the Church. And that is why she extends her pastoral care even to infants and, indeed, to every aspect of human life and existence.

Thus as a mediator the Church helps, in all her activities—whether theological, liturgical, or pastoral—to provide not only the context in which, but also the means by which, effective communication and relationship can be achieved by the individual in four dimensions: with God, with one's neighbor, with the world, and with self. For one of the root causes of psychic illness is the fear to love and to be loved, to share beauty and to participate in the happiness as well as sorrow of others. By attempting to help each member to love and to share in every sphere of life, the Eastern Church assists him in overcoming and transcending this fear.

REFERENCES AND FOOTNOTES

1 By the term "Eastern Orthodox Churches," I refer to the following independent and self-governing churches: (a) The Patriarchates of Constantinople, Alexandria, Antioch, and Jerusalem, Russia, Romania, Serbia and Bulgaria; (b) Independent churches which are not not headed by Patriarchs, but rather by an Archbishop or a Metropolitan, such as those of

Greece, Cyprus, Czechoslavakia, Albania, Poland and Sinai. All these churches are in communion with one another. What unites them is their common faith and common liturgy. I do not aim to represent the views of other Eastern churches, such as the Coptic-Abyssinian, the Armenians and the Jacobites. However, the differences between this last group of churches and the Eastern Orthodox are minor, and much of what I have to say about the Orthodox could apply to them also.

2 *The Practice of Psychotherapy* (Collected Works, Bollingen Series XX). New York, Pantheon, 1954, vol. 16, p. 81.
3 *Adversus Haereses*, IV. xxxviii, 3 (Translated by H. Bettenson) in *The Early Christian Fathers*, London, Oxford University Press, 1956, p. 94.
4 *Adversus Haereses*, loc. cit.
5 *Adversus Haereses* IV. xxxvii, 4.
6 Meyendorff, J.: *Orthodoxy and Catholicity*, New York, Sheed and Ward, 1966, p. 127.
7 The distinction between "essence" and "energies" in God was clearly stated in the East by St. Gregory Palamas, a theologian of the fourteenth century, in connection with the Hesychast controversy. Hesychasm (the word means "quietude"), of which Palamas was the chief spokesman, refers to the experience of the Divine and Uncreated Light and to the meditative method of attaining this experience. The Hesychasts developed breathing techniques along with the repetition of Jesus' prayer. Such methods are similar in some respects to Yoga in Buddhism and to *dhikr* in Islam. They taught that such bodily exercises help to attain the vision of God. As they were being accused of materialism, they pointed out that there is a distinction between the essence and the energies of God. God's essence is unknowable and unapproachable, but he is known in His energies since these have come down to us. These energies, however, are God Himself; for they are His actions and revelations to the world. God is fully present in each of His energies. The Light is one of God's energies. Thus the balance between God's transcendence and immanence was struck by Palamas and the Hescychasts.

In his defense of Hesychasm, Palamas did not fall into the Manichaean dualism of spirit and matter, but rather vigorously affirmed the unity of the body and the soul. He said that the term "man" refers to both. Moreover, he affirmed that the principle of Incarnation, i.e. God becoming a man, is at work in human life, and thus man, in seeking catharsis (purification), is not to escape from the body. For since the entire man (including his body) was created by God, one needs the help of the body in the hard task of purification.

8 Gregory of Nyssa: *Oratio Cathechetica* (Magna), 5. Translation by H. Bettenson in *The Later Christian Father*, London, Oxford University Press, 1970, p. 130.
9 *Orationes*, 45. 8, 9. English translation by H. Bettenson, in *The Later Christian Fathers*, p. 101.
10 Lossky, V.: *The Mystical Theology of the Eastern Church*. London, James Clarke and Co., Ltd, 1968, p. 118.
11 *Ibid.*, p. 121.
12 *Ibid.*, p. 123.
13 Runciman, Steven: *The Great Church in Captivity*. Cambridge University Press, 1968, p. 154.
14 Lossky, *op. cit.*, p. 126.
15 Ware, Timothy: *The Orthodox Church*, Baltimore, Penguin Books, 1969, p. 228.
16 Aulen, G.: *Christus Victor*. London, S.P.C.K., 1931, p. 21.
17 For the opposite reason, perhaps, Christ crucified on the cross is a favored representation in the West, both as a concept in literature and as an image in the visual arts.
18 Zernov, N.: *Orthodox Encounter*. London, J. Clarke and Co., Ltd, 1961, p. 94.
19 In the words of the hymn sung at funeral services, the dead person addresses God thus: "I am the image of Thine inexpressible glory, even though I bear the wounds of sin."
20 The concept of man's relationship to nature is not apparent in this verse. However, the view of Eastern Christians concerning this is conditioned by the Incarnation (God's becoming

man), and by Pauline theology in which cosmic redemption and transfiguration are envisaged: ". . . the creation itself will be set free from its bondage to decay and obtain the glorious liberty of the children of God" (Romans 8:21 R.S.V.).

21 *Apophthegmata* (P.G. lxv), Antony. Quoted by T. Ware, *op. cit.,* p. 239.
22 The degree of customary general participation vocally in the worship service by the congregation differs from one church to another. Modern youth movements emphasize, if not actual vocal participation, at least being able to follow and to enter into every phase of the liturgy.
23 The sermon is not unimportant in an Orthodox Church, but it is not central to the service. This may have led some Western Christians to suppose that the Orthodox do not attach a high importance to the Bible. But this is not the case, for the liturgy is permeated with direct Scriptural quotations and allusions, as well as readings—in fact, the whole of the New Testament (except for the book of *Revelation*) is read at Eucharistic services in the course of a year.
24 An icon is a visual representation in color of transformed and transfigured reality. The icon is not an imitation of nature, but rather is a representation of redeemed man. Thus an icon is not realistic; for it is a two-dimensional painting. Realism, as it is seen in some churches today, crept in with the decadence of icon-painting. Accordingly, an icon representing Christ or a saint is believed to show forth the presence of Christ or the saint, in a very similar fashion as the elements of the Eucharist are believed to be changed into the body and blood of Christ.
25 That is the reason why many theologians emphasize that the meaning of the term "orthodox" is "right praise" (i.e. worship), rather than simply "right opinion or belief." Indeed, the liturgy is the heart of Orthodoxy.
26 Of course, this is not possible in those churches, primarily in America where there are no life-size frescoes or small icons of saints along the walls.
27 Again, many churches in America differ by having pews, or at least folding chairs, probably in imitation of Catholic and Protestant practice.
28 The center and climax of every liturgy is the celebration of the Eucharist, not only those celebrated on Sundays, but also those taking place during the week. The Eucharist represents to the believer, through material means, unity with his Lord. Although there may be few people who receive the Eucharist on a particular Sunday, nevertheless it is the center of the worship service.
29 Florovsky, Georges: "The Worshipping Church," an introduction to *The Festal Menaion,* E.T. by Mother Mary and Archimandrite Kallistos Ware, London, Faber and Faber, 1969, p. 21.
30 *Ibid.,* p. 23.
31 French, R. M.: *The Eastern Orthodox Church.* London, Hutchinson's University Library, 1957, p. 158.
32 The Orthodox believe that the child does not have to be separated from the worship service, either because he is still a baby and might disrupt the service or because, as an older child, he needs to be trained in order to understand the church services. For the Eastern Christians hold that the proper training of the baby and the child is his presence at the liturgy, where his "dawning consciousness is trained to accept the privilege of meeting the other world as it there breaks through into this. When he is seven years old, he is expected to make his first Confession, as he learns another side of the matter—his own worthiness and responsibilities." *Ibid.,* p. 160.
33 *Orationes* 40:17.
34 *Ibid.,* 40:28.
35 This sacrament is not reserved in the Orthodox churches for people who are on their death-beds, as in the West (thus it received there the name of Extreme Unction). In fact, in the Eastern churches it can be administered to any who desire it for spiritual

strengthening or to alleviate psychic disturbances, without that person being necessarily bedridden.

36 *Orationes,* 63. Trans. N.P.N.F., (2nd Ser.), VII, p. 416.
37 *The Festal Menaion,* p. 489.
38 *Ibid.,* p. 502.
39 However many Orthodox churches in America for some reason do not practice such a rigorous fast as the churches of Europe and the Near East.
40 Ware, T., *op. cit.,* p. 306.

Part Two
INDIGENOUS AND EMERGENT RELIGIOUS SYSTEMS

CHAPTER 17

MAGIC, FAITH AND HEALING IN MODERN PSYCHIATRY

Ari Kiev

THE DEVELOPMENT OF DISORDERS of mood, thought and behavior in most pre-literate and pre-technical cultures has invariably been explained and treated in terms of one or more of several supernatural concepts relating to taboo violation: witchcraft, the intrusion of harmful objects into the body, and possession by angry or evil spirits. This paper explores some of the forms of these concepts and techniques in pre-scientific cultures and in modern psychiatry as we know it in the West, by way of illuminating certain universal features which seem to appear in all forms of healing.

Taboo Violation

Incest and murder are taboo violations believed almost universally to have deleterious effects on the mind of the perpetrator, bringing punishment in the form of insanity caused by ancestral deities, by God or, as in our own culture, by the individual's conscience.

At one time or another several different theories have prevailed in psychiatry about the development of mental illness caused by a guilty conscience resulting from various taboo violations including adultery, masturbation, and other forms of sexual excess.

For the civilized layman a variety of superstitions have similarly been assigned etiological significance, as for example, walking under a ladder, crossing the path of a black cat or breaking a mirror—each of these in its own way being a form of taboo violation.

Witchcraft

Witchcraft is usually associated with the nefarious activities of others, for example, witches, sorcerers, and black magicians, whose special power or use of sympathetic magic inflicts insanity on the victim. Witchcraft is often thought to be responsible for the introduction into the victim of magical or foreign substances that produce illness by upsetting the natural equilibrium of the body.

The Western psychiatrist, like his native counterpart, has focused special attention on negligent parents, impersonal orphanages, and other sources of emotional deprivation in the early years of life which so alter the psychological equilibrium of the child as to produce permanent effects. The recent interest in the role of early nutritional deprivation in the production of permanent mental retardation is an example of the scientific utility of "witch hunts" which seek to find the culprits and wrongdoers in the child's past.

Can we say then that we don't have a concept of witchcraft in our psychiatric theories? Is there a more nefarious, malevolent person that the schizophrenogenic mother whose oversolicitous and overprotective concern for a schizophrenic youngster are invariably construed as proof positive of "cannibalism," disguised hostility, and oral sadism. Do not the self-sacrificing plaints of martyrdom of such mothers sound very much like the self-accusations of witchcraft which Field found so common in Ghana, for instance?

Spirit Intrusion

Strange behavior is often explained by the presence of an alien spirit sent sometimes by malevolent sorcerers or by ancestral deities as punishment for failure to honor the dead. Haitian peasants, for example, believe a sorcerer can force the *gros bon ange* (soul) from the victim's head by magical means and replace it with the soul of an insane dead man or animal, whose manifestations are then responsible for the erratic behavior.

The belief that powerful forces in the environment can deplete or dominate the individual, shows up in Western psychiatric theory in terms of notions of environmental stresses which are subjectively "harmful" because the individual perceives them as such—so that almost all experiences may, in fact, become potential stressors. The notion of individual susceptibility or vulnerability to stress which is heightened by the individual's failure to act autonomously, independently assuming control over his own destiny, is quite central to psychiatric theory.

Indeed the basic objective of psychoanalysis is to strengthen the capacity of the ego (soul) to master the forces of the superego (environment) and the id (strong frightening impulses).

Community Responsibility

In most traditional cultures, responsibility for illness is attributed to outside forces, as indicated by the notion of witchcraft or spirit intrusion. Rarely is the patient himself viewed as the cause of the problem as in our own emphasis on *the patient's* responsibility for his difficulty.

Thus a common notion in our psychiatry is that the patient didn't assert himself enough or didn't understand how he repeatedly got himself in trouble. While this relates to the notion of taboo violation, it is vague and general and has to do with the development of internalized standards of behavior (conscience) as opposed to externalized or group standards of conduct in non-Western cultures—where the individual assigns more weight to *the group's* judgement about his behavior.

Treatment approaches linked to internalized standards emphasize positive thinking and individual effort as mechanisms for personal growth, maturation, and the resolution of neurotic conflict.

The Evil Eye

Precautions to protect newborn and young children from "the evil eye" seem to be universal. They take diverse forms from the wearing of amulets in the Middle East and red ribbons in Eastern Europe to the insistence of Mexican-Americans that those who "look strongly at," compliment, or envy a child, touch the child to prevent harm from coming to him. Often these notions have to do with the violation of formalized social boundaries which maintain group stability in traditional, tight-knit, well-integrated communities.

The intensity of negative emotions which are assigned etiological significance is the obverse side of the coin of strong integration in close knit traditional communities where intense emotional reactions can have a significant effect on the behavior of the more vulnerable. While these strong emotional drives (such as envy which gives rise to *mal ojo*, or "evil eye," or hate which may result in bewitchment) do also occur in the West, they are considerably diluted down in intensity by virtue of the fact that group processes are not that intense, the individual having some option to avoid group pressures.

Yet it is quite clear that psychiatrists accept the harmful effects of the attitudes and expectations of significant others, as witness the emphasis placed on interpersonal conflict as a source of illness. Certainly a variety of personality theories have developed in our Western culture to explain the incompatibilities of individuals.

Soul Loss

Sudden fright, severe panic states and acute psychosis are often attributed to "loss of soul" or depletion of the spirit, formerly said to be caused by magical powers which have "possessed" the victim.

The depletion of some vital substance appears to be a universal explanation of behavior characterized by fear, anxiety and withdrawal.

In contemporary psychiatric theory much attention has focused on such factors as the etiological role of enzyme deficiencies, avitaminoses, and hypothetical biochemical abnormalities. While such hypotheses are supported by scientific theory, the inclination to accept them is derived in part from the same assumptions as those of native healers.

Prevention and Treatment

Ways of Prevention

Ideas about the causation of mental illness lead, although not always logically, to certain specific solutions to prevent or to remedy mental illness. Many cultures believe, for instance, that undue sympathy on the part of an expectant mother for the sick or the mad may lead to the same affliction in her child. Consequently, expectant mothers are often shielded from such contacts. Precautions to protect newborn children from the evil eye seem to be universal.

A large part of modern psychiatric treatment is designed to assist the patient in learning how to avoid certain difficult people or situations which are likely to prove stressful because of the special idiosyncratic or symbolic significance of the stress to the patient, which to the onlooker often does not appear to have any reasonable or logical basis to it. The psychiatrist, like his native counterpart, is skilled in responding to subliminal, subtle, interpersonal cues and pressures and therefore much of his attention focuses on some of these same processes.

Attitudes in Treatment

Attitudes toward the mentally ill vary with beliefs, economics, resources, and other factors. In some places, the sick blend into the setting as wandering beggars; whereas, elsewhere, they are thought to be divinely appointed and are chosen as medicine men. By viewing psychiatric symptoms as evidence of spiritual tests and special psychic powers, Puerto Rican spiritualists make acceptable such symptoms as hallucinations and delusions. Schizophrenics can often be reintegrated into the community by becoming mediums, their hallucinations serving as a source of prestige. While psychotic patients were once clearly believed to require hospitalization, recent shifts in attitudes toward custodial care have increasingly led in the advanced Western world, to a more tolerant humanitarian approach—

and a recognition of **the value of community care** for schizophrenic patients.

Inadequate, crowded asylums still exist in the modern world and many psychiatrists still view the chronic regressed psychotic as incurable and as insensitive to the horrors of their environment, an attitude not far removed from those communities where insanity is viewed as an indication of bewitchment, and where the sufferer may be cruelly punished to protect the community from the evil within him. The mentally ill (believed to be possessed by frightening evil spirits) were often buried alive in Fiji and New Hebrides, while victims of witchcraft among the Bengala of the Belgian Congo were put to death to destroy the magic in them.

What then of culture-bound relationships and attitudes toward the mentally ill? Where techniques exist for treating the mentally ill, they appear to be meaningfully related to etiological theories and other beliefs and practices. In most societies, these concepts are in fact logically related to the medical techniques used. Where sorcery is suspected, counter-sorcery is used, or elaborate witch hunts are conducted until the culprit is found. Where harmful objects are believed to have entered the body, extraction of the supposed object by sleight-of-hand or **ritualistic exorcism** is attempted. To propitiate, exercise, or coerce unwanted spirits possessing the sick, various cultures have used prayer, sacrifice, fumigation, starvation, heat, frightening, bloodletting, catharsis, and scapegoats. To recover lost souls confession, expiation and purification of the sinner, as well as counter-sorcery and threats against the sorcerer, have been used.

Confessing one's sins to a religiously sanctioned healer or a socially accredited group, provides an emotional catharsis and a reduction of guilt and anxiety for those who have been punished with sickness. The psychotherapeutic search for the patient's errors and the encouragement to work through problems provide a treatment technique consonant with our value system—one which places great weight on autonomy, self-reliance, and individual responsibility. There is, in fact, a large confessional element to psychotherapy. Both the psychiatrist and the patient often believe that the patient must have done something wrong to bring about his emotional difficulties. This does not hold for most traditional cultures, where notions of individual responsibility rarely obtain—the emphasis there being placed on outside forces. Even where taboo violation is considered the cause, few believe that the origin of the difficulty is within the person.

The burden of treatment in Western psychotherapy falls on the patient for **working through his problem.** Treatment failures are often explained by the notion that the patient was not motivated enough or lacked initiative. This relates to the notion of the perfectibility of man and the belief that the patient *can* better himself. For we believe it is our destiny to master the environment.

This attitude contrasts with other cultures. The Mexican curandero, for example, may attribute problems to the fact that the patient was trying too hard, overextended himself, and aroused the envy of his neighbors. The curandero believes that one should not presume on the natural order, but should fatalistically accept things as they are. For him, assertiveness beyond the social norms may lead to problems, while Western psychiatrists have the notion that failure to be self-assertive may really be what leads to problems.

Thus we place great demands on the patient and discourage passivity.

General cultural values also influence the treatment process. *Privacy*, for example, is sanctified in contemporary Western medical practice. Many believe that the value of therapy is dissipated if the psychiatrist answers a telephone call while seeing a patient. In India, on the other hand, the doctor who sees the patient alone is suspect since it is customary to treat patients publicly. In traditional societies, **the group** assumes responsibility for the patient's illness and may insist on sharing decision-making functions with the doctor. Even though religion plays a major role in prescientific psychiatry, the values of scientific obpectivity and the assessment of "psychological facts" are emphasized in Western psychotherapy.

While the goal of pre-scientific psychiatry is primarily **reintegration of the patient into the community** and reaffirmation of the values of the group, **Western psychotherapy concerns itself with the growth and development of the individual and his liberation as a person.** Much as change is viewed as a measure of progress in society at large, so too is it viewed as a value in Western psychiatry.

In most societies, treatment procedures are governed by particular rules and follow **prescribed patterns** comprising the relationships among the healer, the patient, and the group. In the cultural context, the mysteries of illness and healing procedures are rationalized and made understandable, and thus less frightening. The accuracy of diagnosis and the efficacy of the treatment count less here than does the simple fact that anxiety, fear, and doubt, all of which may contribute to an illness by complicating symptoms and reactions, are dispelled.

In their place are substituted the prospect of help and a sense of hope that may contribute directly to the patient's improvement.

Such basic features of all modes of psychological treatment may be more important than the features that differentiate them. The healer in all instances can exert a tremendous amount of **personal influence** and arouse a multitude of emotions in the patient, as well as in the group, during a healing situation. In addition, the healer's ability in most instances to use the beliefs and ideas of the group as a fulcrum for influencing treatment increases the chances for successful reintegration of the patient into the community.

Thus the use of influence to arouse emotion may have therapeutic value. As Ackerknect has written, "The therapeutic achievements of the psychogenetic movement do not necessarily depend upon real etiological knowledge of causal treatment .... It is quite possible that the therapeutic successes are essentially due to the same two basic mechanisms of confession and suggestion which are so little understood and which had been used with such success by the medicine man." (1)

Participation as Therapy

Participation in religiously sanctioned cults whose ceremonies are designed to purge evil spirits and cause possession by a deity, is generally useful in promoting therapeutic emotional reactions through "psychodramatic" opportunities to express inhibited impulses and desires. Often cult members themselves have suffered from mental illness and attain high status from their cult roles and their ability to become possessed. One such cult in Nigeria is the Sopone possession cult. The members are Yoruba women who have previously suffered from mental illness. Possession by their particular spirits during the annual festival is believed to be prophylactic for the members and to ward off illness throughout the rest of the year.

Along these same lines increasing recognition has been given in recent years in Western psychiatry to the value of community support systems, group therapy, patient clubs and other social forms of therapy. Psychiatrists are also increasingly recognizing the value of self-help groups such as Alcoholics Anonymous, Gamblers Anonymous and the newly emerging rehabilitation programs, all of which have been organized and led by individuals who themselves had mastered particular problems. The growth of the encounter or sensitivity movement may reflect recognition of the failure of current methods to really reach people because of the too great impersonality of therapists; it also may reflect a search for charismatic experiences less available in modern life.

Psychotherapy lacks emotion-arousing techniques, placing too much emphasis on cognitive changes and intellectual comprehension. On the other hand as in primitive psychotherapy, it contains many non-specific factors which increase the patient's involvement: the use of powerful symbols, and unconventional style of communication, review of emotionally charged issues which increase anxiety and the patient's amenability to the therapist. Various elements of Western psychiatry appear to have an underlying culture-specific foundation and as such may not be necessarily crucial to the efficacy of the therapeutic process.

The family need not be excluded or viewed as potentially detrimental to the effect of treatment—they may prove very supportive and helpful especially if they are given some role in treatment. Religious values and practices need not be anathema to the development of a reasoning objective ego, capable of coping with reality. Religious activity may supplement psychotherapy and may also provide some philosophical framework for coping with the vagaries and uncertainties of life experiences.

The Therapist's Influence

Much of the therapist's influence derives from his credentials, procedures, and special scientific jargon—which may have more impact on treatment because of their general symbolic value than his scientifically valid interpretations. The use of insight and self-understanding similarly may be less significant because of their accuracy than for their shock value in jolting the patient into restructuring his values and his behavior.

Impressive clinics, elaborate equipment and highly trained psychiatrists satisfy passive, dependent, and magical expectations. They provide a socially sanctioned source of power and a time-honored technique that can arouse the hope of help and increase the patient's suggestibility. The connection of treatment with dominant values, by enlisting the support of the community, further reinforces the patient's faith in the treatment.

On the basis of much observation and training, psychiatrists have developed a theory of disease causation, along with special techniques for diagnosis and treatment. Categories of psychiatric illness conform to clinically recognizable syndromes recognizable in many instances by laymen as outside acceptable cultural norms.

Indeed the psychiatrist like his prescientific counterpart is trained and prepared to tolerate a wider range of human behavior patterns than those in his culture. In addition what he considers to be within his province of study is also reflective of cultural values, a case in point being the question of whether psychopathic behavior, alcoholism, drug abuse and the like constitute mental illness or simply had conduct. Like laymen, psychiatrists often believe that depressive reactions are caused by frustration, a weak brain, or excessive intellectual effort.

Diagnosis is most often made in terms of the patient's conforming with a recognized marginal model of behavior, and not simply in terms of deviation from the norm. When behavior does not fit any psychiatric "thought model," it is often looked upon as criminal, not insane. This applies to such conditions as alcoholism, drug abuse and psychopathy. About all of these, much confusion exists regarding whether or not they constitute psychiatric illnesses.

Diagnosis

Elaborate psychological testing lends an air of scientific credibility to the psychiatrist's diagnostic procedures, but may for many serve the same symbolic functions as devination by water-gazing, automatic handwriting, or card-reading used to distinguish supernatural from natural illnesses by Voodoo priests in Haiti—before treatment begins. To continue the analogy, detailed histories are also obtained by these Voodoo priests to ascertain whether the patient has offended someone or has violated a taboo. Frequently, such a "diagnostic interview" is sufficient to induce the patient's recovery probably as a result of the support and reassurance he derives from describing his difficulties to an interested listener. Whereas a native healer goes through the same steps to determine whether someone had a motive, for perpetrating sorcery out of revenge or whether he was being punished by an angry deity for his transgressions, the modern psychiatrist looks for evidence of interpersonal conflict in his patient or for what amounts to a guilty conscience from norm violation.

Difficult Cases

Frequently the psychiatrist suggests more elaborate treatment when his initial efforts fail, just as Voodoo priests might utilize more elaborate magical maneuvers or sacrifices in the same situation. If all methods fail the psychiatrist's patient may be admitted to hospital for further observation and treatment. While the psychiatrist cannot utilize religious ceremonials and community participation available to the native healer, he does provide patients with a variety of group situations in a highly structured setting and rewards "good" behavior with passes and privileges.

Group Therapy

Group therapy, like native cults, provides a form of social integration for emotionally isolated individuals, by supplying a universal theme, a structured world view, and methods of attaining mental health (grace) that are independent of special personal qualities, save a willingness to have *faith* in the efficacy of the method. In the groups treatment is directed toward physical ills, emotional problems, and social difficulties. While some individuals attend meetings for symptomatic relief, others develop a desire to change their life style; personality and attitudes may be altered in response to the group's values. Meetings are often very emotion-charged with an emphasis on the reiteration of certain group principles of mental health (insights), soul searching, and audience participation.

The group leader, like the Pentecostal minister, Voodoo priest or other group authority figure, often emphasizes the bad habits of the patient and **the value of emotional expression** to reach a state of mental peace. He relies on much anecdotal material, the repetitive use of formula, and exhortation of the group to participate, to stir up what is usually a very excited atmosphere. **Audience participation** includes exclamations of fixed formulae and, more recently with the growth of the sensitivity movement, such things as nude bathing, touching and even sexual excess. The parallels with primitive cult behavior are self-evident.

All paritcipants, especially those who continue this therapy for any length of time, generally agree on the efficacy of such methods for those individuals who believe in their value, who support the conviction that the group experience is crucial for successful results; even skeptics who seek help will often find relief. Obtaining medical help with successful results is thought to confirm **the efficacy of the group's values** and **the skill of the therapist.** Treatment occurs in a highly emotional and supportive setting and is inextricably intertwined with the themes of personal growth and freedom.

Having seen or heard of the treatment method in previous meetings, individuals are likely to have faith in the leader and an expectant attitude toward positive results. As in native cults, or sects, a reduction of self-identity and awareness and a sense of merging with the group are increased by the testimonies of fellow participants in an emotionally aroused atmosphere; this seems to contribute to an increase of positive good feeling, elation, and sometimes exaltation that may contribute to the **therapeutic efficacy** of the meetings. Therapy groups differ from self-help groups such as Alcoholic's Anonymous largely in terms of the training of the therapist, the level of emotion aroused in the meetings, as well as the philosophical or psychological theory espoused.

The psychiatrist like his native counterpart provides his patient with a whole set of "ethno-psychologically suitable," congenial, and culturally recognized defenses against his idiosyncratic conflicts. The psychiatrist provides corrective emotional experience, which leads to a repatterning of idiosyncratic conflicts and defenses toward culturally conventional conflicts and ritualized symptoms. However, the psychiatrist, unlike the native healer, functions in a private, rather than a public, setting, so that the patient's improvement is not publicly acknowledged in a formal sense—which obviously would reinforce public belief in the treatment. There is of course, on an informal level, a patient referral network, as well as opportunities to publicize the results of treatment through publication of personal accounts.

"Magic," Faith and . . . Healing

In conclusion it may be noted that one should not minimize the role of emotional excitation in psychotherapy. Although the psychiatrist does not utilize Voodoo drums, group dances, animal sacrifices and the like, he does *facilitate change* and he does *reduce resistance* and *increase acceptance* of new points of view by establishing a different kind of one-sided relationship with the patient, adopting a special scientific or objective posture, and encouraging the patient to focus on emotion-laden issues.

In most instances the patient's favorable expectations are reinforced by the treatment, setting, and the techniques used, as well as by the psychiatrist's faith in the patient's *capacity to respond* to treatment. At times the psychiatrist's initial pessimism introduces ambiguity into the situation and increases the suggestibility and anxiety of the patient promoting his desire to please the psychiatrist. The connection of patient treatment with dominant culture values further reinforces his faith in the therapy and his expectation of relief.

Like the native healer, the psychiatrist acting as a cultural or *group mediator* genuinely cares about the welfare of the patient and is committed to producing a desirable change in him. By virtue of ascendancy of role and status, as well as the ability to inspire the sufferer's expectation of relief, he can exert pressures on the sufferer. By impressing the sufferer with the importance of a particular procedure, through the use of symbols, a knowledgeable manner, and a systematic approach, he can increase the expectation of relief even further, thereby enhancing the probability of success.

REFERENCE AND FOOTNOTE

1 Ackerknert: *A Short History of Psychiatry.* New York, Hafner, 1959, p. 84.

CHAPTER 18

PRIMITIVE PSYCHOTHERAPY

WOLFGANG LEDERER

ENSCONCED IN THE SAFETY of our own doctrine, and cradled by some therapeutic success, we psychotherapists tend to conclude that our particular theoretical concepts are the cause of and explain our therapeutic effectiveness. We are confirmed in this belief because we associate primarily with members of our own school of thought. It is the purpose of this paper to go far afield to consider certain strange therapeutic methods, and to draw some tentative conclusions as to those basic elements which make psychotherapy effective.

A Case of Sixteenth Century Psychotherapy

The first case is reported in "The Confessions of Jeanne Fery," by Pierre Debongnie. (1)

> In the year of grace 1584, on the tenth day of April, there was presented to Monseigneur the most Illustrious and most Reverent Archbishop of Cambray, Loys de Berlaymont, by Monsieur François Buisseret, Doctor of Laws, Archdeacon of Cambray, and Official to the aforesaid most Illustrious Lord, one Soeur Jeanne Fery, aged twenty years, a native of Solre-sur-Sambre, a professed religious of the convent of the Black Sisters of the town of Mons in Hainaut, in the aforesaid diocese of Cambray; it having been found that she was proved to be troubled and possessed by evil spirits. To the end that it might please the aforesaid Lord Archbishop to recognize the fact and to advise suitable means for her deliverance [p. 223].

Parenthetically, it should be said that while the Archbishop did indeed recognize Jeanne as being possessed by devils, and treated her accordingly, and while the account that follows is couched largely in the language of the exorcists, it is nevertheless true that many persons, even at that time, felt Soeur Jeanne to be insane, and modern Catholic authorities tend to agree with this opinion.

Jeanne Fery was born in 1559 at Solre—sur-Sambre, a small village

---

† Reprinted by special permission of the William Alanson White Psychiatric Foundation, Inc. PSYCHIATRY: Journal for the Study of Interpersonal Processes, August 1959, Volume 22, Number 3, pp. 255-265.
(Copyright 1959 by the William Alanson White Psychiatric Foundation, Inc.)

near Mons. Her childhood was unhappy, for her father was a violent man who drank to excess. Jeanne herself was "gifted with very quick understanding and a good mind" and she had "a tendency to hear and gladly to treat of great and high matters."

One day her father, returning from the tavern at 6 o'clock in the evening, "met his wife who had come out to seek him with her child in her arms and being angry with her, he wished that the Devil might take the child. In virtue of this, the Devil had power to beset and hover about the aforesaid child until she reached the age of four, when he tried to gain her consent to his being accepted and acknowledged as her father" (p. 225). He presented himself to the child as a handsome young man, gave her apples and white bread, with which she was pleased, and, as she later wrote: "Since then I regarded him as my father by reason of the sweet things he brought me; and he spoke to me in the same way until I reached the age of 12 years; and he protected me, so that I did not feel the blows that were given to me" (p. 226).

Jeanne was sent to a convent school, but at the age of 12 was removed to the house of a dressmaker in Mons, there to learn a trade. The devil urged her to take full advantage of her new liberty and, by her account, reminded her that:

> ... I had led the life of a child quite long enough; and I was not ignorant of the fact that I had chosen him for my father when I was a little girl, and that it therefore behooved me to obey him in all things: otherwise he would torture me in ways which he showed me: and that *each person lived in the manner he taught me, but that they would not confess as much to each other* [italics added].
> ... He would give me ... everything I could desire, if I would consent to do what he proposed. ... And as I would not freely consent, he even used great threats towards me. ... I immediately submitted to all that he could ask [p. 226].

Both the phrasing of the italicized passage and later events make it seem likely that Jeanne is here describing her struggle against masturbation—a struggle which she could permit herself to lose honorably, since she could blame her defeat on the threats and the superior power of the devil.

She was then made to sign a document with her own blood, renouncing her baptism, her Christianity, and all the ceremonies of the church:

> This pact being sealed, the paper was folded very small and I was made to swallow it with an orange, which tasted very sweet until I came to the last morsel, and that was so bitter that I scarce knew how to endure it. And since then I have always had a great detestation of the Church, an abhorrence of everything connected with it, so that since then I have sought to flee and to hide myself from her, and have used many insults against her from that time, being inspired in all things by malice and sin [p. 227].

She was in the following years frequently asked to repeat this pact, and, by way of proving her good faith, had to carry out whatever blasphemies and desecrations she could conceive of. She nevertheless re-entered the Convent of the Black Sisters of Mons at the age of 14, there to begin her novitiate. The devils became ever more tyrannical, but allowed her to act and to work modestly, like the others. In this way she aroused not the least suspicion and at 16 was permitted to take her vows and thus to become a nun.

The devils now deemed her worthy of parodying the sacraments which she had received. She did not, however, actually partake in a witches' Sabbath, an act which would have rendered her liable under the provisions of the civil law. The sacrileges she carried out and the sufferings she underwent continued to occur almost entirely within her own mind and body.

Many new devils appeared meanwhile, among them Sanguinary, who came and desired from her "not a dead sacrifice, but living, and of her own body." She wrote later:

> Hearing all this, I at length gave way to their will. Immediately, this evil spirit entered into my body, carrying with him a sharp knife, and transported me on to a table. He made me spread some white linen on the table to receive the blood which would fall from my body, and to keep it forever. When this was done, with great cries and pains he cut a piece of flesh from the outside of my body, and having soaked it in my blood, went and offered it in sacrifice to the evil spirit, Belial. He accepted it, and made me continue this painful sacrifice *for the three following days.* . . . And the wicked Sanguinary always kept the linen stained with my blood, in order that they might have a double signature from me. *They made me offer this sacrifice many times* [p. 234; italics added].

Jeanne's insistence that the flesh was cut "from the outside" of her body is puzzling: no wounds or scars were ever reported on her body, by her or by others. The rest of her account, as to the duration and the repetitive nature of the event, sounds much as if she were discussing her menarche. In the manner of the hysterical girl of today, she had apparently managed to remain ignorant of the facts of life and interpreted menstruation as another act of the devil. She may have added the term "outside" in later years, while writing her account, so as to preserve the supernatural character of the event.

Eventually the devils, changing their tactics, kept her henceforth in despair and tempted her to let them end her life. Through fear of being disgraced among men, and perhaps put to death by a court of justice, she listened to their promptings. She gave them her girdle that they might strangle her, but being unable to do so, they urged her to slit her throat. Each time she attempted to do so, an invisible presence stopped her. The devils would say: "There is some wicked woman in the place who is guarding her." The woman was later identified as Saint Mary Magdalen, through whose intervention the complete deliverance of the possessed nun was accomplished.

Meanwhile, Jeanne, drained of all energy and unable to declare the cause of her obvious ill health, was visited by a doctor, who could make nothing of the case and prescribed remedies that were of no avail. After these events her disturbance of soul may be imagined. "She felt a growing desire to know the truth about the Blessed Sacrament, but when she spoke to priests, the devils took care that, in spite of all her efforts, she did nothing but dispute." Her fears, alternating with displays of arrogance, ended by arousing the attention and suspicion of the nuns. Jeanne was now 25 years old, and these demoniacal happenings had been taking place for more than ten years in the heart of a religious community, under the vigilant eyes of her superiors and companions. It was not, however, until March, 1584, that this strange business was discovered. She was allowed to continue in the convent, and efforts were made to induce her to make peace with God. Both her health and, even more, her character deteriorated. She wrote later:

> When the last days of Lent came, I was sent into the church, where I blasphemed God and cursed my father, my mother, and the hour of my birth. I thought only of despair, or of drowning myself, if I could find the means and the strength. And all this time the devils nourished me with all those meats forbidden by the church and prevented me from following my sisters to the table, detaining me in an attic or a room in order to feed me with the food they would provide. They left my poor body without any human nourishment, and the nuns had great sympathy with me when they saw the color of my face, for I looked more dead than alive [p. 238].

Apparently Jeanne at this point was suffering from a partly depressive, partly hysterical form of anorexia.

Two days after being presented to the Archbishop, on April 12, 1584, Jeanne Fery was admitted to exorcism, and many sessions were held, with interruptions of varying length, until November 12, 1585— a period of 19 months. The interruptions were caused by renewed diabolical offenses and the relapses of the patient. The exorcism continued, however, as a result of the mysterious and frequent intercessions of Saint Mary Magdalen, and the no less direct and frequent interventions of the Archbishop. Her treatment was characterized by many dramatic events. Thus at one point the devils "as much by reason of old injuries which they had inflicted within her body as through new wounds which they made at their departure, cast forth great quantities of blood and putrid flesh." When she begged a doctor to alleviate her sufferings, and it became known how they had been inflicted, she was told that her illness was mortal and incurable. "It was expected that very soon, even within the space of three or four hours, she would die. However, through the invocation of Saint Mary Magdalen *(after the patient had passed out of her body, with her urine, twenty pieces of putrid flesh, which gave off a horrible stench)* the vehemence of her sufferings was appeased and she was back in her former state" (p, 324; italics added).

It seems clear enough that this was a menstrual discharge. One can assume that Jeanne, considering menstruation as a testimony of her pact with the devil, attempted to inhibit or conceal her flow by packing her vagina. This caused retention of the flow during one or several menses, with decay of the uterine content and presumably a concomitant infection. Thus the matter, when finally discharged, contained clots and some tissue, and may well have been putrid. Once the uterus was evacuated, the patient recovered.

At other times she endured agonies, spasms, convulsions, struggles for breath, epileptic fits, and nightly ravings. Several times she attempted suicide in a shallow stream flowing at the bottom of the convent garden, but these attempts were always thwarted by the arrival of the sisters—just in time. In May, 1585, when she was being returned from the Archbishop's house to the convent against the express wish of her holy protectress, she attacked the Archbishop and other ecclesiastics with blows and kicks delivered with such violence that they feared for their lives.

Another phenomenon—a kind of amnesia and aphasia which reduced the patient to a state of infantilism—greatly impressed the exorcist. It appeared from the start, although only fitfully. The devils reduced her for a full day and night to a state of childishness and babbling; she was unable to recognize any person except the nun who watched over her, and showed horror at everything said to her. Moreover, it rendered her for some time dumb, and she wept continually. She was afraid to renounce the devils who had taught her everything she knew, and when the devil who had been her father was to be expelled, she begged the exorcist on her knees to leave her at least this one devil so that she would not fall into imbecility. To console her for the loss of him, the exorcist promised her that *he* would be a father to her. She accepted this and renounced the devil. From that moment she was reduced to complete childishness, ignorant of all knowledge both of God and of creatures, and unable to say anything except "Père Jean" and "Belle Marie," the names of her exorcist and of her holy protectress. A little later she also spoke of "Grand Père," and on further questioning the exorcist understood that she had taken the Lord Archbishop for her grandfather. As to Saint Mary Magdalen, she requested an image of her and, when it was given to her, she began to dress it up, as a child would do, and then held it to her breast as though feeding it.

Some time later she demanded to be brought before the Archbishop and, upon his blessing her, she immediately recovered her speech and said: "Many thanks, Grand Père, you have given me back my speech." She then wished that all her members should be blessed, and when this was done she thanked the Archbishop for having given her back her head and her legs; she could now walk with ease. When questioned about past events, she answered wisely and to the point. The intervention of Saint Mary Magdalen became apparent by means of pieces of paper which, closely folded, were discovered in the patient's mouth. The first of these demanded that, in order to set free Jeanne Fery from the possession of all the devils, she was to be placed that day, "for care and nourishment, in the hands of Loys de Berlaymont, Archbishop of Cambray, in whatever place he is or will be throughout his life"; and that he was to instruct her in the praise of God and to answer for her conscience before God. She thus became the only nun to have an Archbiship for her confessor.

It is evident that Jeanne, at this point, had thoroughly grasped the secondary gains of her illness; and that she was exploiting them to the hilt.

The Archbishop was a man of benign character. When the possessed nun was presented to him, he greeted her kindly and blessed her, and thereafter had her deliverance very much at heart. His intervention was often decisive. She was now kept in his house, with another nun as her guardian. This prolonged stay of a young nun in the house of the Archbishop "could not fail to surprise people," and therefore the Archbishop decided to send her back to the convent and to fulfill his obligation by contributing to her keep. Jeanne immediately suffered a severe relapse and in an ecstatic vision of Mary Magdalen was told that her grandfather, the Archbishop, had incurred the anger of God by sending her back to the convent. She was to return to his house for a year, after which time she would be fully relieved.

The Archbishop twice tried to avoid keeping her in his house and instead sent her food and a priest to shield her from the devils. But she suffered increasing torment, and when the Archbishop visited her to convince himself of her condition, "she was immediately seized by such torment, and her whole appearance was so greatly changed by the vehemence of her sufferings, that the Lord Archbishop, fearing that she might die suddenly, was forced to lift her up from the bed" (p. 251). This event caused him to lodge her thereafter in his house, where she recovered the use of her senses, having no recollection of what had occurred. There she stayed until November 12, 1586, when she took the Archbishop's hand and said: "Today I am restored and returned to my sisters. As to my food, you are discharged of the obligation. Nevertheless, you will have charge of my conscience for the rest of my life" (p. 253).

She had that day one final vision in which Saint Mary Magdalen gave her detailed instructions as to the ceremonies of her final deliverance. During her last conflict all nuns were to pray for her and to continue praying until an hour which the patient herself would determine. They were then to assemble in her room to witness her deliverance. Her room being very small, it was decided to take Jeanne into a bigger room, "for the number and the better convenience of those who would be present." She had a final vision of Saint Mary Magdalen and of a multitude of devils filled with rage and fury. Through the intervention of the Archbishop this last agony was terminated, and her deliverance was complete. It was fittingly celebrated by an elaborate ceremony.

She was now well, and remained so for the rest of her life. Only once more did she draw attention to herself and this through the publication, without consent of the Archbishop, of a long and detailed autobiographical account of her possession. She must have felt that some doubted her sincerity, for she wrote: "Some have expressed the opinion that it was nothing but madness. I protest before God and the whole world that there was not a member of my body which was not bound and subjected to the Devil."

As mentioned before, modern opinion tends to disagree with Jeanne: it was indeed madnes of the sort that today would most likely be labeled a hysterical psychosis. The dynamic structure of her illness lies almost bare, and tempts one to discussion; but for the purpose of this paper the following points suffice.

Jeanne was suffering from a severe mental illness, and from this illness she recovered, presumably at least in part because of the treatment she received. The treatment, based on religious principles, consisted essentially of more or less daily sessions carried on over a period of 19 months. During each session Jeanne was in the presence of one or the other of her two therapists—the exorcist or the Archbishop—to each of whom she developed a strong and affectionate attachment.

This attachment had to be largely resolved before her cure was complete.

Native Psychotherapy on the Gold Coast

The next example is taken from the present-day African Gold Coast. (2)

A belief in witches is currently rampant there. They are thought to be numerous, and to fly at night to assemblies in out-of-the-way places, where they engage in cannibalism. The belief cannot be gainsaid or disproved, for it is not the real, material body of the witch that is supposed to be flying to such gatherings: it is the witch's spirit, her, or his, *Susuma* that is involved. Similarly, it is not the body of the victim that is eaten, but the victim's vital essence, his *Kla*. Although a person's *Susuma* may leave his body without ill effect, the *Kla* cannot leave without causing sickness or death. If the witches steal away a man's *Kla* and cut it up, he becomes mortally sick. If, relenting, they reassemble the parts and restore them to him, he recovers. But an already eaten or mutilated part of the *Kla*—say, its leg—cannot be restored, and the victim's leg will be lost or rendered useless.

What makes this whole matter particularly sinister is the fact that the witches exercise their mischief not on their enemies or on persons against whom they might be expected to harbor a grudge; but, on the contrary, they destroy precisely those nearest and dearest to them—the members of their own village, or their own family.

To meet the danger of witchcraft, numerous shrines have been set up in the forest country. Each one is in the charge of a practitioner of skill and renown, and amounts to a native mental hospital dealing with outpatients as well as long-term, voluntary inpatients. The patients fall into several categories. First, there are the self-confessed witches, moaning of the evil they have wrought; they are agitated and self-accusatory, much in the manner of agitated depressives. Others complain that witches have stricken them with such ills as sterility, blindness, or misadventure. Diagnostically, these are a varied group with a generally paranoid tinge and may include hysteria, psychosomatic illnesses, and, doubtless, some purely organic complaints. Perhaps the most striking of all are those terrified, anxiety-ridden people who, while protesting that they have never done any harm, yet feel themselves being converted into witches against their will. They have the feeling of impending doom so commonly seen in the prepsychotic state.

The practitioner receives all these patients, and puts them through an elaborate "intake procedure." It involves not only much ceremony and ritual, designed to strengthen the prestige of the doctor and to enhance his power of suggestion and reassurance, but also the gathering of a most detailed and searching case history, in the course of which the practitioner ruthlessly ferrets out envies, spites, rivalries, marital troubles, and kinship disputes, laying bare all secrets. Astonishing tales of guilt and misdemeanor often emerge. Then he sums up the situation as he sees it, announces who should confess and apologize and to whom, and gives out advice and reprimand. Confession, it seems, is good for the soul, on the Gold Coast as elsewhere; and some patients promptly recover and go home.

Occasionally, however, a suppliant is kept for a long stay of treatment at the forest compound. There he is given daily therapy and participates in a daily ritual. In such cases a strikingly intense relationship springs up, which the practitioner handles with great skill, referring his own influence over the suppliant back to the deity of the shrine, to whose permanent protection he is now commended.

Here are some case histories, as reported by Field:

> Kofi, a farmer, was received into a practitioner's compound for long-term treatment. When first seen by the author he was miserably thin, terrified and haggard. His malady began, he said, with sleeplessness, short intervals of unrestful sleep being filled with nightmares, during which his Susuma was drawn unwillingly away to join a band of witches. He developed daily periods of blindness and became unable to hear anything except the urging voices of the witches. He also had abdominal pains and his belly was scarred where he had made cuts to let out the evil. He consulted one leech after another and in despair even travelled to a coastal town and saw a European trained doctor, who could find nothing wrong. After a few weeks in the practitioner's compound, with daily ritual and psychotherapy, he recovered his sight and normal hearing, though he was still languid and spent, sitting about on the ground, afraid to go out of the practitioner's sight. But in his presence, he felt a sense of safety and the belief that he was to be rescued. He stayed about a year and the author saw him many times. He gradually grew fatter, lost his hunted look and gained the confidence to go out alone. At the end he was a different creature, with the normal African loquacity and sense of fun. He went home energetic and confident of his power to remain well. (3)

> Kotzo, a literate clerk and a long-term patient, said that his relatives had long been trying to destroy him and had finally decided to make him a witch. They first took away, he said, the use of his right hand, which made him a failure as a clerk. When the author first saw him, the hand was—under the practitioner's treatment—improving, though it trembled severely, especially when he talked about it. He had been to one Government Hospital where he was told that nothing was wrong with him and this had strengthened his conviction that he was indeed being destroyed by witchcraft. After a few months of native psychotherapy in the practitioner's compound, the demons were drawn out of him and he went home well. (4)

Akua, a young woman, felt herself being made against her will into a witch. An older woman came forward and confessed to be doing this. They were both brought to the shrine, where the author saw them together. The girl was skeleton thin and far too weak to walk. She had been ill for four years and had not walked for the last two, but she seemed alert and interested in the proceedings. After formal confession, the witch was purified and made to bless her victim, who was also bathed and purified. After this the girl was given a room in the practitioner's compound. Gradually she improved, put on flesh, learned to walk again and to do her own cooking. She went home quite well and happy. (5)

Unfortunately, no details are provided of the technique used by the practitioner with his long-term inpatients. But Lambo, who describes similar native treatment centers in his own Nigeria, reports a technique used with phobic patients. (6) For example, a patient with a fear of crossing ant trails—and this, in Nigeria, must be disabling indeed—is taken into therapy at one of the native centers. After elaborate ritual has produced a sort of hypnotic trance, the patient is made to do what he fears—in this instance, to cross ant trails. This Pavlovian type of deconditioning is carried out again and again, until the phobia gradually lessens and finally disappears.

A further example of primitive psychotherapy is furnished by Laubscher, who writes of the Tembu of South Africa. (7) He describes a fairly well-structured hierarchy of witch doctors, the most competent of whom are the *Isanuse*, and also a well-structured way of going insane, or *ukutwasa*. A person going *ukutwasa* hears the call of the river people, and he hurries to the river to join them, thereby to gain much secret wisdom and healing power. But the river people live beneath the waters, and thus he has little chance of surviving the experience unless his fellow tribesmen rescue him. If it is then quite clear, from his wild behavior, that he has gone *ukutwasa*, he is taken to the doctor, the *Isanuse*, and accepted into the *Isanuse's* kral, where he may stay and live with him for several years. His presence is carefully hidden from the white authorities who, if they found him, would commit him to a mental hospital. Patients so committed are clearly schizophrenic, with a florid symptomatology, and as a rule deteriorate rapidly and beyond repair.

In the kral of the *Isanuse* a patient's fate tends to be much better; he does not usually deteriorate, and he not infrequently recovers and is returned to his people. In some instances, if he is a gifted person, his *ukutwasa* state and his training by the *Isanuse* even confer upon him special healing powers, and he now becomes an *Isanuse* himself. Indeed, this seems to be the only way to achieve such status.

Laubscher gives no detailed case histories, but includes some brief family histories sent him by relatives of mental hospital patients in answer to a questionnaire. Here are some samples:

> Thank you for your letter. In reply to your questions I can say Robert's father was Ukutwasa, and so was his grandfather. There was none ever suffered from fits. There are witch-doctors in the family, who gather herbs for medicines. Therefore I request you to send him back to his people and their treatments, for we know it's Ukutwasa he has got. He was my father's assistant, as my father was a witch doctor and suffered from the same trouble, and he will also become a witch doctor *if trained* [italics added]. (8)
>
> Ukutwasa was very marked on her mother's side, but on account of being Christians, they never became successful native doctors, or at least not yet. All of them became insane because of not becoming native doctors. (9)
>
> Several of our family have been called to the river. Our elders took care of these relatives and thus kept them from harm, but we children of education are failing to follow our fathers' customs, and we have thus no means of taking care of those who become ukutwasa or are called to the river. *Yes, we have failed* [italics added]. (10)

This last exclamation of despair rings like a severe indictment of modern mental hospital methods that blunderingly interfere with well-tried native practices. Laubscher participated in this interference, even though he expressed the highest regard for the skill of the *Isanuse*. Today Lambo, himself solidly founded both in Western psychiatry and in the culture of his own Yoruba people, can freely admit that the native treatment centers apparently do a better job with functional cases, whether neurotic or psychotic, than he can accomplish with his Western methods of psychotherapy. In view of this and of the shortage of Western therapists, he apparently concentrates on treating organic cases in his mental hospital, leaving the others to the native treatment centers. (11)

In summary of these African accounts, the following points should be stressed: The patients treated according to native methods are emotionally ill, with diagnoses, in Western terms, ranging from hysteria through compulsions and psychosomatic illnesses to depressions and schizophrenia; and they are apparently helped by the psychotherapy to which they are submitted. This psychotherapy takes a good deal of time—months to years; involves daily contact of patient and doctor; and is essentially based on *magic* procedure and rationale. In the course of therapy a close relationship develops, and the patient feels safe in the presence of his doctor; eventually this relationship is resolved, and the patient is thus enabled to leave his therapist.

Zen as a Method of Psychotherapy

The final example in this series stems from the Far East—from

China and Japan, and could have taken place at any time during the past eight hundred years. No adequate case history is available, however—the only one known to me is unsatisfactory from the point of view of this paper; (12) and all authorities on the matter of Zen have agreed that it cannot be written or talked about, and have refused to do so, at least intelligibly. For Zen, a mystic technique, insists, as does all mysticism, that one has to experience it if one wishes to understand it. As in psychoanalysis, one "has to have been there" to know what it is all about.

Having had no chance to experience Zen, I am doubly unqualified to write about it; but a purely descriptive treatment of Zen can be attempted and will suffice for the present purpose. (13)

What is Zen? Not a religion in the Western sense of the word, nor a philosophy nor a way of life, it is perhaps best described as a technique toward accomplishing a certain way of life. Its goal has been simply defined: "To eat when hungry, to sleep when tired." Not too impressive a statement at first glance, but upon longer contemplation it strikes one by the economy and accuracy with which it sums up the purpose of Western psychotherapies: to free the patient of all or most of his neurotic fears and inhibitions, of his doubts and ambivalence; to let him recognize clearly what he wants in life; and to enable him to go after it.

One Zen master expressed the idea more elaborately:

> The person who dallies at the edge of a stream, wondering how best to take the plunge, testing the temperature of the water with his toes and thinking about how it will feel when he is in, soon gets into the habit of putting off the issue.
>
> The Zen disciple must walk quietly to the edge and slip into the water without further ado, without allowing himself time to conjure up fears and anxious speculations as to what it will be like, or to find elaborate reasons as to why he should not get in at once. (14)

How can this admirable goal be accomplished? The technique is derived from the mysticism of Mahayana Buddhism but so much has been discarded and modified that Zen no longer resembles its Indian origin. What is left is spare and simple, like everything about Zen. A student attaches himself to a master for a period of several years. The master, much like the psychoanalyst, does not primarily teach, explain, or give advice. Rather he presents the student with a task that permits of no rational or volitional solution. It may appear as a skill or art, such as archery or painting, flower arranging or sword fighting; or as a patently nonsensical problem that the student must contemplate. Such a problem, called a Koan, might run as follows: "A sound is made by the clapping of two hands; what sound is made by the clapping of one hand?"

Under the frequent supervision of the master, the disciple works on such a problem for several years until he eventually reaches a complete impasse; he realizes that every intellectual solution is futile; yet the problem has become so urgent that it has been compared to a ball of redhot iron stuck in his throat. He feels as futile and helpless "as a mosquito trying to sting a lump of iron." At this point of highest frustration the student may suddenly transcend himself and, at the moment of complete impasse, reach a flash of insight. "Nothing is left to you at this moment," writes a master, "but to burst out into a loud laugh." This laugh, so reminiscent of the laughter of insight in psychoanalysis, supposedly signifies that the disciple now realizes: "There was nothing in it after all." The neurotic complexity of life, particularly as it concerns the authority figure of the master, has suddenly fallen away, and he now sees life clearly and simply. The feeling of liberation, in a rigidly authoritarian culture, is most strongly experienced with regard to authority: the disciple, having treated his master with utmost deference and respect may, upon reaching his *Satori*, his insight, slap the master in the face, and walk away from him without looking back; he is now free of him. The master accepts this gladly, for he takes himself not at all seriously: Zen masters depict themselves in their paintings as grotesque, impish old men, laughing over some trifle; once life is free of fear, it is also free of seriousness and weight. One master, in answer to a reverent student, explained his condition with characteristic wit and brevity: "How wondrously supernatural, and how miraculous this: I draw water, and I carry fuel." We would say: "Now that I have been successfully analyzed, I am leading my ordinary daily life, but without fears and hesitations, without neurotic worries or neurotic ambitions."

In what way is all this relevant? Zen is indeed a method of psychotherapy. Although differently worded, the goals are not unlike those of psychoanalysis. Like analysands, the disciples are by and large gifted people: artists, businessmen, soldiers, and so on, who—far from being severely psychopathic—aim primarily to achieve a simpler and more effective mode of existence. The external situation again involves a long-term association of therapist-master with patient-disciple, and this relationship contains all the elements of resistance, transference, eventual insight, and resolution of transference, which are familiar in analysis—even though in some ways the methods are diametrically opposed. One may say that, therapeutically, Zen stands to analysis as, diagnostically, psychological testing stands to the clinical diagnostic interview. The therapeutic setting, far from encouraging freedom of expression, is most carefully and rigidly structured, and it is within this confined arena—be it now archery or painting or a Koan—that the emotional experience must be accomplished. Where analysis aims to illuminate the unconscious with the clear light of reason, calling this insight, Zen strives to eliminate the intellect, as a noxious interference, from the otherwise free flow of the unconscious. Analysis heightens awareness of self: Zen ideally eliminates self-awareness. Miraculously, the results seem to be the same.

In summary, Zen, too, involves a longterm association of therapist and patient. The patient—in Western diagnostic terms presumably a neurotic—is helped by the association, wherein a strong emotional tie is first formed and then dissolved; but the method, this time, is a mystical one.

It is now time to compare and contrast: What do all these methods have in common? How do they resemble more familiar ones, such as psychoanalysis or psychoanalytically oriented psychotherapy, and how do they differ?

First and foremost, they all work. Regardless of rationale or technique, all these methods seemingly effect real improvement in emotionally disturbed patients. And beyond that, all have certain common elements of technique, that come down to this: they all take a good deal of time—from months to years, with frequent, usually daily, contact between therapist and patient; and as a result an intense relationship springs up between the two, with fairly similar characteristics regardless of setting and place.

Major differences also appear, as to means, techniques, and basic orientation. Far from using psychodynamic theory and aiming at insight, these primitive psychotherapies use magical, religious, or mystic techniques to achieve essentially the same results. This raises the immediate questions: What makes them effective? And why?

Actually one need not go so far afield. There are enough differences among the Western psychotherapies to warrant a search for a common, effective principle. The Freudian therapist may shudder at the doings of his Jungian colleague; each of them may read with bewilderment the publications of the existential analysts; and all three groups may doubt that the phenomenologists can do psychotherapy without a dynamic theory. For that matter, one has only to hear a case presentation by a fellow therapist of the same school to realize that he, at best, works differently; and, at worst, does not know what he is doing. And yet they all get results.

They get results, that is, some of the time. And all have their failures. Admittedly, some patients refuse to improve, whatever the dynamic understanding of their therapists. As Wheelis put it, sometimes "the therapist finds that insight is not, for his patients, the edged tool that it is for him." (15) One is driven to conclude that one's dynamic understanding, however profound and scientific one may consider it, does not on the whole make its possessor a more effective therapist than are the primitives.

Admitted for argument's sake, that this be so—that, from Tokyo to Timbuktu, some persons do effective psychotherapy, whereas psychoanalytically oriented psychotherapy often does not work—then, what is the explanation? Are our psychodynamic concepts wrong, or perhaps heuristically correct, but therapeutically irrelevant? And if so, what is the therapeutic principle? In answer to such a question, this paper can only offer a working hypothesis.

In the examples cited, each of the therapists was an authority of what, in his culture, gave the most certainty, carried the most authority, promised best to relieve anxiety; thus, in a magic society, the magician or witch doctor feels himself to be competent, and is so accepted. In a religious society, the priest feels himself to be the most competent. In a mystic society, the master, and in our own rationalistic society, the scientist, feels himself to be most competent. All of these, in their own societies, feel themselves most close to and most informed of the truth—of reality—as they and their culture conceive of it. Each one is closest to what in his society is most comforting, reassuring, stable, and powerful. This not only renders the therapists able to help others, but gives them the feeling of being themselves relatively safe. They can deal with the unknown, the awe-inspiring, the frightening, because their superior competence in such matters protects them. Thus they, the therapists in each culture, can approach the patient with a minimum of anxiety of their own. I suggest that this is the common, basic therapeutic principle.

Such a hypothesis does not challenge the truth of dynamic theory. In our scientific milieu the therapist, too, must be a scientist, and only what he can observe can reassure him and reduce his anxiety. Precisely because dynamic theory corresponds to something really existing and occurring in the outside world does it reassure the therapist. But the theory, per se, is not therapeutic; nor does the validity of the theory depend on the efficacy of the therapeutic method which derives from it.

It may clarify things to approach the same point from a different direction. As a broad simplification, it can be stated that any psychological illness, on one level, represents a defense against anxiety. Primary anxiety is engendered by the underlying conflict, whatever it may be; and the primary anxiety creates certain changes of the environment, of the self, and of perception which, like an amplifying feedback, engender secondary anxiety and thus a vicious cycle of ever mounting fear and panic. Some recent evidence suggests that such a feed-back system may have a biochemical component, by way of a toxic stress-metabolite. (16) Certainly there is a social aspect. The anxious patient communicates his anxiety, and thereby creates anxiety in others; this in turn changes his social milieu, and his perception of such change justifies to him his anxiety and further increases it. The most awesome example is the patient about to suffer a psychotic break. One may see the spiral of fear within him and those who watch over him grow and accelerate within a few hours; it is plain that his fear stems not only from altered perception, but also from the fear he correctly perceives in those around him.

Such feedback of anxiety is interrupted when the patient encounters a relatively nonanxious person. Some people are naturally so—for example, the occasional nurse in a mental ward who by her very appearance exerts a calming effect on disturbed patients. Others become relatively nonanxious because they feel in possession of learned techniques to handle the patients'—and their own—anxiety; regardless of whether the techniques be magical, religious, mystic, or insightful.

In other words, the therapist is one who, rather than reflecting and thereby augmenting the patient's anxiety, absorbs it, and thus breaks the pernicious feedback.

Nor is it enough to do this once; he must do it over and over again, for months and years, in a setting which renders him more important and more competent to the patient than is anyone else. The patient must come to feel that the therapist, fully knowing and understanding him, can yet manage not to be anxious; he must be reassured that the therapist's equanimity is not mere ignorance of the danger. Fortunately, he has been culturally conditioned to trust in the therapist and his methods. If not, as with a native being treated by a Western psychotherapist, (17) therapy is likely to fail, at least until the patient acquires some confidence in his new doctor.

In our culture, things are even more complex. The dominant source of authority is reason, and the therapist is rationally oriented—or thinks he is; (18) but the patient often is not, and his chief mode of functioning may be magical, religious, or mystic.

The patient who shares his therapist's ability to be reassured by understanding is a good analytic patient and if gifted may eventually become a therapist himself—much as in other cultures the good patient becomes himself a magician, priest, or master.

The patient, however, who functions primarily on a nonrational level is not helped by specific interpretations. He may accept them compliantly and repeat them in his verbalizations, but to him they are magical tools or articles of faith, rather than fragments of insight. Any movement in therapy is not correlated with what the therapist analyzes, but springs nonspecifically from his relative lack of anxiety. Thus, in such cases, the analytic method is more closely fitted to the needs of the therapist than to those of the patient. This is not so bad, if indeed the therapist's equanimity is the chief therapeutic ingredient; but it raises the question as to the feasibility of a procedure better tailored to the patient.

Could he be more quickly, more effectively approached at the level of his own functioning? And could this be done without compromising the scientific integrity of the therapist, without leading him into a swamp of quackery? But this speculation lies outside my paper.

REFERENCES AND FOOTNOTES

1 Debongnie, Pierre: The Confessions of Jeanne Fery. In *Satan* (Compiled by Bruno de Jesus-Marie), New York, Sheed and Ward, 1951, pp. 223–261. By permission of the publishers.
2 Field, M. J.: Witchcraft as a Primitive Interpretation of Mental Disorder, *J. Mental Science* 101: 826–833, 1955.
3 *Ibid.*, p. 831.
4 *Ibid.*
5 *Ibid.*
6 Lambo, T. Adeoye: Neuropsychiatric Observations in the Western Region of Nigeria, *British Medical Journal* 2: 1388–1394, 1956.
7 Laubscher, Barend J. F.: *Sex, Custom and Psychotherapy*. London, Rutledge, 1937.
8 *Ibid.*, p. 330.
9 *Ibid.*, p. 333.
10 *Ibid.*, p. 337.
11 Lambo, *op. cit.*
12 Herrigel, Eugen: *Zen in the Art of Archery*, New York, Pantheon, 1953.
13 Watts, Alan W.: *The Spirit of Zen*, London, John Murray, 1936. Also Suzuki, Daisetz Teitaro: *Zen Buddhism*, New York, Doubleday, 1956.

14 Watts, *op. cit.,* p. 41.
15 Wheelis, Allen: The Vocational Hazards of Psycho-Analysis, *Int. J. Psychoanal. 37:* 171–184, 1956.
16 Hoffner, A. and Osmond, H.: Schizophrenia: An Autonomic Disease. In *J. Nerv. and Ment. Dis. 122:* 448–452, 1955.
17 Lambo, *op. cit.*
18 Reider, Norman: The Demonology of Modern Psychiatry, *Amer. J. Psychiatry 111:* 851–856, 1955.

CHAPTER 19

MASTERS OF METAPHYSICS

ROGER M. LAUER

Psychic counselors thrive in the United States and often serve clients who are anxious, depressed, fearful, insecure, psychotic, or suicidal. These practitioners have beeen described in such popular writings as Daniel Logan's *The Reluctant Prophet.* (1) However, they have been covered only meagerly in the mental health literature, with the best, although dated, account appearing in Steiner (1945). (2)

The following examination of psychic counselors (3) is based upon three years of participant observation in a Pacific coast and a mid-Atlantic metropolitan area—sites which yielded remarkably similar data. Interviews or observations were made of more than fifty practitioners, who primarily served white, middle-class adults. Conversations with other informants suggest that the findings presented herein may have applicability to additional client-groups and to additional locales.

As a community psychiatrist, I engaged in this research out of an interest in learning about non-professionals who advise emotionally distraught people. I was unconcerned about proving or disproving the existence of any occult phenomena. In short, my perspective during fieldwork was clinical and anthropological rather than parapsychological.

Practitioners

In this chapter, I have grouped together as "psychic counselors" those practitioners who offer occult-inspired guidance and who refer to themselves by such titles as spiritual reader, reader, spiritual advisor, psychic medium, psychic, or medium.

These people show much ideological diversity and heterogeneity. They have not independently converged regarding doctrine and lack a national organization which might stimulate and articulate common beliefs.

Some counselors emphasize magic, witchcraft, mysticism, Cabalism, mesmerism, reincarnation, theosophy, spiritualism, shamanism, gypsy lore, yoga, gnosticism, mentalism, hermetic wisdom, rosicrucianism, or other strands of the occult tradition. Some accept mystic teachings of Mexicans, Puerto Ricans, American Indians and other ethnic groups, or propound their own idiosyncratic ideas.

Although psychic counselors do not subscribe to any single, well-defined system of ideas, there are certain core concepts which they, more or less, share.

They believe that humans can show a wide range of psychic talents, either during waking consciousness or during varying degrees of trance. This claim is said to rest not just on unsubstantiated faith, but on irrefutable evidence which they or parapsychologists have gathered empirically.

The specific psychic talents which can be distinguished include the following: Clairvoyance and clairaudience—the perception of sights and sounds in ways beyond normal vision and hearing. Precognition—the foreknowledge of events. Levitation—the rising of a person or object without using physical supports. Telepathy—the communication between minds via extrasensory perception. Mediumship—the communication with "spirits" of deceased persons. Astral travel—the journeys of a human "spirit" after separation from the physical body.

Most psychic counselors view the foregoing abilities as natural (that is, normal and good, not alien or evil), although a few practitioners see them as a mark of divine favor, a god-given gift. Either way, psychic skills are supposed to be accepted with grace and used constructively.

Psychic counselors consider a highly worthwhile use of mystic talents to be the furnishing of information and suggestions for needy people. This is called giving a spiritual reading. The raw data gathered by "tuning in" to the occult may be thoughts and ideas, or may seem to come through a sensory modality. The counselor may see "spirits," symbols, naturalistic visions, or auras (colored emanations from a person which reflect his health and personality). He may hear spoken messages, music, or other sounds. He may smell foods, flowers, perfumes or chemicals. He may feel hot, cold, dry, nauseated, tired, dizzy, stiff, weak, or paralyzed.

During readings, psychic counselors may examine palms, tea leaves, cards or crystal balls; or use numerology, astrology, automatic writing, phrenology, and psychometry. Some counselors claim that these methods facilitate their psychic efforts, but that, if necessary, they could work without any such aids.

The readings themselves can focus upon the past (e.g. prior incarnations, childhood traumas), the present (e.g. current preoccupations and stresses), or the future (e.g. predictions of coming events). Clients can get advice regarding themselves, friends, relatives, any other person, or even a pet.

In my experience, about 75 per cent of psychic counselors are women. This finding may reflect the well-documented phenomena of sex-linked differences in perceiving and thinking (Witkin, et al., 1962).

Nearly all practitioners seem astute, intuitive and quick-witted; they can skillfully pick up and utilize information from clients. Frequently, they have a background in theatre or sales, and come across as articulate, dramatic, emphatic and compelling—that is, as charismatic. Believers in conventional morality, they nevertheless show much tolerance for the deviancies and transgressions of their patrons.

They are less understanding with peers. Although sometimes cordial, helpful and supportive towards one another, more commonly psychic counselors are antagonistic. They compete regarding the extent of their abilities or quarrel over points of doctrine.

To illustrate, here are the barbed comments exchanged by Ronald Fisher and Brenda Lewis at their first meeting. (4) Ronald claimed that a Catholic priest he visualized next to Brenda was her spirit guide. She replied that this was just a minor guide. The major one was White Feather, an American Indian who was very "high" in spiritual terms and who could only be perceived by an exceptional psychic. Ronald disputed the existence of White Feather, then added that Brenda had been a low-class whore in one of her prior incarnations. Such spiteful rivalry is difficult to remedy; there is no accepted large-scale organization which could act to smooth interpersonal interactions between practitioners.

Due to a vulnerability under laws relating to medical practice, fortune telling and fraud, psychic counselors may take a number of precautions. They may consult with a lawyer over the legality of their publicity, fees, promises, procedures, and recommendations. They may, with due regard for prescribed governmental procedures, build religious, educational or scientific organizations as shields around them. They may work closely with more "reputable" community personnel: chiropractors, parapsychologists, hypnotists, masseurs, physical therapists, physicians, mental health professionals, and clergymen. They may even secure training and accreditation in one of these fields. For example, some become ministers, but do not publicize this fact, do not wear religious garb, and do not work within a church. They are covert clergymen who keep ministerial credentials in reserve for possible legal troubles.

A further precaution is that psychic counselors usually state aims which are righteously idealistic: to do good, to give help, to provide useful guidance. Other likely motives often go unsaid: to gain power over clients, influencing their thoughts and behaviors; to become famous, the object of attention and respect; and to earn money.

Regarding the financial motive, some practitioners make their entire living from psychic counseling, while others get part or all of their income from outside sources. The fees charged range from nothing to more than 100 dollars per psychic consultation.

The practitioner in the following anecdote flaunted pecuniary goals, possibly because she lacked the competence and finesse of most other psychic counselors.

Case Example 1: Eva Jansen. A friend told me that Mrs. Eva Jansen, a florist in my middle-class residential neighborhood, was reputed to do spiritual counseling. I visited her shop in hopes of discussing her psychic activities, but was given little opportunity to explain my purpose. I only had time to ask if she was a "sensitive" before this sturdy, sixtyish woman took over the conversation with a long, disconnected discourse about spiritualists, theosophists, low spirits, auras, lunatics, science fiction, hypnotism, income tax, newspapermen, doctors and lawyers. Mrs. Jansen's monologue was a verbal avalanche. It had authority and conviction, but little over-all coherence; her associations were so loose as to appear psychotic.

Next, she showed me through her shop, explaining that a pile of clothes on a back table were waiting to be tailored whenever she could get around to them and that the landscapes on the wall were painted by her. In a small frame near the pictures was a Church of the Master ordination certificate, which went unmentioned.

Suddenly, she ordered me to sit in a chair, lay my palms facing upward in my lap, put my feet flat on the floor—and place 50 dollars on a table. Because of my unwillingness to pay this amount, she berated me: the sum was trifling; I had the money; the spiritual reading to be given would be well worth the cost.

A short while later, she shifted the attack to the many "bad" mediums in the city and their erroneous views on metaphysics. Mrs. Jansen felt superior to them, having secured the "true" answers during the course of progressing spiritually through four lives. Her present incarnation began in Denmark, where she was trained by Gypsies. After emigrating to the United States so as to make her fortune, she encountered many frustrations and was particularly bitter about the people who had taken advantage of her. Looking pointedly at me, she said that cheating still occurs. Clients refuse to pay for readings; some are so corrupt as to give bad checks. Sanctimoniously, she projected the image of a decent, yet poverty-stricken, woman who was constantly defrauded and victimized.

In an abrupt change of topic, she asked, "Are you psychic?" I replied that some mediums had told me so. After peering at me with narrowed eyes for a moment, she triumphantly announced that I would never become a successful medium.

Then she picked up my sweaty palm, inspected it under an enormous magnifying glass, and concluded that I was nervous. I agreed. Continuing her examination, she decided that my lifeline indicated an important occurrence of an unspecified nature at the age of 45.

Losing patience, she finally said, "No more talk without payment." And with that we parted.

Publicity

Psychic counselors make strong statements about their powers in any of a variety of media and settings—boasting of being able to solve many, if not all, personal problems. Some give business cards and propaganda to community personnel who are in a position to supply referrals. Some place ads and write articles in nationally circulated magazines and newspapers, or publish their own newsletters and journals.

On radio and television they may explain their occultist views, demonstrate their skills, and advertise their practices. One enterprising woman, immodestly billed as the Voice of Wisdom, has a daily morning radio show where she talks with people over the phone and supplies psychically-derived advice. Continually, she reminds the audience of her office hours when face-to-face guidance can be secured.

Under windshield wipers, in mailboxes and on doorsteps, some counselors place descriptive flyers with stereotyped phrasing and layout; the following illustrates the genre.

Sister Mary

—Spiritual Reader & Advisor—
Past Present Future

I will tell you just what you want to know about your friends, enemies and rivals—whether your husband, wife, sweetheart is true or false, how to gain the love of one you most desire, how to control or influence the action of anyone, even though miles away. I further guarantee and promise to make you no charge unless you find me superior to any other reader you have consulted.

I GUARANTEE SUCCESS WHERE ALL OTHER READERS FAIL

I give never failing advice upon all matters of life, such as love, courtship, marriage, divorce, business transactions of all kinds. I never fail to reunite the separated, cause speedy and happy marriages, overcome enemies, rivals, lovers' quarrels, evil habits, stumbling blocks and bad luck of all kinds . . . There is no heart so sad or home so dreary that I cannot bring sunshine into it. In fact, no matter what may be your hope, fear or ambition, I guarantee to tell it all before you utter a word to me.

COMPLETE CONSULTATION
Open from 9 a.m. to 9 p.m. Daily and Sundays
For Appointment Phone: ―――――

Occult bookshops serve a population receptive to spiritual counseling. Psychic practitioners use these stores in several ways: giving lectures on the premises; encouraging the bookshop staff to refer clients; and placing notices on the store's bulletin boards, in their directories of metaphysical services and in their newsletters.

Persons with occult interests frequently join with friends in occasional home meetings on spiritual topics, or join established organizations ranging from parapsychological societies to flying saucer (U.F.O.) clubs. Psychic counselors may make contact with the informal circles or the more structured groups: giving talks, participating in experiments, and leading study groups.

Some counselors place ads in the yellow pages of phone books under such headings as Psychic, Psychic Medium, Spiritualist, and Palmist. One metropolitan phone book, which lists only a small fraction of all the local practitioners, contains sixty separate advertisements.

Case Example 2: Mrs. Donner. "I will answer one question free"—was the enticing statement distinguishing Mrs. Donner's ad from the others in the yellow pages. I telephoned her at a time of discouragement over a personal matter, and my mournful, haltingly delivered query was, "How can I get to feeling better?" Over the background sounds of a crying infant and playing children, her quick, emphatic reply was: "Keep active and busy. Don't sit around. Associate with people; go out with the crowd, develop your interests." She seemed familiar with my problem, certain regarding the remedy, and optimistic about the eventual outcome. Furthermore, she exuded gentleness, wisdom and maturity. From a clinical viewpoint, her brief performance seemed praiseworthy and her suggestions seemed appropriate—similar to the advice I or other psychotherapists might offer a depressed patient.

After giving the answer to my question, Mrs. Donner paused and then inquired if a complete reading at a cost of five dollars was desired.

Clients

Those persons seeking help from psychic counselors do not consistently use any one term to refer to themselves, and I have chosen to call them clients.

They are male or female in roughly equal proportions. Typically, they are disturbed by what is to them a serious, immediate and pressing problem: a life crisis (e.g. marriage, birth of a child, bereavement), a personal decision (e.g. about sexual behavior, drug use, jobs, residence, or life style), or a psychological symptom (e.g. hallucinations, insomnia, anxiety). However, some seek help regarding more trivial issues, and a few are just curious about what a spiritual counselor might say.

Numerous clients are hardcore faithful ("seekers" who believe staunchly in psychic powers); others are merely sympathetic or "openminded" about the occult. An occasional person even professes skepticism, but this attitude often is only a veneer covering a desire to believe. Overall, virtually all clients define their problems or concerns as suitable for metaphysical advice. Thus they share a similar world view with psychic counselors.

Many Americans are secretive about receiving psychic counseling because of a fear of criticism. Some feel awkward about visiting a professional reader or lack access to one, and instead secure spiritual guidance from a friend or relative who is considered to be "sensitive."

Treatment

Spiritual readings may occur in homes, offices, hospitals, hotel rooms or other locales; may be given to individuals, families or groups; may take from a few minutes to a weekend; and may be given once or many times. Clinically, the readings serve three different functions.

At the beginning of a treatment session, the readings are used as evidence of psychic skills—to provoke faith, trust and confidence. The counselor brags about and demonstrates his ability to provide accurate information about clients.

Next, readings are used to define a client's problem: his stresses, concerns and symptoms. The source of the difficulty might be said to involve childhood traumas, interpersonal tensions and other factors familiar to mental health professionals, or on the other hand, might involve possession, karma and other spiritual elements. For example, hallucinations and strange perceptions are often explained as an early sign of the development of psychic abilities. Clients seem to get comfort from the labeling and exploitation of ailments. Specifying the problem makes it understandable, commonplace and less upsetting; here diagnosis acts as psychological treatment.

Thirdly, readings are used for direct suggestions, which are often homiletic or platitudinous: take the good with the bad, keep trying, get a grip on yourself, keep smiling, look within yourself for strength and wisdom. In these suggestions, the counselor's warm, concerned, optimistic, confident, sympathetic attitude is probably as important for treatment as is his explicit message.

In addition to giving readings, spiritual counselors may provide any of a number of additional treatment-related services. They may attempt to cure illness by laying on hands (touch healing) or by concentrating upon someone who is not physically present (distant healing). During this procedure, a restorative power is supposedly transmitted which clients are expected to perceive as heat, electricity, or some other form of energy.

Spiritual counselors may try to minimize personal problems and promote maturity by nurturing clients' psychic skills in "self-development" classes. The emphasis is not on reading about others' experiences or indulging in overt action, but rather on introspection: describing one's own feelings, dreams, impulses and intuitions. The teacher examines, judges and interprets these experiences, translating them into acceptable metaphysical language. This language, or argot, contains both religion-based terms (demons, possession, God, angels) and science-based terms (energy, tune in, rate of vibrations).

Other unorthodox remedies that practitioners may proffer include chiropractic, naturopathic diets, message, craniopathy, color therapy, light therapy, zone therapy, polarity therapy, psychic surgery and talismans (such as lapis lazuli stones and copper bracelets).

Next are described two practitioners who offered both psychic readings and other treatment-related services.

Case Example 3: Ludmilla Kosa. Brian Kane, a full-time clinical psychologist and part-time student of the occult, had heard from friends in a parapsychological society about the psychic skills of Ludmilla Kosa. After talking with me, he called and made an appointment for us to receive "treatment."

We arrived at Mrs. Kosa's white frame house (located across the street from a suburban city hall) to find a slender, grey-haired lady, energetically sweeping leaves off the front steps. She greeted us with, "Go right in, boys, I'll be with you soon." Her living room–waiting room contained theosophic and naturopathic journals as well as Pageant magazine. At one end of the room was a worn, green curtain and beyond was a steam bath, a massage table and some esoteric apparatus. In an inconspicuous location on the wall were a healer's certificate from a metaphysical church and diplomas from a school of myopathy and a school of Swedish massage.

After carefully locking the door, Mrs. Kosa chatted with us about our interests and viewpoints, and alluded to recent troubles when a registered nurse had come for help, tape-recorded the session, and then informed the local police. With an undertone of seriousness, Mrs. Kosa asked, "Did you bring any tape recorder?" Her implication was that we, too, were potential spies and troublemakers. Even though previously a common friend had spoken well of us to her, nevertheless, we were mental health professionals and strangers, and she retained some suspicions.

However, further conversation seemed to relax her; she invited us to call her Ludmilla and began discussing her background. Born and raised in a Bulgarian village, she was trained by her mother to carry on a family tradition, going back seven generations, in psychic healing, herbalism, midwifery, necropsy, undertaking and astrology. At age 15, she came to the United States because of a desire to return to what was her home during a previous incarnation. She studied osteopathy for two years, worked as a nurse at Cook County Hospital, learned the intricacies of naturopathic diets, high colonic irrigations, and numerous other religious and health practices.

Seriously ill several times herself, she reported once being miraculously healed after having a vision of Christ perched upon a mountain top. A painting of this scene, done by Mr. Kosa from her description, hung in her bedroom, and she gave us small reproductions of it.

"Who is going to be the first victim?" she asked, explaining this was what all clients were called. Brian went first, and the curtain was drawn behind him.

When my turn came an hour and a half later, I was instructed to undress and cover myself with a towel, while Ludmilla waited in the kitchen. Tucking me into a hot, confining and altogether uncomfortable steam bath, she put cloths soaked in cool water over my head and regulated the inside temperature according to changes in my pulse. After 15 minutes of steam, she turned on a cold needle-shower and told me to wash and dry myself.

Then, Ludmilla went into a state of partial trance to give me a detailed psychic reading. According to her, I was a renegade in temperament and had an appropriate spirit guide—a fierce Viking visible next to me. In one of my 22 prior incarnations I had been a Turkish doctor who was strangled for political reasons. She also made numerological computations with my birth date and explained the meaning of the colors seen in my aura.

After oiling my body, rubbing it vigorously with her hands and with an electrical massager, she went on to wash my feet so as to spiritually cleanse the Christ within me. To invoke the proper reverence during this procedure, she played hymns (including *Alone in the Garden,* and *I Believe in Miracles*) on the phonograph in her kitchen. Since resentments were supposedly interfering with my medical work, she kneaded my belly to extract these negative feelings and then washed them from her own hands.

Ludmilla instructed me on how to gather energy to do healings: look at the sun in the morning for a brief instant and then imagine it deep within the abdomen. At the end of the day, turn off the power by moving the arms upward and closing oneself in the name of God. She predicted that, by following this advice, I would be extremely successful as a healer and physician.

Next, she moved my neck to and fro and then suddenly and forcefully twisted it—producing a fearful, cracking sound, like that of a bone breaking. During my recovery from this procedure, she hung my slipper-enclosed feet onto a vibrating machine for what was reputedly an improved (that is, less painful) form of zone therapy.

Quickly following this was craniopathy. She pressed hard against my skull to "take up the slack," and then moved her hands rhythmically back and forth to induce "pulsations"—a well-known treatment which had been formulated twenty years earlier by a chiropractor. This man was now numbered among Ludmilla's spirit guides, and according to her had explained the technique from the beyond. The guiding principle was as follows. Although autopsies have demonstrated that cranial bones are fused, before death these bones are mobile. Manipulating them can reduce pressure that otherwise might accumulate and cause illness. To enlarge my own medical skills, Ludmilla showed me how to perform craniopathy, and I practiced upon her. After a concluding alcohol rubdown, I got dressed.

Ludmilla told Brian and me that we were both basically healthy, with rosy futures ahead of us, and then said that her fee would be eight dollars. We each gave ten, with Brian complimenting her that the session was well worth the cost.

Later Brian told me that Ludmilla's treatment was superb and her psychic powers were unquestionable. Personally, I was less enthusiastic. Although the spiritual reading was enjoyable and perhaps even enlightening, I disliked some of the physical procedures. A few hours after my treatment, I felt tired and dizzy (probably from salt and water depletion in the steam bath), and had a stiff neck and an aching head—thanks, no doubt, to the manipulations!

Case Example 4: Dave Johnson. Since I have described Dave Johnson's treatment methods in detail (Lauer, 1972), only some highlights will be presented here.

In terms of astuteness and sensitivity, Dave was one of the most outstanding psychics I encountered. He was a short, handsome 45-year-old man who radiated power and certainty. Trained in the occult by Spiritualists, Dave claimed to have secured a deceased, local psychiatrist as a spirit guide—with whose help he could root out people's emotional problems. In addition, he offered to assist people in developing their own mediumistic skills, and was particularly interested in training mental health professionals.

I met Dave through a mutual acquaintance and was a participant observer when he formed a psychic development class for a group of 6 psychotherapists. His stated rationale for such an activity was this:

> Every human being has psychic abilities. Most withdraw from exercising or even recognizing this capacity because it is not "scientific" and because psychic awareness is too stressful. Properly trained, however, psychic ability can be controlled 'til it contributes remarkably to a person's growth . . . . (This class will be for those) professionals who suspect that there is more to "intuition" than subliminal cues.

The class cost 100 dollars per person and lasted for ten consecutive weeks. Pupils discussed Dave's concepts, used his vocabulary and practiced his methods—gaining facility in mediumship and becoming his partisans. Classwork ended in a clearly marked way with a formal graduation ceremony, following which the group went on to receive "psychic therapy." This treatment phase then lasted for an additional ten mornings, and no further fee was levied.

In "psychic therapy," Dave explored our individual backgrounds, explaining how our parents had hurt and warped us. He wanted to expose childhood traumas that were causing present-day psychological difficulties, or in his word to "overcome negative reflex actions."

This goal, of course, was congenial to the assembled psychotherapists.

In his probes, Dave pointed out conflicts, resistances, defenses, and transferences. He used mediumship as well as techniques reminiscent of Freudian analysis, transactional analysis, psychodrama, guided affective imagery, role playing, gestalt therapy, and poetry therapy.

Initially the group members resisted Dave's promptings, but eventually gave in and discussed unhappy memories about their parents. They went on to rail at their mothers and fathers for cruelties, then forgave them . . . and finally accepted them as blameless.

I thought that Dave's treatment had some merit and that it undoubtedly heightened my awareness of certain childhood events. The other group members reported that the "psychic therapy" helped them to achieve greater comfort and peace of mind. They were so favorably impressed that they began referring clients to Dave and used some of his procedures in their own professional practices.

The teacher, too, was pleased with the group. Dave earned money and gained experience in dealing with psychologically sophisticated clients. He built a channel to local mental health professionals by which he spread his ideas and secured referrals. And, lastly, he enhanced his standing with clients by his work as a teacher and treater of therapists. He often would tell people about his work with professional psychotherapists, and used the following statements to advertise one of his public lectures.

> Mr. Dave Johnson is one of the few practising psychics today who combines the talent for psychic reading with developing the same abilities in others. With volunteers from the audience, he will prove that "everyone is psychic."
>
> His sensible down to earth approach, is a refreshing quality, proven very effective in his development classes. By showing people how to overcome their mental blocks, he has aided them to attain inner peace and self-acceptance.
>
> Currently, Mr. Johnson is working with a group of psychiatrists, clinical psychologists, psychiatric social workers and M.D.'s, helping them develop their own clairvoyant and clairaudient faculties. Several psychiatrists, recognizing Mr. Johnson's unique talent, use his services as an adjunct to their own therapeutic techniques. The results have been both gratifying and dramatic.

Psychics and Psychotherapists

Spiritual counselors have certain unacknowledged similarities to mental health professions. Both practitioners offer emotionally distraught clients aid which is based upon esoteric, elaborate metaphysical ideas concerning the causes and remedies of intrapsychic suffering. The concepts of the two fields sometimes even overlap: for example, one mystic defines "spirit" as being the same thing as "ego." In addition, a basic technique which both practitioners use is suggestion. They aim it at changing attitudes and behaviors and give it in a warm, confident, hopeful and earnest manner.

Although a complete census of spiritual counselors in a locality is nearly impossible, such persons, in my experience, seem at least as numerous as professional psychotherapists. Skills and motives vary among the two kinds of practitioners, and among the ranks of either may be found sages, businessmen, missionaries and quacks. From my observations, the results of spiritual counselors seem able to stand comparison with those of psychotherapists. Sometimes, spiritual counselors may bring no benefit or may even cause harm. But frequently they bring quick improvement to emotionally disturbed people, as judged by outside observers as well as by clients themselves.

In short, psychic counselors are commonly found community practitioners who seem to provide psychologically disturbed clients with an oft-times useful service which parallels psychotherapy.

Because of this fact, community mental health workers should, in my opinion, become informed about the activities of psychic counselors. This could take place either as part of education in professional schools or through in-service training. This does not mean that professionals should strive for definitive proof or disproof of these counselors' assertions regarding psychic phenomena, for the metaphysical claims are complex and perhaps impossible to evaluate at the present time. Furthermore, in examining spiritual counselors within a mental health framework, it is immaterial whether their claims are "true" in any scientific sense.

Since mental health personnel and psychic counselors perform similar tasks, cooperation between the two might sometimes bring mutual benefits. Neither party need necessarily accept the other's beliefs or values. The two types of practitioners might help each other with information, suggestions, encouragement and referrals. Either might act formally as consultant, teacher, supervisor or therapist with the other.

Psychic counselors potentially could furnish the community mental health effort with added manpower—rapid, inexpensive intervention techniques and access to previously unreached people. Mental health professionals, in turn, could provide technical assistance and legitimation (as in the case of Dave Johnson) to psychics.

My experience to date suggests that at times collaboration between psychics and psychotherapists may be worthwhile. In addition, there has been some precedent for this viewpoint in the mental health literature. For example, Torrey (1969) has argued the value of indigenous therapists in general and suggested their incorporation in formalized mental health services.

Nevertheless, many factors hinder the development of psychic-psychotherapist alliances—including each party's stereotype of the other as "foolish," "insensitive" or "incompetent." Further research is needed to determine the circumstances when a rapprochement may be feasible in contemporary America. To this end, interaction between the two types of practitioners should be attempted and then carefully evaluated.

Conclusion

Since psychic counselors have a powerful impact on many emotionally disturbed persons, they must be considered important mental health agents. They are persuasive, influential folk-therapists whose activities warrant inquiry by mental health professionals. These counselors seem to provide certain constructive services. And to the extent that they do so, psychic counselors deserve respect and support.

REFERENCES AND FOOTNOTES

1 Logan, Daniel: *The Reluctant Prophet.* New York, Doubleday, 1968.
2 Steiner, Lee: *Where Do People Take Their Troubles?* Boston, Houghton-Mifflin, 1945.
  Author and date in the text of this study indicate the monograph, article, or book referred to (usually in parentheses). Consult the Bibliography at the end of the chapter.
3 This work was begun in 1969 under the auspices of the Langley Porter Community Mental Health Training Program, and the assistance of Dr. Joan Ablon and Dr. M. Robert Harris is gratefully acknowledged. I also appreciate the useful suggestions of Drs. John Hartley, Fred Ilfeld, Dee Lloyd, Ann Maney, Fortune Mannino, Milton Shore and of other staff members of Langley Porter Institute and the National Institute of Mental Health.
  This report does not necessarily reflect the opinions of any of the foregoing individuals, nor the official policy or position of the foregoing institutions.
4 All names have been changed and identities have been disguised.

BIBLIOGRAPHY

1. Lauer, Roger: A Medium for Mental Health. From *Pragmatic Religions: Contemporary Religious Movements in America* (ed. by I. Zaretsky and M. Leone). Princeton, Princeton University Press, 1972.
2. Logan, Daniel: *The Reluctant Prophet.* New York, Doubleday & Co., 1968.
3. Steiner, Lee: *Where Do People Take Their Troubles?* Boston, Houghton-Mifflin, 1945.
4. Torrey, E. F.: The Case for the Indigenous Therapist. *Archives of General Psychiatry*, vol. 20, pp. 365–373, March 1969.
5. Witkin (H. A.), Dyk (R. B.), Faterson (H. F.), Goodenough (D. R.) and Karp (S. A.): *Psychological Differentiation: Studies of Development.* New York, John Wiley & Sons, 1962.

CHAPTER 20

GESTALT, BIOENERGETICS, AND ENCOUNTER: NEW WINE WITHOUT WINESKINS

JOSEPH HAVENS

THE TRUTH THAT SHATTERS

IN THE FIRST SUNBURST of any new religion its initiates are led into a personal experience of shattering Truth. Their habitual ways of knowing are broken open, and a New Self takes shape. The old rubrics no longer work; new and unimagined experiences must be assimilated and affirmed. The world is transformed. Fresh categories of understanding, new modes of living must come into being to contain and to nourish this new man.

We live in an age when "the Truth that shatters" is more likely to originate outside an explicitly religious setting than within one. The "new therapies" of Gestalt, Bioenergetics and Encounter have demonstrated their shattering and transforming power. Yet any lasting system of human transformation—the great religions are the best exemplifications—must find its meaning and its rationale in a total cosmic vision. This vision must not only make sense of the universe; it must contain or be set in a time-line of history and tradition, and it must provide an image of the stages of spiritual growth through which the disciple passes. Our task, our basic theme in this paper is to appreciate fully the "new wine" of the therapies we have mentioned, but to insist on their need for "wineskins."

Experiences of "the truth that shatters" can be found in firsthand personal accounts from almost any religion, especially its early phases. In Christianity we know it, for instance, in the agonies and ecstacies of the earliest Resurrection faith, in the Desert Fathers, in the Franciscans, in the Lutherans' discovery of salvation-by-faith, in the Spiritual enthusiasms of the English Reformation, in the Great American Revivals, and in our own time in the rediscovery of

Pentacostal religion. In this paper we shall draw upon the spiritual tradition of the English Reformation, especially that of seventeenth century Quakers.

We begin with an experiential parallel. My thesis is that the partial shattering of my existing self-image in the following encounter is comparable to the "searchings" and "openings" brought about by the Spirit or the Inward Christ among Reformation Christians.

The incident took place in an encounter group of members of a professional staff. The session had been slow-moving and I found it difficult to get in touch with what I was feeling. Finally a younger staff member and I began to argue about whether the session was getting anywhere. He was the person I liked least in the group. I had felt threatened by him in the past because of his great facility with words and his self-congratulating bravado. Finally, the leader became exasperated, asked us to stand at opposite ends of the room and walk toward each other, doing whatever we felt like when we met. He was particularly insistent on our not planning ahead of time nor controlling at the moment what our actions would be. I remember a kind of fear/excitement in hearing the strong authoritative voice with which he said this. Usually quite controlled, I tried to let happen in accordance with his directive. My antagonist was infuriatingly passive: we stood facing each other for a long time, while I made several gestures trying to evoke a response. Finally, I put my hands on his shoulders, and he followed suit. But when I began to push, he gave only hints of resistance, as if he were teasing. Suddenly I began to shove with all my might, slamming and pinning him against the wall with great force. All of us were stunned; I more than anyone.

It was only as I lay in bed that night that I became aware of how much I *enjoyed* the whole episode. It was not a competitive game I liked, but the deep pleasure of hurting a person I must have hated. I felt again a kind of lust for this uninhibited attacking. Such behavior was at a sharp variance with my picture of myself as a considerate, controlled person. Apparently the *permission* of the leader allowed what was buried in me to find expression in this primitive non-verbal way. I knew theoretically that I had a clenched fist within me, but to recall the *glee* with which I lived it out in the group was a most ungleeful experience!

Not long afterwards I ran across a passage from Quaker history which seemed to echo the essence of my experience, though it was couched in a very different language. Margaret Fell, an early follower (and later wife) of George Fox, wrote:

> Now, Friends, deal plainly with yourselves, and let the Eternal Light search you . . . for this will deal plainly with you; it will rip you up, and lay you open . . . naked and bare before the Lord God, from whom you cannot hide yourselves . . . Therefore give over deceiving of your Souls; for . . . all Sin and Uncleanness the Light condemns. (1)

Both kinds of experiences are immediate, unpredictable, anxiety-producing. Both unmask the public, role-playing, self-satisfied ego and lead to a deeper knowledge and a longing for inner peace on a new level. If my encounter was truly similar to the experience of earlier Christians, then the same claim can be made for some of the self-disclosures of the new therapies of Gestalt and Bioenergetics. (2) (I do not intend by this statement to exclude all other contemporary psychotherapies or modes of personal growth.)

THE NEW THERAPIES

Gestalt (3) was born of the attempts of psychoanalysts Fritz and Laura Perls to make psychotherapy more existentialist, more experiential. My own view of it is deeply colored by my experience of it, and by my teachers. Gestalt attempts to bring to awareness experientially—i.e. in one's immediate feelings and bodily sensations—those aspects or dimensions of the self which have been blocked from consciousness. Psychoanalytic therapists also attempt to increase awareness, but they do it primarily through the mind, through the interpretative word of the analyst. Let us suppose a patient has been kept waiting three minutes for his therapy hour, but his irritation over this is only minimally expressed in the stiff silence with which he enters the room, plus a quick snide comment about, for example, "the smoke in this room." The paradigmatic psychoanalytic response (oversimplified) would focus on the irrationality of this anger: "You're pretty upset for my keeping you waiting only three minutes! Did your father keep you in suspense like this? Can you think of instances where you felt this same kind of irrational anger?" The Gestaltist, on the other hand, uses a wide variety of "games," exercises and procedures to help the patient *experience* more intensely the anger of which he may be dimly aware. He discovers, not only its irrationality, but also its aliveness and its importance in his life, the fact that it is fully a part of *him*. Thus if the patient tried to discount the irritation or pass it off as nothing, the Gestalt therapist could ask him to exaggerate his rigid back and stiff arms. As he did so, he might discover that his fist also begins to clench and his face flush. This experience, carried to its fullest expression, could spontaneously result in a change of self-perception.

Bioenergetics (4) has been developeed by Alexander Lowen and John Pierrakos. It is explicitly an outgrowth and development of the work of Wilhelm Reich, especially his work on *character armoring*. The fundamental thesis of Bioenergetics is that long-standing emotional tension and conflict become lodged in the musculature and physiological processes of the body, and they must be attacked through work on the body. Lowen and Pierrakos begin with a body diagnosis. They note the basic body structure, the stance, the distribution of weight, the position of the head, any asymmetries and abnormalities. They pay considerable attention to breathing patterns, and to facial expression and appearance of the eyes. The therapeutic work focuses essentially on breathing and strengthening exercises, and on emotionally cathartic actions—e.g., pounding the bed using the whole upper body; raising one's arms and hands high and crying 'Mama'. These frequently evoke hitherto unexpressed feelings—crying, deep laughter, fury, cringing fear or sexual excitement. Though the Bioenergetic therapists talk some with their patients, the main work is physical and cathartic. Insight flows from the experiencing of new feelings or sensations in oneself, rather than from the mind of either the therapist or the patient.

Encounter (5) therapy is perhaps better known. Unfortunately, being "in" right now, its abuse is as widespread as its responsible and creative use. Eschewing the psycho-analytic emphasis on past events and psychodynamic analysis, Encounter therapists claim that growth comes through experiencing new modes of being and relating in a situation close to the patient's reality one. He is encouraged to express his feelings to his peers in the group, and to receive their honest response to him. Studies suggest that these feelings move *from* those having to do with, Do I belong here? And Who is in charge?, *to* tenderness and sexual feelings and anxieties about intimacy. Here again, the growth occurs not through "understanding oneself" in any intellectual sense, but in discovering what feelings one has, how one comes across to others, and in trying out new modes of reacting to others.

BEYOND THE ANALYTIC MIND

For me these experiential therapies have revealed my inner self more powerfully than earlier analytic, interpretative therapies. This cutting beneath the thinking mind to immediate emotional reality is an important common factor in the work of the Inward Christ and the new therapies. Here is the report of Stephen Crisp, a Quaker of the seventeenth century:

> Here at the very first of my Convincement [his conversion to Friends] . . . my Wisdom and Reason was overcome by the Truth . . . therefore I received the Truth . . . and defended it with the same Wisdom by which I had resisted it, and so was yet a stranger to the Cross which was to Crucifie me. . . . In this state I continued a Month or two, but then a swift sword was drawn against that Wisdom and comprehending mind . . . . Then . . . Woe, Misery and Calamity . . . opened upon me . . . . I am poor and blind and naked who thought I had been rich and well Adorned . . . . After long Travel. . . and many bitter Tears . . . I waited as one that had hope that God would be Gracious to me. (6)

The experience of the comprehending Mind being shaken by Truth which brings "woe, misery and calamity" was dramatized in a small way for me in the following incident.

During a Bioenergetic session I was lying on a mat after an exhausting work-out over a stool which stretches the abdominal wall and brings about deep heavy breathing. My wife, who has had some training in this work, was encouraging me to continue breathing deeply and allow to come up whatever sounds and facial expressions were pressing for expression. I writhed and moaned for a while. Then gradually I felt my lip curl, and I began to experience in my face a sneer, an expression of utter disgust. It was most unpleasant, and seemed to arise from somewhere deep inside me. I wanted to hide from my wife; I tried to dismiss it all as a temporary mood or as something I had dreamed up to make something happen. No go; I had to admit that somewhere in me lived a demon of nauseous sneering superiority. I was reminded of those "natures of dogs, swine, vipers, of Sodom and Egypt" which George Fox once saw in himself.

As with Stephen Crisp, the revelation of inner poverty and nakedness was not fruitless. The escape of my woeful, sneering demon meant a deepening of the love between my wife and me. Letting another experience the despair and the hatefulness in one does not alienate but brings closer, which is the human equivalent of the Psalmist's cry, "Thou has searched me and known me," yet "even there thy hand shall lead me, and thy right hand shall hold me."

The second parallel is drawn by Aldous Huxley in a letter to Barry Stevens, a student and trainee of Fritz Perls. In an earlier letter to Huxley, Stevens noted in her Gestalt practice that when she would "let go," she would experience a "writhing and moaning and shaking and jumping (hips and shoulders)." Huxley replied:

> This is a phenomenon I have observed in others and experienced in myself, and seems to be one of the ways in which the *entelechy*, or physiological intelligence, or deeper self, rids itself of the impediments which the conscious, superficial ego puts in its way . . . . Beneficent results seem to be obtained when the deeper self sets up this disturbance in the organism—a disturbance which evidently loosens many of the visceral and muscular knots, which are the results and counterparts of psychological knots. Disturbances of this kind were common among the early Friends—and led to their being called Quakers. "Quaking" is evidently a kind of somatic equivalent of confession and absolution, of recall of buried memories and abreaction to them, with dissipation of their power to go on doing harm. We should be grateful for the smallest and oddest mercies—and this quaking is evidently one of them, and by no means the smallest. (7)

Huxley's "somatic equivalents" are confined neither to Gestalt work (they are common in Bioenergetics for instance) nor to Quakerism. They were found among many sectarians of the English Reformation, and are experienced among present-day Pentacostals, Glossolalia groups, and spiritual healers. Being bodily, rather than verbal phenomena, they represent experiential parallels which bridge gulfs of philosophical interpretation.

As a summary of the connection between spiritual self-discovery and therapeutic experience I again quote Hugh Barbour, a historian of the English Reformation who is well acquainted with contemporary psychotherapy.

> . . . The most crucial truths learned by a man who opened himself to the Light are about himself or his "state"; in puritan England this meant his sins, even those the puritan pastors pronounced unavoidable and forgiven. Against such truths a man protected himself by every sort of evasive action, by piety, above all by anger and physical violence. The acceptance of the Light almost always required a lengthy period of inward struggle and grief. In physical appearance, early Quaker meetings included most of the wild behavior of revivals, and their psychological shatterings . . . . There are analogies with mental breakdown and psychotherapy, especially in the supporting role of the Quaker group for its members going through the fires . . . . the way out came unwilled and usually gradually. There was seldom a single crisis of rejecting the past, or of commitment once-for-all to Christ; rather, a daily effort to obey the Light in every leading. Early Friends thus opened themselves to any impulse they did not identify with self-will or sin. The sources of some of these impulses can be recognized by a modern Freudian, but at least the old self and self-image were broken open in the direction of new spontaneity and responsiveness to human situations . . . . The new Quaker life was characterized by steadiness as well as by joy, excitement, and unrestrained affection for fellow Friends. Worship was [a] sort of shared outpouring. . . . (8)

THE NECESSITY FOR WIDER VISION

In trepidation the new Christian tried "to obey the Light in every leading". His concern was not to release his buried potential, but to be sustained by and to become a part of a Person, a Kingdom, a Life dwarfing his weak and fallible self. He demanded to know the facts about himself *in the interest of a wider Truth* which encompassed his personal truth as the ocean the drop of water. It is this broader "frame of orientation and deviation" (Fromm) which the new therapies lack. This lack, I believe, finally truncates the transformations which they bring about.

Evidence for such a statement lies not so much in empirical measures of transformation as in the unsatisfied longings for "something more" among many who have pursued the new therapies. We shall comment further on this below.

Every great religion has its own Wider Vision. This is not the place to describe or compare these. From the standpoint of a critique of the new therapies and finding adequate "wineskins" for them, three elements are crucial. The broader framework must affirm a radical ("at root") inter-connectedness of every individual with all other individuals; it should provide, through tradition, a sense of continuity with the past and with future generations (and hence beyond one's personal death); and it will be the inspiration of a community of fellow seekers which both judges and sustains the individual. We shall try to indicate the pitfalls of the lack of mythology/cosmology, tradition and community in the new therapies, and to indicate how some of them are making the first moves in this direction.

BIOENERGETICS AND PLEASURE

Bioenergetics provides an instance of the way in which brilliant clinical insights and an unusually effective mode of treatment can be inappropriately extrapolated into a total philosophy of life. As we have indicated, Alexander Lowen learned from Wilhelm Reich that emotional disturbance lodges itself in the musculature, shallow breathing, rigid ways of moving, etc.; and that body-oriented therapy is frequently the road to cure. Lowen was deeply impressed with the split between the body, and mind/will, and the inappropriate hegemony which the latter often established over the natural wisdom of the body. Because genuine bodily *pleasure* was the most important single indicator that the mind-body split was healed, Lowen hypothesized that pleasure was the major force bringing about the unity of the self. (9) The development of this idea led eventually to his elevating Pleasure as the central integrating value of human life:

> The domination of the personality by the ego is a diabolical perversion of the nature of man. The ego was never intended to be the master of the body, but its loyal and obedient servant. The body, as opposed to the ego, desires pleasure, not power. Bodily pleasure is the source from which all our good feelings and good thinking stem .... Pleasure is the creative force in life. It is the only force strong enough to oppose the potential destructiveness of power. Many people believe that this role belongs to love. But if love is to be more than a word, it must rest on the experience of pleasure. (10)

Creativity, love, all good feeling and thinking stem from the healthy experience of bodily pleasure. Lowen can create this Imperialism of the Physical and be highly convincing to many because it represents a powerful and necessary corrective to the sick over-valuation of logical thought and ego control in our culture. But precisely because it is a corrective, it is also Western-culture-bound. No society can sustain itself on such an individually-oriented *Weltanschauung*. Body is only a part of a larger whole which we call *person*; and each person is ultimately a part of a larger organism we call society, mankind, cosmos. (11) Given the existing fabric of society, Bioenergetics is an enormously creative and effective therapy, but extrapolated to a total philosophy of existence it fails to encompass the facts of our inter-connectedness and the necessity of our continually renewing and celebrating this wider vision.

I have not dealt here with the work of John Pierrakos, another Bioenergetic leader who in his pioneering investigations of the energy fields of the human body may be providing us with important bridges between biology and the mystical vision of the world as dynamic, interpenetrating fields of energy. (12)

GESTALT AND FULLER AWARENESS

Some Gestalt writers make explicit connections with religious systems of transformation. In a perceptive essay on the implicit philosophy underlying Gestalt (13), Claudio Naranjo deals at length with its great stress on living in the Now. An example will dramatize how far Gestaltists carry their insistence on present-centeredness:

Patient: I don't know what to say now. . . .
Therapist: I notice that you are looking away from me.
Patient: (*Giggle*)
Therapist: And now you cover up your face.
Patient: You make me feel so awful!
Therapist: And now you cover up your face with both hands.
Patient: Stop! This is unbearable!
Therapist: What do you feel now?
Patient: I feel so embarrassed! Don't look at me!

Therapist: Please stay with that embarrassment.
Patient: I have been living with it all my life! I am ashamed of everything I do! It is as if I don't even feel that I have the right to exist! (14)

In Gestalt's stress on living in the present, Naranjo explicitly recognizes the parallel with Christianity:

> When Jesus says, "Take, therefore, no thought of the morrow, for the morrow shall take thought for the things of itself," giving the example of the lilies of the fields [Matt. 6], he is not only saying, "Don't act upon catastrophic expectations," but more positively, "Trust!" While the Christian version is framed in a theistic map of the universe, and trust means trust in the heavenly Father, the attitude is the same as that regarded as the ideal in Gestalt therapy, which may be rendered as trust in one's own capacities for coping with the now as it comes.... Such attitudes bespeak two basic assumptions in the *Weltanschauung* of Gestalt therapy: things at this moment are the only way that they can be; and behold, the world is very good. (15)

Unfortunately the broadly humanistic concern found in some Gestalt writers (such as in this essay, and in some of Perls' more philosophical comments) seems to get lost in the actual work of the Gestalt session. What is more typical is a kind of radical individualism uncorrected by any wider-than-individual frame of orientation. This is perhaps best expressed in Perls' famous "Gestalt prayer":

> I do my thing, and you do your thing.
> I am not in this world to live up to your expectations
> And you are not in this world to live up to mine.
> You are you and I am I,
> And if by chance we find each other, it's beautiful.
> If not, it can't be helped.

That this is a "prayer" reveals its intent: to supplant the Jewish-Christian invocations which assert responsibility for others' lives (*You are your brother's keeper*). As a corrective to the pervasive sense of *duty* to love or to care, I welcome it. It is a fresh breeze in a stale cellar. But the prayer is sometimes taken to mean that we are psychologically and spiritually free and independent of others if we so decide. This is an old American myth, reformulated. It is a myth deeply rooted also in secular existentialism—but it plays neatly into the American spirit. In point of fact we are profoundly and indissolubly inter-connected with each other in our hopes and panics, in our illnesses and our ecstacies—yes even in the fulfillment of one another's dreams and expectations. This is true in economics, in poltics, in family and work relations and, according to recent parapsychological research, in the interaction of multiple organismic, geologic and other field phenomena. Faith (both Christian and Hindu/

Buddhist) affirmed that we are "all members of one body" long before science began to document it. Gestalt and Encounter, in their ingenious and successful methods of bringing new life to individuals, may still fail to lead us into that larger life which binds us to one another. Gestalt has helped us to identify and swim round the nets of expectation which others have set. But in our caution let us not slip into the other danger of tadpoling off oblivious to the sea of other persons which nourishes us.

Fritz Perls shows this interrelatedness clearly in his more philosophical moments.

> We are part of the universe, not separate. We and our environment are one. We cannot look without something to look at. We cannot breathe without air. We cannot live without being part of society. So we cannot possibly look on the organism as being able to function in isolation. So this organism here labeled "Fritz Perls" is a living sum of processes, of functions, and these functions are always related to something of the world he has, the world that we try to describe with the word *now*. (16)

BEYOND ENCOUNTER: THE STAGES OF PILGRIMAGE

I did indicate at the beginning, and in material submitted in supplementary notes, how Encounter can be understood in religious terms. While this paper was being written, a new book by the man whose name is most widely associated with Encounter, William Schutz, came into my hands. It strikingly confirms the basic thesis of the paper, namely, that the "new wine" of the experiential therapies *is* in search of "wineskins." In his Introduction, Schutz tries "to state the philosophy of open encounter in some spiritual terms—life flow, energy cycle—because I feel the spiritual element is central, although I don't understand it very well." He is more concrete in a partially autobiographical chapter, "Mysticism and Spirituality." The insight of

> ... the almost total interrelation of mind, spirit, and body ... has already made important contributions to the open encounter as will be seen in the discussions of the Kundalini and of some of the specific techniques, such as yoga and meditation, the increased use of silence, and personal centering. ...
>
> One point at which the open encounter and a mystical viewpoint are mutually helpful occurs when an encounter is going very deep. After hostility is worked through and differences acknowledged as people reach the deeper layers of personality, the similarity of all men becomes clearer. We are all in the same struggle but using different paths with different defenses. The notion that we are all one is given great meaning at these almost mystical moments in the group's life. (17)

Schutz puzzles over the apparent contradiction between the Hindu stress on detachment from feelings and the demand in encounter to go into them and work them through. His attempted reconciliation leads him to the first statement I have seen in the new-therapy context about *stages*: "Perhaps these methods are not contradictory but represent two stages of human evolution: feelings must be faced directly with awareness and worked through before a detachment can be acquired." (18) This suggests one of the major *deficiencies* associated with almost exclusive emphasis on the here-and-now: a lack of awareness of the *developmental stages* through which man must pass in his spiritual-psychological growth.

A sense of the long road of self-realization creates a personal humility which is sometimes lacking in the human-potential therapies. Some Christian traditions have spelled out the life-long growth in grace as Sanctification; and the more sophisticated Buddhist schools, e.g., Zen, describe various states or levels of enlightenment; but it is the Hindus who have most explicitly delineated life stages within a spiritual world-view. The devotee is first a student under his spiritual teacher. Then follows the householder stage, during which he takes family and job responsibilities and focuses his attention outward. The third stage is that of the contemplative, the forest dweller, who is released from worldly obligations and seeks inwardly for spiritual enlightenment. The final stage, the *sannyasin,* is that of the enlightened one who can wander over the world unattached even to his own individual existence. We need a comparable scheme in the West. (The contemporary psychotherapist moves from the Householder to the forest-dweller Self-realization stage when he begins to do therapy— or whatever—not for the sake of others, but for his own unfoldment. In the modern world the *where* or the *what* of one's actions is less crucial than the motivation and style with which he lives and "works".) To see the bodily/emotional growth of the new therapies as one dimension of a life-long Pilgrimage of Awareness would both heighten the importance of psychological understanding (because it does, for instance, prefigure and point toward mystical awareness) and yet keep it from becoming the final fulfillment it is in some disciples.

Many who have moved through the human-potential obstacle-races and growth-games are now seeking for something beyond them. It is no accident that a number of successful Human Potential Centers—e.g., Cumbres in New Hampshire, Bucks County Seminar House in Pennsylvania, among others—are now closing their doors in order that their founders and leaders may pursue the next step in their own unfolding! No less than forty Esalen Institute regulars went to Chile a year or so ago to study with Oscar Ichazo, a spiritual teacher nourished by the Shinto, Sufi and other spiritual traditions. Some of them are now serious disciples of Ichazo or other spiritual gurus. As a step, a phase of development, then, the new therapies are admirable. As a total view of human existence and its meaning, they fall far short.

TRADITION AND COMMUNITY

The other problem with insistence on the here-and-now is **historical rootlessness**. New therapies are "new" precisely because they have broken sharply with existing traditions—primarily the psychoanalytic tradition. This iconoclasm is an important part of their appeal. But to be unable to see oneself as part of a larger faith, an historical community, and a life-style undergirded by ritual worship and celebration is to put enormous strain on the individual seeker, his teacher and the here/now community. The checks and balances which, for instance, the early Quakers had in the Scriptures and in their local Meetings, provided support for the individual in his choices and decisions, and sometimes restrained a fanatical enthusiasm. To a considerable extent the slings and arrows now being flung at the encounter movement stem from the lack of a guiding and corrective tradition. Gestalt therapy, and possibly Bioenergetics, may suffer similar woes.

It is instructive to note that the Christian setting of some Encounter workshops or retreats,(19) has provided some of this corrective. Behavioral limits—e.g., on "sleeping around", or psychological scapegoating—are more likely to exist there than in other contexts. Though a religion's setting may in some instances provide a built-in caring for the welfare of others which randomly chosen groups may lack, its norms may *also* inhibit freedom of expression and thereby undercut the central dynamic of encounter.

Another deficiency of the new therapies, as we have said, is their failure to provide "communities of fellow seekers which judge and sustain individuals through time." Unfortunately, the contemporary Christian Church, with rare exceptions, does not give us a model in this regard. And, here again, we must note the beginning emergence of correctives: the thrust toward the establishment of more enduring communities among Gestaltists and other human-potential disciples. Fritz Perls' last dream before his death was to create a Gestalt Kibbutz, a genuine community based on **Gestalt principles**.

It is unnecessary to develop here the way in which religious communities have chastened and nurtured and inspired individual seekers. Human-potential-directed communities can, of course, do this; but we must reckon with the fact that in recent history nearly all communities without a *religious* base have collapsed after a year or two. Somehow the goal of individual fulfillment loses its lustre in time, unresolvable personal differences erupt, and sudden demise or slow disintegration follows. Long-term communal life seems predicated on some vision or purpose transcending the lives of individuals. It is significant that Alfred Adler used to guide his patients toward one of the many Socialist groups of Vienna once his therapeutic work with them was over. The success of Alcoholics Anonymous is based largely on the surrender of the drinker "to a Higher Power," and his dedication of himself to rescuing other addicts. The overarching purpose need not be specifically religious, but it must lift the prospect of the individual beyond his own growth.

A CONFLUENCE OF THERAPY AND TRADITION

Eastern religion seems to be preferred among those disciples of the experiential therapies who have become seekers. I am not acquainted with attempts to practice Gestalt or Encounter or Reichian modes of transformation in a Hindu or a Buddhist context—though it is quite evident that some Eastern-religious communes (such as the Lama Foundation in New Mexico) imbibe of the encounter spirit in working through the interpersonal tensions of communal life. There are fraternal bonds between the Zen Monastery at Tassajara and Esalen (just 35 miles apart through the Pacific rain-forest). We have referred to a number of Christian centers where experiential methods are being employed. (20) The following will illustrate this "new wine" at work within a Quaker Christian context. It is an episode in a week-long session at a retreat house, entitled "Encounter and the Spiritual Journey."

On the morning of the fourth day of the workshop Gertrude, who had accompanied her husband, Tony, came to breakfast looking like a zombie. Just before the morning session, in bitter clipped phrases, she told me (the leader) how furious she was with me and with the whole group, her husband excepted. She had slept not at all during the night. She said she would tell the group how she felt when I would let her, and added that she would "have very little to say." In the context of the Quaker Center we preceded the encounter sessions each day with a twenty or thirty minute unprogrammed quiet meeting for worship. An older woman broke the silence, which felt tense and heavy, by describing an image which had come to her: a blossoming tree, deeply rooted in the soil, with birds singing in the higher branches. There was a gash in its trunk, "which may have been bleeding." During the break, while we were rearranging seating, she confided to me that that was not all she had seen, but she was afraid to report the entire vision. During the earlier part of the morning Gertrude had been sitting beside her husband, immobile, her face a death-mask. I worried for her. At the first opportunity I invited her to say what was on her mind. She began, "No one has the right to do to another person what you have done to me. Many of the things which were said yesterday hurt me deeply. I do not believe what you believe. Some of the things which were said could destroy me, could destroy our marriage. I do not trust you, any of you. I trust only Tony. I blame Joe especially for letting these things happen. But I blame all of you for not considering our feelings, for not knowing how vulnerable I was to the kind of things you were talking about yesterday. . . ."

Thus began a slow, boiling diatribe. I feared it would stop too soon, that she would leave and not return. Fortunately, she kept talking. Perhaps she felt the shock her words produced in others. Perhaps as she talked she heard her words sounding too one-sided, too extreme. In any case, she went on, never fully revealing the hurts and fears of earlier years which lay back of her anger, yet gradually making us aware of the self-erected walls which kept her from reaching out. She was slouched very close to her husband on a long sofa. Both by his posture and his words he placed himself in a mediating position—less alienated from us, yet protective and supportive of her. Gertrude described how desperately she needed the love and assurance of her husband, how they had both come to the encounter week hoping for help but finding mostly estrangement and more conflicts. When finally she paused, one or two of the group made overtures, reaching out, in words, to her. I sensed how easily and quickly we might overwhelm her with loving-kindness, born partly of our own uncomfortableness; so I found myself voicing the image that had come to me toward the end of Gertrude's long delivery: "I see Gertrude as a very small person at the bottom of a huge fortress—made of thick walls which she has laid, stone by stone. There are a few chinks in these bastions, through which she can look at us. There is another larger hole through which she can see and reach one other person, Tony. I see her using that opening now. All of us are an advancing army, trying to storm the fortress and 'liberate' Gertrude. But she is frightened, and hides as she sees us coming. The besieging army must wait."

A group member asked Gertrude to forgive him especially for a remark he had made which had hurt her. At first she dismissed this request, "you do not need *my* forgiveness." But when later he came back to it and said he needed her to touch him, she allowed him to move to her and laid her hand on his shoulder. When he then raised her up and embraced her, her face visibly softened, though her reluctance to receive was still evident in her slight drawing back. Gertrude accused us of bringing out and accentuating her "bad side". She declined to say more about what this bad side was, so I asked her husband if he knew. He immediately said yes, which surprised her: "Does it show, even to you?" "Yes," he answered, "I see it quite frequently, but I have been afraid to speak of it. I thought you didn't want to know about it." When he added that he loved her, she visibly relaxed and seemed to come forward toward us.

Shortly after this we fell into a spontaneous worship. The woman who had had the vision of the tree said softly, "I didn't tell you the whole of my vision. The gash in the tree became blood. The tree changed into a cross. It was frightening; but I see now it foreshadowed what was to happen this morning." Several persons expressed gratefulness that Gertrude had stayed with us; others hoped that we might continue to grow toward a reconciliation. Someone voiced his feeling of the inevitableness of our hurting one another in various ways, and of our need for forgiveness. Another began the song, *Spirit of God*, which we had sung together earlier in the week. Someone else began the Lord's Prayer. "Forgive us our trespasses, as we forgive those who trespass against us." Never had I heard these words prayed with such fervor and longing. During this worship period, to our surprise and joy, Gertrude moved into the circle we had formed.

She and her husband stayed through the workshop. By the end of the day following this episode, she was taking full part in the discussions and the party times. She told me at the end of the week that she wanted to go back into therapy, perhaps this time with her husband.

The "wineskin" of tradition we experienced there in the availability of spontaneous silent worship, song, and the Lord's Prayer. Just these corporate rituals seem to allow the universal or spiritual dimension of our encounter to be recognized and integrated and this without diluting the particularity of one person's suffering or another's need for forgiveness. Sometimes in other settings (therapy; non-religious human potential workshops) my wife or I have seen interpersonal experience move toward a wordless awe or wonder which found no way of being responded to or shared by the group. The deeply existential became almost embarrassing. Such moments dramatize for us the need of cradles of spiritual tradition to contain and nurture the "shattering truths" of the experiential therapies.

REFERENCES AND FOOTNOTES

1. Quoted in Barbour, Hugh: *The Quakers in Puritan England*. New Haven, Yale University Press, 1964, p. 98.
2. For further spelling out of the parallels between encounter group experience and religious experience, see my "Religious Awareness and Small Groups" in *The Dialogue Between Theology and Psychology*, (Peter Homan, ed.). Chicago, University of Chicago Press, 1968. Also Clark, James V.: Toward a Theory and Practice of Religious Experience (in Bugental, J. F. T. (Ed.) New York, McGraw-Hill, 1964.
3. For a recent collection of essays by various writers see Fagan, Joan and Shepherd, Irma Lee: *Gestalt Therapy Now*. (Science and Behavior Books, 1970) New York, Harper Colophon, 1971. The "case-book" of Gestalt therapy is, Perls, Frederick S.: *Gestalt Therapy Verbatim*. Lafayette (California), Real People Press, 1969. The most extensive theoretical treatment is, Perls, Hefferline, and Goodman: *Gestalt Therapy*. New York, Julian, 1951.
4. The two most useful books on Bioenergetics are in my view, Lowen, Alexander: *The Betrayal of the Body*. New York, Macmillan, 1967 and Collier, 1969. Also Lowen, Alexander: *Love and Orgasm*. New York, Signet, 1965.
5. I suggest two books as a start in understanding Encounter: Burton, Arthur (Ed.): *Encounter*. San Francisco, Jossey-Bass, 1969; Schutz, William: *Here Comes Everybody*. New York, Harper, 1971.
6. Quoted in Barbour, *op. cit.*, pp. 104–105.
7. Stevens, Barry: *Don't Push the River*. Lafayette (California), Real People Press, 1970, pp. 89–90.
8. Barbour, Hugh: from an unpublished dittoed paper on religious experience, especially of Quakers. About 1969.
9. Lowen, Alexander: *The Betrayal of the Body*. New York, Macmillan, 1967, p. 46.
10. Lowen, Alexander: *Pleasure*. New York, Coward-McCann, 1970, p. 15. This most recent book of Lowen's also most clearly states his general philosophical position.
11. Andras Angyal is a too-little-known personality theorist who takes full account of the inappropriate control which mind and will exercise over bodily functioning, but who also holds the vision of the larger Gestalt which encompasses both. See his *Foundations for a Science of Personality*, New York, Commonwealth Fund, 1941.
12. See Pierrakos' The Energy Field of Man. Institute for Bioenergetic Analysis, 71 Park Avenue, New York, N. Y.
13. See Claudio Naranjo's essay in *Gestalt Therapy Now*. New York, Harper-Colophon, 1971. See "Present-Centeredness: Technique, Prescription, and Ideal."
14. *Ibid.*, p. 56.
15. *Ibid.*, pp. 67–68.
16. See Fritz Perls' contribution in *Gestalt Therapy Now*, p. 30.
17. Schultz, William: *Here Comes Everybody*. New York, Harper, 1971, pp. xviii and 56.
18. *Ibid.*, p. 56.
19. For example, at Kirkbridge at Bangor, Pennsylvania; at the Institute for Advanced Pastoral Studies at Bloomfield Hills, Michigan; at Quaker centers such as Pendle Hill at Wallingford, Pa. and Powell House at Old Chatham, N. Y.
20. Jud, Gerald J.: The Human Potential Movement. *Enquiry*, Dec. 1971–Feb. 1972.

CHAPTER 21

EXORCISM AND PSYCHOTHERAPY: A CASE OF COLLABORATION

E. Mansell Pattison

THIS CHAPTER WILL DESCRIBE an unusual, but successful, method of collaboration across the boundaries of two human systems of guidance. In this case, the psychiatrist, a member of the scientific professional world, collaborated with the native members of a tribal healing culture in order to achieve the successful "cure" of an adolescent girl who was living in the borderland between these two world views.

I. The Indigenous Healer

During the development of psychotherapy in the twentieth century as a scientifically based enterprise, attention was naturally focused upon the acquisition of new knowledge of human behavior, and the refinement of new therapeutic skills based upon that knowledge.

Only in the second half of this century, with the firm establishment of psychotherapy as a discipline and profession, has there been a widening of inquiry into other systems of human help. In part this widening perspective began with a re-evaluation of the helping traditions of the clergy in the Western Judaeo-Christian tradition. After an earlier period of mutual hostility that characterized the first half of the twentieth century, the second half evolved into a period of mutual recognition and rapprochement. It was recognized that many people sought help from the clergy in Western society, and that the clergy were often potent and successful "therapists." Further, it was realized that many of the clergy continued to work within their "religious framework," rather than adopting the "scientific framework" of the psychotherapist. (1)

Hard on the heels of these developments, psychotherapists and anthropologists began to report studies on the role and function of healers working within the world view of the many world religions.

Although there has been a tendency to reinterpret all these methods of healing in terms of the paradigms of psychotherapy, there is ample evidence that all societies have their systems of guidance, their methods of healing, their healers, which are the cultural counterparts of the psychotherapist of Western society. (2)

The indigenous healer is of considerable interest in terms of forging effective working relationships as psychiatry becomes a part of the development of scientific medicine in developing countries. (3) The indigenous healer is of importance as a comparative model of psychotherapeutic methods. (4) And the indigenous healer is important as healing resource within Western society itself. For although scientific psychotherapy is the paradigm among the intellectual elite of the West, there are many groups of people within Western society who do not ascribe to the scientific world view, and who do not seek or accept help from the professional psychotherapist.

Therefore, in this chapter we are concerned with one example of a cultural group where scientific society is foreign, and for whom the indigenous healer remains an important and significant resource.

II. Models of Interaction

Although initial evaluations of the indigenous healer may have been a bit skeptical, those professionals who have had experience in the field have come to respect the functional ability of the indigenous healer. But there is still the question of how to frame working relationships between the psychotherapist, operating within one world view, and the indigenous healer who operates within another world view.

One model is to maintain total separation. In this model the psychotherapist works in his world, while the indigenous healer works in the other. Although one may recognize the existence of the other, because of divergent world views, the two do not see the other as a viable alternative.

A second model is competitive, with one suspicious of or disdainful of the other. Proselytization of clientele is important, in order to demonstrate the truth of one's world view, and the efficacy of one's method.

A third model is the consultative relationship. Here there is an attempt to bring knowledge and skills from one arena into the other. Examples include the current consultative work with Navaho witch doctors, and the highly developed consultative and triage relationship between psychiatrists and witch doctors that has been developed in Nigeria. (5)

While the fourth model might be called the collaborative model. Here one healer works with the other, each within his own sphere, each in his own way, but working in mutual support of each other. In this model one does not attempt to change the world view or skills and methods of the other.

Since there have been few case reports of this latter model, this chapter will present an account of this mode of interaction.

III. Transcultural Diagnosis: Normal versus Abnormal

Other problems aside, one of the major problems for the Western psychotherapist is getting "inside" the world view of another culture. What to our eyes seems aberrant and psychopathological may be expectable behavior in another culture. This becomes even more acute in the evaluation of various altered states of consciousness, which are common experiences in many cultures of the non-Western world, but are seen as foreign to our experiencing of existence. (6)

In the case under discussion in this chapter, we are dealing with an episode that involves perceptions (hallucinations?) of ghosts, agitated behavior that appeared to involve a dissociated state, and beliefs about witchcraft and spirit possession.

Now it is relatively simple to describe this episode in Western clinical psychopathological terms. But what meaning do we give this episode? How do we interpret what is happening? Only when we can satisfactorily understand these phenomena within the meaning context of the culture, can we approach the question of intervention.

The central issue is well put by Erika Bourguignon. (7) She points out that the meaning of behavior is defined by the culture. If the behavior is a culturally defined norm, then although it may be deviant within the culture it is expectable and acceptable. There are culturally specified modes of response. In this sense the person is deviant, but not "sick." Whereas deviant behavior that is not culturally defined is sickness to that culture. Further, the behavior itself may not be the determinant criteria, but rather the *cause* of the behavior.

In the case under discussion there were several interpretations of the behavior. The Western physician made one evaluation, the family in the culture another, while the psychiatrist made still a third. The importance of interpretation, as we shall see, may be most critical.

IV. A Case History

This experience occurred during a period when I served as the psychiatric consultant to the Public Health Service Clinic serving the

Yakima Indian reservation. The Yakima are located on several thousand acres of farming and lumbering land in central Washington amidst the rich agricultural Yakima valley. As on many Indian reservations, these Indian people live in close proximity to white Western culture. Although they have relatively good economic resources, life on the reservation is isolated from the world in which it is located. The reservation culture is in the midst of cultural disintegration. The "long hair" Indians cling to the traditional Yakima mores, while their middle-aged children flounder in bewilderment, not part of the white culture, not part of the Indian. Meanwhile the grandchildren attend the local white schools and watch television in the homes of their grandparents. Here in the middle of two cultures we find our case.

Upon arrival at the reservation one snowy December morning, the young public health doctor grabbed me for an emergency consultation. He had been called to the home of an Indian family the previous night to see an adolescent girl. The family stated that she was crying, frightened, incoherent, running around the house in a state of panic. He reported that upon arrival at the home he found the girl incoherent, babbling, agitated, muttering about ghosts and stating that she was afraid of dying. He gave her an intramuscular injection of chlorpromazine which had calmed her down, and she had gone to sleep. He had made a diagnosis of acute schizophrenic psychosis. Since I was due to arrive the next day, he had requested that the family bring the girl to the clinic for my evaluation and recommendation for further treatment.

Precisely at the appointed time, the mother and daughter appeared. I had worked on the reservation for several years at this time, and was known to the Indian people. I had found good rapport and little difficulty in establishing working relationships with my Indian clientele. But this was a different situation from my usual clinical consultations. Both mother and daughter were sullen, guarded, withdrawn. The girl was a pretty, well developed, adolescent, thirteen years old. She was dressed like a typical high school girl. But she hunched over herself, eyes downcast, barely speaking in audible tones. With great difficulty and much patience her story was told.

The problems began the prior August when Mary (her pseudonym) had gone off to a week-long summer camp for Indian girls, sponsored by the local O.E.O. program. One night, as kids are wont to do at a summer camp, after lights were out and the counselors were in bed, Mary and several of her girl friends went sneaking out of their cabin to frolic in the moonlight among the tall fir trees.

As they ran about in the moonlight they looked up in the trees and saw human figures. These ghost-like figures drifted down from the trees, and the girls recognized them as their tribal ancestors. The girls talked to the ghosts and the ghosts talked to the girls. But after a few minutes the girls became frightened, and they ran back to their cabin, jumped into bed, and hid under their covers.

All seemed safe now. Except for Mary. A ghost followed her into the cabin, jumped on her as she lay in bed, and tried to choke her. She fought and struggled against the ghost, she gasped for breath, she screamed for help. The counselors came running into the cabin, but they could not calm her. Mary was sure the ghosts would kill her, she sobbed and screamed. Finally, the counselors bundled her up in a car and drove back home to the local hospital. When seen in the emergency room she was still in an agitated state and was given an intramuscular tranquilizer shot before being taken home to her parents.

The stage was set, and the pattern from then on to December was rather routine. Mary would go off to high school everyday with ratted hair and teenie-bopper clothes. She would participate in her daily high school activities as any teenager. She was on the honor roll, was a cheerleader, and a student body officer. But when she came home a different Mary appeared. She combed her hair into long Indian braids. She put on long-skirted traditional Indian clothes. Then she would wander about the house as if in a daze. She would see ghosts at the window and cry out in startled fright. She went walking in the fields and saw blood on the ground. She thought the ghosts had killed one of her girl friends. She thought the ghosts would attack and kill her younger brothers and sisters. She would become so frightened and worried that at times she would cry, and scream, and run around the house. At times the parents could not calm her, and they would take her to the hospital for a shot to calm her down. But the next morning she would always get up and go to school like a normal adolescent girl.

The mother and the girl had no explanation for this behavior. They were bewildered. Then the mother turned to me and asked what I, as a psychiatrist, thought of this behavior. Was her daughter crazy? What I observed was a withdrawn sullen girl. But she spoke in a coherent manner. She was logical and realistic in her conversation with me. I stated that I did not know what this all meant, but perhaps the mother might have some ideas.

The mother said she had heard that psychiatrists did not believe in religion. Did I believe in religion? I told her that I thought religion was very important in the lives of people. Did I believe that she had been healed? I told her that many people experience healing, and that she too might have had a healing experience. She smiled, relaxed, and leaned toward me. Look at my face! Do you see any scars? No, I don't. Well, my father healed me. Do you believe that? Yes. Well, he was a witchdoctor; he used to care for the whole tribe. And when I was a girl I fell in a fire and burned my face. And he made a pack of mud with his spittle, and anointed my face and said his prayers, And said I would be healed and have no scars. He said I would have a beautiful face. Do you think he was right? Is my face beautiful? Yes.

The mother was satisfied. She sat back. Then she tensed up again. Doctor? Yes? Should I say this? Maybe I shouldn't. I've never talked about this before. My daughter doesn't know about this, I've never told her. Well. You see, my father, the witchdoctor, he told me that his powers would be passed on when he died. But not his children, not to me. But his powers would be passed on to his grandchildren. And the oldest, this daughter, this girl, would have his powers.

By this time my thoughts about the clinical situation had been stirred. Do you think that Mary's experiences have something to do with your father? Oh yes, she answered. But we don't talk about those things anymore, because, you know, we're Presbyterians now, and people don't believe in witchcraft anymore. But what if they did? I asked. How would you handle something like this?

The mother was now animated, and the daughter was listening intently. Well, we knew what to do. You see, in the old times, when someone was going to be given the powers of the spirits, was to be given the gifts of the witchdoctor, you had to struggle with the spirits. You had to prove you could rule them. Well, what would you do? I asked. Oh, there's nothing we can do. If this were the old times, we would just open the door and let Mary wander out of the house at night. And she would go out and meet the spirits. And she would have to fight with them. And then she would come back with the powers . . . ; or maybe we would just find her out there after a few days, but that's the way it happens. . . .

I see. Well, what do you think about this now? Since this is not the old days, what do you think might be the best way to help Mary now?

Well, you know, doctor, I've been thinking about that. You can't really practice much as a witchdoctor these days. It might be better if Mary were a Presbyterian and didn't accept the gift her grandfather left her.

Well, how would you work that out?

You see, doctor, we have to get rid of the spirits. We have to tell them that Mary doesn't want to fight with them. And then they'll go away and leave her alone. And she'll be O.K.

H'm. Well what do you have to do?

Oh, I don't know how to do that.

Who does?

Oh, grandma does. She and some of the other old women know the ceremony. We all have to get together. And we would dress Mary up in the ceremonial dress, and we have to have prayers, and offerings, and we would anoint her, and say the prayers. . . .

Lest I leave the reader in suspense, at the end of one of the most fascinating experiences in my professional life, I reached an agreement with Mary and her mother. We agreed that it was not appropriate for Mary to attempt to achieve the mantle of power her grandfather had bequeathed her. That would be looking backward. So we agreed that Mary should renounce the legacy and look forward to becoming part of the modern world. The mother agreed to call grandmother and see if she and the other tribal women could conduct a ritual of exorcism that night. I would return in one month. They agreed to see me again at that time.

Now it was January. With some trepidation I awaited their arrival. They came early! They were delighted to see me. I was a great doctor. They had followed my advice. The ceremony of exorcism had been conducted. It had been successful. Mary was healed.

Indeed, since that night of exorcism the strange behavior had disappeared. The mother was happy, Mary was happy, I was happy. Because of my ongoing contact with this tribe, I had the opportunity to follow this family for many months thereafter. Mary remained healthy and happy. No more was she bothered. In contrast to her mien that first cold snowy December morning, when I saw her thereafter she was bright and bouncy, talkative and enthusiastic, like any other energetic adolescent girl beginning to become a woman.

V. Some Religious Observations

As I listened to this story, I thought of an Old Testament story that was identical, and I thought of the universality of human experience.

In the following passage, we read of Jacob wrestling with the angel of the Lord, in order to obtain power over the spirits:

> And Jacob was left alone; and there wrestled a man with him until the breaking of the day. And when he saw that he prevailed not against him, he touched the

hollow of his thigh; and the hollow of Jacob's thigh was out of joint, as he wrestled with him. And he said, Let me go, for the day breaketh. And he said, I will not let thee go, except thou bless me. And he said unto him, What is thy name? And he said, Jacob. And he said, Thy name shall be called no more Jacob, but Israel; for as a prince hast thou power with God and with men, and hast prevailed. . . . And Jacob called the name of the place Peniel; for I have seen God face to face, and my life is preserved. . . . and he halted upon his thigh. (8)

What is remarkable is that over a span of perhaps six thousand years and over three continents we find the same interpretation. The man gains power over spirits by fighting with the spirits. If man wins, he then has special powers, he can command the spirits. He is a shaman, a healer, a witchdoctor. But it is a dangerous business. For to acquire the special powers requires a mortal combat. Jacob won, but he was crippled for life. And as for Mary, she feared her own death, or that of her siblings, if they got in the way of the combat.

In this case, we have the reenactment of an age-old saga: Man in the quest of power over the forces of his life.

VI. Some Psychodynamic Observations

One can look at this clinical experience through the dimensions of scientific psychodynamics. (9) Although we have limited clinical material, we may rough out the following possible interpretations. The mother presents herself as the favored daughter of her father. Father heals her, using his spittle (semen?). Mother continues to frame her acceptability as a person around her external appearance, her beauty, her sexuality. She asks for acceptance as a desirable object from the therapist (father symbol). Daughter Mary appears on the scene at the time of adolescence as a maturing women, hence competitor to mother. Mother does not give approval to daughter to become a sexual mature woman, for that poses a threat to mother. Mary projects the disapproving mother into the hallucinatory ghost object who would kill her. But also the projected forbidden object is the father figure who lays upon her in bed—the incestuous father. Mary wanders in the field and finds blood in the fields (menstrual blood?) where her girl friend was killed. While the sibling competitive rivalry between mother and daughter is projected onto the fear of Mary's siblings being killed by the spirits.

The conflict is resolved. The mother is re-affirmed in her role as woman. She in turn, in concert with her own mother, participates in a symbolic ritual with gives daughter, mother, grandaughter, the sanction and approval to mature, to grow up, to become a sexually mature woman. Daughter Mary is no longer a competitive rival, seeking to gain the exclusive rights and affections of the witchdoctor grandfather (oedipal father). So mother can now allow daughter Mary to become a woman in her own right. Result: daughter no longer acts out the mother-daughter conflict.

VII. A Trans-Cultural Perspective

The case history presented represents many of the issues involved in working across the boundaries of belief systems in different cultures. (10)

Our observations are in concert with the definitive work of Melford Spiro, (11) who has shown how one can look at various possession states and methods of healing from both the Western psychodynamic perspective and from the cultural perspective of the indigenous healer. It is of note that, in Spiro's work on possession, the most common conflict was sexual conflict. Spiro notes that the dissociative state of possession deals with the fear of retaliation, which is certainly true in this case.

But given the fact that we deal with a dissociative state, can we consider this an abnormal state? Here we have an instance in which the particular psychodynamic of family life was acted out in a pattern provided by the culture. Within the cultural set, the behavioral pattern exhibited by Mary was not unusual nor unexpected. In fact, she acted out the cultural norm.

In this instance we can note that the diagnosis of acute schizophrenia is understandable, but inappropriate. However, the family itself was caught in an interesting and pathetic cultural bind. If they had been living within the traditional Indian culture, they would have followed the prescribed patterns of response. We may assume that the deviant behavior would have been appropriately resolved. However, the family was caught between two cultures, between two belief systems. And so the family was immobilized. The behavior of the patient, Mary, was congruent with the belief system of the old culture, while the treatment of the hospitals was congruent with the new belief system.

What provided a significant intervention in this impasse, was a sanction by a scientific professional psychotherapist to an indigenous cultural healer. And that collaborative support enabled this natural system to function and to restore a person to function.

A psychodynamic interpretation of this case intervention might include the possibility of a "transference cure." In this instance the mother experiences reaffirmation of her beauty, her wholeness, her person, from the psychiatrist (witchdoctor—transferential father). She need not feel threatened by her daughter's emerging sexuality, for mother is still the favored one. Then too, the psychiatrist (transference father symbol) enlists the aid of mother (herself now the successful oedipal competitor) to help daughter grow up. And this is allowed because daughter will not be stronger than mother.

Although these psychodynamic speculations may be appropriate and accurate, I do not think that one can conclude that this explains the total interaction.

In my opinion, these psychoanalytic motifs may indicate why this particular intervention was so rapidly catalytic of a therapeutic resolution. The psychodynamic cards were stacked in my favor.

On the other hand, the family had sought medical treatment on many occasions before they came to see me. The medical interventions could have been given the same symbolic ascriptions, which I propose were ascribed to me. And the failure of medical treatment, or the knowledge of the tribal beliefs could have resulted in the family going ahead and conducting the exoricism ceremonies. Yet they had not ostensibly even thought about exorcism.

If this family were fully participant in the Western thought world of the psychiatrist, then I would have considered a typical family therapy model of intervention. But this family was not in my thought world—it only *looked like* they were thinking and living within the Western scientific tradition of medicine. Indeed, they themselves were only conscious of their Western world thought and beliefs. Whether one can consider this solely an *intrapsychic repression* is an interesting problem. My own inclination is to conclude that this family had a higher than usual level of repressive defense structures. But also that idiosyncratic family style was reinforced by the transitional Indian culture in which they live, in which repression of the "old" belief systems is built into the experiential world of living on the reservation.

I seriously doubt that a scientific style psychotherapy intervention would have been of any value at all. Not that one cannot conduct rather typical psychotherapy with Indians living on the reservation. For I did conduct a great deal of straightforward psychodynamic interpretive psychotherapy. But the problem of Mary and her mother was embedded in *the traditional Indian belief system*. I think that psychotherapy with either Mary or her mother around other issues might have been possible and appropriate within the Western scientific frame of thought. But with the acting out of the problem within the framework of the traditional Indian belief system, in order to conduct a scientific psychotherapy, one would have to translate the whole problem from one belief system to another belief system.

The alternative which I followed, was to take the traditional Indian belief system *for real*. To accept the interpretation of cause and effect within that system for real also. And to support an intervention within that system that would indeed be *real*.

My point is that I was not playing a game with this family, conning them, or going along with their ideas as if my system of psychoanalytic interpretation was the real system, while their interpretation was a fake system. No, the traditional Indian belief system and the psychoanalytic belief system are two different ways of looking at and acting upon this life situation. Thus it is possible to maintain *the integrity of both belief systems*. I feel that it was appropriate for a psychodynamic psychiatrist to help by not imposing his system, but by enabling other people to use their own systems of belief.

VIII. Summary

A case history of an adolescent girl is presented. She first reported seeing ghosts, then engaged in agitated dissociative behavior, and presented bizarre fears. The family was part of an American Indian tribe living in a situation that particularly emphasized the problems of living in two worlds. An initial interview with the girl and her mother revealed a family history of shamanism and the belief that the daughter was suffering from spirit possession. The psychiatrist supported this interpretation of the problem and encouraged the family to conduct an exorcism ritual. This was done and the girl immediately became asymptomatic and remained so. This case illustrates the importance of the belief system—the cultural frame of reference—in the interpretation of behavior. The psychiatrist is limited in that he operates within a particular scientific world view of behavior. It is possible and appropriate to help others by enabling them to act within their own world view, even though it is fundamentally different from the psychiatric view.

REFERENCES AND FOOTNOTES

1 These conclusions are based in part on the work of J. D. Frank, S. Z. Klausner, W. Sargant (see also E. M. Pattison). Cf. Bibliography.
2 See A. Kiev (ed.): *Magic, Faith and Healing: Studies in Primitive Psychiatry Today* (New York, Free Press, 1964). Cf. also Chapter 17 of the present volume.
3 Kiev, A.: *Transcultural Psychiatry*. New York, Free Press, 1972.

4. Kiev, A.: *Curanderismo: Mexican–American Folk Psychiatry.* New York, Free Press, 1968.
5. Lambo, T. A.: A Form of Social Psychiatry in Africa. From *World Mental Health*, vol. 13 (1961), pp. 190–203.
6. Tart, C. T. (ed.): *Altered States of Consciousness.* New York, Wiley, 1969.
7. Bourguignon, E.: The Self, the Behavioral Environment, and the Theory of Spirit Possession. In *Context and Meaning in Cultural Anthropology* (M. E. Spiro, ed.), New York, Free Press, 1965.
8. Genesis 32: 24–31.
9. I appreciate the helpful comments on the psychoanalytic meanings of this case by my colleague, Justin Call, M.D.
10. Cf. conclusions from G. Parrington's *Witchcraft: European and African* (London, Faber, 1958) and *Trance and Possession States* (R. Prince, ed.), Montreal, Bucke Memorial Society, 1966.
11. See M. E. Spiro: *Burmese Supernaturalism*, Englewood Cliffs, Prentice-Hall, 1967.

BIBLIOGRAPHY

1. Bourguignon, E.: "The Self, the Behavioral Environment, and the Theory of Spirit Possession" in Spiro, M. E. (ed.): *Context and Meaning in Cultural Anthropology.* New York, Free Press, 1965.
2. Devereux, G.: Normal and Abnormal, "The Key Problem of Psychiatric Anthropology," in J. Casagrande and T. Gladwin, (eds.): *Some Uses of Anthropology: Theoretical and Applied.* Washington, D.C., Anthropological Society of Washington, D.C., 1956.
3. Frank, J. D.: *Persuasion and Healing.* Baltimore, Johns Hopkins Press, 1961.
4. Kiev, A.: *Curanderismo: Mexican-American Folk Psychiatry.* New York, Free Press, 1968.
5. Kiev, A. (ed.): *Magic, Faith and Healing: Studies in Primitive Psychiatry Today.* New York, Free Press, 1964.
6. Kiev, A. *Transcultural Psychiatry.* New York, Free Press, 1972.
7. Klausner, S. Z.: *Psychiatry and Religion: A Sociological Study of the New Alliance of Ministers and Psychiatrists.* New York, Free Press, 1964.
8. Lambo, T. A.: A Form of Social Psychiatry in Africa. *World Mental Health* 13: 190–203, 1961.
9. Parrington, G.: *Witchcraft: European and African.* London, Faber, 1958.
10. Pattison, E. M.: Systems of Pastoral Care. *J. Past. Care* 26: 2–14, 1972.
11. Prince, R. (ed.) *Trance and Possession States.* Montreal, Bucke Memorial Society, 1966.
12. Sargant, W.: *Battle for the Mind: A Physiology of Conversion and Brainwashing.* London, W. Heinemann, 1957.
13. Spiro, M. E.: *Burmese Supernaturalism.* Englewood Cliffs, Prentice-Hall, 1967.
14. Tart, C. T. (ed.): *Altered States of Consciousness.* New York, J. Wiley, 1969.

CHAPTER 22

THE PEYOTE RELIGION AND HEALING

Robert L. Bergman

THE USE OF AN HALLUCINOGENIC drug is so striking a feature of a religion that most outsiders who are at all acquainted with the Native American Church notice almost nothing else about it. Many of them seem to imagine that whatever else there is about the church is the trappings or the excuse for drug taking. In fact, the drug experience to a large extent does give color to the religion, but it is its complex and eclectic, yet harmonious, set of beliefs and practices that give it shape. It is a Christian church, and its ideas, its ways, and its members are from almost every Indian tribe of North America.

The origins of the church are obscure. Lophophora Williamsii, the Peyote cactus, is native to Texas and Mexico and almost certainly its use was discovered in these southern regions, but some of the earliest recorded knowledge of the religion concerns its presence among tribes of the northern United States and Canada. The church is more than a century old, and now probably has more than 100,000 members, and is still growing.

Peyotist Beliefs

The Peyotists believe that the Christian Trinity and the Great Spirit of Indian religion are the same, and that through prayer and communion with God, man's sins are forgiven, he may learn to lead a good life, and he may be cured of illness. The universe is an harmonious creation of which each individual is a humble part and into which he must try to fit himself as harmoniously as possible: all men are his brothers and he must live in peace and charity with them. The earth is our mother and she must be treated with respect and gratitude. Rules of conduct are not sharply or dogmatically defined in detail except that strict abstinence from alcohol is advocated. Humility and brotherly love are particularly strong themes. The weakness and sinfulness of man and his need for God are constantly emphasized in services.

The tie between members of the church is deeply felt and

helping one another in practical and difficult ways consumes much of the time and resources of many Peyotists. In general, other religions—Indian or otherwise—are regarded as good and as all being variations on the same theme. Many Peyotists are active members (and in some cases clergymen) of other churches. They believe, however, that the services of the Native American Church through the use of peyote establish a closer contact with God than do the services of other churches. A common Peyote saying is that the white man prays to God, but the Indian speaks to him face to face. It is believed that God made a special gift of the sacrament, Peyote, to the natives of North America because of their sufferings at the hands of the invaders. The Indian grievance is seen as very great, but revenge is forbidden. Instead, union and redemption of all Indians through religion is promised.

Aboriginally, Indian religion and medicine were the same, and this lack of distinction holds true for the Peyote religion. Until relatively recently, all services were held for the purpose of curing a specific sick person whose family sponsored the meeting. Most meetings are still for this purpose, and most Peyotists use their religion for personal curing whenever they are ill. They also use doctors and hospitals and the two ways are not seen as contradictory. If a patient is cured physically, it is still necessary to cure the underlying cause. This belief is analogous to a recommendation of psychotherapy for a patient who has undergone surgical treatment of a bleeding duodenal ulcer.

Services are also held for such purposes as to pray for a child about to leave for boarding school, to pray for a child on his birthday, to give thanks for the safe return of a soldier from Viet Nam, or to celebrate a holiday. There is always a specific purpose and there may be many. For example, several Navajo Peyotists who work in a community mental health program decided to put on a meeting (the customary name for the service) to celebrate Christmas and to pray for the success of the program. One of the sponsors of the meeting also brought an adopted brother. The brother who is also a minister of the church had been depressed and came to the meeting for help. A couple came a great distance to pray for the recovery of their son who has severe arthritis. These were only some of the purposes of the meeting, all of which were fully discussed during and afterwards among the thirty people who took part.

The Setting

Peyote meetings resemble traditional Indian religious ceremonies more than they do ordinary Christian church services. They are held at the home of the sponsor in an old-fashioned Indian dwelling—usually a tepee or a hogan. The formal service begins at sunset and continues without interruption until after sunrise. Everyone stays through the night. The participants sit in a circle around the edge of the bare earth floor of the structure. A fire is built in the middle. The door is on the East; the minister sits opposite it against the west side of the wall. The altar is made between him and the fireplace. It is a low smooth crescent of wet sand representing the moon, who by Indian tradition is also a mother of mankind. A line drawn in the center of the altar from end to end is the road of life down which we all travel from birth to death. From this line the minister takes his name: road chief. A particularly fine Peyote button is placed at the center of the altar at the beginning of worship and removed at the end.

The worshippers are not divided into audience and performer. The road chief is in charge and leads the service, seeing to it that everything is done properly. He is assisted by several other officers of the meeting, but everyone participates almost equally, praying, singing, drumming, and speaking to the group. Tobacco is smoked not as a casual habit, but as in Indian tradition, in prayer. At the beginning and at several other specified times in the night, corn husks and tobacco are passed around the circle, cigarettes are rolled and smoked during prayer. The smoke rises from within each person and goes out the hole in the ceiling to the sky, as his prayer comes from within him and ascends to God. Similarly cedar incense is burned in the fire as an accompaniment of prayer, and everyone fans the smoke onto themselves to symbolize their wish to participate in the feelings and ideas expressed. At midnight the road chief goes outside, prays and walks around the tepee, blowing his eagle bone whistle to the four directions. Then water is brought in, shared with mother earth and with the people. The various smokes (prayers while smoking), the midnight water and other parts of the order of service give a regular structure to the meeting. Within that form there is considerable spontaneity. Through much of the night, a staff and drum pass around the circle. The person holding the staff sings, accompanying himself with a gourd rattle, and the person next to him drums. Anyone else who knows the song joins in. The songs are traditional Indian music of all tribes with Indian words expressing Christian ideas. There are many times during the meeting when anyone who feels like it can offer a prayer or address the other worshippers. At sunrise there is a morning water ceremony and the meeting ends with the eating of a symbolic meal including meat, corn, and fruit.

Peyote is consumed by all present from shortly after the first smoke until an hour or so before morning water. A group supply is passed around and each person is free to take whatever amount he wishes. This process is repeated during the night and after a certain point everyone is free to use a personal supply of medicine which most bring with them. Eating it is an ordeal. It is served in several forms—all are hard to get down. The extraordinarily bitter taste makes chewing and swallowing difficult, and the most immediate drug effect is nausea and sometimes vomiting.

Peyote contains more than ten alkaloids all of which probably are active psychopharmacologically. The most significant is mescaline. According to Seevers the average peyote button weighs three grams and contains forty-five milligrams of mescaline. Buttons are eaten fresh or dried, ground up or whole, and sometimes are brewed in a tea that is drunk. The amount taken varies from person to person and from meeting to meeting. The range appears to be from three grams of Peyote or forty-five milligrams of mescaline to thirty grams of Peyote or four hundred and fifty milligrams of mescaline. The usual is probably closer to the high than the low end of that range, and it seems safe to say that most Peyotists customarily take what is generally thought to be an effective dose of mescaline.

In the laboratory, subjects have reported a variety of hallucinations and other effects resulting from mescaline. Hallucinations do not seem to be as common among Peyotists. Many say that they have never seen or heard anything of the kind. Most report occasional hallucinations. Commonly, a rainbow of gemlike color is seen in the fire, sometimes the singing seems to take on the quality of a vast choir. One man on first attending a meeting had the thought that it would be interesting to see into his own body. Then he looked down at his crossed legs and indeed could see within them. He sat staring at his pulsating arteries until he saw several beetles walking along the inside of the femoral artery. This vision was frightening and he thought "I don't want to see that," and his leg became opaque again. Reassuring hallucinations are also reported: One man went to a meeting shortly after suffering an injury to his eye. He had received medical treatment but was still worried and in pain. He inquired until he found a meeting and then traveled a long way to go to it because he wanted to pray for his recovery. At Midnight Water, he saw the water bucket coming around to him as a little woman walking towards him. It was a bucket again when it was passed to him, and he dipped some of the sacred water out and held it to his eye. He felt that his eye was drinking and his pain and anxiety were less after that.

The Meeting

The Peyote probably also helps the worshippers to stay awake all night, and also seems to affect their mood. It is very difficult to assess the role of pharmacology in producing the group feeling of a meeting. Enotions are deeply felt and freely expressed. Speakers often cry and there is a great sense of communion with God and the other worshippers. It would be easier to assume that these phenomena are caused by Peyote, for they are not frequently observed in the part of the meeting before any medicine is eaten. It seems likely that the drug does heighten emotionality and make freedom of expression easier, and that each Peyotist initially learns that kind of behavior from his drug experience and is able to repeat it without a drug effect but in the same setting.

"Peyote teachers," the Peyotists say, and they frequently talk of learning about the depths of themselves and their problems. This kind of insight probably is facilitated by the physiologic effect, but it would be a frightening and usually useless experience except for the help that the road chief and the other members give each other. They share insight with one another and help to clarify each other's experience. For example, a man who had just been given an important job in an Indian community reported in a meeting that he felt guilty and anxious about his big promotion and he wondered if he should quit. After some further discussion and prayer, the road chief told him, "The trouble is that you are too proud of being so important. You know that's not right. You have to always remember who you are and where you came from and remember that you have that job in order to help your people. As long as you do that you will know that your having the job is right."

Another meeting was held for a woman suffering from a mild menopausal depression. Older women present described their feelings about aging and the end of child-bearing, and towards morning, the patient's husband said that he had realized that he was partly to blame for his wife's difficulties. "I have been so busy with church work," he said, "that I don't think I've been paying much attention to my companion. It came to me during the night that the reason I've been working too hard is that I've prayed for a lot of people and sometimes they get better, but sometimes they don't, and sometimes they're grateful for what I did, but a lot of times they're not, and so I guess I began to have my doubts about religion, and the more I had doubts the harder I made myself work so I would forget about them."

The newcomer to the church who saw beetles in his leg failed to talk about the experience until several hours later. When he did report what he had seen, the road chief said, "You should have told me about that right away. That was important and we should have prayed about it. You were supposed to learn something important from that." Further discussion revealed that it was the birthday of the man's father whose death several years before still haunted him. Prayers were then offered commemorating the birthday and for the deceased father and grieving son.

These examples may give some idea of what happens intellectually, but what feels much more important is the warmth and closeness experienced among the worshippers, and the closeness to God felt by the group. At the Christmas meeting mentioned before, the sponsor who had brought his brother—the road chief who was feeling depressed—offered the following prayer: "I want to thank you Father for letting me bring my poor brother here to our worship service. I know you've been looking after him and you know the terrible condition he's been in lately. I'm grateful that he could come here with us because I thought maybe we could make things a little better for him—pitiful as we are because I know you will listen to us and help us." The road chief who was officiating said in his prayer, "Father, let something good come to our brother. We know what it's like to work the way he has been. It seems like every road man gets sick every once in a while. He prays for someone all night one night and for someone else all the next night, and once in a while it's too much for him and he ends up on his back and then he can look straight up to you and see where he's going and where his strength comes from."

In the early morning of another meeting an old man spoke to a younger one whose wife had recently died: "I know the road you're walking brother—better than you do yourself, because you're just starting out on it and I walked it a long time before. You'll be coming home in the evening not thinking of anything much and then you'll realize that there's no one waiting for you there and no one to cook your dinner, and you'll cook it yourself and eat it all by yourself, and then you'll think about all the times your companion cooked your dinner and all the time there was someone who took care of you and then you never thought about it or thanked her for it and how she had your children and raised them for you and you never thought about it or thanked her for it, you'll really know what having a wife was like and what you've lost, and when that time comes, I want you to remember me brother because my door is always open for you, and I want you to come and see me any time like that because we need each other."

Insight and deep feeling alone are not enough to account for the helpfulness of Peyote meetings. Other groups who routinely use hallucinogenic agents have reportedly suffered from very high rates of mental illness apparently as a result of their practice. Peyotists, however, do not. The rate of seriously negative reactions to Peyote among Navajo members of the Native American Church is probably less than one per 70,000 ingestions. The difference seems to be that the feelings made available in meetings are carefully channeled in ego strengthening directions. Some of the crucial factors are a postive expectation held by the Peyotists, an emphasis on the real interpersonal world rather than the world within the individual, an emphasis on communion rather than withdrawal during the drug experience, an emphasis on adherence to the standards of society rather than on the freeing of impulses, and certain practices during the meetings.

Peyotists regard Peyote as powerful and beneficial medicine. Meetings are held for curative or other beneficial purposes and the road man is regarded as curer as well as priest. Much of the time in meetings is spent in praying for, and talking about expected benefits of the use of the drug. As in psychotherapy or any other curative ritual, this expectation seems to be an important influence.

In general, Peyotists expect that leading a good life according to their religion will result in greater personal success in the real world. Very few ever mention the possibility that their practices will increase their aesthetic sensitivity or show them a new view of the world—except perhaps a more moral one. It is quite common for a member of the church to cite examples of people who joined, became more responsible and as a result were able to be more successful financially. In many ways, in meetings and outside of them, customary social forces influence the members not to indulge in narcissistic withdrawal or grandiose fantasy.

Though a few people use Peyote religiously outside of meetings, this is an uncommon practice and they seldom do so alone. The whole spirit of the religion seems best characterized as communion— with God and with other men. Meetings are experienced as a time of being close and growing closer to one another. It is acceptable and expected that if someone in a meeting expresses strong feeling that the others present feel it with him and tell him so. If there is any tendency to lose old features of one's identity, there is an equally strong tendency to acquire stronger identity as a member of the group. As a member of the church, each person is assured of his own significance, and of group support for his own needs to be self-assertive in the outside world. The outside world—particularly the world of non-Indians—is seen as difficult but livable, and members expect to be able to cope with it.

Meetings are conducted in a strict and orderly way. Distortions in time sense are counteracted by the various events of the service that take place at precisely defined times of the night. Almost everything is done in a ritualized way that requires attention to the detail of one's movements and speech. The drum, ceremonial tobacco and other important objects are passed only in a certain way. In moving about the hogan or tepee, one walks only in a certain direction. All these details are invested with considerable emotion and some Peyotists say that this keeps them "thinking in the right way." The ceremony is experienced as beautiful, but much of the beauty is the beauty of orderliness. One of the most impressive instances of this orderliness, is the way the fire is tended throughout the night. One man is designated for this task, and is busy with it a great part of the time. Only the straightest pieces of wood are used and are cut to a uniform length. They are arranged in the fire in a specified way and kept straight and true throughout the meeting. The ashes are frequently swept together in a prescribed way and at the end of the service this results in their being in the image of a water turkey—a sacred symbol to the Peyotists because he can fly straight up as they want their prayers to go to God.

Road men are trained to look after people who become excessively withdrawn. If a participant begins to stare into the fire fixedly and seems unaware of the others in the meeting, the road man will speak to him, and if necessary go to him to pray with him. In the process of praying with such a person, he may fan him with an eagle feather fan, splash drops of water on him, and fan cedar incense over him. All of these processes are regarded as sacred and helpful, and it appears to me they provide stimulation in several sense modalities to draw one back to the interpersonal world. Another safeguard is the custom that no one is to leave the meeting. Considerable efforts are made if necessary to prevent someone who has been eating Peyote from going off into the night alone. This factor is probably important too, in the customary activities of the morning after the meeting. Everyone stays together and socializes until well after the time the drug effect is over.

The interaction of Peyotists outside of meetings is probably almost as important therapeutically as the meetings themselves. Most Indian communities today are at least somewhat disorganized and most are poverty-stricken. Though some tribes do not share them, Indians as a whole have high rates of suicide and alcoholism. Many Indian people can no longer live the traditional life of their tribe and have few Indian sources of self-esteem and they find themselves, when they move into the non-Indian world, persecuted, despised and at an educational and economic disadvantage. In this setting the Native American Church presents an enormous contrast. It is hard for a non-Indian to understand the strength of the church because we are not accustomed to strong organizations with little formal structure, but that is the Indian tradition and it is what the Peyote Church is like. In formal corporate structure, the Native American Church of North America is loose-knit and sparsely supplied with officers. Only a few are full time employees. The real strength comes from the informal association of non-professional members.

Road chiefs are highly skilled and highly trained. They learn their business through observing and helping other road chiefs. Occasionally they are given a present or a small fee in return for their services, but they are not a professional clergy. All have other occupations. The members do everything for themselves. They build the tepees and hogans that are their churches. They make the intricate fans, beadwork-covered gourd rattles, staffs, drums, and ceremonial boxes they use in worship. They make the symbolic jewelry by which they recognize one another, and they devote enormous energy to one another's needs. The road chief who ran the Christmas meeting mentioned before drove a thousand miles to get there because his adopted brother asked him to come.

The old Indian way of taking brothers and sisters is followed by the church, and is a considerable source of strength. A Peyote meeting is an ordeal as well as time of communion, and people who live through one together feel close to one another. They often adopt one another as relatives and such relationships are taken very seriously. Many Peyotists go occasionally to the area of Laredo, Texas, where the Peyote cactus grows. Meetings are held there by people of all tribes and all parts of the United States. As a result there are huge extended adopted families stretching across thousands of miles. Many members of such families visit each other for meetings, praying with one another, living with one another, exchanging songs, ceremonial objects, and help whenever needed. Navajo Peyote meetings in Arizona are often held in tepees made by brothers who live in the Dakotas, and the Sioux tepee makers wear Navajo silver waterbird jewelry. Tape recordings are mailed all over the country as Peyotists increase their knowledge of the songs and language of other tribes.

In earlier times, religion was inextricably a part of everything an Indian man or woman did. As the way of life was destroyed, the old religion was impossible, forbidden, and in some instances partially forgotten. For a great many Indians, white religion has become their own and means a lot to them. For others, however, it is important that the Peyote religion is alive, fits their needs, and above all is Indian.

Alcoholism among Indians is a self-fulfilling myth. The drunken Indian is not just a stereotype. Many of the members of the Native American Church are former drunks. Many of them once were in a condition where getting drunk was the only thing they ever did that felt Indian to them. As Peyotists they have regained Indian identity and an Indian group to belong to, and in which to gain respect. To tie the drum and sing all night takes strength and skill. To become a road chief takes years of effort, and winning the respect of a community. These challenges give many Indian people a chance to test and prove themselves after the traditional ways of their tribe have disappeared. All of this is held together by the shared experience of the meeting.

After their night together, the worshippers come out into the dawn breeze. Everyone shakes hands and says good morning. After a few minutes they go back to the ceremonial place for a feast. At such a moment lounging on the bare earth, smiling, joking together, proud of what they did all night, they know they are Indian and they feel their strength.

BIBLIOGRAPHY

1. Aberle, D. F.: The Peyote Religion Among the Navajo (Viking Fund Publications in Anthropology, 42). New York, Wenner Gren Foundation for Anthropological Research, 1966.

2. Bergman, R. L.: Navajo Peyote Use—Its Apparent Safety, *Amer. J. Psychiatry* 128: 6 (December, 1971), pp. 695–699.
3. Hollister, L. E.: *LSD and Related Drugs*. Springfield, Thomas, 1968.
4. La Barre, W.: *The Peyote Cult*. Hamden (Conn.): Shoestring Press, 1964.
5. Slotkin, J. S.: *The Peyote Religion*. New York, The Free Press of Glencoe, 1956.

CHAPTER 23

MYSTICAL EXPERIENCE AND THE CERTAINTY OF BELONGING: AN ALTERNATIVE TO INSIGHT AND SUGGESTION IN PSYCHOTHERAPY

RAYMOND PRINCE

SEVENTY YEARS AGO William James published the first major scientific study of mystical experiences *(Varieties of Religious Experience)*; he described their phenomenology, divided them into categories, and distinguished them from other types of religious experience. Perhaps his most important contribution, however, was that he made mystical experience an intellectually respectable object of study. In the past twenty years, the *weltanschauung* has been increasingly favorable for such studies; scores of publications have appeared discussing these states, their similarities to and differences from other alterations of consciousness (especially those induced by psychedelics), the methods of their production, their neurophysiological correlates, their explanation in psychological terms and their philosophical and religious implications (Tart, 1969).

Some Definitions

What is mystical experience? It may be defined as an alteration of consciousness during which there is a radical change in the everyday sense of self and experience of time and space; the mood is usually euphoric and a feeling of heightened significance attaches to the episode; there is the feeling that words are inadequate to describe the experience. These states vary greatly in mode of onset, intensity, duration and susceptibility to recall. Some occur spontaneously; others represent the culmination of a prolonged quest; still others may be the result of the use of psychedelic substances, or form part of the phenomenology of a functional psychotic episode or a toxic or organic brain disturbance. W. T. Stace, in *The Teachings of the Mystics* (1960), has conveniently divided these states into those in which the awareness of the environment persists—the extrovertive group—and those in which the awareness of environment is lost—the introvertive.

In extrovertive experiences the individual feels himself to have become part of surrounding nature and, in addition to the general mystical characteristics noted above, there is usually a heightened intensity of visual or auditory perception, and a quality that suggests the use of the word "religious". They often light up the surroundings, so to speak, so that many years later these experiences can be recollected complete with the setting in which they occurred. Other terms for them include peak experiences, nature mysticism or adamic experiences: the last of these, for example, suggests that during the episode the world appears as it did to Adam on the day of creation.

Introvertive experiences are more intense and for the most part occur to those who have adopted an ascetic way of life and have practiced meditation or other techniques in order to achieve them. The environment is lost and there remains in consciousness only the sense of one all-pervading aspect; or in the Judeo-Christian and Islamic traditions, the sense of two things, the self and God. Some authors maintain that these two kinds of introvertive experience are identical and that only the interpretation is different; the interpretation of the experience depends upon the pressures of the belief system of which the mystic is part, and to *be* God is anathema in the Judeo-Christian world.

Some authors assert that these various kinds of mystical experience, including both the introvertive and extrovertive, are part of a single continuum of increasing intensity, with aesthetic experiences and adamic states at one end and the high-powered introvertive experiences at the other. But others like Zaehner (1957) see a profound difference between the adamic and monistic experiences on the one hand and the dualistic self-in-the-presence-of-God experiences on the other: according to him, only the latter are of supernatural origin.

Quite apart from their alleged supernatural implications, there has been increasing interest in the potential psychotherapeutic value of mystical experiences. Savage and his associates (1967) have used mystical experiences induced by a single large dose of LSD in the treatment of alcoholics and drug addicts; Pahnke (1970) used a similar technique in preparing terminal cancer patients for death. Asrani (1963) has emphasized that there has always been an awareness of the important mental health implications of mystical experience in Hinduism. As a result of his personal experience he concluded that

> ... mystical experience not only concentrates and balances the mind; it also frees the self from psychological states such as superiority and inferiority, insecurity and fear, doubt and opinion, and egotism. It seems to be a state of perfect mental health, for the mind and its workings become so smooth and unperturbed that the very existence of the mind is not felt at all. ...

Kapleau (1966) provides a number of interesting case histories of improved mental health following enlightenment associated with Zen meditation. In this paper I would like to explore these psychotherapeutic effects further, finding a reply to the question: *Why should mystical states have this beneficent result?* In approaching the problem, I will briefly review some contemporary theories about what is therapeutic in psychotherapy and I will explore the nature of mystical states to determine whether these theories can adequately explain their observed therapeutic effects.

No doubt the most influential contemporary explanation for the value of psychotherapy in the Western world has to do with insight. It is believed that the disproportionate anxieties, hostilities and dependencies that constitute neurosis are disproportionate because of childhood experience. Psychoanalysis is the process of attaining insight into these relevant childhood experiences and the coming to terms with them. In the process the patient makes temporary regressions into his past. He reexperiences situations in his early family and projects his reactivated feelings upon the analyst. The responses of the analyst are different from those of his pathological family members and the patient is able to see his illusions for what they are. In this process, the regressions are of use to the ego in that they permit the patient to experience his disproportionate feelings in the here and now. He actually feels rage towards his analyst-cum-father in the analyst's office and sees that it is without foundation. The final result of this insight is hoped to be the creation of a self-determining individual who can see people and relationships as they objectively are.

In some quarters, it is believed that such insight and independence is the only valid therapeutic element and goal of psychotherapy. When therapeutic results seem to be obtained apart from insight, they are explained as maturations that would have occurred anyway as the result of natural personality growth or as supportive or "transference cures" that work only so long as the patient is in frequent contact with his therapist, or finally that the therapeutic effects are only transitory and symptoms dispelled by suggestion without insight only return under another guise.

But these concepts are being called into question; or perhaps it is more accurate to say that they are being seen as too limited. Although independence and insight are probably still to be regarded as the most desirable goal for some Western patients, most of the world's population is not interested in such insight and, furthermore, most psychoneuroses may effectively be mastered without it. Let me introduce this subject with an example from my own experience in Nigeria (Prince, 1963).

> One of my first patients was a schoolteacher with a walking disorder. When she walked forwards her right leg was stiff and she moved with a severe limp; however, if she ran forward, or walked backward, no stiffness occurred and her movements were normal. Her illness was obviously functional (i.e. the pathology was not in muscles or nerves but in feelings and ideas) and I decided that the best treatment would be intensive psychotherapy aimed at exploring and resolving the fears or hostilities or guilts that were theoretically behind her trouble. She seemed an appropriate candidate for such treatment; she was young, intelligent and spoke adequate English. I followed the technique of psychotherapy I had learned and employed satisfactorily in Canada. I found it quite ineffective. In spite of considerable labour and explanation, I could discover no more than that the illness seemed to be related in some way to an illegitimate pregnancy and that the girl herself attributed her affliction to stepping on some bad medicine planted in her path by the relatives of her lover. I could elicit no significant picture of her relationship with her mother or father or lover, nor any emotionally charged material. After some ten or twelve hours, I abandoned psychotherapy and resorted to drugs and electro-convulsive therapy. There was only temporary improvement, and when Dr. Lambo, the Yoruba Superintendent of the Hospital, returned from leave, I was relieved to turn her over to him, whose patient she had originally been. It was with some amazement that, a short time later, I saw the girl walking quite normally! I asked Dr. Lambo what magic he had used. He said he had simply given her an intravenous sedative and during her drowsy state, had suggested strongly that she would walk. And she walked! Now such a direct command approach is frowned upon in the school of psychiatry in which I was trained; it is said that the symptoms will be relieved only temporarily or that other symptoms will appear to take their place: 'You push it in here and it comes out there' as it were. Whatever one's theories are, the fact remains that she did walk and, from recent reports, is still walking and doing her work effectively. Such an experience is a little hard on one's professional vanity! I soon learned that the much-prized Western techniques of insight therapy are inapplicable when doing psychiatric work among the Yoruba.

This experience is not unique. In recent years a growing number of studies suggest that insight psychotherapy is both culture and class bound (Prince, 1969). Its appropriateness is largely restricted to the upper-income members of the Western world. At the same time it is also clear that the bulk of the emotional disturbances of the non-Western world are being effectively treated by techniques which foster dependence and unreasoned belief instead of insight and independence. In a recently published symposium edited by Ari Kiev (1964), descriptions of the indigenous psychiatric systems of sixteen widely distributed cultures are presented. In spite of their enormous cultural differences, the therapeutic techniques are remarkably similar! I have elsewhere (Prince, 1969) summarized the significant therapeutic elements in these cultures by using the concept of a "cone of authority."

> . . . primitive psychotherapy makes no attempt to provide the patient with insight into his own personality or to render him independent. On the contrary, the common technique is to place him within a cone of authority as it were—he is assigned to the care and control of a benevolent spirit. Important elements in the procedure include: the human representative of the benevolent spirit—the healer-priest with superhuman powers; the healer's demonstration of his powers; the charade demonstrating the destruction or transfer of evil; in some instances the periodic acting out of asocial impulses. In exchange for protection and succor, the patient must provide the spirit with food or other offerings, must behave in certain prescribed ways and follow certain tabus. There is an exchange of freedom for protection. In these systems independence is looked upon as a vice, and the spirits punish the miscreant with illness or other bad luck.
>
> I could perhaps best develop this concept of the cone of authority by means of a figure. Consider a cone of light at the vertex of which is an omniscient spirit who is the source of light. All men within the cone of light are healthy, fertile and prosperous; in the darkness beyond men are dying, or ill and prey to all manner of anxieties. To enter the cone of light requires purification, and to remain requires obedience. Halfway to the base of the cone is the circle of healer-priests who because of their proximity can communicate directly with the spirit, but the common man who rests at the base of the cone can communicate only through the healer. Under special circumstances, the spirit may descend from the apex and mount or enter the healer and speak of spiritual things to the men below; or the spirit may mount the laity directly generating within them and their companions-in-light salubrious actions.

I think this summary is sufficient for our purposes. Because of its importance for what follows, one point however, should be elaborated. As noted, one of the therapeutic steps is the healer's demonstration of his powers. Of key importance in this system is that the patient *believe*. The healer's public image is of course a highly magical one. Berndt's (1964) report of the healers of Northern Australia is typical.

> . . . like his counterparts in other regions, (he) is credited with ability to perform marvellous feats. He can, it is claimed, climb into the sky; render him-

self invisible to ordinary persons and follow them unobserved . . . his association with the supernatural and marvellous imbues him with an aura of special privilege and knowledge. It suggests that his actions in this respect have supernatural backing, that he can draw on a resource of power that is not available to other people.

To bolster his image, many healers give a demonstration of their supernatural powers as a prelude to each healing session. Murphy (1964) described some of the tricks of the Eskimo shaman.

> One shaman . . . was reputed to wrap a walrus skin rope around his neck and to direct two men standing on either side of him to pull as hard as possible until it cut his head off. He would then wrap the head in a raincoat and have someone carry it down to the edge of the ice and throw it into the sea. When the errand was accomplished and the group reassembled, they would find his head was fastened on again. A certain shamaness was said to gnaw her hands until they were bleeding and then with her tongue, to lick them back into wholeness . . . . One shaman could make the parka of his patient rise from the ground and stand up with no one in it and nothing for support.

Mystical States and Psychotherapy

Let us now return to our original question. How do we explain the psychotherapeutic effects of mystical states? Can we account for them by means of the two models we have just outlined?

I believe there is ample evidence that at least some mystical states are psychotherapeutic because of the belief and dependence they engender in accordance with the second of our models. Mystical states frequently occur within the framework of one of the established religions; the subject prepares himself for the mystical experience and expects eventually to achieve it. The presiding spirit is the Holy Ghost or Christ or Kali etc.; the spiritual director takes the role of the healer-priest; the sacrifice of worldly interests or of the sexual life takes the place of the tabus and sacrifices imposed by the deity in exchange for which the latter provides protection and succor. To make the parallel clear let us consider the well-known example of Blaise Pascal, the seventeenth century mathematician and savant. A few days after Pascal's death, his servant found sewn into his master's doublet a description of his profound mystical experience:

> The year of grace 1654, Monday 23rd November, day of St. Clement, Pope and Martyr and others in the martyrology of Rome, the eve of St. Chrysogonus, martyr and others etc. From about half past ten in the evening till about half past twelve—FIRE—God of Abraham, God of Isaac, God of Jacob, not of the philosophers and the learned. Certitude. Joy. Certitude, emotion. Sight. Joy. Peace. God of Jesus Christ, My God and thy God. Your God will be my God.

Forgotten of the world and of all except God. He is only found in the ways taught in the Gospel. The sublimity of the human soul. Just Father, the world has not known thee but I have known thee. Joy, joy, joy, tears of joy. I do not separate myself from thee. They left me behind, me a fountain of living water. My God, do not leave me. Let me not be separated from thee eternally. This is eternal life that they should know thee the only true God and him whom thou hast sent. Jesus Christ—Jesus Christ. I have separated myself from him; I have fled, renounced, crucified him. Let me not be forever separated from him. One is saved only by the teaching of the Gospel. Reconciliation total and sweet. Total submission to Jesus Christ and to my Director. Continual joy for the days of my life on earth. I shall not forget what you have taught me. Amen.

Unfortunately many biographical details which would be helpful for our analysis are not available. We do not, for example know the full extent of Pascal's neuroticism before the "feu." He is however always spoken of as sickly and he suffered what is described as "dyspepsia and a kind of paralysis." Although he was a religious man, particularly from the time of his conversion to Jansenism at the age of 23, he was neither a recluse nor an ascetic. There is also a story about his narrow escape from death in a carriage accident shortly before his mystical experience at the age of 31.

After his experience he lived intermittently at the Port Royal monastery where he at least partially observed its rule though he never joined the order. His health and peace of mind are said to have improved at this time. He became very charitable and at one point gave his house to the poor and went to live with a sister. He developed a rather extravagant asceticism, for example he would not permit anyone to discuss a woman's beauty in his presence and another sister reported that he disliked seeing her caress her children. It was after his *feu* that he composed his remarkable *Provincial Letters* and his *Pensées* (Saintsbury, 1911).

In spite of this limited information I believe that a good case can be made for placing the psychotherapeutic effect of Pascal's experience within our pattern of belief and dependence. We have a man of neurotic temperament whose symptoms were probably intensified by his narrow escape from death; his *feu* clearly had a powerful noetic quality—"certainty. . .certainty. . . I shall not forget what you have taught me"; his experience was such as to substantiate beyond any doubt what he had already believed, though heretofore with far less intensity: complete submission to Christ and to his spiritual director. All the elements of the cone of authority are present, the only variation on the theme (and this variation seems common to the higher religions) is the method of verifying supernatural involvement in the system. It will be recalled that in the more primitive cultures, proof was afforded by conjuring tricks of the healer-priest or the demonstration of supernatural powers during possession. In the case of Pascal and with most higher religious systems, such manifest phenomena are not common. Instead, proof of the supernatural is afforded by the nature of the mystical experience or by personality changes that result at the time of entry into the cone of authority. The importance of this kind of assurance can be seen in the following account attributed to Ramakrishna (Isherwood, 1965) whose experience can also, I believe, be fitted into the cone of authority model. The passage describes his yearning to experience communication with Kali:

> ... There was an unbearable pain in my heart, because I couldn't get a vision of Mother. Just as a man wrings out a towel with all his strength to get water out of it, so I felt as if my heart and mind were being wrung out. I began to think I should never see Mother. I was dying of despair. In my agony, I said to myself: 'What's the use of living this life?' Suddenly my eyes fell on the sword that hangs in the temple. I decided to end my life with it, then and there. Like a madman, I ran to it and seized it. And then—I had a marvellous vision of the Mother, and fell down unconscious.... It was as if houses, doors, temples and everything else vanished altogether; as if there was nothing anywhere! And what I saw was an infinite shoreless sea of light; a sea that was consciousness. However far and in whatever direction I looked, I saw shining waves, one after another, coming towards me. They were raging and storming upon me with great speed. Very soon they were upon me; they made me sink down into unknown depths. I panted and struggled and lost consciousness.

I believe it will be clear that in at least some cases, the psychotherapeutic effects of mystical states can be adequately accounted for within the framework of more primitive modes of psychotherapy—the integration of the individual into a supportive religio-social network with periodically reinforced convictions and significant sacrifices balanced by significant benefits. The chief difference between the primitive modes and the more advanced is the difference in the methods of generating conviction: in the former, visible magical proofs are common, or possession states furnish proof; in the latter, conviction is engendered by the noetic quality of the subjective experience. Thus far then no new therapeutic principles need be formulated.

Let us now turn to the question of insight. Can the psychotherapeutic effects of mystical experiences be attributed to insight using that word as the psychoanalysts do and as I have defined it earlier? I maintain that they cannot. Mystical states do not furnish this kind of insight. I do not know of any instance of a mystical state resulting in, for example, the recognition of an oedipal situation! Some states, particularly as experienced by women, are expressed in frankly sexual imagery:

> I had a great desire . . . to receive the kiss from the Lord, and that I would be embraced with the love of his arms, and that he would take hold of me with a grip into my heart. And this was fulfilled on me one night. I was given to understand that God wished to accomplish it on me . . . . And then the grip was so powerful that I felt it for a long time, waking and sleeping . . . . (Moller, 1965).

But even supposing we have in such instances, including the famous ecstasies of St. Teresa, the expression of incestuous father-daughter fantasies, there is no insight in the subject's mind as to the real identity of the "Lord." The situation is more akin to the "acting out" that the analysts describe. Such acting out without insight is dismissed as having no therapeutic value, but whether or not this is so, (2) it is clear that there is no insight.

We have seen then that mystical states do not bring insight, but that at least some of them fit clearly within the pattern of the cone of authority. The question is then, are there mystical states with psychotherapeutic sequelae which cannot be so placed? I believe there are. Some of these states occur spontaneously and apart from any religious structure. It is true that some of the subjects, because of the disruptive effects of their experience, seek outside advice and help; and because of the more or less specifically religious quality of the experience many seek help from religious advisors; in these circumstances they may find their way into a cone of authority. But let us consider some examples where the subjects do not. The case of Bucke is well known (Bucke, 1901).

> All at once, without warning of any kind, I found myself wrapped in a flame-colored cloud. For an instant I thought of fire, an immense conflagration somewhere close by in that great city; the next, I knew that the fire was within myself. Directly afterward there came upon me a sense of exultation, of immense joyousness accompanied by an intellectual illumination impossible to describe. Among other things, I did not merely come to believe, but I saw that the universe is not composed of dead matter, but is, on the contrary, a living Presence; I became conscious in myself of eternal life. It was not a conviction that I would have eternal life, but a consciousness that I possessed eternal life then; I saw that all men are immortal; that the cosmic order is such that without any peradventure all things work together for the good of each and all; that the foundation principle of the world, of all the worlds, is what we call love, and that the happiness of each and all is in the long run absolutely certain. The vision lasted a few seconds and was gone but the memory of it and the sense of the reality of what it taught has remained during the quarter of a century which has since elapsed. I knew that what the vision showed was true. I had attained to a point of view from which I saw that it must be true. That view,

that conviction, I may say that consciousness has never, even during periods of the deepest depression, been lost.

Two other examples from my own records of the experiences of ordinary people make the same point. I give these in the subjects' own words:

> At the age of twenty-one I had an experience in which I was in a state of ecstasy lasting about three days with an acute awareness of everything and a feeling of unutterable joy and happiness for which there was no outside reason. Since I am a very unexcitable person, matter-of-fact and never subject to either ups or downs in mood—this was a most remarkable experience, almost as if I were "one" with my maker—this way of feeling seemed to involve me in a responsibility for everyone, which I feared to accept, so I deliberately "tuned out"—the experience was never repeated. I am now 52, working mother of two teenagers with an alcoholic husband—the experience has helped me all through life.

> I am twenty and I had two intense experiences. The first was in the mountains of British Columbia; the second in Banff, Alberta. The deepest beauty I have ever experienced in my life was the overwhelming urge to throw myself into a creek on the mountainside so that I might become part of it all. At the same time I was conscious of my obligation in this life which held me back. The intensity of happiness and awareness is impossible to justly describe to anyone who has not had similar experiences. They are experiences I can bring to mind at any time as if they only happened moments ago. The memory of these two experiences have given me strength to continued through difficult periods of my life. The feelings of ecstasy cannot be compared to any other feelings of joy in this life. It is only since my last strong experience in Banff that I have been able to live a socially acceptable, constructive and independent life.

Lacking insight and without the religio-social structure, what accounts for the lifelong increase in ego strength reported by Bucke? In an earlier paper Savage and I (1966) expressed the view that:

> ... mystical states represent regressions to very early periods of infancy. The basic characteristic—that of ecstatic union—suggests a regression to early nursing experience. Possibly the variation in phenomenology represents variations in depth of the regression to earlier or later types of nursing experience. It is possible too that the outcome of the experience—either the successful return to the real world or the entry into psychoses—depends in part upon whether these early feeding experiences were pleasurable or frightening.

Conclusion

In examining these experiences of Bucke and others (particularly in Western cultures) one is impressed by reports of first hand experience of cosmic beneficence. There is the assurance that at the heart of things there is something that is good. This is not a knowledge arrived at by logic, but first hand experiential knowledge which I think can be quite well explained as a regression to early pleasurable oral experience. That early experience was of course before the creation of the world, as it were, in the primal chaos long before there was self and other and before space or time and before there were objects. It is conceivable that this first hand regressive experience of goodness could have a psychotherapeutic effect. I know of no similar kind of effect in other psychotherapies and therefore would consider that it is a distinct psychotherapeutic principle, quite distinct from insight and authority and dependence.

Another closely related element which appears strongly in these texts is the assurance that man is not alone and separate but is linked in some very intimate way with the rest of the universe—inanimate nature, the animal world, other men—All. Of course, this is an idea that can be arrived at rationally. But arrived at by logical argument the concept seems to have little meaning. It is cold comfort to know that the supernovae, the trees and I are all made of the same stuff! But with the regression to a primordial ego structure with more fluid boundaries so that one can actually experience unity with nature, the idea takes on much more reality and significance. One really knows that one is part of the All because one was there.

It should also be noted that the assurance of being one with the All, in addition to nullifying the sense of alienation that reputedly afflicts modern man, may lead to other psychological changes. As one subject explained:

> Before the experience I was full of petty resentments and jealousies and had many fears—particularly of certain little bugs that crawl on the cellar floor. In the experience I felt I was part of everything and loved everything. I tried out the thought of having one of those bugs crawl on my arm and I wasn't afraid anymore. But also I felt one with all animals and I couldn't possibly eat any of them or even kill bugs. Even now, long after the experience I have no interest in eating meat—I suppose I might be sick if I tried. It is a sort of extension of the idea of cannibalism. On the whole though, since the experiences, I am much more placid and don't care about a lot of things that seemed so important at one time—you know the latest fashions, and keeping up with the Joneses and having a horse for the children to ride and having a house in the country and all that.

It is no doubt a combination of these factors that provides the therapeutic effect of mystical experiences: the knowledge that the self is part of the All and therefore is in some sense immortal; that the fundamental nature of the All is beneficent; and most important, that these beliefs are indubitable because they derive from immediate experience.

REFERENCES AND FOOTNOTES

1 For all references consult the Bibliography at the conclusion of this study. Author's name and publication date indicate the monograph, article, or book referred to in the text (usually in parentheses).
2 Studies in primitive psychiatry would, it seems to me, call this tenet into question. Acting out, without insight, within socially sanctioned situations does seem to have therapeutic value. The acting out of female roles in annual masquerade festivals by men damaged by witchcraft seems to have some therapeutic value in impotence, etc. Such therapeutic effects fit within the cone of authority patterns (Prince, 1964).

BIBLIOGRAPHY

1. Asrani, U. A.: A Modern Approach to Mystical Experience, *Main Currents of Modern Thought, 20*: 15–20, 1963.
2. Berndt, C. H.: The Role of Native Doctors in Aboriginal Australia. In Kiev, Ari (ed.): *Magic, Faith and Healing*, 1964 (see below), pp. 264–282.
3. Bucke, R. M.: *Cosmic Consciousness/A Study of the Evolution of the Human Mind*, Philadelphia, Innis & Son, 1901.
4. Isherwood, C.: *Ramakrishna and His Disciples*, New York, Simon & Schuster, 1965.
5. James, William: *Varieties of Religious Experience*, New York, Longmans, Green and Co., 1902.
6. Kapleau, P.: *The Three Pillars of Zen*, New York, Harper & Row, 1966.
7. Kiev, A.: *Magic, Faith and Healing*, New York, Free Press, 1964.
8. Moller, H.: Affective Mysticism in Western Civilization, *Psychoanal. Rev. 52*: 117–130, 1965.
9. Murphy, J. M.: Psychotherapeutic Aspects of Shamanism in St. Laurence Island, Alaska. In *Magic, Faith and Healing*, 1964, pp. 53–83.
10. Pahnke, W. N.: The Psychedelic Mystical Experience in the Human Encounter with Death, *Psychedelic Rev. 11*: 4–13, 1970.
11. Prince, R. H.: Western Psychiatry and the Yoruba: The Problem of Insight Psychotherapy. *Conference Proceedings, March, 1962, Nigerian Institute of Social and Economic Research* (pub. 1963), pp. 213–221.
12. Prince, R. H.: Indigenous Yoruba Psychiatry. In *Magic, Faith and Healing*, 1964, pp. 84–120.
13. Prince, R. H.: Psychotherapy and the Chronically Poor. In *Culture Change, Mental Health and Poverty* (J. Finney, ed.), Lexington, University of Kentucky Press, 1969, pp. 20–41.
14. Prince, R. H. and Savage, C.: Mystical States and the Concept of Regression, *Psychedelic Rev. 8*: 59–74, 1966.
15. Saintsbury, G.: Blaise Pascal, *Encyclopoedia Britannica*, Eleventh Ed. (1911), Vol. 20, pp. 878–881.
16. Savage, C.: Psychedelic Therapy and Personality Maturation. In *Do Psychedelics Have Religious Implications?* (ed. by D. H. Salman and R. H. Prince) Montreal, R. M. Bucke Memorial Society, 1967.
17. Stace, W. T.: *The Teachings of the Mystics*, New York, Mentor Books, 1960.
18. Tart, C. T.: *Altered States of Consciousness*, New York, Wiley & Sons, 1969.
19. Zaehner, R. C.: *Mysticism, Sacred and Profane*, Oxford, Clarendon Press, 1957.

CHAPTER 24

RELIGION AS A MEDIATING INSTITUTION IN ACCULTURATION

The Case of Santeria in Greater Miami

Joan Halifax and
Hazel H. Weidman

INTRODUCTION

This chapter describes some of the specific situational, cognitive, perceptual, and psychodynamic factors we believe to be operating in the efflorescence of an intricate religious system within the Cuban community of Miami, Florida. Santeria, a syncretic religion derived from West African forms of worship, is the focus of our investigation. This religion can be considered in its present setting as a "crisis cult." (1) Certainly, it is proliferating more in Florida than it did in Cuba. If we accept La Barre's hypothesis that a majority of religious movements occurring in the arena of acculturation occupy varying positions on a continuum between the purely nativistic and the accommodative, (2) then Santeria in Miami would be placed at the accommodative end of the scale.

The social facts are as follows: (a) rapid acculturation as a consequence of displacement of large numbers of Cubans into the United States, (b) minority status of the acculturating group, and (c) social ambiguities inherent in the acculturating situation as well as psychological ambivalence about them.

This chapter describes the way certain strategies within Santeria help resolve some of the adaptive problems experienced by the Cuban. The hypothesis advanced is that specific psychological processes, such as denial, projection, and dissociation, which many Cubans commonly rely upon in ego-defense, can be ego-integrative within the context of this religious system. These defense mechanisms are seen as being used constructively within a traditional institutionalized framework to allow the individual to achieve a progressive adaptation within his community. The function of this religion, then, is presented as providing a means of structuring a new reality for its followers.

The discussion proceeds as follows: First, there is a description of the community "in process." Second, some of the key elements involved in value conflict are outlined. Third, Santeria is described to reveal its existential and pragmatic orientation, and to suggest the ways in which both "distancing" and "explanatory" aspects of projction function in the religion. Fourth, divination by the santero is examined as a ritual which has important therapeutic functions. Finally, there is an analysis of the emergence and role of this religion as a mediating factor in the acculturative situation.

THE COMMUNITY "IN PROCESS"

Since 1959, Cuban nationals have been coming to the United States in great numbers. The first migration represented the wealthier Habaneros, (3) some of whom brought their fortunes with them. By a majority, however, the Cubans arriving in the past decade have come from the lower middle class, bringing with them the desire for upward mobility and the hope of returning to Cuba one day. In these past ten years, more than 400,000 Cubans have made their way to the United States. (4) Over half have settled in Dade County, Florida, bringing the Cuban population of the county to well over 200,000. This represents one fourth of the total population. Demographers estimate that the Cuban population of South Florida will reach 450,000 within the next ten years. (5)

Although the government of the United States has given material aid and encouragement to the Cuban, some very basic problems have emerged in recent years. Perhaps they can best be illustrated by demonstrating the discrepancy between the Cuban's perception of his destiny in this country and the perception of the host. Since the beginning of the sixties, many Cubans have referred to themselves as "exiles," implying that they intend to return to their country in the near future. Yet the Anglo community has consistently referred to the Cuban national as "refugee," a term having the more negative connotation of "intruder" or "uninvited guest." The significance of this discrepancy and the need for its resolution become more salient every day as the possibility of return to Cuba grows more remote. The Cuban survives, and in many cases survives in style, in his "temporary" homeland. Yet, he has often suffered humiliation and disappointment in his new environment. Language and values set him outside the American norm. Beside the loss of his country he has experienced a loss of status and often the loss of loved ones. Loss, separation, and value conflict combined with economic uncertainty in an environment often perceived as hostile have contributed to increased anxiety for many individuals.

VALUE CONFLICT

The encounter of specific, contrasting American values with traditional Cuban values provides a clearer picture of the extent to which social ambiguities and psychological ambivalences are implicit in the acculturative process being experienced by many Cuban exiles in Southern Florida. While Kluckhohn and Strodtbeck outline five dimensions along which social groups assume one or another position to "solve" the five basic orientation problems of man, (6) only the *Relational* value orientation is examined here. We believe that it is this particular Cuban value orientation which has undergone the most significant change in the present setting. The patterns under discussion are drawn from the literature, conversations with Cubans, (7) and from participant observation. (8)

The dominant Cuban relational value-orientation has been that of *Lineality,* where authority passes from parent to child, from priest to congregant, from santero (9) to initiate, from dictator to citizen. The dominant social configuration in Cuba reflects esteem for one's elders and loyalty to one's family. The primacy of the family binds an individual into an intimate continuity with an historical successional past and an ordered present.

Collateral and *Individual* orientations also occur within the dominant *Lineal* configuration. *Collaterality* exists in the form of exclusive peer groups that are based in friendship and loyalty. These peer groups secondary to the family,—can be classified by age, sex, profession, status, or region. *Collateral* and *Individual* orientations can functionally exist without paradox. This is seen when the laterally extended friend-group is temporarily incorporated into the extended family of one of its members. The group itself then becomes subject to the authority of that family. Another example of co-variant co-existence occurs in the case of idiosyncratic behavior, which is tolerated with the confines of the clan as long as it represents no threat to the continuity of the family. In fact, the Cuban parent may inform his child that he, the child, is different from and better than everyone else, thereby reinforcing the child's sense of individuality and high self-esteem. This message, however, is set within the frame of the family so that all family members enjoy a feeling of uniqueness and worth together. (10)

The family forms the basis and model for all relationships. It is within the family network with its linear authority and historical continuity that individuals experience a familiar sense of indentification and can be supported. Yet, it is this system that has suffered the most in the present setting.

The American relational system is the obverse of the Cuban one in that individual goals have a primary over those of any lineal or collateral group. This autonomy is based in competition and goal-orientation. The feeling of possessiveness experienced by the loyal and nostalgic Cuban, is weaker in the middle class "mobi-centric" American as he moves in and out of jobs, in and out of homes, and in and out of families with relative ease.

Kluckhohn and Strodtbeck point out that a society which is Lineally or Collaterally oriented, with a first order preference for *Present* time orientation and *Being* activity orientation (as is Cuban society) will encounter severe problems in introjecting the values of the American middle class, with the following dominant orientations: *Individual* (relational), *Future* (time), *Doing* (activity) and *Mastery-over-nature* (man-nature). Particularly will this be so if change in the *Relational* orientation occurs too rapidly. (11)

The *Relational* value orientation has been one facet of Cuban culture most difficult to maintain in the United States. Economic pressures, the emancipation of the Cuban female, and the school system have all contributed to the stress load on the *Lineally*-oriented extended family. Other support systems are emerging, however, one of which is the unorthodox Afro-Cuban religion, Santeria.

Santeria—Foundation and Characteristics

The foundations of Santeria were brought to Cuba by West African slaves during the seventeenth century. A process of syncretism occurred over several centuries as social interaction between blacks and whites developed, and whites became increasingly involved in African religion. (12) The African belief in the existence of ancestral ghosts (i.e., the Egungun), was similar to the spiritism popular in Cuba during the nineteenth century. The adulation of Catholic saints meshed with the worship of African gods called "orichas." Catholicism, spiritism, animism, (13) and animatism (14) syncretized into what is called "Santeria" or oricha worship.

The Orichas

Santeria reflects the Yoruba world view, and its saints, or orichas, are African is style and concept. Unlike the distant and moral saints of the Catholic church, the orichas are complex and very human personifications of nature. Lydia Cabrera says of these dieties: "The saints are the same here and in Africa. The only difference is that the orichas like to eat and dance; yours are contented with incense and do not dance." (15) Under Miss Cabrera's wit lies a mountain of truth.

The Yoruba do not conceive of the world as a conflict between good and evil forces. Rather the forces that inhabit this world are close to the individual, are part of him, and can be bribed into working on his behalf or protecting him. By forming the right alliances, one can manipulate his universe and thereby master it. When favor with a divinity is lost, an individual who was formerly protected may become the target of forces that could cause him misfortune or even death. The central purpose in life, then, is to form the proper relationships with the spirits. The maintenance of these relationships occurs within the context of the religion by means of multiple rituals.

Everyone has an oricha, or saint, which is the guardian of his "head." A person does not ordinarily know which diety has his "head" however. Frequently, an individual begins to question "ownership" when he feels uneasy about certain aspects of his life or when others imply such "ownership."

The santero is one who has the ability to determine an individual's oricha, but he must be sought out by a client for this purpose. The santero performs a "registro," or divination with cowrie shells, and learns the name of the oricha that is beginning to make its presence known. Generally, the oricha bears some resemblance to his "hijo" or "son" and is an appropriate fit in terms of personality characteristics and/or behavior. This has important bearing on the expressive aspects of existential Santeria.

The Existential Emphasis

The existential nature of Santeria is one of its most striking characteristics. Emphasis is placed on the ability of the devotee to define his existence within the framework of the religious cosmology. There is constant affirmation of "beingness" whereby an individual experiences a degree of freedom and expressivity that he could not otherwise enjoy. Yet his freedom is circumscribed by his responsibilities to the orichas and his loyalty in implementing their directives.

It is through the oricha and its many "caminos," or roads, that an individual can move beyond the limits of socially acceptable behavior. Dissociation in the form of trance occurs in the course of ceremonials, and "possession by one's saint" implies that the individual is no longer himself. "I feel Shango tonight," may be the sanctioning prelude to sexually aggressive behavior in the trance state. "Eleggba was in my head when I stole the wallet," displaces the responsibility of action from the individual to the capricious trickster saint. In both sacred and secular contexts the displacement of responsibility provides an individual the opportunity to behave in ways and express feelings that, ordinarily, would be beyond the bounds of propriety. His circumstances then, depend entirely on the nature of his present relationship with the saint.

The Pragmatic Focus

Problem solving and an action orientation are central to the operation of the religion. The devotee concerns himself with his current problems on this earth, whether they lie within the realm of love or health or money. His suffering in whatever form it takes, is in the here and now and is frequently interpreted as a "falling out of favor" with the orichas. To right the situation an individual curries favor with his saint. Acts of propitiation and appeasement are carried out to obtain power, to preserve order, and to insure health, happiness, and success in the present time, not to pave the way to heaven.

The Psychodynamic Base

For the Cuban involved in Santeria the immediate nature of the relationship with the orichas provides a concrete and familiar set of reference points in a world that reflects less order than it did previously in Cuba. The "reality" of the new world in the United States is not yet determined. It contains many ambiguities which, at times, make it seem threatening and chaotic. The tendency for many individuals under such circumstances is not to look within the self for resources or guides to behavior which might lead to clarification and definition of a new "reality." Rather, the pattern is to turn to a "higher" source of authority, secular or sacred, for assistance. When secular figures of authority are not recognizable, are inaccessible, or non-functional, the powers which dominate the sacred realm may offer greater potentialities in this regard.

The world view of Santeria provides a particularly appealing cognitive system within which such social and psychological uncertainties may become more meaningful and structured. It is a guidance system which builds upon psychological processes of denial and projection in its advocates. It supports and utilizes constructively the two related but slightly different aspects of ego-defense described by Weidman and Sussex as the "explanatory" and the "distancing":

> In the intra-psychic system . . . escape, avoidance or 'distancing', is implemented by the use . . . of repression and denial. . . . Projection and dissociation are among the mechanisms by which repression and denial are maintained. . . . The mechanism of projection accomplishes two related but slightly different functions. It is, in one sense, part of an explanatory system by which the culture defines the nature of the universe and leads to a view of the self as more 'acted-upon' than as 'actor'. It is also a mechanism by which the ego defends itself against the conscious acknowledgment of impulses and feelings which, if expressed and acted upon, might call forth a retaliatory response from the potentially destructive environment. (16)

Santeria defines the individual as more "acted upon" than as "actor" and thus provides "the reason" for the Cuban's increased sense of powerlessness—a powerlessness which accompanies the fact that traditional behavioral "keys" do not always fit new social "locks." The religion also allows the intra-psychic "distancing" by which the ego defends itself against guilt or overt recognition of undesirable inclinations or affect.

In our view, feelings of guilt inevitably enter the picture in any acculturative situation. (17) At one level of awareness or another guilt accompanies the inability to carry out traditional patterns of behavior or to meet traditional sets of expectations. Guilt also accompanies feelings of inadequacy associated with "not knowing" the new rules of the game. (18) When the new rules of the game are learned and they conflict in the fundamental ways described above, i.e., at the level of basic value orientation, guilt mechanisms are compounded and their functioning greatly complicated.

Quite in line with traditional ways of defending the self and the good name of the family, such feelings tend to be handled by the Cuban through repression, denial, and projection. Unfortunately, the patterned projections of the past do not apply in the new setting; nor do the institutionalized ways of channeling and coping with them have the same "goodness of fit." Unpredictable political regimes, regional factions, and old family rivalries are no longer entirely appropriate "sources" of dys-ease or misfortune. Status hierarchies are shifting. Some have collapsed. Key figures of authority are not always identifiable. Santeria provides alternatives in this regard. The defense mechanisms of denial and projection are left intact. In the religion they are, in fact, reinforced, and the orichas become "causal agents" in the maintenance of the individual's sense of well-being.

The entire institutional form, Santeria, rests upon processes of denial and projection in its adherents. It defines sources of responsibility as lying within the supernatural realm and, therefore, supports the "transfer" of guilt in the individual to loci outside the self. This kind of "distancing" is primary. Another kind of "distancing" is involved in the effort to deny unacceptable impulses and feelings, and this, too, is supported within Santeria. The existential emphasis in the religion allows expression of such impulses and feelings. Dissociation is the means whereby expression becomes possible, but denial and "disavowal of ownership" is maintained by the explanatory aspects of projection. The rationale for behavior in the trance state is, of course, "possession by the saint." Furthermore, the "explanatory" aspect of projection, which clarifies through pronouncements and commands of orichas, reduces feelings of anxiety associated with a still ambiguous new "reality." This explanatory and directive process is highly developed within the pragmatic focus of the religion and operates through the ritual of divination.

In our view, reliance upon denial and projection can be ego-integrative for an individual within the context of Santeria. For example, denial and projection underlie the states of trance dissociation that occur in ceremonial context. Such psychological processes serve to enhance the individual's sense of mastery by separating the acceptable "me" from the unacceptable "not me" and then allowing the return to "self" again, refreshed through the catharsis of "acting out" or indulging repressed, denied, or unconscious impulses. A person is further strengthened by the knowledge that his saint has "mounted" him and, therefore, has a personal interest and investment in his well-being. We believe that the Cuban's sense of "place" and "mastery" in his new world is enhanced in other ways in the religion, but it is the relationship with the oricha, through the santero acting as intermediary, that is particularly important in this regard.

THE SANTERO AND DIVINATION

The role of the santero in Santeria is a central one. This priestly figure functions not only as mediator and medium between humans and other-than-humans but, also, as personal counselor, healer, and visionary. One of the most frequent devices he uses in relating to his "clients" and the supernatural is divination, of which there are many forms. It is the function of divination that suggests the santero's role as "change agent" and "therapist" for many Cubans in the Florida setting.

As diviner, the santero employs rituals intended to mobilize the supernatural to reveal the unknown. Divination is performed when an individual wishes to understand the "inexplicable" or threatening, to insure gratifications of various kinds, both positive and negative in character, or when he must make a decision which he feels unsure about or incapable of making. (19)

It is the process of divination which guides the metamorphosis from "self as acted-upon" to "self as actor." The individual becomes involved in "initiating" behavior the moment he decides to go to a diviner. In this step he has exercised an option which represents a beginning effort to alter some aspect of his life. The process of divination brings specific issues into clearer focus. Through the voice of the oricha, the balance of cognitive and perceptual ambiguity is tipped to one side or the other. Feelings of ambivalence in a particular problem area are resolved, and appropriate affective response becomes possible. Freedom to act is the immediate consequence, and the initial actions taken are guided by the santero.

The client is always advised to perform certain rituals, harmless in themselves but usually involving sacrifice of some sort. Again, the individual exercises an option to follow directions or not. Usually, he does, and this strengthens his resolve to effect change. The propitiatory offering to the client's saint diminishes the sense of vulnerability in two important ways. It alleviates guilt associated with prior inability to act, and it reduces anxiety associated with feelings of powerlessness. The offering serves to establish or reaffirm an alliance with the diety. It represents an act of obeisance. But, because of the nature of reciprocal obligations involved in Cuban patterns of gift-giving, it also puts the recipient, i.e. the oricha, in a position of indebtedness. The individual is, in effect, "buying" power, a fact which may be reflected by greater confidence in subsequent relationships and activities.

This suggests the manner in which cognitive inputs from observations and experiences in a new setting may be "processed" through divination to alter perceptions and to change behavior. (20) The diviner, as spokesman for the supernatural, deflects responsibility from the individual onto the dieties. Often the oricha sanctions probing behavior which extends the field of individual experience. If significant others should comment or criticize, the indvidual remains blameless. The saint, through a santero, has guided him. Frequently, his actions represent changes in or transformation of previous behavior appropriate in Cuba but not in the United States. (21) Consensual validation from the santero and other advocates of the religion provides additional support for new behaviors and relationships which, under other circumstances might increase anxiety or induce guilt. Because they are set within a traditional sanction system, however, they are legitimized.

SANTERIA—A MEDIATING INSTITUTION

The emergence of "oricha worship" in Miami's urban Cuban community comes at a time when the family system is under severe acculturative stress. Space limitations have not permitted discussion of the structural aspects of Santeria; nevertheless, it is important to note that it replicates the kinship system in many respects. Part of the appeal of Santeria may relate to its appearance as a social form closely resembling the traditional, *Lineally*-oriented family. Inside the familiar, hierarchical structure, however, ritual provides a context that allows flexibility and alternate modes of behavior necessary for healthy adaptation.

Santeria functions as a mutagenic setting, a testing ground for the adoption of new values and behaviors. As such, it is assisting in the creation of a social fabric that is neither Anglo nor traditionally Cuban. The existential and pragmatic nature of the religion make it possible for individuals to define a new reality while meeting immediate needs. New proscriptions and prescriptions evolve in the wake of consecutive crises.

The individual's sense of mastery does not emerge from immediate and direct action upon his environment, however. Instead, it emerges obliquely, as he becomes involved in manipulating his universe through an increasingly structured network of relationships with the santero, other followers of Santeria, saints, and the supernatural. Until a set of relatively stable, acceptable values and cognitive structures are incorporated by the Cubans, the religion will exist as a mechanism of translating the threatening and potentially destructive into the meaningful and constructive.

SUMMARY

In the last decade there has been displacement of large numbers of Cubans into South Florida with consequent rapid acculturation. This has produced many areas of conflict and ambiguity in cognitive and perceptual sets for Cubans in Miami. The accompanying ambivalence has led to perceptions of self as vulnerable and environment as threatening. These processes have been interpreted as leading to a potential disorder in ego functioning. Traditional means of coping can no longer be organized in the same way as was possible previously in Cuba; yet denial and projection continue to serve Cubans as predominate modes of ego-defense.

Such a set of circumstances is potentially generative of increased rates of emotional disorder. For example, if in the absence of clear-cut social support systems, an individual increasingly relied upon projective mechanisms in an attempt to maintain ego-integrity, an extensive delusional system could evolve over the course of time. (22) It has been argued, however, that the Afro-Cuban religion, Santeria, functions to subvert this kind of regressive process. It does, indeed, reinforce the reliance upon denial and projection in ego-defense but builds constructively upon these psychological processes and, consequently, provides the means for a progressive adaptation in the acculturative situation rather than a regressive one. (23)

Santeria in South Florida is seen as reflecting a social configuration similar to that of the *Lineally*-oriented extended family. As such it offers a familiar alternative support system at a time when the family itself, as well as other traditional institutions, values, and behaviors are under pressure of change. It provides the degree of stability and direction necessary to ease the transformations occurring at the interface of two social systems which tend to meet with friction. Its major therapeutic function lies in its role as a mediating institution which builds upon traditional psychological processes to sanction new modes of understanding, perceiving, feeling, and behaving. In brief, Santeria is described as playing a central role in the structuring of a new "reality" for many Cubans in Miami.

REFERENCES AND FOOTNOTES

1 La Barre, Weston: Materials for a History of Studies of Crisis Cults: A Bibliographic Essay, *Current Anthropology*, Vol. 12, no. 1 (February 1971), pp. 3–44.
2 *Ibid.*, page 21.
3 "Habaneros" are Cubans from Havana.
4 *Health Care Needs and Resources for the Spanish-Speaking People in Dade County*, Comprehensive Health Planning Council of South Florida, March 1, 1971, p. 3.
5 *Ibid.*, p. 4.
6 Kluckhohn, Florence and Fred Strodtbeck: *Variations in Value Orientation*, Evanston: Row, Peterson, 1961. According to Kluckhohn and Strodtbeck, the five basic orientation problems of man are to find answers to the following questions: (1) What is the character of innate human nature? (2) What is the relation of man to nature (and supernatura)? (3) What is

the temporal focus of human life? (4) What is the modality of human activity? (5) What is the modality of man's relationship to other men?

Whatever variation occurs in the "replies" given, the position taken represents a value orientation, the classification of which corresponds to each of the questions as follows: (1) *human nature* orientation, (2) *man-nature* orientation, (3) *time* orentation, (4) *activity* orientation, and (5) *relational* orientation. The value orientation concept is important but complex and requires the reader's full attention, both to this and other chapters in the present volume.

7 Dr. Mercedes Cros Sandoval made an invaluable contribution to this section.
8 Participant observation was carried out by the first author of the present study.
9 The santero is the priest in Santeria.
10 Such feelings of uniqueness and worth may be contradicted in other ways by virtue of the fact that any hierarchical system *de-values* those on the "deference" side of respect relationships. This is very similar to the Burmese case examined in detail elsewhere. Cf. Hitson, Hazel M. and Daniel H. Funkenstein: Family Patterns and Paranoidal Personality Structure in Boston and Burma, *International Journal of Social Psychiatry*, Vol. 5, no. 3 (Winter 1959). The point to be made here is that the basic contradiction between individual "worth" of children and "low status" of children within the family hierarchy of respect relationships contributes to the level of ambivalence built into Cuban personality. It has been argued, in fact, that such social ambiguities, in combination with other factors, are systematically related to primary reliance upon denial and projection in ego–defense. In this regard cf. particularly, Weidman, Hazel Hitson: "Cultural Values, Concept of Self, and Projection: The Burmese Case," in William Caudill and Tsung-yi-Lin (eds.): *Mental Health Research in Asia and the Pacific* (Honolulu, East–West Center Press, 1969), pp. 259-285.
11 Kluckhohn, Florence and Fred Strodtbeck: *op. cit.*
12 Sandoval, Mercedes Cros: Lo Yoruba en la Santeria Afro cubana. Unpublished doctoral dissertation, University of Madrid, Madrid, Spain, 1966.
13 "*Animism*—belief that all events of the material world are affected or controlled by supernatural entities, such as ghosts, spirits, or witches," from Beals, R. L. and Harry Hoijer; *An Introduction to Anthropology*, 4th ed. 1971, p. 674.
14 *Animatism* is defined as "the belief that inanimate objects are capable of sentient action and movement" (from Beals, R. L. and Harry Hoijer, *op. cit.*, p. 674.
15 Personal communication with first author, Joan Halifax.
16 Weidman, Hazel Hitson and James N. Sussex: Cultural Values and Ego Functioning in Relation to the Atypical Culture–Bound Reactive Syndromes, *Internatioinal Journal of Social Psychiatry*, Vol. 17, no. 2 (Spring, 1971), pp. 83–100.
17 This subject has been discussed extensively in a previous paper by the second author, Hazel H. Weidman, entitled, "Shame and Guilt: A Reformulation of the Problem," presented at the 64th Annual Meeting of the American Anthropological Association, Denver, Colorado, Nov. 18–21, 1965.
18 A classic illustration of this point comes from the Psychiatric Institute of Jackson Memorial Hospital. A Cuban psychiatric patient complained to the first author, John Halifax, that his major problem was not knowing the "rules of the game" in America. He said, "In Cuba, we have a rule book; it's all written down how to behave. But here you have no rule book; so I'm always getting in trouble." The implication in the context of this discussion was that he was being punished for breaking rules he did not know or understand.
19 In this regard, see Wallace, Anthony F. C.: *Religion, An Anthropological View*, New York, Random House, 1966. Wallace defines divination as a technological ritual "intended to control various aspects of nature, other than man himself, for the purpose of human exploitation" (p. 107). He states that divination is performed "when a decision must be made that the actor feels should be based on more information than is available or on more valid principles of judgment than he commands. In such a situation, divination is intended

to provide the missing information or principle of judgment by direct, if apparently arbitrary, advice from supernatural authority" (p. 108).

20 For an important discussion of the place and function of divination in several different cultural settings see Park, George K.: "Divination and its Social Contexts," *Journal of the Royal Anthropological Institute*, XCIII (1963), 195–209, reprinted in William A. Lessa and Evon Z. Vogt, (eds.): *Reader in Comparative Religion*, 2nd ed. New York, Harper and Row, 1965, pp. 381–392. Park makes many observations similar to those introduced here. However, he stresses that "divination has as its regular consequence the elimination of an important source of disorder in social relationships" (in Lessa and Vogt, p. 382). In our view divination within the context of Santeria also has as a consequence the elimination of an important source of disorder in ego-functioning.

21 For example, C., a 40-year-old upperclass Cuban woman was told, through cowrie shell divination, to seek employment. This directive contradicts the traditional Cuban conception of the woman's role in the family. Yet, setting and circumstance make new patterns of behavior necessary for survival. In this case divination provided the means whereby a critical life decision was made when information, experience, and resolve were insufficient.

22 Weidman, Hazel Hitson: "Anthropological Theory and the Psychological Function of Belief in Witchcraft" in Thomas Weaver (ed.): *Essays on Medical Anthropology*, Athens: University of Georgia Press, 1968, pp. 23–35.

23 Weidman, Hazel Hitson and James N. Sussex, *op. cit.*

Part Three

PLURALISM: MULTIPLE SYSTEMS

CHAPTER 25

THE MAN UPSTAIRS

Harry C. Stamey

A REVIEW OF THE LITERATURE of religious and psychiatric thought as they have related down through history affords an interesting study. For a long time the two disciplines were closely allied and indeed most psychiatric disorders were considered to be an indication of disturbance in a person's spiritual life. Beginning with Freud and his followers, however, these two disciplines took divergent paths and, in fact, seemed to assume positions which were quite opposed to one another. Many people began to think of psychiatry as being anti-religious and there was a period of time when such was obviously the case. In a recent paper I reviewed the literature pertinent to this problem and found that a less passionate and more objective study of the interaction of the two disciplines has been undertaken by modern writers. (1) Nonetheless, a considerable degree of bias remains. Most writers make some vague reference to accepting religious concepts as an integral part of a mature personality but feel that in most people it is used as a defense or a device to meet infantile needs. (2) Labarre, an anthropologist, took perhaps the strongest position and I thing his statement bears repeating here. He says, "Religion is in most people a hodgepodge of amateur cosmology, oedipus complex, private superstitions and neuroses, fossil folklore, threatened narcissism, earnestness, yearning for love, conformity, distorted views of themselves and of mankind in general, good will, cowardice, guilt, infantilism, and impulses to common decency." (3)

Such statements, plus observation of current therapeutic endeavors in the literature and in colleagues, have led me to believe that there still exists in the thinking of psychotherapists a marked ambivalence toward religion. This ambivalence has prevented or hindered objective efforts to fully understand the topic and to use this understanding to help patients. If this area of thought is puzzling to scientists who have been trained to evaluate and deal with ambiguities, what effect must it have on the untrained person, particularly one who is troubled?

PSYCHOLOGICAL IMPORTANCE OF RELIGION

With this background in mind, let us attempt for a moment to put aside to the greatest degree possible any bias which might exist in our minds and to explore religion and its importance in our society and therefore in our patients.

First of all, it seems clear that anyone who reads history cannot deny the impact of religious concepts on the early development of our country (or for that matter any other country or society). It is equally difficult to dismiss the importance of these forces in our society today. On the current political scene the subject is seldom discussed honestly and openly. In recent past we elected a Catholic president and it would seem that this denominational qualification would have been abolished as a factor in our elections. However, we have still not elected a Jewish president and it will probably be difficult to do so. Even more to the point, it is not unforeseeable that we might have a Negro or perhaps a woman as president sometime, but it is inconceivable, given the current thinking of people, that a man could ever be elected president of this country after stating flatly that he is a practicing atheist.

All sorts of changes have been made in our secular literary productions with almost no words or customs being taboo or unprintable. Nonetheless, it is very rare that the word "God" is not capitalized, or even the personal pronoun "He" when it refers to God. One could say that this is simply a literary custom that people just haven't fractured as yet but one could state with equal conviction that even our liberal writers are a bit afraid of the consequences of meddling in these matters. It interests me as I write this to realize that I, too, have continued to capitalize "God," and, in fact, will continue to do so, but I will utilize from now on quotation marks around the word "God" when I mean to indicate a neurotic, symbolic use of that word.

At any rate, all of these things seem to indicate the tenaciousness, and at times the irrationality and emotionality, with which people hang on to religious thoughts. The persistence of this trait would seem to indicate some need for it. People want the security and the structure of a religious code and in many ways, as I will point out later, it is frequently a healthy situation.

And there is a certain logicality to religious thinking. I say this because, after all the arguing is finished and all the philosophizing and theorizing and scientific obsessing is over with, we are still left with the fact that there are many things in this would which cannot be explained. The idea of a super being looms large as the only possible answer. It seems at first blush to be an easy answer, and this causes some people to grasp it readily while others rebel against it. Objective examination, however, makes us realize that we can neither prove nor disprove the existence of such a being. This renders it inadvisable for therapists to come on to patients with a superior, learned air. We must realize that we are dealing with a subject about which we are no more likely to be right than they are. In other words, what seems like idiosyncratic or at times even delusional ideas on the part of patients must be reconsidered in this light.

CLINICAL OBSERVATION

Having thoroughly confused the issue with this background, I would now like to get to the point of this chapter. Clinically, I think that we can see times in which religious thoughts are indeed a strong part of a person's mature, adaptive, personal characteristics. Some individuals who seem to be quite mature and who seem to possess a large degree of mental health judged by any of the many criteria that are available to us, seem to have this same approach to their religious thoughts. There is an adequate mix of optimism, reality orientation, doubt, ability to tolerate that doubt, indecision, acceptance of a certain degree of dependency needs, plus a zest for further exploration and growth. In other words, they are as mature in their religious thoughts as they are in other areas of their lives.

The degree to which people achieve this position is relative. There are some who cannot approach this level of maturity and in these people "God" seems to clearly enter into their neurotic problems. Once again, I think that we can see a marked similarity between their ideas about "God" and their ideas about other factors in their lives. In other words, their religious ideas and thoughts can be recognized as clearly defensive, purposeful and often symbolic of wider conflicts and must be understood and treated as such.

In recent years there have been movies, song titles, and all sorts of public references to "the Man upstairs," usually referring to the question of whether or not he likes us or is on our side. This is seen clinically in patients' ideas about "God" which reflect their dependency needs, relationship to authority figures, omnipotent feelings, guilt, etc.

THE "MAD AT GOD" SYNDROME

I became interested recently in treating depressed patients in whom religious thoughts had a real significance in the causation of their symptoms. In the previously mentioned paper I described a type of depression which was usually seen in middle-aged Protestant women. They were people who had always lived exemplary lives, being superego dominated, and in adolescence this superego had become personified by the church and by "God". These women seemed to live their lives for their "God" and seemed to be willing to do anything provided it was in the name of their religion. They showed the usual reaction formations as a basis for their personalities and they came across as very friendly and jolly, often described as "salt of the earth" people. Sometimes in late middle age depression overtook them. Evaluation revealed that there was a lot of repressed anger in these people which was directed at "God." They had lived their lives on the premise that they had a contract with "God." The terms of this contract, welded at the time of burgeoning adolescent impulses, were that the patients promised to be good and to do as "God" commanded, and in exchange for this price they would be taken care of, ultimately to receive their just reward. As time passed they began to wonder when the reward was coming. As in other depressions, symptoms seemed to come at a time when their families were leaving and when they no longer seemed needed by anyone, as younger people crowded in and replaced them in their social activities. Their questioning slowly changed into a conviction that the promised reward was not forthcoming. This resulted in tremendous anger at "God" with a feeling that he had welched on the deal. However, the very characteristics of this tremendously omnipotent authority figure rendered the patients impotent to do anything about their anger except to turn it upon themselves and become depressed. Successful therapy could be carried out by helping them to mobilize these feelings, perhaps directing their anger against another more acceptable object, and to make slight adjustments in their dependency relationships with their "God".

RELIGION AND SYMPTOMS

Interest in this syndrome brought increasing attention to the role of religion in the psychic life of patients. Could such problem areas have a causal role in other types of symptoms? As I explored this I became more convinced of the earlier statement that a person's religious life reflects his general level of personality development. In fact, I believe that if one can really evaluate in detail the patient's attitude toward "God", one will usually find a replication of his attitudes toward his parents and of the methods which he has developed to handle these attitudes. Hopefully as a child grows, he will introject parental dictates and parental traits which he finds acceptable and useful. He will integrate them and make them a part of his personality, modifying them so that there is harmony between these introjections, stored in his superego, and other aspects of his mental functioning. Sometimes, however, an incomplete type of introjection seems to take place. For one reason or another the parental ideas are not completely acceptable but neither is the patient able to reject them or modify them. They are taken in almost in toto but then transferred onto "God". The patient somehow refuses to make them a part of his own basic personality and will not take responsibility for them. He handles this paradox by setting up a strong belief in "God" whose omnipotence takes the place of the parents. Thus he does as his parents dictate but refuses to accept full responsibility for the ideas. Of course, he postpones a direct confrontation.

The need for this is based upon the child's interpretation of his parental situation and it varies with each patient. I can see, for example, that one patient might have such strong dependency needs on his parents that the only way he can give them up is to establish another, more socially acceptable figure upon whom to lean. He will often be an adequate, hardworking person but always in a dependent, somewhat self-denigrating role. This was the primary mechanism which I saw in my depressed patients.

Perhaps the patient's view of the parents was that they were extremely harsh, punitive, authority figures and he couldn't tolerate the constant guilt that would come if he made them a part of his own superego prototype. If he could transfer this feeling complex onto "God", perhaps he could occasionally ignore Him or even hide from Him, thus getting a bit of relief. In some ways this is a good bit more healthy than the complete introjection of this harsh conscience and, in fact, this is probably the mechanism most commonly contributing to religious thought.

Some people completely reject the domineering parent and refuse to consider any "God" as a possibility. Thus we see that almost any sort of mechanism might exist and the exact connection with certain clinical syndromes is uncertain at this time. The dynamics are often the same as those found in many other neuroses, but with "God" as the omnipotent figure, a figure with whom the patient cannot deal tangibly and openly, the troubles are often magnified.

RELIGION IN PSYCHOTHERAPY

As the therapist becomes aware that religious thoughts are playing a role in the patient's symptoms, he must keep several principles in mind. As already mentioned, many patients do have idiosyncratic ideas about "God" that are symbolic and neurotic. Secondly, these ideas probably reflect, either directly or inversely, his attitude towards his parents and his relationship with them. Thirdly, and perhaps most importantly, the therapist may have some biased religious ideas of his own and, these will definitely affect his thinking about his patient.

Of course this danger exists in dealing with any sensitive topic in psychotherapy, but we are usually taught during our training to deal with most such areas openly and directly and to acknowledge our hangups. Sexual feelings, hostility problems, and other emotion-laden conflicts are met and explored and hopefully solved in ourselves before we are turned loose upon the public. Such cannot be said about religion. Very little has been done in most training programs to even consider the matter, at least until fairly recently. Psychotherapists as a group tend to be more liberal, which is probably as it should be, but this sometimes becomes solidified into a type of rigid "liberality" when it comes to matters of religion.

For example, we are all aware of how irritated non-psychiatric physicians frequently become with a patient in whom they can find no organic, treatable illness and whom they promptly label as a "crock". We know that this is because of their own anxiety in dealing with an unknown situation and their frustration at having their professional competence placed in jeopardy. A psychotherapist, faced with a patient's stubborn resistance based upon religious ideas which the therapist cannot comprehend or handle, might react in the same way. He might, on the other hand, defend against this irritation by being overly gentle. Either way his own anxieties and distortions can't help but come through to the patient and interfere with therapy. Therefore, we owe it to ourselves and our patients to go back to the drawing board of self analysis to deal with these problems more completely before we attempt to handle them in patients. More effort should be exerted in training programs to assure that this work is done in embryo therapists.

THERAPY

Suggestions concerning the practical handling of therapy are scarce in the literature. Most writers make a plea for the understanding of various organized religions and their principles. I feel that this is useful but probably only from the standpoint of gaining rapport with the patient. We must show an interest in the patient's religion through an effort to understand his professed religious thoughts. Certainly his anxiety levels will be decreased if he feels that he does have a therapist who at least has made the effort to become knowledgeable with the dogmas of his church. This serves, however, only to get a foot in the door in the way of rapport, and offers little insight into the patient's mind and conflicts. His true religious thoughts are probably nowhere near those professed by the church to which he belongs or professed by him verbally.

It often helps to admit that we don't know much about the dogmas of his denomination. This may get him to attempt an explanation of his religious feelings. The more he talks, the more his actual feelings about "God" will emerge. Then we can begin to get behind this facade to find out what he really thinks about the man upstairs, whether he likes him or not, whether he is afraid of him, dependent upon him, or whatever.

We have to get him to talk about "God" as a person and gradually we try to remove the quotation marks from around the word. The patient will be very fearful of anything critical of "God" or anything which threatens to take away his dependency upon "God". He will feel guilty about angry feelings or negative feelings directed Heavenward. We have to use all sorts of techniques to get around these inhibitions, but I have found that very gradually beginning to talk about "God" is most helpful, in that simply using the word seems to defuse some of the anxiety.

It is interesting parenthetically to note how difficult certain words are to use in everyday conversation. Certainly "God" is one of these words, and "love" seems to be another one. I have found in my patients that "God", "love" and "hate" are very difficult for them to talk about in anything but a very superficial manner. The ambivalence is very easily seen and these patients, as well as many psychotherapists, tend to shy away from the direct use of the words. Running through all this, of course, is magical thinking about the power that the words have, coupled with a tendency to equate the use of the words with some sort of action predicated upon the feelings. These people very seldom see the difference between thoughts and actions.

As we get the patient to use the word, and as we get him to talk about "God" almost as a real person, we can gradually deflate "God" a little bit, occasionally seeming in the patient's eyes to tempt God's wrath right in the therapy hour. And in doing so, we subtly give the patient permission to do the same thing. Agreeing with the patient, for example, that he ought to feel angry if he believes he was treated unfairly gives him support for allowing his angry feelings to come out. Sometimes we have to go about this obliquely, such as mentioning that "fate" seems to have given him a bad deal, or "life certainly has been nasty to you, hasn't it?" At a later time, these words can be gradually supplanted by the word "God" and we get more directly into the discussion. Once this entire subject has been somewhat detoxified the patient's irrational thoughts can be handled in the same fashion that we would handle difficulties in any other area.

TROUBLE

There are two factors which render this type of treatment very difficult to carry on with the correct degree of restraint. The first is, of course, the tremendous power that the term "God" has. As mentioned before, people automatically think of "God" as a super human, super powerful, omnipotent being who can hurt with a flick of his little finger. This is enhanced by society's general attitude toward religion. These patients usually travel in religious circles and their environment does not understand any attempts at changing religious faith but encourages them to simply have more faith and to continue in the paths of religiosity that they have trod in the past. Anyone who questions "God" is considered to be an enemy and in league with the devil. Thus the behaviorist technique of society works against our therapeutic efforts.

The second factor, already mentioned, lies in the therapist's own ideas. Any deviation from complete objectivity will be picked up by the patients who are extremely sensitive to this because of their own ambivalence, and it will result in trouble.

These two factors differ little from those that operate in any other situation in which the patient has strong feelings and the therapist has unresolved conflicts in the same area. We must make every effort to treat patients' religious thoughts as just one more aspect of his personality, no more and no less. We should come on with the humility which I think is appropriate in an area in which the patient has every bit as much chance of being correct in the final denouement as does anyone alse, and we must allow him to have his feelings. If we feel that there is a strong neurotic component to them we must do our best to help him be a bit more realistic within the limits of his defensive tolerance. Our patients need their religious beliefs or they wouldn't have developed them in the first place. Our task is to modify them so that the patient can live with them, being careful above all to avoid taking too much away.

Jerome Frank discussed some of these matters in a recent article concerning therapeutic factors in psychotherapy. (4) He listed six features which are common to all psychotherapies, one of which was that we give the patient a rationale, or myth, which includes an explanation of the cause of his problems and methods to help him. He uses the word "myth" to denote a rationale of human behavior (and psychotherapy) that is not subject to disproof. I would certainly agree with this. I would take the idea a bit further and state a basic premise, namely, we must be careful not to take a myth away from a patient unless we are certain we have a better myth with which to replace it. It is entirely possible that his religious faith, certainly a myth in Frank's terms, may be serving him far better than any myths which psychotherapy might offer him.

REFERENCES AND FOOTNOTES

1 Stamey, H. C.: The "Mad at God" Syndrome, *American Journal of Psychotherapy*, 25:93, 1971.
2 Woollcott, Philip, Jr.: Pathologic Processes in Religion. In Pattison, E. M. (ed.): *Clinical Psychiatry and Religion*. Boston, Little Brown, 1969.
3 Labarre, W.: Religions, Rorschachs and Tranquilizers, *American Journal Orthopsychiatry*, 29:688, 1959.
4 Frank, J. D.: Therapeutic Factors in Psychotherapy, *American Journal Psychotherapy*, 25:350, 1971.

CHAPTER 26

PSYCHOTHERAPY AND THE "NEW MORALITY" AS SOURCES OF PERSONAL VALUES†

C. Marshall Lowe

MODERN MAN HAS to a large extent lost faith in the older systems of belief that provided meaning and psychological structure for his forebears; he therefore finds himself plunged into an experience of alienation and self-doubt. The anxiety and despair that have been the result of the loss of traditional types of faith have produced a crisis for man in both the religious and psychological aspects of his life.

The theologian is likely to ascribe the bewilderment of modern man to the loss of traditional religious symbols. The psychologist, on the other hand, is likely to describe the so-called emancipated individual as experiencing an identity crisis, or as having difficulty in formulating a consistent and coherent concept of self. While the theologian and the psychologist use different terms to describe the inner state of modern man, theology and psychology both attempt to interpret many common aspects of the contemporary individual's inner world. Both disciplines must therefore deal conceptually with the experience of a modern man who feels bewildered and alienated in a changing world where social guidelines can no longer be experienced as believable or reliable.

The Need of the Individual for a System of Personal Values

Underlying both the contemporary individual's loss of religious belief and his psychological difficulty in discovering an identity is his difficulty in formulating a system of values that is personally satisfying to him. Elsewhere, I have described values as attempts by the individual to gain an experience of an inner psychological unity that will enable him to encompass psychologically virtually the whole

---
† Reprinted by permission from the *Journal of Religion and Health*, Volume 8, No. 4, July, 1969.

of his life experience. (1) It is through values (as also through rather more specific social attitudes) that man learns to impose order and structure upon the world that he experiences at birth as a blooming, buzzing confusion. On the basis of such a schema or psychological blueprint, the individual establishes for himself an implicit set of priorities, which help determine what his purpose shall be. Gardner Murphy has thus described values as canalized drives that provide anchor points for goal-seeking behavior. (2) It is upon these psychological anchor points that man fashions a cosmology or general outlook on life that enables him to find spiritual and religious meaning and significance in his existence.

Man rather universally seeks to create an orderly and goal-directed life for himself. Every individual must find a system of attitudes and values that will enable him to arrange hierarchically his choices and experiences so that he can fashion for himself a schema or inner psychological core that will enable him to confront with confidence a world he experiences as being structured and predictable. It is obvious, therefore, that as older systems of faith and sources of belief cease being acceptable as sources of value, man must find a new rationale for his choice of values. Without some justification for his moral choices, it is apparent that man must experience the terror of an unstructured existence in a society so anomically without form that the individual falls prey to the alternative forms of that existential sickness foretold by Kierkegaard of bland indifference or hopeless despair.

Psychotherapy and the "New Morality" as Sources of Values for the Contemporary Individual

Values are (as we have seen) attempts by the individual to create an inner experience of his existence that is uniquely his own. But even though such values are both personal and individualistic, the individual is, in the learning of such personal values, never completely self-taught. As he seeks to fashion his own unique cosmology, he is inevitably influenced by the social *Zeitgeist*. Within the Western world, personal values have to a major extent been formulated out of various aspects of a general Judao-Christian tradition. In the past, therefore, individuals have been largely dependent upon the moral practices and beliefs of a so-called Christian culture for both their religious and psychological outlook upon the world.

Since modern man has to a large extent lost faith in older sources of belief, it is evident that he must search for new sources of values. Man is no longer unquestioningly willing to give assent to authoritarian and dogmatic religious creeds. Similarly, he is increasingly likely to reject traditional social moralities. He seeks instead for new types of attitudes and beliefs that will enable him to find meaning and significance among the changing social mores of the contemporary world. Contemporary man relies upon a number of different sources of direction in his search for personal values. Many individuals still find traditional types of faith to be meaningful. Others continue to find direction in political ideologies and other types of secular beliefs. There are, however, a significant number of individuals who find that these traditional sources of direction do not provide personal meaning and direction.

We shall in this paper consider two sources of values that appear to be of major current significance. Because of their contemporary importance, these new sources are able to address themselves effectively to those individuals in modern society who have become estranged and alienated from older sources of value.

The first source of contemporary values for the bewildered individual is psychotherapy. The psychotherapist has, as a moralist, taken over many of the social roles once performed by the theologian and the moral philosopher. While the psychotherapist is commonly thought of as a scientist trained in psychiatry or one of the behavioral sciences, it is inevitable that his own personal values as to what is basic in human nature profoundly influence his conception of what is wrong with man, his choice of methods in treating those problems, and the definition of mental health that he sets before his client as being the goal or purpose of treatment.

The second new source for values is found in the contemporary theological and philosophical movement popularly formed the "new morality." There are many individuals who, having rejected more traditional authorities, also refuse to become beholden either to the psychotherapist or to that interpretation of the nature of human life derived from the behavioral sciences. They seek instead to find values that have personal significance from more traditional theological and philosophical sources. This attempt to replace the older creedal orthodoxies of theology and moral philosophy with open systems of thought that possess personal meaning and, significance seems to be the broad common denominator for that rather diverse ideological movement called the "new morality."

How Psychotherapy and the "New Morality" Both Function as Sources of Values

Psychotherapy and the "new morality" are the result of two rather different fields of study. They are based upon quite divergent types of thinking, and their appeal is to quite different types of individuals. While at first glance these obvious dissimilarities would appear to defy attempts at comparison, there are, upon thoughtful reflection, important similarities between these two systems of thought. Both psychotherapy and the "new morality" have become some source of values for individuals who have become distrustful of older types of moral dogma. Psychotherapy and the "new morality" share a concern for providing the contemporary individual with a value-orientation that is both meaningful and significant in the following ways.

By providing man with a more individualized set of values. The contemporary individual finds it more and more difficult to derive values that have personal meaning from the customs of his culture. The diffuseness of modern society makes it less likely that his culture will provide him with a satisfying set of social roles. As a result, modern man is to an ever increasing extent thrown upon his own inner psychological resources. Since the fashioning of a set of personal values tends to become a "do-it-yourself" affair, the social ferment that has accompanied recent ideological and moral changes can be regarded as being the birth pangs of a more differentiated and and authentic kind of individuality. The result has been an increased need for man to maintain fidelity to his own personal value-orientation.

The significance of an increased individuality in personal values can be appreciated best by following historical trends. Western civilization during the last thousand years has been witnessing a forward movement from the rigidly prescribed morality of a feudal society where morals are enforced by supernatural sanctions to an open society where there is an increasing tolerance for diversity of values.

The decline of the Middle Ages was accompanied by the breakup of a traditional or closed morality that forced the subjugation of the individual to the general social will. The Renaissance ushered in an age of what by almost any standard must be judged to be an era of self-reliant individualism. Nevertheless, the new individualism does not appear in retrospect to have long remained as genuine as the ideologists of the period often imagined. Instead, the spontaneous nature of the new cultural forms took on an increasingly stilted nature with the passage of time. During the Age of Reason, man sought to realize his individuality through an exaltation of his rational powers that at times approached intellectual pretense. The individual came increasingly, therefore, to nourish the illusion that he was so completely set apart from culture that he was completely self-made and rationally self-determining. As a result there was, during the Age of Reason, a moral sameness, the basis for morality now being the shared ideology of basic truths that were assumed to be self-evident. Post-feudal individualism consequently had about it a stereotyped moral imprint resembling the mass-produced character of forms stamped out by a cookie cutter.

Contemporary man has suddenly become more sophisticated in his thinking about himself. Dietrich Bonhoeffer describes modern man as suddenly having come of age. No longer is the contemporary individual willing to be blindly subservient to the rigidly encapsulated system of religious belief that Bonhoeffer terms a *deus es machina*. And similarly he refuses to be swayed any longer by the polemics and apologetics based upon philosophical abstractions. Bonhoeffer describes man as possessing an independence produced by new knowledge of a universe whose mastery has become a much more reasonable challenge.

As he has come of age, modern man has also gained insight into his place in society. He has learned that he must achieve a resolution of the need for social solidarity that dominated the Middle Ages with the need for self-reliant individualism that has more recently been the dominant social morality. Thus within our own century man has become aware of the dynamic tension between the need for the individual to experience his own personal value system and the opposing press of a social morality imposed from without that seeks to enforce adherence to the mores of the culture.

Psychotherapy can be regarded as the first vehicle that modern man has chosen in his search for a personal freedom that allows him to choose his own unique set of values. Psychotherapy can justifiably be described as man's search for a more genuine experience of selfhood. Phillip Rieff, in his book *Freud, the Mind of the Moralist*, uses the phrase "the psychological man" to describe the awareness of newly individualized man of his need to reconcile the seething turbulence of emotional arousal with the demand by society that he conform in an orderly fashion to the requirements of various social institutions. Rieff associates the emergence of the psychological man with the advent of psychoanalysis. Accordingly he describes the successful patient in psychoanalysis as one who "has learned to withdraw from the painful tension and assent and dissent in his relation to society by relating himself more affirmatively to his depths." (3) He concludes, therefore, that Freud's significance lay in providing a negative community that limits the power of the culture to strangle the individual's quest for personality. In his recent book *The Triumph of the Therapeutic*, Rieff traces modern concern for this psychological man as it has evolved with various post-Freudian therapeutic systems. He describes this triumph of the therapeutic in general terms "as a profound effort to end the tyranny of primary group moral passion by learning to live more distinctly from one another. (4)

Different therapeutic processes seek a more genuine type of individuality in quite different ways. Amidst the broad diversity of a proliferating number of different types of psychotherapy there is, however, a broad common denominator: the enhancement and enrichment of the individual personality. Such a concern is seen in the Rogerian or client-centered concern for an increasingly positive self-regard. In client-centered therapy, the individual is encouraged to express his own individual feelings in what is classically described as a hothouse atmosphere in which the enhancing personal warmth of the therapist is an antidote to the coldness of an impersonal society. Concern for the enhancement of individuality is even more obvious in the newer existential therapies. Here the therapist is much more overt in focusing the client's attention upon the individual responsibility he must take for asserting his freedom in a responsible fashion and finally, an enhancement in individuality can be seen as a basic goal in behavioral or learning theory therapies. By freeing the client from the inhibitions produced by anti-therapeutic types of social learning, behavioral therapies enable the individual to gain a greater degree of self-control over his environment.

It is also the aim of the "new morality" to increase man's sense of individual freedom in his choice of values. Such an emphasis seems to be equally prominent in both theological and humanistic interpretations of the "new morality." The "new morality," as it has been embodied within Christian patterns of thought by such theologians as Fletcher (5) and Robinson, (6) has placed emphasis upon a Pauline interpretation of Christian freedom: Man is freed from subservience to the law to gain spiritual freedom. When so justified by faith, the individual is freed from legalistic and moralistic concerns so that he may fulfill the Augustinian admonition to love and do what he pleases or (as Fletcher translates the phrase) "to love with care and then what you will, do." (7)

Theological efforts to establish an *agape* or love ethic that guarantees a respect for individuality finds an echo in secular interpretations of the "new morality." While secular new moralists seem less concerned than their theological counterparts with transcendental aspects of human personality, they are equally opposed to a conventional morality that judges individual human worth on the basis of degree of adherence to social conventions. Henry D. Aiken thus describes the primary attitude of secular "new moralists" as believing that "moral experience is something wholly real, but its reality is wholly personal." (8) He describes these "new moralists" as being dissatisfied with the social game as it is conventionally played, and therefore as being concerned with replacing conventional morality with a moral code that is more experientially derived. Instead of being based upon the expectations of others, Aiken sees "new morality" as being built upon what he terms "first-person responsibilities." Morality in this way becomes a personal discovery, as moral principles become first-person precepts for the guidance of one's conduct through the maze of one's life.

By helping the individual find an identity and sense of selfhood. When the individual is uncertain as to what set of values he should espouse, he finds it difficult to know who he is. Some theorists have conceptualized this inability to find a stable identity as being due to a failure to discover a coherent system of social roles. Others have described such a failure in terms of the inability of the individual to develop a concept of self that is able to draw the different aspects of his behavior into a consistent pattern. Rather recently existential thinkers have described the problem as one of finding meaning and significance so that one is able to experience a freedom of choice over one's destiny.

Those sources of identity that have in the past supplied individuals with a sense of meaning and significance are lacking in contemporary Western culture. In a traditional society, man was able to define the nature of self through his membership in the tribe or the clan. Since he could identify with a social group, the individual hardly found it necessary to look within himself for the meaning of life. Instead, he gained a sense of significance from the strength of a group whose destiny transcended his own. Similarly, man experienced little problem in finding meaning and a sense of significance during the recent period of history in which his values were greatly dominated by his faith in reason. The individual now sought to gain a substantial amount of detachment from his culture, but instead he gained a sense of significance through the achievement of those values that were sanctioned by the Protestant ethic. Man now to a large extent could evaluate himself by the values of the marketplace, the result being what Erich Fromm describes as a marketing orientation that has required the individual to judge his own worth in terms of the value placed upon his abilities by the marketplace. (9)

There are among contemporary youth signs of an increasing dissatisfaction with an identity dependent upon recognition by others. A reaction against the values of economic achievement appears to be occurring, and new sets of values that emphasize being rather than doing are emerging. As modern youth seek to become more genuinely individualistic, they seek an identity based upon neither the values of an achievement-oriented activism, nor recognition by others. Instead, they seek an identity based upon their own stabilizing sense of wholeness or inner coherence as part of what Erikson terms a search for fidelity.

Both psychotherapy and the "new morality" can be regarded as attempts by contemporary man to replace a moral code based upon the expectations and demands of others with a more personal morality that is more personally meaningful. A broad common denominator that unites what would otherwise be highly divergent types of therapy is, however, the task of helping the individual find a satisfying value orientation that will help him to gain an enriched experience of his nature. As divergent as different schools of therapy are in both goals and methods, the aim of virtually every method is to help the individual gain control over his life. Psychotherapy does this either by helping the individual grasp his identity or sense of inner selfhood or by teaching him significance. The "new morality" can be regarded as a reaction against what Aiken calls a morality based upon "my station and its duties." (10) The sanctions for such an "old morality" are incurred through various obligations demanded by the various institutional relationships and practices in which his social life is involved. The "new morality" replaces the demands of so-called institutional establishments with what Aiken describes as a process that is akin to the Socratic search for self-understanding.

By relying upon the case study approach for understanding of the individual. The contemporary individual's heightened need for his own personal value orientation may be due in large part to his fear that, without fidelity to his own values, he will be ground down by the depersonalizing forces of a mass society whose organizational complexities constantly subordinate each member's need for individuality beneath the bureaucratic demands of institutional establishment. Indeed, many forms of contemporary social protest can not unreasonably be interpreted as attempts by individuals who feel alienated and depersonalized to confront so-called establishments with their own needs to be dealt with as individuals and not merely as atoms in an undifferentiated social mass.

It is in reaction to the greyness of the commonality characterizing so much of modern life that modern man seeks the sharpened awareness of differences that occurs through a search for values. It is in this spirit that both psychotherapy and the "new morality" can be regarded as attempts at redressing a social balance that gives short shrift to individual differences. Both seek to accomplish this through awareness of the unique circumstances in each person's life. It is, in other words, possible to interpret each one as being a reaction against those dehumanizing tendencies in modern thought that depersonalize man by interpreting his behavior in terms of abstract economic, social, or political principles.

The use of the case study approach has rather obviously been an essential part of the professional lore of the psychotherapist. Ever since Freud instituted the practice of psychoanalysis, clinicians have regarded the case history method as essential to gathering together all the relevant variables of a patient's past that bear upon his present situation. The case study is, in fact, essential to the understanding of the underlying psychodynamics basic to every type of therapeutic procedure. Indeed, it is on the basis of the case study approach that therapy can be differentiated from advice-giving. While the advice-giver moralistically applies a bromide or truism derived from experience with situations that possess surface resemblances, the therapist, by contrast, attempts to fashion his therpeutic responses into insight that reflect an understanding in depth of the unique human situation of the particular patient.

While the use that the "new morality" makes of the case study is not quite so obvious, it will upon reflection be found to be as essential to the "new morality" as it is to psychotherapy. The unique circumstances of each ethical decision must be carefully weighed in the balance. It is appropriate that Joseph Fletcher chose to entitle his already classic exposition of the "new morality" *Situation Ethics*. The basic concern of the "new morality" is, indeed, with the application of moral principles to the particular social situations. Fletcher's book is therefore appropriately interspersed with illustrative case material. It is significant also that Bishop Pike in a more recent book entitled *You and The New Morality: 74 Cases* (11) almost completely abandons a topical presentation, and relies almost entirely on a case-presentation arrangement.

Conclusion

The major thrust of this article has been that the modern individual finds that traditional types of philosophies and theologies no longer provide him with a satisfactory cosmology. Without such a general outlook on life, the individual has the giddy experience of being a rather ephemeral self in a fluid and shifting world. We have, therefore, in this paper reviewed the parallel ways in which psychotherapy and the "new morality" attempt to provide modern man with meaningful and comprehensible answers as to who he is and what is the meaning and significance of his existence.

Psychotherapy and the "new morality" have both done much to help modern man discover a system of values that is both meaningful and personally satisfying. Psychotherapy and the "new morality" are, however, for somewhat different reasons limited in their ability to change decisively the general moral style of contemporary society. Psychotherapy is expensive and time-consuming, and only a small minority of the members of contemporary society can avail themselves of its benefits. And as the author has pointed out, the practice of psychotherapy is itself rent by a multiplicity of value-orientations that make competing and conflicting claims for moral truth. There are also serious practical limitations to the "new morality" as a source of values. In its theological context it depends upon a biblical concept of *agape* that is somewhat less than universally understood in contemporary society. In addition, the principles of the "new morality" are often difficult to apply in real life. One critic has, therefore, charged that using the "new morality" as a guide to ethical actions is as frustrating as trying to grasp a greased pig.

There is a very real danger, therefore, that the psychotherapist and the "new moralist," in spite of good intentions, will both fail to become authoritative sources of values unless each can further enrich his own grasp of the ultimate nature of human behavior. The concerns of the psychotherapist and the "new moralist" complement one another. Each can contribute in different ways to the individual who seeks a more personal set of values, and since there is a significant amount of overlap to ultimate concerns of the psychotherapist and the "new moralist," it is obvious that they should have much to say to each other. It would seem appropriate, therefore, for them to work together in helping man secure a more authentic type of individualism. If this takes place, the likelihood is increased that men will be able to advance through a period of moral ferment and uncertainty to a new type of culture in which humanistic, theological, and psychological values can find a more authentic fulfillment.

REFERENCES AND FOOTNOTES

1 Lowe, C. M.: *Value–Orientations in Counseling and Psychotherapy: The Meanings of Mental Health.* San Francisco, Chandler, 1969.
2 Murphy, G.: *Personality.* New York, Harper, 1947.
3 Rieff, P.: *Freud, the Mind of the Moralist.* New York, Doubleday, 1961, p. 362.
4 Rieff, P.: *The Triumph of the Therapeutic.* New York, Harper, 1966, p. 243.
5 Fletcher, J.: *Situation Ethics: The New Morality.* Philadelphia, Westminster Press, 1966.
6 Robinson, J. A. T.: *Honest to God.* Philadelphia, Westminster Press, 1963.
7 Fletcher, *op.cit.*, p. 79.
8 Aiken, H. D.: The New Morals, *Harper's*, 236 (1413) : 58–72, 1963.
9 Fromm, E.: *Man for Himself.* New York, Rinehart, 1947.
10 Aiken, *op.cit.*
11 Pike, J. A.: *You and the New Morality: Seventy-four Cases.* New York, Harper & Row, 1967.

CHAPTER 27

HUMANISTIC PSYCHOLOGY, THERAPY. RELIGION AND VALUES

JOHN A. HAMMES

TODAY THE SEARCH for meaningful solutions to the human condition and the problems of life is a prevalent theme. This chapter presents a sketch of the contemporary value crisis, some current responses of humanistic psychology, psychotherapy, and religion, and suggestions toward the alleviation of value confusion, whether in the present or the future.

THE CONTEMPORARY AGE

Our present society has been described as passing through the *age of anxiety* and the *age of meaninglessness*. Today it appears to be in the throes of an *age of valuelessness,* in the sense of questioning the validity of traditional value systems and failing to find a satisfactory substitute.

Rollo May (1950) has presented a classical work on the age of **anxiety.** In later works he describes contemporary man in terms of T. S. Eliot's *hollow man,* devoid of a personal center, suffering as well from a loss of communication with others and with nature. Individual insignificance in an anonymous world leads to apathy, frustration, and violence (May, 1953, 1967, 1969; Gilula *et al.*, 1969). Keniston's noteworthy study of contemporary youth reflects on the theme of alienation in society. Our age manifests estrangement, non-involvement, fragmentation, despair, loneliness, and unfulfillment (Keniston, 1965). Alienation has even become a way of life (Keniston, 1968). Tillich (1952) has probed anxiety in terms of existential thought. Anxiety appears in three forms: the anxiety over *fate and death* (ontic anxiety); the anxiety of *emptiness and meaninglessness* (spiritual anxiety); the anxiety of *guilt and condemnation* (moral anxiety). Although Tillich relates these forms of anxiety to different periods of Western civilization, they can also be related to a personal time perspective. That is, moral anxiety aptly describes anxiety of the past, spiritual anxiety that of the present, and ontic anxiety that of the future.

Meaninglessness in the present age has been the theme of Frankl and the basis of his school of logotherapy (Frankl, 1963, 1966). He characterizes man as living in an existential vacuum of inner emptiness and ultimate meaninglessness. This existential vacuum, if unresolved, leads to existential neurosis, the collective neurosis of our time, characterized by a planless attitude toward life, a fatalistic helplessness, mass rather than individual thinking, and fanaticism (Frankl, 1966). Phenix (1964) relates the loss of meaning in contemporary society to the spirit of universal skepticism, depersonalization through societal specialization, and transience. He further describes the assaults on various realms of meaning. For example, meaning in language is threatened by ambiguity, self-evident truths of mathematics and science and construed as arbitrary, traditional forms of art, music, and literature have been fragmented, and absolutes have been reduced to changeable pragmatic expedients. Kemp (1967) points out that uncertainty and unawareness of where meaning can be found in life leads to horizontal living, a term he borrows from Tillich. Contemporary man runs after superficial goals without depth or true significance. To avoid confrontation with ultimate meaning, one seeks escape in busy activities, diversion, and even repression. Cole (1966) describes the world as being sick, and the germ is meaninglessness. The bizarre and grotesque aspects of modern art, music, and literature reflect this sickness. Keniston (1965) lists four types of alienation related to contemporary meaninglessness: (a) "cosmic outcastness"—the loss of connection with a divinely or metaphysically structured universe that "cares" about man; (b) "developmental estrangements"—a sense of the loss in individual life of ties and relationships that can never be recreated; (c) "historical loss"—a loss due to rapid, worldwide, and chronic social change; and (d) "self-estrangement"—a lack of contact between the individual's "conscious self" and his "real self," manifest in a sense of unreality, emptiness, flatness, and boredom.

From the age of meaninglessness man passes into the age of **valuelessness**, a consequence not inevitable but certainly descriptive of modern society. Confusion over values has resulted from the rejection of the past and lack of hope for resolution in the future. Pessimism, skepticism, and relativism dominate contemporary thought. What is left is only the present which, because of contingency and transitoriness, is of little consolation in a search for enduring values. The lack of a shared myth has let to a shattering of community, the ascendency of technological values, and the replacement of final values with instrumental values (Baier and Rescher, 1969; Keniston, 1965). Relativism prevents total commitment, for fear of allegiance to a false cause, and leads to a plethora of values, each held with only the certainty that tomorrow all will change (Cole, 1966). Empiricism reigns supreme in a technological era, leading to depersonalization, dehumanization, and social destructiveness (Reich, 1970; Roszak, 1969; Sanford and Comstock, 1971). And accelerative change in all phases of contemporary life forecasts a disease that has been called "future shock" (Toffler, 1970).

THE AGE OF THE ID

Changes in value systems are reflections of human interests, concerns, and goals at a given time in history. These in turn stem from the basic make-up of man, which has changed very little over the past few thousand years. Therefore, values can be classified in terms of human nature—namely, spiritual, mental, and physiological dimensions. At one time in Western civilization, man's value system centered on God. It was a time when Faith reigned supreme and theology, as queen of the sciences, embraced the past, present, and future from the perspective of eternity. Man, recognizing his finitude, acknowledged his God and Creator as the Alpha and Omega of human existence. Descriptively, this era could be characterized as the *age of the Superego*.

With the emergence of the Reformation and Renaissance, man became autonomous, independent, creative. Faith gave way to reason, theology to humanistic philosophy, with an emphasis on the past and present dimensions of time. It was the time of enlightenment, the *age of the Ego*. Soon thereafter the industrial revolution ushered in the age of technology and the mechanization of man. Empirical and experimental science figured highly in the evolution of values, and the consequent rule of technical reason.

The contemporary revolt against technology began with the younger generation and thence spread throughout society. Technology has become the scapegoat, rightly or wrongly, of all that is evil in society. The rebellion against the depersonalization and dehumanization of man has resulted in an emphasis on feeling, sensualism, emotion, passion, and immediate experience. Pleasure, sex and drugs are prevalent themes in contemporary living. With the rejection of the past and the future, comes the focus on the present. There is no tomorrow, so enjoy today. Man, turning away from both Faith and Reason, seeks his purpose, goals and values in affective hedonism, arationality, concupiscence. He has arrived at the *age of the Id*.

APPROACHES TO THE VALUE CRISIS

One purpose of the present paper is to evaluate the contributions of humanistic psychology, psychotherapy, and religion toward the resolution of the present value crisis. A sketch of the humanistic movement in psychology and psychotherapy is first appropriate, followed by a look at their relationship to religion. Finally, a common meeting ground will be examined, and its application to values.

Humanistic Psychology

Existential psychology can be used as a term to embrace both humanistic psychology and existential psychotherapy (May, 1961; May, Angel, and Ellenberger, 1967). With historical roots in existentialism and phenomenology, humanistic psychology was an attempt to humanize psychology and return to the discipline that behaviorism had rejected (Misiak and Sexton, 1966). In America the movement has declared itself to be the Third Force in psychology, in contrast with psychoanalysis and behaviorism. Maslow and and Sutich in 1961 founded the American Association for Humanistic Psychology, recently renamed the Association for Humanistic Psychology, and described the movement as an attitude rather than a school. It is concerned with topics such as love, creativity, self-actualization, meaning, responsibility, and values (Bugental, 1967; Severin, 1965; Sutich and Vich, 1969). The first American symposium on existential psychology was held at the Cincinnati APA Convention in 1959 (May, 1961). A related event was the first symposium held by the APA Division of Philosophical Psychology at Rice University in 1963, contrasting behaviorism and phenomenology (Wann, 1964).

Themes of the Cincinnati symposium included phenomenological experiencing, will and decision, the centered self, affirmation, self-actualization, anxiety, guilt, and death. Papers were presented by May, Maslow, Feifel, Allport, and Lyons (May 1961). The Rice symposium was rather a kind of debate on the merits and demerits of phenomenology and behaviorism. Contrasting views were presented on the nature of consciousness, predictability, modeling, objectivity, rationality, uniqueness, relativity, and potentiality of man. Participants included Koch, MacLeod, Skinner, Rogers, Malcolm, and Scriven (Wann, 1964: Hitt, 1969).

Other contemporary works in the area of existential psychology have been penned by Allers (1961), Buhler and Massarik (1968), Burton (1967), Byrne and Maziarz (1969), Giorgi (1970), Lyons (1963), Rogers (1969), Ruitenbeek (1962), Strasser (1967), and Van Kaam (1966).

Existential Psychotherapy

Existential psychotherapy, or existential analysis (*Daseinanalyse*), is usually associated with the leadership of Ludwig Binswanger and Medard Boss (Misiak and Sexton, 1966; Hall and Lindzey, 1970; May, 1967). It opposes reductionism, rejects positivism, and emphasizes personal responsibility and freedom. The primary theme is man-in-the-world, for existential analysis is a monistic point of view, in contrast with the dualistic separation of man from his environment. Man's relationship with the world (*Umwelt*), his fellowman (*Mitwelt*), and himself (*Eigenwelt*) are the existential modes explored as the therapist attempts to enter into and experience the world of his patient. The existentialist view that man creates his essence through existing, that is, by actualizing his potentialities, is the basis for existential guilt, the failure to do so (Knight, 1969). Several case histories of existential analysis are presented in detail in a work by May, Angel, and Ellenberger (1967).

The version of existential psychotherapy probably best known in this country is *logotherapy*, so-called by Viktor Frankl to distinguish it from Binswanger's existential analysis. In contrast to Freud's "will-to-pleasure" and Adler's "will-to-power," Frankl (1963) stresses the "will-to-meaning". Man lives in three dimensions, somatic, mental, and spiritual, the latter distinguishing man as human. In addition to human spirituality, two other characteristics are essential to Frankl's theory, those of freedom and responsibility. The essence of logotherapy is to make man more fully conscious—thereby increasing his freedom—and as a correlative, to have him accept responsibility for his freedom. Furthermore, man lives by three kinds of values—creative, experiential, and attitudinal (Frankl, 1966). Creative values refer to productivity and achievement; experiential values include the experience of the good, the true, the beautiful; and attitudinal values embrace one's orientation to the tragic triad of human existence, that of suffering, guilt, and death (Frankl 1966, 1967). Attitudinal values are the most important, for these give meaning and significance to human misery, and reflect the spiritual posture of man. For Frankl, freedom and responsibility go together; man is responsible to himself (conscience), to others, or to God. Since logotherapy sees in responsibleness the essence of human existence, value decisions are left to the patient. A famous Frankl dictum is *live as though you were living for the second time* and had acted as wrongly the first time as you are about to act now (Frankl, 1966).

Although Frankl conceives of his use of the term "spiritual" as broader than the term "religion," his philosophy of human nature is compatible with theistically oriented therapy (Ungersma, 1961).

Existential Psychology and Religion

Existential psychology has been defined as embracing humanistic psychology and existential psychotherapy. Religion will be considered here as generally a theistic orientation, and specifically as the Christian tradition. What relationship, then, has developed among these areas? First, it should be noted that there need be no conflict between science and religion, for the two are mutually complementary disciplines (Barbour, 1966; Bube, 1968; Raughley, 1962; Armerding, 1968; Teilhard de Chardin, 1959). Secondly, psychology as a science is reconcilable with religion (Strunk, 1959, 1962; Pruyser, 1968; Allport, 1950; Spinks, 1963; Bakan, 1966; Havens, 1968; Doniger, 1962). Thirdly, the established truths of psychology are compatible with those of the Christian tradition (Hammes, 1971).

Within psychology, the existential trend has the greatest significance for religion. Humanistic psychology, with emphasis on creativity, freedom, potential, and the dignity of man, prefaces the way for religious psychology (Strunk, 1970; Homans, 1968; Hillman, 1967). Of the various perspectives in psychotherapy (Patterson, 1966; London, 1964; Sahakian, 1969), it would appear that existential psychotherapy, in its stress upon human finitude, fulfillment, confrontation with death, and the search for meaning to existence, leads to spiritual emphases and pastoral counseling (Rudin, 1968; Aden, 1968). Finally, a therapeutic approach that lends itself readily to a Christian development is that of Frankl (see also Leslie, 1965; Tweedie, 1961; Ungersma, 1961).

The Common Ground of Meaning

The plague of meaninglessness in modern life has already been discussed. Meaning can be considered a basic human need (Weisskopf-Joelson, 1968; Maddi, 1970). The concept of ultimate meaning is not new. The three primary questions of man's origin, purpose, and destiny have intrigued theologians and philosophers for centuries. The personal confrontation with these questions is necessary in the quest for meaning, and resolutions are essential to human happiness. The three areas of humanistic psychology, psychotherapy, and religion share common interest in the ground of meaning. The humanistic viewpoint, rejecting reductionism and mechanism, opens psychology to the study of the human interest in ultimate meaning. Although most psychotherapeutic perspectives attempt to induce patient insight into proximate and immediate meanings, and whereas existential therapy fosters concern in past as well as present meaning, it is Frankl's logotherapy that centers on *the crucial pivot of ultimate meaning*. Meaning as essential in psychotherapy was recognized in earlier days. Jung defined psychoneurosis as ultimately the suffering of a soul which has not discovered its meaning, and emphasized the necessity of knowing the meaning of personal existence. He went further to say that the basic problem of almost all of his patients over thirty-five years of age was finding a religious outlook on life (Jung, 1969). With respect to religion, this discipline is by its very nature concerned with the relation of man to God and the ultimate meaning of human existence.

ULTIMATE MEANING, ABSOLUTE VALUES, AND RELATIVISM

Returning to the essential theme of this paper, the value crisis, it will be contended that the search for ultimate meaning is actually a search for absolute values, which in turn give structure and direction to human aspiration and growth. Two questions arise here. What are these absolute values and can they be attained? Absolute values are based on ultimate or absolute truths. What is the ground of absolute truth and ultimate being? Does man have the capability of discovering it? Let us consider the respective responses of humanistic psychology, psychotherapy, and religion to these questions.

Humanistic psychology, as one might suspect, is a contemporary expression of the philosophy of humanism. Humanism is essentially the rejection of God and the affirmation of man, in that philosophy has meaning in man alone. Man is the measure of all things (Kurtz, 1969). Humanism in ethics is known as naturalism (Bourke, 1970; Sahakian, 1968). Humanists accept the death of God and the assertions that human existence is probably a random evolutionary occurrence, that death is completely terminating, and that all values are but human creations (Kurtz, 1969). Humanistic psychology, as represented in the writings of Royce, Fromm, Maslow, and May maintains the philosophy of humanism in the relativity of values. Absolute values, therefore, are considered non-existent or at least humanly unattainable. Royce (1964) contends that man is encapsulated by his finiteness and is consequently condemned to a search for ultimates without ever possibly realizing them. Bertalanffy (1967) stresses human creativity in value formation, and that as an open system man will continually evolve different values in the future. The rejection of God and any value source other than man is most clearly presented in Fromm (1969) in his comparison of the authoritarian and humanistic conscience. Maslow (1962, 1964) advocates a naturalistic science of human values, to be based on experiential and experimental evidence. May (1953), sharing Fromm's rejection of authoritarianism, stresses man's creative conscience in value affirmation, thereby appearing to support relativism.

The same thread of relativism runs through contemporary psychotherapy. Rational, learning, psychoanalytic, perceptual, and existential approaches emphasize the humanistic basis of values and a consequent relativism (Patterson, 1966). The new development of Gestalt therapy is decidedly a naturalistic perspective (Pearls, 1969; Fagan and Shepherd, 1970). It is probably this relativistic conviction that partially accounts for value neutralism in the therapeutic and counseling situation. However, there has come the realization that the silent or non-committal value attitude of the therapist is in itself a communication to the patient. A preferable position has been to teach the client at least *some* ways of *evaluating the value worth of alternatives,* leaving the final choice to him (Rogers, 1969; Williamson, 1965; Pattison, 1969; Junell, 1969). Even this approach is not value-free, however, in that it presupposes value criteria whereby alternatives are to be judged.

Finally, in religion and theology there has crept the trend toward relativism. The contemporary death-of-God theology reflects the degeneration of some versions of Christian theology into the misty realms of immanentism and atheism (Fabro, 1968; Barnette, 1967).

VALUES AND THE FUTURE

Relativism and continual value change appear to be the tenor of the future. While humanization of technology rather than its obliteration is agreed upon by all, predictions of future value change are diverse (Baier and Rescher, 1969). Reich (1970), condemning the evils of industrial society (Consciousness I), and the failures of the corporate state (Consciousness II), sees hope in American youth (Consciousness III). The values of Consciousness III are bohemian, as reflected in the life-style, uninhibited freedom, drug use, and total immersement in the sensuality of the present. Reich's optimistic prophecy that Consciousness III will bring joy and salvation to the world is not shared by his critics (Nobile, 1971). In contrast, a picture of doom is presented by Toffler (1970). With the so-called death of permanence and emergence of accelerative change in all phases of contemporary life, comes a new challenge to human survival. Unless man learns to cope quickly, contends Toffler, he will succumb to the disease of "future shock."

Biogenetic knowledge provided by science and technology figures prominently in today's value crisis (Haselden and Hefner, 1969; McLean, 1968). What directions should human evolution follow? Should the ethics of religion (Barbour, 1970), humanism (Fromm, 1968; Kurtz, 1969), or science (Skinner, 1971) prevail in the determination of man's future?

CONTEMPORARY HUMANISM AND CHRISTIAN HUMANISM

The consequences of humanistic relativism are skepticism and pessimism. The existential conclusion of the absurdity of existence is a clear example. The paradox of relativism is, of course, the contention that all things are absolutely relative. Again, if man alone is the measure of all things, then truth, certitude, and value are as diversified as human opinion, and who then has the right to set forth his value system as the model to be followed? The hope of humanistic philosophers and psychologists for a value system universally agreed upon and acceptable to all, appears doomed. Their aspirations are to be greatly admired, but a value system contingent upon man alone, without sanction or validity beyond man himself, has little possibility of being universally acknowledged and accepted as binding upon men everywhere.

The alternative to a relative basis of values is one that is nonrelative or absolute, that is, one grounded in unchanging objective reality apart from subjective human opinion. That man has the natural capacity of attaining absolute certitude has been demonstrated elsewhere (Hammes, 1971). For present purposes this point will be assumed. It is then in the use of this capability that man can probe ultimate meaning and ultimate, absolute values. This brings the discussion to religion, specifically *the Christian perspective*. It should be noted that Christianity can be conceived of as true humanism (Reid, 1970) in that it embraces man in the fullness of human dignity. Not only does the Christian synthesis include the well-made points of contemporary humanism; it goes beyond the merely human to the significance of man's immortality and eternal destiny. Naturally, if Christianity is the basis for the correct theology, philosophy, and psychology of man, it would follow that contemporary humanism lacks the perspective necessary to arrive at a value system fully comprehensive of and appropriate to the nature of man. Furthermore, careful scrutiny of the objections of humanistic psychologists to the Christian interpretation indicates their opposition to be based on abuses of Christianity—e.g. religious wars, inquisitions, imposition of ecclesiastical authority on the individual conscience, etc. True Christian humanism was summed up by its founder in the two-fold commandment of *love of God* and *love of neighbor*. No humanist, relativistic or otherwise, objects to this precept. But unless it is authentically validated on ground outside of man, it will never receive universal acknowledgement and allegiance, or even invite total commitment. Many basic Christian precepts have parallels in other theistic theologies, so it is not remiss to say that a universal value system can be predicated on such common ground. The anchoring point is theism. Once God is ruled out, the only alternative is that of contemporary humanism, relativism, and the present stalemate over values.

RECOVERY OF THE SENSE OF ABSOLUTE VALUES

Contemporary humanism as a basis for a stable value system has failed, as witness the value confusion presently reigning. Christianity, and theism in general, have been abused; and these abuses have resulted in historical failures. What is needed is a fresh examination of Christianity, in terms of the communication and application of Christian doctrine. What is desperately needed is a recovery of *the sense of absolute values*. It this is achieved, other goals of recovering human dignity and humanizing technology will occur, not as direct efforts (Fromm, 1968; Wallia, 1970; Toffler, 1970; Reich, 1970; Barbour, 1970) but rather as a natural consequence of a truly Christian perspective.

What are some possible roles that humanistic psychology, psychotherapy, and religion can play in the recovery of a sense of absolute values? Humanistic psychology can continue its direction of exploring the characteristics that mark man as distinctively human—e.g. self-reflection, freedom, responsibility, creativity. It can add further the study of human behavior patterned after a belief in Divine Providence, the response of faith and love of God, the recognition of being created in the Divine image, and the directive of loving others as oneself is loved. Psychotherapy, particularly existential therapy, can study means of communicating the sense of absolute values in the therapeutic and counseling setting. Obviously, any imposition of values is a violation of human freedom, but cannot values be openly discussed with alternative choices fully explored?

Such a phase in therapy would not be introduced, of course, until the patient is capable of self-determination in the decision-making process. It should be unnecessary to add that in some instances a person's misinterpretation or at least inappropriate interpretation of religious concepts and values has in itself led to crippling emotional problems (Schneiders, 1965; Van der Veldt and Odenwald, 1952; Mowrer, 1967). These instances, however, illustrate the abuse, not the use, of religious principles in value formation.

As noted, the two-fold challenge to theism in general and Christianity in particular is the clarification of absolute values and the communication of their validity to a skeptical world. If this challenge is not effectively met, the alternative of relativism will continue to reign and eventually lead to complete moral chaos. Man must come to realize that he is not an autonomous intelligence in a mindless universe. God, the Alpha and Omega, is alone the ground of ultimate value, ultimate meaning, and ultimate being. Man may discover the purpose of all things beneath him, but without God he will never discover his own significance and meaning. Only with God can he transcend his finitude and achieve the eternal destiny for which he was created.

NOTE

For all references appearing in the text consult the Bibliography which follows. Author's last name and publication date indicate book or article to be consulted in each case.

BIBLIOGRAPHY

1. Aden, Le Roy: Pastoral Counseling as a Christian Perspective. In Homans, P. (Ed.): *The Dialogue between Theology and Psychology.* Chicago, University of Chicago Press, 1968.
2. Allers, R.: *Existentialism and Psychiatry.* Springfield, Thomas, 1961.
3. Allport, G. W.: *The Individual and His Religion.* New York, Macmillan, 1950.
4. Armerding, H. T.: *Christianity and the World of Thought.* Chicago, Moody Press, 1968.
5. Baier, K. and Rescher, N. (Eds.): *Values and the Future.* New York, Free Press, 1969.
6. Bakan, D.: *The Duality of Human Existence: An Essay on Psychology and Religion.* Chicago, Rand McNally, 1966.
7. Barbour, I. G.: *Issues in Science and Religion.* New Jersey, Prentice-Hall, 1966.
8. Barbour, I. G.: *Science and Secularity.* New York, Harper & Row, 1970.
9. Barnette, H. H.: *The New Theology and Morality.* Philadelphia, Westminster, 1967.
10. Bertalanffy, L. von.: *Robots, Men, and Minds: Psychology in the Modern World.* New York, Braziller, 1967.

11. Bourke, V. J.: *History of Ethics,* esp. Vol. II: *Modern and Contemporary Ethics.* Garden City, Image Books, 1970.
12. Bube, R. H. (Ed.): *The Encounter Between Christianity and Science.* Grand Rapids, Eerdman's, 1968.
13. Bugental, J. F. T.: *Challenges of Humanistic Psychology.* New York, McGraw-Hill, 1967.
14. Buhler, C., and Massarik, F.: *The Course of Human Life.* New York, Springer, 1968.
15. Burton, A.: *Modern Humanistic Psychotherapy.* San Francisco, Jossey-Bass, 1967.
16. Byrne, E. T. and Maziarz, E. A.: *Human Being and Being Human: Man's Philosophies of Man.* New York, Appleton-Century-Crofts, 1969.
17. Cole, W. G.: *The Restless Quest of Modern Man.* New York, Oxford University Press, 1966.
18. Doniger, S.: *The Nature of Man in Theological and Psychological Perspective.* New York, Harper & Bros., 1962.
19. Fabro, C.: *God in Exile: Modern Atheism.* New York, Newman Press, 1968.
20. Fagan, J. and Shepherd, I.: *Gestalt Therapy Now.* Palo Alto, Science and Behavior Books, 1970.
21. Frankl, V. E.: *The Doctor and the Soul.* New York, Alfred A. Knopf, 1966.
22. Frankl, V. E.: *Man's Search for Meaning.* New York, Washington Square Press, 1963.
23. Frankl, V. E.: *Psychotherapy and Existentialism.* New York, Washington Square Press, 1967.
24. Fromm, E.: *Man for Himself: An Inquiry into the Psychology of Ethics.* Greenwich, Fawcett, 1969.
25. Fromm, E.: *The Revolution of Hope: Toward a Humanized Technology.* New York, Bantam Books, 1968.
26. Gilula, M. F., and Daniels, D. N.: *Violence and the Struggle for Existence.* Boston, Little and Brown, 1969.
27. Giorgi, A.: *Psychology as a Human Science: A Phenomenologically Based Approach.* New York, Harper & Row, 1970.
28. Hall, C. S. and Lindzey, G.: *Theories of Personality* (2nd ed.) New York, Wiley, 1970.
29. Hammes, J. A.: *Humanistic Psychology: A Christian Interpretation.* New York, Grune & Stratton, 1971.
30. Haselden, K. and Hefner, P. (Eds.): *Changing Man: The Threat and the Promise.* Garden City, Doubleday, 1969.
31. Havens, J.: *Psychology and Religion: A Contemporary Dialogue.* Princeton, Van Nostrand, 1968.
32. Hillman, J.: *Insearch: Psychology and Religion.* New York, Charles Scribner's Sons, 1967.
33. Hitt, W. D.: Two Models of Man. *J. Amer. Psychol., 24:* 651–658, 1969.
34. Homans, P. (Ed.): *The Dialogue between Theology and Psychology.* Chicago, University of Chicago Press, 1968.
35. Junell, J. S.: Can Our Schools Teach Moral Commitment? *Phi Delta Kappan, 8:* 447–451, 1969.
36. Jung, C. G.: *Psychology and Religion: West and East.* Vol. II of *The Collected Works* (2nd ed.) Princeton, Princeton University Press, 1969.
37. Kemp, C. G.: *Intangibles in Counseling.* New York, Houghton Mifflin, 1967.
38. Keniston, K.: *The Uncommitted.* New York, Dell Publishing Co., 1965.

39. Keniston, K.: *The Young Radicals.* New York, Harcourt, Brace & World, 1968.
40. Knight, J. A.: *Conscience and Guilt.* New York, Appleton-Century-Crofts, 1969.
41. Kurtz, P.: *Moral Problems in Contemporary Society: Essays in Humanistic Ethics.* Englewood Cliffs, Prentice-Hall, 1969.
42. Leslie, R. C.: *Jesus and Logotherapy. The Ministry of Jesus as Interpreted through the Psychotherapy of Viktor Frankl.* Nashville, Abingdon Press, 1965.
43. London, P.: *The Modes and Morals of Psychotherapy.* New York, Holt, Rinehart, & Winston, 1964.
44. Lyons, J.: *Psychology and the Measure of Man: A Phenomenological Approach.* Glencoe, Free Press, 1963.
45. Maddi, S.: The Search for Meaning. In Arnold, W. J., and Page, M. (Eds.): *Nebraska Symposium in Motivation, 1970.* Lincoln, University of Nebraska Press, 1970.
46. Maslow, A. H.: *Religions, Values, and Peak-experiences.* Columbus, Ohio State U. Press, 1964.
47. Maslow, A. H.: *Toward a Psychology of Being.* Princeton, Van Nostrand, 1962.
48. May, R. (Ed): *Existential Psychology.* New York, Random House, 1961.
49. May, R.: *Love and Will.* New York, Norton, 1969.
50. May, R.: *Man's Search for Himself.* New York, Norton, 1953.
51. May, R.: *The Meaning of Anxiety.* New York, Ronald, 1950.
52. May, R.: *Psychology and the Human Dilemma.* Princeton, Van Nostrand, 1967.
53. May, R., Angel, E., and Ellenberger, H. F. (Eds.): *Existence.* New York, Simon & Shuster, 1967.
54. McLean, G. F.: *Philosophy and the Future of Man: Proceedings of the American Catholic Philosophical Association, 1968.* Washington, American Catholic Philosophical Association, 1968.
55. Misiak, H. and Sexton, V.: *History of Psychology.* New York, Grune & Stratton, 1966.
56. Mowrer, O. H.: *Morality and Mental Health.* Chicago, Rand McNally, 1967.
57. Nobile, P.: *The Con III Controversy: The Critics Look at the Greening of America.* New York, Simon & Shuster, 1971.
58. Patterson, C. H.: *Theories of Counseling and Psychotherapy.* New York, Harper & Row, 1966.
59. Pattison, E. M.: The Development of Moral Values in Children. *Pastoral Psychology, 20:* 14–30, 1969.
60. Perls, F.: *Gestalt Therapy Verbatim.* Lafayette (Calif.), Real People Press, 1969.
61. Phenix, P. H.: *Realms of Meaning; A Philosophy of the Curriculum for General Education.* New York, McGraw-Hill, 1964.
62. Pruyser, P.: *A Dynamic Psychology of Religion.* New York, Harper & Row, 1968.
63. Raughley, R. C. (Ed.): *New Frontiers of Christianity.* New York, Association Press, 1962.
64. Reich, C.: *The Greening of America.* New York, Random House, 1970.
65. Reid, W. S.: Christianity: The True Humanism. *Christianity Today,* 1970, *14,* 9–11.
66. Rogers, C.: *Freedom to Learn.* Columbus, Charles E. Merrill, 1969.
67. Roszak, T.: *The Making of a Counter Culture.* Garden City, Doubleday, 1969.
68. Royce, J. R.: *The Encapsulated Man: An Interdisciplinary Essay on the Search for Meaning.* Princeton, Van Nostrand, 1964.
69. Rudin, J.: *Psychotherapy and Religion.* Notre Dame: University of Notre Dame Press, 1968.

70. Ruitenbeek, H. M. (Ed.): *Psychoanalysis and Existential Philosophy.* New York, Dutton, 1962.
71. Sahakian, W. S. (Ed.): *Psychotherapy and Counseling.* Chicago, Rand McNally, 1969.
72. Sahakian, W. S.: *Systems of Ethics and Value Theory.* Totoway, Littlefield, Adams & Co., 1968.
73. Sanford, N., Comstock, C., & Associates: *Sanctions for Evil.* San Francisco, Jossey-Bass, 1971.
74. Schneiders, A. A.: *Personality Dynamics and Mental Health* (Rev. ed.) New York, Holt, Rinehart, & Winston, 1965.
75. Severin, F. T.: *Humanistic Viewpoints in Psychology.* New York, McGraw-Hill, 1965.
76. Skinner, B. F.: *Beyond Freedom and Dignity.* New York, Alfred A. Knopf, 1971.
77. Spinks, G.: *Psychology and Religion: An Introduction to Contemporary Views.* Boston, Beacon Press, 1963.
78. Strasser, S.: Phenomenologies and Psychologies. In Lawrence, N., and O'Conner, D. (Eds.): *Readings in Existential Phenomenology,* Englewood Cliffs, Prentice-Hall, 1967.
79. Strunk, O.: Humanistic Religious Psychology: A New Chapter in the Psychology of Religion. *J. Pastoral Care, 24:* 90–97, 1970.
80. Strunk, O.: *Readings in the Psychology of Religion.* Nashville, Abingdon Press, 1959.
81. Strunk, O.: *Religion: A Psychological Interpretation.* Nashville, Abingdon Press, 1962.
82. Sutich, A. J., and Vich, M. A. (Eds.): *Readings in Humanistic Psychology.* New York, Free Press, 1969.
83. Teilhard de Chardin, P.: *The Phenomenon of Man.* New York. Harper & Row, 1959.
84. Tillich, P.: *The Courage to Be.* New Haven, Yale University Press, 1952.
85. Toffler, A.: *Future Shock.* New York, Random House, 1970.
86. Tweedie, D. F.: *Logotherapy and the Christian Faith. An Evaluation of Frankl's Existential Approach to Psychotherapy.* Grand Rapids, Baker Book House, 1961.
87. Ungersma, A. J.: *The Search for Meaning: A New Approach in Psychotherapy and Pastoral Psychology.* Philadelphia, Westminster Press, 1961.
88. Van der Veldt, J. H. & Odenwald, R. P.: *Psychiatry and Catholicism.* New York, McGraw-Hill, 1952.
89. Van Kaam, A.: *Existential Foundations of Psychology.* Pittsburgh, Duquesne University Press, 1966.
90. Wallia, C. S. (Ed.): *Toward Century 21: Technology, Society, and Human Values.* New York, Basic Books, 1970.
91. Wann, T. W. (Ed.): *Behaviorism and Phenomenology: Contrasting Bases for Modern Psychology.* Chicago, University of Chicago Press, 1964.
92. Weisskopf-Joelson, E.: Meaning as an Integrating Factor. In Buhler, C., and Massarik, F.: *The Course of Human Life.* New York, Springer, 1968.
93. Williamson, E. G.: Value Orientation in Counseling. In Severin, F. T.: *Humanistic Viewpoints in Psychology.* New York, McGraw-Hill, 1965.

CHAPTER 28

PSYCHOANALYSIS AND RELIGION: A METAPSYCHOLOGICAL APPROACH TO RELIGIOUS DATA†

EDGAR DRAPER

IT HAS BECOME POPULAR in our day to call psychiatirsts all kinds of names—even if one is not seeing such. These names would include wig picker, head shrinker, nut cracker, witch doctor, couch doctor, nerve doctor, and I would like to add another—"nervous doctor." I am anxious not only because I am expected to write something of importance and interest, that is bad enough, but I am nervous over the task I have set before myself. Namely, to write about a subject that comes within the framework of not one but two emotionally charged areas, religion and psychoanalysis. If one does not have a strong opinion about religion, politics or psychoanalysis, it does not mean he is unprejudiced, but likely asleep. My problem is not only to steer around those stands or positions one may take in relationship to religion or psychoanalysis, but also steer by the peculiar interrelationships between religion and psychiatry.

Having indicated what I am not going to write about, I need to give some hint of where we *are* going.

As much as I might wish to avoid the choppy waters of some highly vested interests and opinions regarding religion and psychoanalysis, I cannot sweep into foreign territory without having cited along the way a few familiar landmarks. These will include a brief look at the historical relationship between religion and psychoanalysis and at certain current views of practicing psychiatrists about religion. Then I would like to present an examination of religion as it is experienced by a patient from the vantage point

---

† Versions of this paper were presented to the Research and Training Staff of the Institute for Psychoanalysis of Chicago (1967), to the American Psychoanalytic Association's annual meeting in Boston (1968), and to the Association for Clinical and Research Studies of Ypsilanti State Hospital (1969).

of psychoanalytic theory. The first task, then, is to understand the meaning that religion has to the minds of individuals, and its implications for research. I intend then to present an analytic case, illustrating both the psychological assessments of religion and the therapeutic implications of understanding religion as experienced psychologically.

Introduction

The relationships between religion and psychoanalysis historically have been characterized more by heat than light. Pathways of communication between the two have been slippery, difficult, at times explosive and at others seductive. Freud's early works, *The Future of an Illusion* and *Totem and Taboo* have been interpreted by some as overt powerful attacks on religion. Freud's own evangelistic hopes to bring his hard won clinical findings and theoretical positions to the gentile world were partially dashed by the desertion of Carl Jung. Although Jung was apparently more interested in relating religious, especially Christian, concepts to "depth psychology" he has been questionably hailed as an "apologist" for "Christian psychoanalysis." Erich Fromm's analysis of these two men's positions in *Psychoanalysis and Religion* finds Freud the far more "religious" man than Jung! Fromm feels that the important aspects of the spirit of religion are more closely allied to Freud's general positions than Jung's (whether Freud saw it or cared to acknowledge that or not!).

Antagonists of Freud, carrying to the extreme, have viewed his theories and discoveries not as a scientific psychological system, but as a new philosophy. For instance, McClelland in the *Princeton Bulletin* analyzed the Freudian movement as "The New Church of the Unconscious." He found the parallels between the early Christian movement and psychoanalysis striking. These included a hero worship, a group of dedicated disciples with an evangelism, philosophy, seminaries, a salvation, a holy scripture, a brotherhood, a way of life, etc. Critics have accused Freudians of philosophizing without using the tools of philosophical discipline, running behind clinical skirts when in trouble. If a cause they have, Freudians have not always helped it, either in relationship to philosophical critics or peers in medicine or psychiatry. For example, at a large psychiatric meeting held at Michael Reese Hospital, Chicago, the head of a psychoanalytic institute presented a paper entitled "The Three Superegos of the Western World." To my great shock a member of the audience introduced his comments on the paper by saying,

"We all know that psychoanalysis is a Jewish science"! To my still greater amazement no one commented on his remark. Such a position can only undermine whatever scientific contributions might be available in psychoanalytic concepts and practice, since Einstein hardly gave us the Jewish theory of relativity! Or if the commenter said with tongue in cheek, "Psychoanalysis is a Jewish science," he may have viewed psychoanalysis as a Jewish reply to Christian Science!

But if there have been battles and antagonisms and alienations, there have also been "ecumaniacs" who have overdiligently sought to perform a marriage between depth psychology and liberal religions.

In short on both theoretical or philosophical levels, as well as clinical or practical levels, states of high tension periodically spring up. However, these are two great arenas of human experience, of concepts and contributions: religion and psychoanalysis are likely here to stay, even if only to co-exist!

How do practicing psychiatrists view religion? I personally have encountered at least four attitudes which are not limited to analysts but spread across the broad field of psychiatric practice. Although there is no official "canonical" psychoanalytic position concerning religion, I know of analysts whose views range through the whole spectrum and farther than the following:

First, there is the highly polemic position in which religion, *any* religion, is viewed as neurosis or psychosis, as part of an individual sickness and therefore, the object of therapeutic attention, the counterpart of sin to the preacher or cancer to the surgeon—to be eradicated!

Second, there is another position of psychiatrists (often Catholic) no less polemic but certainly less aggressive, which in effect states, "Religion is out of my territory and to be avoided; leave it to priests."

A third position, perhaps more popular than either of the above, could be stated in this way: "Patients' religious interests are for the most part *unimportant* unless they form trappings on which neurosis or psychosis is hung."

A fourth position, to which I would adhere, would state that none of the above positions is adequate. In the treatment of patients religion is neither to be (1) destroyed, nor (2) avoided, nor (3) ignored as unimportant. I would not consider it *categorically* sick, nor a foreign body in someone else's domain, nor irrelevant. Rather, like any *other aspect* or the patient's intimate, personal life, *convictions require psychological understanding*.

Early in his prolific life Freud stated "dreams are the royal road to the unconscious," and indeed in the practice of psychoanalysis dreams remain "royal." But in other forms of therapy and *particularly* in diagnostic work, other avenues to the unconscious are readily recognized, whether it be in projective tests such as the Rorschach, in associations, symptoms and behavior, or the intriguing blips of the unconscious revealed through early memories. Especially, then, in diagnosis I would assert that a patient's religion is not to be *destroyed, avoided* or considered *unimportant* since it is so intimately personal. We consider it to be a hitherto largely neglected "royal road" to understanding the patient.

One may have some concern that my position places emphasis on "understanding" as reductionistic of religion. But in many instances for the patient to understand *why* he believes, may or may not change *what* he believes and in any case certainly does not change reality. For example, in political campaigns it becomes only *useful* to the voter to know why he choses one candidate over another. Thus a vote for Eisenhower because, unbeknownst, he struck a paternal heart string was not an enlightened vote. No more rational was the convention delegate whose unresolved competition with his father tossed his vote to Kennedy in nomination over Stevenson because it meant victory of a young man over an older man; nor in 1968, to vote for Nixon because his running partner resembled Ed McMahon! In short, *understanding of oneself,* politically or religiously is not reduction nor destruction, necessarily.

To get to the heart of the matter: my hypothetical position states that religious beliefs, interests, and activity are intimately personal, individualized, and forged out of a person's *whole* life experience, past and present; that the individual within any formal religious group continues to interpret individually and personally whatever his church or denomination has set before him throughout his life history; that the impact therefore of the particular religious group to which he has been life-exposed will present only a great array of possibilities for belief from which he chooses without awareness, influenced by the whole of his life experience including childhood.

What I consider to be a man's own personal individualized religion has been expressed through the words of the author of the book of Proverbs who stated, "As a man thinketh in his heart, so is he." (Proverbs 23:7) What is the heart? In Cruden's *Concordance for the Bible* it is defined: "The word heart is used in scripture as the seat of life or strength; hence it means, mind, soul, spirit or one's entire emotional nature and understanding."

Thus, keeping our hypothetical position in mind if we can learn a man's "heart religion," we ought to be able to know him. It is not enough to know simply a man's denomination preference or even the idol he worships with his heart, but to know the *details*. To know something of a man's personal religion—not what he parades, pretends, or talks about to his priest, rabbi, or minister—but his unguarded personalized life philosophy (including religious elements), is psychologically "a royal road" to understanding *him*.

Very simply, then, if one can learn what specific tenets or religion are of importance to a person at any one particular time in his life, one can learn of his current crisis, his struggles of development, his character structure, and make accurate clinical and psychodynamic diagnoses. It is not simply current crisis or major life occasion that influences what is important in a person's religion to him. The struggles associated with stages of life maturation influence such choices. For example, could anyone affirm that his current life philosophy is the same today as it was when he was in school? In adolescence or childhood? Will his life philosophy or religious interest of today be the same twenty years hence? The point is, what is religiously meaningful to an individual changes with time and experience even though his formal religion remains the same.

From another frame of reference, the history of theology can be written around the contribution of *individuals*, whether they be saints, heretics, reformers or rejuvenators. The more one learns of the lives of people like Luther, Calvin, Wesley, Augustine and Tillich, the easier it is to understand their theological contributions in their life perspectives. As far as we are able to tell, God hasn't been changing during these centuries, but concepts *about* him, influenced by the times, have indeed been changing. This can be observed in historic individuals, who were living out and declaring their own personal interpretation for which the time was ripe, as easily as in the new evangelists for the "God is dead" theologies.

To make the intent of this paper as clear as possible, its goal is to examine the phenomenon of religion as it is expressed primarily in clinical data through the various lenses of the several metapsychological points of view. (1) Marjorie Brierly states my position succinctly: "The psychoanalytic conception of psychological reality does not involve any mystical assumptions. All the phenomena that, since the time of William James, have been called the 'varieties of religious experience' are subjectively real and there can be no doubt of their psychological importance. But, insofar as investigation has shown up to the present, those experiences are capable of the purely psychological as distinct from a mystical explanation." (2)

In the light of this perspective, I would then define religion as a system of beliefs, practices and customs rooted in a culture, with a historical tradition which offers a *Weltanschaaung,* moral code and facility for social communion between adherents. It is geared to address itself to life's great problems and, psychologically, has the power of attracting cathexes of the *individual* that inspire worship or awe, command attention or respect at all stages of his life cycle from childhood to senescence. To remain in the category of living religions it must have a repertoire of need-satisfying provisions for its membership.

Case Presentation and Interpretation

A colleague, knowing of my interest in the study of religion, told me of an analytic control case that he had recently terminated. He had been struck repeatedly by the multiplicity of religious forms brought up in the analytic material. By contrast, my own analytic cases could only serve for vignette demonstration. But this one of his sounded replete with opportunity for a review of the patient's religion with a metapsychological eye. With his permission to study his extensive notes and with his personal collaboration, I have come to know the case, I believe, as well as one could without seeing the patient. Further, the case, as his and not mine, offered anonymity and special appeal to the goddess of objectivity who knows the power of influence of an analyst's special interest on his patient's material. After a brief summary of the case, I will attempt to bring the perspectives of the various metapsychological systems to bear on its religious elements.

The patient was a 23-year-old, single graduate student in microbiology, referred for analysis by his professor who had himself had analytic treatment. He presented himself as a poised, good-looking, boyishly pleasant young man in ivy-league attire with three complaints. First, he had a peculiar difficulty working at his research in that he found himself unwittingly prolonging tasks as though thereby prolonging his life. It was not unusual to complete a project "only to find a crucial error right in the middle." His work inhibition was also characterized by procrastination and "small, subtle mistakes." Secondly, he experienced great discomfort around women, even in casual situations, finding himself insulting and defensive. He avoided any kind of sexual activity but especially intercourse which up to his entry into analysis had "eluded" him. Finally, he had vague but persistent fears of death which seemed ever present in the background.

He grew up in a large town in southern Illinois that served as center for a rural area. His father was school superintendent and principal during the patient's entire pre-collegiate education. The father personally arranged "the best possible training opportunities" for his only son. This special place subjected the patient to repeated physical and verbal attacks by older children and tougher peers. He came to accept these somewhat stoically, since he wanted to preserve father's good name, "to be the best guy in school," to be courageous and "a cut above" other kids, a status dear to his mother especially. Fundamentalistic religion was in the air, both in the community and in the family. Father was a church "pillar" and taught the men's Bible class. The entire family never missed the frequent and regular revival services that were characterized by physical gyrations, shouting, hyperventilation, fainting and occasional bedlam, which the patient viewed with a mixture of great curiosity, revulsion, awe, and at times, terror.

He was born on Christmas day, eight years after his nearest sibling, a sister. His other sibling, a sister ten years his senior, used to "soul kiss" her brother "for practice." In his infancy he was often bound hand and foot with stockings to prevent him from thumb and toe sucking. He remained in the parental bedroom until he was four. Mother shared her bath with him through his first seven years, but at this age suddenly excluded him. "Running around naked was a habit with her, too." Disobedience brought switchings in the pantry by his mother. Mother was never content with his achievements and the patient, too, persistently expected something better of himself. She was described as a proud woman, fearful that anyone would make a fool of her or the patient. Mother was "sick in bed" at monthly intervals. Both the patient and his sister repeatedly feared for her life "while father never seemed concerned." The patient felt that his mother's death would be God's punishment should it happen and blamed God for anything that went wrong with her or himself. When he was nine, mother had gynecological surgery "as an aftermath of child bearing that put an end to her womanhood." He recalled that as a youngster he repeatedly fantasied the invention and use of a "soul gun" that was capable of shooting down and destroying souls permanently that were on their way to heaven and eternal life.

Early in the analysis it was learned that the patient had experienced a severe learning block with the theoretical aspects of molecular biology which contradicted the Bible and his beliefs. He was about to fail until he came under an unusual tutelage offered by his referring professor. The "tutorials" took place in the professor's home and consisted of various punishments for failure to assimilate new material. The "penances" ranged from performing repeated physical exercise to submission to floggings that lasted until, climactically, as the patient put it, "my ass bled." The method overcame the patient's resistance to learning evolutionary theory (!) but also eventuated in the patient's referral, as well. He chastised the professor to the analyst for hypocrisy "because he got as much out of it (whippings) as I did, but pretended it was for my own good." The professor's hypocrisy stimulated the recurrent thought that father's religion was a hoax, as well as the memory of a repeated event during his school days: seeing father criticize girl cheerleaders exposing their panties by standing at the edge of steps above where the boys *and* father stood.

The early analytic course was stormy. The patient initially successfully evoked sadistic counter-transference communications from the analyst which produced shameful confessions of aborted sexual escapades by the patient. One of the trying developments was the patient's productions on the couch of histrionic gyrations when he thought himself to be in "deep analysis." In such states, he huffed and puffed, thrashed about, demonstrated clonic and tonic movements, yet maintained consciousness throughout and reported feeling excited.

At the termination of his patient's four years on the couch, the analyst concluded that a major theme in his course was that of self defeat and masochism. Hyperstimulation through exposure to repeated primal scenes and through the mother's and sister's seductiveness together with fright of the female genitals provided half the stimulus for oedipal retreat. The other half was supplied by the image of a powerful, manipulative, undemonstrative father who quietly ran the school system, town, church and family. His retreat from oedipal heat and dangers of competiton was to the relative safety of a symbiotic oral sadomasochism with the mother. But here, of course, separation worries flourished in adulthood in the form of extinction fears. The patient attempted at first successfully to make the analyst his "sadistic sweetheart." He also became convinced of the importance of his role as a control patient to the analyst. He considered his own outcome to be instrumental in the success or failure of the analyst's career.

The Topographical Point of View

Inherent in Freud's topographical model as outlined in the

classic seventh chapter of the *Interpretation of Dreams* are not only concepts of the realms of unconscious, preconscious and conscious thinking. There also are elucidations of primary and secondary processes and the place of the primitive mental mechanisms (symbolization, condensation, displacement and *transference*). (3)

In consideration of mental functioning, to think of transference in the grossly restricted sense of the therapeutic situation, or even as expanded to include the transfer of old psychological cathexis from a parent to a present person not in the therapeutic situation, is to see only the top of the transference iceberg. Freud reminds us in the famous seventh chapter: "We learn from the neuroses that an unconscious idea is as such quite incapable of entering the preconscious in that it can only exercise any effect there by establishing a connection with an idea which already belongs to the preconscious, by transferring its intensity on to it and by getting itself 'covered' by it. Here we have the fact of 'transference,' which provides an explanation of so many striking phenomena in the mental life of neurotics. The preconscious idea, which thus acquires an undeserved degree of intensity may either be left unaltered by the transference or it may have a modification forced upon it, derived from the content of the idea which effects the transference." Freud added that a repressed (unconscious) idea resembled that of an American dentist in his own country who could only practice under the license (cover) of an M.D., a stalking horse, who gave the dentist a ride. He noted that dream residues not only borrow something from the unconscious (the instinctual force of the repressed wish) they offer something in return, that is, the necessary point of attachment for a transference. Freud made it clear that the phenomenon of transference is a normal mentation process. It does not wait for nor need an analyst to come along. It operates in dream formation. We would add in "religious formations," too. Thus a patient's transference may attach to a theological concept, a belief, a dogma, a priest, a saint, a ritual, a prayer, a set of beads, an ethic, an order, a tradition, a sacrament, a fellowship, a hymn, a Bible verse, a story or character, a disciple or charismatic person, like Jesus, Buddha or Mohammed.

Religion as an external trapping to accommodate transferences was ever handy to our patient from his earliest years. The fundamentalist brand of religion in his experiences offered its revival services as a new focus for his intense scoptophilic interest secondary to exposure to repeated primal scenes with their excitement, curiosity and fright. He could never allow himself as a child to get too close to the altar where the participants' occasional ecstatic activity took place. Whether one agrees with Kris that ecstatic inspiration is a sexualization process of preconscious mentation or not, (5) for *this* patient his reaction to it clearly indicated he responded to the excitement, gyrations and groans as a derivative of a sexual scene. The patient later attempted to bring the same reflections of his intensive and lengthy primal scene exposures with their frustrations and stimulation into the analysis in repeated attempts to enter "deep analysis" through his hyperventilation, twitchings, and so on, all simulating the primal scene and his sawdust trail observations.

With its great variation of theological formulations, his religion provided a self-modified system of belief that early had held the Bible as God's own Word, never to be contradicted. It was a natural place to find out what his silent but powerful earthly father wanted him to do. As he grew older, his education prompted doubts. His father's hypocrisy made him consider the whole religious business a hoax. But his fear of disbelief in the Bible and God provided the block which kept him from accepting concepts like the evolutionary principle in microbiology. This held sway until he got "tutored" into a *new* system by an *old* teaching technique. His masochistic submissive interests sought out a sadistic and hypercritical professor. Besides reviving old pantry pleasures with the mother that followed being "bad," transfer to a more powerful figure and system of beliefs became possible in microbiology, until he attempted to do the same thing with the theory and principles of psychoanalysis with his analyst as the new power.

His chronic thanatophobia found a natural harbor in his religion's concept of an after life. He learned of hellfire and damnation in regular Sunday dosages. In his oedipal battle he made God (father) more like the devil, responsible for anything that went wrong, especially the possible death of his mother who was regularly "hurt" in the marital bed. Mother's being sick (with dysmenorrhea) without father's worrying, as well as her sexual subjugation to the father, made the patient's image of God a threatening one. His own inventive theology provided him with a "soul gun" as the most dangerous weapon imaginable giving him the power to shoot down his enemies (like devilish parents and a misbehaving sister). His castrative fears at the hands of a woman were accentuated by mother's naked demonstrations and openness about her monthly period. The dangers to women out of the sexual act or its consequences gained impetus with his early knowledge that childbirth had resulted in mother's gynecological operation. He recalled for a long time he could "never look into that matter."

There were two aspects to his death fears. His vague fear of *hell* had roots in his oedipal fear of father's retaliatory actions for competition, success or completing things. There were hellish (castrative) dangers, too, in a woman's genitals. His fear of the latter was so strong that a very important and creative experiment in his graduate studies was axed because of his inability to touch a plumbing fixture at the right time that needed manipulation. "It looked so much like a woman's crotch I couldn't get near it." The other aspect to his fear of death was extinction, which appears to have been an extension and perpetuation of his separation anxiety that was only allayed by continually reestablishing a sadomasochistic hyperstimulating relationship. His regular regressions to oral-sadomasochistic expressions from the dangerous oedipal struggle kept alive the extinction (separation anxiety) and hell-fire (castration anxiety) fears. Although he added his own unique theological alterations, like his soul gun, the patient's religious world was ready with its invitations to transference.

In short, religion's multiple provisions acted as a psychological hat rack for our patient. A religious service, the Bible and the doctrine of an afterlife were members of a veritable stable of "stalking horses."

The Psychodynamic Point of View

Freud's major works about religion must be considered too generalized a treatment of the subject to qualify as dynamic. (6) In these he looked for broad principles that would be applicable to the masses. But, in the data of his cases, he could be and was definitive about the interplay of internal psychological forces that make dynamics come alive.

In his careful study of the "Wolfman" he took pains to translate the meaning of religion for his patient as a little boy. He linked concepts of ambivalence and obsessive acts dynamically with the religious acts of kissing holy pictures, the making of the cross, and repetition of "God-shit" thoughts. The sadomasochism of the passion story, hating God, getting the Holy Ghost and his identification with Christ as submissive to the will of God the Father, all became understood in the revealing light of psychoanalytic dynamics. (7)

Schreber's religious preoccupations, Freud understood, reflected "a method in his madness." In a man who had been no believer in a personal God before he became ill, Schreber's voluptuous affair with and marriage to the God of the "anterior and posterior realms" who could offer "male and female states of bliss" found earthbound explanations in Freud's enlightened perceptions. (8)

One of the most fascinating dynamic constellations in our patient was his identification with Jesus. Born on Christmas, the only son and raised like an only child, he was treated as unique from the start. His mother's superhuman expectations, her own compensated grandiosity as a "cut above" all others, her unreasonable eroticized attention and stimulation, and her need for a sadomasochistic partner helped to set the stage. At the same time, there was father's silent authority, special (and somewhat corrupt) management of his son's schooling in his own system, and his expectation that his son show the courage and the equanimity to rise above the punishings administered by understandably aroused older and tougher peers at school—all endured "for *his* sake." Entering then as he did in analysis, small wonder he attempted immediately to reestablish a sadomasochistic relationship, to try to get beaten or induced into "deep analysis," to find submission to "ANALYSIS" as a new belief system and to heed mother's repeated warnings about people, especially Jews "who want to make a fool of you and take your money." (Crucify you.)

Late in the analysis, the patient reported he felt an enormous fear about completing his thesis and some day ending the analysis. The analyst asked, as was his custom, "What's that got to do with us?" The patient replied in disgust, "Oh, Jesus Christ!" The perceptive analyst said immediately, "Maybe so!" "Well," said the patient, "*He* sure went through a lot for *his* old man! Jesus was afraid to grow up and leave his father, too. I've been telling you that for two months. I recall my father telling our class in first grade that he'd be *our* father. That made me mad. I felt, 'God damn it, I'm already your son.'"

The Economic Point of View

A grand place (besides the phenomena of scrupulosity, religious delusions and religiosity) to witness the economic aspects of religious operations is in conversion episodes. The ego is overwhelmed either transiently or more permanently in such episodes. Whether transient or more permanent confusion results, does not depend on the immediate energetic explosiveness of the experience, but on its management by the individual. This depends on the health of the ego prior to such experiences and, more particularly, its capacity for draining and filtering energetic charges through channels of neutralization as described so well by Hartmann. (9)

The repetitious trauma of our patient's primal scene exposures extended well into the psychologically sensitive period of oedipal development. After expulsion from the parental bedroom, he found the ready nesting place for his attempts to work this trauma through (or keep it alive?) in the now *holy* rolling he viewed always from the rear of the church with great awe, curiosity, and agonizing anxiety. He apparently never lost interest in revival services until late adolescence when he submitted to the sexualized thrashing acted out with his professor. On the couch he repeatedly drummed up pseudo-orgiastic attempts as described earlier. These were often evoked out of relatively "benign," extra-analytic encounters with his analyst that stimulated resurgence of primal scene material and acting-in. Toward the end of his course, the analyst reported that the patient for the first time began to make distinctions between his belief system in molecular biology and his sexual and aggressive drives. These had been amalgamated with first his religious system, then his theoretical molecular biology, and finally in his unsuccessful attempt to create a belief system out of psychoanalysis, which, of course, offered itself for analytic working-though.

The Genetic Point of View

Freud pointed without hesitation to childhood development as the important source of religious expressions. (10) However, in the analysis of the individual we cannot be content with generalizations of phylogenetic inference as he insisted on, nor be limited to one developmental stage (phallic) or to one or two types of formal religious groups to give the fullest credit to genetic understandings of religious expression. It would appear that for any one individual, each of his psychosexual stages casts its shadow on his religious choices, identifications and cathexes.

Freud thought that the fear of death was little more than the superego's intimidation of the ego. (11) For our patient this certainly applied, *sometimes*! During those periods of life and of the analysis when oedipal competition was aroused, either by heterosexual wishes or by a possible completion or success, his fear of death and hell breathed new life, fed by castration anxieties. In adulthood, his fear was characterized by punishment, retaliation, dire consequences and damage to his genitals. As a child, fears of hell fire were breathed down at him through the nostrils of shouting, evangelistic, guilt-arousing preachers. *But* at times of greater regression, his death fears took on a different coloring, that of extinction, fed by separation anxieties. When he felt the death sting of possible loss of the mother as a near-symbiotic sadomasochistic partner, he sought desperately to re-establish such a relationship to preserve himself and avoid the terror of loss of identity. In that early eroticized relationship he felt alive, needed, and thereby protected from oblivion. His soul gun seems to have been a neat combination that reflected his ambivalence toward both parents as well as a defense against his projected fears of each of them as dangerous figures at different stages of his development.

The evolution of our patient's belief system, colored right along by pre-teen developmental influences, has been noted. In addition, adolescence as a developmental stage forced his primitive Biblical beliefs into doubt and reflected his emancipation wishes from parents. He made mighty casts looking for a purpose, orientation, and self respect and finally landed the more consistent and culturally acceptable ideologies, first of molecular biology (with a little help) and then "PSYCHOANALYSIS," which led him paradoxically to treatment and, hopefully, a more complete emancipation.

The Structural Point of View

Completing his chapter on "Some Integrative Functions of the Ego," Hartmann writes: "Though all these comments are tentative and, of course, very incomplete, I cannot close this section without a reference to the psychological significance of religion. Religions are (*among other things*) objectivations of a value scale. We are familiar with Freud's genetic derivation from a single source of the elements which are integrated in religious systems, namely, their attempts at consolation, at explanation of the unknown, and at creating a system of ethical imperatives. The continued influence on the human mind and the synthetic achievement of religions rest on their integrative imagery and on their being tradition-saturated, socially unifying wholes which are fed by the contributions of all three mental institutions (ego, id, superego) and provide a pattern, accessible to many people, for satisfying the demands of all three institutions. Religions are the most obvious attempt to cope with these mental institutions and with social adaptation (through forming communities) by means of synthesis." (13)

Freud was quite aware of the dual aspects of the superego that serve as approving as well as disapproving. Further, he hints at the possibility that there may be inherent (could we say "autonomous?") superego possibilities. Freud's persistent rooting in the biological, his interest in the life and death instinct theories, his taking for granted as a given the moral and evil nature of man, offer the same kind of background for autonomous superego possibilities as were present for the basis of the development of autonomous ego functioning. One could entertain speculative possibilities of secondary autonomous superego functions as, for example, might be seen in the "yes-no", "good-bad" dichotomies, or in the readiness for shame and guilt or in what appears to be a need to obey, be trained, or gain approval. But abandoning speculation for the surer ground of Hartmann's autonomous ego functions, we will strive now for illustration more than completeness.

Our patient embraced religious song cathexes that offered examples of both *conflict-free* and *conflict-burdened ego functioning*. As a boy when the patient felt appreciated and loved by the father his Sunday School song, "Jesus Loves Me, This I Know" became a tune of joyous expression and thanksgiving, slipping out of conflictual pathways and untouched by repression. It meant, "Father loves me and Jesus does, *too*." Being loved, appreciated and secure built memory traces as important as being unloved, unappreciated, insecure and abandoned. (Response to these positive experiences can be carried off in a religious context whether one celebrates the mass, feels "lifted" in congregational chorus, breathes the gladness of old traditional feasts, or shares the fun of caroling Christmas tidings.) For our patient this very same song, however, was expressive of morbid consolation in feeling unloved by anybody else except a member of the Holy Family. This was a different and definitely conflicted story. At those times the song meant, "Well, at least *Jesus* loves me."

If one is preoccupied on hearing "Onward Christian Soldiers" with the vindictive holy wars and crimes in the name of Christ or the Malleus Malificorum, he will miss its potential for a growing boy's need to express and enjoy his aggression particularly if other outlets do not present themselves. For our patient, the hymn was not only a chance to blast his father (with the latent approval of the religious system), it was an enjoyed outlet not unlike the necessary games of "cops and robbers," "Cowboys and Indians," and the whole sports arena. While our patient excelled at sports as did his father, winning in direct competition, as in golf, was too much to ask. But, how well he could sing, "Onward Christian Soldiers, Marching as to War!"

Conclusion: The Adaptive Point of View

The adaptive point of view includes those propositions that concern relationships to the environment. There is the assumption that every point in the life cycle of an individual calls for psychological states of adaptation (which insure survival, and mesh with that individual's particular society) and that there are mutually influential exchanges between the society and that individual.

If I have had to be precise before with other systems of the mind regarding the place of religion in intrapsychic processes, I have to be doubly cautious now when we come to the adaptive point of view. Care must be mustered to ensure that intrapsychic adaptation is not confused with cultural or societal adaptation wherein sociological, anthropological, philosophical, aesthetic, but, above all, historical perspectives must be the judges about such things as "survival values" in religion for civilization.

Freud's major works on religion, even though extrapolated and contributed to by his clinical observations, move well out of the range of analytic science on to his philosophy and his personal point of view. When Freud, however, moved from his generalizations about religion to specific cases, psychoanalytic principles of scientific status became obvious. In regard to the "Wolfman", after carefully delineating a number of psychodynamic clarifications of his patients' religious cathexes, Freud added, "Apart from these pathological phenomena it may be said that in the present case religion achieved all the aims for the sake of which it is included in the education of the individual." It offered a restraint on his sexual impulsions "by affording a sublimation and a safe mooring." It lowered the importance of his patient's family directly yet without isolation through "access to the great community of mankind." The untamed and fear-ridden child became social, well-behaved, and amenable. "So it was that religion did its work for the hard-pressed child by the combination which it afforded the believer of satisfaction, of sublimation, of diversion from sensual processes to purely spiritual ones, and of access to social relationships." (14) These observations move us, most definitely, from symptomatic religious cathexes into the realm of adaptive possibilities that systems of religion can afford the individual.

Hartmann indicates, "At one point we may be interested in the pathology of a process, in its genetic relationship to adaptation disturbances and, at another point, in the positive adaptation value it gains in another context (conflict and health). Our vantage point determines which aspect of the process will assume importance." As an example, he chooses fantasy. At one point in life, this active process is within the limits of normal ego development. Even though adults may never give it up totally, "From the point of view of mental economy it is a very different matter when a fantasy replaces an important piece of reality in adults than when this occurs in a child." Hartmann adds further, "A rigid view of mental health to the contrary notwithstanding, the healthy adult's mental life is probably never free of the denial and replacement of some reality by fantasy formation. Religious ideas . . . are examples." (15)

Because fundamentalist religion was in the air, our analysand had to breathe it in. It was part of his infantile, latent and adolescent world. The adaptive potentials offered to our patient by his particular exposures to religion include the following examples:

In handling the traumas of primal scene hyperstimulation, he found the revival services ready to offer holy rolling as a substitute toward which he could regulate his closeness and involvement, as an "acceptable" scoptophilic opportunity ("everybody's doing it"), as a shared problem with the whole congregation ("same boat" consolation), as displacement of his own sexual excitement, as a regular activity offering some possibility for working through or mastering the trauma and in these services (aimed at cleansing the soul) a source of potential forgiveness for his "crimes."

The God idea offered him some safe distancing for his rivalry with the father. It partially freed him from his own guilt consequent to both the assumed responsibility for hurt he caused mother by being born and the hate and envy he held for father in the latter's "damaging" intimacies with mother.

His identification with Jesus allayed his concerns about being special and accepting suffering, gave him (by precedent) an idealistic possibility for flights into adolescent asceticism and rebellion, offered consolation for feeling isolated, abandoned and "above" earthly pleasures, and helped "explain" the persistent gnawing of expected perfection.

The Bible gave him black and white directions for which he sought in vain from his father, gave him a belief system to be at times tested or doubted and at others adhered to.

His fears of death were blamed on his "protestant ethic" diverting attention from their more personal sources in separation and castration anxieties. This same belief system earlier had given consolation and partial reassurance with its eternal life and heavenly home premises. In spite of the wide variety of theological or dogmatic possibilities, his own creative fantasy life led him to dream up a soul gun for further protection.

In summary, aspects of this patient's religion served as a stable of stalking horses for over-determined and shifting cathexes, as affective and cathartic outlets, as repeated opportunities for working through traumas, as an organizational system of belief and orientation for viewing the world and for instinctual need satisfaction, as a reservoir of mythical materials inviting his own creative fantasy, and as a treasure house of religious exposures that presented adaptational possibilities at his several stages of development and life crises.

Religions apparently have an antiquity as old as historical man. Religions have come and gone. Living religions survive only because they meet man's needs and die when this function stops. Freud has pointed out the constancy of instinctual arousals in the human organism which are continually searching for satisfaction. (16) The wealth of variety for religious choice within any great living religion offers special service to the mind in health and illness, (17) with instinctual satisfaction as one such service. My task has been to demonstrate the general services to mental functioning offered by religion as viewed from each of the metapsychological systems. (18) And, for our patient, to paraphrase President Kennedy's words, psychologically speaking, "Ask not what you can do for your religion, but what your religion can do for you."

REFERENCES AND FOOTNOTES

1 Rapaport, D. and Gill, M.: The Points of View and Assumptions of Metapsychology. *International Journal of Psychoanalysis*, 40: 155, 1959.

2 Brierley, Marjorie: Further Notes on the Implications of Psychoanalysis: Metapsychology and Personality. *International Journal of Psychoanalysis*, 26: 106, 1945.

3 Freud, Sigmund: The Interpretation of Dreams (1900). Standard Edition of *The Complete Psychological Works of Sigmund Freud*, London, Hogarth Press, 1953, vol. 5, pp. 506–623.

4 Arlow, Jacob: A Psychoanalytic Study of a Religious Initiation Rite, Bar Mitzvah, *Psychoanalytic Study of the Child*, vol. 6, 1951.

5 Draper, E. et al.: The Diagnostic Value of Religious Ideation. *Archives of General Psychiatry*, vol. 13, 1965.

6 Kris, E.: On Preconscious Mental Processes. *Psychoanalytic Quarterly*, 19: 557, 1950.

7 Freud, Sigmund: The Future of an Illusion. Standard Edition, vol. 21; Civilization and Its Discontents, Standard Edition, vol, 21; Moses and Monotheism, Standard Edition, vol. 23; Totem and Taboo, Standard Edition, vol. 13; Group Psychology and the Analysis of the Ego, Standard Edition, vol. 18.

8 Freud, Sigmund: From the History of an Infantile Neurosis (1918), Standard Edition, 17: 7–125, 1955. See also: Notes Upon a Case of Obsessional Neurosis, Standard Edition, 10: 235.

9 Freud, Sigmund: Psychoanalytic Notes on an Autobiographical Account of a Case of Paranoia (1911) Standard Edition, 12: 9–85, 1958. See also Hartmann, Heinz: *Ego Psychology and the Problem of Adaptation*. New York, International Universities Press, 1958.

10 Hartmann, Heinz: A Contribution to the Metapsychology of Schizophrenia. *Psychoanalytic Study of the Child*, 8: 184, 1953.

11 Freud, Sigmund: Three Essays on the Theory of Sexuality, Standard Edition, 7; Leonardo Da Vinci and a Memory of His Childhood, Standard Edition, *11:* 123; New Introductory Lectures on Psychoanalysis, *22:* 164, 167, 169; Preface to Reik's Ritual: Psychoanalytic Studies, Standard Edition, *17:* 262; The Future of an Illusion, Standard Edition, *21:* 18–20.
12 Freud, Sigmund: The Ego and the Id, Standard Edition, *19:* 57, 58. See also Hartmann, Heinz and Loewenstein, R. M.: Notes on the Superego, *Psychoanalytic Study of the Child, 17:* 79, 1962.
13 Hartmann, Heinz: *Ego Psychology and the Problem of Adaptation.* New York, International Universities Press, 1958.
14 Freud, Sigmund: From the History of an Infantile Neurosis, Standard Edition, *17:* 114.
15 Hartmann, *op. cit.,* pp. 16–18.
16 Freud, Sigmund: Instincts and Their Vicissitudes, Standard Edition, *14:* 118, 119.
17 The Psychic Function of Religion in Mental Illness and Health, vol. 6, Report no. 67. Group for the Advancement of Psychiatry, January 1968.
18 Draper, Edgar: Religion as an Intrapsychic Experience. *Cincinnati Journal of Medicine,* vol. 50, 1969.

CHAPTER 29

RELIGIOUS PROBLEMS OF COLLEGE STUDENTS

Truman G. Esau

As a generalization, college students in the United States are indeed religious but not in conventional terms. It is out of an explanation and elaboration of this statement that I will develop the thesis of this chapter. The notion that the average American college student is religious might seem absurd. Certainly the literature on the psychological and psychiatric problems in college students does not lay heavy emphasis upon their religious lives. On the surface, they do not appear as a group to attempt to deal with their problems through religious means. I think college students are intensely value-oriented, to the point of a religious fervor. In this sense, many elements of a religious nature are handled. The generation gap, the intense confrontations of our days over social issues, the overt testing, and often rejection, of the prior generation's values are not only matters for psychological concern, but our society as a whole struggles with these matters.

I would like to examine the background to some of these statements. We well know and recognize in adolescent development that one of the crucial issues or tasks that the adolescent must fulfill in order to achieve maturity is the formulation of *a value structure* with which he can live. Accomplishing this reduces the turmoil in the adolescent's conflict. Thereby he resolves the struggle between his wishes, parental prohibitions and reality structure. It is when the adolescent comes to a modicum of resolution as to what standards he will own as his own that he achieves some degree of internal harmony. This, of course, is not necessarily restricted to the teenager. It is frequently a recurrent and continuing theme of the college age years or later also. We have come to view this process of adolescent turmoil as a somewhat beneficial period for out of it will come personhood with parental instruction given its appropriate historical place. Perhaps never before in the short history of our republic have we observed so much freedom for the adolescent to test these issues out in overt fashion.

A TIME OF TRANSITION

Religious formalism is not typically as important in the background of the average college student today as it was at the turn of the century. This is probably a mixed blessing, however, as we will see in subsequent discussion. Value diffusion and confusion has marked the last decades. The great surges of church attendance and membership are not necessarily representative of personalized religion; they have often been part of a value decay. I would argue that even the doctrinaire religious position makes an easier target for an adolescent to deal with than value confusion and ambivalence. Later I will try to examine specific responses that represent my observations in clinical practice with regard to different groups. However, I would point out here that the working through of value structure for the student from a rigid background is distinctly different from a student whose background has not had religiously formulated value structures. For this latter student, there is trouble identifying the opponent. But value-oriented, all of these students are.

In these initial remarks, I'm drawing similarities which are more or less common through all the college age group, themes that connect the diverse experiences that I have observed clinically, dependent upon different cultural and family backgrounds. I would dare state that at the cornerstone, values for the majority of these students is the doctrine of relationship. I have observed that the affect hunger for belonging undercuts all of the cultural diferences. It is the one consistent theme in their whole culture; it is the one place that we all meet. We are products of and subject to a distancing society. The present young adult group is attacking this with a vengeance. The fervor of transition in the last fifteen years is astonishing. The hippy movement, communal living, Jesus freaks, drug subculture and other group phenomena point to sincere, although often misguided, attempts at belonging which has not arisen out of family life. The reasons for this are legion, but the experience of this hunger is almost universal among college students. I would further contend that this placing of relationship at the cornerstone of a value structure is derived in part from a decaying religious background. Even when the present college student's parents did not have a religious orientation and commitment for themselves, they often had guilt feelings because they had rejected a conservatism in their parents and after all, feeling guilty about something verifies its importance to a growing child. I am not blankly defending the forms in which relationships are and have been sought in recent years by college students but I would point to the essential health and the acknowledgement of the need of this kind of relationship. The bitterest experiences arise out of the young adult who fails to find what he is seeking through drugs, communal living or other new sociological developments.

In attempting to deal with the diversity of cultural-religious backgrounds, I will describe composite syndromes which contain the essential elements as I see them in clinical practice of college students' value conflicts as presented in psychotherapy. I draw these experiences from a vantage point of psychotherapy which needs identification at this point. It has become my conviction in years of experience with college students, who represent a majority of my clinical practice, that their fantasies about family are not reliable. The information that I will convey according to the clinical pictures and vignettes that I will describe do not come from the prejudice of the college student but from direct exposure to his family. It is in the family that my clinical explorations have taken place and therapy has been carried on. There are exceptions of course for there are those students who have severed so finally from their families that to include them in psychotherapy would be impossible. Even sometimes in these situations, families may be available for anamnesic verification. I do not mean to indicate that it is my conviction that college students must maintain warm relationships with their parents, but it is my conviction that the parting of the ways must be honest, open and understood for the maximum mental health of the student.

If one were to take the fantasies and prejudices of the college student seriously, most parents would seem unlikely allies for a psychotherapeutic process. But most college students have sufficient doubts about their hostilities so that they will work at therapeutic exploration with the family. Even more significantly, the wish to belong either has not died or it has traversed through a series of abortive attempts to find substitute families. This need to belong is not neurotic and is not relieved by or supplanted by psychotherapy. In fact, this need to belong is mostly intensely human and its denial effects many malignant psychiatric symptoms. There is agony for the student who has to face up to the fact that his need of belonging was either not met in earlier years or may not be met because of limitations, incapacities and deprivations in the parents themselves. The task of therapy for such a person often becomes a containment of dependency wishes to avoid seeking substitute retionships with eventual formation of more healthy peer relationships.

I would further add some observations about the transference phenomena in such family diagnostic and family therapeutic ventures. When the young adult's parents are part of therapy, the therapist is not in line for the usual transference formation. His role becomes more real. In fact, the tendency to formulate a transference relationship in the presence of one's parents becomes the occasion for interpretation. The emotional need is brought back to the parent-student relationship rather than being developed in the therapist-patient relationship. Perhaps the family as a whole may have a transference reaction with the therapist but the goal of therapy is clarification of their relationship and as long as they assign a legitimate role to the therapist, this is acceptable.

Moving now into the clinical syndromes, I would point out that these syndromes do not correspond with specific religious orientations. To make a direct correlation between religious doctrine and psychological illness or health would be folly. I consider religious integrity to be a positive contributor to mental health. I think that the positive correlation betweeen these two can be demonstrated. The determinants of psychological distress occur or are built into the personality in days before religious doctrine is perceivable by the child. Therefore, it is really the relationship of the parents' value structure, including what is seen in religious terms, and child-rearing that becomes the critical issue. Some conservative groups, especially in Protestantism, wishfully think and hope that spiritual health offers some insurance for mental health. I don't think that this is demonstrable clinically. To explain this in depth, of course, would require an exploration of what is meant by spiritual health and mental health and this digresses from the main topic of this chapter. Suffice it to say that the child comes to experience the God of his parents in terms of the emotional relationship that the parents have to him. Their views of and transmission of authority, tenderness and forgiveness tend to form the emotional expectation of the child toward the parents' God. Perhaps one parameter of the spiritual health would be a positive correlation of the parents' verbalizations about religion and their emotional attitudes toward the child. This could be illustrated in a negative way by the father who staunchly proclaims the Protestant idea of Grace and the love of God but in a contradictory way holds God out as the one who will punish the child with ultimate rejection for his misdeeds.

Let us turn then to perhaps the largest group most representative of students in our culture at this time. This is the student whose parents have themselves gone through value diffusion and confusion.

VALUE DIFFUSION IN COLLEGE STUDENTS

In my experience, this group is represented by students from "liberal" homes, typically suburban, typically affluent and typically religious in form, but not in content. This can be true of Protestant, Roman Catholic or Jewish religious backgrounds. A brief description of the parents' value setting points to the fact that they have usually deviated rather widely from their own parents' religious backgrounds. Very often this has not been worked through at the emotional level with the student's grandparents and so there is chronic tension, distancing and guilt feelings in these relationships. These parents have typically held onto the form of the grandparents' religion, perhaps moving to more liberal wings of their religious structure and it has ceased to have much personal meaning for them. Other values have become ascendant. These include competition, getting ahead, putting the other guy down and the assumption that affluence and financial security are sufficient for relationship development. The ideals which the student has been expected to live by are those that maintain the middle class image, place success at the pinnacle of achievement. Human relationships are very important but as means to an end, not for purposes of intimacy. The marriages of these students' parents are often fraught with distress. Often the home has been religiously split from its inception. This is representative of the way they handled the emancipation from their own parents. They tended to take the position the religious affiliation was not important and so they crossed religious lines in marriage. This has often served to keep the in-laws apart who in turn put pressure on the primary family. The mother of this family typically has yearned for belonging and intimacy from her husband, but his world does not allow much of this in his pursuit up the stairway of success.

The net effect to the college student has been a lack of guidelines as to what is beneficial and what is detrimental in human relationships. This student yearns for something that he *can depend upon*. In the presence of the success orientation, he has turned to his peer groups for substitute family experience during adolescence. This often ended in the "blind leading the blind." Sexual experience has been premature, painful and disillusioning. Drug utilization is very high. Perhaps at the core of the self-image of this student is the question of whether anything is of value, especially whether *he* is of any value. If he is of no value, anything goes and it usually does. If this syndrome should lead to a frank psychiatric disorder, the student's expectation from the parents is one of blame because he has not fulfilled their image of success. His wrath and disillusionment abound as does his despair. However, what he does not see is that very often his parents are not happy with the pattern as well. He knows that their marriage is in trouble, but he doesn't know that it may still mean something to them. It becomes the task of the psychotherapist to explore these questions with the possibility that they can salvage something, because there really is something of importance underneath all of this: they do care for each other.

What I have described thus far does not appear to be very religious in its content or perception in the student's mind and I think this is true. I would argue, however, that the self-value that the students seek from family is positively related to something the parents did not destroy in their flight into success. Very often, one or both of the parents are greatly heartened when their young-adult child brings to the surface the vacuousness of what they espoused. This isn't really what they want. In fact, therapy sometimes will bring the grandparents as well into therapy in a three-generation exploration. At times one corollary to this kind of therapy is a clarification in religious identification and observance. Although it is not a goal of therapy, it is one way that people do find to express common values. There are enlightened religious groups in our communities which see this deterioration in the American family and actively reach out to resolve it. My observation of these churches is that they are few in number but extremely exciting and provocative places when the leadership of the church does allow the family to expose its agonies.

The next syndrome I will describe also cuts across denominational lines. It is not unique to any given religious group and doubtless does not exist because of religious observances. I refer to the psychological-religious problems of the overly dependent student. The latter may be male or female although the characteristics for each is somewhat different. I think it is worthy of discussion as a group in itself. Its uniqueness is in the dominance of the mother in the home. In the previous authority diffusion and confusion we observed the child who had been presented contradictory information about authority and values, in fact, there was the suggestion that there was probably no authority that was really reliable. In this present syndrome, authority is reliable but it's invested in the mother and this is of great conflict both to the male and to the female child. If mother also happens to be religious, the student's conflicts are often expressed in religious terms.

DOMINANT MOTHER SYNDROME

The characteristic presentation in this situation was a background in which mother was really also father. The problem multiplied because there was a father in the scene whom the child wanted to be more significant. Mother, usually as an extension of her own mother, was the dominant one. She was typically not a very feminine person and covered her own anxiety with pesudo-strength, strength which is expressed at the expense of the children. She was very strong in what she considered right and very forthright in her penalty for infraction. She has typically seen her child as an extension of herself and his or her good behavior vindicates and gratifies herself. I will avoid the more frank feminization in the male, because I'm really not trying to focus on frank psychiatric pathology such as homosexuality. What I would point to is the existential despair that emerges in the male college student from such a background. He frequently drifts toward a dropout status, formulates goals very poorly. He will frequent religious meetings, seeking support and understanding from religious leaders. This will develop a variety of responses. In some instances, he is frankly utilized because he obeys so well. His utilization of the religious structure of the college community isn't really authentic. He turns religious observance and structure into a mother substitute, looking for guidance and approval from them as a maternal surrogate. His psychological conviction and religious clarification are vague indeed. If he should drift into the office of a mental health professional, it's usually with depression, aimlessness and his experience there tends to be shortlived. He tends to seek answers from others, not from himself. As the risk of loss of therapuetic contact is already great, I have come to take the position that with passive dependent individuals, I want to see mother early in process. I don't mean see her early if she lives within short commuting distance but wherever she lives. Too much is at stake for him to risk a negative therapeutic outcome. Some attempt to break into the family patterns is necessary in the hopes that he can externalize some of his hostility of his mother's obsessive overprotection. Quite a different person emerges if one is successful in this. It may not be possible for this student to face up to his mother's domination but this cannot be presumed. Apathy, apparent lack of anxiety, an interpersonal clinging are not always reliable indicators of what is possible. The father should be present in the family conferences as well because any positive movement on his part to counteract his wife's control would have enormous benefit to his son. The interesting thing that sometimes develops is that the son comes to see his own religiosity as just a further maternalization. I think psychotherapists are prone to let such a student's religious life "go down the tube" with mother. Perhaps this is inevitable sometimes but a destruction of a value system does not deal with an interpersonal relationship. People need values. This needs to be pointed out to the student for, in his fervor to rid himself of mother's control, he may assume that all control must go. A therapist may rejoice in the flash of victory as he sees self-identity arise in such a person, but he is not fully mature until he has formulated a value structure of his own which would include clarification of his religious orientation and observance. Psychotherapists themselves have been so prone to avoid religious issues that they sometimes get in the way of the maturing process in their patients. An interesting sidelight at this point is the frequency with which mental health workers have themselves come from quite religious backgrounds. One wonders whether the mental health profession is not a substitute for religious performance in dynamic terms for some of us. (1)

The female college student whose mother has been dominant often has a malady as intense and distressing as the male. An overly strong mother does not assure an adequate feminine self-image. Quite to the contrary, it is often eroded because the girl cannot be herself. By that, I mean she cannot choose to identify with those parts of her mother's character she wishes as she emerges into adulthood but is under an obligation to become a carbon copy. The necessity of mimicking mother produces a sterile kind of personality with profound self-doubt. She is usually socially inept and prone to seek mother substitutes in her peers and the adults on campus. She destroys these very relationships from within though because she asks for too much. She often asks for a repeat of the relationship she had with mother. This may be out of a fear of asking for something different, that is violating the mother's code that "you must represent me," or, if she does dare to violate the mother's prerogatives, she may form a highly positive transference reaction with adult women with which they are uncomfortable or which take on homosexual overtones. This girl's religious experience is usually perfunctory and mimicking of mother's and has little value to herself. It's very common that her father has not supported her in the manner that she needed; in fact, his disdain for his wife may have been expressed toward his daughter by displacement. Another alternative is that he may have turned to her for the affection that he did not dare seek in his wife. This frequently has incestuous overtones. This has been particularly true in my experience with students from low socio-economic backgrounds whose attempted college education is a first for the family. The parents' marriage has usually been horrendously bad and father has often made overt sexual advances toward his daughter, not necessarily unbeknown to the dominant mother. This is ofttimes present in families of the most conservative religious structure. Such a girl's real hope of resolution comes in an alliance with a therapist who will help her face up to the truth of the situation and confront mother in the process. Mother is so strong that such students do not ordinarily have a conviction that they have dealt with mother unless they have done it out in the open. Although it is not common for such a mother to openly acknowledge her contributions to the problem, it does result on some occasions. Of course, it is best if she can set her daughter free. In any event, the daughter must develop controls over the father or she is likely to avoid all male relationships or duplicate incestuous type relationships in the ones she does develop. It has been my experience that a number of these persons have had a short term but intense relationship of a very positive nature with someone who saw the tragedy of the situation. It could be an aunt, a grandparent, or somebody in the church structure. So little was offered within the family that a great deal was made out of the identification with these substitute love objects. They often can form the nidus of health from which the person can grow into self-respect.

Of all of the groups I have described thus far, this particular one has less working through the family structure than any of the others. This is because of the mother's absolutism. A change for her would be even greater than for her child. But her presence is vital in the opening up of the process. These students are particularly loathe to be honest about how bad it really was and some fresh re-exposure to this is often very helpful. Obviously, the religious experience of this group of students has been and will be conditioned by the overmaternalization and the identification of this maternalization with religious life.

Thus far, we have looked up two broad categories. In the first of these, religious observance failed to provide a consistent value structure. Resultant diffusion and confusion of values often produced in these students a wish for clear and reliable authority patterns, including those represented in religious convictions. The personality of these students has been influenced by the absence of religious values. In the other category, religion was the handmaiden of maternalization and almost incidental to that process. I will now turn to those students who have come from far more conservative, religiously oriented homes. It's a truism to state that values of parents always influence the personality development of their children. Religious values are especially significant when they are given a central place in the life of the family. The family which centers its value structure around religious convictions is going to communicate its meaning of life, the importance of the child to the parent and the whole authority structure in religious terms. It is very difficult in such a setting for the child to differentiate parental religious convictions from parental personality patterns. Expectations from God and the parent are interchangeable.

AUTHORITARIAN RELIGION AND PERSONALITY

The students that I have seen from a Roman Catholic background find the religious structure of their families extremely important in their perception of life and themselves. As the reliability of authority in this group has been questioned, the Catholic family has tended to move from formalism with its dutiful character of worship to a more thought-provoking one. The church no longer represents to this typical family the same kind of reliability which was so important in former years.

I have observed a variety of patterns that represent paths that Catholic students turn to in struggling with these issues. One pathway is represented by the student whose only defense against the shaking of the reliability of authority is passivity and dependency. His symptoms may include apathy, motivational immobility and his personality will lose vibrance, vigor and aggressivity. Having been instructed that obedience to the pattern is the norm, he is bereft of adequate guideposts when there is internal conflict within the religion and family. For fear of losing acceptance, he retreats into some form of inertia. This is not usually represented by frank depression but a sense of lostness. In contrast, is the Catholic student who moves very rapidly toward emancipation and becomes caught up in the opportunities in his religious community for change. But what he at first embraced with relish because it seemed to relieve him of many burdens later may turn to the service of splitting in his personality. His intellectual pursuits, stirred on by the loosening of authority patterns, ofttimes are in conflict with his dependency needs which relate to parents who continue to adhere to a more traditional value form. This may evidence itself in a dissociative pattern or even frank psychosis if the rift is deep enough. I would add, however, that in my experience it is not changes in religious structure alone which are responsible for schizophrenic illness in such situations. There are schizophrenogenic patterns in the "pre-religious" era of childhood.

My clinical experience in authoritarian religious structures has been in contact with conservatism in Protestant groups and I will devote myself more extensively to this group as a consequence. I would refer you to E. Mansell Pattison's publications in this area. (2) Conservative Christianity has developed strong convictions about the nature of man and has labored hard to implement these convictions in child-rearing. There is confusion in conservative Protestant anthropology with regard to the relationship between personal value and original sin. In this struggle, emotion is deprecated while intellectualism is exalted. There is a basic contradiction between the concept of Grace, unmerited love from God, and expectation of punishment. Historically this confusion has been reinforced as the Church and family have threatened the child with God's authority to maintain loyalty to the group. In this respect, the very conservative Protestant groups share similar conflicts with other minority groups. Aggression is especially pointed to as a difficult area. Intellectualization and aloofness are products of this. Passivity is another common defense against aggression. Parallel to the necessity of repression of aggression is the necessity of repression of erotic drives. There is much confusion in adolescents of this subculture as often little preparation has been given to the experience which the adolescent faces.

A WISH FOR ACCEPTANCE

In summary, there is a basic ambivalence about the value of the child in the extremely conservative Protestant groups. This ambivalence is perceived by the child with consequent doubt of the reliability of his relationship to his parents. Very often the verbalizations within such groups would raise doubts about his value because of the stress that is placed on the consequences of deviation from the behavioral norms that are expected. This is backed up with theological precepts about the nature of sin which leave the child in a position of wonder about his own nature. He's threatened with rejection, temporal and eternal. In opposition to this, his parents may be relatively healthy persons and give him a clear emotional message that he is of value. Usually in such situations the emotional relationship with the family will prevail over the religious tyranny when therapy is necessary.

There are several clinical pictures which come out of this pattern. It is no theoretical notion to me that sexual distortion and primitive religious observance are often allied. This has been demonstrated over and over again to me in the lives of students coming from extreme fundamentalistic backgrounds, especially where the socio-economic structure is low. The child is caught between the manipulative stimulation of the parent in the sexual area and the extreme authority in a religious vein. The typical effects of this struggle are severe depression with suicidal intent or severe psychic splitting. The severe depression arises out of uncertainty of self-image. A tenacious dependency struggle is often coupled with this as the student still seeks the approval of a very authoritative family structure. He can only perceive that to hate himself is one way of achieving such approval. This student commonly accepts inappropriate responsibility for sexual stimulation and finds it impossible to defend himself against these injustices. Hospitalization is sometimes essential to confront this family situation in an open manner. The abject horror that might be evoked in the therapist's feelings is not sufficient support to enable such a student to change his relationships within the family. No amount of sympathetic support usually lasts long as his wish for acceptance is so profound.

In a family confrontation, however, a student can bring his or her need for recognition directly to the parents and have an open demonstration that he is important or is not important. Then the necessary emancipation may begin. The course upward though to self-respect is arduous and difficult. This student has often learned well that he belongs to the family and the self-depreciation which they have taught him and which they in fact feel about themselves is normative. Curiously enough, many of these students do not reject the religious patterns that they have been exposed to. Rather they try to find relief within it and it has been my observation that someone identified with that religious structure who will take a stand with them against the family can often be most beneficial in effecting emancipation. There is a serious treatment problem in the dependency which often accompanies such a relationship.

Toward the other end of the socio-economic spectrum are those students from more affluent families. Religious conservatism is their way of life also. But the student is in conflict with the family's allegiance to more materialistic goals. These students see their parents' religion as divested of significant meaning because it does not alter their relationships to social problems of our times, but rather seems to support the parents' socio-economic standing. There may be very firm adherence to the group's behavioral norms. The taboos that are prohibited by the conservative group may be religiously adhered to but it comes through to the student as a form. What they miss in the parents is authenticity of emotional relationship. This emotional relationship is missing in the religious area as much as any other. It's very tempting in the clinical situation to overidentify with the student's hostility toward such a pattern and assume that he will be free by rejecting them, the possibility which he often presents. Ofttimes when this alternative is pushed too far, the student will end treatment because he cannot tolerate the guilt of having rejected those he really does care for. This is often correlated with the fact that the parents have in a parallel fashion given him something very authentic although they have not lived up to it in a way that the student needs. Family confrontation is essential in this regard. I take as a rule of thumb to never accept judgment about such a family without seeing for myself. Of particular significance is the pastor's child from a conservative background. He has grown up with the conflicted notion of how important the individual is, how essential love is, and yet he has seen himself and the rest of the family sacrificed at the altar of Christian duty imposed on his father by the church's expectations or by himself. He has been unable to deal with this effectively because to attack the system is to attack God for all this is done by God's authentication. (3)

With rare exception, the children of middle class conservative Protestant backgrounds still hope for relationship with their parents, when caught in the value struggles I have described. Very soon in therapy they want the possibility of honest candor with their parents. As further evidence of the double message given to children in this subculture are the evidences of psychic splitting observed in routine MMPI evaluation of incoming students at Christian colleges which I've been involved with for the last ten years. This psychic splitting is not usually of a schizophrenic nature. In the usual follow-up diagnostic evaluation and sometimes therapy, the psychic splitting represents the conflict between the parents' emotional message that the child really is important and the contradictory message that the child must live for God and is in danger of jeopardy because of sin. The parents' adherence to a behavioral pattern in the church, which they do not always believe in themselves but must insist on in the child to remain a loyal member of the group, further intensifies this conflict. It typically comes to the surface in middle or late adolescence or young adulthood. It can show itself in severe hysterical behavior and not uncommonly in acute schizophrenic syndromes. However, the investment of the therapy in honestly looking at the pattern and honestly hearing the child's conflict about his own value quickly dissolves the acute schizophrenic pattern.

Religious ideation often becomes a significant content of psychotherapy in the communication between these students and their parents. It's the coded way in which they have understood each other in the past, and now this must be decoded so that they can find something that is more real in it or elsewhere. These students have frequently thrown aside the doctrinaire, intellectualized theology. However, they have retained something of the integrity and value in the value system, mainly that they are of importance. I have been frequently gratified by the readiness with which such families have accepted this challenge. What often appears is a parental recognition of the person in their child and a putting of religious doctrine into that perspective. Contrary to what might be anticipated, these students and their families do not typically turn the church into a scapegoat but remain in it with renewed insight for change. There is consistency in the pattern whereby these students do not resolve the problem by rebellion, by destruction of the religious structure, but by coming back to the family for the clear message of their importance, even in religious terms.

CONCLUSION

In this paper I have taken the position that college students in the United States are indeed religious creatures. Their religion however often deviates significantly from that of their parents. Typically, where the parents' religious patterning has been vague and for social implications rather than religious implications, the student seeks some solidity of value structure with which to identify. He has suspected his parents because of the lack of consistency but he still hopes in the possibility that he is of value to them. This student welcomes family involvement in a therapeutic process.

In another group, the maternalization of religious systems seems to parallel maternalization in the American family. I have described some facets of the travail that these students experience in becoming persons.

Finally, I have described more conservative religious groups and some of the influences on personality development that have been evident therein. In all of these, values are extremely important to the typical student, albeit he may have rejected what he considered theological , intellectualized orientation. What he desires though perhaps is the best that the religious structure could offer, namely, a means by which within the family relationship he can come to find that he is of value, deal with the vagaries of his own existence and find reliability in human relationships. These families do assume that they belong to each other and this cannot be easily erased in the life of one of their children.

REFERENCES AND FOOTNOTES

1 Henry, Wm. E., Sims, John H., Spray, S. Lee: *The Fifth Profession*. San Francisco, Jossey-Bass, 1971.
2 Esau, Truman G. and Cox, Richard H.: "The Mental Health of Ministers' Wives and Families" in Pattison, E. Mansell, (Ed.) : *Clinical Psychiatry and Religion*. Boston, Little Brown, 1969.
3 Pattison, E. M.: Ideological Support for the Marginal Middle Class: Faith, Healing and Glossolalia. In Zaretsky, I. and Leone, M. P. (Eds.) : *Pragmatic Religion: Marginal Religious Movements in America Today*. Princeton, Princeton University Press, 1972.

BIBLIOGRAPHY

1. Blaine, Graham B., Jr.: *Youth and the Hazards of Affluence*. New York, Harper, 1966.
2. Blaine, Graham B., Jr.: *Emotional Problems of the Student*. New York, Norton, 1964.
3. Erikson, Erik H.: *Insight and Responsibility*. New York, Norton, 1964.
4. *Group for the Advancement of Psychiatry*, Report No. 60, "Sex and the College Student," 1965; Report No. 68, "Normal Adolescence," 1968; Report No. 78, "The Field of Family Therapy," 1970.
5. Howells, John G., (Ed.) : Chapter IV of *Theory and Practice of Family Psychiatry*. New York, Brunner/Mazel, 1971.
6. Pattison, E. M. (Ed.) : *Clinical Psychiatry and Religion*. Boston, Little Brown, 1969.
7. Pattison, E. M.: Ideological Support for the Marginal Middle Class: Faith, Healing and Glossolalia. In Zaretsky, I. and Leone, M. P. (Eds.) : *Pragmatic Religion: Marginal Religious Movements in America Today*. Princeton, Princeton University Press, 1972.

CHAPTER 30

ETHICS AS THE MORAL CODES MEN LIVE BY AND THE ESSENTIALS OF HUMAN WELL-BEING

SYLVANUS M. DUVALL

THE CONCERN OF ETHICS is with standards and norms of conduct; how people *ought* to act, and what is more or less worth while (values). Its task is to provide the principles and standards that constitute the basis of morality, and that determine relative importance.

TRADITIONAL AND FUNCTIONAL APPROACHES TO ETHICS

Traditionally, the whole field of ethics has been seen as best expressed in the verbal statements of recognized authorities, individual or corporate. Thus Christian ethics is identified with the ethical "teachings" of the Bible, or of Jesus, or of the Church as interpreted by major Christian leaders and church bodies. On this basis, Christian ethics is seen as centered in love, with the Fatherhood of God and the Brotherhood of Man as major corollaries. Unloving conduct, such as war or racial discriminations, is rejected as clearly un-Christian. The failure of Christians to live up to the teachings of their faith, in no way affects their validity as constituting the nature of Christian ethics.

The functional approach insists that the ethics of any group, individual or institution be judged by its functioning content, not its "advertising claims." Christian ethics, like a car, should be judged by its performance, not by appealing statements in the brochures. By their "fruits," not their "teachings," shall ye know them. True, Christian ethics should not be judged by the behavior of some Christians. But deliberately chosen policies in which people act as Christians, including the Crusades, the Inquisition and the innumerable wars of religion, are the most reliable indications of the nature of Christian ethics. Likewise, the ideals of our Revolutionary ancestors are best determined, not by statements made in some document, but by the kind of government they set up after they gained control.

INTERPRETING THE VERBAL BEHAVIORAL DICHOTOMY

Discrepancies between the verbal codes that are professed and the functional codes by which people actually live, are commonly seen as "hypocrisy"—a deliberate attempt to deceive. This explanation, while sometimes true, is often superficial and misleading. Societies and individuals alike are torn between conflicting values and value systems, each of which is genuinely cherished. "Hypocrisies" may be primarily devices, however regrettable, to adjust such inner conflicts.

Awareness of such discrepancies varies widely. Some, blithely unaware of them, idignantly deny that they exist. The more insightful are in a tougher spot. They "acknowledge and bewail their manifold sins and wickedness," often in agonizing frustration. They have tried so earnestly and so futilely to overcome them.

Frankly recognizing that we humans have two kinds of moral standards, often in conflict with each other but each sincerely held, has important advantages. To begin with, we will know better what to expect of others and of ourselves. Knowing the actual content of Christian ethics, or the "American Dream," can protect us from disillusioning or even damaging expectations. An awareness and acceptance of ethical dualism may make us feel more kindly toward others. Dropping the demand that people live up to non-functioning moral standards can help to prevent undue exposure and reduce resentments. It would also reduce our own pious self-righteousness. None are quite so hypocritical as those who denounce the hypocrisies of others most vehemently. Best of all, it would facilitate the development of possible expectations and more valid ethical norms.

Functioning codes are called folkways, customs, manners or mores, depending upon their importance. In simple societies, these social expectations are so built into the behavioral practices of people that few verbal statements are necessary. In more complex societies, contractual agreements and legal requirements may be verbally stated. But by far the greater number, and the most important part of such codes are a vast network of behavioral responses that function with a minimum of conscious attention.

Those codes are sustained mainly by conditioning and sanctions. The experiences of children living under the direction of adults often so internalize cultural demands that they are observed as a matter of conscience. A second major support, and a part of the conditioning process, is sanctions, rewards and punishments. In times of rapid change, and among groups not themselves well acculturated, much of what was "taken for granted" no longer can be, with resulting uneasiness and social disruptions. What once was picked up from the experiences of ordinary living, must now be carefully formulated and deliberately taught, or it will be lost to oncoming generations.

HOW TO IDENTIFY THE CODES MEN LIVE BY

Determining the mores of any culture is a highly technical and involved task. The following suggestions may be helpful. The codes men live by can be identified as follows:

1. By programs and the allocation of resources. To know what any institution, such as a church or a school really stands for, disregard its "creeds" and resolutions. Look at its budget and its programs. To determine what is important in any society, note what it gives its attention to and spends its money for.

2. By functioning sanctions. Note what will get you into real trouble, or win strong approval. Regard official awards with suspicion.

3. By what people do when they have a chance. We know that our revolutionary ancestors did not believe in "democracy" because when they had control, they denied the ballot to about 90 per cent of the white adults and tried to put the Presidency, the Senate and the Supreme Court beyond the control of the voters. They had some concern for freedom because they did adopt a Bill Of Rights.

MAJOR ETHICAL CODES THAT MEN LIVE BY

Any classification of ethical codes will inevitably be somewhat arbitrary. The following may prove helpful.

The Moral Is What I Want

Discounting, but by no means rejecting idealistic professions, the major ethic of most people is seen in terms of what they want or wish to avoid. This assumption includes hedonism, but is more comprehensive. Far more improtant than comfort and pleasure, and sometimes even life itself, are such psychic satisfactions as acceptance by others, feelings of dignity and worth, and meaningful identifications. Conversely, the major evils are such psychic pains as shame, guilt, embarrassment, loneliness, frustration and boredom.

Nor are such ethical values necessarily "selfish." The well-being of friends, loved ones, and sometimes even "humanity," are real wants for some, whether their basis be "healthy" or "neurotic." Altruistic values are as real and may be as potent as "selfish" values.

Basing morality upon what people want has real advantages. It simplifies definition and identification. People may not know what they *need*, but they usually know what they want. Since moral demands grow out of human motivations, inner tensions and pressures for "hypocrisy" become minimal. Moral demands are more likely to be within ethical capacities.

On the other hand, identifying the *moral* with the *desired* has obvious limitations. Although this ethic need not be selfish, it often, if not usually, is. People tend to regard anything they can get as their "rights," whether they be king, nobility, organized labor, or on relief. One result is a flagrant lack of concern for the rights of others, whether they be peasants, consumers or taxpayers.

Most serious, striving for what we want is often self-destructive. Self-*interests* are often in basic conflict with self-*welfare*. Note how eagerly young men flocked to the banners of Napoleon, to leave their bodies on the fields of Waterloo, and for what? A valid ethic must rest upon something far more substantial than the often chaotic caprice of ardent feelings.

Ethical Fundamentalism, Sometimes Called "Legalism"— The Moral As What Is Right

Morality is seen as embodied in self-validating propositions, sometimes called "laws" and sometimes called "principles." These may be not only unrelated to, but even destructive of human values. They are to be observed because they are "right." They constitute the basis of primitive tribal taboos, and the absolute immutable "moral laws" of such notables as Calvin and Kant. The essence of this ethic is a dogmatism.

In recent years, "laws" as a basis of ethics have come into disrepute and have widely been replaced by "principles" such as "love" or "democracy." The result has been greater flexibility, but no greater objectivity or realism. Among less desirable results have been *moralisms*—morality with its consequences amputated.

Moralism tends to classify conduct into *Virtues* (The Good Guys), such as honesty, love, justice and compassion, and *Sins* (The Bad Guys), such as greed, prejudice, hatred and deceit. Such distinctions have considerable merit. "On balance" love is better than hate, and honesty than deceit. But not always. Under some circumstances, what is sincerely regarded as "love" can be disastrous, and deceit highly beneficial. The basic evil of moralism is its refusal to look at consequences; we must *always* do what is "just" or "democratic"; we must "serve" others, regardless of the situation or the probable results.

As soon as people become morally concerned, they tend to become inveterate liars about the areas of their concern. A common form is extravagant promises. Advocates of free public schools in this country asserted that whenever a school opened, a jail would close. President Wilson promised that if only "Kaiserism" would be defeated, we would have a world safe for democracy. The Prohibitionists in all sincerity made sweeping promises of how crime, political corruption, poverty and even insanity would be reduced by the adoption of their program. Recently a prominent reformist assured us that if only Congress would appropriate enough money for relief, "it would solve every problem of the poor." Much literature dealing with social reform is riddled with distortions, if not downright lies. In some instances, this is frankly acknowledged, and defended as the only way to arouse the public.

As a lubricant of human relationships, deceit has a real place. But it is a bad foundation for the erection of a building or the determination of a social policy. Much of the frustration and failure that attend efforts to "do good," result because the advocates of such efforts have lied, first to themselves, and then to others about both the costs of their endeavors, and the results to be expected. If by some miracle ethically concerned persons decided to be basically honest they would demand and attempt far less, and accomplish infinitely more.

Equalitarian Inclusiveness

Until recently in this country, sizeable groups, conspicuously but not exclusively Blacks and women, were regarded as inherently inferior and excluded from important rights and opportunities. In addition, social and economic failures tended to be rejected, often with contempt. Lately, however, those ethical assumptions have been extensively reversed. The rejected are often seen as victims, rather than as unworthy. One result has been ardent and surprisingly successful efforts to include these disadvantaged on a more equal basis. This ethical thrust has had two main prongs: (1) the push for *Rights*—to vote, to hold office, to be freer from discriminations and to compete with others on a basis of greater equality; and (2) increasing economic support for those who have failed to make the grade. Equalitarian inclusiveness has become the most influential functioning ethic in America today.

The achievements of this ethic have been impressive. Millions of people have been freed, not only from external repressions, but from "self-fulfilling" inner attitudes that often resulted in unwarranted self-rejection. However, along with such gains, have come losses that ought clearly to be recognized.

Equalitarian inclusiveness has helped our people to recognize that pigmentation and sex are distorted and often evil bases for inequalities, and that much "failure" is learned. In so doing, it has also often blurred the distinction between real and often inborn differences in abilities, in incentives and in concern for the common good. When important decisions are involved, assumptions of equality can be disastrous, whether we are building a bridge or formulating a social policy.

Rights gained by the disadvantaged have often been at the expense of the rights of those who support them, of those who have even become their victims!

In helping the disadvantaged to enjoy our affluence, equalitarian inclusiveness has failed to protect such gains from threats of irresponsible fecundity and inordinate demands that already threaten the financial solvency of some cities. Moreover, measures for the benefit of the disadvantaged have been pushed without adequate concern as to how these will affect the security and the survival of society.

Morality as Obedience to Authority

This standard of morality is, in part, the basis of ethics of ancient monarchies, authoritative churches, the military, and Communist and fascist dictatorships. Morality consists in doing as you are told by those in authority over you. The cardinal sin is heresy and disobedience.

Like legalism, this basis of ethics provides definiteness and certainty in an age of confusion, and greatly simplifies a complex world. An additional advantage is a flexibility that legalism lacks.

The basic defect is that of all dictatorships. It offers no protection against the stupidities and the iniquities of those in authority. However noble may be their avowed intentions, those in control are usually corrupt and never infallible. When people blindly do "as they are told," there can be no adequate checks on shameless exploitation or disastrous blunders. Those who can only obey, can only contribute as tools of society. Authoritarian societies waste, or even destroy, much of their resources. Domination also increases resentments, nonetheless real because they are underground, or even repressed into the "subconscious."

The shores of time are strewn with the wrecks of former dictatorships, once proud and towering vessels that have foundered on the rocks of the distorting ethics of blind obedience. Add to them we can. Restore them we cannot.

The Holy Cause

By far the most virile and influential ethic of our times, if not of all time, is "the Holy Cause." This was the motivating ethic for the seizure of Russia and the amazing conquest of China by the Communists. It enabled Hitler to transform a discouraged, beaten people into a force powerful enough to threaten the entire world. It has inspired the Viet Cong to fight a major military power to a standstill. In any list of viable ethical theories, the Holy Cause would be among the most prominent.

This ethic identifies morality with some "Cause," often seen as crucial for human welfare and rooted in imperative demands of reality itself. The spirit is definitely religious; the ideology quasi-theological. The promotion of this cause overrides all other considerations, and merits supreme devotion. In the Holy Cause ethic, *this* end justifies any means. Hence, the often complete absence of honesty, and the ruthlessness that is so baffling and shocking, especially to liberals. Whenever the fires of fervent faith burn fiercely (as they still do among the Communists of Viet Nam), there is a sacrificial devotion that rages like a forest fire and that can be both as disastrous and as difficult to contain.

Causes vary widely in their comprehensiveness. Some, like Abolitionism, the Populist Movement, Prohibition or Women's Liberation, are limited to some one reform. Others, like fascism and especially Communism, seek to reorganize the whole of society, including its ideologies. In the competitive struggle for the minds of men, the newer and more inclusive ideologies have considerable advantage. Some Christians have striven valiantly to present the "Cause of Christ" as the "better answer" to the human predicament. Unfortunately for such efforts, Christian theology has never developed, or seriously attempted to develop, an ideology that convincingly interprets social process. (Splinter Adventist groups such as Jehovah's Witnesses have moved toward this.) Despite repeated assertions that religion must include the "whole" of life, Christian churches are not and, as now constituted, cannot be committed to any program beyond limited reforms. As a theology, Communism has this advantage: it includes an interpretation of social process and clearly defined social programs.

The psychological bases for the power of the Holy Cause have been vividly presented in Eric Hoffer's *The True Believer*. However we may question his particular analysis, his basic thesis is essentially sound. People support Holy Causes, primarily to meet their own emotional, and often neurotic or psychotic, needs.

Such motivations can make a dictatorship virile. Dictatorships such as those of the Czars, the French Monarchy before the Revolution, and the Batista regime in Cuba enjoyed no such emotional support and were, therefore, like all régimes that must depend mainly upon coercion, decadent and doomed. Hitlerism and Communism relied extensively upon repression, but they had something more; widespread, enthusiastic public support. As a Holy Cause succeeds, it no longer offers a fulfilling mission, and morale declines. This has become clearly evident in Russia and to some extent in China. The régime then becomes only another oppressive dictatorship.

The basic defect of the Holy Cause ethic is its dogmatism that makes the solution of human problems more difficult. The diagnosis of human problems is highly technical. Resolving them is safe, but only if approached with cautious experimentation. It is so easy to make bad conditions worse. Liberal critics of society are less dangerous because they are less likely to practice what they preach. Ineffective denunciations and futile resolutions become substitutes for ruthlessness in conduct.

"Hard Core" radicals operate without such checks of hypocrisy. Neurotic needs often inspire them with unrealistic hopes. From such hopes come impossible demands for an ideal society. Worst of all, they *act* rather than merely talk. The results can be disaster. Even if defeated, inevitable disillusionments result in disruptive recriminations, bitterness and resentments. Granting control to the most dogmatically distorted and power-hungry will result not in a good world, but in catastrophe.

WHERE DO WE GO FROM HERE?

Sound ethics results not from some one good code, but from sound processes for formulating codes. We need ethical codes for a variety of relationships. Like anything else, codes sometimes break down, wear out, or become obsolete. Codes must not only be formulated, but revised and kept in good repair. The following are offered as guide lines.

The Moral as the Beneficial

When Hitler occupied the Rhineland on March 7, 1936, driving him out might have cost many innocent lives. Since the territory was German, it would have been an injustice. It could also have prevented the second World War. The basic question of ethics is not what is "just" or "right," but what will do more good than harm. The moral is the beneficial.

When people "hypocritically" fail to live up to their ideals, the fault may be with the ideals rather than the people. Not too long ago, morality required that sex feelings and interests be repudiated for "purity." Current moralists today often demand a comparable rejection of "greed" and hostility. Altruism and "service to others" have taken the place once held by "purity."

Seeing *the moral as the beneficial* will raise questions about such current ethical dogmas. "Service to others," far from being always a virtue, can encourage infantile dependency in others. Supporting a day care center may be a way in which church people evade the more demanding responsibility of providing sound ethical guidance regarding more crucial and more thorny issues. An undue repression of hostile feelings can harm, not only personalities but good human relationships.

Deceit is certainly dangerous, but can be ethically desirable. The person with convictions contrary to those of his group sometimes should boldly state them and suffer the consequences. But he may thereby cut himself off from any possibility of changing them. It might be best to pretend conformity, so that he can work quietly and more effectively for his ideals. Often, if not usually, the interests of ethics are best served by working *with* people rather than by breaking with them.

"Hypocrisy" may also be necessary to enable a person to get along with himself. We often hold conflicting moral values. Sometimes we best progress morally by holding ideals that we cannot live up to as "beliefs," but that can become goals toward which we may strive. "Hypocrisy" is dangerous and even costly. Often these costs can and should be reduced. But it may be the only way we know of preserving, and making progress toward, higher moral ideals.

People Are Funny That Way

In determining what is beneficial, many have assumed that a world without suffering and pain, failure or risk would be a good world. Such hedonism is a superficial and often distorted misinterpretation of human need. We rightly question Freud's "death wish." But as mountain climbing, dangerous driving and a love of war so abundantly illustrate, conflict, risks, suffering and their frustrations are often eagerly sought. As "soap operas" and classic drama demonstrate, tragedy can be highly entertaining. The use of drugs and other self-destructive conduct may be a response to a world that has become more safe than many find comfortable. People are what they are, not what others take for granted that they "must" be.

Be Willing to Take What You Can Get

In ethics as on Wall Street, the "hogs" lose out. In the old days The Prohibitionists demanded more sobriety than Americans were willing to accept. Today if relief payments require more altruism than the tax payers find tolerable, they will jeopardize the whole program. Demands for justice cannot successfully go much beyond the power to implement them. A sound ethic must be adjusted to the capacities of those for whom it is intended. To be effective, the morally concerned must learn to take what they can get.

SOME BASIC ETHICAL PRINCIPLES

The Principle of the Larger Situation

People have long recognized that grabbing *short run* advantages can work against *long run* goals. The basic problem, however, is not of time, but of scope. Conduct and policies intended to achieve some one result, produce also a whole "package" of other results not intended, and often not foreseen. Well-meaning people have been dismayed at the raft of unanticipated evils that resulted from the "good" they sought. Costly housing programs have destroyed communities. By attracting more people into the area, they have depressed wages and increased unemployment. By providing good housing for those who failed to use it well, they have increased slum conditions. Likewise, bestowing "rights" upon the oppressed who lacked discipline, has increased crime and social disruption. The answer is not to avoid programs for social welfare. It is to recognize the large situation—that is, if we do *this* we must also do *that*. Morality is to be determined, not by some one result, but by the desirability of the total results in a larger situation.

This principle requires a willingness to accept necessary evils. "Larger situations" are complexes of goods and evils, often so intertwined as mutually to support each other. A badly needed power plant may increase pollution. Concern for the rights of criminals may reduce the rights of their victims. The basic defect of "situation ethics" was a failure to make clear that "situations" are extensive and highly complex contexts, not individual episodes. The basic moral question is not whether this particular act or result is *good* or *bad*, but the desirability of the totality of results that constitute the larger "package."

The Principle of Probable Consequences (Life Requires Rules).

It is wrong to run a red light, even if no one gets hurt. Why? Because as a policy, this would increase accidents. Likewise, sex codes should be determined by the social consequences of conduct if adopted as a general policy. Current allocations of property and income cannot be justified on the basis of either merit or need. But attempts to improve them by private theft, or even by social policy, could produce economic chaos.

Rules and regulations, like shoes or a girdle, can be harmfully constrictive. They are also essential. Few people are able to appraise the desirability of policies of conduct. Even for those who could, doing the investigation necessary to determine the morality of each of the innumerable decisions we must make each day, would be an intolerable burden. The only effective way is to decide in advance— by observing rules. Rules also perform other functions. They help us to know what to expect of one another. Without rules, no competitive sport would be possible. "Love" cannot eliminate the need for water safety regulations, traffic lights or rules for other human activities.

The Principle of Balance

The problem is not to eliminate change, but to avoid capsizing. On July 24, 1915 the excursion steamer *Eastland* overturned at its dock in the Chicago River with a loss of 812 lives. Waving good-bye to friends, the passengers had crowded the side nearest the dock. This imbalance of weight caused the ship to capsize. There is certainly nothing immoral about being on one side of a ship or the other. The wrong was in upsetting the balance. Morality regarding a social policy may not depend upon which side we are on. It may consist primarily in avoiding any sudden upset of a balance. As Aristotle pointed out, the essence of the Good Life and the Good

Society is a "Golden Mean," an equilibrium sufficient to prevent capsizing.

The Devil Is an Angel Who Has Gotten Out of Line.

As Milton so classically indicated, an angel who goes beyond his proper place can become a devil, and Paradise is lost. The morally concerned endanger their goals by giving to some one ethical angel, a greater position than is safe. Justice is certainly one important ethical angel. But to make it the only, or the decisive moral consideration, can be disastrous. The Viet Nam War resulted, mainly because a concern for justice to a small nation overrode other moral considerations. A "just and durable peace" is a contradiction in actualities. Greater "justice" for the disadvantaged has resulted in social disruptions that threaten justice for others. Like any angel, justice must be kept in line.

Love and compassion are angels whom we rightly revere and support. Yet uncontrolled love with its "service" ideal can spoil children and encourage paranoia and dependency. Compassion is directly responsible for one of our most threatening problems—the "population explosion." Our virtues may be more dangerous than our sins. Even our most cherished and important angels must be carefully watched and rigorously controlled.

The Crucial and Ultimate Ethical Question Is Social Survival.

All men are fellow travelers upon the same one ship: our physical earth and the civilization that makes human relationships tolerable. The great danger is that we shall be so preoccupied with squabbling over who is to have what staterooms, or over conditions of labor among the crew, or over doing good to the miserable, that we shall not give enough attention to the safety of the ship itself. Yet if this ship is torn apart by disastrous conflict, or founders because people are too selfish or unduly concerned with correcting evils, nothing else will make much difference! In the past, many forms of life and a number of civilizations have flourished, only to perish for reasons unrelated to "moral worth." The paramount issue for all ethically concerned persons must be social survival.

Ethics Has Theological Dimensions.

The conditions for human well-being and survival are set by the God who embodies the realities that determine human destiny. Ethics has theological dimensions. In much liberal religion, however, God is essentially the postulate of a baptized ethic, at best ornamental, and at worst, misleading. Despite some recognition of "demonology," current theology has failed to come to grips with the ethical challenges of "Darwinism."

The Durants do not offer their *The Lessons of History* as a treatise on theology. Yet like Paul and Calvin, they have faced the human predicament in its transcendental dimensions with stalwart realism. The following quotations are offered without endorsement or rejection, to indicate the kinds of theological issues that must be faced to establish a valid ethic.

> The laws of biology are the fundamental lessons of history. (p. 18)
> Life is competition. . . . Cooperation . . . is a form of competition. (p. 19)
> Life is selection. . . . Inequality is not only natural and inborn, it grows with the complexity of civilization. (p. 20)
> Freedom and equality are sworn and everlasting enemies, and when one prevails the other dies. . . . Utopias of equality are biologically doomed. (p. 20)
> In the last 3,421 years of recorded history, only 268 have seen no war.
> Violent revolutions do not so much distribute wealth as destroy it. (p. 72)
> The first condition of freedom is its limitation. (p. 68)
> Competition compels the capitalist to exhaustive labor, and his products to ever-rising excellence. (p. 59)
> Every economic system must sooner or later rely upon some form of the profit motive to stir individuals and groups to productivity. (p. 54)
> Nature and history . . . define good as that which survives, and bad as that which goes under. (p. 46)

Relevant Scientific Knowledge as a Basic Ethical Essential

Understanding human needs and how to meet them, and determining the nature of the total situation and the effects of behavioral policies upon human welfare require a high level of scientific knowledge. Furthermore, such knowledge must be relevant to the matter at hand. A highly trained surgeon may be no more able to build a bridge than anyone lese. A high level of "education" may leave a person no better qualified to cope effectively with a social issue than the merest novice. Few if any colleges have ever seriously attempted to educate for social leadership.

In the Area of Human Relationships, We Live in a Pre-Scientific Age.

When Albert Schweitzer decided to serve mankind as a physician, he first qualified himself by an adequate medical education. No one assumed that his good intentions and his eminence as an organist and a scholar would be enough. Those who would cure social ills often do not know enough even to see the need for technical competence. Most reformists have no more business to engage in social action than they have to practice dentistry. With cancer, we see the need for research by competent authorities. In social reform we squander billions without any serious attempt at research, or even pilot experiments. We shall not make significant progress in solving human problems until we become as scientific about them as we are about heart transfusions and the construction of bridges. The one commandment of the God who determines human destiny of which we may be most sure is this: THOU SHALT BASE THINE ETHICAL JUDGMENTS UPON THE BEST SCIENTIFIC KNOWLEDGE AVAILABLE.

CONCLUSION

A major need of our day is sound guidance regarding personal conduct and social policies. Traditional ethics cannot provide such guidance because it is geared primarily to the verbal statements of authorities, rather than to actual functioning codes. We must break new ground.

The major functioning codes have great merit, but also serious defects. None is adequate. The two most influential ethics, *equalitarian inclusiveness* and *the Holy Cause,* are not safe. None of them seriously attempts to provide for social health and survival.

The great, and as yet hardly begun task, is to see ethics in terms of the beneficial, and the beneficial in terms of social survival. Formulating ethical codes on such a basis is a highly complicated and demanding technical task. To it we must commit, not only our sincere idealism, but our best scientific resources.

BIBLIOGRAPHY

1. Bach, George R. and Wyden, Peter: *The Intimate Enemy.* New York, Morrow, 1968.
2. Callwood, June: *Love, Hate, Fear, Anger.* New York, Doubleday, 1964.
3. Durant, Will and Ariel: *The Lessons of History.* New York, Simon and Shuster, 1968.
4. Forrester, Jay W.: *World Dynamics.* Cambridge, Wright-Allen, 1971.
5. Hoffer, Eric: *The True Believer.* New York, Harper, 1951.
6. Lundberg, George A.: *Can Science Save Us?* New York, Longmans, 1961.
7. Mumford, Lewis: *The Pentagon of Power.* New York, Harcourt, 1970.
8. Olsen, Marvin E.: *The Process of Social Organization.* New York, Holt, 1968.
9. Snock, J. Diedrick (Ed.): Values in Crisis. *Journal of Social Issues,* vol. 25, no. 1, January, 1969.
10. Tannenbaum, Abraham J. (Ed.): Values, Attitudes and Behavior, *Journal of Social Issues,* vol. 24, no. 1, January 1968.

CHAPTER 31

CAN RELIGION AND PSYCHOTHERAPY BE HAPPILY MARRIED?

An Experiment in Education

PAUL W. CLEMENT
AND NEIL CLARK WARREN

DURING MOST OF ITS MODERN HISTORY, American psychology has treated religion as a taboo topic (Douglas, 1966). Organized religion has tended to take an equally aloof stance toward psychology. The distance these disciplines have maintained between themselves is frustrating and puzzling. Both are concerned with human behavior and the nature of man. And because of this common interest, they would seem to be vital partners in a common effort. Although such has not been the case for the most part, some changes have occurred in recent years suggesting a gradual movement toward increasing amounts of cooperation. The present chapter focuses on some of the problems encountered when one attempts an integration of religion and psychology.

Definition of Terms

Integration

For general purposes the term "integration" can be defined as the organization or bringing together of various components into a harmonious complex or whole. To date we have identified four general types of integration: (1) conceptual-theoretical integration, (2) integration through research, (3) integration in professional practice, and (4) intra-personal integration. Specific examples of each of these modes will be given later in this chapter.

Religion

"Theology," rather than "religion," is the term more often used in our own efforts at integration. Religion, however, is the broader concept, and it incorporates theology. Religion consists of a complex of human behaviors: (1) a theology or system of beliefs about God or Divine Power; (2) a code of ethics which guides a person in his relationships with others; (3) a philosophy which shapes the way a person views himself and his place in creation; (4) modes of worship such as praying, singing of hymns, giving sacrifices; (5) a community of people who share similar beliefs, ethical codes, philosophies, and modes of worship.

Psychotherapy

There are dozens of systems of psychotherapy, each having its own definitions. Two of the more widely known of these systems, behavior modification approaches and client centered therapy, were developed largely by psychologists on the basis of careful empirical research and systematic observation. These two general systems are most representative of the basic approaches of the present writers.

What is perhaps central to all behavioral techniques is the use of a systematic approach to change human behavior in the direction of goals which have been stated by one or more of the parties who are engaged in the therapeutic process. There is a sense in which the whole *raison d'être* of this system is to see the behavior of the client change. Client centered therapy on the other hand focuses on relationship. It is the "process" of therapy which is important for this orientation. When client and therapist engage in productive process, the outcome of therapy is nearly always positive.

The goals for most behavior modification approaches fall under the following three categories: (1) to increase some behaviors, (2) to decrease other behaviors, and (3) to maintain the remaining behaviors. Those behaviors which need to be increased can be called "deficits." A particular behavior may be deficient in that it does not occur with sufficient frequency, duration, intensity, or at specified times. Lack of social assertiveness or rarely saying good things to oneself are examples of behavioral deficits. Those behaviors which need to be decreased can be called "excesses." A particular behavior may be excessive in that it occurs too often, with too great intensity, or at the wrong times. Frequent complaining, fear of public speaking, and frequent self-critical statements are examples of behavioral excesses. It is highly important in this orientation not only to focus on changing a client's behavioral deficits and excesses, but also to help him maintain his behavioral assets. A particular behavior is considered to be an asset when it occurs with acceptable frequency, intensity, or at desired times.

Performing one's daily work, being relaxed around other people, and having realistic and obtainable goals are examples of behavioral assets.

In client centered therapy, as we mentioned, the relationship between client and therapist is central. The manner in which the therapist relates to the client and the style with which the client relates to his own experience become the most significant aspects of therapy. Therapy outcome has been shown to be significantly influenced by the presence or absence of certain therapist qualities. These have come to be known as the therapeutic triad and include: (1) nonpossessive warmth, (2) accurate empathy, and (3) genuineness. When a therapist is nonpossessively warm, accurately empathic and genuine in his relationship with a client, positive outcome is virtually assured. When these qualities are absent, however, deterioration is likely to occur. It has also been demonstrated that the style with which the client participates in therapy is of great importance. If the client deals with that part of his experience which has immediate importance for him, if he always includes himself in what he is processing, and if he relates to his experience in subjective rather than objective ways, the outcome of therapy is likely to be positive.

Psychology

For the purposes of this chapter, psychology is defined as the study or science of human behavior. Psychology is the science underlying psychotherapy. Scientifically based psychotherapy borrows concepts and methodology from psychology. The systematic development of more effective psychotherapies is contingent on the development of a better understanding of variables which change and maintain human behavior.

Thus, although "psychotherapy" is a key concept throughout these readings, it is our contention that it will ultimately prove to be more productive to focus on psychology. Psychotherapy relies heavily upon developmental psychology, learning theory, personality theory, etc. To narrow our concern to psychotherapy alone will likely lead to limited gain, but to broaden our scope to psychology in general and to concern ourselves with the integration of religion and psychology is to create considerably more possibilities for relationships of mutual benefit to both disciplines.

The doctoral training program in clinical psychology of which we are a part is explicitly committed to exploring the relationships between religion and psychology in theory, research, and practice.

Since the fundamental purpose of our program is directly related to the theme of this volume, most of the material in the remainder of this chapter comes from our experiences at Fuller Seminary. Although some of our problems in trying to integrate psychology and religion may be unique to our particular situation, we believe that most of them will be encountered by most individuals and institutions who engage in the integrative task.

Integrating Religion and Psychology

Conceptual-Theoretical Integration

In general, psychologists and theologians have failed to carry on long-term, meaningful dialogues concerning the interrelationships of their theoretical systems. There need to be places where such interactions are officially encouraged, so that psychologists and theologians can begin to investigate the theoretical significance of both disciplines. Such dialogues will lead to raising questions as to how psychological data might appropriately influence theological propositions and how Biblical studies and theological concepts should modify psychological theories.

We have already uncovered numerous alternative models which provide unique perspectives on the overall relationship of theology and psychology. At this point in our development we strongly encourage flexibility in this regard. Some of us think that psychology and theology are orthogonal systems—that is, independent and uncorrelated. If this be true, there cannot be a Christian psychology anymore than there can be a Christian geology or physics. Others of us assume that insofar as the subject matter and intention of the two disciplines overlap, psychology and theology can be thought of as essentially the same discipline. With this in mind, some people are hoping eventually to develop a single, unified, conceptual-theoretical system combining data and ideas from both branches of knowledge. Still others think that what a man needs to hear and think comes through theology and that psychology should become involved in helping a person appropriate and apply these theological truths. So there are many ideas about the correct or appropriate way in which psychology and theology should be related. The following-up on these ideas is often a painfully difficult task. We are of the opinion that we have just begun to grapple with the issues.

One way of fostering conceptual-theoretical integration is to have a psychologist and a theologian jointly chair seminars in which psychology and theology students participate. The following are the titles of some such seminars which have been held in recent years: The Problem of Suffering; Dualism of Flesh and Spirit; Human Spirit and Holy Spirit; Schleiermacher; Sin and Forgiveness; Theological Anthropology; Theological and Psychological Assessment of Behavior; Death; Behavior Modification of the Spirit; and *Beyond Freedom and Dignity.*

Conceptual-theoretical integration is fraught with many difficulties. First, the dialogue between psychology and theology is impeded by the different languages of these two disciplines. Second, these and other differences often cause one discipline to undervalue the other or to worry about the worth of itself. Such negative sets interfere with free, open communications. Third, some theologians talk in terms of ultimate truths. "Ultimate truths" are foreign to psychology and tend to "put off" psychologists. Fourth, there are not many psychologists and theologians who have a serious interest in integrating the two disciplines. Fifth, some psychologists and theologians feel that we are not yet ready to take on conceptual-theoretical integration because the individuals attempting the integrating do not know enough about both disciplines. Sixth, some feel that other modes of integration should be dealt with *before* we move into the conceptual-theoretical realm.

Although all of the above problems exist, few people would deny that more dialogue has taken place between psychologists and theologians during the last few years than has probably occurred at any other time in history. Although few answers have been provided, many problems on the conceptual-theoretical level have been identified. The major area of progress has been the posing of critical questions which need to be answered.

Integration through Research

As indicated earlier in this chapter, American psychology has tended to treat "religious behavior" as a taboo topic. Fortunately, during the 1960's attitudes began to change. Several national organizations came into existence which are interested in applying the methodology of the social sciences to the study of religious behavior and experiences. Some of these are the Society for the Scientific Study of Religion, the Religious Research Association, the Christian Association for Psychological Studies, the Academy of Religion and Mental Health, the American Catholic Psychological Association, and the Religious Education Association. Many individual psychologists have become active in these organizations, but most university psychology departments have continued to avoid research on religious processes. Research centers are needed where students can be trained in the specific problems of research on religious experiences.

"Normal adults" are probably the group least often studied by psychologists (Bischoff, 1969), but they are a major target population for any serious study of religious behavior. Normal adults do not seem very interested in having their religious experiences or any other private events studied by psychologists. Because of the special sensitivities people have about their belief systems, they are especially suspicious of the would-be investigator. On the other hand churches provide access to normal adults more readily than almost any other social institution. Churches are excellent sources of subjects for most developmental psychologists, because the church is the only major social institution which is designed to deal with the person *throughout* his life span, from the cradle to the grave. Religious communities have unique contributions to make to the psychological development of most people. Clinebell (1965) listed six such contributions: (1) they provide for a periodic renewal of basic trust; (2) they develop a feeling of both horizontal and vertical belonging; (3) they provide a viable philosophy of life; (4) they help the person transcend himself; (5) they provide procedures for dealing with many of the developmental and accidental crises of living; and (6) they foster personal growth and social change.

Integration through Professional Practice

For many decades most psychotherapists have tried to deny the effects of their personal belief systems upon their clients. Existing data suggest, however, that the therapist's value system does have a direct impact on his client's behavior (Rosenthal, 1955; Welkowitz, Cohen, and Ortmeyer, 1967). London (1964) has given the most extensive attention to this problem area. These studies suggest the need to examine how the psychotherapist's practice is affected by his personal beliefs, but we touch upon some very sensitive areas when we raise questions concerning the effects of religious commitment upon professional practice. Although such questions have been sidestepped in the past, they should no longer be avoided.

Whereas theology seems to affect therapeutic practice mostly in the area of values and therapeutic goals, psychology seems an especially appropriate resource for the applied areas of theology—e.g., preaching, pastoral counseling, religious education, etc. Psychologists have helped develop the area of motivational research for the field of advertising. Might they not do the same for the field of organized religion? What ethical, practical, and theoretical problems would be involved in such a venture?

We have no ready response to these questions, but we are committed to looking for answers. One direction in which we are moving is to take advantage of the special religious backgrounds of our students. Most of our students at Fuller have come from evangelical, conservative Protestant churches. The people who belong to such churches represent a unique subculture within American society. This particular subculture has been highly suspicious of the mental health professions and has avoided coming for professional consultation. Much of this "paranoia" is due to the fact that the typical psychotherapist does not "speak the language" of these religious groups. We want to produce clinicians who do speak the language of these special groups. Psychology and other mental health professions have learned the importance of sending people with special training and backgrounds to work with minority ethnic and racial groups. We can afford to use the same wisdom in approaching the various religious populations.

In the past churches have played a very important role in the total life of each community. There is some evidence, however, that this influence is decreasing rather rapidly on the American scene. We believe that the time has arrived for the establishment of church consultation centers which are designed to help the church better meet the psychological, social, and spiritual needs of the surrounding community. Such centers should be staffed with highly trained psychologists and other professionals who are psychologically sophisticated, but who are also aware of the special problems confronting the church of today.

Although the Los Angeles basin probably has as many institutions for training psychotherapists as any metropolitan area in the country, there have been no institutions in the area which are suitable for training students in church consultation. There are some community mental health centers which are willing to consult with churches, but typically the center and its staff are not well informed concerning, nor sympathetic with, the special problems of the church.

In order to provide an appropriate training base for our students, the Church Consultation Service was established in July, 1969 under the direction of Dr. H. Newton Malony. It provides students in psychology with a model of the kind of services they can offer after they have received their Ph.D.'s. Faculty and students are available to provide consultation regarding a wide range of problem areas. One area of consultation is the performance of consumer surveys and social psychological research. Specific examples of such consultation would be (1) assessing the attitudes of church members regarding specified church programs, (2) evaluating the meaningfulness of the worship services, (3) surveying community needs, and (4) designing and testing the impact of experimental worship services. A second area of consultation concerns therapeutic services within the church. Specific examples of this mode would be (1) consulting with pastoral counselors, (2) conducting workshops on therapeutic strategies that may be used by clergymen, (3) training and supervising lay counselors, and (4) helping resolve conflicts within a church staff. A third area of consultation involves teaching and training programs for the members and staff of a church. Specific examples of this mode would be (1) seminars in program development, (2) parent training workshops, (3) seminars on sex and family life education, (4) workshops for Sunday School teachers on methods of handling children with behavior problems, and (5) training in the "therapeutic triad." A fourth area of consultation involves program development, especially finding ways of utilizing the church's human and physical resources for delivering psychological services to the community. Specific examples of such services are (1) a day care center for seriously disturbed children, (2) a recreation program for senior citizens, (3) a Head Start program, (4) a half-way house for various clinical populations, and (5) lay "pastoral care teams."

If psychologists and theologians *or* clinicians and clergymen do not cooperate in attacking their common problems, society suffers. As indicated earlier in this chapter, the mutual mistrust of therapists and clergymen has hindered cooperative programs which would meet the needs of the clergyman's parishioners and the psychotherapist's clients. There is great need for a special kind of clinical psychologist who is uniquely equipped to act as a bridge between the clergy and the various mental health professions. The churches are a *sleeping giant* which has incalculable potential for delivering mental health services to almost every community, large or small, throughout the country. Unfortunately, most journal articles and books on community psychology have overlooked these human and physical resources. Most clergymen and laymen have little understanding of how a psychological consultant may be of value to the church; therefore, those individuals and agencies who wish to engage in church consultation must first educate their prospective clients in how to utilize psychological consultation.

Intra-personal Integration

Unfortunately, talking about personal religious conflicts in the typical graduate program in clinical psychology is unacceptable. The acceptance and understanding which are present when one is discussing conflicts in the areas of sex, dependency, or aggressive feelings suddenly disappear when personal religious problems are mentioned. The typical academic culture tends to inhibit rather than to enhance the clinical student's integrating his psychology with his personal theology.

This state of affairs contrasts with the fact that many students enter graduate school experiencing from mild to intense conflicts in the area of their religious beliefs. Quite often they have become anxious as undergraduates when what they were learning in psychology seemed to be clashing with the religious belief systems taught to them by their family and church. Presumably this type of student would like a graduate program in which he can openly work on integrating all of his thoughts and feelings without having one or more parts of his personality rejected by his professors and peers.

One way of facilitiating intra-personal integration is to participate in weekly encounter groups in which exploring one's spiritual conflicts is explicitly encouraged and supported. Intensive clinical supervision, when conducted by a therapeutic person, also may aid in promoting personal integration. Having well-integrated faculty members expose themselves psychologically to their students also seems to aid the integrative task. A part of this exposure process should be to require each faculty member to demonstrate his forms of psychotherapy and other professional practices to his students.

Can Religion and Psychotherapy Be Compatible?

People often ask us, "Can a young Graduate School of Psychology be happily married to a conservative School of Theology." We have no prophets who can tell us for sure, but we can promise a large number of provocative encounters between the two for as long as the marriage lasts. And the marriage is producing an increasing number of vigorous offspring who are committed to the proposition that religion and psychotherapy can and will be compatible.

Although our own integration effort is only six years old, we feel that excellent groundwork has been laid. We are gearing up for an exciting and promising future. Our initial efforts have convinced us that attempting to integrate theology and psychotherapy is a task worthy of our most determined commitment.

BIBLIOGRAPHY

1. Bischoff, L. J.: *Adult Psychology*. New York, Harper & Row, 1969.
2. Clinebell, H. J. (Jr.): *Mental Health Through Christian Community*. Nashville, Abingdon Press, 1965.
3. Douglas, W.: Religion. From *Taboo Topics* (N. L. Farberow, Ed.) New York, Atherton Press, 1966, pp. 80–95.
4. London, P.: *The Modes and Morals of Psychotherapy*. New York, Holt, Rinehart & Winston, 1964.
5. Rosenthal, D.: Changes in Some Moral Values Following Psychotherapy. *Journal of Consulting Psychology 19:* 431–436, 1955.
6. Welkowitz, Joan, Cohen, J. and Ortmeyer, D.: Value System Similarity: Investigation of Patient-Therapist Dyads. *Journal of Consulting Psychology 31:* 48–55, 1967.

CHAPTER 32

TRANSCENDING THE ROLE OF PSYCHOTHERAPIST†

VIN ROSENTHAL

1. WOULD YOU BUY A USED CAR FROM ME?

It has been a delight to discover, as I have this summer, that I can be a *psychotherapist in sandals*. I wonder if this is almost the same as saying that Hans Eysenck was right? *Of course* all sorts of "therapies" work, just as all sorts of styles of painting, music and literature and other art forms "work." While this may appear to give little support to those who prefer to view psychotherapy as a science, I do believe in the scientific process; in fact, what my discovery about being a therapist in sandals has led me to is a further affirmation of my hypothesis that I may, indeed I must explore and experiment.

Like a true scientist, I am less interested in counting and measuring minutae than I am in taking great pains to know what I am doing, in being aware of how I change what I am doing, and in taking responsibility for understanding what happens in relation to those changes. After completing my formal psychotherapy training, I was reminded by my professor that if I did anything but client-centered therapy I was to remember that I had not been trained to do it. In a way he was right, but what I really had been trained to do was to think and feel deeply, seriously and carefully about psychotherapy and what I was doing with it. Nothing is clearer to me than that over the years I have changed my notions about the purpose of psychotherapy and how it may be done; not just modified my way of being a therapist but *transformed*, like a frog turned into a prince.

Now the *role* of the psychotherapist is the *assumed* character taken by a person who has contracted to perform certain prescribed, task-

---
† Paper read at the Symposium "Psychotherapy As A Secular Calling," American Psychological Association Annual Meeting, Washington, D.C., September 4, 1971.

oriented skills in order to achieve goals mutually agreed upon between himself and another person. The expertise he presumably possesses is an amalgam of percepts, concepts and behaviors more or less agreed upon by members of his professional group and more or less systematically organized; to be employed at appropriate times with appropriate intensities during the course of his interaction with the other person. There is nothing wrong with a role *per se*. But let us not confuse *role* and *goal*. (1) It is my experience that I can enter into a contract with another person in which the goal (or function) of the interaction is whatever the seeker wants to accomplish but without our entering into roles. The function—or duty, or special action—I agree to perform with the person who seeks my help is to be authentic and act in good faith with that person who is thinking about or engaged in the struggle of modifying, changing or transforming his life. My purpose in being a therapist is to help me live a good life. To achieve my end I believe I must work towards being a person whose *natural* way of being corresponds to the function I contract to perform as a therapist, so that "me" and "therapist" are integrated. If I truly am this way, I have integrity and a chance to live a good life. That is simply the way it is.

Now there are problems with its being this way. Sometimes I feel I am a prick or trickster; (2) a wheeler-dealer, expedient huckster going through the motions and saying the right words, wondering whether I really care deeply about the other person, or whether I should; wondering whether I enjoy the safety of the time-limited intimacy of therapy because of my own reservations about closeness. Sometimes I don't trust myself. My way seems self-conscious, posed, acted, calculating. I monitor myself in sneaky secrecy, later playing back what I have recorded to see when my self, caught unaware, is different from the way I hope and want myself to be. (Sometimes when I am with a fellow seeker, focusing on him, I suddenly become aware that an unselfconscious self has been at work; I can trust that "me" to be closer to how I really am.)

Sometimes I have an impulse to abandon the other person, to kick him out, to shut myself off when he confuses, frustrates, pains me. Sometimes I'm vain, pretentious, scared and pompous. In one way my value is that I'm really no one that special, just another hopeful journeyer; if I can make it as well as I have, having been as screwed up as I've been, why can't you! Then the other person usually moves toward his goal. But then I think about what a great therapist I am; I'm no longer a fellow sufferer and I distance myself. Then the other person usually doesn't move toward his goal. Sometimes I want to be loved by the other yet not asked by him for anything beyond what is natural and spontaneous for me to give; and I want for me not to ask of him anything beyond what is natural and spontaneous for him to give. This is part of the paradox of therapy: I am dependent upon the patient for my very existence as a therapist, and therefore for that measure of my self-esteem which derives from my being a therapist; yet to be effective and uncorrupted by the demands of the patient, my self-esteem must be independent of him. If I don't care, I can't help him; if I care too much, that is, if I want too much for myself, I can't help him. Only by letting him alone can I really be with him and help him, yet letting him alone feels like I'm not doing what I'm supposed to be doing. It's like learning not to slam down your brakes on icy pavement.

So I want to give up the role and be me; even though I sometimes do feel like a prick, at least this way it is out in the open where I have a better chance of dealing with it than I would if I hid behind a role; even though I run the risk of being frightened and getting hurt by the intimacy which comes with giving up the role, it's better than leaving huge hunks of myself outside the space I share with the other. Sometimes I run back into the role and when I do, I know I run the risk of spoiling it for the other person. Yet from this ebb and flow we experience together part of what being alive is all about. Right now I'm feeling pretty good, on a hilltop where I can glimpse my worthiness. I know I got here only with the help, support, affirmation of others. When I reached this place I discovered I had been worthy all the time, without doing anything to earn it and without the help of others. A woman said to me the other day: "I don't like men with bare feet and sandals but you're okay with me."

2. GENESIS, 32: 25-29.

There I was, alone in the night. All of a sudden, from out of nowhere a man confronts me and we begin to wrestle: We struggle strongly for hours and I grow confused and exhausted, but he's unable to overcome me. He puts fierce pressure on my body and I feel it strain; still I will not give up! Even though I do not understand what our struggle is all about and though I sense he means me no harm, it feels important not to stop. Finally he grunts to me, "let me go, it's getting on to morning." And I strain back, "I won't until you bless me!" And he asks me, "What's your name?" And I tell him, "Jacob." And he says: "From now on you shall be called 'Israel,' for you have striven with God and Man and you have prevailed."

I frequently have this fantasy during a session with a fellow seeker: Suddenly bolting upright and in one motion flipping my nail-studded red leather Georgian wing-back chair into a graceful arch over my head, out through the sealed windows: Give me air! *followed by a deep sigh, a sign to cease; though the wrestling goes on and on inside my body; until my door opens again and once more it's two on the mat.*

3. MYSELF AS MEDIUM

One day I was feeling great, just back from a workshop in which I had witnessed my moving further toward my next piece of business, leaving others alone. A fellow seeker and I were engaged in a mutually delightful confrontation in our group and I was glad to be back from my workshop in such high spirits. She was declaring her independence and I felt good about it, though sad because I knew that meant it would not be long before she left. Suddenly, for no apparent reason, I began to question myself, my genuineness, my adequacy as a therapist. It was a painful, deep, even physical struggle and what distressed me most was my unwillingness to share with my group what was happening inside me. Just as suddenly I found myself looking up at the one member of the group who as yet had said nothing this night. "Have you something to say to me?" I asked. Then, as if the question awakened him, he poured forth an excretion of pain, reliving how difficult it had been for him during my recent absence and how he had slipped back into old, bad ways of feeling and behaving.

As I massaged his back, my own spirits sank and fell further until I could visualize my own hopes of worthiness reaching the bottom of my own barrel of depression and anomie. At bottom, a familiar theme: Obviously I was unfit to be a therapist.

Again there followed an abrupt shift in awareness and mood. I realized what was happening: It was *his* misery I was experiencing; as though I were a medium in a seance, his voice and experience were speaking through me and my body. I described aloud to him the sinking feelings I mysteriously had begun to experience just prior to asking him if he had something to say to me. As I spoke, he identified parallel feelings within himself. Somehow I had picked up the inner message he had been sending.

4. BRIDGE OVER TROUBLED WATERS

*"Like a bridge over troubled waters,
I will ease your mind..."*
Simon and Garfunkel

Whenever I write, I absolve myself of having to present the most polished paper ever written on the most original ideas ever expounded. Maybe I am just a *schlepper* reinventing unconditional love in a new language, but I am now in the process of learning how to leave others alone. I think at its best this means: "Take from my presence, my being whatever you, fellow seeker, need or want to take from me." Where I am most of the time is becoming more and more aware of catching myself trying to impose on or influence someone, trying to get him to be someplace it would be more comfortable for *me* for him to be.

For example, a student in my class, sitting right next to me, obviously was doing homework for another class. I found myself getting angry. My impulse was to scold her. Then I realized she really was living out what I had asked of my students: to be as honest with me as they can about where they are with me at this moment. I expressed my appreciation for her direct, non-symbolic, non-verbal message and she elected to join the group—for the first time—about three weeks later: after having been left alone, after having been alone, she chose to come into the group the hard way, via a "break in" during a mini-marathon.

5. HAIKU

One snowy Winter day, on a plane flying somewhere, I wrote a haiku—that magnificently simple seventeen syllable poem form expressing with deceptive ease the essence of Japanese Zen Buddhism.

The man in the next seat was a Japanese. I wanted to share my haiku with him but I felt too embarrassed to do so. How presumptuous of me, a Westerner, to express myself in this most Japanese way.

I thought of my decision not to share my haiku as an example of how often I don't let myself be the way I want to be. Then I decided to let myself be. The man most graciously accepted my gift. He especially appreciated its reference to his being far from his homeland. As a return gift he said he felt his publishing company should publish my haiku. Here it is:

*Rising . . . sunshine through
snowfog; descending . . . will I
see sun shine again?*

6. BUSHY-BEARDED VIN ROSENTHAL

a fucking word-chef
preparing a verbigeration
topped with a Caesar's dressing
slobbering over each plump tomato slice,
staining every lettuce leaf a sickly, pale green.
Pity not
this poor lemon
for its sweetness
is sometimes all I've got.

I do want to tell the truth, yet I *can't*
tell you how ugly you look to me;
not merely unattractive, but bordering on the grotesque
  that Hapsburg lip,
  your mustache,
  mushy, fleshy cheeks and jowls;
  fat, pot-bellied nose;
  enormous cow eyes looking out
  from under painted lids heavy
  with spikey lashes.

As for me, I want to dive into a pond of lukewarm words,
lose myself in their self-contained, unverifiable wavy existence;
later, lying bareass on a beach of wit, puns, rhymes and fancy,
well-heeled on well-turned phrases which answer to no one but
    themselves;
self-validating, denying any reality beyond the boundaries
of this nudist camp fence. Posted on the sign as you enter:

DON'T EXPECT ME TO PAMPER YOUR NEUROSIS
and
  YOU'RE COMING HERE TO BE WITH ME,
THAT'S EXACTLY WHAT AND ALL YOU'LL GET!

7. " 'DON'T JUST DO SOMETHING,' BUDDHA SAID, 'STAND THERE!' " (3)

"*During the lifetime of the Buddha his followers did not separate out his person from his teachings. His own way of being and his relations*

to those who came to him was so much a part of his teachings that to believe in him was to grasp his doctrines . . ."
Sheldon B. Kopp
Four Oriental Metaphors From A Psychotherapist

What if you discover that I am a person in whose presence you can experience greater joy, deeper pain, more hope about your own possibilities, fuller appreciation of being alive. What if my very existence and our way of being together encourages you to feel less alone, more in touch, bigger, freer, more able to uncover the something in nothing.

I enjoy deepening my experiences with others, especially with those who seek after truths about themselves. This is a means by which my end is served. My joy is reunion (love) with my fellow journeyers, reduction of my loneliness and isolation, seeing my existence affirmed by experiencing my impact on others and feeling their impact on me. I invite others to join me in such a venture as I have discovered that it makes a great deal of personal sense to me and I believe it may prove meaningful and useful to them. My own life has been revolutionized by the search and struggle and I feel it has been worth the negative consequences attending all revolutions.

Over the years I have come to learn that psychotherapy, for me, is not what I was taught it was. I stumbled along and found it was a way of life discovered by an individual who sees in it potential for creating meaning in his own life. Later I found it was the struggle for discipline of my own identity. Finally I learned that psychotherapy does not exist at all except distributively as one dialogue at a time.

Now I am aware of a futher transition, looking now into myself as into an infinity of mirrors, recognizing the most immediate image as the me I feel and think myself to be; further images look less like "me," though my essence is clearly embedded in them; straining to glimpse momentarily the most distant image: it gives the feeling of a saffron-robed monk wandering with a begging bowl.

What if you discover that I am a person in whose presence you can experience greater joy, deeper pain, more hope about your own possibilities, fuller appreciation of being alive. What if my very existence and our way of being together encourages you to feel less alone, more in touch, bigger, freer, more able to uncover the something in nothing.

What if I actually could become such a person.

REFERENCES AND FOOTNOTES

1 Many thanks to Ruth Cohn for a walk in Central Park which helped me think this out.
2 Scher, Jordan M.: "Trickster Counters Trickster—Seeking Healer and Healing Seeker," *Voices*, The Art and Science of Psychotherapy, Vol. 7, no. 3, Fall 1971.
3 Comment by Daniel Berrigan, *Psychology Today*, April, 1970.

CHAPTER 33

THE PSYCHOTHERAPIST AS PRIEST, PROPHET, HOLY MAN, "RELIGIOUS" EDUCATOR AND PERSON†

JULES BARRON

PSYCHOTHERAPHY IS OUR METIER. It is a profession that is particularly susceptible to a wide variety of orientations, approaches and jargons. When I first read the title of this symposium, I thought of its history and the multitude of philosophies that have emerged from and been applied to psychotherapeutic practice. Broadly, psychotherapy has been regarded as a science, an art, a human event and a religious experience.

The concept implied in the title of this symposium seems to be an attempt to bring together something of the religious or spiritual and the human. This is a radical departure from earlier efforts to follow a more strictly scientific model or, at least, what was believed to be scientific.

Generally a "calling" refers to one's occupation or trade. In religious circles it has been used in ways that suggest the presence of some voice or spiritual force that determines the direction of one's life work. (It may also be interesting to note that "calling" denotes a state of sexual excitement—used particularly in regard to the female cat.) Perhaps reference to *secular calling* is intended to bring the spiritual down to earth where man lives as a psychobiological being.

The second part of our topic—the therapist as priest, prophet, holy man, "religious" educator and person intrigues me. I am not sure whether the intent is that the therapist be all of these or some combination thereof. Nonetheless it is a big mouthful with very significant implications in terms of the therapist's role, image, style,

---

† Adapted from the Chairperson's *Introduction* to the Symposium "Psychotherapy As A Secular Calling; The Psychotherapist As Priest, Prophet, Holy Man, 'Religious' Educator and Person," American Psychological Association Annual Meeting, Washington, D.C., September 4, 1971.

values and relatedness. We are confronted not only with the scientific functions of the therapist, but with his moralistic functions as well. There is a strong flavor of a Secular Priesthood emerging in the psychotherapeutic arena.

Religion and its human agents—priests, prophets, rabbis and pastors—were used in connection with supernatural forces to affect man's existence and wordly matters involving his human condition, health, goals, relationships, sexual behavior. Commonly, the function of the priest was to mediate between human beings and one or more deities. The priestly job was to facilitate the individual's ability to adapt, to adjust within the framework of a particular ideology and explicit value system. An authoritarian model of relatedness was usual and submissive, obedient behavior was expected. "Self-realization" and the "good life" were based on obedience rather than autonomy, on submission to dogma rather than through questioning and exploration.

While religion clearly has involved a system of values and taboos, psychotherapy, until our recent history, *less* clearly has involved these as well. The psychotherapist also has tried to influence man's behavior and the nature of his existence. However, his orientation, his methods, his style and his values have been, for the most part very different and often antithetical to that of the religionist. We have come to recognize that rather than the therapist being without values in his work—which originally was in an effort to be truly scientific—his values may be different, covertly expressed and, indeed, affecting the nature of his professional work. Even the selection of psychotherapy as an occupation suggests the presence of values. Based on his values, the psychotherapist selects his orientation, his methods and style of being as a way of influencing the behavior of others. And it is in the area of methods and particularly of goals, that the therapist has differed from the religious leader. Goals in psychotherapy involve improving one's human condition rather than accepting the status quo, searching for a more comfortable life, freeing oneself from the chains of anxiety or prisons of fear, self-actualization, growth, and the like.

Both religion and psychotherapy may be characterized by a search for meaning which variably has been in ultimate, futuristic or existential terms but with critical differences in meanings. Such meanings have been related and pertinent to man's role and place in his cosmos.

In recent times we have been witness to radical changes in therapeutic language and behavior. We have also seen radical alterations in the language and behavior of many disciples from the pantheon of religion. There has been a very perceptible crossing over of one discipline into the other. A bridge between two worlds has been created.

The religious leader has been trying to partake more fully of the secular world and its fruits. The psychotherapist has been trying to deal with his spiritual and human values in connection to his work. In each case there is evidence of the need to be more human and recognized as such.

Perhaps the change in therapeutic language, the crossing over into religious dialect, the adoption of spiritual terminology and concern about values reflects a search for a more personal identity and feeling of community rather than an institutional identity or professional detachment. This is especially evidenced by the use of such terms as *prophet* and *guru* rather than *priest* or *rabbi*. The priest is vested with his authority through sacred tradition as part of an institutional arrangement. His charisma is bestowed upon him. The prophet's position is a result of a personal charisma. Like the guru he is an interpreter and propagandist of the faith, whatever it may be. The apostles served a similar function. *Apostle* from the early Greek tongue literally meant "messenger" or "one sent forth." The voice of the prophet usually claimed to "speak for" a deity. This certainly would lend to his charismatic state and add weight to his words. However, whatever his tools, it was his personal self that was primarily involved in his experience, in contrast to being an institutional agent.

n short, the priest receives charismatic authentication from the religious institution, the therapist from his professional definition and institutional affiliations and the prophet or guru from his personal being. Of course, at this point we may question whether the nature of the image and charisma effected by any of these roles result in some form of deification that leaves less room for the person. If, indeed, being a real person in therapeutic work is considered to be desirable and helpful to the patient, then it must be determined whether the therapist as a secular priest or prophet is merely changing one robe for another.

I believe that the changes we see taking place in religion and in movements in psychotherapy are ways of finding more significance on the personal and human level of being in opposition to the importance achieved as an institutional or professional agent. This striving is notably reflected in the form of the humanistic movement in psychotherapy. For the most part, I suspect that each therapist would tend to regard himself as humanistic in his work, if not the bearer of the humanistic label.

In our revolutionary times our major concepts regarding God and Man are being questioned. Throughout time gods have varied in their forms depending upon the sociology of man and the human condition. In a literal, formal and sociological sense, man has been polytheistic, monotheistic, and henotheistic. Psychologically, man has been polygamous with regard to his deistic inclinations. Perhaps this parallels his human relations, such as may be seen in many marital experiences. The very meaningful and current trend shows man (which includes therapists and women) struggling for personal meaning and worth that is truly his own as a human being and a function of his humanness rather than divinely given.

What is the meaning of all this in connection with psychotherapy as a science and as an art? What are the truly therapeutic forces in the psychotherapeutic relationship? Must there be Gods in the form of Man or Man in the form of God? Is it desirable that the therapist be seen as the priest, prophet, educator or person? Let us listen to some personal answers.

CHAPTER 34

PROPHETS AS PSYCHOTHERAPISTS, AND PSYCHOTHERAPISTS AS PROPHETS†

SIDNEY M. JOURARD

THIS SYMPOSIUM IS an extraordinary happening. Psychotherapists have sought, since before Freud, to ally themselves with science and to regard psychotherapy as a scientifically grounded skill. Connections with religion were regarded as anathema. Yet, a strong affiliation with religion may be found in many of the great psychotherapists; Freud's connection to the Jewish mystical tradition has been documented by Bakan. Fromm, though not theistic, is an Old Testament scholar whose studies influence his work. Jung, of course, was the son of a clergyman. The religious streak in Whitaker and Warkentin is obvious. Paul Tournier is patently a Christian psychotherapist. Frankl's logotherapy seeks a kind of religious conversion, and we know that Carl Rogers intended a career in the clergy. Hobart Mowrer has been insistent upon a view of psychotherapy as a moral "turning."

For many years I prided myself on my secular approach to the understanding of human suffering and my intervention therein. But the thinker whose work most influenced me beyond my initial training was Martin Buber, and so in spite of the fact I had no formal instruction in being a Jew, there was and remains an Old Testament flavor to my thinking, writing and ways of being. And, so, after a recent visit to Israel, I began to read the Old Testament for the first time. I am finding it a fascinating, extraordinary document about the struggle of some prophets and leaders of a recalcitrant people to become human beings freed from the idolatry of place, tribe, family; whose worship of their deity is not in words, sacrifice or ritual, but through *living in a way*, a way that is informed by Divine

---
†Paper read at the Symposium "Psychotherapy As A Secular Calling," American Psychological Association Annual Meeting, Washington, D.C., September 4, 1971.

Ecology, Divine Public Health, and Divine Interpersonal Science. When this stiff-necked people fell away from living in the way prescribed by *JWH*, their punishment was swift and terrible. I prefer, however, not to regard defeat in battle, famine and disease and other evidences of the Lord's wrath as evidence of the Lord's wrath; rather, they seem to be outcomes of not paying attention to long-range consequences of one's present ways of treating the weak, the lowly, the strangers in one's midst, the soil, the waters, the animals, and oneself.

The ancient Hebrews were as vulnerable as Portnoy is today to the temptations of Canaanite *shiksas,* who inveigled them into copulatory rituals that were thought to keep the soil fertile—and even if they didn't, it is difficult for vital people to turn down a romp when it is gladly offered. It is important to assure the growth of crops, but not at the cost of neglect of larger questions: "How is life possible? How can I live amicably with people younger, older, of different culture and tradition?" The laws and ordinances proclaimed by Moses, and amplified elsewhere in the Old Testament can be viewed as answers to this question, supposedly announced by JWH and which, if followed, would lead to multiplication of one's seed (an index of grace no longer needed) and improvement in the quality of existence. In short, to live in the Way—being like God—*was* worship and redemption, the choice of life over death.

The prophets, beginning with Moses, and through Elijah, Elisha, Jeremiah, Isaiah, Amos, Ezekiel, Hosea and others, sought to bring an entire people back into the way when they preached. Their preachings were not bland and they were not, themselves, seeking to be liked—there was no Dale Carnegie school in those days. When they were not preaching to masses, they were, some of them, in a position analogous to "The President's Analyst," or those of our colleagues who work for Rohrer, Hibler and Replogle—consultants to men of power and decision, so that the latter will not destroy their companies or cause the loss of profits. The prophets were *unpaid* and unsolicited consultants, in many cases, to the kings of Judea and Israel, reminding the latter that they were supposed to rule in godly ways. They were not at all like Machiavelli who was advisor to his Prince, seeking to help him maximize his control over the people. The Old Testament prophets wanted their kings to rule by the example of an upright existence, not through cunning, bribery, mystification and threats.

The prophesies that were presented often grew out of visions. The prophets were, in some ways, ecstatic men, with vision informed by imagination. The biblical records are not complete enough to provide a basis for understanding how an ordinary person became a *navi*. Some cataclysmic crisis, perhaps suffering, experienced by them as an encounter with God, induced them to abandon their former conventional existences, driving them to proclaim the evil, suffering and injustice to which others were blind and indifferent. We can infer that they were not totally in the thrall of their culture and of the prevailing, conformist ways of seeing, construing, valuing and behaving. If God spoke, then they could hear where all others were deaf. They could see what was there. They could see that if kings and people continued to behave in the ways they were behaving—worshipping the work of human hands, mistreating widows, orphans, strangers in their midst, pursuing pleasure through eating forbidden foods and indiscriminate screwing—dire consequences would follow. Since life was insecure in those days, we don't today have to say that God smote the people whom he smote. A human, livable existence in those days called for continuous vigilance, continuous attention to the basic conditions that made life possible in the face of a hostile physical environment and hordes of hostile cultures. The teachings of Moses were explicit descriptions of these conditions.

The prophets, like Ralph Nader, told it like it was. They were like divine agronomists, military advisors, family counselors, ecologists, public health officers and muckraking journalists, pointing to, and reminding and showing others a better way, if not the "Right Way."

Over the years I have been examining and reexamining psychotherapies and psychotherapists from the standpoint of different models and metaphors. The one model most compelling for me over the past ten years is that of exemplar, or role-model of authentic existence. Now the very term authentic existence means more than simply living in truth and choosing one's existence. It also implies increasing enlightenment, so that one can make choices compatible with life, growth and self-actualization. Psychotherapists in increasing numbers have been taking their own lives and growth seriously, seeking to authenticate their professional contacts by themselves being exemplars of the quest for growth, truth and self-fulfillment. And they are seeking, some of them, to share their visions and knowledge with masses of others; to function, in short, as prophets outside the consulting room.

The psychotherapist, according to this view, embodies part of the way of a prophet, that of being an exemplar of the way of life he wishes to invite others to follow for their own good, and, by implication, for the good of the community. And he is a prophet when he points out the truth about destructive behavior. Old Testament prophets were desirous that the polyglot aggregation of Hebrew tribes might overcome their limited and autistic perspectives and become a people, a community called Israel, united under one God, living in exemplary ways as a beacon and example to all mankind. An extraordinarily modest ambition. A modern psychotherapist—insofar as he can see connections between and implications of usual ways for people to be and sickness, social disorganization and stultified growth and madness on large scale—can tell individual patients or seekers *what* he sees. And he can prophesy in market-places, before temples and in the places where people work; and modern prophetic psychotherapists have access to the press and the mass media—TV, movies, etc. to present their diagnoses and prescriptions.

According to Abraham Heschel, a prophet is extraordinarily sensitive to evil; he feels fiercely, he sees injustice and indifference to evil and refuses to excuse or to ignore it. He shrieks of what he sees. He pays attention to what others regard as trivialities, too obvious to note, but which signify a person or a people hell-bent on self-destruction, or destroying the very conditions that make life possible. Prophets are not mealy-mouthed; they do not write the bland pablum of Norman Vincent Peale. A prophet is, without compromise, committed to the highest good of which man is capable, and he mourns, castigates and incites in order that mediocre men might rise to those heights. Like the *outsiders* of whom Colin Wilson wrote, the prophet sees too much, hears the groans of pain to which others are deaf. Yet the prophets have a compassion for mankind and they seek to invite all men to take responsibility for the fate of man and life in this place and time. The prophets feel the blast from heaven, they inveigh against callousness, indifference and yet take no pleasure in the lot to which they have been called. Prophets are seditious, cranky, threats to the status quo.

This is the way Heschel answers the question, "What manner of man is the prophet?" I see adumbrations here, as I said, with Colin Wilson's *outsiders*—the raw nerve-endings of our times: the Lawrence of Arabias, the Nijinskys, the characters who never could be swallowed up by the hypocrisies and false values of their times, but who, as Wilson points out, were destroyed because they lacked insight and didn't know what was going on. What psychotherapist measures up to the stature of a prophet rather than a mere *outsider?* Which is a true and which is a false prophet? Wilhelm Reich, I feel, was a *prophet manqué,* who had magnificent revelations to share, but he was arrogant in a way that perhaps the prophets were not. I suspect he was ruined by his upbringing in a Germanic culture, which made him wish to be appreciated as a genius. The prophets were not on an "ego trip." Brock Chisholm, after World War 2, became a prophet at risk of reputation. He preached against the teaching of myths to children so they would not be vulnerable to incitements to war. Israel Charney, a colleague in psychotherapy whom I have not yet met but whose writings I have sampled, seems to fill some of the job description of a prophet. He is sensitive to the violence of our time, to the viciousness that prevails in marriage, in families; Auschwitz can be foreseen in the German family structure. Ronald Laing and Aaron Esterson, both psychotherapists, are prophets in their writings, pointing out how the family serves as a place within which some members are sacrified to the mental hospital rather than allow the cosmetic image of a happy family to be besmirched. I presume to prophesy, as I have in print, that cosmetic family structures are responsible for physical disease, including cancer. I suppose I have had a prophetic function, too, in my writing about research and therapy as exploitive and adjustive disciplines, striving to find more humanistic and liberating ways for psychologists to be.

The psychotherapists whom we consider great—I have argued—are great not because of their theories, which are efforts to scientize existential courage and enlightenment—but they are great because their lives were threatened by some aspect of facticity and they learned how to tame, to transcend it, and could teach others how to be free and upright in the face of doting, destructive parents, addiction to heroin, or lack of awareness of others' destructive games. But many of the writing psychotherapists overstate their cases and believe that God has told them *the* reason why everyone suffers, and has confided the best and rightest solution. The plethora of oversold theories and techniques in individual and group therapy, in encounter groups and in Primal screaming, in gestalting, rolling, yoging, meditating, to me is evidence of arrogance and false prophesy. Look at the prophet, not his methods and words, to see if he knows how to live.

The fact that seems obvious to me about life in the time of the Old Testament prophets is that no one knew how to live in a way that would sustain life for self and others; and no one knew how to live in a way that would foster growth of more than a brutish few of man's infinite possibilities. The statutes, commandments, ordinances that Moses received "from God" may be regarded as the inventions of a highly imaginative and intelligent and compassionate man. Perhaps God spoke through him. Moses fascinates me—how did he (or they) arrive at a statement of ways to live in that time? Perhaps being reared in a civilized culture (Egypt) without being *of* it was a factor. Moses' writings and teachings were the equivalent of the writings of Dr. Spock, Ralph Nader, Rachel Carson, Adelle Davis, Mohandas Ghandi, and other contemporaries (Hobart Mowrer, George Bach) who have tried to help people live in viable ways. Failure to live in a viable way is to court disease, stultification and death. This is as true today as it was in biblical times. The prophets could be viewed as existential teachers who were horrified at the ways people, through lack of leadership from the responsible authorities, were behaving daily, ways that courted disaster and which already were yielding full measures of suffering for some. The prophets could not be indifferent to suffering and injustice and they addressed kings directly, urging them to mend their ways and to do what they were anointed to do.

Today's psychotherapists treat individually and in encountering groups with people who suffer, with people of stultified growth, with people who, simply, are not living right for themselves and possibly not right for others. The therapist is prophetic insofar as he has learned, and authenticated in his very being and presence, viable ways to live—what the ancients may have called righteousness. If they invite others to change their ways and threaten them with dire consequences if they do not, they are being as much prophet as the times admit. The prophets tried to make men realize their freedom to choose and to choose to change from "sin" to righteousness. A psychotherapist who is not as sensitive to self-destructive behavior and who is not committed to learning and living and leading in viable ways, is neither prophet nor therapist.

One of the defining characteristics of the Old Testament prophets was the idea that the one true God, *Jaweh,* spoke through them. This, I believe, is a metaphor signifying that the prophet was able to achieve a perspective on his culture, on the behavior of self and others which enabled him to see what those embedded could not see. The psychotherapist in modern days must be capable of achieving such an outsider's perspective, of attaining what Buber calls "distance," but he must also have the capacity to "enter into relation," in order to have his vision and message heard. In modern terminology, an effective psychotherapist, like an effective prophet, can detach himself from prior ways of being and then return into community with one other, or many others, and share his vision. But I hold the hypothesis that the prophetic psychotherapist and the psychotherapeutic prophets are effective to the extent to which they embody, in their very *being*, the ways to live that are most compatible with life together in this time and place. It is not possible, I argue, for a true prophet to preach one way and live another. This may require that the psychotherapist in his prophetic function (which is not incompatible with healing) may be, for the moment, a very irritating, infuriating person who discloses the truth that hurts, that fosters guilt, anxiety, and intense suffering. But, like the prophets, he does not confront for the joy of inflicting pain, but out of profound concern. If the therapist, like the prophet, is angry, it is because there is something to be angry at. We can view Carl Rogers' wrath at certain dehumanizing aspects of graduate and undergraduate education and his promulgation of encountering as "a Way," as a case of a therapist "gone prophet."

Frank Shaw, my late friend whose ideas are not widely enough appreciated, viewed talent in phenomenological-behavioristic terms: talent was a matter of a specialized fascination with something in the world that one could not resist tinkering with in order to make it "right." We might look afresh at prophets and psychotherapists in order to discern whether they might resemble one another in terms of talent thus defined. It is clear that the therapist and the prophet are fascinated by "sin"—pathology-producing behavior—and by suffering: they cannot neglect it in self or in others. It is as if they are receiving sets turned in permanently on the wave-length most interesting to them. But the fascination is not a passive one. No psychotherapist I know of, and no prophet who is recorded could resist responding to the sufferer (the prophets felt God's suffering), in spite of the fact that many therapists claim that indifference to whether one is helping the other is, paradoxically, the best way to be helpful. Prophet and therapist alike will not rest until they are doing what they deem best to remedy the situation. We have no evidence that therapists who see what a patient is doing wrong and simply say, "Stop doing that, and start living right," have a lower success rate than any other kind of therapist. I can verify that with certain people who have consulted with me, I have behaved as much like a prophet as like a contemporary therapist: "If it makes you sick—and it does, why don't you stop doing it? Start to stop doing it right here in my office, because I find it sickens me."

The wheel has turned full circle. Beginning several decades ago, men of the church turned to psychology and psychiatry to learn how to function better as pastoral counselors. As time went on, increasing numbers of clergymen dropped out of the church and turned toward a more humanistically oriented career in psychology or counseling, because they felt they could not be true to the prophetic motives that perhaps directed them to a religious career. Less prophetic clergymen who stayed in the church made use of many of the techniques of Madison Avenue and folksy, non-threatening flattery.

Now, it seems to me that growing numbers of working psychotherapists are moving increasingly toward a prophetic and utopian vision of the good society and may become a new kind of churchman. It will be interesting to see where some of us go next.

CHAPTER 35

IS THE SMALL-GROUPS MOVEMENT A RELIGIOUS REVOLUTION?†

O. Hobart Mowrer

ONE OF THE DEFINITIONS of a "calling" which Webster's *Unabridged Dictionary* gives is: "One's usual occupation; vocation; business; trade." I am sure this is *not* the meaning intended by the word "Calling" in the title of this symposium. Much closer surely is this definition: "A divine summons, or prompting to a particular act or duty." But in a telephone conversation with Vin Rosenthal some months ago, it was clear that by "calling" he did not mean anything supernatural or divine but something entirely secular, of this world, humanistic, so the second of the definitions I have quoted from Webster doesn't apply precisely either.

What the word "calling" in our title has come to mean to me is a type of activity or behavior which one engages in, as Webster says, from a "prompting to a particular act or duty," and from which one may or may not derive his livelihood. For some persons, their job or occupation is a means of making money and nothing more, with little or no intrinsic urgency or interest. In our sense, such an occupation is definitely not a "calling." By contrast, it seems that for many—perhaps most—persons who are today seriously engaged in psychotherapy, either on a professional or a peer-group basis (as, for example, in Alcoholics Anonymous), there is a strong sense of "prompting" and "duty," something which they believe is eminently useful and in which, one way or another, they want to have a part.

During the early decades of this century, when individual psychotherapy was developing (largely on the model of the physician seeing a patient in private or a priest hearing a confession), it seems that many psychotherapists were interested in what they were doing and curious about the underlying causes of personality distur-

---

† Adapted from a paper read at the Symposium, "Psychotherapy As A Secular Calling," American Psychological Association Annual Meeting, Washington, D.C., September 4, 1971.

bances; but it is doubtful if there was any very strong sense of "calling" as we have just used that term. However, as we began to gain a clearer idea of the motives which take persons into individual psychotherapy and as we saw laymen forming mutual-help or peer groups of various kinds, a new way of thinking about and responding to this entire situation began to emerge. Gradually we began to see that the common, underlying problem was *human alienation*; that is, a condition of loneliness, fear and separation from one's fellow human beings. And it also became increasingly clear that this personal isolation was growing to near-epidemic proportions because the traditional institutions of home, church, school and neighborhood—as a result of various technological changes and dislocations—has become unstable and no longer provided a sense of personal identity, human and emotional intimacy and cosmic meaning for great numbers of people.

In the late Nineteenth Century, when physicians began to see increasingly large numbers of patients who were suffering from assorted ailments and agonies which had no demonstrable organic basis, the French neurologist, Jean Martin Charcot, suggested, for want of any better nomenclature, the term "neurosis" which was soon widely accepted and is still in common use. However, the nonmedical psychoanalyist, Erik Homberger Erikson, has suggested an alternative and more apt expression, namely, *identity crisis,* which is gradually beginning to replace the term "neurosis." Paradoxically, this is occurring at a time when an increasingly sure neurological foundation is being established for some types of personality disorders which are generally but inaccurately known as "psychoses" because it now appears that, to some extent at any rate, there are true "neuroses"; and considerable headway has been made in developing successful biochemical remedies for these conditions. However, no such neurological basis or biochemical treatment has been found for most persons who are today suffering from so-called "neurosis" and it is clear that a change in conceptualization and terminology is indicated. Erikson's expression "identity crisis" seems to be much more descriptively accurate and diagnostically precise. If this latter type of phenomenon is not truly neurological but interpersonal and existential in nature, then *sociological* rather than medical means of remediation or redemption are called for.

If, as we now have reason to suspect, a person who is suffering from or undergoing an identity crisis is in such a state because of personal isolation, alienation, or disconnection, the salient practical question is: What can be done to help such a person regain a sense of human affiliation? Or, how does one assist persons who feel humanly separated and alone to recapture a feeling of togetherness, community, of being interpersonally "plugged-in"? Even while psychotherapy still was being conducted on an almost exclusively individual or dyadic basis, it gradually became clear that, regardless of rather wide divergences in the nature of the psychotherapeutic techniques employed, the factor that seemed to be most generally helpful and common was something that came to be known simply as *relationship*. This observation would seem to have special meaning and importance: If a formerly lost, detached, alienated person, through so-called individual psychotherapy, becomes closely and meaningfully related to another person, this effect could conceivably derive its special significance because this one close, rewarding human relationship or connection serves as an entry back into a larger community or group of Significant Others (to use Sullivan's apt expression).

The next question which logically could have been asked is this: Might not re-entry into or recovery of community be more expeditiously achieved directly rather than through the mediation of an individual known as a "therapist"? Oddly enough, this question seems not to have been asked, at least not in any very explicit or compelling way. And the phenomenon of *group* therapy, which has come into such prominence in the past decade or two and is largely replacing classical forms of individual therapy, was not developed consciously and systematically but was discovered more or less accidentally or inadvertently.

There are today two basic forms of group therapy, the one conducted by professionally trained leaders and the other which operates without professional leadership and involves mutual-help or peer group. Professional group psychotherapy, as is now well known, was developed as a substitute for individual therapy for psychiatric casualties during and after World War II because of a shortage of "trained personnel," with the expectation that, for any one patient, it would be considerably less effective than individual therapy but perhaps, in the aggregate, more helpful than the equivalent amount of time spent with just one patient. To almost everyone's astonishment, it turned out that most patients seemed to profit more from group therapy than they would have if they had been in individual treatment.

And the prototype for mutual-help or peer-group therapy is, of course, *Alcoholics Anonymous* whose history is well known and does not need to be repeated here. But the moral was again the same: an effect, namely the successful cultivation of sobriety, which had rarely been achieved by means of individual professional treatment became a commonplace in this remarkable "fellowship of men and women who share their experience, strength and hope with each other that they may solve their common problem and help others to recovery from alcoholism" (A.A. Creed).

Now what, if anything, does all this have to do with religion—or with a "religious revolution"? There is a common misconception about religion which easily could prevent us from seeing an important and vital implication here. For many persons the term "religion" implies theism or belief in a deity of some sort. But there is no necessary association here. Our English term religion comes from the Latin term *ligare* which means "connection"; religion, therefore, literally and explicitly means *reconnection*. And that, in the *interpersonal sense,* is certainly what group therapy is mainly about. Thus it can be said that all or at least most group therapies are highly religious in their basic nature and objectives, and whether they are or are not also theistic (as Alcoholics Anonymous is but many other types of groups are not) does not alter or detract from their basically *religious* character.

The title of this paper asks: "Is the small-groups movement a religious revolution?" As just indicated, it is not at all difficult to show, since it is concerned with the reconciliation or re-connection of alienated human beings, that this movement is essentially and and pre-eminently religious. The question that remains to be answered is in what way this movement is also "revolutionary." Many considerations could be mentioned pertinently in this connection but two will suffice for present purposes.

In the first place, in traditional churches the religious or reconnective aspect has for many centuries been mainly *vertical*, that is, between man and God. In the contemporary small-groups movement reconciliation is horizontal or humanistic, between man and man, with only a secondary or no concern at all with the man-deity relationship. Presently there is a powerful and pervasive revivalistic trend in this country involving Fundamental or Conservative Christianity which is having a particularly powerful appeal to young people (cf. *Time Magazine* cover story for June 21, 1971). Here theism is dominant and interpersonal reconciliation of second-order importance. Whether this wave of Revivalism will eclipse the contemporary small-groups movement, which essentially is secular, or prove to be only a transistory phenomenon remains to be seen. But in any case it is clear that the small-groups movement—whatever its ultimate destiny—*is* revolutionary in that it essentially is secular, whereas Christianity, whether of the traditional or currently revivalistic form, is otherworldly, supernaturalistic and theistic.

The other point has to do with the difference in the degree of personal self-disclosure which is a dominant feature of the small-group movement and is much less conspicuous in latter-day Christianity.

The Christian Church started out as a small-groups movement—the House Church of Apostolic or so-called Primitive Christianity (*see, The Chicago Theological Seminary Register,* December, 1970) — in which there was a very high degree of personal self-disclosure, which was known by the Greek term *exomologesis,* to the other members of a particular small group or congregation. The small group meeting in individual homes and practicing, along with exomologesis, *restitution* and *koinonea* (mutual concern) characterized Christianity until the beginning of the Fourth Century, A.D.; at which point (following the Council of Nicaea) confessions began to take place privately and by the end of the 12th Century, at least in the Western branch of the Church, self-disclosure or confession before a small group had disappeared completely, according to the best evidence presently available.

By the 16th century the vitality and integrity of Christianity were so badly eroded that the Protestant Reformation took place. But it did not perform the function which was most needed, elimination of private or so-called sealed confession and restoration of the practice of full and unflinching self-disclosure and personal openness in small groups, which had given the Early Church so much of its power to change human conduct and quiet turbulent emotions. Instead of re-establishing open confession, the Protestant Reformation "sealed" confession still further by substituting prayer for human interchange of any sort. The contemporary small-groups movement, although not nominally Christocentric or even theistic, seems to be affecting the type of change in this connection which the Reformation should have undertaken but did not; and for this reason, combined with the shift from supernaturalism to secularism already mentioned, this movement deserves to be called not just a "reformation" but a more radical transformation or *revolution.*

If this view of the situation is essentially valid, there are good grounds for referring to contemporary psychotherapy of both the professionally led and the peer-group varieties as a true calling, prompted, as Webster suggests, by a sense of duty and significance which greatly transcends the incentives involved in an ordinary vocation or profession. What the practical implications of these developments will be we cannot at present confidently say, but they can hardly avoid being momentous.

CHAPTER 36

THE PSYCHOTHERAPIST AS PRIEST†

E. Mark Stern

A PRIESTLY CALLING manifests itself in providing mediation between man and the superindividual community. That is, the only authentic advance any person makes is that which weds him to a larger sense of himself. The lines and divisions between each person and the other are at best descriptive.

A yearning for a comprehensive sense of participation may lie at the center of a person's propulsion in both the social and spiritual spheres. It is as if identity can only continue to take shape as it ceases to make boundaries the *sine qua non* of experience.

Boundlessness happens when borders are transformed into frontiers. Each other then becomes a possibility for a new sense of oneness. This openness for which a new level of appreciation comes into being most often happens *via* the intercession of a person willing to nullify the emphasis on raw conflict and replace it with understanding. The psychotherapist is in a unique position to provide this mediation.

It was with a startling sense of freshness that Clifford Beers far back in 1908 quoted the superintendent of a state hospital as follows: "After all, what the insane most need is a friend." (1) On the level of mediation, a friend is the stranger who keeps faith with the possibility of surprises. In the case of the psychotherapist, the surprises he bears witness to offer alternative transpersonal perspectives.

The newly perceived interpersonal reality becomes effective when it elevates concerns beyond the need for being-in-the-world *sans* encounter with the other. Indeed, it reshapes the horizon so that divisions between people and people are seen within the scope of what Alfred North Whitehead termed "activity and process." (2) Whitehead was interested in proceeding beyond Newtonian physics which, according to his best knowledge, stated that "Each bit of

---

† Paper read at the Symposium "Psychotherapy As A Secular Calling," American Psychological Association Annual Meeting, Washington, D.C., September 4, 1971.

matter occupies a definite limited region," and that "The essential relationship between bits of matter is purely spatial." (3) Likewise, in a post-Newtonian humanistic psychology, the transpersonal happening is probably much more than the stasis of each consciousness.

All mechanical models ignore the embryology of a larger field of conscious awareness which can potentially transform each separat vision. Teilhard de Chardin noted that "multiple centers of reconstruction" which were once thought to have "radiated independently of one another probably do much more." "We can now realize," he continued, "that their apparent plurality (just as that of the isolated groups of cells are formed in a living tissue that is healing) soon joins up and fuses together when it is seen as part of the coherent and integral picture of a universe that is in full process of being made organic." (4) This humanistic emphasis speaks of the celebration of awareness; i.e., when individual consciousness becomes the wholeness of community a man can finally shout "Amen!"

The psychotherapist, friend and entrepreneur of vital surprises, presides over a vital liturgical function. This objectification of a subjective desire for authentic harmony is brought about when the psychotherapist reacts as part of the entire synergistic process. He sacramentalizes awareness as he proclaims his own place in the patient's world. In this way he embodies the true meaning of conversion or spiritual leap: he literally re-discovers himself and the patient in illumination. Or as an ancient Chinese text proclaims: "The light of human nature shines back on the primordial, the true. (5) Thus, the therapist sees any and all infusions of consciousness as proof that superindividuality is a viable possibility.

The psychotherapist is the friend who declares that participation with the other is the tacit fact of life. At the same time, he notes that to have become separated from the other may have been an initial enterprise in the service of the ego. After all, Adam and Eve were to have chosen consciousness above all in their taking leave of the womb-Garden. According to Genesis, "Yahweh God said, 'See, the man has become like one of us, with his knowledge of good and evil.'" (Genesis 3:22) This trend toward individuation, considered within the framework of a social universe, is an authentic attempt at mapping the field of relationships. That is, I can only be in relationship to the whole, ot the superindividual gestalt, if I first seize a position with a name. Adam is the name each person takes, with obvious variation, since Adam is a field of consciousness. However, Adam is soon discovered to be a pair, (See Genesis 2:22) and eventually the primordial symbol for parenthood. (See Genesis

4:1) Nevertheless Adam is never lost to the superindividual transpersonal field. This paradox is best celebrated by the playwright Ugo Betti who announced: "Each soul is like a tiny drop without which the whole world would thirst."

Thus, for the psychotherapist and his patient, each life event must be celebrated as an enlargement of experience. This clearly indicates that experiences of greater wholes can be comprehended. Awareness of participation in more sophisticated superindividual gestalts arises from what Michael Polanyi terms "connoisseurship." That is, responsiveness to the possibilities of living requires a tacit experiential dimension. Polanyi noted that "Connoisseurship, like skill, can be communicated only by example, not by precept." (6) Thus, within the psychotherapeutic relationship, an apprenticeship begins to take place. As the therapist handles all material offered to him by the patient he becomes ideally positioned to embody total regard for the person's quest for participation.

The witnessing of a leap toward superindividuality is the healing mission within which the therapist stands as the representative of the expanded community. He carries through his sacramental task as he responds to the patient's concerns in a way which indicates that these concerns are palpable components of an expansive participation. Within the scope of his own connoisseurship the therapist lends credence to personal struggles and interpersonal conflicts as constituent elements of the developmental matrix. For example, a patient approached a therapy session with misgivings about hardly ever feeling understood by the most significant people in her life. She was treated by her therapist as a person striving to get across a message which had potential vitality to offer to those who only would hear. She felt that the therapist too responded to her in many ways characteristic of those dearest to her. He acknowledged the sense of aloneness that this could bring. He then suggested that he would try to listen to her as someone who virtually could change his life. He requested that she try to afford him equal sensitivity.

The patient was asked to note when she felt most in contact with the therapist. In addition it was recommended that she pause when she felt most alone and isolated, and that she try to associate such feelings with periods in her life when she saw herself as solitary and lonely. Also, that she try to align herself spiritually with other people she felt also stood alone.

This simple exercise provided the patient with an opportunity to identify her own plight with a friend who had committed suicide, with her father who felt trapped in his marriage and who had spent years identifying himself with stray dogs and other helpless animals, and also with the therapist whom she felt for the first time she saw as "a voice crying in the wilderness." But most important, she came to consider each position as a possibility of more fully being-in-the-world. At the same time she felt a new camaraderie with other life styles thus providing more of a meaning to her own. This sense of new relatedness was not unlike what William James called "love-systems" which he stated form an "ensemble" and are somehow "unifying the world." (7) Thus the therapeutic situation had enabled her to proceed along new avenues of superindividual awareness. "The ear that heard me," states Job, "blessed me."

The type of tacit learning involved in authentic therapeutic encounters allows for a more dynamic appreciation of the live space between people. To paraphrase and transpose an earlier quotation from Whitehead: The essential relationship between organisms is not purely spatial, it is as alive as the organisms themselves are. A substantial appreciation of this vital participation provides a perception of the sacredness of all experience. It is as if the therapist becomes priest by eliminating distinctions between rational and mystical states and between those conditions labeled sacred and profane. In true fashion he regards his patient as a participant in communion with all life. Likewise, as an historian of human psyches, he is enabled to view life styles as archetypic and in so doing grants total respect to each re-presentation of the cosmic gestalt. During times of peak recognition of the vitality of social linkages and superindividual phenomena, the therapist takes on the mantle of the redeeming and restorative mission of spiritual healer, since this vocation is best fulfilled by those who, in whatever psychodynamic system, recognize what Teilhard de Chardin saw as "the spark leaping the gap between God and the universe *through a personal milieu.*" (8)

The mediating function of the priesthood becomes realized in the psychotherapeutic mission not because it considers itself the duly accredited and spiritually endowed representative of God. Rather, the mediation is simply an open consciousness of what may ultimately be possible between people. It is on some levels what Thomas Hora defines as intercessory prayer, i.e., "The beneficial, loving radiancy reaching out of one human consciousness for the welfare of another." (9)

How "reaching out" takes place, or whether in fact it is always verbal must remain the product of each therapist's connoisseurship. J. B. Rhine, in suggesting a possible pastoral dimension in the counseling and therapeutic relationship, recommends a sensitization to the possibilities of "the extrasensory or, more inclusively (of) the parapsychical interchange." He rightly questions the dependable effectiveness of such possibilities. He does feel, however, that "Their main value now is in reminding us that people have a more intangible side [and that] the counselor and his client both have it." The psychotherapist, according to Rhine, "is a little more receptive in his approach if he is merely sure that he does not know it all." At this point "a bit of telepathic intuition . . . could change the picture. This helps the non-religious counselor to feel like the sincerely religious one—appropriately humble." (10)

Humility grants both therapist and patient a reverence for all experience. To mediate then means to be open to whatever comes forth from the patient, and to see this coming forth as having radical Immanence within the human community. In contemporary terms, it is the therapist, in whatever guise, who celebrates the forces of dynamic energy between people and people, and between people and events. This takes him beyond Otto Fenichel's view of therapy as the objectification "of a struggle between certain unconscious impulses (which reveal themselves relatively more clearly in analysis than in ordinary conversation) and certain resistances of the ego, which likewise are unconscious to the subject or become apparent to him in distorted form only:" (11), to what Josef Goldbrunner terms "the immediacy of experience." (12) It is in the latter view that "depth psychology broadens the reality of psychic life and thus uncovers a new realm of the reality of creation for systematic investigation." (13)

It would be proper to say that each insight felt and experienced within the psychotherapeutic relationship is a liturgical celebration of "the reality of creation." Beyond the possibility of happenstance, creation is the product of a covenant between the Source of all being and the existents in the universe. As such, the office of priest-therapist is to bear witness to the psychological complexities of this covenant—to view all of the potentials as the real outcomes of encounter.

The struggle between the conscious and unconscious parts of man is the quest for cognition. All such struggles become personified in the interactions of the community. Thus, it is not merely some unconscious primary process which vies for control of a relatively established ego. It is rather the license and depth of freedom that the patient may see in others. Therefore, the psychotherapist never parts from actual experience. He assists his patient in the task of looking for completion by trying to see what the other expresses as part of the Whole that he himself participates in. Each person, then, is creation personified. The therapist's recognition of a supreme quest makes him proper heir to the priestly offices of Melchizedek and Aaron. And through these good offices, it would be safe to conclude, that a true reverence for the experience of the patient becomes a humanizing factor in the world.

Finally, the therapist as priest continually prays. His prayer is one in which the established stimulus-response bond is abandoned and replaced by a conception of life which is always filled with authentic surprises. This prayer is formless and open-ended. It is, after all, a total responsiveness to the other. From this responsiveness comes a recognition of the other's unique creative potentialities which are possible only through interaction with the expansive community. It is enough for the therapist to celebrate and to bear witness to these surprises.

REFERENCES AND FOOTNOTES

1 Beers, C. *A Mind that Found Itself*, New York, Longmans, Green and Company, 1917, p. 318.
2 Whitehead, A. N. *Nature and Life*, London, Cambridge University Press, 1934, p. 36.
3 *Op. cit.*, p. 181.
4 Teilhard de Chardin, P. *Activation of Energy*, New York, Harcourt Brace Jovanovich, 1971, p. 255.
5 From "The Face Turned to the Wall" in Wilhelm, R. *The Secret of the Golden Flower— A Chinese Book of Life*, New York, Harcourt, Brace and World, 1962, p. 77.
6 Polanyi, M. *Personal Knowledge—Towards a Post-Critical Philosophy*, New York, Harper and Row, 1962, p. 54.
7 James, W. *Pragmatism*, Cleveland, World Publishing Company, 1955, pp. 93, 94.
8 *Op. cit.*, p. 147.
9 Hora, T. *In Quest of Wholeness*, privately printed, 1968, pp. 100-101.
10 Rhine, J. B., "Pastoral Dimensions in Counseling and Psychotherapy," (An Exploration), in *The Journal of Pastoral Counseling*, Vol. 5, No. 1, 1970, p. 9.
11 Fenichel, O. *The Psychoanalytic Theory of the Neuroses*, New York, W. W. Norton and Company, 1945, p. 24.
12 Goldbrunner, J. *Realization—Anthropology of Pastoral Care*, Notre Dame (Indiana), University of Notre Dame Press, 1966, p. 94.
13 *Op. cit.*, p. 111.

CHAPTER 37

THERE'S NO TURNING BACK

Irma Lee Shepherd

As I have dwelt upon the bringing about, the writing of this paper, I have come to call it "The Relentless" paper, or my paper on "Relentlessness." Letting it shape itself as if it were clay under the guiding, responding hands of a potter has been difficult—bordering at times on agony, for in this task, I have had to open myself to its content, its theme, enter into its process, the process of being—of becoming more aware of the process-stream of my own person, my own life. That which has shaped me into the therapist-person I am at this moment, I believe I share with all mankind—over all time—that is, the struggle for the comprehension, understanding, acceptance, commitment and involvement in that process which I can only call That Which Is.

Each human being at some time ponders on his being, some only dimly nudged by observations of birth, meeting, death. Others are more profoundly grasped by their restlessness and drawn back again and again into the deep plumbing of their own depths—the pushing of their limits to know and feel their being. Their searching expressions come to us in myth, metaphor, poem, prayer, song, preaching, treatise, and of late in the outpourings in therapy tapes and transcripts—each an account of a lifelong odyssey into that realm one goes into because it is ever just there.

The writings of the ages carry a parallel persistent theme: what happens to man when he will not follow his promptings or when he avoids hearing the quiet persistent call into and with the process? Jesus said it very well. "The kingdom you seek is within you." and "He who once puts his hand to the plow and turns back is not fit for the kingdom of God." I have found that being a psychotherapist is like that. There is no turning back from the process of becoming the free, open, powerful, aware, whole human being that I some-

---

† Paper read at the Symposium "Psychotherapy As A Secular Calling," American Psychological Association Annual Meeting, Washington, D.C., September 4, 1971.

times am. This has meant persistently refacing every door of life I closed in order to survive childhood's pain, facing each, opening each, and going in. The unopened doors we call symptoms, sin, unfinished business, tensions, dis-ease, dis-order, anxiety, all learned ways of protecting but limiting my being, stifling my energy, my potentiality, my reality. To sit in the presence of another human being painfully opening his own doors is to risk feeling a powerful fist pounding on my closed door and then to hear an answering scream from the me inside who wants release from that prison, freedom from those limits to expand into that inner-outer realm that in swelling moments of joy I know reaches and transcends the stars and makes me for a moment infinitely free.

Often, I do not have the courage-support to open a door and I turn away, only to find in the days, weeks, succeeding years through the pushings of dreams, depression, actions and consequences, the impact of other persons that I have cornered myself, narrowed my possibility of choices of movement until in despair or agony or dull emptiness, I own that I am there where I did not want to be, facing that unopened door with now no choice but to die or to go in. The relentlessness of this shaping pushes me to the point of surrender to That Which Is, to my own powerful drive for wholeness. For a time, that which follows this yielding is the peace of full-being with little energy lost in defending in fighting, energy that now merely illumines me—shining, clear, white, pure, essence, being. For the time there is the resolution of paradox upon past paradox: man—God; temporal—eternal; inner—outer; material—immaterial; life—death; pain—joy; struggle—peace.

In these years of struggle, the most relentless dawning of knowing has slowly overtaken me and now with doubting and smiling I take hold of this possibility: If I do not yield to my more real self now, the Relentless Process is very patient. It will continue waiting until I yield, waiting lifetime after lifetime after lifetime. The wise strugglers of the East recognize this openly, that the Universe evolves continuously and man must continuously unfold in higher levels of consciousness and unity.

Hermann Hesse gives an elegant and poignant expression of his understanding and appreciation of the process in *Siddhartha*. Siddhartha was drawn away as a young man from his wealthy and high station in life by the appeal of the teachings of Brahman and tried to lead the ascetic holy life of a Samana, denying of flesh and emptying of Self. Following a meeting with Gotama Buddha, Siddhartha could no longer seek to escape from himself. He had to explore his sensuous humanness to his fullest knowledge, to experience relating to other persons, to know the loving surrender to the daily struggles of all humankind, the ecstacy and pain of loving and mating, being loved, parenting and then losing his son, grieving and coming to the humility of knowing and respecting what less developed, ordinary human beings experience. He found that in all these ways he was not better than they; that he, too, was a man and that he was different only in his knowing of the unity of all life. The surrender to this reality opened the way to his deeper knowing and his becoming, then, powerfully valuable to those who met him. In his later years, many sought him out for the profound-touching-knowing he made available by his presence as he spent his days ferrying people across a river. This account, to me, so clearly parallels the life-long training process involved in being and becoming a therapist, a process, relentless, redeeming, and rejoicing. At that moment of commitment, of most powerful surrender to the Relentless, of turning loose, of giving in, of accepting destiny—I know—and am known. That Which Is smiles me. I cannot turn back.

INDEX

A

Aaron, 457
Abraham, 112, 114, 156
Absalom, 113
Absolution, prayer of
    at the end of the sacrament of confession, 213
Acceptance
    (*see also* Catharsis)
    analyst's attitude of, 309–310
    child's longing for, 398–401
    of therapist
        based on his competence, 250
    of primitive belief system considered, 294
    of things as they are, recommended, 230
    step necessary to those who would help others, 460
Acceptance of the self
    in human existence, 39
Acculturation
    adjustmtnt to culture conflict, 321–326, 328–329
Ackerknert, 231
"Acting out"
    enjoyment of open hostility, 269
    of family problems(s), 292
Action(s), good
    enriching the *next* life, or incarnation, in Hindu belief, 170
"Activity and process"
    erasing divisions between people, 452
Adam
    consequences of the Fall of, 200
    Christ as the new, 206
    man's guilt through, 200–201
Adamic state, in Mystical experience, 307–308
Adler, Alfred, 280
Adoption
    godparents' "spiritual," in the Eastern Orthodox Church, 208
Aesthetic awareness
    and extrovertive mystical experience, 308
Affiliation, human
    gradually regained through therapy, 448
"Affirmation and denial"
    Christian Science, in, 79
Afterlife
    Orthodox belief in, 199
    not stressed in Christian Science, 74

Afterlife, Mormon teaching regarding, 98
Age
    not a factor in the gift of grace, 208–209, 210–211
Age, respect for
    the Eastern Orthodox Church, in, 208
Aged, or old
    kindness to, 189
Aggression
    relieved through Catharsis, 115–116
Akiba, Rabbi, 114
Akua
    made victim of a witch, 245
    unable to walk, 245
    witch purified and victim cured, 245
Alcohol
    abstinence in Peyote religion, 296
Alcoholic Anonymous
    creed, 449–450
    example of group therapy, 231–234, 449–450
    involving peer group(s), 450
    religious character of, 450
    sobriety, successful cultivation of, 449
    theistic, 450
Alienation
    as isolation, or separation from fellow human beings, 448
    causes in American life, 448
    contemporary syndrome, 168, 177
    fear in, 448
    loneliness in, 448
    problem of near-epidemic proportion, 448
    relieved by personal consultation, 448
    as a lifelong process of disintegration, 209
    explained as part of Orthodox belief, 209 ff.
    from God, 200, 216
    Hindu answer to the problem of, 178–179
    overcome through therapeutic quest of oneness with divine essence, 178–179
    from God, man's sense of, 95
    result of original sin, 200
    widespread problem in American society, 448
All, assurance of being one with the, 317
Allport, G. W., 38
Almsgiving
    in Islam, 157
    in the Eastern Orthodox Church, 215

Al-Mureed
  seeker after truth, 159
Alone
  leaving the other fellow, 431
Aloneness, patient's
  cause of, 454
  relieved through interrelating with other sufferers, 455
Amaterasu, Sun-Goddess in Japan, 125
Ambivalence
  freeing mental patient from, 247
"American dream," 404
American Indian
  belief system (traditional), 293–294
  culture, example of, 287–289
  growth in self-esteem of, after Peyote meetings, 296, 301, 304–305
  caught between two cultures, 287
  living in close proximity to white Western culture, 287
  reliance on mystical teachings of, 255
  reservation culture disintegrating, 287
American Psychological Association, 439, 447, 452, 458
Amida
  (see Buddhas), 131
  Buddha of Healing, in Japan, 125–126
Amitabha
  becoming a Bodhisattva, 126
  Buddha invoked by Mahayana Worshippers, 124
  compassion rather than reward for good deeds, to followers of, 126
  contemplative Buddha, 125
  contrasted with Gautama, 126
  faith and devotion to, in Mahanaya Buddhism, 126
  infinite light of, 126
  leading light in Mahayana theology, 126
  less popular in India, 126
  perfection, striving to attain, 126
  prayers to, 126
  presiding over Sukhavati, the Happy Land, 126
  receiving followers at death in Paradise, 126
  teachings of, emphasized in China, Japan, Nepal and Tibet, 126
  wisdom, leading believers to Reality-Itself, 126
Amor concupiscentiae (self-gratification)
  as opposed to *amor benevolentiae*, 21
Amore, Roy C., 142–155
Amos, 440
Analysis
  the professional's recurring need for analysis, 458–459
Analysis, Freudian
  use of, in group therapy, 265
Analytic method
  better suited to therapist than to mental patient, 252
Ananda (ecstasy), 175
Ancestor worship
  cult in early Chinese religion, 181
Ancestors, Chinese, 180–181
Angel, wrestling with the, 429–430 (see also Jacob)
Anger, God's
  Father rebuking His people, 113 (see also Reward and retribution, divine)
  Old Testament record of, 440
Animism
  in early Chinese culture, 180
Animal **magnetism**
  (see "Malicious Animal Magnetism")
Animal world,
  Eastern Orthodox attitude toward, 213–214
  respect for the, 215
Anorexia, hysterical, 239
Anselm, Saint, 201
Anthony of Egypt, 202–203
Anxiety
  absorption of, 251
  cases of, among Gold Coast patients, 243
  changes in patient's environment, 251
  communication of, patient's, 251
  cumulative effect of, 251
  defense against, patient's, 251
  existential, derived from lack of faith, 58–59
  increased in patient who observes fear in his associates, 251
  inducing chemical reaction in patient, 251
  lack of, in Zen man, 138
  narcissism as source of, 134
  perception, effect on patient's, 251
  primary, 251
  secondary, 251
  self, effect(s) on the, 251
  social aspect(s) of, 251
  stage in Sufism, 159
  therapist's attitude toward patient experiencing, 251
Anxiety, freedom from
  psychotherapy's goal, 436
Anxiety, ontological
  a residue, 43
Anxiety state(s)
  caused by depletion of vital substance, 228
Apostle
  definition of, 437

Approach to mentally ill, new
to listen and to minister, 52–53
Aquinas, T.
on prudence, 17–18
Arab
characteristic use of exaggerated statement, 158, 164
Arabic, 157, 164
Arahat (saint)
higher stage (fourth) in Nirvana, 147
Arastch, A. R., 138, 140
Arhat, in Theravada Buddhism
definition of, 123
Aristotle
on man, 17
Asceticism
and introvertive mystical experience, 308 (*see also* Meditation)
Gautama's, 119
Hindu
Brahmanism, 172
exclusion of the aesthetic, 175
opposition to Tantric indulgence (*see* Control, in Tantric yoga), 176
redemption from rebirth, leading to, 171
rejection of the senses, 175
retreat from the world (*see also* Monastic ideal), 175
saints, sayings and writings of the, 172
synthesis of poetic-religious thought, 172
various degrees of, 171
Vedantism, 172
in India, 119
Pascal's, 313
strong flavor of, in Christian Science, 86
Ashoka, 142
Asrani, U. A., 309, 318
Assimilation
of unfamiliar experiences, 268
Astral travel
definition of, 255
Astrology
use of, in psychic counseling, 255
Asylums
conditions of, 229
Atonement
(*see also* Redemption)
Day of (*see* Yom Kippur)
Attitude(s) of mind
"Protestant" healing, in, 49
Augustine, Saint, 35, 200
Aulen, G., 201
Authority
obedience to, as an ethical code, 408–409

Authority, source of
patient's, 252
psychotherapist's, 252
Authority, the Church's
flexibility of, in Eastern Orthodoxy, 203
Automatic writing
use of, in psychic counseling, 255
Avalokita
appearing as Prince of Indian ancestry in rich raiment, 128
Bodhisattva, 127–128, 129
Buddha, many-armed, 128
came to earth 300 times in human form, 128
connected with Amitabha Buddha, 128
diety answering prayers of the childless or the distressed, 128
description of, 128
female form of, in China, Korea, and Japan, 128
many-armed diety, showing compassion to mankind, 128
mercy or pity, personification of divine, 128
omnipresent savior of the distressed, 128
Avalokitesvara
"the Lord who looks down from heaven," 128
Avoidance
of potentially stressful situations, 228
Awareness
celebration of, 453

B

Baasher, T., 162–163
Bach, George, 444
Bandura 34
Banff, Alberta, 316
Baptism
in the Eastern Orthodox Church, 206–209
Barbour, Hugh, 273
Bar Mitzvah, 114
Barron, Jules, 435–438
Basil the Great, 205, 210–211
Becker, E., 136
Becoming
man in a state of, 197
process of, 458–459
Behavior, human
illumined by modern psychotherapy, 118
Behavior
meaning defined by particular culture, 286
psychotherapist's concern with, 436
therapeutic influences on, 436
Behavior, pathological
explained in terms of magic and the supernatural, 225–226
role of, in psychotherapy, 134

Behavior patterns, parents'
  influence on children, 113
Being, infinite
  one with, 119
Being, Supreme
  offering security, 3
Belief
  "right," in Buddhism, 121, 122
Belief system
  importance of the, in interpretation of culturally conditioned behavior, 294
  pressures on mystic, in interpreting experiences, 308
  translation from one system to another, 294
Believers, Community of (*see also* Community, Church)
Belonging, sense of
  in a church community, 89
  in Judaism, 114
"Beloved community"
  goal of, 39–40
Benares, Hindu center, 120, 121
Benedict, Ruth, 66–67
Bereavement (*see* Mourning)
Bergman, Robert L., 296–304
Berndt, C. H., 311–311, 318
Berque, Jacques, 157–158
Betti, Ugo, 454
Bhagavadgita, 174
Bhaktivedanta, Swami, 173
Bharati, Agehananda, 167–179
Bhikku, 121
Bible, 112–113
Bible
  as the revealed Word of God, 91
  literal interpretation of, 91
  sufficient guide for man's conduct, 91
Bibliography (*see* end of individual Chapters, esp. 364–368)
Biochemical abnormalities (hypothetical)
  as explanations for mental ills, 228
Biochemical component
  anxiety-induced, in the patient, 251
Bioenergetics, 268 ff.
  body diagnosis, 271
  breathing patterns noted, 271
  drawbacks in larger perspective of individual's interrelatedness and larger Vision, 275
  effective as therapy, 275
  insights derived from feelings, 271, 272
  mind-reliance minimal, 271
  new therapy, 268, 272
  outward expression of hitherto unexpressed feelings, 271, 272
  personal experience of base, sneering side of self in session of, 272
  pleasure principle in, 274–275
  recommended exercises in, 271
Birth
  painful, to the Hindu believer, 170
Birth, death, and rebirth cycle
  (*see also* Rebirth)
  in Hindu belief, 170, 171
  in Jainism, 171
  interrupted by Hindu meditation leading to mind's release, 170
  uninterrupted, according to Hindu belief, if mind release is not achieved, 170
Bishop, Mormon
  duties and responsibilities, 99–100
Blessed Sacrament
  Jeanne Fery's questions regarding, 239
Blindness
  case history (*see* Kofi)
  cases associated with witchcraft, Gold Coast, 243
Bloodletting
  primitive therapeutic method, 229
Bloomfield Hills, Michigan, 273
Blyth, R. H., 138, 140
Bodhi tree, 120, 132
Bodhisattva, 124, 126–129
  Avalokita, 127–129
  concept arising out of the historical buddha, 126
  definition of, 126
  liberating the world from all suffering, 127
  Manjusri, 127–129
  object of devotion in Mahayana Buddhism, 126
  postponement of the bliss of Nirvana to alleviate the suffering of others, 126
  savior of others, in Mahayana Buddhism, 123, 126–129
  supernatural being attaining Buddhahood, 126–129
  supra-historical, mythical element in Mahayana Buddhism, 126
Body
  functions of, as the work of God, 111
  only one part of person, 275
  physical reactions to tension, esp. in individual's musculature and stance, 271, 274–275 (*see* Bioenergetics)
Body of Christ, the Church as the, 203
Boisen, Aaron, 52

Bonhoeffer, Dietrich, 35, 45
Book of Mormon, II Nephi, 99
Boston, Massachusetts, 77,
Bourguignon, Erika, 286
Braden, Charles S., 78, 79, 83
Brahmá (Creator), 177
Brahman
  cosmic essence in Hinduism, 119, 121, 175, 178–179
  Siddhartha following teaching(s) of, 459
Brith, the, 114
British Columbia, 316
Brother(s)
  men as, 296
Browning, Donald, 32, 45
Buber, Martin, 439
Bucke, R. M., 315–316, 318
Bucks County Seminar House, Pennsylvania, 278
Buddha
  (*see* Gautama)
  as Reality itself (or Absolute Reality), assuming many forms, 124
  compassion, filled with, 124
  Four Great Events
    Birth, 121
    Enlightenment, 121
    Paranirvana, passing into, 121
    Preaching of First Sermon, 120–121
  Gautama first called, 120
  historical, 131 (see Gautama)
  later theological descriptions of the, 124
  many manifestations of the, 124
  Middle Way, the, 121
  teaching of, 122
  Trikaya, three-fold body of the, 124, 131
  wisdom, filled with, 124
Buddha-sásana
  "Teaching of the Buddha," 142–143
"Buddha Field," 126 (*see* Sukhavati)
Buddha, the
  his life and teaching all one, 432–433
Buddhism, esp. 129–130
Buddha(s)
  Amida, Buddha of Healing, in Japan, 125–126, 131
  Amitabha, invoked by Mahayana Buddhists, 124, 125–126 (*see* Amitabha)
  Avalokita, personification of meditation, 127, 128–129
  Bodhisattvas, saviors in Mahayana Buddhism, 123, 124, 126–129 (*see* Bodhisattva)
  contemplative (*see* Dyani), 124, 125
  Dyani, 124, 125
  female-formed, esp. in China and Japan, 128
  Gautama (see main entry)
  historical (*see* Manushi), 125
  Light-givers, 125
  Maitreya, Future Buddha, 129
  Manjusri, a Bodhisattva, major author of salvation, 127, 128–129
  Manushi, 124, 125
  many, in Mahanaya Buddhism, 123, 124, 129, 130
  O-Mi-To, Buddha of Healing, in China, 125–126
  supernatural being(s), varying in number, 123
  Vairocana, bringer of salvation, 125
Buddhism
  (*see also* Buddhism, Mahayana; Buddhism, Theravada; Buddhism, Zen; *and* Zen)
  among great religions, 117
  and modern psychotherapy, 129–130
  as a system of human guidance, 142
  asceticism in, 119
  born in Nepal, India, 118
  compared to psychotherapy, 153
  compared to other religions, 118
  compared to psychotherapy, 118
  defeat of, during Muslim conquest of India, 143
  escape or *moksha,* 119
  for laymen, 152
  Four holy truths, 120
  (*see also* Path)
  eightfold Path, the holy, 121, 122
  Gautama as Buddha, "the Enlightened One," 118–122
  (*see also*) Gautama
  Hinduism, reaction against, 120
  in Muslim mysticism, 159
  India, born in, 118–119
  Indian religious system, 133
  karma, role of, 119
  liberation from rebirth, basic belief in, 171
  man's bondage to rebirth, 171
  meditation in, 120, 153
  multiplicity of Buddhas and forms of Buddhas, 124–129
  "Path," 151–154
  practiced by monks, 152
  Reality (Absolute) behind earthly appearance of the Buddha, according to later thelogy, 124 ff.
  rebirth, role of, 119
  redemption, man's rather than God's, 130
  self-acceptance in, 118
  self-knowledge in, 118

self-realization in, 118
split into two branches (see Theravada and Mahayana), 122
Zen, branch of Mahayana, 118
Buddhism, early Indian
schools in, located throughout India, 143
Buddhism, Mahayana
altruistic ethics in, 123–124, 130
Amitabha, Buddha of Contemplation, Compassion and Healing, 125–126
Amitabha, invocation of Buddha's name, 124
becoming a *Bodhisattva,* 123
beginning of, 123
Bodhisattva, a "savior" of others, who postpones Nirvana for himself, 123, 126
branches like separate religions, from Buddhism, 123
Buddha, characteristics of the, according to later theology, 124
compassionate attitude toward other followers, 123, 128, 130
compassionate wisdom, as revealed by Amitabha, 126
contemplative Buddhas (see Dyani), 125
Dharma, the Way, 120
deliverance from suffering, 120
Dharmakaya (Body of Truth), Buddha as, 131
doctrine of salvation by faith in a Buddha, 124
ethical interpretation of the world, 130
faith, emphasis on, 130
faith in Amitabha less emphasized in India than in China, Japan, Nepal and Tibet, 126
"Great Raft or Great Career," 122
higher ideal in, 123
historical Buddhas (see Manushi), 125
images, worship of, 124
located mainly in China, Japan, Korea and Tibet, 123
many saviors in, 123, 124, 129, 130
meditation, role of, 120
Nirmanakaya (Manifested Body), Buddha as, 131
Nirvana postponed for the sake of releasing others from *Tanha,* 123
other Buddhas, 123–129
paradise, 130
patient (suffering man) transformed into perfect being, 130
prayer and contemplation rather than good works required in this life, 126 (see Amitabha)
proclamation of, central, 126
Reality, Absolute, the Buddha as, 124
Reality-Itself in, 126
religious fervor in movement, 124
ritual, reliance on, 124
salvation, emphasis on, 118, 123, 124
salvation, many authors of, 124
salvation of others to be admitted into Nirvana, 123
Sambhogakaya (Accommodated Body), Buddha as, 131
self-realization in, 129–130
seven categories of, 123–124
solution offered to human frailties and social ills, 130
suffering humanity transformed into perfect beings, 130
Trikaya, doctrine of the, 124, 131
Zen, as branch of, 118
Zen technique derived from, 247
Buddhism, Theravada, 122–123, 130, 143–155
Buddhism, Theravada
Arhat, individual overcoming power of desires, 123
asceticism ("renouncing the world") in, 122
baed on self-effort, 122–123, 130
becoming an *Arhat,* 123
Buddha, historical, 118–122
Buddha's attainment of enlightenment, 124
followers located mostly in Ceylon, Laos, Cambodia and Thailand, 123
continuation of earlier Buddhism, 122–123, 124
four stages in, 146–147
Gautama, Buddha or "the Enlightened One," 118–122 (see Gautama)
guide to conduct, 143, 154
history of, 142–145
long adopted as major religion of countries of Southeast Asia, 143
Noble, Eightfold Path, 147–149
non-theistic system of belief, 143
original Buddhism, continuation of, 122–123
psychological approach in, 142 ff.
seeking one's own release from the power of *tanha,* 123
self-effort in, 123, 130
source of strength in overcoming evils of life, 143
"The Way of the Elders," 122
Buddhism, Zen,— (see Zen)
intuition, viewed as, 130
Buhler, Charlotte
values in therapy, 56–57

Bultmann, R., 167
Bunam, Simcha, 116
Burns, D., 153

C

Cabasilas, N., 199–200
Cairo, 161
"Calling"
  either renumerative or unrenumerative, 447
  peer-group counseling, a true, 451
  professional leadership in psychotherapy, a true, 451
  prompting to particular act, duty or profession, 447
Calling of the Christian
  to the monastic vs. the secular life, 200
Calling, sense of
  psychotherapist's, 435, 436
  strong motivation in "helping" professions, 447
Calvinism (see Puritanism)
Calvin, J., 200
Cambray, Archbishop of
  236, 239–242, esp. as grandfather figure, 241
Cambray, France, 236, 241
Cancer patients, terminal
  use of mystical experience(s) in preparation for death, 308–309
Cannibalism
  Momism as, 226
  witches', 243
Cards, consultation of
  reliance on, in psychic counseling, 255
"Care of souls" (iatros tes psuches)
  the Shepherd's concern, 56
Carnality, sin of, 176
Carson, Rachel, 444
Catharsis
  emotional release in Jewish life through ceremonials and Holy Days, 115–116
  group experience, in observance of Jewish rituals, 115
  in Bioenergetics, 271
  in Encounter groups, 269, 271
  Mormon experience of forgiveness at "fast and testimony" meetings, 102
  primitive therapeutic method, 229
  through confession, 229
Catholic authorities
  opinion of
    on Jeanne Fery case, 236
Catholic tradition in counseling
  updated to cover various areas of counseling today, 15

Catholicism
  Cuban, 320–329 passim
Cautery (Kayy)
  magical treatment method in the Near East, 160
Centering, personal
  to stress complete interrelation of mind, spirit and body in the individual, 277
Ceremonial life
  in Judaism, 110, 114
  participation in, 199
  religious observance(s) and obsessive act(s) parallels between, 114
  symbolic of group philosophy, 114
Ceremony
  (see also Ritual)
  on patient's admittance to shrine hospital, Gold Coast, 244
Ceylon, 175
Chai, Ch'u, 180–194
Chai, Winberg, 180–194
Chang, C. C., 136
Chanukah (see Hannukah)
Chaos, primal
  mystic's reality going back to time before the Creation of the world, 317
Charcot, Jean Martin
  and neuroses, 448
Charity
  emphasized in Judaeo-Christian moral action, not in Hindu religion, 169
  not encouraged in Christian Science, 84
"Charity"
  not entered in index of Christian Science Manual, 84
Charity,
  or compassion
    in Buddhism, Mahayana, 128
    in Mormon life, 100–101
    represented in many-armed Buddha(s), 128 (see also Avalokita)
Charms
  to ward off evil spirit(s), 160
Chassidim, the 116
Chien (insight)
  in Chinese Zen, 137
Chih (wisdom), 188
Child
  confirmation after baptism, in the Eastern Orthodox Church, 207 (see also Chrismation)
  in Jewish family, 112–113
  inclusion of, in the (Eastern Orthodox Church), 204, 206–209, 220
  independence from parents, 208

influenced by his environment (the liturgy) and his community (the Church body) for good, 209–210
protected by his patron saint (after whom he is named), 207–208
received as church member and communicant, in the Eastern Orthodox Church, 207, 208–209
Childhood
unhappiness in, 237
insight, gained from psychoanalysis, into the client's relevant experiences during, 309
incidents from patient's, projected on analyst during therapy, 309
Western psychiatrist's fascination with early, 226
bringing up our, xii
Koran's legal provisions on behalf of, 157
psychiatric help to, as a Mormon social service, 101
China
Buddhism in, 125, 126
land of Confucianism, 183
Zen in, 246–247
Chinese, early
basic religious beliefs of, 180–181
Chinese political order, ancient
sanctioned by divine power, 182
Chinese ritual practices
less emphasized in Chou period, 182
Chinese thought
continuous tradition of aiming at the highest type of life, 194
ethical, basically, with later stress on self-fulfillment 193–194
humanism and naturalism, blend of, 193
Chiropractor(s)
psychic counselors' contact with, 256
Chisholm, Brock
example of dedicated modern "prophet," 443
Chou dynasty
Chinese kings, 181
Chou kings, carrying out Mandate, 181–182
Chrismation
in the Eastern Orthodox Church, 207
Christ
as Reality or Spirit to which mystic gives himself, 312, 313
as Redeemer, 93
as Savior, 93
in Adventist theology, 93–95
in man's redemption, 91
victory over Death, 213

Christ-centered life
both *in* the world and withdrawn from "the world" (monastic), 200
Christ, divinity of
denied by Mary Baker Eddy and Christian Science, 72
Christ, the Inward
comparison of religious motivation and the new therapies, 272–274
in the reformed individual, 269
(The) Christian
as psychotherapist, 56
Christian
definition of a, from Evangelical viewpoint, 58
Christian ideas
at Peyote meeting(s), 298
"Christian" in Christian Science,
interpreted as religious doctrine—absolute, perfect, final, 72–73
Christian Science
"absolute consciousness of good," level of treatment, 80
"Affirmation and denial," 79
"argument," level of treatment, 80
as a religion, 73–74
as a system of healing, 73, 75–76
attitude toward mental illness, 75
attitude toward social ills, 83–84
basic theological principles, 73
care of body, 74
critical appraisal of, 72–86
denial of pain or suffering, 80
Eddy, Mary Baker, influence of (*see* main entry)
examples of type of healing in, 76
feminine bias in, 77
healing of ills, sins, fears and wants, 73
helping new members, 78
"Mental and silent argument," 79
no social gatherings outside of church services, 84
practitioners, 76–80
number of, 77
readers, 77 (*see also* Teachers, *below*)
spiritual nature of man in, 74
teachers, 76–77
"wholeness" of man, 74
Christian Science Journal, esp. 82
Christian, the new
and the "Wider Vision" of the Person of God, 274
Christian view of God and man
psychologist's need for a formulation of the, 61

Christians, first
  Resurrection faith, impact of, 268
Christianity
  among great religious, 117
  and healing, 49
  emphasizing righteousness and self-sacrifice, 170
  in Muslim mysticism, 159
  liberal versus conservative, in college students' background, 390–395
  Pfister's defense of, 61
  Primitive, 451
  revivalistic trend in, 450
  small groups movement in early, 450
Chrysostom, Saint, 205
Chuang Tzu
  one to the books of Taoist thought, 191–192, 193
Chung (conscientiousness)
  state of being completely honest with one's self; part of Jen, 184–185
Chung Yung
  Doctrine of the Mean, 183
Church affiliation
  individual steered away from, 90
Church of Christ, Scientist (*see* Christian Science), 72–88
Church of Jesus Christ of Latter Day Saints, 98–107
  (*see also* Mormonism *and* related topics)
  Mormon leaders
    able to endure "all things," 99
    blessed with the "gift of discernment," 100
    divinely authorized, 99
    inspired in guiding Church affairs, 99
  Mormon programs and services
    adoption services, 100
    blessing of the sick, Mormon leaders', 100
    foster home care, 100
    guidance services, 99, 104
    hospital system, 101
    mentally ill, ministry to, 100
    pre-baptism interviews, Bishop's, 100
    pre-marriage counseling, 100
    recreational activities, providing, 99
    Relief Society, Mormon women's auxiliary, 101
    religious education and leadership training, 98, 102
    social service agencies, Latter-Day Saints, 100
    visits in homes, Bishop's, 100
    welfare agency, 100–101
  Mormon values and beliefs
    devotion to "light and truth" of God, 99
    "Doing good" to all men, 99–100
    Eternal life, individual goal of, 98
    Exaltation, goal of personal, 98, 101, 105
      (*see below* Man, perfectibility of)
    God-like, becoming more, 98 (*see below* Man, perfectibility of)
    "Gospel life" as set forth in the Bible and Mormon scriptures, 98, 105
    humility, Christlike, 98–99
    love of God and neighbor, 98
    man, perfectibility of, 98, 105
    obedience to teaching of Church leaders, 98
  Mormon way of life
    compassionate service, 99
    family life, father's leadership in, 99
    fast and testimony, monthly encounter, 102
    "Gospel life," joy in, 98–99
    identification with fellow Church members, a strong feeling of, 102
    meetings, frequent attendance to, 99
    prayer and inspiration, 99
Church of the Master, 257
Church, the
  as God's house, 204
  as Heaven on earth, 204
  as one channel for healing powers, 216
  as the redeemed community in Orthodox belief, 202
Church, pastoral function of the
  in Orthodox belief, 206, 207–208, 209, 210–211, 212–213
Church, Roman Catholic, 237
Church(es) (*see under* individual denomination *or* belief system)
Circumcision, 114
"Claims"
  of patient to the (Christian Science) practitioner, 75, 79
Clairaudience
  definition of, 255
Clairvoyance
  definition of, 255
Clement, Paul W., 417–426
Clergy, members of the
  psychic counselors as ordained, but inactive, 256–257
  psychic counselors' contact with, 256
Clergymen as therapists
  often very effective, 284
  working within own religious framework rather than scientific one of psychotherapy, 284

Client
  attitude(s) of, 21–24
  "innerview" of, 23
  self-reorganization, 23–24
  therapist's relationship with the, 428
Client (s)
  available for psychic ounseling, 254
  emotionally distraught, 254, 260
  need for therapy in population at large, 254
Client-therapist relationship, 248–249, 251–252
Cline, Victor B., 106, 107
Clinebell, Howard, 32, 45
Clinical Pastoral Education movement 52–53
Collaboration, a case of
  between indigenous tribal methods of healing and psychotherapy, 284–290
  evaluated by family in its own cultural setting, 286
  exorcism, ritual of, 290
  girl's behavior at home, 288
  girl's behavior at school, 288
  girl's illness described, 286–289
  healer working with therapist, therapist with indigenous healer, in mutual support, 285
  integrity of both systems upheld, 293–294
  outcome, 290
  patient's history, 286–290
  patient's symptoms, 284, 287–290
  psychiatrist's interpretation, 290–291
  psychodynamic observation, 291–294
Commandments
  fulfillment of, basic to Jewish faith, 109
  commandment, fourth, 92
Commandments, The Ten, 91–92
Commandments, The Ten
  church's role regarding, 91
  fulfilled in love through Christ, 95
  guide in relationships, 91–92
  importance in the Seventh-Day Adventist Church, 95
Commitment
  depth of, experienced by the Mormon believer, 103
Common-sense advice, 259, 261
Communal living, 389
Communion
  (see also Eucharist, the)
  feeling of, at Peyote meeting(s), 300–301, 302–303, 305
  with God, in Peyote cult, 296
  as high point of the church service, in the Eastern Orthodox Church, 205
Communities
  lack of positive, contemporary, xiii

Community
  little emphasis on, in Christian Science, 83–85
  psychic counselor's contacts with the, 256, 258
  re-integration into, aided by the group, 231
Community care of the mentally disturbed
  movement toward, in the Western world, 228–229
Community, Church
  in Orthodox belief, 206, 207–208
  salvation of the individual within the according to Orthodox belief, 202–203
Community, sense of
  in fellow seekers for Truth, 274
  heightened for alienated patient, if contacts are multiplied, 449
  in profession of psychotherapy, 449
  "prophetic" psychotherapist's, 445
  therapeutic prophet's, 445
  vital need of Encounter participants, 279–280
Community, the "healing"
  effect on patient, 64
Community, the redeemed
  in Orthodox belief, 202
Competitiveness, morbid
  setback in individual's full functioning, 138
Compulsion (s)
  cases of, in native African treatment centers, 246
Condolences, formal presentation of
  as social obligation, 163
Conduct
  "right," in Buddhism, 121, 122
"Cone of Authority"
  concept in primitive therapy, 311–313
Confessing one's "sins"
  in psychotherapy, 229
Confession
  before small groups, in early Christian Church, 451
  importance of, in psychotherapy, 229
  patient's recovery after, 244
  private or sealed, 451
  psychotherapeutic value of, 229
  therapy on the Gold Cost, 244
  treatment for loss of soul, 229
  use of, in group participation to allay fears, 231
Confession, sacrament of
  (see also Forgiveness)
  as a healing of the soul, 213
  forgiveness from one's neighbors required first of all, 212
  in the Eastern Orthodox Church, 212–213

Confessor
  in the Eastern Orthodox Church
    layman at times consulted first, 213
    priest not necessarily from the confessant's parish, 213
Conflict, interpersonal
  in Encounter groups, 269, 280–282
Confucius, 132
  accepting of Fate, as long as one did his best in life, 185
  cultivated mind, 184
  ethical system centering about man and man's duties to other men, 183–187 *passim*
  high moral tone of life, 187
  life ideal of, 183–187
  role of Jen in thought and experience, 184–185
  testing way of life (his *tao*) during travels, 185
  "this-worldly" emphasis in his thought, 184
Confucianism, 183–190
Confucianism
  afterlife, silence on the, 183
  among great religions, 117
  ceremonial and sacrificial practices, observed within, 183
  changes in, historical, 183–184
  ethical and political, stress on the, 183
  Heaven, reverence of (*see* T'ien), 183
  humanistic, 190
  influence of Mencius on, esp. 190
  lofty intellectual ideals set forth, but not as a religious system, 183
  moral values, stresson, 183
  not popular with Taoism
    ethical programs and man-directed action, called "against Nature," 192
  origins and influence defined, 183–184
  religious comfort derived from, 183
  service to others and self-cultivation encouraged, 187
  still dominant in Chinese thought today, 183
Congregation
  composed of living and of departed saints, 205
"Congruence" (See Rogers, Carl), 38
Conscience, 67–68
  as internalized standard, 225, 227
"Conscious" and "unconscious"
  psychological terms, 38 (*see also* other terms and phrases)
Consciousness
  where we are, ix, xii
Conservative-Evangelical Christian
  a definition, 57–58

Conservative Protestantism (*see also* Seventh-Day Adventist Church)
Consolation after death, 301–302
Consummation, spiritual
  in Hindu meditation, 169–170
  in Tantric tradition, 177
Contact with others, 433
Contemplation
  Chinese Zen attitude toward, 135
  Hindu ideal, 170
  more important than action, in Hindu belief, 170
  stages in Hindu sannyasin's seeking, 278
  Zen, 247–248
Contemplative, Hindu
  mystical experience of, 179
Continuity, sense of
  in small towns, turn-of-the-century (twentieth), ix, xi
Control
  central requirement for Hindu to escape the travail of rebirth, 174
  important in Yoga, 174
  in ritualistic copulation, 177 (*see also* Tantrism)
  in Tantric ritual of the Five M's, 176
  of mind, in Hindu wishing to be liberated from rebirth, 170, 171, 174
Convention
  use of five forbidden elements to break down, 176–177
Conversion
  basic concept, 89–90
  psychological interpretation of, 63
  "spiritual leap," in therapy, with awareness from patient and therapist, 453
Conversion after despair, 44
Conze, E., 127, 131, 154
Cooperation (*synergeia*) with God, man's in Orthodox belief, 200
Copulation, ritualistic
  Canaanites', 440
  Maithuna, 176–177 (*see also* Five M's)
Corey, Arthur, 79
"Cosmetic image"
  of happy family, 443
Counsel
  as first act of prudence, 18
Counseling
  and the normal personality, 16
  attitude of acceptance in, 25
  between healer and patient, 211–212
  definition of, 18
  during penance, 212–213
  in Christian Science "treatment," 78–80
  in Roman Catholicism, 15–24

informal character of, 17
objectivity in, 21
process and dialogue, 18-24
related to learning, 24-27
relationship between client and counselor (*see also* Counselor)
relationship between client and counselor, 21-23, 24
steps in, 24
Counseling, pastoral
of interest to churchmen today, 446
Counseling, psychic
(*see also* Counselor(s), *psychic*)
consultation regarding client's present problems, 256, 259-260
giving a spiritual reading, 255
lack of established doctrine in, 254, 256
methods used, 254-256, 259-260
occult, "tuning in" to the, 255
prediction of coming events, 256
questioning regarding client's childhood traumas and past experiences, 255-256
sample case studies, 256, 257-258, 259-260, 261-264, 264-265
treatment in, 260-265
types of client usually reached
an occasional skeptic or a secretive individual, 260
anxious or fearful, 254
disturbed individuals suffering from hallucinations, anxiety, or insomnia, 260
hard-core faithful, who are "seekers" after mystic truth and what the practitioner will reveal, 260
individuals caught up in a life crisis, 260
insecure or suicidal individuals
persons about to make a decision, 260
psychotic or depressed individuals, 254
the openminded and sympathetic, 260
victims of idle curiosity and publicity, 260
Counseling, spiritual
Arab psychiatrists' reliance on intuitional approach, 165
segment of the population interested in, 259
Counselor
characteristics of a good, 20-23
cleansed or "scrubbed" for counseling session, 21-22
reasoning ability or "power," 22-24
response from, 23-24
self-giving of, 22-24
Counselors, psychic
availability as therapists to unreached people, 266
background and training, 256
compared in effectiveness to psychotherapists, 265-267
eclectic in knowledge and approach, 255, 257
number of, 266
peer relationships
non-supportive of one another's counseling efforts, 256, 257
peer relationships among
professional rivalry, 256
qualifications and characteristics
self-confident, 259
survey of services overdue in the community, 266
Counselor(s), psychic
core concepts of
acceptance of client's psychic resources, 255
acceptance of mystic teachings as basis of practice, 255
basic value of "reading" the client, his past, present and future, 255-256
benevolent aim as being basic to their practice, 257
claim to educational, social and professional advantages to bolster status, 256-257
fee payment required for service rendered, as in any other profession, 256, 257
obligation to advise client or to suggest solutions to his problems, 255
positive gains from intense sense awareness and mystic divination, 255-256
reliance on client's psychic (or God-given) abilities and talents, 255
reliance on extrasensory perception, 255
utilization of information from drift of conversation with client, 256
lack of central professional organization, 254, 256
medium, 254, 255
need for support within the community, 267
non-professional, 254-257
principles and techniques, 254-257
acceptance of psychic powers, in practitioner *and* client, as basically good, 255
claims backed by empirical evidence rather than system or theory, 255
constructive use of the occult as "God-given," 255
physical reactions in practitioner influencing message or solution offered client, 255
practitioner's ability viewed as God-given; development or happening as a "mark of divine favor," 255

refutation of the existence of any evil or alien influence in psychic phenomena, 255
reliance on trancelike states (*see also* Trance), 255
publicity, 258–259
qualifications and characteristics
charismatic, with strong personalities, 256
often possessing theatrical or sales background, 256
tolerant of clients' shortcomings and transgressions, 256
upholders of conventional morality, 256
reader, 254, 258–259
spiritual advisor, 254
women practitioners, percentage of, 256
Cox, Harvey, 35, 45
Cox Richard H., xix–xx, 2–12
Craniopathy, use of, by psychic counselors, 263
Creation
liberal Protestant view of the, 36
Creation, God's
man's share in, 196–197
Creature(s), God's
love for, 199
Crisis theology
esp. 43–44
Crisp, Stephen, 272
Cross, the
shown empty (in the Orthodox Church), 201
shown with Christ crucified (in the West), 219
symbol of the Christian believer's four-way relationship, 202
Crystal ball(s)
reliance on, in psychic counseling, 255
Cult(s)
Cuban, with Catholic overtones, 319–320, 321–322, 324–326, 328–329 *see* Santeria)
fertility, Canaanites,' 440
Cultural attitudes
important in therapy, 229–230
Culture
absorption with one's, 134
liberation from bondage to one's, 138
mono-valued, x
Culture context
conditioning of patient in, 251–252
therapist's understanding and dominance of, 250
Culture, primitive
faith and healing in, 225–236
Cumbres, New Hampshire, 278–279, 283

Cure
of illness, among Peyote beliefs, 296
Curran, Charles A., 15–31, 67

D

Dai, Bingham, 118, 132–141
Dakin, Edwin, 80–81
Damascus, 161
Daughter
mother-dominated, 395–396
Daughter-parents relationship, Jewish, 113
David, 113
Davis, Adelle, 444
Davis, Will B., 80
Death
beyond control; source of fear, 6
Bodhisattva liberating believer from the terrors of, 127
Christ's victory over, 213
in Buddhist teaching, 122, 127
in the Eastern Orthodox Church, 213
Jewish ritual following, 114–115
man not finally overcome by, 216–217
outlook on, in the Estern Orthodox Church, 219
the risen Christ overcoming, 201–202
threat to our "wholeness," 6
sense of tragedy regarding, in the Eastern Orthodox Church, 217
Debongnie, P., 236, 252
Dedication
of a life to enrich other lives, 433
Deer park
location of Gautama's early conversions, 120, 121
Deficiency, enzyme
factor in loss of psychological equilibrium, 228
Deification in Christ, of the believer
in Orthodox belief, 202
Deities, ancestral
causing insanity, 225
Deities, Chinese
earth, 180
grain, 180
moon, 180
mountains, sacred, 180
objects of Nature as, 180
Deities, Chinese
rain, of the, 180
rivers, sacred, 180
stars, 180
sun god, 180
Supreme Deity (the Lord-on-High), 180–181
(*see Ti*)

wind, of the, 180
Deities, heavenly and earthly, in Chinese religion, 180–181
Deity, shrine
　doctor's appeal to the, in treatment of Gold Coast patient(s), 244
Delusion
　extinction of, in Nirvana, 146, 150
Dementia, senile, 162
Democracy
　declared but not practiced, 405
Demon
　believed to help release Hindu individual from Karma, 171–172
Demonstration
　in Christian Science, 75
Denial, psychological
　as defense mechanism against pain and threats to the ego, 80
Dependency needs, man's
　limitations of religion based on, 109
Dependency needs, man's
　limitations of religion based on, 109
Depression
　cases of, in native African treatment centers, 246
Depression, feelings of
　patient's identification of, in others, 454–455
Deprivation, child's
　as cause of psychic ills, 226
Desire
　end of, as goal of Buddhist "Way," 121, 122
Despair, xv
　"dipping down" to the bottom, 43–44
Destructive elements in man
　judgment of, 39
Detachment, professional
　thought less important than feeling of community and personal helpfulness, 437
Devil (*see* Satan), x, 414
Devil, the
　ceremony of driving out, in (Eastern Orthodox) baptism, 207
　renunciation of the powers of, in (Eastern Orthodox) baptism
(The) Devil, or personification of evil
　in Mary Baker Eddy's experience, 81–84
Devil(s)
　possession by, 236, 237–238, 239, 240, 241–242
Dharma (*see* Hinduism)
Dharma (the Way)
　Buddha's teaching(s) regarding, 120, 122, 124, 127, 144, 152
Dharmakaya (Body of Truth), Buddha as
Diagnoses, minister's vs. psychiatrist's, 9–10

Diagnosis
　understood as dispelling patient's fears, 230–231
Diagnosis, spiritual
　in Christian Science practice, 78
Dilthey, 35
Dimension, experiential
　seen in patient's responsiveness to the possibilities of living, 454
Discipline
　asceticism, 119
　cf. science (*knowing*) to, 30–31
　liberation from master, in Zen, 248
Disciple-master relationship
　compared to Client-therapist relationship, 248–249
　in Zen, 248–249
Discovery and overcoming of self
　Siddhartha's, 460
Discussion, doctrinal
　discouraged in Christian Science circles, 83–84
Disorders, behavior
　explanation of, 225
　in primitive society, 225
Disorders, personality
　underlying causes of, 447 ff.
Dissociation, psychological, 286
Dissonance, cognitive, x
Distance
　ideal attained by psychotherapist in order to have his message heard, 445
Disturbed individual(s)
　accepted in the community, 228–229
　thought to be divinely appointed, 228
Doctor
　(*also see* Healer)
　appeal to local (shrine) deity, in treatment of patient(s), 244
　patient's relationship with, in Africa, 243, 244–245, 246
　power of, in Gold Coast shrine hospital, 244
　skill(s) of native African, 243, 244–245, 246
Doctrine
　Seventh-Day Adventist Church, 90–96, esp. 91
Doctrine and Covenants, 99
Doctrine, fundamental Christian
　basic Christian Science beliefs compared to, 72–73
Dogma, submission to
　religious leader's traditional perspective, 436
Doubt
　stage in Sufism, 159
　freeing patient from, in psychotherapy, 247

Doubt regarding potential of self
  freedom from, at first stage of Nirvana, 147
Draper, Edgar, 369–387
Dream analysis
  clues in patient's non-verbal behavior, 140
  Freud's contribution to psychotherapy, 133
  in Zen meditation, 140
Drug subculture, 389
Drug taking
  in Peyote worship, 296, 299–300, 302, 303–304, esp. mescaline dosage, 299
Duality of man
  dramatized in the sacraments, 206–207, 209
  emphasized in Orthodox belief, 206, 209
  Manichean belief, 219
Dualism
  in the self-in-the-presence-of-God experiences of the mystic, 308
Dukkha
  Theravadin word for anxiety, 122, 147
Duvall, Sylvanua M., 403–416
Dyani Buddhas (contemplative), 124, 125

E

Earth
  as Mother (in Peyote cult), 296
Easter celebration
  joyousness of, 201–202
  midnight service in Eastern Orthodox Church, 202
Eastern mystics
  wisdom from, 459
Eastern Orthodox Church (*see* Orthodox Church, Eastern)
Ecology, 439–440
Ecology movement
  a "now" trend, xii
Ecstasy
  being one with one's Maker, 316
  measuring scale of, in Hindu meditation, 175
  experience of mystical
    in Eastern Orthodox liturgy, 205
Ecumenical representation
  among viewpoints sampled, xix
Eddy, Mary Baker, 72, 73, 77–78, 79, 80–84, 85, 86
Education
  in Seventh-Day Adventist Church program 95
Education, professional
  dehumanizing abuses and tendencies, 445
Effort
  "right," in Buddhism, 121, 122

Ego
  "egoless," in Japanese Zen, 134
  liberation from the, in Zen Buddhism, 138
  mastering the forces of the superego and the id, 226
  not intended to be "master of the body," 275
  role of the, 226
  "spirit" likened to, 265–266
Ego-defense
  by way of joining Santeria, 329
Ego-ideal
  compared to God's image in man, 93–94
  twentieth century, x, xiv
Ego-preoccupation
  block in patient's therapy, 134
  blocking Zen meditation, 134
  lessened progressively in effective psychotherapy, 138
  liberation from, as first step to meditation, 134
  setback in individual's full functioning, 138
  source of man's suffering, 134
Ego-strivings
  preventing patient's adaptation and flexibility, 134
Ego-striving (s)
  expressed by patient in therapy, 135
  renounced or suppressed by Zen monk, in meditation, 135
Egoism
  philosophy in Taoism, having the individual and his self-concerns as basis, 191
Egypt, 444
Eightfold Path, the holy, 121, 122
Elijah, 440
Eliot, Sir Charles, 123, 125
Elisha, 440
Ellis, A., 57
El-Mahi, T., 161–163, 166
Emaciation
  case history (*see* Akua)
Emergence of "self-image"
  versus repressed feelings, 38
Emotion (s)
  in conflict with reason, 18
  intensity of, in closely-knit communities, 227
Encounter
  abuses widespread, 271
  contrasted to outlook of Hindu mystics, 278 (*see also* Zen)
  esperiencing new modes and new feelings, 271
  ideal group, description of, 279
  in religious terms, 268–269, 277, 279–282, 283

lack of guidance and corrective tradition in, 279
new therapy, 268, 271, 277
personal experience (s) of emotional release in, 269, 270–271, 280–282
with Quaker overtones, example of, 280–282
Encounter, 268 ff. (*see also* Encounter groups *and* Encounter, open)
Encounter group (s)
spontaneity of members' reactions, 269
too many high-flown theories, 443
Encounter, open
mystical moments in, 277
philosophy of, 277
spiritual element foremost, 277
Encounter workshops
behavioral limits imposed, 279
Encounters, therapeutic
called to mind in therapy to mark "the sacredness of all experience," 455
Enlightened man
definition of, 138
"Enlightened One"
Buddha who marked Path for his followers, 142, 143 (*see* Gautama)
Enlightenment
element (s) of genuine, 136
goal of Zen, 137
levels of, in Zen, 278
short cuts to, not usually countenanced in Zen, 137
time factor involvtd, in Zen, 137–138
Enlightenment,
Night of
Gautama's (Buddha's) experience, 120
under the Bodhi tree, 120
Enthusiasm, spiritual
during English Reformation, 268–269, 273
occurring in periods of religious ferment, 268
Enstasy, yogic, 177, 179
Environment, alleged insensitivity to
in psychotics, 228
Envy
handicap to individual's adjustment in society, 134
source of "evil eye," 227
Erikson, Erik, 38, 49–50, 112, 116, 448
Esalen Institute, 279, 280
Esau Truman G., 388–402
Escape
Indian religion (s) in, 119
Moksha, in Buddhism, 119
E.S.P. (*see* Extrasensory perception)
Essence, cosmic, 178–179

Esterson, Aaron, 443
Eternal life vs. temporal life
in Orthodox belief, both worlds together, 206
Ethic, Protestant
effect on Hinduism, 168, 176
limitations of, in later Hindu practice, 173
Ethical standards encouraged in Chinese kings, 182
Ethics
and men's "codes," 403, 410
Christian, 404–409
connection with psychotherapy, 117
emphasis on, in Judaism, 108–109, 111–113, 114
in Mahayana Buddhism, 130
of Buddhism, for laymen, 152
some basic principles, 412–414
stressed in Mahayana Buddhism, 130
Ethic of Love, 39–40
Ethnic group (s)
practices of, in psychic counseling, 255
Eucharist, the
as high point of the Eastern Orthodox liturgy, 205
definition of, 220
Evangeligal defined, 58–59
Evans, Harrison S., 98–97
Evil
(*see also* Sin)
actions (evil karma) weighing down the soul, 148
Buddhist symbolic idea of, 148
Christ's victory over the forces of, 201–202
defilement, Indian notion of, as opposed to purity, 148
denounced by Hebrew prophets, 440–441, 442–443
denounced by today's "prophets," 441, 442–443, 444
felt and seen sensitively, by therapist, 442, 445–446
not a reality in Christian Science doctrine, 73
performance of bad actions, in one life, carried to some future life, according to Hindu belief, 170, 171
prophet's refusal to excuse or ignore, 442
reality to most religions, 10
struggle of Good with, 163
"Evil eye," the
effect of, on the individual, 227
protection of children from, 228
"Evil wish," undoing an
magical treatment method in the Near East, 160–161

Exaltation
   goal of Mormon Gospel of life, 101, 105–106
   emotional role in primitive cults; effective also in psychotherapy, 235
Exemplar, therapeutic
   role model of "authentic existence," 441
Exiles, Cuban
   statistics and prospects, 319, 320–322, 329
Existence, authentic (see Exemplar, therapeutic)
Existential analysis, 249
Existentialism
   influence on psychotherapy, 34
   anguish and uncertainty in the human predicament, 168, 179
Exomologesis, 451
Exorcism, 236, 239–240, 241, 242–243
   (see also Spirits, casting out of)
   during baptism, according to Orthodox practice, 207
   Eastern Orthodox rites of, 211–212
   in Buddhist groups, 154–155
   ritual of, paralleling Western psychotherapeutic treatment, 292–294
   ritual used to extract supposed spirit intrusion, 229, 290
   special gift for, in chosen Eastern Orthodox priests, 211–212
Exorcist(s)
   called on by village Buddhists, 144
Experience
   a psychotherapist's deepening of, 433
Experience, mystical
   emerging often *outside* established religion(s), 268
   emphasis on, in Hinduism, 179
   in open encounter, after hostility has been worked out, 277
   of oneness with God, 179
   healing rooted in, 216
Extrasensory perception, 255
Extreme Unction, 220–221
Extrovertive mystical state
   description of, 308
Ezekiel, 440

F

Faith
   basic factor in psychotherapy, 50
   justification by, 92
   man's need to believe and to worship, 4
   pathway of, in Mahayana Buddhism, 130
   total commitment to religious answer(s), 7

Faith, traditional
   threatened by analysis of unconscious motivations, 33
Faith and healing, primitive
   influence on modern psychiatry, 225–236
Faith, individual's
   strengthened through therapy, 90
Faith healing, in Mormon Church, 100
Faith, role of
   in coping with life's problems, 89
Fall, consequence of the, 93
False prophecy
   in contemporary psychotherapy, 443
Family
   college contacts as substitute for, 390–391
   role of the, 321–322
Family life
   Jewish emphasis on, 111–113
   Mormon, 99
   nurturing individual's value system, 111, 113
   personal relationships within Jewish family unit, 111–113
   solid base for survival of Jewish people, 111
   "togetherness" emphasized, in Jewish home, 111–112
Family member(s), individual
   "sacrificed" to mental hospital to preserve appearances, 443 (see "Cosmetic image")
Family structure, German
   Auschwitz predictable as outcome, 443
"Fast and testimony" meetings, in Mormonism, 102
Fasting
   for reconciliation with God, 215
   in Islam, 157
   in the Eastern Orthodox Church, 212, 214–215
     exception, 221
   in the practice of healing, 211
   religious significance of, 215
   to aid man's reconciliation with God, 212
   to show humility toward nature, 215
Fate
   acceptance of, in Jen, 186
   according to Confucius, 185
Father
   importance of relationship with child, psychologically, 112
   role of, in Jewish family life, 112–113
Father-daughter relationship
   Saint Theresa's story, 314
Father figure
   therapist as, in psychoanalytic and therapeutic process, 112

Father-son relationship
  Abraham-Isaac, 112–113
  David mourning for Absalom, 113
  Hebrew culture, in, 112–113
Fear
  anxiety-induced, in patient, 251
  caused by depletion of vital substance, 228
  feedback of, in anxiety cases, 251
  in anxiety patients
    handling of, 251
  in patient's associates
    effect on patient, 251
  of counseling or of seeking therapeutic help, 103
  patient's, in psychotic break, 251
Fear of loving and being loved
  as a root cause of psychic illness, 218
Fear (s)
  influences in Mary Baker Eddy's life, 80–81
Fear (s) and inhibitions
  source of man's suffering, 134
Fear (s), neurotic
  freeing patient from, 247
Federn, 138
Fees
  for treatment by Christian Science practitioners, 77–78
  legality of, in psychic counseling, 256
  non-payment of, in psychic counseling field, 258
  psyment of
    in psychic counseling, 257, 258, 260, 264
Fell, Margaret, 270
Fenichel, Otto, 456
Fery Jeanne
  admitted to Archbishop for pastoral counseling 239–242
  case study, 236–243
  confessions of, 236, 242, 252
  consenting to the Devil, 237–238
  exorcism sessions, 239–240, 241, 242–243
  prayers and blessings, effect of, 239, 240, 241, 242–243
  renouncement of devils 240–241, 242
  signing pact with the Devil, 237
  spiritual recovery, 242
  tempted and "possessed" by the Devil, 237–239, 241–242
  testimony, later, 238, 242
  treatment, based on religious principles, 242–243
  under physician's care, 239–240, 241
Feud (s), village
  information regarding, for patient admittance to Gold Coast hospital (s), 244

Field, M. J., 244–245, 252
"Final cause" *versus* "efficient cause," discussion of, 60
Fingarette, H.,138, 155
"First thought"
  compared to "free association," 136
  in Zen meditation, 139 (*see also* Free Association)
Five M's (*see* Mada; Maithuna; Mamsa; Matsya; and Mudra)
Five M's, 176–177
Food, forbidden in Hindu diet
  mada (wine); *mamsa* (meat); *matsya* (fish); and *mudra*, 176 (*see also* Five M's)
Forgiveness (*see also* Penance)
  according to Orthodox belief
    granted by God, not the confessor, 212
  Christ's gift, 94
  humility toward nature, 215
  of early invaders, by American Indians, 297
  of sins, in Peyote cult, 296
  repentance toward the poor, 215
  service of, before Lent (in the Eastern Orthodox Church), 215
Forgiveness, asking for
  from the "community," 212
Forgiveness, man's search for
  from fellow men first, then from God, 109–110
Forgiveness-of-sins
  doctrine explained, 58
"Forgiveness" vs. "acceptance," 9
Formalism
  attitude toward religion, 399
Fortune telling
  legal difficulties regarding, 256
Four Books
  holy scriptures of the Chinese people, 183
Four-way relationship of Eastern Orthodox believer with God, Self, Neighbor, and Nature, 218
Fox, George, 270, 272
Fragmentation
  man's state of, 4, 7–8
  offering and finding solution(s) to, 4
  the ultimate pain, 6
Frankl, Viktor, 51, 53, 439
Fraud, danger of
  in psychic counseling, 256
Free association
  basic in Zen philosophy, 133
  "first-thought" principle, from Zen, 139

Freud's contribution to psychotherapy, 133
in Zen mediation, 139-140
Freedom
Freud's defense of religious, 109
in Zen (see Zen ideals)
perfecting of individual's, at third stage of Nirvana, 147
Zen leading to, 133-134
Freedom, man's
according to Orthodox belief, 198, 200
in Orthodox Church worship, 203-206,
Freud, Sigmund, xiii, 8, 57, 133, 168, 178
dream analysis in therapy, 133
Ego and Id, prototypes of, in early Muslim culture, 163
founder of modern psychotherapy, 133
founder of psychoanalysis, 110
free association in therapy, 133
Jewish mystical tradition, connection with 439
"mésalliance with agnostic forces," 61
religion, 109, 114, 116
Friend
defined, especially in counseling field, 452
necessity for someone to confide in, 116
(see Quakers)
Friendship
need of mentally disturbed for, 452
Fright (see also Panic)
Frightening
primitive therapeutic method, 229
Full being, the peace of
after release from complexities and incertitude, 459
Fuller Seminary, Pasadena, California, 425
Fumigation
primitive therapeutic method, 229
Fundamentalism
ethical, 406
reflecting conservative Christianity, 450
revivalistic, 450
definition of, 58
Fundamentalism, religious
Freud's condemnation of, 109
Fundamentalist Churches
Seventh-Day Adventist Church, 90 ff.
Funeral rite
in the Eastern Orthodox Church, 217
Fromm, Erich, 113, 116, 274
Fromm, Erich
Old Testament Scholar, 439
Frustration
period of, in Zen, 248

Frustration(s) and anger
handicap to individual's adjustment in society, 134

G

Gadallah, F., 162, 166
Gandhi, Mahatma, 168, 172, 175, 444
Gautama Buddha, 459
Gautama
Asceticism, 119
Bodhi tree, meditation under, 120
childhood and youth, 119
Gautama
converts, first, 120
decision to share discoveries with men, 120
Dharma, or discovery of the Way, 120
Dharma (the Way), teaching about, 120
"Enlightened One," or Buddha, 118
fasting, 119
historical Buddha of the Sakya clan, 131, 143
Holy Truths, the Four, 120
karma, thoughts regarding, 119
leaving home (Great Going Forth), 119
life-death-rebirth cycle, thoughts regarding, 120
Gautama
marriage, 119
meditation under the Bodhi tree, 120
Middle Way, the Buddha's ideal, 121
mortification, bodily, 119
Night of Enlightenment, 120
paranirvana, passing into, 121
preaching of first sermon, 120-121
son, birth of a, 119
suffering, deliverance from, 120
suffering, understanding of human, 120
teaching evil doers right path, 146
teaching of, summary, 122
yoga, experience with, 119
Gautama, Siddhartha (see also Buddha)
historical Buddha of the Saka clan, 118-122, 130-131
Genesis, 112, 453-454
orderliness of God's universe, 60
Gestalt
actual experiences of, esp. 270-271, 275-276, 277
compared to psychoanalysis, 270, 271-272
definition of, 270
existentialism in, 270
individualistic, xix
new therapy, 268, 272-273, 277
rootlessness of movement, 279
shortcomings of, 278
too many high-flown theories, 443

Ghana (see Gold Coast, African)
  witchcraft in, 226
Ghosts
  fears and hallucinations, 288
  spirits of the dead in Hindu life, 144
Glasenapp, 153
Glossolalia, 273
Gnosticism
  in modern psychic counseling, 255
Goal (s)
  common, of Zen and Psychotherapy, 136
  psychotherapeutic, 40–41
  therapist's, and anticipated outcomes, 37–38
God
  a right relationship with, 39
  absolute reality of, in Christian Science, 73
  as confidant, 115
  as creative power of renewal and healing, 40
  as Father, 113
  as Healer, 59, 95
  as "Significant-Other," concerned with man, 93
  as the Man Upstairs, 335–340
  attributes of, acc. to Christian Science, 73
  concept of a personal, 91
  energies of, 219
  essence within the believer, stressed in Hinduism, 179
  faith in, according to Eastern Orthodox Church, 206, 218
  faith in, essential to Jewish belief, 109–110
  healing relationship with man, 40–41
  Kingdom of, within the believer, 216
  man's duty toward, according to Judaism, 109, 110
  man's need for, 297
  name of, added to Westernized versions of Hinduism, 173
  praise of, in Eastern Orthodox liturgy, 205
  prayer to, in Jewish faith, 110
  proof of the existence of, not essential to Hindu belief, 178–179
  punishment or reward from, 110
  service of, in Jewish faith, 109
  soul's union with, 159
  speaking through Moses, 444
  speaking through the prophets, according to Biblical account, 441
  speaking to, 297
  unity of, in Islam as in Judaism and Christianity, 156
God-Adam-Eve relationship, some parallels, 453
God (s)
  varying in form, according to the human situation and "the times," 438

God, image of
  distorted after Adam, not destroyed, 200
  intellect, mind or spirit in the, 198
  kept alive in man (according to Orthodox belief), 209
  man able to realize potential in the, 196
  man's soul in the, 197
  Orthodox fathers and theologians in disagreement regarding, 197
god-is-dead, xv
Godparents, role of
  in the Eastern Orthodox Church, 207, 208
Gold Coast, African
  confession expected of patients, 244
  early release of mental patients, 244
  native psychotherapy on, 243, 244–245, 246
  research in witchcraft, 243–245
  ritual expected of patients, 243–244
  Shrines, for use as native mental hospitals, 243–244
  treatment of patients, 244
Goldrunner, Josef, 456
Good
  affirmation of, in Christian Science texts, 86
  cultivation of the, in Jen, 185
  in man's nature, 132
  struggle between Evil and, in mental illness, 163
  the, 20
  the, performance of in one's life, 170, 171
  what is harmonious with nature, according to Mencius, 188–190
Good life, the, 169, 172, 296, 435
Goodness
  innate to man's nature, according to Mencius, 187
  of God, man a potential sharer in, 198
  of God, meditation upon, 199
Gospel
  life in the Mormon Church, 98, 105
  spreading of the, by Seventh-Day Adventist Church, 95
Gotama (see Gautama)
Grace
  God's, man able to receive, 200, 209–210
  natural objects as vehicles of, 213
  versus "works," 92
Grandmother role, 290
Great American Revival(s), 268
Great Spirit, 296
Greed
  extinction of, in Nirvana, 146, 150
Gregory of Nazianzus, 198, 109, 211
Gregory of Sinai, 200
Grief (see also Mourning)

Gros bon ange (soul)
    replaced by another, who can bring harm; primitive belief in, 226
Group
    analysis vs. individual psychotherapy, 449
    catharsis, 115
    influence, 227
    judgement, reliance on, 227
Group
    participation in healing, 231
    the, following prescribed patterns, 230
    the, pressures of, 227
    the, reliance on beliefs, convictions, of, 231
    the, role of in society, 230
    the, therapy conducted by, 231
Group therapy
    advantages over individual treatment, 449
    developed after World War II, 449
    discovered accidentally, 449
    example of effective, 264–265
    interrelatedness of members and leader, 231
    long used all over the world; only recently in Western medical practice, 230
    mutual help among peers, 449
    patients' preference for, 449
    vs. individual therapy, theories regarding, 443
Growth, human
    theory of, 117
Growth, psychological
    religion's contribution to, 89–90
Guidance
    defined, 41–42
Guidance
    human, 3–14
    in Sufism, 159 ff.
    modern man's need for, xi, xii
    systems, variety of, xix
    systems, Western, function of, 284–285
Guiding and approved principle
    the healing ministry, 46
Guilt
    Christian therapist's views on, 59 *ff.*
    cleared through subject's repentance and God's gift of forgiveness (I John 1:8-9), 68
Guilt
    collective (*see also* Catharsis)
    factor in mental illness, 225
    feelings, described, 66–67
    feelings, release of, 244
    individual made to feel responsible for his own difficulties, 229
    irremovable through scientific therapy systems, 68
    problem of, 104
    real or neurotic? discussion of, 65–68
    reduction of, after confession, 229
    relief from, 9–10
Guru, 119
    and prophet, "speaking for" deity, 437
    in Hindu yoga practice, 169, 172
    more accessible than "rabbi," 437
    not a mediator, 172
    role of, described, esp. 172
Gypsies
    lore, in psychic counseling, 255
    training of psychic counselor by, 257

H

Haiti
    sorcery in, 226
Halifax, Joan, 319–331
Hallucinations
    from Peyote use, 299
Hallucinogens
    use in Peyote belief, 296, 299–300, 302, 303–304 esp. dosage, 299
Hammes, John A., 355–369
Hannukah, 115
Happiness
    Jewish family's role in achieving, 112
    marriage as fulfillment, 112
    parents' safeguarding of children's, 113
    promises of, xix
"Happy Land"
    Paradise or *Sukhavati* of Amitabha, 126, 130
Hare Krishna, 173
Harmony
    authenticated in therapist's "seeing the whole" (*see also* Wholeness)
Hate
    analysis of, in Buddhist meditation, 153
    extinction of, in Nirvana, 146, 150
    source of "evil eye," 227
Havens, Joseph, 268–283
Healer
    native, use of, in Islam, 162–163
    personal influence of, in helping the patient, 231
    priest and therapist, 216, 273
    priest, association with supernatural, 312
Healer, indigenous
    and Western therapist compared, 235
    association with the supernatural, 311–312
    collaboration of psychotherapist with, showing mutual support, 285
    demonstration of powers early in patient therapy, 311

earning respect of psychotherapist(s) trained in Western methods, 285
in touch with "patients" who are nonaccepting of Western methods, 285
prescribing routines to the patient, 311
relying on superhuman skills and authority-prestige rather than insight therapy, 311
respected in his own society, 285
serving "patients" who are non-accepting of Western therapeutic methods, 285
viewed as comparative model of psychotherapeutic methods, 285

Healing
Buddha of, 125–126 (see Amitabha)
demonstration of, 78
differences between psychological and spiritual, 96–97
distant, 261
gift of, in Orthodox priests, 211–212
of ills, sins, fears and wants, acc. to Christian Science practice, 73
of psychosomatic ills, 75–76
powers of the Isanuse, 245, 246
psychotherapy as art of, 117

Healing, spiritual, 210
by appointed Orthodox priests, 211–212
as practiced in the Sudan, 163
Church's role in, 208–209
differences in Christian Science practice, 80
effect of Buddhist meditation, 153–154
effected through the Holy Spirit by the dedicated healer, 212
effectiveness of, in Muslim world, 162–165
examples in Christian Science practice, 76
guides and written materials provided by the Eastern Orthodox Church for, 212
in counseling during the sacrament of confession, 213
practice of, within the Peyote Church, 296–306
private nature of Christian Science practice, 80
skill-development in, 263
through confession and counseling, 213
through the Eastern Orthodox Church, 216
use of reading in Christian Science practice, 80

Healing, touch, 261

Heart, The (Al-kalb)
seat of knowledge, intuitively gained, in Sufist division of "psyche," 159

Heaven
better life *not* stressed in Hinduism, 171
ethical force in Chinese religious belief, 182
in Buddhism, 152
in Chinese worship (see *T'ien*)
reverence for, in Confucianism, 183

Heaven and man
Chinese theory of the Unity of, 183

Heaven, Tao of
in Chinese thought, reaching for the sublime, 194

Hebrew tribes
becoming a people, 442

Henotheism
as religious system suited to the human condition and "the times," 438

Heroin addiction
therapeutic freeing from, 443

Heschel, Abraham, 442–443
Hesse, Hermann, 459
Hibler, 440
Hillel, 114
Hiltner, Seward, 32, 45

Hinayana
Little Vehicle, in Buddhist movement, 143

Hindu mysticism
therapeutic effects of, 309

Hindu teaching(s)
(see also Hinduism; Meditation, Hindu; *and* Yoga)
as alternative to Western psychotherapy, 168, 178–179
man's bondage to cycle of birth and rebirth, 169
not compatible with modern therapy, 174
release from Karmic bondage, 169–172, 177
tutorship of a guru, 169, 172
withdrawal of mind from objects and from sense perceptions, 169

Hinduism, 278
(detachment)
among great religions, 117
and the human predicament, 167–179
as way of life among Indian villagers
belief in role of the supernatural—demon, witch or whimsical god—in individual's fate, 171–172
belief in witchcraft's role in individual's fate, 171–172
contemporary interpretation of, 172–173
asceticism in, 119
asceticism in, 171
authentic, uncluttered with social and ethnic complexities, 168 ff.
authoritarian character of, 174
Brahmin tradition in, 172, 173, 179
brand of simplistic, 168, 173
circle of devotees, or *engagé* Hindus, as interpreters of, 167, 170, 171–172, 177, 179

compared to Western religion(s), 170, 178–179
contemplative religion, 170, 172–173, 179
contrasting belief systems in, 171
   gnosticism *vs.* agnosticism, 171
   monism, 171
   monotheism and polytheism, 171
   theism and atheism, 171
description of modern belief system of, 172
emancipation sought through meditation and mind release, 170
existential knowledge of God in the seeker for truth, 179
fascist tendencies in, 167–168
genuine, non-Westernized, 168, 178–179
goal of
   present existence not stressed, 171
Hinduism
goal of, immediate
   redemption from rebirth, 171
grassroot vs. Westernized, 167–168, 173
indigenous, 168
indulgence, sensual, in, 171, 176–177, 178
intellectual search for Truth not stressed in, 171, 178–179
liberation from rebirth, basic belief in, 171
limitations of contemporary, 173–174
meditative religion, 171, 178–179
modern versions incompatible with psychotherapeutic ideals of Wstern sicnce, 174
monastic ideal in, 170
moral effort, not central in, 171
not a system of logic, but of belief, 172, 179
official in modern India, 173
popular, not complementary to modern therapy, 173–174
practice of yoga or meditation in, 168, 169–170
simplistic, modern brands of, 168
total-solution, exaggerated claims of, 167
use of word "God" in, 173
Yoga, as achieving freedom from rebirth, 171
engagé, narrow circle of, 167, 170, 172
percentage of at grass-roots level, 171
stadards of morality among middle-class, 175
Hippie movement, 389
History, Hebrew
   interpreting of Old Testament record of, 440
Hitler, A., 168
Holy Cause, the
   and what it can lead to, 409–410
Holy Days, Jewish
   Atonement, Day of (*see* Yom Kippur, *below*)

group catharsis, as a form of, 115
Hannukkah (Chanukah), 115
Passover, 115
Pentecost, 115
Purim, 115
Rosh-ha-Shonah, 115
Yom Kippur (Atonement), 115
Holy Ghost
   as Reality or Spirit to which mystic gives himself, 312
Holy-roller(s)
   theorizing about, 443
Holy Spirit, guidance of the
   in the Eastern Orthodox Church organization, 203
Holy Truths, the Four
   of Buddha, 120
Holy Unction, the sacrament of
   in the Eastern Orthodox Chuch, 210
Homeostasis
   in natural man, 133
Honig, Emanuel M., 108–116
Hora, Thomas, 455
Horney, K., 40, 133, 140
Hosea, 440
Hospital(s) (*see also* Treatment centers)
Hostility patient's
   drawback in therapy, 134
House Church of Apostolic Christianity, 451
Hovey, Stanton L., 106, 107
Hsing (practice)
   in Chinese Zen, 137
Hunt, Robert D., 106, 107
Hu Shih, 135, 140
Hudson, B., 159, 166
Hui-neng
   Patriarch in Zen Buddhism, 132, 135
Human nature, basic goodness of
   psychotherapy, belief held in, 133
   Zen, foundation of, 133
Human-Potential movement, 278–279, 280, 283
Human-transformation process
   viewed as resting on openness and caring, 44–45
Humanism
contemporary *versus* Christian, 363–364
in Chinese belief, emphasizing interrelationship of man and nature, 182–183
in liberal Protestant theology, 33–37
in religion
   Freud's defense of, 109
non-Christian,
   interest in Indian religion(s), 167
Humility
   psychotherapist-priest's, 456

Husband, duties of Jewish, 111
Hutchinson, K. D., 137, 140
Huxley, Aldous, 272-273
Hyder, O. Quentin, 70
Hymn (s)
 Easter (in the Eastern Orthodox Church), 201, 203
 mood music, psychic counselor's, 263
Hynotic experience
 trance-like state, in Zen, 136
Hypnotist (s)
 psychic counselors' contact with, 256
Hysteria
 cases of, in native African treatment centers, 246

I

I Ching, Book of Changes, 132
I-Thou encounter
 man-God approach, 218
Ichazo, Oscar, 279
Icon, definition of, 220
Iconostasis, 204
Icons
 in the Eastern Orthodox Church, 204-206, 207-208
Id
 age of the, 357-358
 role in individual's destiny, 226
 role in mental illness, 163
Ideal
 a psychiatrist's, 433
Identification
 of man with Christ, 94
Identification, group
 in Judaism, 114
 psychological need for, 113-114
Identification of individual
 with his surroundings, 136
Identity
 man's search for, 452
"Identity crisis"
 aided by human interrelationships, 449
 Erikson's term, 448
 more interpersonal than neurological, 448
 sociological rather than medical remedy, 448
Identity, loss of
 in contemporary patient's alienation from surrounding value system (s), 117, 178
 meaning in Hindu theology, 173, 178-179
Identity, man's
 (see also Individuality)
 within the group, 218
Idolatry
 Hebrews' liberation from, 439-440

Illnesses
 caused by outside forces, 226-227
 of "mental origin," acc. to Christian Science, 73
Illumination
 after "peak" experience in therapy, 44-45
 joint insight, in therapy, as rediscovery is effected, 453
Imago Dei (see God, image of)
Image, God's
 man created in, 94
 man restored through Christ to, 94
Immersion, in baptism
 in the Eastern Orthodox Church, 207
Immortality
 applied to the Buddha (who "never dies"), 124
 in Mahayana Buddhism, 124
 man's share in (according to Orthodox view), 196-197
Impersonal treatment
 third level of Christian Science treatment, 79-80
Inadequacy
 the psychotherapist's feelings of, 430
Incarnation (s), prior
 focus, on, in psychic counseling, 256, 263
Incest
 taboo violation with alleged deleterious effect on perpetrators of crime, 225
Incompatibility
 explained by personality theories, 227
Independence, achieving
 the client's goal, 430
India
 (see also Nepal)
 birthplace of Buddhism, 118-119
 Buddhism in 126
 current cultural situation in, 167
 puritanical tone of official culture in, 175
 twentieth century leadership in, 172
Indian music
 at Peyote meeting (s), 298
Indian religious tradition
 Western misunderstanding of, 175-176
Individual
 action of the, within the Eastern Orthodox Church, 205
 alienation of, acc. to Christian Science, 83
 control over his own destiny, 226
 each, a part of the harmonious universe, 297
 domination of the
  by stress, 226
 effect of the "evil eye" on the, 227
 failure to control own destiny, 226

in search of God through self, 216
interrelated with the (Church) community, according to Orthodox belief, 203, 205
in the Eastern Orthodox Church
  choice of his own "father confessor," 213
  liberation of the person after therapy, 230
  man as, Orthodox emphasis on, 195, 198
  Mencius on the importance of the, 189
  modern patient's insistence on being treated as, 230
  reaction to environmental stress, 226
  role of sacraments in the life of the (according to Orthodox belief), 208–210
Individualism
  on becoming a "whole" person, 402–403
Individuality
  of decision-making patient, disregarded in contemporary versions of Hinduism, 174
  in the Eastern Orthodox Church body, 206
Individuation
  process in life, "mapping the field of relationships," 453–454
Indra
  god of sky and storms, in ancient India, 170
Indulgence, sensuous
  (see also Tantrism)
  among feudal elite in medieval India, 175
  in Tantric tradition, 171
  no place for, in Judaeo-Christian ritual and belief system(s), 173, 178
Informality
  of worship in the Eastern Orthodox congregation, 203
Inhibition(s)
  freeing patient from, in psychotherapy, 247
  sexual, caused by religious repression, 110
Injections and prescriptions
  use of, in Arab countries, 163–164
Injustice
  contemporary prophets' attack on, 444
  denounced by Hebrew prophets, 441
Innocence, cultural
  contemporary loss of, ix
Insight
  as "Wisdom" in Buddhism, 129
Insane, the
  Koran's provisions for, 157
Insanity
  as punishment for taboo violation(s), 225
  in Jeanne Fery's medical history, 236, 240, 241, 242
Insight
  basic qualification of prophet and psychotherapist, 442–443

considered necessary, in the past, to effect disappearance of symptoms from patient's disorder, 309–310
conversion parallel in psychology, 90
effect on individual after psychotherapy, 309
how tapped in psychoanalysis, 133
in analysis, 249
in Buddhism, 121, 151
not essential to successful therapy in most areas of the world, 310
psychological parallel to conversion, 89–90
"right," in Buddhism, 121, 122
self-revelation in, and after, therapy, 139–140
stage at end of counseling, 19
state of, in Hindu meditation, 169–170, 175, 179
Taoist striving for the real things, like faith and contentment for himself, 193
therapy based on, 252
types of, from mystical experiences, 312–316 passim, esp. 314–315
Zen student's, 248
(see also Satori)
Insight(s)
  of psychiatry, reinforcing goal of Judaism, 116
Insight(s), psychotherapeutic
  liturgical celebration, as, 456
Insight therapy
  case history (in Nigeria), 310
  not favored among indigenous and primitive societies, 310
Insight (satori experience)
  translated into every-day living, 137
Intake of patients
  procedure in Shrine hospitals, Gold Coast, 243–244
Integration needed, xix–xx
Integrity, line of
  established between man and fellow men, 11–12
"Integrity of self"
  restored in patient, made more deeply aware after treatment, 38–39
Intellect
  limits of, in Zen, 248
Intellectual probing
  discouraged in authoritarian Hindu systems, 174
Intercession
  God's, in human affairs, 110
Interrelatedness, human, 277
Introvertive mystical state
  description of, 308

Intuition
  in Zen, 130
  in Zen meditation and psychotherapeutic ministration, 139–140
  role of, in the Hindu quest for the Absolute, 178–179
  yogi's, in Hindu contemplation, 179 (*see also* Yoga)
Intuitional approach to Psychotherapy
  advantages of, 140
Involvement, personal
  in the act of worship, 205
Irenaeus, Saint, 196
Isaac, 112, 156
Isaiah, 440
Isanuse, or Native doctor
  care of the *ukutwasa*, 245
  in South Africa, 245
  in-patient (s) in his kral, 245
  practice of primitive psychotherapy, 243, 244, 245–246
  professional skill(s) highly regarded, 246
  training of another, 245
Isherwood, C., 314, 318
Ishmael, 156
Isipatana, Deer park, the Buddha's, 121
Islam
  among great religions, 117, 156–165
  code for living, 157
  heritage from Judaism and Christianity, 156
  number of adherents, 156, 165 (*see* footnote)
  origin and meaning of name, 156
Isolation
  feelings of, during therapy, connected with low moments in patient's experience, 454
Israel
  beacon to the rest of the world, 442
  ideal community Hebrew people grew into, 442
  kings of, 440
  visit to, 439
Israel, brotherhood of
  sense of belonging among Jews, 114

J

Jacob, 156, 429–430
  wresling with the Angel of the Lord, 290–291
Jahweh, 453
  in Old Testament record, punishing His people, 440
  speaking to Hebrews through His prophets, 444
Jainism
  liberation from rebirth, basic belief in, 171
Jainism
  man's bondage to rebirth, 171
James, William, 116, 307, 318, 455
Janet, Pierre, 73–74
Jansenism
  Pascal's conversion to, 313
Japan
  Buddhism in, 125, 126, 128
  Zen in, 246–247
Jealousy, interpersonal
  information regarding, for patient admittance to Gold Coast hospital (s), 244
Jen
  according to Mencius, becoming a natural feeling from the heart, as opposed to Yi, 187
  compassion for the suffering of others, 188–189
  freeing man from anxiety, 186
  importance of effort by the individual, 185–186
  secondary to Yi, according to Mencius, 187
Jen and yi
  no longer encouraged in the Taoist philosophy, 192
Jen (Human-heartedness)
  altrusim (*shu*), 184
Jen (Human-heartedness)
  central concept in the thought of Confucius, 184 ff.
  conscientiousness (*chung*), 184–185
  cultivation of goodness in the whole community, 185
Jen (Human-heartedness)
  flexibility of, 184
  ideography of word, 184–185
  love for the other fellow, 184–185
  maintaining faith with one's self, 185
  natural feeling of positive good will, from the heart, 185
  other definitions, 185
  positive practice of, vs. negative practice of, 184–185
  practical ideal, 184
  practice involving both conscientiousness and altruism, 184 (*see* Chung *and* Shu)
Jen-minded
  showing concern for the whole of humanity, 186
Jeremiah, 440
Jerusalem
  holy city of Islam, 158

Jesus, 156
  acknowledge as personal Saviour and Lord, 58
  central unifying source of Christian life, 46
  coming again, teaching on, 58
  diagnostic method used 9–10
  life, death and resurrection of, 58
  on the Kingdom of God, 458
Jesus as Healer
  emphasized by Mary Baker Eddy, above the historical Jesus, 72
Jewish family
  morality nurtured within, 111–113 *passim*
  personal relationships within, 111–113
Jesus-freaks, xi
Jesus freaks, 389
Jews (*see* Judaism; Religion, Jewish)
Job, 455
Johnson, Paul E., 46–55
Joint commission of Mental Illness and Health findings, 53
Jonathan, 113
Jourard, Sidney, 38, 439–446
Judaeo-Christian ethics
  emphasis on love of neighbor, 276
Judaeo Christian world
  ecumenical atmosphere of, 167
Judaism, 108–116
  alley of psychiatry, 108, 116
  among great religions, 117
  Atonement, Day of, 110
  balanced lifestyle, without extremes of self-mortification, 109
  Bar Mitzvah, 114
  Birth, the, 114
  brotherhood of man, impelling adherents to social action, 114
  catharsis experienced on Holy days and festivals of, 115–116
  ceremonial life in, 114–115
  Circumcision, 114
  Commandments, obedience to the, 109
  continuity of tradition, as Jewish people's inheritance, 113–114
  dynamic life process, 108
  emotional resilience among adherents, 114
  faith in God, 109–110, 113, 115
  family life, emphasis on, 111–112
  fundamental principles of, 109–116
  goal of, 108
  group consciousness in, 113–115
  Hannukah (Chanukah), 115
  Holy days, observation of, 115–116
  humanistic orientation of, 116
  moral responsibility within, 113
  Passover, 115
  Pentecost, 115
  philosophy defined, 108
  philosophy marking milestones in individual's experience, 114–115
  Purim, 115
  quest of, for direction and meaning, reinforced by psychological insights, 116
  Rosh-ha-Shonah, 115
  self-realizing influence on adherent, 108
  synthesis of philosophical influences, 116
  total experience of the Jewish people, 108, 114, 116
  values conducive to mental health emphasized, 108–109
  Yom Kippur (Atonement), 115
Judaism, Conservative, 110
Judaism (*see also* Rabbi(s) *and* Religion, Jewish)
Judea, kings of, 440
Jung, Carl, 38, 57, 195, 439
Jungian therapy, 249

K

Kali
  as Reality or Spirit to which mystic gives himself 312, 314
Kamasutra, 175
Kannon
  (*see also* Avalokita)
  Female-formed Buddha in China, Japan and Korea, 128
Kapleau, P., 309, 318
Karm
  cause and effect, 119
  definition of, 171
  individual responsible for releasing himself from, 170, 171, 172, 174
  main concern of doctors of Hinduism, 172
Karma
  moral actions helping to determine what rebirth or re-incarnation an individual will have, 145, 154–155
  outlook on, in grass-roots Hinduism, 171–172
  other being—demon, witch, or god—responsible for individual's release from, 171–172
  release from past, in Tantric ritual(s), 177 (*see* Copulation, ritualistic; Five M's; *and* Tantrism)
  teaching *not* emphasized at grassroot level of Hindusim, 172

Karmic bondage (see Karma)
　release from, in Hinduism, 169–172, 177
Kassapa
　non-believer in Karma, 146
Ketuboth, 111
Khajuraho, 175
Khalil, Issa J., 195–223
Khartoum, Sudan, 161
Kierkegaard, Soren, 38, 168
Kiev, Ari, 225–235, 311, 318
Kimball, Spencer W., 99, 107
King, W. 153
Kingdom of God
　existing within the (Eastern Orthodox) Church, 206
Kings, line of Chinese
　favored by Heaven and ordered to rule, 182
Kirkbridge, Bangor, Pennsylvania, 273
Kla (vital essence)
　cut up by witches, 243
　loss of, causing sickness or death, 243
Klassen, William, 63
Kluckhohn, Clyde, xiii
Kluckhohn, F. and F. Strodtbeck, 322–326, 329
Knowing and being known, peace of, 460
Koan, use of, 136, 137
Koan (task)
　in Zen 247–248, 249
Koestler, A., 172
Kofi
　case history of blindness, 244
　susama's (spirit's) withdrawal to a band of witches, 244
　treated successfully in shrine compound, 244
Konarak, 175
Kondanna, 121
Koran, 156 ff.
Koran
　Arabic language original, 157
　deeds and ritual emphasized, 157
　fatalism in, 157
　legal code, with provision for dependent members of society, 157
　memorization of, 157–158
　reward and retribution concretely referred to, 157
　the Glorious, God's message to Islam, 156
　tolerance toward sexual activity, 157
　used therapeutically, 161–162
Kotzo
　case history of paralysis, 244
　hand paralyzed by witches, 244
　psychotherapy and ritual drive out demons, 244
　successful cure, 244

Kuan-Yin, 128 *(see also* Avalokita)
Kyoto, site of Koryu-ji Temple, 129

L

La Barre, Weston, 319
Laing, R., 44, 168, 177, 443
Lama Foundation, New Mexico, 280
Lambo, T., 245, 246, 252
Lao Tzu
　one of the books of Taoist though, 191, 192–193
Laotze, 132
Laubscher, B., 245–246, 252
Lauer, Roger M., 254–267
Laughter
　in Zen *satori,* 248
　of insight, in psychoanalysis, 248
Law
　fulfilled in Christ, 95
　psychic counselors' consultation with the, 256
Law of God
　man's life ordered according to the, 91
　Ten Commandments as the, 91
Lawrence of Arabia, 442
Leader, Church
　no Pope in Eastern Orthodox Church, 203
Laymen
　presence of, by the sickbed, 210
　role of, in the Church of Christ, 78
　use of, in group work, 265
Laymen's group(s)
　formed to aid in informal therapy, 448
Learning
　as commitment, 25–26
　defined, 27, 29
　developing a new self through, 28–31
　related to Counseling, 25
　theory, "incarnate-redemptive," 25
Lecky, P., 38, 133, 140
Lederer, Wolfgang 236–253
Leifer, R., 177
Lent
　breaking the fast of, 239
Letter to the Romans, 47
Levitation
　definition of, 255
Lewis, Sinclair, x
　esp. Main Stree, x
Li (reverence and respect), 188
Liberal Protestantism and Humanistic Psychology
　collaboration between, 37 ff.
　collaboration between, 41–42, 44–45
Liebman, J., 115

Life
   as a journey, in Buddhism, 130
   experience of, in Buddhist meditation, 153
   form and order in, 30
   questions about
      answered by Buddhism, 118
      religion, fulfilled through, 117
   source of pain, not bliss, to the Hindu believer, 170, 172
   suffering in, according to Buddhist teaching, 122
Life-death-rebirth cycle, in Hinduism, 120
Life potential
   for most part, untrapped, 51
Life, quality of
   religion, lifted by, 117
Lifestyle
   adopting a better, 89
   Hebrews', before and after Moses, 440
   how to choose *the,* xii-xiii
   or, way-of-being-in-the-world, xii
   proper balance without self-mortification or other excesses, in Judaism, 109
   simplified after analysis, 248
   simplified after Zen experience, 248
   Zen, 247-248
Light
   as a symbol of new life after Christ's resurrection, 202
   in Church and home at Easter (Eastern Orthodox Church), 202
Light, God's
   Quaker experience of shattered self before, 270
Light, the Divine
   in Eastern Orthodox worship, 214
   on Nature, 214
Lingua (phallic symbol of Shiva), 177
Liturgy
   attitude of the worshipper toward
      in the Eastern Orthodox Church, 204
   given a central place in Orthodox belief, 200, 203-213, esp. 205-206
   nature cycle vs. Church year cycle in, 214
Logan, D., 254, 267
Logotherapy
   defined, 51
   Frankl's, 57
Lophophora Williamsii (Peyote cactus), 296
Lossky, V., 198-199, 200
Lourdes, 80
Love
   source of emotional health, 134
   in Sufism, 159
   within the church community, 89

Love, conjugal
   (*see also* Marriage)
   duties of, in Jewish life, 111
   nobility of, in Jewish life, 111-112
Love, God's
   in Christian Science doctrine, 75
   shown cradle to grave through the Sacraments, 206
Love, law of
   Christ's interpretation of the Ten commandments, 95
   obedience in spirit rather than according to the "letter," 92
Love paternal
   Jewish teaching regarding, 112-113
Love, psyical
   Bible on, 110-111 (*see Song of songs*)
   Talmud on, 111
"Love systems"
   increased interrelatedness as aids to patients, 454
Lowe, C. Marshall, 344-354
Lowen, A., 271, 274-275
LSD
   inducing union of mind and body in "trip" or mystical state, 175
LSD, limited dosage
   in treatment of alcoholics and drug addicts, 308
   to induce therapeutic mystic state in selected (often terminal) patients, 308-309
Lun Yii
   Confucian Analects, 183, 184, 187
   pioneers of the Taoist movement, 191
Luther, Martin, 47
Luther, 200
   his religious experience, 50
Lutherans
   Salvation-by-faith, discovery of, 268

M

Machiavelli, 440
Mad-at-God syndrome, the, 337-338
Mada (wine), 176 (see Five M's)
Magic
   modern practitioners of, 254
   parallels in modern psychiatry, 225-236
   supernatural powers over natural forces, 225
   treatment by, in African countries, 246
   (*see also* Sorcery)
Mahayana
   Great Vehicle, in Buddhist movement, 143
Mahanaya Buddhism (*see* Buddhism, Mahanaya)

Mahayana heaven(s)
  populated with transcendental beings, 124
Maithuna (ritualisitc copulation), 176, 177 (see Five M's and Copulation)
Maitreya
  awaiting next appearance, 129
  salvation, bringer of, 129
  future Buddha, 129
Majnunoon, patient classification in the Sudan, 161–162 (see also Psychoses, functional)
Mali, Republic of (see Sudan)
"Malicious Animal Magnetism" (M.A.M.)
  correct handling of, 83
  in Mary Baker Eddy's life experience, 81–84
Mamsa (meat), 176 (see Five M's)
Man
  a dynamic view of, 195–202
  as moral being, in Judaism, 108
  as the son of God, 92
  attainment of perfection in Christian Science, 73
  becoming like God, 92, 94–95
  brotherhood of, fundamental conviction of the Peyote Indians, 296–297
  considered artificial in his ethics, politics, theories and other doings, 192 (see Taoism)
  freedom of, in Orthodox belief, 200
  holistic nature of, 91
  "Man of no-rank," Zen ideal, 138
  physical attraction of, 111
  potential destiny of, 196
  responsible partner in his own redemption, 11
  rival or competitor with God, 200
  state of, before the fall, 200
  state of perfection of, acc. to Christian Science, 73
  Tao of, in Chinese thought, 194
  unity with Nature, 317
  unity with the rest of humanity, 317
  viewed as an "icon" in the Eastern Orthodox Church, 216
  Western, vulnerability to stress, 226
Mandate of Heaven, Chinese (see *T'ien-ming*)
Manjusri
  a Bodhisattva, personification of thought, knowledge, and meditation, 127, 128–129
  represented in Zen temple, 128
Man's nature
  innately good, according to Mencius, 187
Manual of the Mother Church of the First Church of Christ Scientist, in Boston,
Massachusetts, 77–78, 80–81, 82–86 *passim*
Manushi Buddhas (historical), 124, 125
Mara, 121
Margolis, Joseph, xiv
Marhaz Al-Mushahada, Witness before God, in Sufism, 160
Maristan, 161
Marriage
  and Mary Baker Eddy, 82 83
  divine institution of, 112
  husband's obligations, in Jewish, 111
  Jewish wife's rights, upheld within, 110
  personal fulfillment in, 111–112
  roles of husband and wife within, 111–112
  viciousness within, 443
Mary Magdalen(e), Saint
  intercession of, in Jeanne Fery's case, 239–242
Massage
  use of, by psychic counselors, 263
Maseed, Sufi
  Muslim institution for therapy and treatment of mental symptoms, 161–162 (see also Methods, treatment)
Maslow, A., 34, 46
Masseur(s)
  psychic counselors' contact with, 256
Master
  authority figure in Zen, 248
  leader of a mystical group, 250
  role of, in Zen, 248
Material, man's reference to himself as an "illusion" acc. to Christian Science, 73
Materialism
  commonly attributed to the West, 172, 175
Matsya (fish), 176 (see Five M's)
Matter
  occupying "definite limited region" of reality, 453–454
Matter-Body-Evil
  as products of "mortal," or erroneous, mind, acc. to Christian Science, 73
Matthew, Saint, 82, 98
Maturation (see Growth)
Mawhumoon, patient classification in the Sudan, 161 (see also Neurotics)
Maya
  in Hindu belief illusion of time and space, 170
Meaning, creating
  in one's own life, 433
Means of Livelihood
  "right," 121, 122
Mecca
  Islam's holy city, pilgrimage to, 157, 158

Mediator
  (see Redeemer)
  unavailable in Hindu belief, 172
Medical explanation (s)
  for emotional instability, 228
Medicine
  little reliance on (by Christian Scientists), 74
Medicine, role of
  in the healing of the sick according to Orthodox belief, 210–211
Medina, Saudi Arabia, 158
Meditation
  art of, in Buddhism, 153
  basic in psychotherapy, 139
  daily practice recommended, 139
  Gautama's, 120
  in Buddhism, 149, 152–153
  in general religious context, 153–154
  in Theravada Buddhism, 149
  insight, joined with, 135
  in Zen, 139
  "no thought" in Zen, 139
  practice of monks and growing number of laymen, 149
Meditation
  rather high-flown theories of, 443
  "right," in Buddhism, 121, 122
  Stages in Hindu, 278
  Tantric, 176–177, 178
  therapeutic function of, 149, 153, 277
  to restore spontaneity, 134
  withdrawal from the world, 154
Mediation between man and God
  religious leader's traditional goal, 436
Meditation, Hindu
  involving both "body" and "mind," in higher reaches of process, 174
  practiced therapeutically, 168, 178–179
Meditation, Zen
  and "free association" compared, 135–136
  detachment in, 139
Medium, serving as, 258
Medium, the psychotherapist as, 430
Mediumship
  definition of, 255
Meeting, Peyote
  drums, 298
  fire tending, 298
  night, taking place at, 298
  participation in prayers, 298
  purpose (s) of the, 297–298
  religious service, 297–298
  songs, traditional, 298
  symbolic eating of meat, corn and fruit, 298–299
  tobacco smoking ceremonial, 298
  water ceremony, 298
Melchizedek, 457
Milieu, patient's
  personalizing, 455
Member (s), church
  equality of (in the Eastern Orthodox Church), 208
Mencius, 187–189, 193
  all things complete in oneself, 189
  believer in Yi (Righteousness), 187
  considered man innately good, 187
  definition of the Good, 188–190
  differences in men due to environment, 188
  doctrine of the goodness of man, 187
  human nature, affected by externals of life, 188
  Jen, coupled with Yi, focal point of thought, 187 (see Jen and Yi)
  man becoming one with Heaven, 190
  not only goodness, but perfection, as final goal (s) for man, 190
  perfecting goodness by showing compassion, 189
  "seeking in oneself," 189–190
  stress on the importance of the individual, 189
Menarche (see Menstruation)
Meng Tzu
  Book of Mencius, 183, 187–188
Menninger, K. 57
Menstruation
  in Jeanne Fery's medical history, 238, 240
"Mental and silent argument"
  in Christian Science, 79
Mental health
  as goal of psychotherapy and religious meditation, 150–151, 152–154
  definition of, 10
  emphasized in Judaism, 108
  literature, 254
  Mormonism's contribution to, 101, 105, 106
  mystical experience in Hinduism, conducive to, 309
  psychiatrys goal, 105
  psychologically healthy foundation given to Jewish children, 113
  therapeutic goals in, 40
  understanding of, in Buddhism, 150–151, 152
  Western concept of, 152
Mental health agents
  psychic counselors as, 167
Mental health professional (s)
  psychic counselors' contact with, 256

Mental hospitals (see also Treatment centers)
Mental hospitals, modern
  indictment of methods in, 246
Mental illness
  (see also Insanity, Psychoneurosis, Psychosis and Schizophrenia)
  and the clergy's responsibility to the sufferer, 104, 105–106
  caused theoretically by guilty conscience from taboo violation, 225
  Christian Scientist attitude toward, 75
  community attitudes toward, 228
    in the Belgian Congo, 229
    in Fiji, 229
    in New Hebrides, 229
  community responsibility for prevention, 228–229
  community responsibility for treatment, 226–227
  defense against anxiety, as a, 251
  Mormon viewpoints on, 104
  occurring after taboo violations, 225
  secondary status in Christian Science practice, after physical, or bodily illness, 75
  theory of, in Islam, 163
  thought of as being caused by outside forces, 226–227
  treatment of, through psychiatry, 108
Mentalism
  in psychic counseling practice, 255
Mescaline (see Hallucinogens and Peyote drug)
Mesmerism
  in modern psychic counseling, 254
Message(s)
  received by psychic counselors, in client consultation, 255
Metaphysics, Masters of (see Counselor(s), psychic)
Methods, treatment
  determination of, according to culture context of patient and his surroundings, 162
  in psychic counseling
    legality of, 256
  insight, relying on, 251
  isolation and set feeding pattern, 162
  magical, 251
  Muslim practice, effectiveness of, 162–163
  mystic, 251
  native Muslim, in both religious and magical therapy, 160–162
Methods, treatment
  new, theoretically better for mental patient, 252

  religious, 251
  religious instruction and prayer, 161–162
Methods, treatment
  rest and quiet, 161–162
  tradition, reliance on precedent(s) within the patient's culture, 165
Mexicans
  reliance on mystical teachings of, 255
Mexican-American
  protective attitude toward the child, 227
Miami, Florida, 319
Miamonides, 114
Micchā
  wrong path in Theravāda, 145–146
Middle Way, the
  Buddha's ideal, 121
Mimesis
  in learning, 29
Mind
  Al-Akl in Sufism, not mentioned among four faculties of "Psyche," 160
  as opposed to Body, in Indian tradition, 174
  conscious withdrawal from sense objects, 169
  in bondage, according to Indian belief, 169, 174
  in Buddhism, 151
  outwardly directed tendencies of the, to be curbed in Yoga meditation, 169, 174
  released from sense objects, as through yoga and meditation, 169, 170
Mind and body
  healing of, 78
Mind and body together, in unity with the Absolute, 174–175
Mind, mortal
  in error, 73
Mind, original or pure
  called Buddha nature, 132
  return to, in practice of Zen, 139
Mind, (the) Eternal
  dominant in Christian Science doctrine, 73
Miscellaneous Writings, 80
Moench, Louis, 104
Moksha
  escape or release, 119
Momism
  harmful mother-domination, 226, 292
Monastic ideal
  in Hinduism, 170
Monasticism
  as separation from the world, in Buddhism, 152
Monasticism Christian
  in Eastern Orthodox Church, 200

Monism
  and the unity of Ultimate Reality in the mystic's vision, 308
  basis of Hindu theology, 178
Monk, figure of a
  in a psychiatrist's dream, 433
Monk, Zen
  alone with his problem (s), 135
Monotheism
  as religious system suited to the human condition and "the times," 438
Morality
  Buddhist teaching regarding, 147–149
  some definitions, 403–410 passim
Morality
  violation of, 225
Moreno, J. L., 53
Mormonism
  admonishment to seek out the poor and the suffering and to minister to same, 101
  and mental health, 101, 105, 106
  as a way of life, 98–107, esp. 98–99 and 102 (see entries under Church of Jesus Christ of Latter-Day Saints)
  cooperation in treatment of the emotionally ill, 104
  individual's personal development encouraged, 101, 105
  obedience to divine commandments imposed, 105
  outreach efforts of Church members relied on, 99–100, 104
  responsibility to assist all members toward exaltation, 101, 105
  value orientation in, 98, 105
Mormonism and psychiatry
  evaluation of frontiers and common ground, 105
Moreno, J. L., 53
Morality, Mormon standards of, 105
Moses, 114, 156
  first in great tradition of Hebrew prophets, 440
  teachings of, 441, 444
  trained in civilized culture of Egypt, 444
Moses' law and ordinances
  answering questions about life, and how to live it, 440
  commandments and statutes "from God," 444
  offering a Way for the Hebrews, 440
Mosque, worship in the, 204
Mother
  appellation of God in the Lord's prayer, Christian Science version, 72
  dominance syndrome, 394–397
  possessiveness of, 226
Mother Church, Boston, 77
Mother-daughter relationship
  in adolescence years, 286–290, 292
Motif (s)
  psychoanalytic, dictating intervention by healer, priest or psychotherapist, 293
Motivation
  analyzed in Buddhist meditation, 153
Motivation, patient's
  "low" when treatment fails, 229–230
Motives (see also Will)
  "right," in Buddhism, 121, 122
Mourning
  encouraged in the liturgy for the dead (of the Eastern Orthodox Church), 217
  formal expression of grief by the bereaved, in Jewish ceremony, 114–115 (see also Death)
Mourning or grief
  open expression after death of loved one, 163
Moustakas, 38
Mowrer, Hans, 439
Mowrer, O. Hobart, 444, 447–451
Mrs. Eddy: The Biography of a Virginal Mind, 80–81
Mudra (supposed aphrodisiac), 176 (see also Five M's)
Muhammad (Mohammed)
  prophet of Islam, messenger of God's will to the Muslim, 156
Muhji, 159
Munzer, Thomas, 48
Murder
  as taboo violation, 225
Murphy, J. M., 312, 318
Muslim
  belief in one God, 156
Muslim world
  effect of modernization on, 165
Muslims
  number of worshippers, 156, 165 (see fotenote)
Mystic teachings
  use of, by non-professional guidance practitioners, 255
Mystical experience
  Adamic states in, 307–308
  and psychotherapeutic insights, 314
  as outgrowth of church affiliation, 312
  as regression to early childhood, 316
  awareness of the environment, 308 (see Extrovertive)
  definition of, 307–309

during participation in sacraments and liturgy, 199
explanation for observed therapeutic effects of, 309, 312–316
giving perspective on petty goings-on in daily life, 317
good, reassuring, dependent on subject's own testimony, 317
immediacy, sense of, 307, 312–313, 317
in Western culture, 312–317, esp. 316
inability to express, 307, 312–313
intensity of, 307, 308, 312–313
liberating individual from psychological states, 309
non-awareness of the environment, 308 (see Introvertive)
parallel to primitive religious experiences with therapeutic results, 312
regression primordial ego structure, 317

Mysticism
in modern psychic counseling, 254
in Zen Buddhism, 132
psychotherapeutic value of, 308–309, 312–316
soul's union with God, a central theme of, 159
(see also Experience, mystical)
Muslim (see Sufism)

N

Nader, Ralph, 444
Nahmanides, 111, 114
Nara, site of Buddhist temple, Japan, 125
Narcissism
source of neurotic anxiety, 134
Native American Church
(see Peyote Religion and Peyotist Church), 296–306
size of, 296
Nature
Eastern Orthodox attitude toward, 213–216
man's relationship to, 219–220
worship of objects from, in early Chinese culture, 180
Nature, idealization of
self-sufficient, uncreated part of life, spontaneously expressed, in Taoism, 191
Nature, oneness with
goal of Zen meditation, 137–138
in trance-like state, 136
Naturalism, 193
Neo-Hinduism, 174
Neoplatonism
in Muslim mysticism, 159
Nepal
Buddhism in, 118, 126

Neuroses
ailments described, 448
liberation from, in Western psychotherapy, 247
many cured without insight therapy, 310
Neurosis
compared to obsessional acts in religious observances (Freud), 114
isolation, feeling of, within individual, 113
powerful contemporary, loss-of-meaning, 51
product of sexual repression, as, 110
so-labeled by Jean Martin Charcot, 448
Neurotic(s)
Muslim treatment of, at Masheed, 161
New life
growth into, 51
New methods
attempt(s) at, xix
"New Morality," the
and psychotherapy, 344–352
Newtonian physics, 452
Nibbana (see Nirvana)
Nicaea, Council of, 451
Nietzsche, Friedrich Wilhelm, xv
Nigeria, 231, 285, 310
Nigeria, Federation of, 245
"Night of Enlightenment" (see Gautama)
Nihilism, xv
Nijinsky, Vaslav, 442
Nirmanakaya (Manifested Body), Buddha as, 131
Nirvana
after stay in the "Pure Land," 126 (see Sukhavati)
as goal of Theravada Buddhism, 146–147, 152
attainment of, in Buddhism, 123
bliss of, 125
bringing peace, psychological release, 147
Buddha essence, 123
entrance into, postponed (see also Dyani Buddhas)
erasing of anxiety, craving, and hatred, 147
extinction of unhealthy motivations in, 146–147
goal of the "Middle Path," 121
Manushi Buddhas in, 125
overcoming of man's evil motivations, 147
peace of, highest Theravada ideal, 123
postponement of, on the part of Mahayana Buddhists, 123
Non-western culture(s)
offering alternatives to scientific systems, xiv
"No-self"
in Buddhism, 151

No-thought
  method of meditation, 135
  practice of, in every-day life, 139
  principle in Zen outlook, 133, 139
Non-anxious person
  calming effect of, on mental patient, 251
Non-attachment
  principle of Zen teaching, 133–134
Non-delusion, non-greed, non-hatred
  states conducive to progress along Theravada "Path," 150–157
Non-form
  principle of Zen outlook, 133–134
"Normality"
  according to Orthodox belief, becoming more godlike, 197
  not essential as a goal of therapy, 196
Noss, J., 124, 131
Numerology
  use of, in psychic counseling, 255
Nursing care
  of anxiety cases, 251

O

O-Mi-To, Buddha of Healing, in China, 125–126
Obedience to God and an adjustment to man
  religion's traditional stress, 436
Object intrusion
  into the body, 225, 225–226
  producing imbalance in the subject, 226
Objectivity, strictly "scientific"
  psychotherapist's traditional approach, 436
Observation, participant
  of psychic counseling facilities, 254–257, 265–267
Observance, religious
  enriching the *next* life, or incarnation, in Hindu belief, 170
Occult
  "tuning in" to the, 255
Occult bookshops, 259
Occult phenomena
  belief in existence of, 254
Occult, use of the
  in psychic counseling, 254
  "tuning in" to the client's vibrations, 255
Oden, Thomas, 32, 45, 59–60
Oedipus myth, 112
Ojas, 177 (*see also* Copulation, ritualistic)
Old age
  as part of human suffering, 122, 127
Old methods
  revision (s) of, xix

Old Testament, 11, 86
  record of a people's search for ideal community under God, 439–442
Oneness with the Absolute
  man's life, leading to, 178
  man's peak experience, 175
  mystical experience of, 179
"Openness to others"
  capacity to live in love toward them, 39
Orichas
  and "saints," 321–329 *passim*, esp. 323–324
Orientation
  present-time values in American life, 322
Orientation, Western, twentieth-century
  where most of us are, ix
Orthodox Church, Eastern
  acceptance of the findings of medicine and biology, 195
  as mediator in restoring man's wholeness, 218
  basic understanding of psychology and therapy within, 195
  beliefs and practices of, 195–221
  beliefs and practices
    "afterlife" begun here on earth, 199
    age, respect for, 208
    alienation from God, 200, 216
    almsgiving, 215
    animal world, respect for the, 215
    autonomy of 203
    baptism and role of the godparents, 206–209
    channel of spiritual healing, 216
    child received early into membership, 207, 208–209
    Chrismation, rite of, 207
    of Christ-centered life, the, 200
    Church, the, as mediator in restoring man's wholeness, 218
    Communion of Saints taking part in worship, 203–204
    Community, the redeemed, 202
    confession, 212–213
    of consequences of the Fall of Adam, 200
    of contrast between *person* and *individual*, 198–199
    of contrast with Reformed theology, 197
    corporate worship, emphasis on, 204–205
    counseling availability of, 211–212, 213
    of Cross shown empty, 201
    death, attitude toward, 217–218, 219
    of deification, as the goal and destiny of man, 197, 198
    definition of, 220

deification in Christ of the believer, 202
description of, 218–219
dimensions of the believer, 218
Doctrine of grace, 198 ff.
of Doctrine of grace, 198 ff.
of Doctrine of nature, 198–199
duality of man, emphasis on, 206, 209
of Easter celebration, 201–202
ecstasy experienced in worship, 205
Ecumenical Council, 203
of "energies" of God possessed by saints and men in union with Him, 197, 200
eternal and temporal life together in man, 206
Eucharist, high point of church service, 205
exorcism, rites of, 211–212
fasting, 211, 214–215
four-way relationship in, 202, 218
freedom of the individual in Church worship, 203–206, esp. 205
of freedom of man, 200
funeral rites, 217
God as Farther within the church community, 206
God, "energies" of, 219
God, praise of, 205
God's image, teaching regarding, 200
goodness of God, 198
of grace and nature contrasted, 198, 200
healing, 210, 210–212
Holy Spirit, guidance of the, 203
Holy Unction, sacrament of, 210
house of God, the church as the, 204
of hymn singing, 201 ff.
icons, hanging of, 204–206, 207–208
Individual's relationship with the (Church) community, 203, 204–205
individual worship rather than ritual, 204
individuality within the corporate whole, 206
Kingdom of God within the believer, 216
laity and clergy together, 203
Liturgy, place of, 203–213
love, God's, shown cradle to grave through the sacraments, 206
of man created to participate in the divine life, 196–197
of man, doctrine of, 196–202
man's alienation from God, 216
of man's cooperation with God, 200
man's state *before* the Fall, teaching regarding, 200
members, equality of, 208
of monasticism, a special calling, 200
nature, attitude toward, 213–214
others, attitude toward, 212–213
participation of children in, 204, 206–209
of participation in sacraments and liturgy, 199–200
pastoral function therein, 206, 207–208, 210–211, 212–213
penance, 212–213
personal involvement in the act of worship, 205
"possession," or psychic ills, 211
prayer, 203–204, 205
prayers after birth of a child, 207
priest as "spiritual father," 213
recognition of man's individuality, 195ff–196
reconciliation with God, self, neighbor *and* nature, 202
redemption as transfiguration of all nature, 213
of redemption through Christ, 201
sacramental view of the world, 216
Sacraments, effect of the, 207, 208–210, 214
Sacraments, importance of the, 206, 209–210, 218
saints, attitude toward the communion of, 204, 207–208
saint(s), paying tribute to the, 204–206, 207–208
salvation, 200–201, 202, 213
Satan, teaching regarding, 200
Second Coming, Christ's, 206
sick, care of the, 204, 210–212
of sin as alienation from God, 220–201
suffering, easing of, 210–211
of the risen Christ victorious over Sin and Death, 201–202
therapeutic aspects, 215–216
of therapeutic treatment of the "healthy" as well as the ill, 195
Transfiguration, liturgy of the, 214
Trinity, doctrine of the, 199
Trinity's place in Christian life, the, 199
unity of the faith, emphasis on, 203
wholeness, man's restoration to, 195, 202, 217–218
of world, sacramental view of the, 216
of worship, joy in, 201–202
worshipper's attitude toward the liturgy, 204

Osteopathy
  preferred to medicine by Christian Scientists, 74
Others
  concern with, 19 (*see also* Altruism)
  lack of concern for (in Christian Science), 83–85

Others, concern for
  characteristic of the enlightened man, 138
  Confucius' driving purpose, 184 (see Jen)
  modeled on Christ's forgiveness of the individual, 95
  ethical duty of adherents of Judaism, 114
  Gautama's decision to share discoveries with other men, 120
  ideal of Judaism and psychotherapy alike, 109
  in the Eastern Orthodox Church, 212–213, 214–215
  in the practice of Jen, 184–185
  interconnectedness of individual with all others, in a great religion, 274
  natural to man in his goodness, 189
  rabbinic, 109–110
  therapist's, 250–252, 436–445
  therapeutic, 460
Outler, Albert, 32, 45

P

Pahnke, W. N., 308–309, 318
Pain
  as a reminder of Death, 6
  denial of (in Christian Science), 80
  emotional, definition of, 5
  emotional, philosophies and systems to alleviate, 6
  emotional, relief sought in Mormon bishop's interview, 103
  etiology of, 5
  experienced by patient, as psychotherapist unveils the truth, 445
  in birth and in life, to the Hindu believer, 170
  physical, definition of, 5
  physical, man's search for cures, 6
  reactions to, 3–4, 5–6
  succession of episodes causing, 6
  threshold, in modern, Western societies, 5
  threshold, in non-Western, primitive parts of the world, 5
Pali (original) Buddhism, 123
Palmist, 259
Palms, examination of
  reliance on, in psychic counseling, 255
Panic (*see also* Anxiety *and* Fear)
  from "soul loss," 227
Pantheism
  Sufism, certain variations of, 159
Paradise
  Buddha Field, in Mahayana Buddhism, 126, 130
  in Buddhism, 130
  Sukhavati, "Pure Land" of Amitabha, 126, 130
  unreal to the Hindu believer, as happiness is not achieved, 170
Paralysis
  case history (*see* Kotzo)
Paranoia
  cases of, among Gold Coast patients, 243
Parapsychologist(s)
  psychic counselors' contact with, 256
Parents
  oversolicitous, 443
  protective role of Jewish, 113
  punishing *versus* loving, 391
  role of Jewish, as teachers of morality, 113
Participation, patient's
  "how-to," or apprenticeship, "within the psychotherapeutic relationship," 454
  in life events, reported and celebrated in therapy, 454
Pascal, Blaise
  Certainty and Joy, a statement about his mystical experience, 312–313
  Christ, complete submission to, 313
  conversion to Jansenism, 313
  mystical experience of, 312–314
  neuroticism, extent of, 313
  Pensées, thoughts on God and man, 313
  Provincial Letters, 313
  sacrificing worldly interests and giving to the poor, 313
  vision, a reaffirmation of what he already believed, 313
Passover, 115
Past behavior patterns
  breaking away from, in Encounter groups, 269
Pastoral Counseling Movement, 53
Pastoral function
  of the (Eastern Orthodox) Church therapeutic effect of the Sacraments, 207, 208–210
Patanjali, 169
Path
  Buddhist, compared to psychotherapy, 151–154
  Buddhist contrast to Western religion(s), 142
"Path"
  acts of merit in, 149
  goal of, in Theravada Buddhism, 142, 150–151
  healthy mental state needed for progress along, 150–151

leading believer out of samsāra, 145
liberating Theravadin from ten fetters, 147
lifestyle of giving rather than harming, 147
practice of Wisdom in, 149
progress on the, achieved through various areas, 147–149
three stages in, 147
Path (s)
how to choose a way, xvi–xvii
Pathological behavior
discouraged, "stopped," in the therapist's office, 445–446
Patient
attitude toward priest, in Eastern Orthodox practice, 211–212
calmed by therapist's composure, 251
communication from, 133
exonerated from behavior disorder, 226–227
experiential quest in Hindu meditation, effect of, 178–179 (see also Therapeutic Quest and Oneness with the Absolute)
freed by modern psychotherapy to find out what he wants in life, 247
"good," 252
helped by the *process* of meditation, more than by end result, 179 (see Therapeutic Quest)
in dialogue with his therapist, 135
in residence
near priest practicing healing, 211–212
in therapy, compared to Hindu contemplative, 179
making own value decisions, 57
non-rational level of communication, 252
own effort important in therapy, 143
rage reaction against psychoanalyst, 309–310
reassured with prayer, 162
regression during re-experiencing of childhood incidents, 309
reliance on Judaeo-Christian values, effect of, 178
reliance on practitioner's (healer's) faith rather than his own, 79
without religious affiliation or conviction, 177–178
Patient attitudes
concerns now, leading to participation later, 454
efforts at communication watched, as evidence of potential vitality, 454
Patient exonerated
from any part in the cause of his illness, 227
Patient in therapy
explains and learns to cope with his past behavior, 135

how helped by Zen meditation, 139–140
Patients
complaining of being stricken by witches, 243
Patients, native
treatment in Gold Coast shrine hospitals, 243–244
Patient-therapist relationship
intensity of, 249
Pativedha
realization of the Truth in Buddhism, 142
Pattison, E. Mansell, ix–xvii, 284–295
Paul, Saint, 106, 107
Peace
longing for inner, in personal religious experience, 270
Peace of mind defined, 103
Peace with self
after analysis, 248
after Zen experience, 248
Peal, Norman Vincent, 442
Pearl of Great Price, Moses, 99
Peel, Robert, 75, 78
Penance
comparison between Eastern Orthodox and Roman Catholic rites, 212
in the Eastern Orthodox Church, 212–213
through fasting, esp. 215
(see also Confession)
Pendle Hill, Wallingford, Pennsylvania, 273
Pentecost, 115
Pentecostal minister and Voodoo priest incantation techniques compared, 234
Pentecostal movement
rediscovered today, 268–269, 273
Perception
changes in mental patient's, 251
Perfection
attainment of, in Mahanaya Buddhism, 126
in man, acc. to Christian Science, 73
Perls, Fritz, 270, 272, 277
Perls, Laura, 270
Person
deification of, as process, 197
each man a (according to Orthodox belief), 197
man as microcosm, 199
man fulfilling his God-given "image," 199
man in his historical setting and situation, 199
on being and on becoming a, 433–434
the child as, in the Eastern Orthodox Church, 208–209
Personal problems
psychic counselor's ability to solve, 258

Personality
  change in, 151
  development in integrated family unit, 111–113
  father's role in shaping child's, 112
  Jewish family upbringing, influence of, 113
  theories of, 227
Personality change(s)
  resulting from mystical experience(s), 314
Personality disorders
  some types treatable biochemically, 448
Personality, individual
  limited by fears and inhibitions, 134
Personality integration
  counseling area, 15
Personality, normal
  definition of, 138
  outgoingness in, 138
Pessimism, xv
Peyote
  cactus, 296
  practice of medicine, or personal curing when ill, 297
Peyote drug
  benefits derived, 299–300, 302–303, 305
  composition of and effect of, 296, 298–304 passim, esp. 299
  consumption of, at Peyote meeting, viewed as sacramental, 297, 299, 301–303, 305
  group supply for meeting participants, 299
  hallucinogenic, 296, 299–300, 302, 303–304
  minimum effects after consumption, 299–300, 302–304 (see also Time-element)
Peyote meeting
  counseling together, 300–303, 305
  incense-burning, 298
Peyote Religion, 296 ff. (see Peyotist Church and Native American Church)
Peyotist attitude toward
  hospitals, 297
  other religions, 296–297
  their "brothers," 296, 297, 300, 301–303, 304
Peyotist Church
  (see Peyote Religion and Native American Church), 296–306
  membership in other churches, 297
  membership within, 296
  rules of conduct, 296
Pfister, Oscar
  reply to Freud, 61
Phallus, symbol of the god Shivā in India, 177
Phenomenologist approach, 249–250
Philosophy
  connection with psychotherapy, 117
  selflessness in individual, 138–139
  some trends, 362–364 (see also Bibliography), 365–368
Philosophy of life
  associated with an organized church, 89
  meaningful to the individual, 89
Phobia
  case history in Nigeria, 245
Phrenology
  use of, in psychic counseling, 255
Physician
  as father figure, 164
  characteristics of the Arab, 164
  respected among Arabs, 164
  treatment of young Arabs by, 164–165
Physician as priest, xiv
Pierrakos, J., 271, 275
Pilgrimage of Awareness
  need for lifetime design, instead of short-range therapies, 278
Place, or setting
  secondary consideration in treatment or healing, 79
Platform Sutra, 133–134, 135, 139
Pleasure
  as central integrating value of human life, 274–275 (see Bioenergetics)
Plurality of "centers of reconstruction," fused, 453
Poem, sharing a, 431
Polanyi, Michael, 35, 454
Polygamy
  sanctioned in Islam and by the Koran, 157
Polytheism
  as religious system suited to the human condition and "the times," 438
Port-Royal Monastery, 313
Portnoy, 440
Possession
  by angry or evil spirits, 225
  illness (psychic disturbance) as, 211
  spirit intrusion, 226
Powell House, Old Chatham, New York, 283
Practitioner, Christian Science
  characteristics and standards, 76–77
  consciousness of own perfection as affecting sufferer's health, 79
  fees for, 77–78
Prajna samadhi (Wisdom or Insight), 135
Prayer
  after birth of a child, according to Orthodox practice, 207
  before treatment, 162
  for the sick, in the Eastern Orthodox liturgy, 210

in Christian Science "treatment," 78–80
in Eastern Orthodox Church services, 203–204, 205
in healing, 211–212
in Peyote cult, 296–297
Jewish attitude toward, 110
psychotherapist's, 457
substitute for "small-group" interchange, 451
to aid man's reconciliation with God, 212
Prayer(s)
Koran passage recited in Arabic during, 157
Prayer and sacrifice
in primitive cults to ward off unwanted spirits, 229
Precognition
definition of, 255
Predicament, human
Kierkegaardian anguish in the, 167–168
Prepsychotic state
feeling of impending doom, 243
Presbyterians, 289
Pride
as neurotic defensiveness, 38–39
Priest
calling as, 452
changing role of, in contemporary religion(s), 436–437
leader of a religious community, 250
mediator between man and Deity, 436
role within religious institution, 437
Priest and therapist
as mediator(s), 452
Priest as physician, xiv
Priest, role of the
as "spiritual father," in the Eastern Orthodox Church, 213
in Eastern Orthodox Church, exorcism rites, 211–212
ministry to the sick, 210–212
sacrament of penance, 212–213
Prince, Raymond, 295, 307–318
Privacy
basic right in Western doctor-patient consultation, 230
emphasized in Western medical practice, 230
"Private Meeting" in Mary Baker Eddy's experience, 81–82
(The) Problem
diagnosis of, 8–10
existing within man, 12
man's formulation of, 4–8
treatment of, 10–12
Problems
as spiritual disturbances, 335

Problems, man's
basically religious, 3
involving "right" and "wrong," 3
Problem-solving
in Zen, 247–248
Problems, marital
information regarding, for patient admittance to Gold Coast hospital(s), 244
Proclamation(s)
basis of religion(s), 117
Promise
of liberation from suffering
in Buddhist scriptures, 127–128 (see also Bodhisattva)
Prophecy, Moses type of,
offering a "Way," 444
operative in contemporary American life, 444
Prophet
function of, 437
more charismatic than "priest," 437
Prophète manqué, portrait of a modern, 442–443
Prophetic vision
in psychotherapy, 446
Prophet(s)
dedicated to warning and mending ways of kings and leaders, 444
determined to uplift men from mediocrity to highest good, 442
not conforming to culture of their time, 441
not egocentric or out for publicity, 443
seditious cranks, 442
threats to status quo, 442
Prophets, Hebrew
consultants to kings and men of power, 440
crisis-induced conversion(s) of, 441
forthright preachers, 440
God speaking to His people, 441
imaginative, often ecstatic, *navis*, 441
opponents of evil in society and among individuals, 441
other occupations along with call from the Lord, 441
role defined, 440–443
Protestant community effort
toward rehabilitation of the
disturbed, the sick and the lonely, 53
Protestantism
and psychotherapy, 46
four dynamic principles
Call to a vocation in the world, 48, 53
Live by faith, 47, 49
Openness to truth, 48, 52
Priesthood of all believers, 47–48

separatism in, 46
spiritual community, 47
Protestantism, liberal
(see Liberal Protestantism and Theology, liberal Protestant)
Credo, 42
Proverbs, 113
Psalms, 115, 272
Psyche
four faculties in, according to Sufism, 159–160
disturbance of the
(see also Exorcism and Possession)
treated as "illness," 211
Psyche, man's
disintegrative forces at work on, 209
Psychiatrist
as "father symbol," 293
objective for the individual patient, 105
community point of view presented, 254
the faith of a, 107 (see book title)
the Western focus on patient's early experiences, 226
Psychiatry
as practiced in the Sudan, 162–163
attitudes toward religion, 105, 106
goal(s) of, 108
in collaboration with primitive faith and healing practices, 225–235
primitive factors, influence of, 225–236
"witchcraft" as belief in theories that parallel primitive concepts, 226 ff.
Psychic, 256, 258, 259
Psychoanalysis
and religion, 369–385
and the economic point of view, 380–381
and the genetic point of view, 381–382
and the psychodynamic point of view, 379–380
and the structural point of view, 382–383
and the topographical point of view, 379–380
and Voodoo compared, 233–234
attainment of selfhood through patient regression, 309–310
basic objective(s) of, 226
compared to Gestalt, 270, 271–272
definition of, 309
Freudian, 249
goals of, esp. 309
non-Freudian, 168
objective of, 226
process outlined, 309
Psychoanalyst
(see Psychoanalysis, Psychotherapist and Therapist)

"accepting" responses from patient, 309
father-role with patient, 309
frequency of patient contact with, 309–310
Psychodynamic theory, 249, 250
Psychodynamics, 291–292
Psychology
Buddhist, 152
Buddhist meditation and depth, 153
existential influences on, 34–35
generally at odds with modern Hinduism, 174
humanistic, 33–34
isolation from religion and ethics, 154
nature of man and human behavior, study area of, 417
not compatible with authoritarian Hindu tradition, 174
Theravadin, 147, 150–151, and 152
Psychology and religion
attempts at integrating, 417–425
early twentieth century relationship between, 33
humanistic basis in both systems, 116
increasingly compatible fields of study, 417, 425
integration of goals in Judaism, 109
mutual goals, 33–34
Orthodox view endorsing cooperation between, 196
partners in effort to understand nature of man and human behavior, 417
Psychology, depth
and Buddhist meditation, 153
Psychology, modern
humanistic trend in, 443
Psychometry
use of, in psychic counseling, 255
Psychopathy
in Muslim world, linked to struggle between evil and good, 163
Psychosis
acute, attributed to "loss of soul," 227
cases recognized as suffering from, 246
functional, treated according to Muslim therapy, 161–162
hysterical, 242
Psychosomatic ills
cases of, in native African treatment centers, 246
Psychotherapeutic movement
an impoverishment, lack of commitment, xiii
Psychotherapist
(see also Therapist)
a professional, 284
ability to help others, 250–252

accomplishments in today's drug scene, 443
and prophet compared, in function and dedication, 442-433, 446
anger at dehumanizing aspects of our culture, 445
appeal to the client, 428
as an outsider, with proper perspective on his patient(s), 444
as change agent, 51
as churchman, 446
as friend, esp. 453
as medium, 430
as priest, 452-457, esp. 455-457
as prophet, 441
as receptive listener, esp. 454-455, 458-459, 460
as spiritual healer, 454-457
aware of his own behavior pattern, 444
awareness of his own "place in the patient's world," 453
being, high-level quality of, 445
better versed in religious dialect and the spiritual welfare of patient(s), 437
communicating and receiving, 430
communication difficulties with patient, 252
concerned with others' behavior, 444
consulted by lost moderns, xi
contact with reality and actual experience maintained throughout assistance to patient, 457
contemporary achievement of, 443
culture context, understanding of, 250
curious and observant, regarding non-Western cultural patterns and their effect on behavior, 284-285
deeply analytical, 427
definition, 427-434
failing to reach the client, 428-429
father role, 112
function of the, 428
giving child courage to stand up to "doting" parents, 443
having capacity to "enter into relation," 445
helpful at the right time, 429
in what ways "prophetic," 445
inadequacy, feelings of, 430
interaction with a client, 428
interest in things religious and "prophetic," 446
listening stance and correct handling of patient's quest (*see* Participation), 454
mastery over situation, 250
measure of greatness among, 443
minimum auxiety in, 250
modeling way of life for others, 441

objective attitude toward the client, 429
overcoming own early psychological problems, 443
perspective on his own culture, 444
pointing out the truth about destructive behavior, 441, 444, 445-446
present-day goals and ideals, 435-438
"prophesying" to individual patients what he sees, 442, 445-446
prophetic outlook on the meaning and direction of social patterns, 444-445
qualifications as a salesman (used car), 427 ff.
rational level, operating on, 252
reducing patient's fear, 251
religious background of, 439
representative of Western society, 285
representing "the expanded community," with perspective on patient's quest, 454
"role" of the, 427
scientist, confidence as a, 250-251
sensitivity to evil, 442, 445-446
showing "connoisseurship" to patient by his example and lead during therapy, 454
some open to charge of "false prophecy," 443
"telling it as it is," 441, 445
twentieth century scientist, 284
up's and down's of a, 428
viewing both complexities and potentials of encounter, 456
what is expected of a, 250-251, 252, 428, 432, 433
Psychotherapists and spiritual counselors interaction needed, 267
Psychotherapy
(*see also* Psychotherapist *and* Therapy)
achieving independence from, patient's goal, 309
alienated individual helped on one-to-one basis, 449
an amoral approach, xiii
and Buddhism, 129-130
and ethics, 117
and philosophy, 117
and religion, 117
and the Eastern Orthodox Church, 195-221
and wisdom about life, 117-118
and Zen compared, 133-140
art, as an, 435, 438
as a religious system, xiv
as a science, 439
as guiding patient back into the world, 154
as part of a world-view, xiv
as the religious system of contemporary man, xiv

available mainly to rich members of Western society, 310–311
basic objectives of
　acceptance increased, 235
　change facilitated, 235
　resistance reduced, 235
basic problems in, 448 (see Alienation and other related topics)
behavior, illumination of human, 118
compared to the Buddhist Path, 151–154
compared to Zen, 247
confessional element in, 229
contemporary stress on personal-level, humanizing influence, 438
contemporary values in, xiv
creation of self-determining individual, therapist's goal, 309
dedicated to repair of human breakdown, 64
definition of, xiv
dream analysis, role of, 133 (see also Freud)
early involved in critical re-evaluations of Judaeo-Christian helping traditions, 284
encouraged in the Seventh-Day Adventist framework, 95–97
examination of beneficent factors therapeutically, 309–312
example of ineffective use of (in Nigeria), 310
existential viewpoint, 359–361
"false prophecy" in, defined, 443
free association, role of, 133, 135
goal of, 109, 195
goals compared to those of Judaism, 109
guiding patient back into the world, 154
happening, or human event, as a, 435
humanistic theories regarding, 32, 33–41, 43–45
impact on modern life, 117
improving the human condition, 436–438
influence of Zen training on, 139–140
informal, 293
insight, how tapped, 133
intuitional approach to, 139–140
isolation from religion and ethics, 154
modern, ally of Buddhism, 118
native, 243 ff.
orientation now based on selected values, 436
originally cut off from religion, 439
parallels with Zen Buddhism, 132
past role in undermining faith, 90
patient's attitude toward, 250
peer-group variety of
　"calling," a true, 451
phenomenologist approach, 249–250
(mind-healing)
　practiced from primitive times, 49
prepared to apply new knowledge about old therapeutic methods, 284
presently interested in acquiring new knowledge regarding human behavior in any cultural context, 284
primitive, basic elements, 236–253
types of
　primitive, effectiveness of methods, 249
professional jargon of, 437
professional leadership in,
　"calling," a true, 451
Protestant, 49–50
psychodynamic interpretive, 293
refinement of new therapeutic skills, a continuing concern, 284
religious experience, as, 435
results of, 250
return to religious outlook, 446
role of religion within, 108
science, as a, 435, 438
search for alternative(s) to, 168
secular calling vs. religious experience, 435
"selflessness" as goal of, 138–139
self-motivation for good sought, 105
self-realization, developing, 129–120
sense of community in the profession of, 449
sixteenth century case, 236–243, esp. 242–243
small-groups
　"calling," a true, 451
　importance for the future, 451
some twentieth century views, xiv–xvii
still too impersonal and intellectual to reach and deeply motivate patient, 231–232
strong sense of "calling" in, 447
subconscious, role of the, 133
traditional Western goals of insight and independence, still subject to change, 310
unconscious, role of the, 133
value orientation in, 105
value system in, 117
Western contrasted to primitive, 244, 245, 246, 249–250
"working through" process at the end, 137
Zen Buddhism as a system of, 132
Psychotherapy and religion
　a re-evaluation, xiv–xvi
　interrelationships, ix, xiv, xv
　crossing over, between the two disciplines, 437–438
　differences in outlook, noted, 436
　goals increasingly alike, 436–437
Psychotherapy and religion more compatible
　contemporary humanistic psychology and theological concerns studied

Psychotherapy, attitude(s) of
  man's individuality formed by particular historical situation, 196
  man's "normality" not essential as a goal, 196
Psychotherapy, types os
  primitive
    time element in, 249
  Western
    purpose of, 247, 251, 252
    schools of, 249–250
    scientist's reliance on reason, 251
    emphasis on the individual rather than on group interplay, 230
    scientific objectivity stressed, 230
    sessions not usually interrupted, 230
Psychotics
  custodial care of, 228–229
  insensitivity to environment, 228–229
Psychotic break, 251
Public health
  religious outlook on, 439–440
Publicity
  advertising of services in communication media, 258–259
  legality of, in psychic counseling, 256
  psychic counselor's, 258–259
Puerto Ricans
  reliance on mystical teaching of, 255
Puerto Rican spiritualists
  views of, 228
Purim, 115
Puritanism
  influence on beginnings of Christian Science, 82, 86
  sexual inhibitions caused by, 110
"Purity of heart," 38 (see Kierkegaard, Soren)

Q

Quakers, 48
  experience of, compared to modern group encounter, 269
  "Friends" to other Quakers, 273
  in spiritual context of the Reformation, 269–270
  obedience to God's Light a daily effort, 273
  open to non-sinful inner impulses, 273
  reverence for the Eternal Light, 270, 273
  sense of tradition, balancing enthusiasm with reliance on the Scriptures and the Meeting, 279
  shaken by their own inadequacy before God, 270, 273
  "Quaking," 273, 274
Quest, man's
  in spiritual realm, 452
  in social sphere, 452
Questions
  Western modern man's, xi
Quimby, Phineas, 81

R

Rabbi(s)
  not therapists, 108
  teachers of religious values, 108
Racy, John, 156–166
Radhakrishnan, S., 172
Ramakrishna, account of
  ecstasy, 314
  Kali, communication with, 314
  longing for vision of Mother, 314
  mystical experience, with great intensity of perception, 314
Rapprochement between psychology and religion reasons for, 33–37
Rativedha
  realization of the Truth in Buddhism, 142
Reaction, patient's
  immediate in psychotherapy, 139
  intuitively, to his self, his life situation, his attitudes, 140
Reading
  daily practice among Christian Science laymen, 78
  during Christian Science church services, 78
Reading, giving a spiritual
  in psychic counseling, 255
Reality—Itself
  according to Amitabha, 126
  compassionate wisdom in Mahanaya Buddhism, 126
Reality, Ultimate
  in Hinduism, 119
Re-assuring the patient
  technique used in explaining his symptoms, 230
Rebirth
  after following wrong path (Miccha), 146
  after suicide, according to Hindu belief, 172
  cessation of, in ecstatic state, 175
  doctrine less emphasized among Indian villagers, 171–172
  Hindu liberation from, 170, 171, 175
  in Christianity, 170
  in Hinduism, 170, 171, 175
  in Jainism, 171

Index

liberation from, in Jainism, 171
samsara, known as, 119
Rebirth, cycle of
  changed to cultivation of Zen outlook, 133
Receptive, on being, 427–434
Reconciliation
  based on integrity of self, 38
  man in need of, 216
  with God, 202–203, 206, 212
  with himself, 202
  with his neighbor, 202–203, 212
  with nature, 202, 215
Redemption
  (*see also* Salvation)
  as transfiguration of all nature (the entire natural order, 213
  Eastern Orthodox concept of, 201
  in Buddhism, 130
  of American Indians, 297
  of man through Christ, 213
  through attainment of moral good, 169
  through yoga, 169, 172
Redemption and Worship
  Hebrews' choice of life over death, 440
Redemption, story of the
  represented in icons in the Eastern Orthodox Church, 204
Re-evaluation
  after Counseling, 24
Reformation
  Protestant, 451
    not enough of a "revolution," 451
    original Church, failure to restore, 451
    small groups, not enough reliance on, 451
Reich, Wilhelm, 443
  body-oriented therapy, 274, 280
  "character armoring," 271
Reincarnation
  one of doctrines in modern psychic counseling, 254
Re-integration, patients'
  into the community, 231
Rejection
  child's fear of, 398–401
Relationship
  consultative
    between indigenous healer and Western practitioner, one solution, 285
    therapeutic significance of, 34
Relativism
  study of Absolute ideas, Ultimate meaning, 361–362
Relentless Process
  pursuing, 459
  surrender to, 460

Religion
  alienated human beings, appeal to, 450
  and psychiatry, confrontation after Freud, 116 (*see also* Freud)
  and symptoms, 338–339
  "as a universal obsessional neurosis" (Freud), 114
  as psychodrama, 231
  as the surest guide, 3
  central importance of, in people's lives, 288–289
  compared to psychology, 89
  definitions of, 117, 450
  effect of authoritarian, 397–398
  Freud on, 109, 114, 116
  horizontal (man-man) relationships in, 450
  individual believer's requirements of his, 274
  in the psychotherapist's office, 446
  inheritance, viewed as, 113–114
  inhibitive sexually, 110
  interpersonal stress, 450
  nature of man and human behavior, a central concern, 417
  offering answer(s) to ambiguity man faces, 6–8
  offering explanation(s) for unusual or unfortunate happenings, 144–145
  providing the means of enriching life, 117
  psychic counselors' training or ordination in churches, 256–257
  psychotherapy, 33, 435–436
  recent changes in orientation, 437
  reliable base for Encounter groups and experimental communities, 280
  role of, as compared to that of psychotherapy, 436
  selflessness in individual, 138–139
  study from clinical data, and some conclusions, 373–376
  taboo topic to American psychology? 417
  the place of, in psychotherapy, 338–343
  traditional dependence on system of taboos and values, 436
  twentieth century views, xiii–xv
  vertical (God-man) relationships in, 450
Religion, American Indian
  and the early practice of medicine, 297
Religion and psychotherapy
  cooperation between, 90
  interrelationships, xi, xiv, xv
  goals increasingly similar, 436
Religion, Chinese
  pre-Confucian, 180–182
Religion, client's

psychotherapist's basic respect for, 104
context of tradition needed to balance emotional excesses, 268
Religion, human agents in
priest, rabbi, minister, pastor, guru and prophet, 437
Religion
Jewish (see Judaism)
celebration of life, as a, 114-115
ethical behavior patterns emphasized, 108
one aspect of Judaism, not synonymous with it, 108
pathological factors or extremist behavior avoided in, 108-109
quest for meaning found by the people in, 116
values, basic spiritual guidance in, 108
Religion (s)
multiplicity of, xix
Religious experience
one with man's practical and social life (according to Orthodox belief), 195
Evangelical's, viewed as part of training, 59
Religious leader
as therapist, 41-42
Religious leader (s)
increasingly better informed about secular affairs, 437
Jewish, (see Prophets, Hebrew)
Religious life
compatibility of Hindu, with science and technology, 174
contemplative in Hinduism, 170
righteous and self-sacrificing in Christianity, 170
sex in, 178
Religious system (s)
drug experience within, 296
Renan, Ernest, 113-114
Renunciation
Zuhd, mystical stage in Sufism, 159
Replogle, 440
Repression
as a defense mechanism, 293
Repression, intrapsychic, 293
Research
in psychology, only recently undertaken by religious leaders, 417
psychoanalytic, declared at times exploitive, 443
Resignation
stage in Sufism, 159
Resistance, patient's
reduced through therapist's use of intuitional approach, 140

Resources, spiritual
to end man's fragmentation, 4
Response
instantaneous, spontaneous, 136
Responsibility, patient's
for his own illness, 227
for his own wrongdoing, 229
to get well, in the Western world, 229-230
Resurrection
celebration of the, between Easter and Ascension Day, in the Eastern Orthodox Church, 202
Revelation
liberal Protestant doctrine regarding, 36
or "wisdom" in Buddhism, 129
Revivalism
fundamentalist, 450
small groups within, 450
theistic, 450
transitory or permanent? 450
widespread, 450
youth appeal, 450
Revolution
philosophical-religious, xi
religious, 447, 450-451
social-cultural, xi
Reward
the psychotherapists's, 433
Reward and retribution, divine
belief contrasted to personal responsibility for one's actions, 110
Biblical pattern, 112-113
Jewish belief in, popular, 110
Rhine, J. B., 456
Richards, Stephen L., 104
Ricoeur, Paul, 148
Rieff, Philip, xiii, xiv
Right thinking
use of, in Chrisitan Science practice, 80
Righteousness, way of
for modern man, 444
upheld by contemporary psychotherapists, 444
Ritual
in treatment of Gold Coast patients, 244
proper performance of, in Chinese worship, 180
Rivalries, family
information regarding, for patient admittance to Gold Coast hospital (s), 244
River (s)
Chinese deities of the sacred, 180
River people
calling tribesmen to secret rites and wisdom, 245

in South Africa, 245
onset of insanity, agents of, 245
Road chief, Peyote minister, 298
Roberts, David, 32, 45, 61
Roberts, Oral, 80
Rogers, Carl, 37, 38, 44, 54, 55, 57, 133, 140 439, 445
Rogers, William R., 32–45
Rohrer, 440
Role, transcending a, 427–434
Roman Catholicism
    open to new modes, not responsible for any one viewpoint, regarding counseling, 15
Romans, Letter to the, 67
Rose, Louis, 85
Rosenthal, Vin, 427–434
Rosh-ha-Shonah, 115
Rosicrucianism
    in psychic counseling practice, 255

S

Sabbath
    celebrating man's kinship to God, 92
Sabbath keeping
    in relationship to God, 92
Sacrament(s)
    communal character of, in the Eastern Orthodox Church, 209–210
    rites attending man's birth, life and death, 206
Sacraments
    importance of, in the Eastern Orthodox Church, 206, 214
    impoverishment of, in recent Church development, 214
    in the Eastern Orthodox Church, numberless, 206–207, 214
    mystical experience during, 199–200
Sacrifices
    in exchange for blessings (in Chinese worship), 181
    proper performance of, in Chinese worship, 180
Sage
    or "Ideal Man," in Chinese thought, 194
Saint(s)
    Hindu, 172-173 *passim*
Saint
    icon or representation of, 207, 208
Saint, the patron
    child's protector, 207–208
Saints, as leaders in group worship
    in the Eastern Orthodox Church, 205–206
Saints, communion of
    child's introduction to, in the Eastern Orthodox Church, 207–208
    fellowship in the, 207–208
    taking part in Eastern Orthodox worship services, 203–204
Saints, veneration of
    in the Eastern Orthodox Church, 204–206, 207–208
Salt Lake City, Utah, 100
Salvation
    (*see also* Redemption)
    according to Orthodox belief, 213
    and psychotherapy compared, 38–41
    bringer of, 125 (*see* Vairocana)
    by faith, according to the Lutherans, 268
    by grace, within Buddhism, 118
    divine authors of
    in Mahayana Buddhism, 118–126 *passim*, 130
    drama of, 201–202 (*see also* Eastern celebration)
    ideal of, in Bodhisattva's compassion, 127–129
    of the individual as part of the Orthodox Church community, 202
    Orthodox doctrine of, 200–201
    restoration to inner integrity, 40
    though the morally good life, 168, 172
Samatha (Meditation), 135
    Eastern Orthodox worshipper's attitude toward, 204, 207–208
Sambhogakaya (Accommodated Body), Buddha as, 131
Sambodhi, 121
Samma
    right path in Theravada, 146
Samsara
    illusion replacing objects in Hindu trance, 170
    part of Buddhist belief which explains individual's circumstances, 145
    wheel, or stream, of rebirth, 119, 127
Samyasin ("Enlightened One")
    stages of contemplation, to reach Enlightenment, 278
Sangha
    Buddhist monks and disciples, 144
Sangharakshita, B., 124, 126, 131
Sanity
    control, by the mind, of one's destiny, according to Hindu practice, 174 (*see* Control)
    radical standards of, imposed by today's intellectuals, 174

Sanctification
  growth in faith, 278
  in the Christian life, 278
Sanskrit
  Buddhist scriptures in, 123
  use of terms "body" and "mind," 174
Santeria
  Afro-Cuban religion in Miami, 319–326, 328–329, esp. 322–325
Santero
  leader of the Santeria, known for teaching and divination, 322–323, 326–329
Sarnoff, Irving, 67
Sarte, Jean Paul, xv
Satan
  pact with, 237–239
  tempting man to become "like God," 200
Sati (mindfulness)
  meditation practice in Buddhism, 149
Satori
  insight coming to Zen student after long adherence to his master, 248
  Zen disciple's freedom from master, achieved through insight, 248
Sato, K., 134, 140
Saturday
  observed as the Sabbath, 91
Saudi Arabia, heart of Muslim world, 158
Savage, C., 308, 316, 318
Savior(s)
  many in Mahayana Buddhism, 124, 126, 130
Schechter, Solomon, 110
Schizophrenia
  cases of, among African tribesmen, 245, 246
Schizophrenics
  given status in the primitive community, 228–229
Schizophrenic(s)
  rehabilitation of, 228–229
Schneider, Delwin B., 117–131
Schuz, 277–278, 283
Science
  as the Truth in Christian Science, 72–73
  supplementing the task of religion, 90
Science and Health with Key to the Scriptures, 72, 77, 78, 86
"Science" in Christian Science
  not to be tested as any other science, but accepted as already demonstrated, 72–73
Scientist
  expert in a field of knowledge, 250
Scripture
  Genesis 32:25–29, 429
Scripture references
  Mark 9:29, 212
  Luke 17:21

Second Coming (of Christ), 206
  belief in the, 91
Secret, The (Al-Sirr)
  highest faculty, locus of "Witness," in Sufist division of "psyche," 160 (see Marhaz Al-Mushahada)
Seeker(s)
  one seeker among other, xvi–xvii
Self
  a New, birth of, 268
  concern with, 19
  fulfillment of, psychotherapeutically, 118
  not permanent entity, but one in flux (see Nirvana), 147
  questions about the human, 117
Self-acceptance
  Buddhism, by means of, 118
"Self-actualization" (Maslow), 34
Self-actualization
  individual's, 441
  psychotherapy's goal, 436
  through new attitudes, 31
Self-assertion
  lack of, in the patient, 227
Self-awareness
  eliminated in Zen, 249
  emotionally experienced (see Gestalt), 270–271
  heightened in analysis, 249
  in group experience, 269, 271
  long road to, 278
  mind-revealed, 270 (see Psychoanalysis)
Self-discipline
  in Christian Science, 82, 85–86
Self-effort
  basis of Theravada Buddhism, 122–123, 130
Self-esteem of the American Indian
  growth in, after meetings with Peyote brothers, 296, 301, 304–305
Self-esteem, patient's
  increased through therapist's use of intuitional approach, 140
Self-exaltation
  relinquished, 153
Self-examination
  post-therapy, by the patient, 139
Self-forgetfulness
  mark of healthy personality, 138
Self-giving
  of counselor, 22–24
Self-image
  shattering of the old, in Encounter group(s) 269
  transformation of, in religious experience, 269

Self-involvement
  in on-going task, 138
Self-knowledge
  Buddhism, by means of, 118
Self, love of (see also Egoism and Narcissism)
Self-realization
  as a religious goal, 435
  Buddhism, by means of, 118, 129–130
  emphasized in Judaism, 108
  in Orthodox belief, 199
  sense of humility on the long road to, 278
Self-reliance
  demanded of the patient in psychotherapy, 229
Self-reliance, man's
  in Judaism, 110
Self, The (Al-Nafs)
  seat of base emotions, guide to evil, in Sufist division of "psyche," 159
Selflessness
  essential concept in psychotherapy, 138–139
  Zen concept, defined and evaluated, 138–139
Sense perception
  mind's withdrawal from, in highest type of Hindu religious practice, 169
Sensuous craving
  freedom from, at second stage of Norvana, 147
Serenity
  characteristic of Christian Scientist, 84
Seventh Day (The), 92
Seventh-Day Adventist Church, 89–97
  attitude toward the Creation, 92
  origins, 91
  place of Christ in, 93–95
  tenets, 90–95
Sex
  (see also Indulgence, sensuous)
  (see also Love, physical)
  and religion, 178
  Freudian reference to, 178
  In Tantrism, 176–177, 178–179
  Jewish teaching(s) on, 110–111
  purity of sexual union, blessed by God, 111
  education in the Jewish home, 111
Sexual drive(s)
  expression of, in ritualistic practice, 176–177, 178–179
  represssion of, in Judaeo-Christian belief systems, 178
Sexual intercourse
  (see also Copulation, ritualistic)
Sexual repression
  advocated by Puritanism, 110
Shabbath, 112

Shakti, role of
  in ritualistic copulation, 176
Shaman (medicine man)
  giving demonstration of his skills as healer-priest to his Eskimo villagers, 312
Shamanism, 294
  in modern psychic counseling practice, 254
Shang
  conquest of the, by Chou rulers, 182
Shang Ti
  Ruler in Heaven, 180
  ritual in honor of, 180
  Supreme deity in China, 180, 181
Shaw, Frank, 445
She chi
  altar of earth and grain, 180
  as center of the state, in Chinese religion, 180
  as protector of military expeditions, 180
Sheikh, Sufi
  as adviser to Muslim seeker, 159
  therapist role among mentally ill, 161–162
Sheikha
  Muslim woman therapist, esp. in Zar ceremony, 161
Shepherd, Irma Lee, 458–460
Shih Chi (see Ssu-ma Ch'ien)
  Historical Records, 190
  Taoist Historical Records, 190
Shivā (Destroyer), 177
Shrine deity
  protector of patient at shrine and therafter 244
Shrine hospitals, Gold Coast
  administered by native practitioners, 243–244
  doctor, or native practitioner, in charge, 244
  doctor's prestige in, 244
  intake of patients, 243–244
  mental hospital(s), native, 243, 246
  patients in, 243
  witches' victims, for, 243
Shrine(s)
  Gold Coast (see Shrine hospitals, Gold Coast)
Shu (altruism)
  concern for others; part of Jen, 184
  sympathy for one's fellow man, 184–185
Shu *Ching*
  Chinese *Book of History,* 181
Sick
  prayers for the, 210–212
  sacrament of Holy Unction for the, 210
Sick, care of the
  in the Eastern Orthodox Church, 204, 210–212

Sick, cure of the
   in Peyote services, 297
Sick, the
   Koran's provisions for, 157
Sickness
   suffering, as source of, 122, 127
Siddhartha (see Gautama)
"Significant Others," 449
Silence
   practice of, for purposes of self-awareness, 277
Simon and Garfunkel, quotation from song by, 431
Simplicity
   Taoist ideal of life, 193
Sin
   (see Evil)
   as alienation, 37
   as pathology-inducing behavior, 445
   Eastern Orthodox view of, 200–201
   liberal Protestant view of, 37–39 passim
   man wounded by, 202, 237
Sin (s)
   (see also Pride)
   confessing one's, in psychotherapy, 229
Sin, or sickness? xiv
Sisters, Black
   of Mons, 236–242
Skidmore, C. Jay, 98–107
Skinner, B. F., 8
Small-groups movement, 447–451
Small-groups movement
   in early Christian church
      confessional in character, 451
      meeting in homes, 451
      mutual concern for members, 451
      source of new life and inspiration, 451
Small-groups movement today
   confessional function of, 451
   humanistic, chiefly, 450
   need in the Christian church increasing, 451
   revolutionary, 450–451
   secular or religious? 450
   self-disclosure emphasized, 451
Smith, Joseph, Prophet of Latter-Day Saints, 99, 101
Social obligations, man's
   emphasized in Judaism, 110 ff.
Social problems
   lack of concern for, in Christian Science circles, 84–86
   solutions to, in Mahayana Buddhism, 130
Social service agencies, Latter Day Saints, 100
Social values, American

Christian Science's close identification with, 73–74, 86
Society
   service to man and, basic to Jewish faith, 109–110
   prophetic vision of the good
      working psychotherapists moving toward, 446
   value system of
      effects of, 134
"Sociology of man," the
   gods varying in form and concept to fit, 438
Song of Songs, 110–111
Sophisticated ideas
   in Chou period of Chinese kings, mixed with superstition, 181
Sotah, 111
Soul (s)
   importance of each, in enlarged experience of all, 454
Soul
   "no-self" in Buddhism, 151
   union with God, in Sufism, 159
   doctrine of the
      not present in Christian Science teaching, 74
Soul loss, 227–228
   treatment for, 229
Soul searching
   encouraged in Mormon bishop's interviews, 102
South Africa, 245
Speech
   "right" (truthfulness), in Buddhism, 121, 122
Spirit, or god
   believed to help release Hindu individual from Karma, 171–172
Spirit (s)
   alien, 226
   casting out of, Scriptural basis for, 212
   dependance upon, in exchange for protection, 311
   explaining good or bad happenings, in Hindu life, 144
   overcoming of, 289
Spirit
   intrusion (see Possession)
   The, seat of good qualities, opposed to "self," 160
Spirit Guide, psychic counselor's claim to a, 264
Spirit, the Great, 296
Spiritual quality
   commonly attributed to the East, 172

Spiritualist, 257, 259
Spiro, Melford, 292, 295
Spock, Benjamin, 444
Spontaneity
  quality needed in Zen, 134
Spufford, Belle S., 101
Ssu-ma Ch'ien, author of Historical Records (Shih Chi), with first mention of Taoist School, 190
Stace, W. T., 308, 318
Stack-Sullivan, H., 168
Stamey, Harry C., 335–343
Status, loss of, 320–321
Status quo, encouraging patient to accept psychotherapist's traditional goal, 436
Seiner, L., 254, 267
Sterility
  cases associated with witchcraft, Gold Coast, 243
Stern, E. Mark, 452–457
Stevens, Barry, 272
Stress, environmental
  viewed as "harmful" by the individual, 226
Stress-metabolite, toxic
  biochemical component in anxiety cases, 251
Stress prevention
  in patients, 228
Strupp, Hans, 63
Students, college
  religious problems of, 388–402
Sudan, 161
Suffering
  (see also Pain)
  as a "falling out of favor" with orichas (or "saints"), 324
  Bodhisattva taking on burden of, 127
  Buddhist belief regarding, 121, 122
  contemporary prophets' concern with, 444
  death, 122
  denial of, in Christian Science, 79, 86
  easing of, through prayer, 210–211
  ego-desires, caused by one's 122
  existence as, in Buddhist teaching, 122
  Gautama's deliverance from, 120
  Hindu outlook on, 172
  how shared and diluted in encounter groups, 281–283
  in Buddhism, 121–122
  in Mahayana Buddhism, 130
  in Zen Buddhism, 133–134
  intrapsychic, therapists' varying views on, 265–266
  old age, 122
  patient's ego-preoccupation, brought on by, 134
  Platform Sutra on human, 133–134
  psychotherapists motivated to relieve, 445
  psychotherapy providing man with strength and patience to endure, 195
  secular approach to, 439
  sickness, 122
  struggle to maintain individuality among men, 122
  temporal nature of human existence, 122
  Hebrew people's
    recorded as "evidences of the Lord's wrath," 440
    regarded as consequences of laxity in protection of the weak, 440
Sufi Sheikh (see Sheikh, Sufi)
Sufism, 159–161
  pantheistic ideas in, 159
  psychology of, 159
  three stages of, 159
Suggestion
  as therapeutic method, 231
  in Christian Science, 85–86
  in healing, 75
  in Muslim magical therapy, 161
  technique used by therapists, both lay and professional, 266
  to enhance doctor's power and prestige, 244
Suicide
  ruled out, in Hindu belief system, 172
Sukhavati (Pure Land), 126
Sullivan, H. S., 133, 141, 449
Summa Theologica, 31
Sun
  Buddha, 125 (see Vairocana)
  Goddess, in Japan, 125 (see Amaterasu)
Sung dynasty, 137
Superego
  rigid, punitive in neuroses and certain types of religious observances, 114 (see Freud, Sigmund)
  role in mental illness, 163
  role of the, 226
Superindividuality
  as therapeutic goal, 454
Supernatural, therapy by control of the (see Magic)
Superstition(s), 225
"Surprises" from patient
  accepted by friend, 452
  recognized by therapist-become priest as evidence of unique creative potentialities, 457
  welcomed by therapist, as widening range of insight, 452–453, 457

Susma (spirit)
  witch's, 243
Symptom reduction
  secondary goal in therapy, 40
Symptoms
  unopened doors, looked upon as, 459
Synagogue
  role of, secondary to Jewish family's, 111
Syncretism
  in Santeria religion in Southeastern United States, 319 ff.
Synergeia (cooperation), 200
  (*see* Cooperation)
Szasz, T., 168, 177

T

Ta Hsiieh
  Great Learning, 183
Taboo violations
  examples of 225–226
  factor in mental illness, 225
  parallel with modern patient's lack of control over his own environment and circumstances, 227
Tabu(s) and sacrifice(s)
  represented in mystical states by a sacrifice of worldly interests or by a renunciation of sexual life, 312
Taftazani, A., 159, 160, 166
Taittiriya-Upanishads, 175
Talmud, 109–113 *passim*
Talmud
  rules of conduct in, 111–113
Tang hsia i nien
  "first thought..." in Zen, 136
Tanha (Craving or Desire)
  source of suffering, 122, 123
Tantric meditation, 176–177
Tantrism (*see also* Meditation, tantric)
Tantrism, 171, 176–177, 178
Tantrism
  allying individual's religion and sexual orientation, 178
  central position of sex in ritual(s) of, 178
  consumption of forbidden foods in ritual, 176, 177 (*see* Five M's)
  control in ritualistic copulation (*coitus reservatus*), 176–177
Tantrism
  guided sensual experimentation in, 178
  liberation from rebirth, through psychic power in yogic enstasy, 177 (*see* Copulation, ritualistic; *and* Ojas)
  old solutions to modern man's psychological problems, suggested by, 177, 178–179

Tao
  the path of natural spontaneous events, upheld by early Taoist followers, 191, 192
Tao (Path), the great
  everything a part of, in Zen, 136
Taoism, 190–194
Taoism
  among great religions, 117
  Chinese philosophy, 132
  individual life and state of nature stressed, 190
  influence of thought widespread among Chinese people, 191
  influence on Zen Buddhism, 132–133
  "letting things take their own course," 192
  message to "cherish what is within you," and shut out what's without, 192
  only good aspects of Nature seen, 192
Taoism and Confucianism
  both expressing philosophical concern of the "Sage" and the Ideal Man, 194
Taoism and Confucianism compared, 190, 192
Taoist School
  (*also see* Taoism)
  based on the Tao (Way, or way of lfie); early opposed to Confucius' social codes, 191
  made up of men who "shunned the world," to maintain their own purity, 191
  self-interest and personal life upheld, 191
Tao-teh Ching (see LaoTzu)
  exalting the Tao and idealizing Nature, 191
  (*also see* Nature, idealization of)
Task at a time, one
  in Zen, 247–248
Tathagata, 121
Taylor, A. E., 58
Tea leaves, reading of
  reliance on, in psychic counseling, 255
Teacher
  stepping down to man-level, 31
Teacher(s)
  in Christian Science, 76–77
Teilhard de Chardin, 453, 455
Telepathy
  definition of, 255
Telepathy, or thought transfer
  disavowed in Christian Science, 79
Tembu, the, 245
Temple(s)
  Hindu, in India
    erotic sculpture of, 175, 177
Temple, ancestral
  of ruling Chinese dynasty, 181
Temple, William, 36

Temptation
  of Hebrews, by the Canaanites, 440
Tenderness and intimacy
  stirred in Encounter groups, 271
Terminology, religious
  adoption of, by the therapist, 437
"Testimony of the material senses"
  not considered "reality" to Christian Science, 73
Thanksgiving
  (*see also* Catharsis)
  prayer for, in Eastern Orthodox liturgy, (*see also* Transfiguration), 214
Theological dimension, approximation of
  in the therapeutic relationship, 40
Theology
  definition of, 7
  later Buddhist, 123
  liberal protestant positions in, 32, 35–37, 38–45
  naturalistic, 36
Theology, Indian
  contrast to Judaic, Christian, and Islamic beliefs, 171
  Monistic thrust of, 178
Theosis (*see* Deification)
Theosophy
  practiced by psychic counselors, 254, 257
Therapeutic dimension
  in religious experience, 216
Therapeutic method(s)
  strange, 236 ff.
Therapeutic principle, 250
Therapeutic process
  Christian Science practice of, 76–80
Therapeutic quest
  emphasis on seeking rather than thing sought, 179
  in Hindu meditation and practice, 178
  toward unity with the supreme cosmic Being, 178 (*see also* Oneness with the Absolute)
Therapies, culturally conditioned
  translation from one system to another, for the same patient, 292–294
Therapies, new
  powerful and revolutionary, 268, 271–272
  self-discovery and emotional release found in, 270–273, 277
  short road to human-potential goals, in contrast to the way of the mystics, 278
  shortcomings, 279–280, 283
  spiriual dimension, limitations of, 274
  "working through" negative feelings, 278

Therapis (religious leader)
  qualities of, 41–42
Therapist
  (*see also* Counselor and Psychotherapist)
  attitude toward patient experiencing anxiety, 251
  definition of function, 251
  example of cure through direct order to patient under sedation (in Nigeria), 310
  "gone prophet," 445
  independence and insight, two main goals for patient in analysis, 310
  influence of, 436
  influential in restoring patient's confidence, 232–233
  moral guidance from, 436
  patient's confidence in, 251
  priestly functions, 455, 456–457
  process of being and being a, 460
  projected image, 435
  prophetic role of, in modern times, 444
  qualities of a good, 34–37, 38, 41–42, 90, 96
  role of, 435, 437–438
  role within profession and affiliation, 437
  style, a question of, 435
  task of, 436
  value orientation of, 435–436
Therapist and clergy
  division of labor and responsibility, 104
Therapist, attitude of the
  on the Christ-model, 95
Therapist, Christian
  and positive regard toward client, 68–70
  "educator" role, 57
  God helping, always, 70
  interpretation of over-all pattern of behavior, 60–61
  living his faith; keeping channels open for God's healing, 59
  offering patient added resources, 62–63
  role of prayer (silent) during session, 63–64
Therapist (*Hakhamin*)
  Israel's Wise Men, 56
Therapist-become priest
  emphasizing patient's communion with all life, 455
Therapist or healer
  personal influence of, 231
Therapist-patient relationship
  in depth, 455–457
Therapist(s), physical
  psychic counselors' contact with, 256
Therapy
  (*see also* Phychotherapy)
  as an art style, 427

as a science, 427
as a way of giving, 433
Buddhist, 153
client-centered, 427
culturally conditioned in the Arab community, 165
culture context of, 250
daily, in treatment of Gold Coast patients, 244, 246
group-initiated, group-conducted, 230, 233–235
how practiced, 427 ff.
  (*also see* Counseling
in church (es), 446
individual's motivation for entering, 448
in the Arab East, 163–164
needed by the therapist, 41
paradox of the art of, 429
peer group, 449
religious dimension in, 216
symptom reduction in, 40
total-solution, limited success of, 167
Therapy and Tradition, confluence of, 280–283
Therapy as Human Transformation
rediscovery, 42, 43–44
responsibility, human
for decision and action, 34
Therapy *before* and therapy *now*
how the practitioner can maintain an integrated personality, 428
Therapy, description of
as a "caring relationship," 43–45
Therapy, psychic
techniques taught a group of psychotherapists, 264–265
Therapy results (in Christian Science)
influenced by the therapist's state of mind, 79
Therapy, social forms of
increasingly used in Western world, 231
Theravada Buddhism (*see* Buddhism, Theravada)
Theresa, Saint
incestuous fantasy, 315
Thinking, feeling and behavior
re-integrated, 12
Thomas, Saint, 17–18
Thorner, Isador, 86
Thought, change of
in Christian Science, 85–86
Ti, Supreme (Chinese) Deity, 180 (*see* Shang Ti)
Tibet, 125, 126
Tantrism in, 178
T'ien
Heaven, or Divine power, 181

T'ien-ming, Chinese Mandate of Heaven, 181
T'ien Tzu
Chinese king, "the Son of Heaven," 181
Ti (the Lord-on-High)
blessing and protection from, 180
Supreme (Chinese) Deity, 180 (see Shang Ti)
Tilak, B., 172
Tillich, Paul, 32, 35, 40, 43, 45, 167
Tillich, Paul, xv
esp. The Courage to Be
Time-element
contrast between short-duration "new" therapies and the long Path of Zen mystics, 278
effect of all-night meeting on Peyote worshippers, 303–304, 305
in primitive psychoanalytic methods, 249
in therapy, 251
marked difference in duration, between Eastern search for Truth and Western therapies, 278
shortened by use of intuitional approach in therapy, 140
Timelessness
applied to the Buddha ("is never born and never dies"), 124
in Mhayana Buddihism, 124
Torrey, E. F., 266, 267
Tournier, Paul
Christian psychotherapist, 439
Town, small
twentiety-century, American-style, ix, xi
Toxin(s), biochemical
in patients, 251
Tradition
continuity of, in a great religion, 274
cradles of, needed in new therapies, 279–280, 283
in Jewish family life, 113–114
reliance on, in treatment of youth problems in changing society, 165
Training Course and Self Help Guide, Mormon Bishops', 100
Trance
Hindu mind-withdrawal from objects or from sense perceptions, 169
dissociation, 324
illusory character of objective world in, 170
induced in Zen training, 136
in Hindu yoga or meditation, 169–170
insight achieved through, 170
psychic counselors' use of, in consultation, 255, 263

Trance
  reliance on, in psychic counseling, 255
  viewed positively in Hindu religion, 169–170
Trance inducement
  use of, questionable, 136
Transcultural diagnosis
  normal vs. abnormal, 286–290
Transference
  of patient's dependencies and hostilities to counselor-father image of the therapist, 309–310
Transfiguration, Liturgy of the
  in the Eastern Orthodox Church, 214
Transformation, human
  process of, 42–44
  through modern psychotherapy, 118
  through religious faith, 117
Treatment
  away from patient, 79
  by native healer vs. by modern psychiatrist, 228–233
  Gold Coast, consisting of daily ritual and therapy, 244
  impersonal in Christian Science practice, 79–80
Treatment center(s)
  native African
    consulted for neurotic or psychotic disturbances, 246
Treatment methods
  parallel in psychotherapy and in "religion," 11–12
Treatment techniques for the mentally ill
  in primitive societies
    catharsis, 229
    exorcism, ritualistic, 229
    frightening, 229
    fumigation, 229
    prayer and sacrifice, 229
    scapegoats, 229
    witch-hunt, 229
Treatment
  selected to reassure the patient and to win over his capacity to respond, 231
Trikaya
  three-fold body of the Buddha, 124, 131
Trinity, doctrine of the
  each of three Persons, retaining his unity, 199
Trust
  mutual between patient and therapist, 454
  vs. distrust, in the very young child, 50
Truth
  as a goal in Buddhism, 142
  each seeker for himself, 172

  experience of, contrasted to individual believer's own limited truth, 268–269, 274
  Hindu seeker(s) after, 179
  individual discovery of, 268
  therapeutic effect of search after, in patient, 179
Trying "too hard"
  patient's dilemma, 230
Twain, Mark, 72, 84, 88
Tzu-hua (self-transforming)
  one basis of easy-going Taoist philosophy, 192
Tzu-jan
  totality of spontaneity of things, in Chinese Taoist philosophy, 191
Tzu-wang (self-forgetting)
  one basis of easy-going Taoist philosophy, 192 (*see also* Tzu-hua)

U

Ukutwasa (insane)
  in South Africa, 245
  rescued by fellow tribesmen, 245
  taken to native doctor, 245 (*also see* Isanuse)
  "called to the river," 245, 246
Unitarian-Universalist Christianity,
  faith that nurtured Christian Science, 72
Unity
  of body of believers in Christian and Hindu/Buddhist world, 276–277
Unity of man
  body, mind and spirit together, 95
Umn-Dubban, 161
Unconscious, role of the
  in Buddhist meditation, 153
  in Indian psychology, 153
Understanding
  offered by therapist, 452
Union ecstatic
  experienced in mystic state, 316
Unity of all Life
  Siddhartha's knowledge of the, 460
Unity of Heaven and Man, central thesis in Chinese belief system(s), 183
Universe
  harmony of the, a Peyote belief, 296
University of Wittenberg, 47
Upanishads, 119

V

Vairocana
  contemplative Buddha, 125
Vahanian, Gabriel, 34, 35
Vayhinger, John M., 56–71

Value conflict
  traditional belief *vs.* folkcult, 321–322, 323–329
Value Crisis
  some approaches, 358–361
Value orientation
  patient's, in therapy, 178
  psychotherapist's, contemporary, 436
Value system, modern
  based on self-reliance, 229
Value systems, 8–10
  in conservatism, 400–402
  individual's need for a personal, 344–345
Values
  an in-depth study of contemporary, 346–355
  change in, from counseling, 19
  expression of human, in psychotherapy, 118
  hurting a person's, considered in therapy, 56
  in counseling, 19
  parents' endowment of, to the child, 112–113
  practical knowledge regarding, in psychotherapy, 117
  recovery of the sense of absolute, 364–365
  religious, 177–178
Values and the future
  conclusions on continual value change, 362–363
Van Buren, Paul, 35, 45
Vedic sacrifice
  observed in Hindu ritual, 170
Vine and the Branches
  parable of the, 46
Violence, sensitivity to
  needed in out time, 443
Vipassana (Insight), 135
Virtue
  more important than sacrifice in Chou religious thought, 182
Vishnu (Preserver), 177
Visit(s) to the sick, 212
Vivekananda, N. D., 172
Vocabulary, psychologist's professional reflecting ethical concerns, 60
Voodoo priest's incantation
  compared to psychotherapist's repetition of insights, 234

W

Walsche, R., 153
War, incitement to
  "taught" by exposing children to certain myths, 443
Wardell, Walter I., 72–88 esp. 77
Wardwell, Walter I., 72–88

Warkentin, 439
Warren, Neil Clark, 417–426
Way
  truth, in search of, 117
Way of life
  (see also Lifestyle)
  psychotherapist's, reflected in his work, 445
Way of the Elders,
  name of original Theravada movement, 143
Weber M., 168, 179
Weidman, Hazel, 319–331
Well-being, human
  Buddhism, in, 117
  Christianity, in, 117
  Confucianism, in, 117
  Hinduism, in, 117
  Islam, in, 117
  Judaism, in, 117
  Taoism, in, 117
Weltanschauung, 275
Wescott, M. R., 137, 141
Wesley, John, 49
Wheelis, Allan, xv, 250, 253
Whitaker, 439
Whitehead, Alfred North, 452–453
Whittier, J. G., 124
Wholeness
  being open and receptive to, 452
  contribution of Monasticism to, 200
  Death as a threat to, 6
  in an orderly life, 91
  in incarnate-redemptive learning, 26, 31
  in Theravada Buddhism, 142
  individual consciousness becoming, 453
  man's adherence to, 4–6, 7–8
  man's longing for, 4–5, 7–8
  man's, achieved through interrelated experiences, 195
  man's, body-spirit continuum, 218
  mans, compatibility with Eastern Orthodox viewpoint, 195
  man's, in Seventh-Day Adventist faith, 95
  of personality in Catholicism, 25
  person's drive toward, 459–460
  restoration to, 25, 202, 217, 218, 292–293
Wholeness of self
  restored through affirmation of responsibility religious *and* psychological, 37
Wholeness redefined
  to include religious reality, 10
Wholeness (unity)
  of Hindu believer with the supreme cosmic being, 178
Wieman, H. N., 40
Wife, duties of Jewish, 112

Wijesekera, O. H., 145
Will
  God's, surrender to, in Islam, 156
  role of the, in Christian Science, 86
Williams, Daniel Day, 32, 45
Wilson, Bryan, 74, 78, 84
Wilson, Colin, 442
"Wineskins"
  for new wine of contemporary therapies, 268, 277, 282–283
Wisdom
  cultivation of, in Theravāda Buddhism, 154
  deep realization of Buddhist doctrines, 149
  hermetic, use of, in modern psychic counseling practice, 255
  in Buddhism, 121, 129, 149
Witchcraft
  (see also Witches)
  American Indian beliefs regarding, 289–290
  concept in modern psychiatry, 226
  danger of, 243
  Gold Coast, African, 243–
  inflicting insanity on the victim, 225–226
  modern practitioners of, 254
  modern psychiatric theories, 226
  protection from, 243
  shrines or hospitals to combat, 243
  spirit intrusion, 225
Witch doctor
  American Indian testimony regarding, 288–290
  role in magic society, 250
Witch doctors
  Navaho, 285
Witchdoctor(s)
  in South Africa, 245
Witches
  belief in, 243
  believed to help release Hindu individual from Karma, 171–172
  cannibalism, 243
  characteristics of, 245
  destruction or mutilation of victim's vital essence, 243
  Gold Coast, 243
  night wandering, 243
  victims of, 243, 244
  for root cause of instability in a child's past, 226
Witkin, H. A., 256, 267
Witness
  in Islam, 157
Wolpe, 34
Woman
  beauty of, 110–111
  "helpmate" and conscience to her husband, 112
  high regard for, in Jewish life and Scripture, 110–111
  Koran's legal provisions for, 157
  number of, in psychic counseling field, 256
  virtue of, praised in Talmud, 112
Women, Muslim
  double standard, 158–159
  education of, 158–159
  modernization of, 158–159
  traditional role of, 158–159
Women's rights
  equality of the sexes maintained in Jewish scripture, 112
  in marriage, according to Judaism, 110
  in Talmudic law, 111
  in the Jewish home, 112–113
  sexually, 110
  stressed in Jewish religion, 110
"Working through"
  by patient psychotherapy, end of process of, 137
  during therapy and the process of salvation compared, 42–43
  principle in the new therapies, 277–278
  stage in self-awareness, 277–278
Workshops (see Encounter workshops; also Retreats)
World
  no withdrawal from the, in Christian Science, 74
  sacramental view of, in Eastern Orthodox Church, 216
  "the Other," interdependence with this world, in Chinese worship, 181
World-view
  a new, science-oriented, xi
  psychic counselor's and client's, 260
World view (weltanschauung)
  needed for our times, ix, xii
Worldly concerns
  Hindu dissatisfaction with, 169
Worship
  corporate act of, emphasized in Eastern Orthodox Church, 204–205
  freedom of the individual in, Eastern Orthodox Church, 203–206
  in the Eastern Orthodox Church, 201–202, 205
  natural objects used in Eastern Orthodox, 214
  personal involvement in, 205
Worshipper's attitude toward the liturgy in the Eastern Orthodox Church, 204

Wu-wei
  way of no-action in Taoism, 192 (see also Tzu-wang)

Y

Yahweh (see Jahweh)
Yakima Indian reservation, Washington, 287
Yi
  doing right thing, without looking for profit, 187
  human way, 187
  important moral force to Confucius, 187
  proper way to conform to, according to Mencius, 187
Yoga
  (see Meditation, Hindu)
  calisthenics with spiritual overtones repudiated as, 169
  central role in Hindu practice, 168, 169, 170, 171, 172-173, 174, 177, 179 *passim*
  control very important in, 174
  definition of, 169
  Gestalt interpretation, 169, 277
  Gautama's experience with, 119
  in psychic counseling practice, 255
  no intercession or mediation available to the Hindu worshipper, 172
  Tantric (see Meditation, Tantric), 176-177
  too many high-flown theories regarding, 443
  Westernized versions of, 169
Yom Kippur, 115
Yoruba
  "world view," 318, 323, 328
Yoruba people, 246
Young, Bicknell, 83-84
Youth
  counselor's or therapist's dilemma in advising, 164
  good treatment of, 189
  Muslim doctor's reliance on cultural precedent in treating psychological problems of, 165 (see also Sheikh, Sufi)
Yung Chu
  recluse of Taoist School, apostle of Egoism, 191 (see also Egoism)

Z

Zaddik, 116
Zaehner, R. C., 308, 318
Zar, The
  Muslim ceremony to drive out evil spirit and satisfy a wish, 161
Zen
  acceptance of life's realities, 247
  and psychotherapy, 137-138
  as method of psychotherapy, 248-249
  Chinese brand of, 133, 134-135
  communication between master and student, 247, 249
  compared to modern psychotherapy, 247
  conscious existence, appreciation of, 247-248
  contemplation in, 247-248
  detachment in practice of meditation, 139
  definition of, 247
  derived from mysticism of Mahayana Buddhism, 247
  frustration from long dependence on intellect, 248
  goal(s) of, 137-138
  goals of, compared to goals of psychoanalysis, 248-249
  human nature, theory regarding, 132
  ideal of selflessness, 138-139
  insight revealed to student, 248
  intellect, limitations of, 248
  intuitional approach to psychotherapy, 139-140
  koan, use of, 137
  meaning of, 134
  method, mystical character of, 249
  method of psychotherapy, as, 246-253
  mystic technique, 247
  no-thought, basic principle of, 133, 139
  non-attachment, basic principle of, 133-134
  non-form, basic principle of, 133-134
  path of discipleship, 247
  philosophy, Far-Eastern, 247
  purpose(s) of, 132
  school, branching off from Mahayana Buddhism, 118
  selflessness as a practical goal in, 138-139
  simplicity and forthrightness in, 247-248
  spontaneity in, 134
  task, assignment of 247-248 (also see Koan)
  technique displayed in, 247
Zen, Chinese
  acceptance of all thoughts that come to mind, 135
  Chien (insight), in, 137
  Hsing (practice), in, 137
  importance of detachment in, 135
  importance of translating insight into everyday experience, 137
  meditation defined, 135
  "plain feeling" in, 136
  practice of No-thought in, 135
  ritualistic Indian meditation, revolt against, 135
  satori experience transferred to every-day living, 137

wisdom or insight, defined, 135
Zen ideal(s)
  creativity, liberated, 138–139
  enlightenment, from meditation, 137–138
  essential to individual's full functioning, 138–139
  freedom for the individual, 139
  selflessness, basic, 138
Zen, lessons from
  in psychotherapeutic practice, 139–140 (*see also* Dream Ananlysis, Free Association, **Insight,** *and* Reaction, patient's)

Zen man (*see* Enlightened man)
  non-anxious, taking life as it comes, 138
Zen meditation
  beneficent therapeutic effects of, 309
Zen monk
  controls or suppresses behavior, 135
Zen training
  psychotherapy aiding, 138
Zinzendorf, N. L., 49
Zuhd (renunciation and resignation)
  in Sufism, 159
Zwingli, H., 48